IP Design for Mobile Networks

Mark Grayson

Kevin Shatzkamer

Scott Wainner

pg6 20db/decade > $\frac{10 mi}{1 mi} = \frac{1}{100}$

Cisco Press

800 East 96th Street

Indianapolis, IN 46240

IP Design for Mobile Networks

Mark Grayson, Kevin Shatzkamer, Scott Wainner

Published by:
Cisco Press
800 East 96th Street
Indianapolis, IN 46240 USA

Printed in the United States of America

First Printing June 2009

Library of Congress Cataloging-in-Publication Data

Grayson, Mark, 1965-
IP design for mobile networks / Mark Grayson, Kevin Shatzkamer, Scott Wainner.
p. cm.
ISBN-13: 978-1-58705-826-4 (pbk.)
ISBN-10: 1-58705-826-X (pbk.)
1. Wireless LANs. 2. Wireless Internet. 3. Mobile computing. 4. TCP/IP (Computer network protocol) I. Shatzkamer, Kevin, 1978- II. Wainner, Scott. III. Title.

TK5105.78.G73 2009
621.382'12--dc22

2009020541

ISBN-13: 978-1-58705-826-4

ISBN-10: 1-58705-826-X

Warning and Disclaimer

This book is designed to provide information about the evolution of mobile technologies and networks to the All-IP architecture. Every effort has been made to make this book as complete and as accurate as possible, but no warranty or fitness is implied.

The information is provided on an "as is" basis. The authors, Cisco Press, and Cisco Systems, Inc. shall have neither liability nor responsibility to any person or entity with respect to any loss or damages arising from the information contained in this book or from the use of the discs or programs that may accompany it.

The opinions expressed in this book belong to the authors and are not necessarily those of Cisco Systems, Inc.

Trademark Acknowledgments

All terms mentioned in this book that are known to be trademarks or service marks have been appropriately capitalized. Cisco Press or Cisco Systems, Inc., cannot attest to the accuracy of this information. Use of a term in this book should not be regarded as affecting the validity of any trademark or service mark. The following copyright block applies to Figure 7-29 through Figure 7-35 of this book:

Corporate and Government Sales

The publisher offers excellent discounts on this book when ordered in quantity for bulk purchases or special sales, which may include electronic versions and/or custom covers and content particular to your business, training goals, marketing focus, and branding interests. For more information, please contact: **U.S. Corporate and Government Sales** 1-800-382-3419 corpsales@pearsontechgroup.com

For sales outside the United States, please contact: **International Sales** international@pearsoned.com

Feedback Information

At Cisco Press, our goal is to create in-depth technical books of the highest quality and value. Each book is crafted with care and precision, undergoing rigorous development that involves the unique expertise of members from the professional technical community.

Readers' feedback is a natural continuation of this process. If you have any comments regarding how we could improve the quality of this book, or otherwise alter it to better suit your needs, you can contact us through email at feedback@ciscopress.com. Please make sure to include the book title and ISBN in your message.

We greatly appreciate your assistance.

Publisher: Paul Boger

Associate Publisher: Dave Dusthimer

Business Operation Manager, Cisco Press: Anand Sundaram

Manager Global Certification: Erik Ullanderson

Executive Editor: Mary Beth Ray

Managing Editor: Patrick Kanouse

Development Editor: Kimberley Debus

Project Editors: Jennifer Gallant, Seth Kerney

Copy Editor: Water Crest Publishing, Inc.

Technical Editors: Eric Hamel, Kirk McBean, Rajesh Pazhyannur

Editorial Assistant: Vanessa Evans

Book Designer: Louisa Adair

Composition: Bronkella Publishing LLC

Indexer: Ken Johnson

Proofreaders: Jennifer Gallant, Seth Kerney

Americas Headquarters
Cisco Systems, Inc.
San Jose, CA

Asia Pacific Headquarters
Cisco Systems (USA) Pte. Ltd.
Singapore

Europe Headquarters
Cisco Systems International BV
Amsterdam, The Netherlands

Cisco has more than 200 offices worldwide. Addresses, phone numbers, and fax numbers are listed on the Cisco Website at **www.cisco.com/go/offices.**

About the Authors

Mark Grayson is a Distinguished Consulting Engineer at Cisco with responsibility for leading its mobile architecture strategy. He has more than 15 years of experience in the wireless industry. He holds a first-class honors degree in electronics and communications engineering from the University of Birmingham (England) together with a Ph.D in radio communications and has been granted more than 50 patents in the area of mobile communications.

Kevin Shatzkamer is a Customer Solutions Architect at Cisco with responsibility for long-term strategy and architectural evolution of mobile wireless networks. He has worked at Cisco and in the mobile wireless industry for nine years, focusing on various technologies ranging from GSM/UMTS to CDMA networks, packet gateway, network-based services and security, video distribution, Quality of Service, and end-to-end design theory. Kevin has 16 pending patents related to all areas of work. Kevin holds a bachelor's in engineering from the University of Florida and a master's of business administration from Indiana University.

Scott Wainner is a Distinguished Systems Engineer at Cisco, providing design and consulting support for the major U.S. service providers and enterprises. He joined Cisco in 1999 and has led the architectural development of next-generation IP/MPLS services while applying his innovative efforts toward the development VPN technologies and virtualized services. Scott consults with providers in the development of managed services while guiding Cisco in the development of critical IP technologies, such as session-border controllers, virtual private networks, and multimedia distribution systems. His latest development efforts have focused on group-encrypted security architectures for broadcast/multicast content and network virtualization for the enterprise VPN. Scott has most recently started architectural development of integrated services using IP Multimedia Systems. Prior to joining Cisco, Scott was the Director of Product Development at Qwest and Engineering Manager of Global IP Services at Sprint/GlobalOne. He has been active in the networking industry for more than 23 years, including participation in the IETF and IEEE.

About the Technical Reviewers

Eric Hamel is currently working as a system architect in the Service Provider Systems Unit (SPSU) at Cisco, specifically on femtocell technology. He has been at Cisco for eight years, with previous Cisco experience as a Consulting Systems Engineer for service providers covering mobile network architecture (GSM, UMTS, and LTE) with specific focus on voice and signaling, packet data gateway infrastructure, and policy control solutions. Prior to Cisco, Eric worked at France Télécom for four years on mobile core network and was actively involved in standardization activities (ETSI, 3GPP). Eric has filed multiple U.S. patents in his area of expertise (mobile charging, policy, and so on).

Kirk McBean is currently working as an architect for mobile wireless networks at Cisco. He is actively involved in providing input to the Cisco strategy for mobility. His current focus is mobile network architecture, product definition, and product development for mobile technologies such as 4G/LTE and femtocell. Kirk has been with Cisco for 10 years and over the years has supported large customer deployments of IP/MPLS technologies ranging from MPLS L2/L3 VPN to planning complex ATM to MPLS migration strategies. Kirk holds an engineering degree from Pennsylvania State University and enjoys spending time with his wife Evalee and their two children, Sydney and Kira.

Rajesh Pazhyannur, Ph.D, is currently working in the CTO group of the Wireless Technology Group at Cisco. His current activities include indoor cellular solutions such as femtocell and distributed antenna systems, focusing on systems architecture. He has more than 15 years experience in telecommunications industry. He holds nine issued patents and has been published in numerous publications. He is an avid long distance runner and lives with his wife Ishita and daughter Saniya in northern California.

Dedications

Mark Grayson: I dedicate this book to my amazing family, who were unfortunately abandoned on many nights and weekends in order to provide the time for this manuscript to be completed. To my wonderful wife, Sharon, for all the support and encouragement, and to my two sons, Charlie and Harry, who provide the welcomed diversions from a self-absorbed focus on mobile architectures. I would also like to thank the many friends, co-workers, and mentors who, over the last 20-odd years, have helped me achieve so much.

Kevin Shatzkamer: This book is dedicated to my entire family—Jerusha, Emma, Benjamin, and Nathaniel—without whom I would never have had the constant distractions, but also the overwhelming support, during my work on this book. It is for you that I do everything that I do. To my brother, Jason, who pushes me to excel in everything that I do and makes life one big competition. To all my colleagues at Cisco—who constantly make my work environment challenging and a constant learning experience.

Scott Wainner: This book is dedicated to my children—Craig, Brett, Natalie, and Caroline. You are cherished more than you will ever know, and I thank God that He has entrusted you to me. To Julie, you are the love of my life. God blessed me with your presence, smiled, and said "Now watch him soar." To my dad, Tom Wainner, you are an awesome role model—one I aspire to mimic every day. In memory of my mother, Zenith Wainner, I feel your comforting presence with me all the time. What joy you brought to my life. To my family, friends, brothers and sisters in Christ, and colleagues, thank you all.

Acknowledgments

We'd like to give special recognition for the tremendous support we received inside Cisco in writing this book—especially our management team and co-workers. Their expert knowledge was invaluable in the development from the very onset of the book's outline.

Writing a book takes a tremendous amount of patience, discipline, and of course, time. We would like to extend our gratitude to Mary Beth Ray, Cisco Press Executive Editor, for her patience with missed deadlines and rework required to bring this book to fruition. Her assistance through the entire process has made the authoring of this book a rewarding experience.

Most of all, we would like to thank the many standards organizations, technologists, and mobile experts that have contributed to mobile network evolution. Without your hard work in striving for the best of the best, we would not have had a book to write.

Contents at a Glance

Contents

Icons Used in This Book

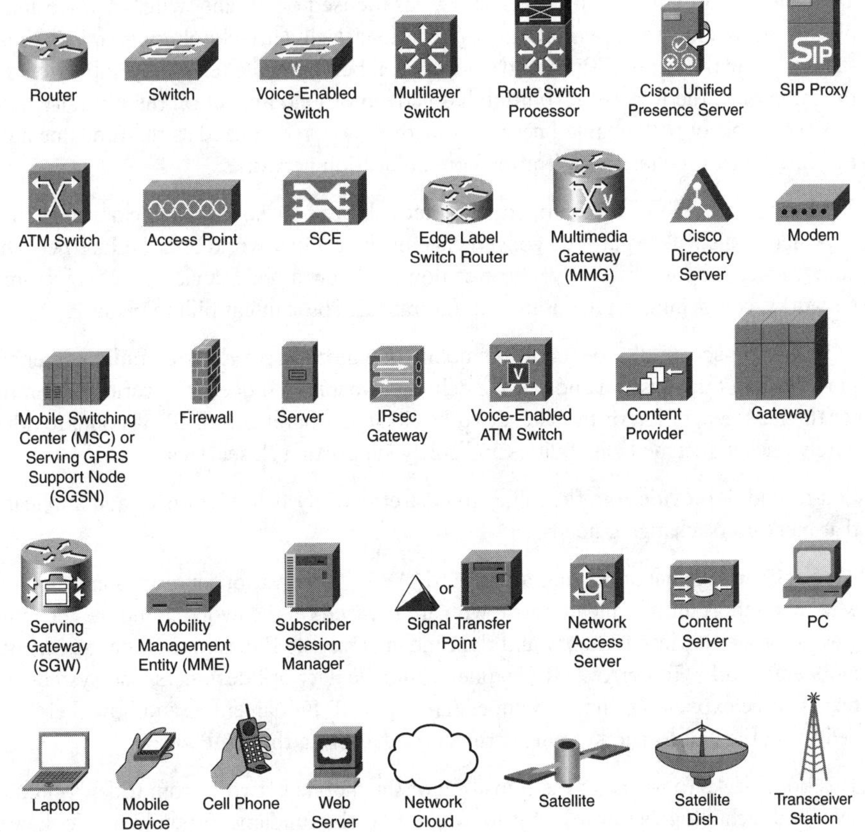

Command Syntax Conventions

The conventions used to present command syntax in this book are the same conventions used in the IOS Command Reference. The Command Reference describes these conventions as follows:

- **Boldface** indicates commands and keywords that are entered literally as shown. In actual configuration examples and output (not general command syntax), boldface indicates commands that are manually input by the user (such as a **show** command).
- *Italic* indicates arguments for which you supply actual values.
- Vertical bars (|) separate alternative, mutually exclusive elements.
- Square brackets ([ ]) indicate an optional element.
- Braces ({ }) indicate a required choice.
- Braces within brackets ([{ }]) indicate a required choice within an optional element.

Introduction

The cellular world, for much of its history, has focused on circuit-switched voice and simple text messaging as its two primary applications. Cellular technology is tremendously successful, with over half the world's population being mobile telephony subscribers. At the same time, the Internet revolution has had a profound impact on the diversity of services accessible over IP-enabled networks, with IP now recognized as the fundamental building block for all next-generation communication networks.

The next step in the evolution of the Internet will be to make it available anytime and anywhere. This will require the convergence of the cellular world and the Internet. This convergence is being driven by a host of powerful new mobile devices, high-speed mobile networks, compelling applications, and flat-rate all-you-can-eat billing plans.

IP is now impacting all aspects of the mobile operator's network, from radio bearer support through transmission and service delivery capability. Indeed, the various definitions for the next generation of mobile networks all align around an "all-IP" vision, providing purely packet-switched capabilities and solely supporting IP services.

End-to-end IP provides the flexibility to cost-effectively deliver services and applications that meet users' changing needs.

As today's mobile networks migrate toward "All-IP," with various interim steps along the way, it is important to educate those who are focused on the evolving mobile technologies on proper IP design theory and the fundamental role IP has in their next-generation mobile networks. Tomorrow's RF engineers, mobile network designers, and system architects will be expected to have an understanding of IP fundamentals and how their role in delivering the end-to-end system is crucial for delivering the all-IP vision.

This book seeks to focus on the transition of the mobile network from today's circuit-switched technologies toward a future where IP is the fundamental building block integrated into all aspects of the network. This IP transition begins with function-specific migrations of specific network domains and ends with an end-to-end IP network for radio, transport, and service delivery. This book looks at the transition from both the standards and design theory perspective.

Who Should Read This Book?

This book is not designed to provide an all-inclusive reference for evolving mobile networks to Internet Protocol (IP). This book is intended to increase the reader's understanding of the current and target state of mobile networks, and the technology enablers that assist mobile operators' migration.

This book assumes at least a basic understanding of standard networking technologies, including the Internet Protocol itself. Many concepts are introduced in order to give the reader exposure to the key technology trends and decision points impacting today's mobile operators. The book does not give recommendations on which of these technologies should be deployed, nor does it provide a transition plan for a mobile operator. Each mobile operator is expected to evaluate the technologies and make decisions based on their own criteria.

This book is written for many levels of technical expertise, from network design engineers and network planning engineers looking to design and implement mobile network migrations toward an all-IP future, networking consultants interested in understanding the technology trends that affect their mobile service provider customers, students preparing for a career in the mobile environment, and Chief Technology Officers (CTOs) seeking further understanding of the value IP technology brings to the mobile network.

How This Book Is Organized

Depending on the level of technical depth required, this book may be read cover-to-cover or be used as a reference manual for IP's role in mobile network evolution. The book is designed to be flexible and enable you to move between chapters and sections of chapters to cover just the material that you need more work with.

The book is divided into three parts.

Part I, "Cellular Networks and Standards," provides an overview of how IP is being integrated into mobile systems, including RF, radio systems, and ceullular networks. Part I includes the following chapters:

- **Chapter 1, "Introduction to Radio Systems":** This chapter provides an introduction to various radio technologies, and wireless technologies used to transport IP over radio bearers, an important foundation for expanding into IP design theory for mobile networks.
- **Chapter 2, "Cellular Access Systems":** This chapter provides an overview of legacy mobile radio systems, including GSM, UMTS, and cdma2000, presenting details of how IP services have been overlaid on top of circuit-switched architectures.
- **Chapter 3, "All-IP Access Systems":** This chapter provides an overview of the "All-IP" Access systems and standards. IP as a fundamental technology for future mobile access systems is discussed.

Part II, "IP and Today's Cellular Network," provides an overview of IP, the technologies used for transport and connectivity of today's cellular networks, and how the mobile core is evolving to encompass IP technologies. Part II includes the following chapters:

- **Chapter 4, "An IP Refresher":** This chapter is intended to level set understanding of IP technology and design theories in order to provide a foundation for expanding into IP design theory for mobile networks.
- **Chapter 5, "Connectivity and Transport":** This chapter discusses the technologies involved in connectivity and transport for mobile networks over various media.

- **Chapter 6, "Mobile Core Evolution":** This chapter provides details on how the mobile core network is evolving, describing how IP connectivity is provided over mobile networks, as well as how IP is being used to transport the circuit-switched core network.
- **Chapter 7, "Offloading Traditional Networks with IP":** This chapter discusses the evolution of today's TDM-based technologies to IP through offload scenarios for the mobile backhaul network.

Part III, "The End-to-End Services Network," provides an overview of the end-to-end services network based on IP, including context awareness and services. Part III includes the following chapters:

- **Chapter 8, "End-to-End Context Awareness":** This chapter discusses the concept of Intelligent IP Networks to extend core functionality and provide intelligent delivery of traffic to mobile subscribers.
- **Chapter 9, "Content and Services":** This chapter discusses the evolution of content and services from circuit-switched technologies to IP-based technologies, and the evolution of the service framework from the Intelligent Network (IN) to service delivery platforms and the Intelligent Multimedia Subsystem (IMS).

Chapter 1

Introduction to Radio Systems

Because radio systems have fundamental characteristics that distinguish them from their wired equivalents, this chapter provides an introduction to the various radio technologies relevant to the IP design engineer. The concepts discussed provide a foundation for further comparisons of the competing mobile radio access systems for supporting mobile broadband services and expanding into IP design for mobile networks.

Many excellent texts concentrate on the detail of mobile radio propagation, and so this chapter will not attempt to cover radio frequency propagation in detail; rather, it is intended to provide a basic understanding of the various radio technologies and concepts used in realizing mobile radio systems. In particular, this chapter provides an insight into how the characteristics of the radio network impact the performance of IP applications running over the top of mobile networks—characteristics that differentiate wireless networks from their fixed network equivalents.

In an ideal world, radio systems would be able to provide ubiquitous coverage with seamless mobility across different access systems; high-capacity, always-on systems with low latency and jitter; and wireless connectivity to IP hosts with extended battery life, thus ensuring that all IP applications could run seamlessly over the top of any access network. Unfortunately, real-world constraints mean that the radio engineer faces tough compromises when designing a network: balancing coverage against capacity, latency against throughput, and performance against battery life. This chapter introduces the basics of mobile radio design and addresses how these tradeoffs ultimately impact the performance of IP applications delivered over mobile radio networks. In Chapter 2, "Cellular Access Systems," and Chapter 3, "All-IP Access Systems," we use these concepts to differentiate the competing mobile access systems defined for supporting mobile broadband service offerings.

Spectrum

Radio Frequency Spectrum is a key distinguishing factor used to compare alternative mobile radio systems. Radio spectrum for communications ranges from approximately 30 Hz (termed Extremely Low Frequency [ELF]) to above 100 GHz (termed Extremely High Frequency [EHF]). Because of its capability to provide very wide area coverage and penetrate sea water, ELF has been used for global systems for providing low-rate submarine communications. EHF, on the other hand, can be used for Line-of-Sight (LoS) microwave communications. Table 1-1 shows the complete range of radio frequency spectrum used in communication systems and provides some examples of spectrum use.

Table 1-1 *Radio Frequency Spectrum*

Band Name	Frequency Range	Example Communication Use
Extremely Low Frequency	3–30 Hz	Submarine communications
Super Low Frequency	30–300 Hz	Submarine communications
Ultra Low Frequency	300–3,000 Hz	Underground communications
Very Low Frequency	3–30 kHz	Navigation
Low Frequency	30–300 kHz	AM broadcasting
Medium Frequency	300–3,000 kHz	AM broadcasting
High Frequency	3–30 MHz	Shortwave broadcast; amateur radio
Very High Frequency	30–300 MHz	Private mobile radio; FM and television broadcasting
Ultra High Frequency	300–3,000 MHz	Television broadcasting, cellular radio, and wireless LANs
Super High Frequency	3–30 GHz	Wireless LANs; point-to-point and point-to-multipoint microwave
Extremely High Frequency	30–300 GHz	Point-to-point microwave

Table 1-1 highlights how the characteristics of the different bands of the radio spectrum vary. In general, the lower the frequency, the better the range (for example, in the extreme case, a single ELF transmitter is able to cover the entire planet), but the bandwidths available are limited (for example, the same ELF systems typically provided a global system with total system capacity below 50 bps). Conversely, EHF systems can provide incredible capacity, but they incur significant attenuation by atmospheric effects due, for example, to extreme humidity, rain, or molecular absorption, and thus are prone to significant losses in non-Line-of-Sight (LoS) deployments.

In between these extremes is the "sweet spot" for the radio spectrum for conventional mobile systems, with the Ultra High Frequency (UHF) band ranging from 300 MHz to 3 GHz and providing what many consider to be the best compromise between usable bandwidths and propagation characteristics required for wide area coverage.

As a consequence, the UHF spectrum is a scarce resource with many competing users. In order to rationalize spectrum usage, the Radio Communications Sector of the International Telecommunications Union (ITU-R) has identified key bands that can preferably be used for International Mobile Telecommunications (IMT) operation. These IMT bands cover operation for the following:

- **IMT-2000 systems:** Covering legacy "3G" technologies, including Wide Band Code Division Multiple Access (WCDMA), cdma2000 1xrtt technologies, and most recently WiMAX.
- **IMT-enhanced systems:** Covering those systems offering improved mobile broadband services, including High-Speed Packet Access (HSPA) and EVolution-Data Only (EV-DO) technologies.
- **IMT-advanced systems:** Covering those systems offering very high-rate mobile broadband operation, including rates in excess of 1 Gbps to low-mobility users.

Note In Chapters 2 and 3, we provide more detail describing alternative mobile radio access systems; it will become apparent that none of the current competing systems, including WiMAX and Long-Term Evolution (LTE), meet the minimum requirements for IMT-advanced systems.

The spectrum for use by the IMT-2000 technologies was first identified by the ITU at the World Administrative Radio Conference (WARC) in 1992 and further augmented at the World Radiocommunication Conferences (WRC) in 2000 and 2007. Even when spectrum has been identified for use by IMT systems, it might not be available for sole use of mobile radio systems. However, the identification of spectrum by ITU-R, as illustrated in Table 1-2, provides equipment manufacturers with guidance on the range of frequency bands that are likely to be used in deploying IMT services, hopefully leading to economies of scale and consequential decrease in the overall cost of production of specialized IMT equipment.

Table 1-2 *IMT Spectrum Allocations*

Frequency Range	Regional Rules
450–470 MHz	All regions
610–790 MHz	Nine countries in Region 3 (Asia and Australasia): Bangladesh, China, Rep. of Korea, India, Japan, New Zealand, Papua New Guinea, Philippines, and Singapore

continues

Table 1-2 *IMT Spectrum Allocations (continued)*

Frequency Range	Regional Rules
698–790 MHz	Region 2 (Americas)
790–960 MHz	All regions
1,710–2,025 MHz	All regions
2,110–2,200 MHz	All regions
2,300–2,400 MHz	All regions
2,500–2,690 MHz	All regions
3,400–3,600 MHz	No global allocation, but over 80 administrations in Region 1 (Europe and Africa), plus nine in Region 3, including India, China, Japan, and Rep. of Korea

Even with the 885 MHz of spectrum allocated to IMT across all regions, as indicated in Table 1-2, the ITU has performed an analysis of the growing requirements for spectrum to address IMT deployments. ITU-R report M.2078 contains the results of that analysis, both for "legacy" systems in terms of pre-IMT systems, IMT-2000 systems, and IMT-enhanced systems that are already being deployed, as well as the spectrum that will be required for future IMT-advanced deployments. These results indicate that although the combined allocations of WARC-1992, WRC-2000, and WRC-2007 are sufficient for legacy deployments, the new IMT advanced systems are expected to require up to 420 MHz of additional spectrum to be allocated by year 2015 and up to 840 MHz of additional spectrum to be allocated by year 2020.

ITU-R Report M.2078 uses the service categorization defined in ITU-R Report M.2072, "World mobile telecommunication market forecast," which includes seven service categories, as shown in Table 1-3, including services at speeds of up to 100 Mbps for *super high multimedia* services!

Table 1-3 *ITU Mobile Service Categorization*

Peak Bit Rate	Service Category
< 16 kbps	Speech
< 128 kbps	Multimedia messaging; low multimedia, low rate data
< 384 kbps	Medium multimedia
< 2 Mbps	High multimedia
< 10 Mbps	Very high multimedia
< 30 Mbps	Ultra high multimedia
< 100 Mbps	Super high multimedia

If the ITU estimates prove accurate, it is evident that future World Radiocommunication Conferences will be required to define increasing spectrum allocations for future IMT operations. These systems will be less telecommunications-focused and increasingly data-centric as capabilities evolve toward supporting super high multimedia service offerings.

Propagation

Because of its relative scarcity, mobile systems are required to re-use the allocated radio spectrum across a particular network of cell sites. Radio frequency signals need to propagate between the cell site antenna and the mobile wireless terminal. As the signals propagate, they exhibit a path loss as the emitted energy is dispersed over an increasing area. Estimating the path loss is critical in determining both the coverage provided by a single cell site and the bandwidth available to the IP services offered in that cell coverage area.

The benchmark of propagation loss is that of free space—in other words, the loss in a region that is free from all objects that might absorb or reflect the radio energy. Because the emitted energy from an isotropic antenna is dispersed over the surface of a sphere (with the transmitting antenna at the center of the sphere), the received energy is inversely proportional to the surface area of the sphere ($4 \pi r^2$, where r is the radius of the sphere), as illustrated in Figure 1-1. Using this approach, you can see that the free space path loss follows an inverse square law with changing distance from the antenna, r.

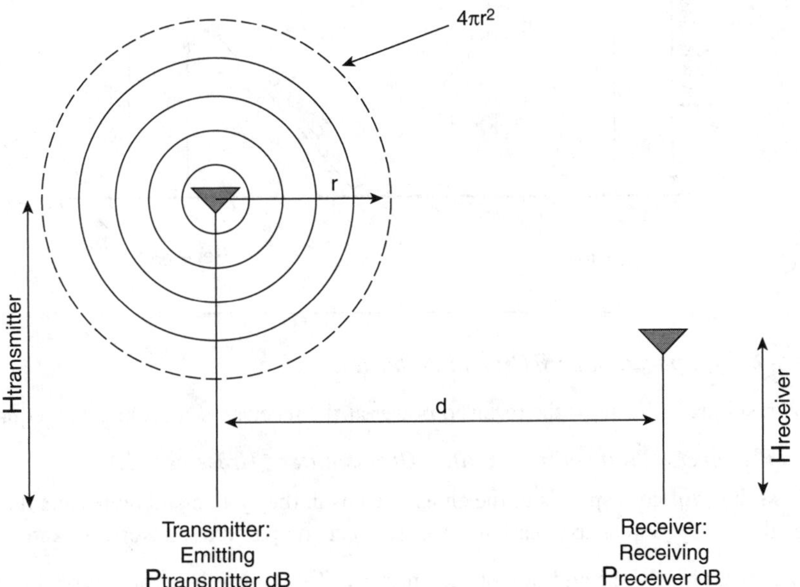

Figure 1-1 *Free Space Loss*

Radio propagation is often defined in logarithmic ratios, termed decibels (dB). When referring to power, a decibel is defined as follows:

$$X \text{ dB} = 10 \text{ Log}_{10}(X/X0)$$

Because path loss is an important quantity in defining the coverage and capacity of mobile radio systems, a useful unit used to compare different environments is to define the decrease in received power over a "decade," where a decade corresponds to an increase in the order of magnitude of distance—for example, when going from 1 mile to 10 miles, 10 kilometers to 100 kilometers, or 13 furlongs to 130 furlongs. Using such an approach and the inverse square law, you can see that the free space loss is equivalent to a path loss of 20 dB/decade; that is, the power received at 10 miles from a transmitter is 100 times less than the power received at 1 mile away from the same transmitter.

Outdoor Coverage

Unfortunately, cellular networks are not built in free space and instead need to accommodate reflections from the ground. Figure 1-2 shows such a model illustrating a direct path between transmitter and receiver as well as a ground reflection.

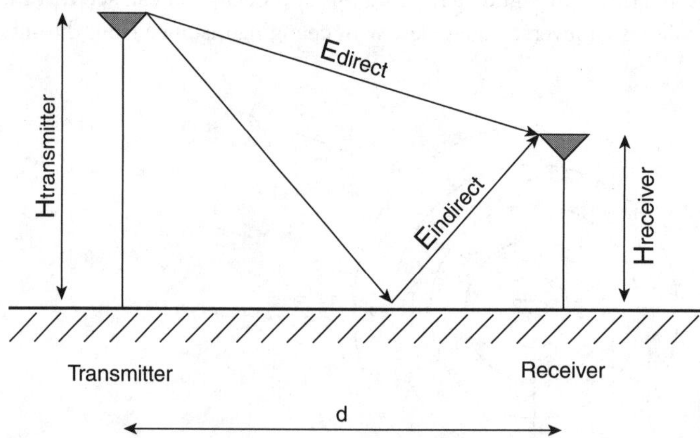

Figure 1-2 *Propagation with Ground Reflection*

The resulting estimate of the received power at the receiver is approximately equal to:

$$Preceiver = Ptransmitter * Gain * (Htransmitter * Hreceiver/ d^2)^2$$

where the *gain* corresponds to the antenna gains in the system and represents the directionality of the antennae radiation patterns when compared to an isotropic antenna.

Counterintuitively, the addition of the ground reflection produces an inverse fourth-power relationship between the power at the receiver and the distance, *d*, between the transmitter and receiver. Instead of the received power diminishing at a rate of 20 dB/decade as predicted by a free-space model, mobile communication systems frequently exhibit received power diminishing at a rate approaching 40 dB/decade as the receiver moves away from the transmitter.

Note The received power is also a function of the square of the product of transmit and receive antenna heights. This is why cellular antennas have conventionally been located on hilltops and raised high on towers, and if you are in a region of poor coverage, why it is often better to try receiving cell phone service on the top floor of a building.

Empirical modeling of radio propagation has been performed by Okumura[1] and Hata.[2] The typical urban Hata model defines the distance (*d*, in meters) related propagation loss as follows:

$$(44.9 - 6.55 \, \mathrm{Log}_{10} \, (h \; base\_station)) \, \mathrm{Log}_{10} \, (d)$$

Using an example 10-meter base station height, the empirical data indicates that the actual path loss should decrease at ~ 38 dB/decade.

This means that when moving from 1 kilometer to 10 kilometers away from a base station antenna, the signal will in fact decrease by a factor approaching 10,000. Although this allows for the scarce spectrum resources to be re-used as neighboring cell site emissions are rapidly attenuated, it also ensures that the cellular designers are constantly battling to provide improved coverage with lower path loss while limiting the number of cell sites required to cover a particular area.

Frequency-Dependent Propagation Loss

We can see from Table 1-1 that in general terms, lower frequencies propagate better than higher frequencies. This intrinsic property has resulted in different systems competing for the sub 1 GHz frequencies, which offer improved propagation characteristics compared with other IMT spectrum allocations.

For example, recent analysis of propagation in the UHF band has been performed,[3] indicating that there is a 26.7 dB increase in path loss when comparing IMT systems deployed in the IMT-defined 698–790 MHz band with those deployed in the 2,500–2,690 MHz band.

Given a typical macro-area propagation loss of 38 dB/decade, it is evident that a change in operating frequency from 698 MHz to 2,500 MHz needs to be compensated by decreasing the cell radius by a factor of $10^{(26.7/38)}$ or five times! The maximum throughput of an individual cell is bounded and will be reduced as the ratio between the wanted signal and the interfering signals decreases. In a lightly loaded system, the interfering signals will be low and hence lower frequencies can provide service over a large coverage area. We describe such deployments as being *coverage limited*, where the performance of the overall system is limited by the attenuation of the wanted signal.

However, as load increases, neighboring cells generate more interference and more cells will be needed to provide the required capacity. In such circumstances, the system becomes limited by interference. We describe such deployments as *capacity constrained*, where the rapid adoption of higher bandwidth IP services means that the maximum attainable cell radius is artificially reduced—for example, by reducing the maximum power—in order to support the required teletraffic density.

The same characteristic that allows a lower frequency signal to propagate over increased distances now also results in the increased effects of interference, as the emissions from neighboring cell sites are similarly attenuated to a lesser degree because of the lower frequency. Hence, the inherent advantages of operating at lower frequencies, which provided improved coverage in a lightly loaded system, diminish over time as the capacity increases.

When these characteristics are coupled with the fact that larger bandwidth allocations are often available at higher frequencies, it is evident that the optimum choice of frequency that delivers the lowest total cost for a specific radio system is a complex tradeoff.

Note The same analysis that indicated that 698 MHz systems had a 26.7 dB advantage in terms of path loss over 2,500 MHz systems also shows that as the 698 MHz systems become capacity constrained, they suffer deteriorating performance compared to the 2,500 MHz systems. For example, they fail to support coverage requirements exceeding 700 kbps/km^2, even in dense urban environments, compared to the 2,500 MHz systems that were able to support capacities in excess of 5 Mbps/km^2.

Fast Fading

Whereas the previous analysis concentrated on propagation in ideal free space or with simple two-ray models, the reality is that mobile radio systems operate with a variety of obstacles and reflections both between and around the base station and mobile terminal, as shown in Figure 1-3. The combination of the disparate propagation paths is called *multipath*—where the transmitted signal arrives at the receiver from various directions over a multiplicity of paths, with each individual path having its own electrical path length and degree of attenuation.

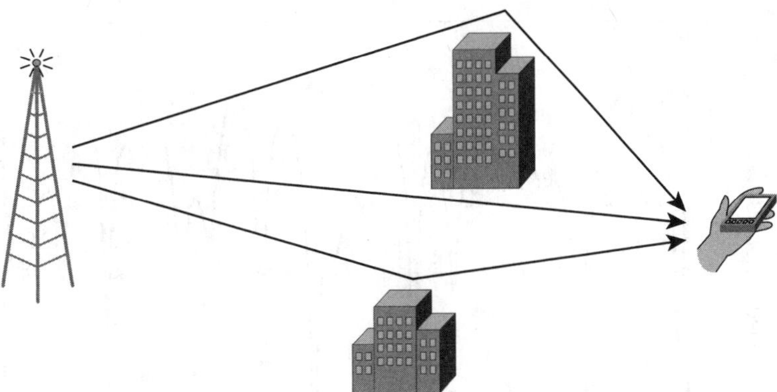

Figure 1-3 *Multipath Propagation*

The variation in path delay caused by the different reflections (termed *time dispersion*) creates distortion in the received signal. This distortion causes the signal from consecutive data intervals to interfere with each other at the receiver, a characteristic termed *Inter-Symbol Interference* (*ISI*). For example, in the Global System for Mobile (GSM) system, the data interval is ~3.9 µs, but operation needs to continue in extreme multipath environments where the time dispersion may approach 20 µs (corresponding to ~6 km difference in path length between the direct path and longest reflection), a scenario that may be experienced in extreme hilly locations with reflections from distant hilltops. In such circumstances, ISI means that at the receiver, a single data interval will be interfering with up to five successive data intervals.

Another consequence of the multipath reception is that different paths can combine constructively or destructively, which will lead to rapid changes in the received signal levels over time, termed *fast fading*, as shown in Figure 1-4. If each multipath component is independent of the others, the Probability Density Function (PDF) of the envelope of multipath components follows a Rayleigh distribution, and the rapid fluctuation in received signal level is termed *Rayleigh fading*. These short-term fluctuations of the Rayleigh fading envelope are superimposed on the long-term distance-related path loss, as defined by the preceding outdoor coverage model.

Just as fast fading generates time-varying changes in the received envelope, the same process can generate frequency-selective fades. This phenomenon creates nulls in the frequency response of the channel. Figure 1-5 illustrates a 15 dB null in the middle of the transmitted signal bandwidth, which may impact signal reception.

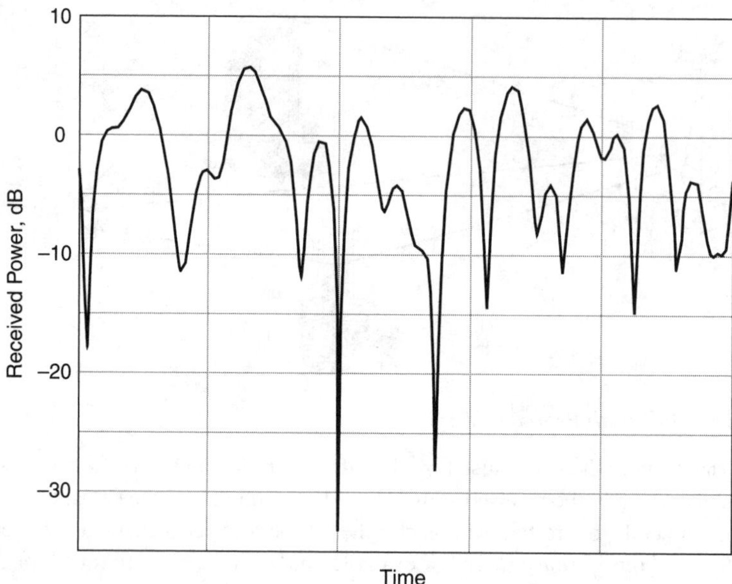

Figure 1-4 *Time-Varying Rayleigh Fading Envelope*

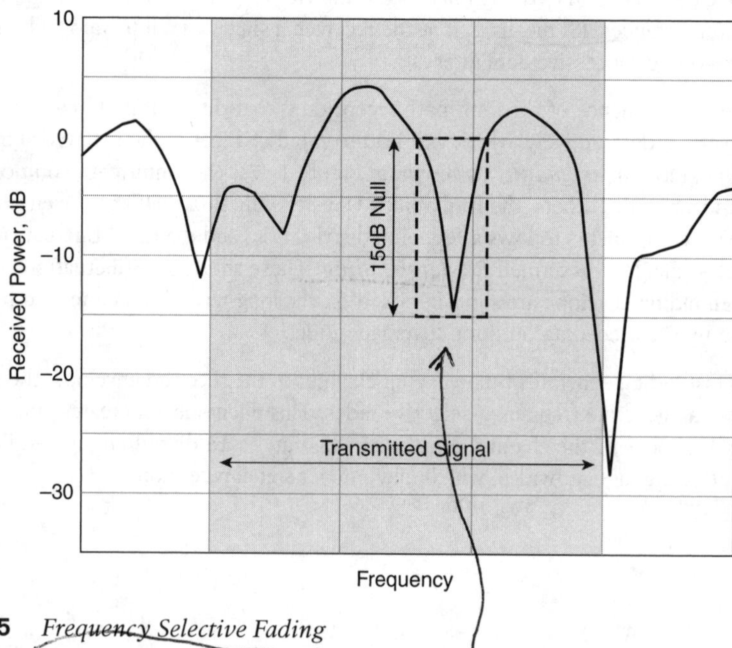

Figure 1-5 *Frequency Selective Fading*

Conversely, if the path lengths of the multipath components only vary slowly, as is normally the case with services delivered to a pedestrian user, flat fading can be experienced. This results in extended periods of time where destructive interference can produce particularly poor propagation conditions. Unless mitigation techniques are employed, the user of IP services may face extended periods where service is substantially degraded.

Shadowing and Building Penetration Loss

Although the first cellular radio systems were designed for vehicle-mounted systems, the mass adoption of cell phone technology has resulted in an increased usage by users located within buildings. JD Power (www.jdpower.com) reported that 2006 was the first year in which indoor wireless call transactions exceeded those made outside, and Telephia[4] reported that indoor viewing contributed 22% of total Mobile TV usage; this trend is set to continue.

Providing coverage to indoor users from outdoor base stations results in an additional Building Penetration Loss (BPL), as signals are required to propagate through the walls, floors, and windows of a building. The penetration loss experienced is dependent on the building materials, window coatings, building orientation, and transmission frequency. In order to provide for 90% in-building coverage, typical mean propagation losses have been shown[5] to be in the range of the following:

- 11 dB for a residential building with plywood wall construction
- 16 dB for a residential building with external brick type construction
- 30 dB for an office building with brick wall construction

BPL is one extreme example of the long-term statistical variation in the mean signal level termed *shadowing*. Because the statistical nature of such slow fluctuations results in the local mean having a Gaussian (or normal) distribution, such shadowing is often termed *log-normal fading*. The standard deviation of the log-normal distribution varies depending on the user's environment. A measurement campaign[6] conducted on behalf of the GSM Association (www. gsma.org; a trade body representing the GSM community) examining 3G coverage concluded that the log-normal standard deviation ranges from 10 dB in rural environments, to 12 dB in urban environments and 13–18 dB in indoor locations. This means that the radio engineer has to combat both the BPL, lowering the mean signal, and an increased spread of signal levels, associated with log-normal statistics, if IP services are to be offered to indoor users.

Historically, indoor coverage has typically been provided as a by-product of radio planning for good outside coverage. However, the increasing adoption of mobile broadband IP services by indoor users highlighted previously indicates that this will likely need to change. Indeed, a study for Signals Research Group (www.signalresearch.com) indicates that if a cellular network is planned with a 98% Probability of Coverage (PoC) to an outdoor voice user, the same network will be able to provide around a 70% probability of providing coverage for delivering a voice service to an indoor user. However, if the service is IP-based and requires a higher data rate (for example, 144 kbps or 384 kbps), the research indicates that the probability of indoor coverage falls to around 40% or 30%, respectively, in an urban environment, or to 26% to 16% in a rural environment, as shown in Table 1-4.

Table 1-4 *Probability of Coverage by Bearer Type*[7]

	Dense Urban	Urban	Suburban	Rural
Outdoor Probability of Coverage	98%	98%	98%	98%
Indoor Probability of Coverage				
12.2 kbps	67%	70%	72%	68%
64 kbps	50%	70%	72%	68%
144 kbps	41%	39%	34%	26%
384 kbps	31%	28%	22%	16%

As mobile services evolve from low-rate voice and short message-centric services toward higher-speed IP services, the challenge of providing reliable indoor service will become increasingly challenging. It may be likely that simply providing an increasing cell density in order to accommodate the 11 to 30 dB of building propagation loss is uneconomical and that the cellular service providers will be forced to adopt alternative approaches to providing reliable indoor mobile broadband IP services.

Note ITU-R Report M-2078 includes data on teletraffic density and macro-cellular coverage area per radio environment. In this report, Building Penetration Loss is assumed to decrease the urban cell coverage from 0.65 km^2 to 0.10 km^2, to decrease the suburban cell coverage from 0.65 km^2 to 0.15 km^2, and to decrease the rural cell coverage from 0.65 km^2 to 0.22 km^2.

Modulation

Modulation is the process of encoding information onto one or more radio frequency carriers. Digital modulation can encode information into the phase, frequency, or amplitude of a carrier, or use a combination of such techniques. One of the most common techniques of modulating a carrier is with Binary Phase Shift Keying (BPSK), where information is encoded by changing the phase of a reference carrier. Figure 1-6 shows an example of a BPSK waveform with modulated phase. Each encoded bit corresponds to either a phase shift of 0 degrees or a phase shift of 180 degrees. In this example, if a phase shift of 0 degrees represents the encoding of bit "0," and a phase shift of 180 degrees represents the encoding of bit "1," the waveform in Figure 1-6 encodes the seven-bit sequence 0100100.

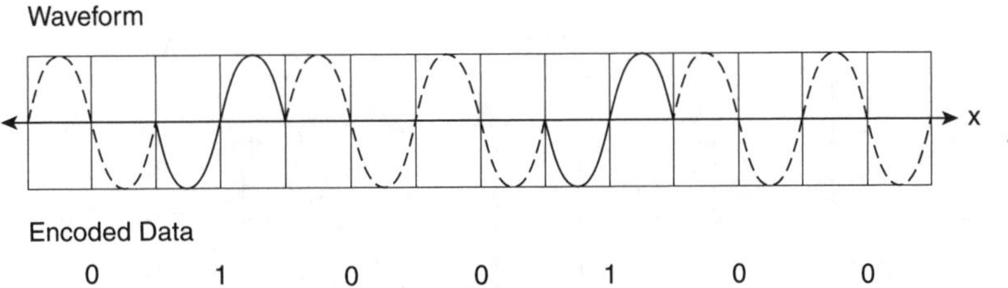

Figure 1-6 *Binary Phase Shift Keying Waveform*

Whereas BPSK encodes a single bit of information in each symbol, Quaternary Phase Shift Keying (QPSK) uses four possible phases to encode two bits of data per symbol. Figure 1-7 shows an example of a QPSK waveform:

- A phase shift of 0 degrees can be used to encode the two bits "00."
- A phase shift of 90 degrees can be used to encode the two bits "10."
- A phase shift of 180 degrees can be used to encode the two bits "11."
- A phase shift of 270 degrees can be used to encode the two bits "01."

Using this encoding scheme, the waveform in Figure 1-7 encodes the 14-bit sequence 00101101000111.

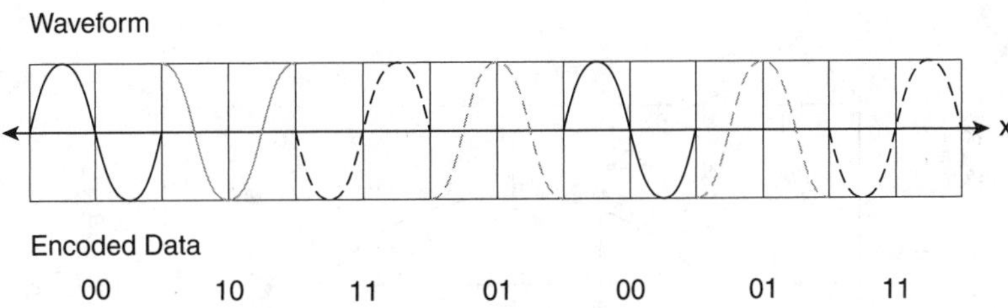

Figure 1-7 *Quaternary Phase Shift Keying Waveform*

Another way of representing the modulation schemes is using a constellation diagram, which displays the modulated waveform on a two-dimensional quadrature and amplitude axis. On a constellation diagram, BPSK and QPSK will be shown as the individual phases used to encode the information (two phases in the case of BPSK and four phases in the case of QPSK), as shown in Figure 1-8.

Obviously, because two bits of information are encoded in each symbol of QPSK compared with the one bit of information with BPSK, QPSK is able to transmit more information in the same time interval. One class of higher-order modulations makes use of a combination of Amplitude and Phase modulation and is termed Quadrature Amplitude Modulation (QAM). Figure 1-9 shows the constellation diagram for a 16-QAM signal, where now four bits of information are encoded in a single symbol.

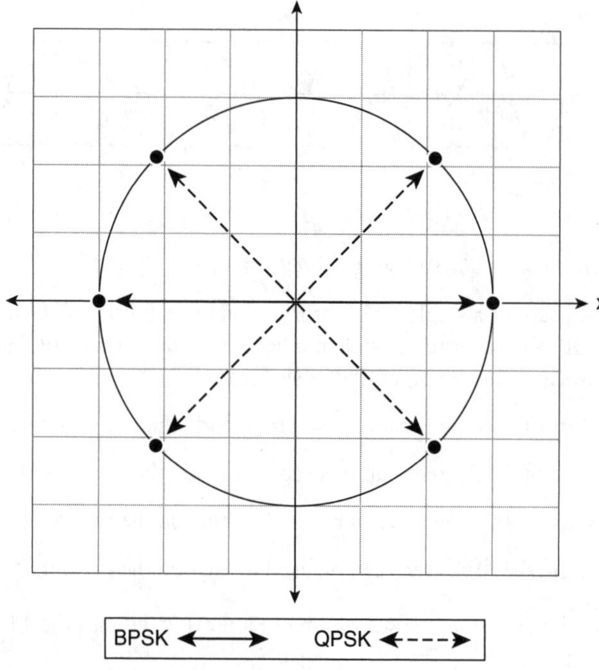

Figure 1-8 *Constellation Diagram for BPSK and QPSK*

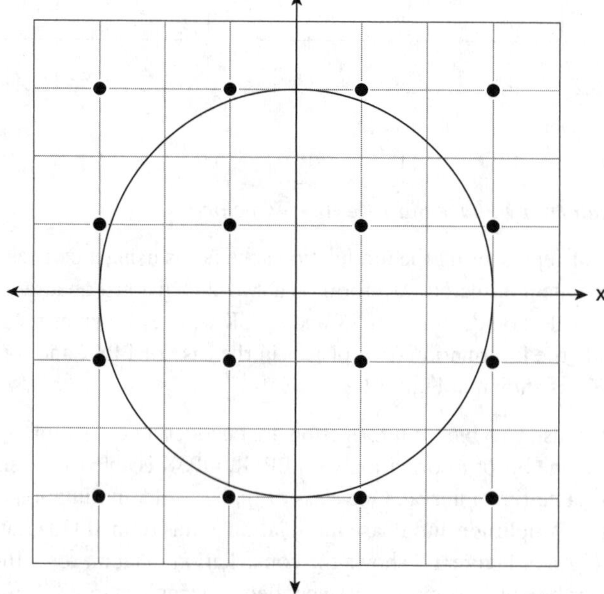

Figure 1-9 *Constellation Diagram for 16 QAM*

The more advanced mobile radio systems may include 64-QAM modulation, where six bits of information are encoded in each symbol, or six times the information encoded in the basic BPSK waveform. The IEEE 802.16 specification[8] used by the WiMAX system includes an option for 256-QAM modulation, where eight bits are encoded in each transmitted symbol.

The higher the order the modulation, the more data that can be encoded in a waveform and the greater the transmission speeds offered to the IP applications that utilize the mobile radio network. However, the higher-order modulation schemes are also more susceptible to impairments by noise and interference, leading to an increased probability of errored data being recovered at the receiver. As the distance between the mobile terminal and the base station increases, the Signal-to-Noise Ratio (SNR) or Carrier-to-Interference Ratio (CIR) will fall at around 38 dB/decade. Therefore, it is important to understand how the different modulation schemes perform in the presence of decreasing SNR ratios. A high-order modulation scheme that provides high speed throughput when the user is located in the vicinity of a base station actually performs worse in terms of the error-free throughput as the terminal moves away from the base station.

Figure 1-10 compares the Bit Error Rate (BER) of five different modulation schemes in the presence of Additive White Gaussian Noise (AWGN). Because a single symbol of 256-QAM modulation transmits eight bits of information compared with the single bit of information transmitted with a single symbol of BPSK modulation, the performances are normalized by plotting the BER against the ratio of Energy-per-bit (Eb) to Noise Power Spectral Density (No), or Eb/No. Eb/No is related to SNR by scaling for the bandwidth in which the SNR is measured, B, versus the data rate of the modulation scheme, R, where:

Eb/No = SNR * B/R

Consider a mobile radio system designed for a nominal BER operating point of 10^{-2}, and assume that the base station has a constant energy per symbol, independent of which order modulation is used. If the radio planner has set the transmit power such that at 1 kilometer from the base station, there is 16.5 dB of E_b/N_o at the 256-QAM demodulator, Figure 1-10 indicates that the BER operating point has been achieved. As the user moves away from the base station, the BER of the 256-QAM demodulator will degrade. If the user moves a further 459 m away from the base station to 1.459 kilometers away, using the Hata model, the carrier would be attenuated by an additional:

38 log10 (1.459) = 6.2 dB

If the modulation is unchanged, the E_b/N_o will be decreased to 10.3 dB and Figure 1-10 indicates that corresponding BER would degrade to over 0.07, or over seven times that at the nominal operating point.

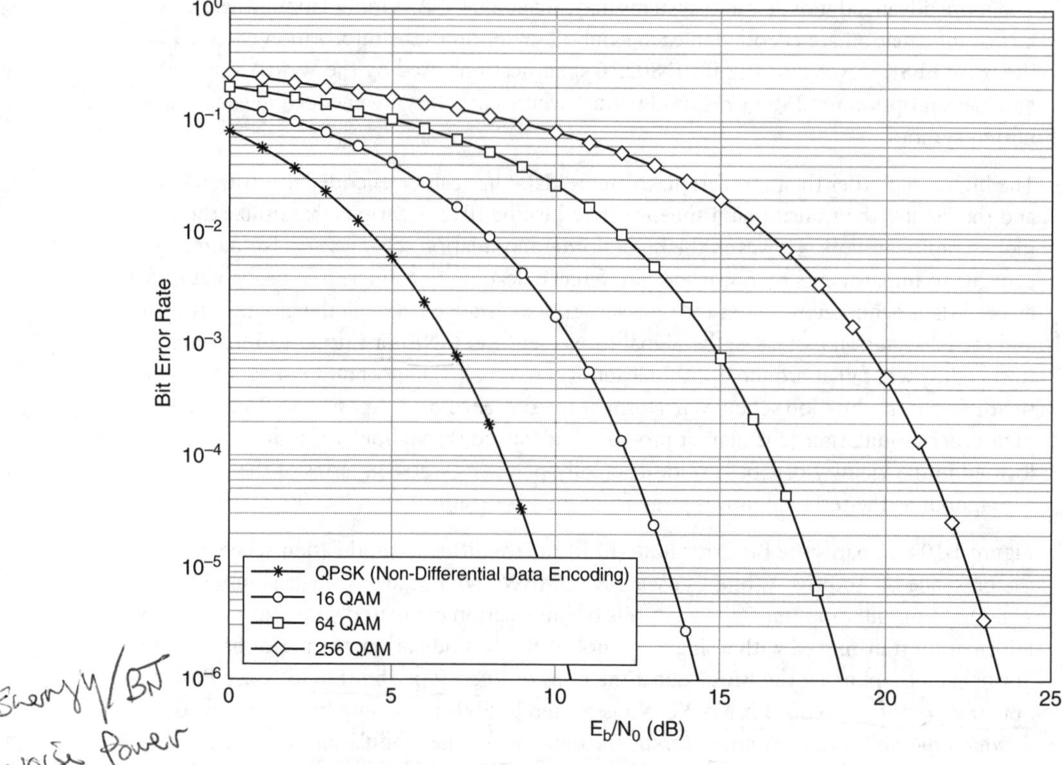

Figure 1-10 *BER Performance in AWGN of Different Modulation Schemes*

Now, if instead the modulation is decreased from 256 QAM to 64 QAM while keeping the symbol energy constant, since Eb/No is a normalized measure of the energy per symbol to noise spectral density ratio, there will a corresponding increase in E_b by a factor of:

$$\text{Log}_2 M$$

where *M* is the number of alternative modulation symbols.

Therefore, decreasing the order of modulation from 256 QAM to 64 QAM will increase the E_b/N_o by:

$$\text{Log}_2 256 / \text{Log}_2 64 = 1.33 \text{ or } 1.24 \text{ dB}$$

This means that by moving a further 459 meters away from the base station and switching modulation schemes, the E_b/N_o available at a 64-QAM demodulator is 11.5 dB, which, according to Figure 1-10, is sufficient for the nominal operating BER of around 10^{-2} to be maintained.

As the user moves further away from the base station, the path loss increases such that when the user is 2 kilometers away, the Hata model indicates that the 64-QAM BER would degrade to 0.07. The increase in path loss can be compensated by switching to 16-QAM modulation, such that the nominal BER is maintained at 0.01.

Finally, as the user approaches the edge of coverage at 2.75 kilometers away from the base station, the path loss will have increased by almost 17 dB compared to the nominal 256-QAM operating point at 1 kilometer. However, by switching to QPSK, the nominal BER is maintained.

Figure 1-11 summarizes the coverage by modulation type using the AWGN results of Figure 1-10 with the 38 dB/decade Hata model. The results highlight that even when the system is designed to operate with 256-QAM modulation, over half the cell is only able to receive data modulated with QPSK.

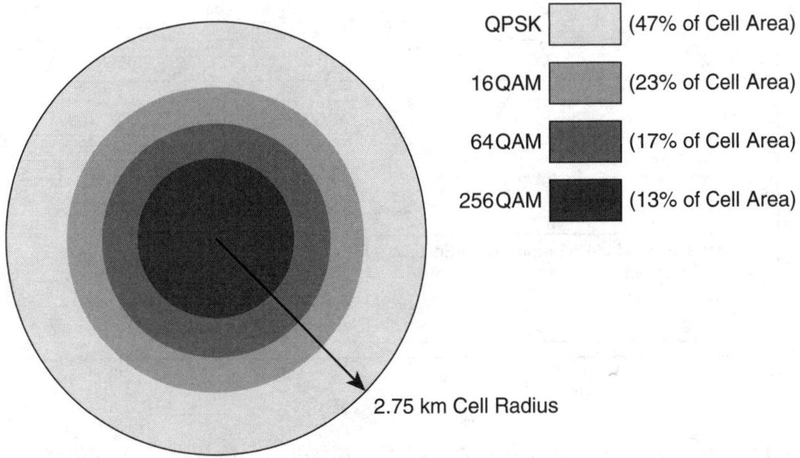

Figure 1-11 *Cell Coverage by Modulation Type for a Nominal BER of 0.01 in AWGN*

Unfortunately, by switching modulation schemes to keep the BER constant, the throughput achievable has been reduced by a factor of four from the original eight bits per symbol when operating at 256 QAM (when the use was in good coverage) to the two bits per symbol (when operating at the cell edge). In the downlink, this offset in throughput could be countered by applying a disproportionate amount of base station power to those users at the cell edge, resulting in increased interference in neighboring cells. Unfortunately, the same approach is often not possible in the uplink, where the device is peak power limited because of its power amplifier design. As a consequence, the IP design engineer needs to factor in the decrease in IP throughput able to be supported by those users located toward the cell edge.

The decrease in cell performance is further exacerbated by the impact of fading on the BER performance. The deep nulls characteristic of Rayleigh fading cause the BER to dramatically increase, as shown in Figure 1-12. The required Eb/No necessary to deliver the nominal un-coded BER increases by the order of 8–10 dB, decreasing the maximum achievable coverage of the cell in AWGN conditions from 2.7 kilometers to 1.5 kilometers.

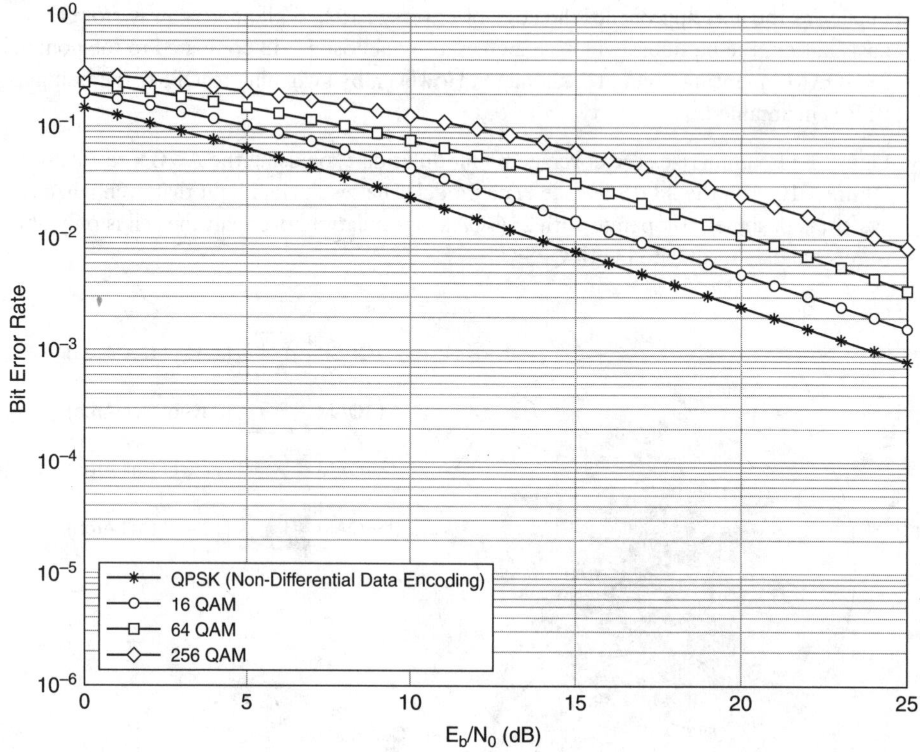

Figure 1-12 *BER Performance of Different Modulation Schemes in Rayleigh Fading*

Multiple Access Technologies

Although a simple modulated carrier may be sufficient for supporting a point-to-point communications link, mobile radio systems are characterized by their ability to support multiple users using a common communications resource. Multiple access techniques define how the communication resources are partitioned between the different users.

Figure 1-13 illustrates the various techniques for partitioning the radio resources, which are as follows:

- **Time Division Multiple Access (TDMA):** Each user is allocated a particular time interval when they have access to the communications resources.
- **Frequency Division Multiple Access (FDMA):** The communication resource is partitioned into separate carriers, and each user is allocated a subset of the overall frequencies when they have access to the communications resources.
- **Code Division Multiple Access (CDMA):** All users can use the same frequency at the same time but are isolated by a separate pseudo-random code that they use to spread their information.

- **Space Division Multiple Access (SDMA):** Isolation between communications resources is achieved using smart antenna techniques that generate directional antennas for each user.

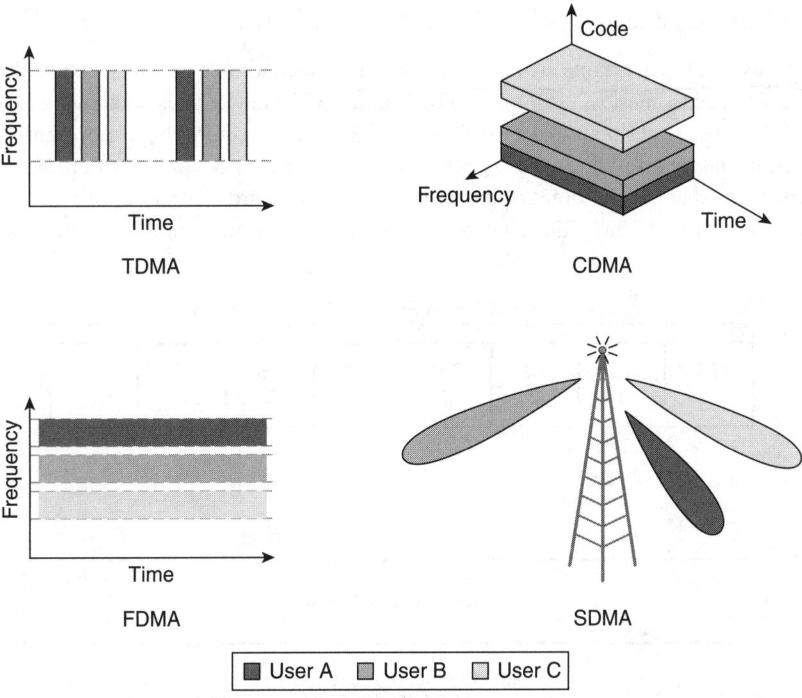

Figure 1-13 *Multiple Access Techniques*

Frequently, communications systems will use a combination of multiple access techniques; for example, the General Packet Radio Service (GPRS) system uses a combination of TDMA together with FDMA, and the High-Speed Downlink Packet Access (HSDPA) system uses a combination of CDMA together with TDMA.

Time Division Multiple Access

Time Division Multiple Access (TDMA) allows a number of users to share a communication resource by segmenting the resource into time slots and allocating each individual time slot to one user at a time. A communication resource may be dedicated to either transmission or reception, in which case two sets of frequencies are required to support bidirectional communications. Because of the frequency separation between transmit and receive resources, this technique is termed Frequency Division Duplex (FDD). The GSM system is one example of a communications system that uses TDMA with FDD.

Alternatively, a communication resource can be dedicated to transmission and reception, in which case there needs to be clear demarcation in time between those timeslots allocated to transmission and those allocated to reception. Because of the time separation between transmit and receive resources, this technique is termed Time Division Duplex (TDD). The Digital Enhanced Cordless Telecommunications (DECT) system is one example of a communication system that uses TDMA with TDD.

GSM uses a TDMA frame structure of 60/13 milliseconds (4.615 milliseconds) that is split into eight timeslots (TS0 to TS7) of length 0.577 milliseconds, as shown in Figure 1-14. Because timeslots cannot overlap, TDMA systems require the use of tight synchronization and guard periods, during which no transmissions occur. For example, Figure 1-14 shows that a GSM timeslot includes 8.25 bits of guard period out of a total timeslot duration of 156.25 bits, equivalent to over 5% of the overall communications resource.

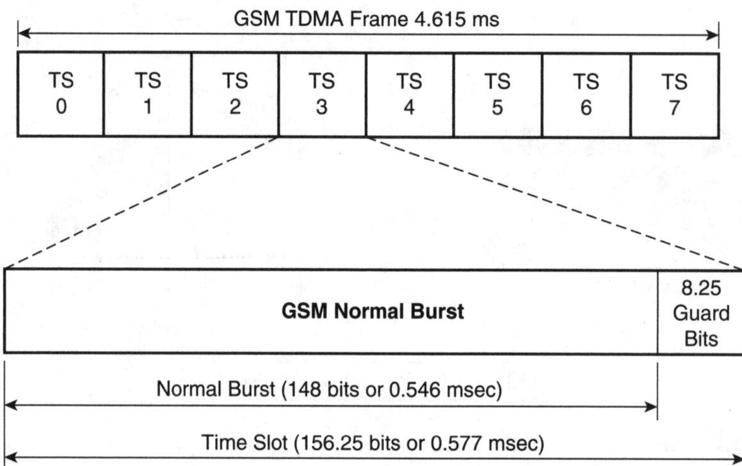

Figure 1-14 *TDMA Frame Structure*

When sending information, each user will be allocated one or more timeslots for transmitting and receiving information. In this way, users with more information to send can be allocated a larger percentage of the shared communications resource in order to support higher transfer speeds. Figure 1-15 highlights the multislot capability of the GSM system, where multiple timeslots can be allocated to a single user.

The figure shows the basic timeslot allocation of a single timeslot for receive (Rx), one for Transmit (Tx) and another timeslot for monitoring neighboring cells (Mn). The single timeslot operation is able to support 14.4-kbps service. Because GSM operates in FDD mode, a terminal can use a single radio, which can be switched between receive and transmit operation, allowing time to re-tune the oscillator frequency between bursts. The eight-slot TDMA frame allows different combinations of transmit and receive timeslots. The 2 + 2 configuration highlights how two timeslots can be allocated to reception and transmission, increasing the aggregate throughput to 28.8 kbps. Alternatively, the allocation may be asymmetrical with Figure 1-15 also showing a 3 + 1 multislot configuration that, assuming each slot can support 14.4 kbps, is able to support transmission speeds of 43.2 kbps in the downlink.

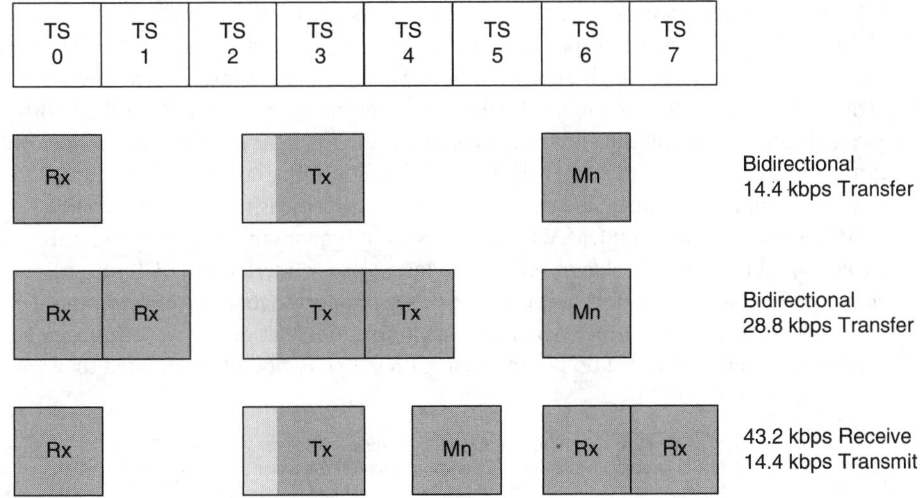

Figure 1-15 *TDMA Multislot Configuration*

Frequency Division Multiple Access

Frequency Division Multiple Access (FDMA) allows a number of users to share a communications resource by segmenting the resource into separate subcarriers and allocating individual subcarriers to one user at a time. In traditional mobile radio systems, a user was allocated a single subcarrier at any one time. For example, in the GSM system, a single user is allocated a 200-kHz channel during a particular time duration (corresponding to a TDMA frame). Because a large cell site will likely support multiple subcarriers, the same timeslot can be occupied by different users accessing using different subcarriers. Figure 1-16 shows three users simultaneously accessing via Timeslot 3, with each accessing via a different subcarrier.

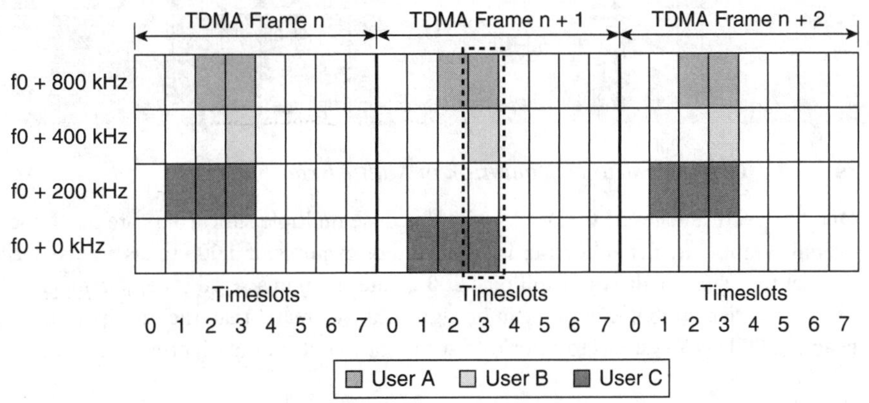

Figure 1-16 *Traditional FDMA Access*

Whereas traditional FDMA systems have operated in single-carrier mode, more recently FDMA techniques have been applied to multicarrier systems. In contrast to GSM, where a user is only allocated a single subcarrier at one particular time instant, a multicarrier FDMA user can be allocated multiple subcarriers, or tones, at a particular instant with each subcarrier being modulated independently. If the frequency separation between subcarriers is selected to be an integer of the modulating symbol rate, the tones are said to be orthogonal to each other, and the multiple access scheme is termed Orthogonal FDMA (OFDMA). With OFDMA, a receiver with optimum sampling and perfect frequency synchronization is able to reduce the Inter-Carrier Interference (ICI) to zero. Figure 1-17 shows the receiver outputs for five separate orthogonal tones over time. The figure shows that at the correct sampling instant, the contributions of the neighboring tones sum to zero and hence do not interfere with the reception of the wanted tone.

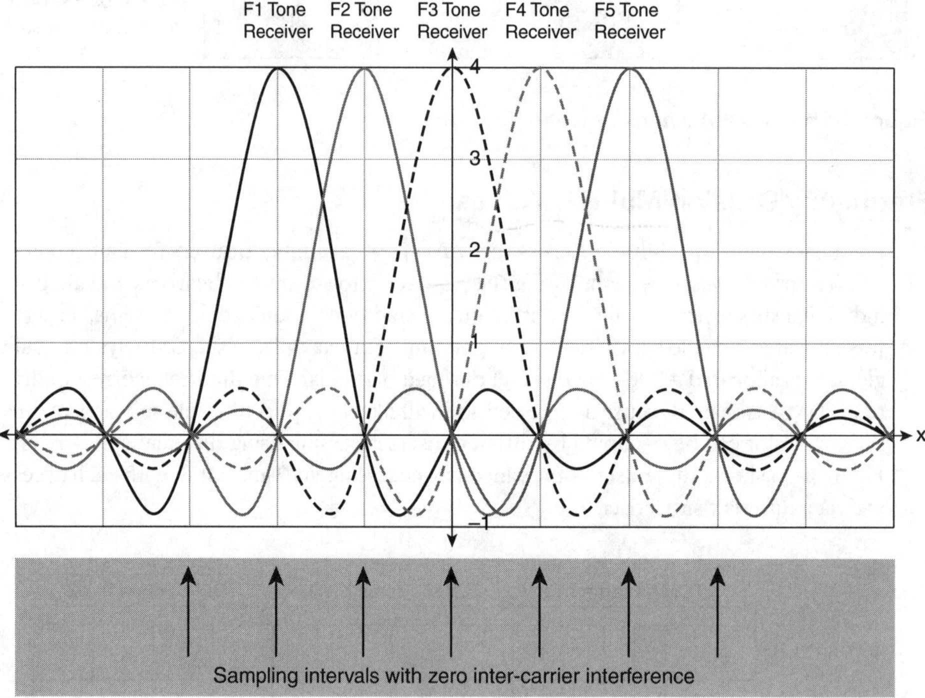

Figure 1-17 *Orthogonal Tone Separation in Multicarrier FDMA*

One of the advantages of OFDMA is that because multiple subcarriers are used, the overall symbol rate per subcarrier is reduced. For example, if 1,000 tones are used, the parallel tone symbol duration will be 1,000 greater than in a serial tone system, and this new subcarrier symbol duration can be significantly greater than the multipath duration, enabling OFDMA systems to offer robust mitigation of multipath effects.

Another advantage of OFDMA systems becomes apparent as the bandwidth/number of tones increases such that the channel experiences frequency selective fading. In such circumstances, the fading experienced by the tones at the lower end of the channel bandwidth will be de-correlated with the fading experienced by the tones at the upper end of the channel bandwidth, such that the effects of frequency selective fading are diminished.

Figure 1-18 shows an OFDMA system with 15 kHz subcarrier separation. The figure highlights how OFDMA enables users to be assigned multiple subcarriers in particular timeslots.

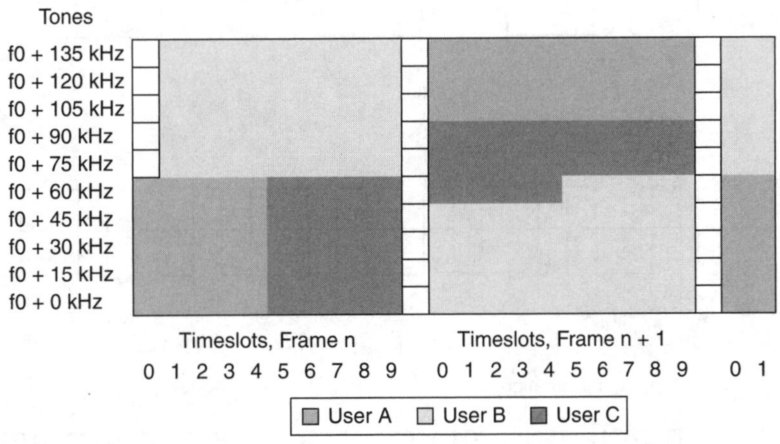

Figure 1-18 *Multiuser Operation in OFDMA*

Unfortunately, one of the disadvantages of OFDMA systems is that a handset transmitter needs to be able to transmit parallel tones simultaneously. The combination of these individual tones combine to generates a time waveform with a high Peak-to-Average Power Ratio (PAPR). A high PAPR places additional requirements on the linearity of the power amplifier. Linearity is normally increased by de-rating a particular amplifier, leading to decreased efficiency. Although inefficient or more expensive power amplifiers are not necessarily critical issues for the base station designer, they do pose challenges in the uplink where a decrease in terminal transmitter efficiency might decrease the maximum transmission time or lead to degraded uplink performance/coverage compared to the performance of single-carrier systems. In Chapter 3, we introduce techniques used by OFDMA-based mobile systems for reducing PAPR.

Code Division Multiple Access

Code Division Multiple Access (CDMA) is the key multiple access technology used in today's third-generation cellular systems, being the foundation for both 3GPP's WCDMA and 3GPP2's cdma2000 wireless systems and their respective evolutions to support mobile broadband data. CDMA operates by using special spreading codes to artificially increase the symbol rate of the information to a chip rate of the spreading code; the information to be transmitted is logically exclusive-ORed with the spreading code. (Exclusive-ORing is a logical function where precisely one input must be 1 [true] for the output to be 1 [true].) Figure 1-19 shows an example of spreading factor of 8 (where Td, the information bit duration of the original data, is 8 times Tc, the chip-timing duration).

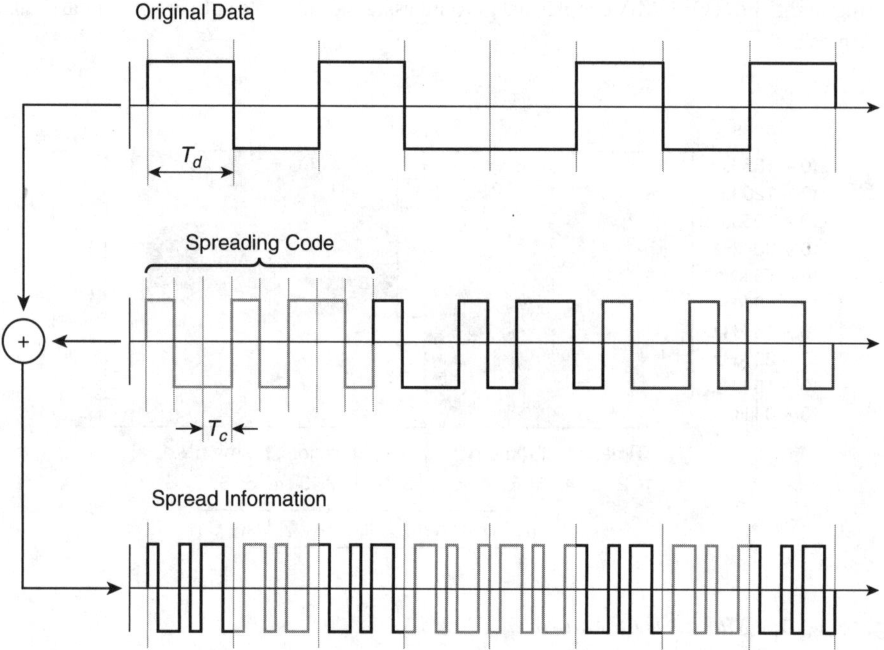

Figure 1-19 *Spread Spectrum Operation*

The spreading codes have special orthogonal properties that allow a particular user's information to be recovered from the composite waveform. Figure 1-20 shows an example of orthogonal spreading codes. Here, eight codes are shown with zero cross-correlation properties. The cross-correlation of two sequences is calculated using the vector product of two sequences.

When correctly synchronized, the vector product of sequence S1 and sequence S2 is equal to zero, as shown in Figure 1-21.

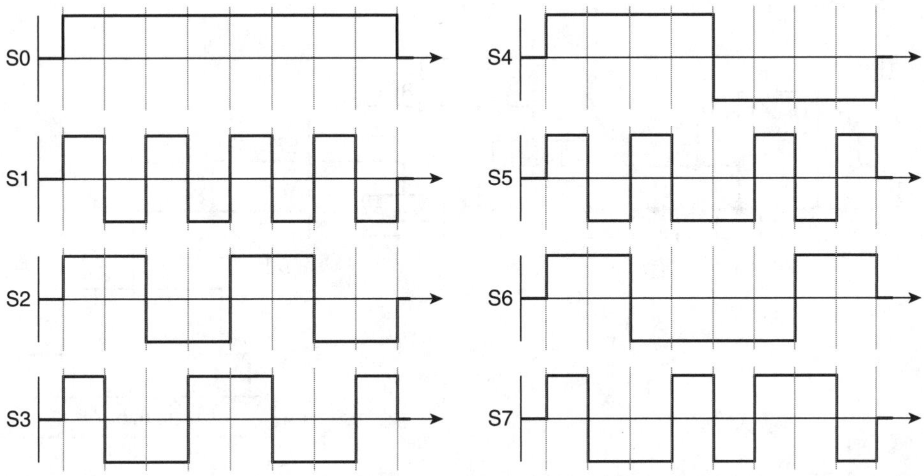

Figure 1-20 *Orthogonal Spreading Sequences*

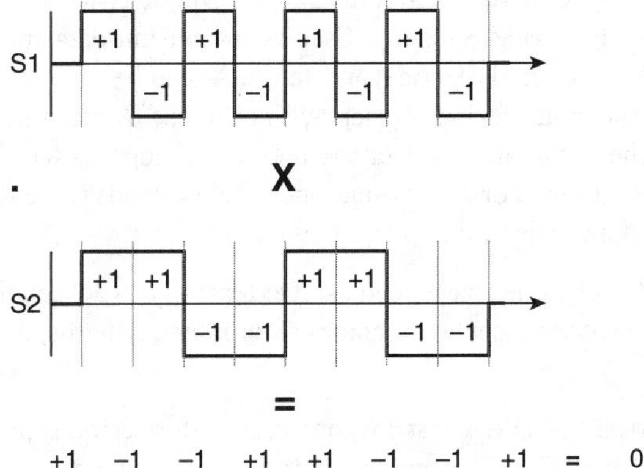

Figure 1-21 *Sequence Cross-Correlation Calculation*

Because of the good cross-correlation properties, each user can be allocated a separate spreading code and the receiver is still able to recover the original data from the combined waveform.

Instead of defining the use of fixed spreading codes in a system, Variable Spreading Factor (VSF) codes can be used. The different spreading factors result in different code lengths and allow different source rates to be effectively combined while still preserving orthogonality between the different users/sources. This is achieved by using an Orthogonal Variable Spreading Factor (OSVF) code, which can be represented by a code tree together with smart code allocation. Figure 1-22 shows a code tree that has codes up to 64 bits long.

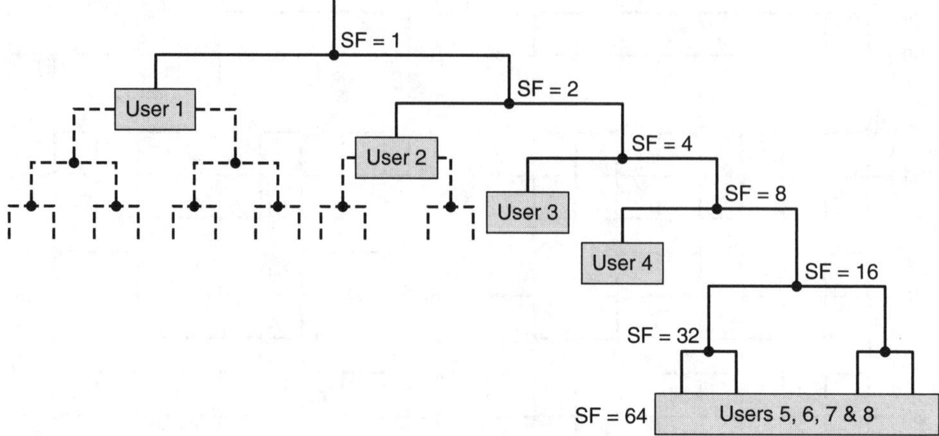

Figure 1-22 *Orthogonal Variable Spreading Factor Codes*

The code tree shows how eight users have been allocated different codes corresponding to different spreading factors. User 1 has been allocated a code with spreading factor 2 (SF=2). The rate at which User 1 can transmit data will be twice as fast as User 2, who has been allocated an SF=4 code. Similarly, User 2 can transmit data at a rate double User 3, who has been allocated an SF=8 code, and so on. As can be seen, the adoption of OVSF codes allows for the multiplexing of users with different IP data rate requirements. Note, however, that if the instantaneous data rate needs to change, as will frequently be the case during an IP session, corresponding functionality needs to be defined, which enables the spreading code to be updated in real time.

Although CDMA techniques have been used extensively in 3G cellular systems, they do have some unique challenges when it comes to supporting high-speed IP services, as follows:

- **Power Control:** In CDMA systems, one user's information signal is another user's noise source. If all CDMA users transmitted at the same power level, the base station will be able to decode those signals from those users near to the base station, whereas those signals from distant users will be perturbed by high levels of interference (the so-called near-far problem). In order to solve this, CDMA systems must include fast power control; for example, in UMTS, the power control is updated 1,500 times per second.[9] The efficiency of any power control system will decrease as the burstiness of traffic increases.
- **Low Spreading Factor Support:** Many of the advantages of CDMA are apparent only for high spreading factors. As the IP bandwidth requirements increase, the spreading factors decrease, leading to a decrease in CDMA efficiency.

Space Division Multiple Access

Space Division Multiple Access (SDMA) is an emerging technology for improving the throughput and capacity of mobile wireless systems. SDMA involves using advanced antenna systems and spatial signal processing to isolate the communications resources between multiple users, enabling those users to operate in the same channel simultaneously. Figure 1-23 shows how an eight-element base station is able to calculate the spatial signatures of the two users, effectively allowing re-use of the same frequency within the same cell.

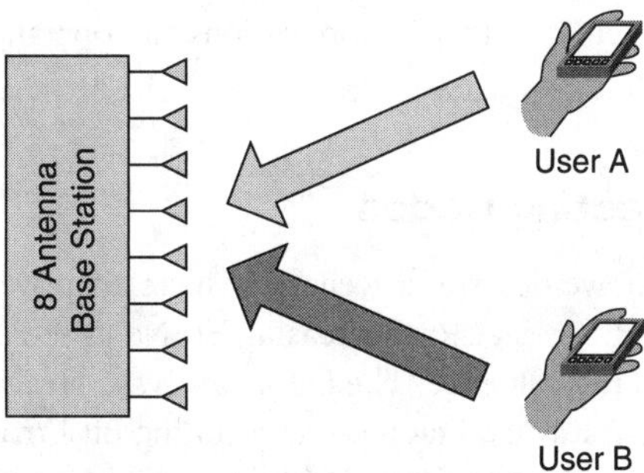

- Capture the spatial signatures of User A and User B.
- Based on the signatures of User A and B, construct the optimal Beam Forming weight A and B.
- Apply the weight A and B to the uplink data streams of User A and User B.
- Joint detect data streams of User A and User B.

Figure 1-23 *Space Division Multiple Access*

It is anticipated that SDMA and Adaptive Antenna Techniques will be used for a variety of purposes in future mobile broadband systems, including the following:

- **Limiting co-channel interference:** The directional antenna patterns of SDMA decrease the downlink interference to other users in the same and neighboring cells, improving overall throughput.
- **Improving coverage:** The directional antenna gains of SDMA allow any Adaptive Modulation and Coding thresholds to be moved further away from the cell center, allowing more users to benefit from the throughput associated with higher-order modulation.
- **Stabilizing multipath:** The latest Multiple-Input Multiple-Output (MIMO) techniques take advantage of multipath propagation. SDMA techniques can be used to stabilize the multipath environment in outdoor environments, allowing an increasing percentage of macro-cellular users to benefit from MIMO gains.

SDMA techniques are not without their challenges. At the very least, conventional SDMA techniques rely on reciprocity between the uplink and the downlink channels. Although this is the case for Time Division Duplex (TDD) operation, where the same carrier is used for uplink and downlink transmission, the same is not true for Frequency Division Duplex (FDD), where there is a large frequency offset between the downlink channel and the uplink channel.

Combating Radio Impairments

This section introduces techniques that can be used to mitigate performance degradations, increasing the likelihood that IP applications can operate in such imperfect environments.

Forward Error-Correcting Codes

In the previous section, we described scenarios where adaptive modulation can be employed to minimize the effects of decreasing Eb/No as the user moves away from the center of a cell toward the cell edge. The fading analysis, however, has shown that when the channel suffers from Rayleigh fading, the resulting Bit Error Rates are significantly higher than those experienced in simple Additive White Gaussian Noise (AWGN) environments.

Forward Error-Correcting (FEC) codes add redundancy to the original information bits in a deterministic fashion, such that the receiver can correct and detect a certain subset of the errors received due to noise and interference impairments. FEC codes are characterized by their code rate, *R*, which indicates how much redundancy is added to the original information:

$$R = i/(i + r)$$

where *i* and *r* denote the number of information and check bits, respectively.

For example, a 1/3 rate FEC code transmits three coded bits for each information bit ($i=1$, $r=2$), and a 3/4 rate FEC code transmits four coded bits for every three original information bits ($i=3$, $r=1$).

The FEC operation decreases the probability that an IP packet will be received in error, reducing packet error rates and any delay associated with packet retransmission. However, the use of FEC coding effectively reduces the IP throughput, because the redundancy bits do not convey any new information. As a consequence, in order to enable systems with optimum throughput, systems that use adaptive modulation frequently define the use of adaptive FEC, which is a parallel technique where the amount of redundancy allocated to FEC coding is altered according to the prevailing channel conditions. The radio designer defines a range of FEC coding rates in order to accommodate different channel conditions. For example, in good propagation environments, the probability of a bit error will be low, so a high-rate code can be used (little additional redundancy added to the source information bits). Conversely, at the edge of a cell, even when using the lowest-order modulation, the probability of bit error might be high, so a low-rate code should be used.

The combination of adaptive modulation and adaptive FEC is termed Adaptive Modulation and Coding (AMC). Chapters 2 and 3 provide more details regarding the use of AMC in different wireless standards. As one example, 3GPP's High-Speed Downlink Packet Access (HSDPA) supports coding rates raging from 0.14 to 0.89.[10] When adaptive coding is used together with QPSK and 16-QAM operation, the nominal data rates supported can range from 68.5 kbps up to 12.779 Mbps, as shown in Table 1-5.

Table 1-5 *HSDPA Adaptive Modulation and Coding*

Modulation	Number of HS-DSCH*	Effective Code Rate	Instantaneous Data Rate
QPSK	1	0.14	0.07 Mbps
QPSK	1	0.27	0.13 Mbps
16 QAM	2	0.38	0.72 Mbps
16 QAM	5	0.65	3.10 Mbps
16 QAM	15	0.89	12.78 Mbps

*HS-DSCH = High-Speed Downlink Shared Channel

AMC is increasingly being adopted as a technique used to improve the overall throughput of next-generation mobile radio systems. This is important information for IP designers who need to accommodate transport over cellular systems; there might be a significant difference in the throughput available to those users in the good coverage toward the center of a cell and those users located at the edge of coverage.

Mitigating Multipath Effects

You can combat multipath effects using a variety of techniques, including the following:

- **Using channel equalization techniques:** Channel equalization involves estimating the impulse response or the multipath channel, and applying the inverse of this impulse so as to minimize the effects of Inter-Symbol Interference.

- **Using spread spectrum techniques:** Spread spectrum systems spread the signal energy over a wide band by decreasing the symbol duration by the processing gain of the system. The wide bandwidth makes spread spectrum systems more immune to narrow frequency nulls generated as a result of multipath fading. In CDMA systems, multiple correlator receivers, sometimes called *fingers*, are then used to independently decode the individual multipath components in the receiver. The contribution from all the correlator receivers are then combined (using a *Rake* receiver) in order to leverage the energy dispersed over different multipath components.

- **Using systems of parallel tone modems:** In OFDMA systems, the information to be transmitted is converted into a large number (*N*) of parallel streams. Each stream is used to modulate a narrow band subcarrier, with the overall transmission being comprised of *N* finely spaced subcarriers. The effective symbol rate of each of the subcarriers is decreased by a factor of *N*, resulting in the symbol duration being increased by a factor of *N*. If the new subcarrier symbol duration is significantly greater than the multipath delay spread, only a small guard period needs to be used in order to mitigate the effects of ISI and a simple receiver can be used to recover the original information.

- **Using frequency selective transmission:** In conventional systems, the frequency selective channel response can be combated by using frequency hopping. Frequency hopping systems use a pseudo-random hopping sequence to repeatedly change the carrier frequency of the transmitted modulated waveform. The pseudo-random sequence is known by the receiver, which synchronizes the sequence phase with the transmitter. If a slowly moving user is unfortunate enough to be positioned at a location of destructive interference for one frequency, there is a good probability that the location will not suffer destructive interference after the next frequency hop. In multicarrier systems, frequency selective multiple access can be achieved by smart allocation of tones. For an individual user, those tones that are exhibiting constructive interference are allocated in preference to those exhibiting destructive interference.

- **Interleaving:** The time-varying nature of Rayleigh fading, as shown previously in Figure 1-4, results in errors being generated in bursts corresponding to the nulls in the amplitude of the received signal. Unfortunately, Forward Error-Correcting (FEC) codes are not suited for correcting bursts of errors. Consequently, interleaving is a technique that is used to randomize the location of errors, ensuring that, even in the presence of multipath, the bit errors at the FEC decoder should be more uniformly distributed.

Note An unfortunate characteristic of interleaving is an increase in the end-to-end delay. For example, the GPRS system[11] interleaves one Radio Block over four consecutive TDMA frames. With one TDMA frame lasting 4.615 milliseconds, the use of the interleaver in GPRS to combat burst errors adds an additional 18 milliseconds to the packet transmission delay.

Radio systems frequently employ a range of techniques for mitigating multipath interference. For example, the GSM system includes a combination of equalization, frequency hopping, and interleaving in order to combat Rayleigh fading and Inter-Symbol Interference.

Complexity of Multipath Mitigation

As mobile radio systems move to increasingly supporting mobile broadband IP services, the overall peak throughput speeds required to be supported necessarily increase and the symbol durations correspondingly decrease. As data speeds increase, the use of a pure-spread spectrum Rake receiver technique is challenged, because the increase in speeds necessarily requires the spread spectrum processing gain to be decreased. The performance of the Rake receiver is dependent on a minimum processing gain, below which its performance becomes suboptimal, resulting in an error-floor that cannot be mitigated.

This has caused 3GPP to define the use of additional equalization techniques, previously avoided in 3G systems because of their computation complexity. Analysis[12] has shown that such advanced receivers can improve the performance of HSDPA in the pedestrian environment, increasing the average throughput from around 30 kbps to 90 kbps when the user is located at the edge of a cell and from around 700 kbps to 1,200 kbps when the user is located near the center of the cell.

The problem with relying on equalizers to combat the impairments generated by multipath propagation is their complexity, which rises rapidly with system bandwidth. Complexity comparisons have been performed by Van Nee and Prasad,[13] contrasting the implementation of a 24-MBps modem realized using a Gaussian Minimum Shift Keying (GMSK) serial modem (a type of frequency modulation used by the original GSM system) and an OFDM multicarrier implementation. The analysis estimates that in terms of multiplications per second, the equalization of the single-carrier GMSK system is ten times more complex than the Fast Fourier Transform (FFT) required for OFDMA reception. The OFDMA FFT complexity grows only slightly faster that the product of the bandwidth-delay spread product—that is, a function of the relative amount of Inter-Symbol Interference, compared to the equalizer-based solutions that have complexity growing at the square of the bandwidth-delay spread product.

As IP data rates increase, transmission bandwidths will increase further, and OFDMA's advantage over single carrier will more than likely continue to grow.

Smart Scheduling

Previous voice-centric mobile radio systems used deterministic scheduling; for example, these systems used a round-robin procedure, where the system would attempt to use a range of techniques to combat the multipath fading conditions experienced in the allocated scheduling interval. The move to data-centric mobile radio systems enables the radio design engineer to leverage the increased jitter tolerance of IP applications by defining the use of smart schedulers. Smart schedulers leverage the fact that when considering IP data transmissions in a multiuser system, some users may be momentarily disadvantaged by being located in a region of destructive multipath interference, whereas others will benefit from being located in a region of constructive multipath interference.

Techniques termed *multiuser diversity* are used to segment the resources on a time basis; during each time interval, the system is able to determine the instantaneous fading environment on a per-user basis. This information is used to decide which user to serve in each time interval. Compared to the deterministic round-robin scheduler, which would expend power to provide a degraded service through the deep fading nulls (for example, using a low-order modulation and high coding rate), the smart scheduler expends the same amount of power, offering higher throughput to a more advantaged user (for example, using a high-order modulation and low coding rate). Because of the time-varying nature of the multipath fading, the users who were momentarily disadvantaged will most likely find themselves being served at some later time when their multipath fading resulted in constructive interference. Figure 1-24 shows the scheduling to two users based on their respective instantaneous fading characteristics, showing how both users are served using a smart scheduler. Because transmission power is used more efficiently, the system throughput of the multiuser diversity smart-scheduling system increases over the case of the simple deterministic scheduler.

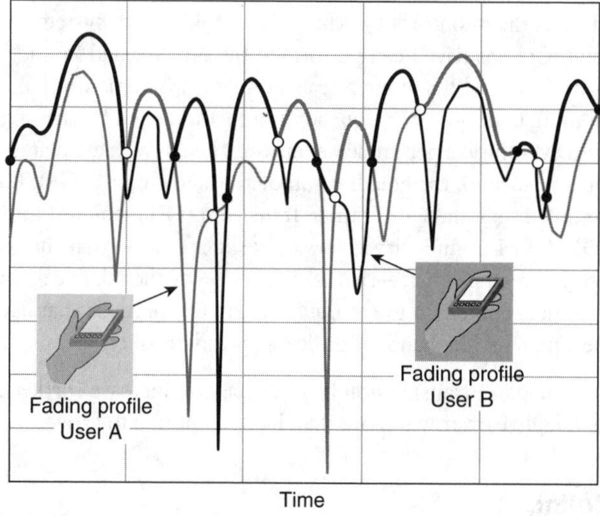

Figure 1-24 *Smart Scheduling Using Multiuser Diversity*

The scheduling algorithm defines how the shared radio resources are divided between the multiple users in a cell. These algorithms can be characterized by the scheduling metric (M_n), which is used to determine which of the n users to allocate radio resources to in the timing interval. If r_n is the instantaneous rate that a user n can support, a *Maximum C/I* scheduler will set the scheduling metric M_n equal to r_n, so as to dedicate resources to the user with the highest r_n value, as demonstrated previously in Figure 1-24. A *Maximum C/I* scheduler ensures that the throughput of the cell is maximized as resources are dedicated to a small subset of users in preferential coverage. Unfortunately, those users who are experiencing less-preferential propagation conditions (for example, those located at the edge of a cell) will be starved of resources.

In order to normalize the scheduling metric and remove the effects of wide-ranging propagation losses across a cell, the Proportional Fair (PF) scheduler has been defined, which uses a scheduling metric M_n equal to $r_n/Avg(R_n)$; R_n is the average data rate for user *n*. This then equates to scheduling users "at the top of their fades" but also ensures that those users in disadvantaged locations would have their scheduling priority increased over time as $Avg(R_n)$ slowly decreases.

Under optimum conditions and for best-effort traffic, HSDPA simulations have shown that the proportional fair scheduler offers up to 130% capacity improvements over round-robin scheduling. However, as the user speed increases, the fading environment becomes less temporally stable, and so the scheduler is less likely to be able to estimate the instantaneous r_n achievable during the subsequent scheduling instances and the benefits of PF scheduling diminish.

The adoption of smart-scheduling algorithms impact the average delay experienced by the transmitted IP packets. Typically those schedulers that optimize throughput result in degraded delay characteristics. In the extreme example of the Maximum C/I scheduler, certain users will be starved of resources, and the associated packet delay will continue to increase until the user changes location. Consequently, smart schedulers normally define a Discard Timer, which specifies the maximum queuing delay after which the scheduler will drop a packet.

Figure 1-25 illustrates the results of performed simulations[14] of the HSDPA queuing delay per TCP segment in a typical low-speed environment using a Proportional Fair scheduler. The results show that optimization for mobile broadband services requires careful tradeoffs between cell throughput and packet delay characteristics.

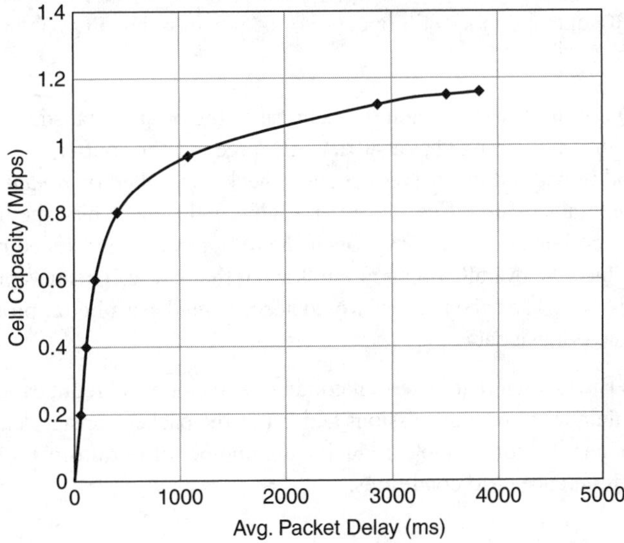

Figure 1-25 *HSDPA Proportional Fair Throughput versus Average Queuing Delay*

Automatic Repeat Request

Because degraded conditions might still generate a residual BER even after FEC decoding, additional techniques need to be applied in situations where error-free transmission is important. In conventional 3G data services, the Radio Link Control (RLC) layer has traditionally been the location where Non-Real-Time (NRT) services could receive error-correction capabilities. In UMTS, the RLC can operate in Acknowledged Mode (AM), which uses Automatic Repeat Request (ARQ) functionality. In RLC-AM operation (the default mode for packet-based services), error-detection capabilities together with a selective repeat operation for error correction are defined.

The centralization of the network-side RLC functionality in traditional mobile radio systems results in substantial retransmission delays between this and the peer RLC functionality in the radio terminal. These delays further degrade the performance of the RLC operation with the mean packet delay increasing as a function of BLock Error Rate (BLER). Typical mean packet delays due to UMTS RLC-AM operation can easily be shown to be in excess of 150 ms,[15] unfortunately leading to interactions with timers integrated into higher-layer protocols such as TCP. In Chapter 9, "Content and Services," we provide more detail of how TCP can be optimized for wireless operation.

To combat the excessive delays of centralized ARQ processing, more recent mobile broadband systems including High-Speed Downlink Packet Access (HSDPA), EVolution Data Only (EV-DO), and WiMAX have all adopted Hybrid-ARQ (H-ARQ), which integrates FEC functionality with the ARQ process.

Note In addition, to reduce the retransmission delays, the newly introduced H-ARQ functionality in these mobile broadband systems is typically located in the base station. Centralized ARQ operation may still operate to recover from H-ARQ failures.

The H-ARQ re-transmissions might be identical to the original transmission, called *chase combining*, or if the receiver has a sufficiently large memory buffer, the retransmission might instead provide additional redundancy/check bits, called *incremental redundancy*. If the original transmission used i information bits and r check bits, the first transmission would have a coding rate of $i/(i+r)$. Now if the re-transmission included r_{add} additional redundancy bits, the overall coding rate following the first re-transmission would be equal to $i/(i+r+r_{add})$ and the receiver would accordingly have a better probability of recovering the original data.

Simulations have shown that in certain conditions, incremental redundancy can decrease the average number of re-transmissions and hence the packet transfer delay compared to chase combining,[16]—for example, reducing the number of re-transmissions by 4 for low carrier-to-interference ratio conditions.

Diversity Combining

Diversity combining is used to combine the multiple signals received over different fading multipath components. The concept holds that if the fading experienced by the different components is independent, the chances of different signals received over diverse paths experiencing deep fades simultaneously is dramatically reduced; if the probability of a single Rayleigh fading signal experiencing a fade in excess of 20 dB is 1%, the probability that simultaneous fades in excess of 20 dB will occur on two independent signals is 0.01%. The diversity in a system is characterized by the number of independently fading diversity paths or branches, also known as the diversity order. There is a diminishing combining gain as the diversity order increases, where the greatest degree of improvement in performance is achieved by going from a single-branch system (no-diversity) to a second-order system with two diversity branches.

Note The Hybrid-ARQ combining techniques described in the previous section are examples of time-diversity. If the different re-transmissions are separated in time by a period greater than T_s, where $Ts = \lambda/2V$ and V is the user's velocity relative to the base station and λ is the wavelength of the carrier frequency, the signals will be de-correlated and diversity gains will be obtained.

Antenna diversity refers to the use of spatially separated antennas for generating the independent signals necessary for delivering diversity combining gains. The antenna separation required to generate uncorrelated signals has been shown to be equal to 0.4 λ at the mobile.[17] At the base station, measurements have indicated that horizontally spaced antennas need to be separated by 10–30λ for the correlation between antennas to be less than 0.7.[18]

Antenna diversity has been primarily used in the uplink on cellular systems. More recently, mobile receive diversity has been added to EV-DO and HSDPA systems, where it has been shown to assist in increasing data rates and sector capacity—for example, increasing the sector throughput from 1.24 Mbps with EV-DO Revision 0 to 1.5 Mbps with 2-Receive forward link diversity.[19]

Spatial Multiplexing

Many of the techniques described in the preceding sections concentrated on attempting to mitigate the degradations generated by the multipath mobile radio channel. *Spatial multiplexing* is a technique that looks to leverage the separate multipath components, using each as an independent channel to enable multiple data streams to be transmitted at the same frequency but over different spatial channels. Because the spatial multiplexing procedure requires multiple receive and transmit antennas to realize the multiplexing gains, the technique is often referred to as *Multiple-Input Multiple-Output (MIMO)*. Spatial multiplexing techniques have been adopted by IEEE 802.11n, IEEE 802.16e/WiMAX, HSDPA, EV-DO, and LTE radio systems.

Figure 1-26 shows an example of a 4x4 MIMO system, so called because of the four transmit and four receive antennas. In general, an array of N_{tx} transmitting antennas and N_{rx} receiving antennas can provide a spatial multiplexing order of SM_{order} = MIN (N_{tx}, N_{rx}), which allows SM_{order} parallel streams to be simultaneously transmitted, effectively increasing the spectral throughput by SM_{order}.

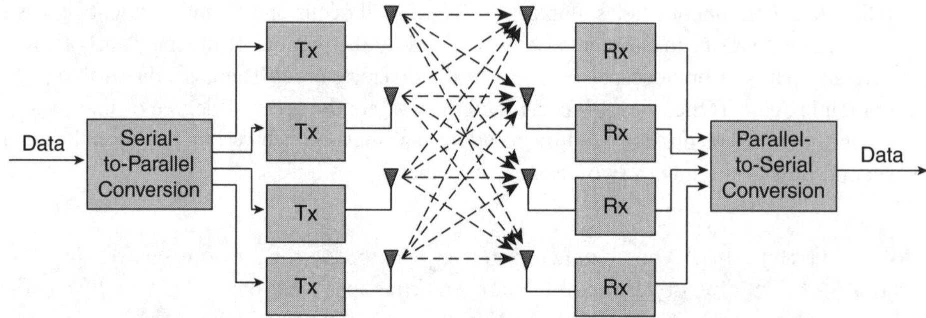

Figure 1-26 *4x4 MIMO Spatial Multiplexing System*

The capacity enhancements of spatial multiplexing requires a certain Signal-to-Interference-and-Noise Ratio (SINR) that enables sufficiently high SINRs on the parallel streams to achieve the overall increase in throughput. Simulations[20] have indicated that the SINR needs to be greater than 12 dB to achieve the gains promised by spatial multiplexing.

Note The very high throughput figures often used in marketing mobile broadband services that rely on MIMO operation will only be available to those users experiencing high SINR, and will thus typically be available to less than 10% of users in a particular cell. This, coupled with the use of AMC, will increase the disparity in mobile broadband services offered to those users in good coverage toward the center of a cell and those users at the edge of cell coverage.

Below these levels, the same MIMO concepts can be re-used to enhance coverage using Space Time Codes (STC), where instead of transmitting different data over parallel streams, a single stream of data is replicated and transmitted over the multiple antennas such that the transmit sequences from each antenna are orthogonal. Figure 1-27 shows an orthogonal Space Time matrix used for a rate-1 STC with two transmit antennas; the figure demonstrates how the matrix is used to map the streams of modulated symbols to the different antennas over time. The gains obtained using Space Time Coding with N_{tx}=2 transmit antennas and N_{rx} receive antennas is equivalent to providing a diversity order of $2N_{rx}$[21].

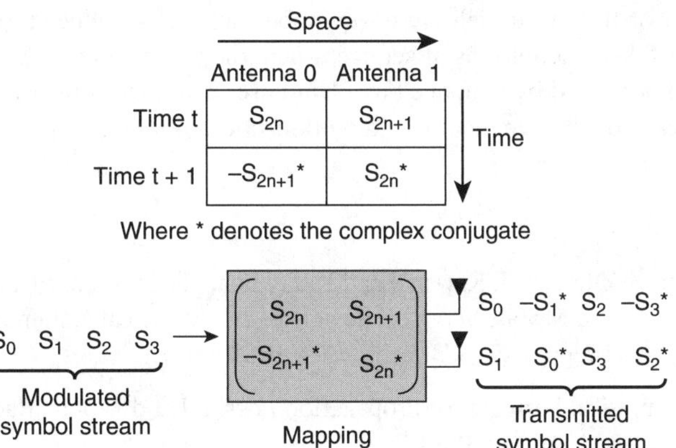

Figure 1-27 *Space Time Coding*

This leads to the definition of systems that use Space Time Coding techniques when the SINR is low to extend the reach of mobile radio systems and spatial multiplexing techniques when the SINR is high in order to increase the spectral efficiency and throughput delivered by mobile radio system.

Note WiMAX has defined its own MIMO nomenclature, specifying the use of 2x2 antenna configurations for both Space Time Coding, which in WiMAX is termed "Matrix-A," and spatial multiplexing, which in WiMAX is termed "Matrix-B."

Summary

The evolution of cellular systems from legacy car phone-centric systems, created to deliver narrow band voice services to outdoor users, toward systems optimized for the economical delivery of high-bandwidth IP services to users located both outdoors and indoors, creates significant challenges for the radio engineer. A level of background is necessary to understand the key compromises faced when trying to design a system, carefully balancing those characteristics that impact the performance of IP services supported by the latest mobile broadband systems.

Compared to legacy systems where service availability could be defined in binary terms (either voice service was available or not), the range of techniques used to increase the peak throughput of mobile broadband systems leads to an increasing disparity between services delivered to different users; the operation of Adaptive Modulation and Coding, Hybrid-ARQ, multiuser diversity, and spatial multiplexing are all techniques that preferentially benefit those users in good coverage conditions compared to those experiencing worse conditions.

The designer of IP services delivered over mobile networks will need to increasing adopt a more probabilistic definitions of service, where the throughput, latency, and jitter characteristics experienced by a mobile broadband user may vary considerably across the cell coverage area and between indoor- and outdoor-located users.

Endnotes

[1]Y. Okumura, E. Ohmori, T. Kawana, and K. Fukuda, "Field Strength and Its Variability in VHF and UHF Land Mobile Service," Review of the Electrical Communications Laboratory, Vol. 16, pp. 825–873, Sept.–Oct. 1968.

[2]M. Hata, "Empirical Formula for Propagation Loss in Land Mobile Radio," IEEE Trans. VT-29, pp. 317–325, August 1980.

[3]http://www.wimaxforum.org/technology/downloads/comparative_analysis_of_spectrum_alternatives_for_wimax_networks_with_scenarios_based_on_the_us_700_mhz_band.pdf.

[4]http://www.agbnielsen.co.nz/Common/Files/Downloads/TAMWise_03_2006_press.pdf.

[5]O.W. Ata, "In-building Penetration Loss Modeling and Measurement in Suburban, Urban, and Dense Urban Morphologies," IEEE Int. Symp. on Antennas and Propagation, pp. 779–782, July 2005.

[6]http://cnfrs.institut-telecom.fr/pages/pages_evenements/journees_scient/docs_journees_2008/GATI-JS08.pdf.

[7]http://www.signalsresearch.com/Mobile%20Broadband%20Wireless%20Aug%2007.pdf.

[8]IEEE Std 802.16-2004, "IEEE Standard for Local and Metropolitan Area Networks—Part 16: Air Interface for Fixed Broadband Access Systems," October 2004.

[9]3GPP TS 25.214, "Physical Layer Procedures (FDD)."

[10]3GPP TS 25.321, "Medium Access Control (MAC) Protocol Specification," RTS/TSGR-0225321v5d0.

[11]GSM 43.064, "Overall Description of the GPRS Radio Interface."

[12]A. Ghosh and R.A. Kobylinski, "Advanced Receiver Architectures for HSPA and Their Performance Benefits," Texas Wireless Symposium, pp. 49–53, 2005.

[13]R. Van Nee and R. Prasad, "OFDM for Wireless Multimedia Communications," Artech House, 2000.

[14]P.J.A. Gutierrez, "Packet Scheduling and Quality of Service in HSDPA", Ph.D. thesis, Aalborg University, 2003, http://kom.aau.dk/ADM/research/reports/PhDThesis_Pablo_Ameigeiras.pdf

[15]N. Enderle and X. Lagrange, "Radio Link Control-Acknowledged Mode Protocol Performance Modeling in UMTS," 4th Int. Workshop of Mobile Wireless Communications Network, pp. 332–336, 2002.

[16]Performance Comparison of Chase Combining and Incremental Redundancy in HSDPA, 3GPP TSG RAN1, TSGR1#17(00)1428, www.3gpp1.org/ftp/tsg_ran/ WG1_RL1/ TSGR1_17/Docs/PDFs/R1-00-1428.pdf.

[17]W.C.Y. Lee, "Mobile Communications Engineering," McGraw-Hill, 1982.

[18]L. Aydin, et al, "Reverse Link Capacity and Coverage Improvement for CDMA Cellular Systems Using Polarization and Spatial Diversity," IEEE Int. Conf. on Comms., Vol. 3, pp. 1887–1892, 2002.

[19]"Beyond 3G, Part II (the CDMA2000 & 1xEV-DO evolution)," Signalsahead, Vol. 2, No. 16, August 31, 2005, http://www.signalsresearch.com/Links/ Signals%20Ahead%200831.pdf.

[20]Na Wei, "MIMO Techniques for UTRA Long-Term Evolution," PhD Thesis, Aalborg University, 2007.

[21]S.A. Alamouti, "A Simple Transmit Diversity Technique for Wireless Communications," IEEE J. on Sel. Areas in Comms., Vol. 16, No. 8, pp. 1451–1458, October 1998.

Chapter 2

Cellular Access Systems

This chapter builds on the introduction to radio systems outlined in Chapter 1, "Introduction to Radio Systems," and demonstrates how the various techniques have been used to develop mobile access systems. The chapter describes how cellular access systems have traditionally decomposed functionality between radio base station elements and base station controller equipment, with legacy Time-Division Multiplexing (TDM) or Asynchronous Transfer Mode (ATM)-defined interfaces between the two. The chapter then describes how IP is fundamentally impacting these access systems in two distinct ways, as follows:

- **IP in the transport network:** Access System interfaces are increasingly being defined using IP protocols and thus the significance of IP in the transport network is increasing.
- **IP over radio bearers:** The wide-scale adoption of IP-based mobile services is causing a re-architecting of the access systems away from hierarchical voice-centric circuit-switched services toward being optimized for IP-based services.

Note Whereas this chapter focuses on how the influence of IP is changing Access System design, Chapter 6, "Mobile Core Evolution," defines the corresponding core network aspects that are necessary for delivering end-to-end IP services over the Radio Access Network (RAN) toward the mobile device; the access system deals with the physical and link layer specifics of the radio system, whereas the mobile core network deals with access-agnostic Layer 3 signaling and upper-layer service support.

The cellular access systems described can be defined as follows:

- **Pre-IMT-2000 systems:** Specifically, the Global System for Mobile communications (GSM) and its enhancements, namely the General Packet Radio Service (GPRS) and Enhanced Data Rates for GSM Evolution (EDGE), used to provide IP service capability.

- **IMT-2000 systems:** Includes Wideband Code Division Multiple Access (WCDMA) (often referred to as Universal Mobile Telephone System, or UMTS), as well as the competing cdma2000 1xRTT system.
- **Enhanced IMT-2000 systems:** Includes the evolution of WCDMA systems to support High-Speed Packet Access (HSPA) and the evolution of cdma2000 1xRTT to support EVolution Data Only (EV-DO) high-speed packet capabilities.

The evolution of the access systems described in this chapter will clearly demonstrate how IP is increasing in relevance to the traditional cellular network designer, both from a transport and services perspective. Chapter 3, "All-IP Access Systems," will then provide detail of those access systems that have been designed as end-to-end IP systems.

The GSM Access System

The GSM system was designed in the late 1980s and originally comprised a Base Station Subsystem (BSS) and a Network Switching Subsystem (NSS). Figure 2-1 shows the Mobile Station (MS) connecting to the BSS over the *Um* interface and how the BSS can be further decomposed into a Base Transceiver Station (BTS), which is controlled by a Base Station Controller (BSC) with the *Abis* interface connecting the two. The BSS interfaces to the NSS over the *A* interface. The NSS has since been renamed the Core Network, and Chapter 6 provides detailed description of the Core Network.

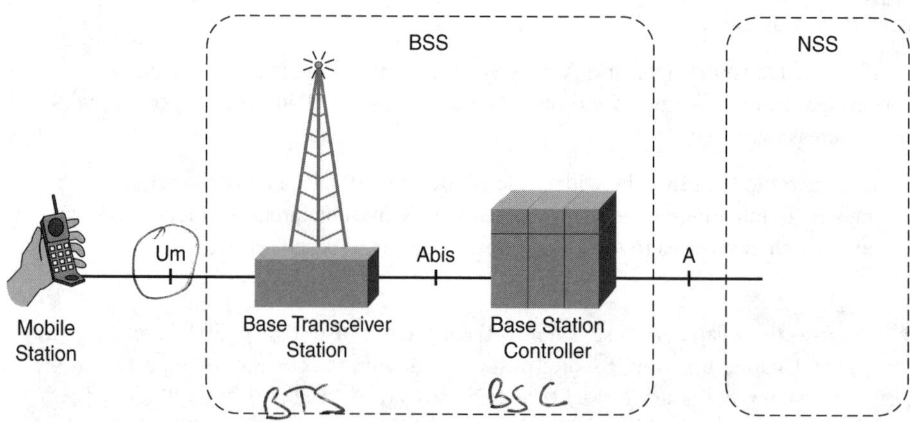

Figure 2-1 *GSM Base Station Subsystem and Interface Names*

The BTS includes all the radio equipment for supporting the physical layer channels, including modulating and demodulating signals to/from the MS over the Um interface, as well as channel coding and encryption. The BSC will typically manage tens, and in some deployments hundreds, of BTSs. The BSC handles control and bearer-plane traffic to and from these BTSs, as well as operations and maintenance messages. The BSC also includes some elementary switching capability, which enables it to map between terrestrial connections to the NSS and logical radio channels toward the BTS. This switching capability is used to support the handoff of channels between neighboring BTSs when a mobile station moves from one cell to another, as well as between different channel configurations controlled by the same BTS.

Protocol Architecture of GSM Access System

The GSM BSS defines the protocol stacks between the MS, BTS, and BSC, as shown in Figure 2-2.

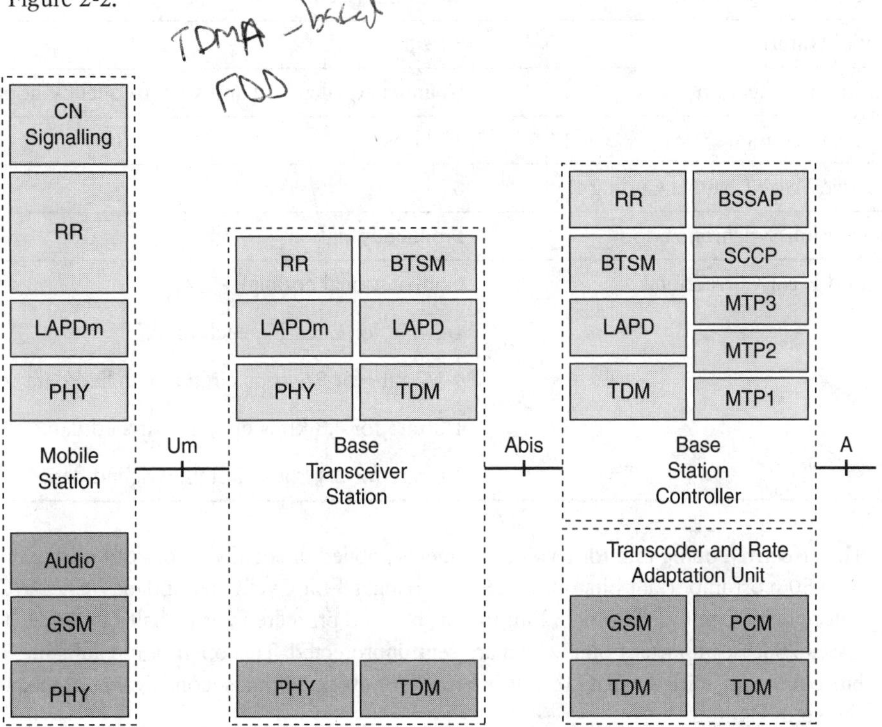

Figure 2-2 *GSM BSS Protocols*

GSM Physical Layer

On the Um interface, the physical or PHY layer uses a Time Division Multiple Access (TDMA)-based FDD system, where each voice user is nominally allocated one out of eight slots within a TDMA frame. The other key attributes of the GSM Physical layer are shown in Table 2-1.

Table 2-1 *GSM Physical Layer Attributes*

Duplex	**FDD**
Channel Bandwidth	200 kHz
Modulation Type	Gaussian Minimum Shift Keying (GMSK)
Multiple Access Technique	TDMA
Time Slots per TDMA Frame	8
TDMA Frame Duration	4.615 milliseconds
Symbol Duration	3.69 μs
Multipath Mitigation	Channel equalization and slow frequency hopping
Voice Source Rate	13 kbps
Effective Voice Channel Coding Rate	0.57
Base Station Synchronization	Frequency only
Forward Error Correction	Convolutional coding: 1/2 rate for Class I speech bits ~ 1/2 rate for 9.6 kbps circuit-switched data 1/3 rate for 4.8 kbps circuit-switched data 1/6 rate for 2.4 kbps circuit-switched data

The effective coding rate for a voice channel is applied unequally across the source bits, with 50 most important bits out of 260 receiving a 3-bit Cyclic Redundancy Check (CRC) before being combined with 132 important bits and protected with a half-rate code. This leaves 78 least-important bits, which are sent unprotected. This operation results in 456 bits being transmitted across the air interface for every 20 milliseconds voice frame, as shown in Figure 2-3.

In the GSM system, the PHY layer is additionally responsible for performing the encryption—in other words, ciphering is only defined to be performed between the MS and the BTS.

Note Chapter 6 describes the signaling exchanges by which the core network authenticates the user, and Chapter 8, "End-to-End Context Awareness," defines the authentication algorithms and how shared keying material is generated for use by the stream ciphers.

½

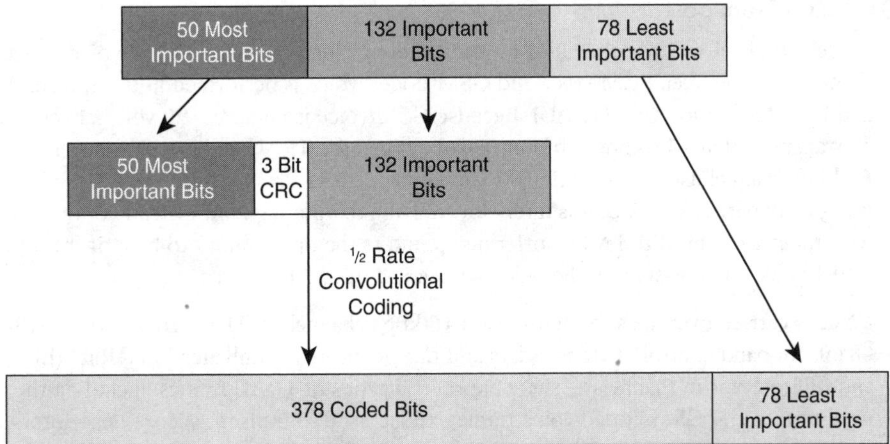

Figure 2-3 *Speech Coding over GSM Um Interface*

GSM Signaling

Signaling messages are sent over the Um interface using the LAPDm protocol (as defined in GSM 04.06), where m indicates a modification of the ISDN-defined Link Access Procedures on the D channel (LAPD) to account for layer 2 transmission over the radio interface.

The establishment, maintenance, and release of the physical radio connection, including those required for signaling transport as well as voice traffic channels, is performed by the Radio Resource (RR) management sublayer. The RR layer is also responsible for management of connection modification—for example, during handover operation. The physical channel is managed by the BSC using the BTS Management (BTSM) Protocol (as defined in GSM 08.58).

In terms of signaling to the core network over the A interface, the GSM BSC supports the BSS Application Part (BSSAP) signaling protocol (as defined in GSM 08.06). BSSAP is sub-divided into the Direct Transfer Application Part (DTAP) and the BSS Management Application Part (BSSMAP) (as defined in GSM 08.08). Figure 2-2 indicates that BSSAP is a Signaling Connection Control Part (SCCP) user, which is Signaling System #7 (SS7) protocol transported using Message Transfer Part (MTP).

Note Chapter 9, "Content and Services," provides more detail on SS7 and how IP is being used to replace the lower-layer MTP functionality for transporting SS7 signaling messages over IP networks, as well as how signaling gateway functionality has been defined to allow SS7 and IP application interworking.

GSM Voice Transport

Voice is transmitted over the GSM physical radio channel using a 13-kbps voice codec. Transcoding between PCM voice and GSM-coded voice is performed in the Transcoding and Rate Adaptation Unit (TRAU). Because GSM voice is compressed, voice channels can be transported in a 16-kbps sub-multiplex between the TRAU and the BTS, instead of the 64-kbps channel used for traditional PCM transport. As a result, even though the TRAU is logically part of the BSS, it is rarely located at a remote BSC but instead co-located with the more centralized MSC, offering operators the opportunity to benefit from the 4-to-1 voice compression on the links between MSC and BSC sites.

Voice is carried over the sub-multiplexed 16-kbps channels in TRAU frames (see 3GPP TS 08.60, "In-band control of transcoders and rate adaptors for Enhanced Full Rate (EFR) and full-rate traffic channels"). There are several types of TRAU frames, including those used to transmit GSM-coded voice frames, those used to transmit silence descriptors, and those used to transmit idle speech frames between silence descriptors, as well as those used to transmit a repeating idle signal when a particular channel is not assigned to call transport.

Note Even though no radio transmissions are made during silent and idle periods, redundant information is nevertheless required to be transported across the backhaul Time Division Multiplexed (TDM) network. Chapter 7 describes how IP technology can be used to optimize the legacy RAN transport by compressing the information sent across the Abis interface.

GSM Short Message Service

The mandatory support of Short Message Service (SMS) capability in the first phase of GSM has led to the subsequent explosion of *texting*, where users exchange short 140-byte messages capable of transporting 160 7-bit characters. Longer messages are supported by concatenating multiple user data fields (up to 255 times).

Note The phenomenal success of texting led Ovum (www.ovum.com) to predict that over 2.8 trillion messages will be sent in 2010. Chapter 7 will describe how IP can be used to scale the transport of SMS services.

The SMS service is a store-and-forward service; Chapter 6 provides additional details of how the message service is realized from a core network perspective. From an access system perspective, the transmission and reception of SMS messages typically uses a Standalone Dedicated Control Channel (SDCCH), which is a signaling channel whose bit rate is equivalent to 598/765 kbps (or just over 780 bps).

GSM Circuit-Switched Data

From its infancy, GSM was meant to support more than simple voice communication and defined the concept of tele-services. Circuit-Switched (CS) data was then defined for supporting a range of data oriented applications, including dial-up email access.

As we have seen, 456 bits are used to transmit 260 bits of coded information every 20 milliseconds using a Full-Rate (FR) voice codec. When operating in CS data mode, the same 456 bits are used to transmit 240 bits corresponding to a Radio Link Protocol (RLP) frame. The RLP is defined in GSM 04.22[1] and specifies the support of Non-Transparent (NT) data, where additional Automatic Repeat reQuest (ARQ) procedures are used to overcome the loss of CS data frames. Figure 2-4 shows how the RLP data entity for non-transparent data is actually located in the core network. Rate Adaptation function RA1' is used to map the synchronous data rates onto the GSM air interface, and Rate Adaptation function RA1 is responsible for mapping the data stream into data frames that can be sent over the TDM-based A interface.

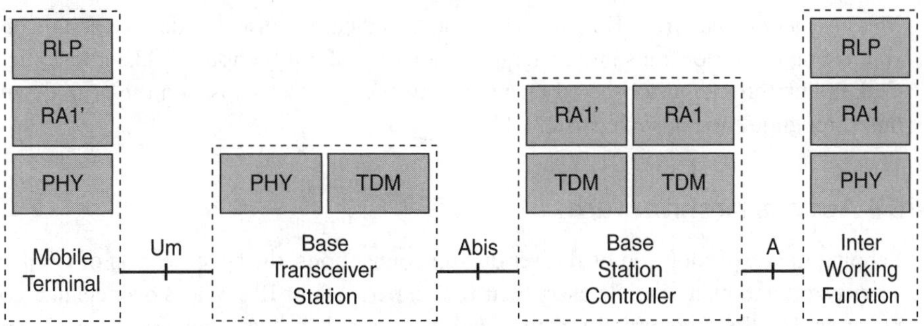

Figure 2-4 *GSM Circuit-Switched Data Protocol Stack*

GSM-RLP is based on an adaptation of High-Level Data Link Control (HDLC) for use over cellular networks and specifies that 48 bits out of the 240-bit RLP frame correspond to header and Frame Check Sequence (FCS), leaving 192 bits for user data, equivalent to a throughput of 9600 bps.

The typical configuration has RLP supporting Non-Transparent data services, where the RLP is responsible for guaranteeing error-free transmission by requesting re-transmissions of frames received in error. This results in the throughput of RLP diminishing as the channel error rate increases. Simulations[2] indicate that with a mean frame error rate of 10%, which is typically satisfactory for supporting voice service, the actual RLP throughput decreases to below 6000 bps.

High-Speed Circuit-Switched Data

In an effort to increase the speed of CS data transfer, the GSM system was evolved to support High-Speed Circuit-Switched Data (HSCSD). The HSCSD definition included two key functionalities, as follows:

- **14.4-kbps support:** By reducing the FEC overhead, HSCSD increases the data transmitted in a single timeslot to 14.4 kbps, compared to the original 9.6-kbps rate. Note that the 14.4-kbps bearer will be more susceptible to radio interference and noise compared to the original 9.6-kbps bearer.
- **Multislot support:** By allowing a user to be allocated more than one transmit and one receive timeslot within a TDMA frame, the aggregate data throughput for a particular user can be increased.

Refer back to Figure 1-17 in Chapter 1, which shows an example of a single device being allocated two transmit timeslots and two receive timeslots, which corresponds to an HSCSD configuration capable of supporting 28.8 kbps.

Measurement results from HSCSD deployment[3] indicate that with a device capable of supporting three-slot transmission (equivalent to a peak throughput of 43.2 kbps), the peak uplink throughput observed on a real network was 23.3 kbps, and the peak downlink throughput was observed as 27.9 kbps.

GPRS Access Architecture

Echoing the early adoption of IP over dial-up connections, the specification of CS data services offered many mobile users their first experience of IP services over cellular connections. The GSM community recognized, however, that there were a range of IP applications that were ill-suited to the dial-up model and thus set about standardizing a packet-based system optimized for bursty traffic patterns and asymmetrical flows, termed the General Packet Radio System (GPRS). GPRS allows radio resources to be allocated only when there is data to be sent, with the resources being released when there is no more data to send.

A clear requirement was for the GPRS architecture to co-exist with legacy voice, SMS, and CS services; the decision was made to use an overlay approach for introducing packet data services. In particular, the BSC functionality was augmented with Packet Control Unit (PCU) functionality. The PCU provides a physical and logical data interface to the BSS for packet data traffic, directing data traffic to the GPRS network. Packet data is transported over the air interface to the BTS, and then from the BTS to the BSC in the same way as a standard GSM call. However, at the output of the BSC, the traffic is separated; voice is sent to the Circuit-Switched Core Network and packet data is sent to a new element called the Serving GPRS Support Node (SGSN) via the PCU over a Frame Relay interface, as shown in Figure 2-5.

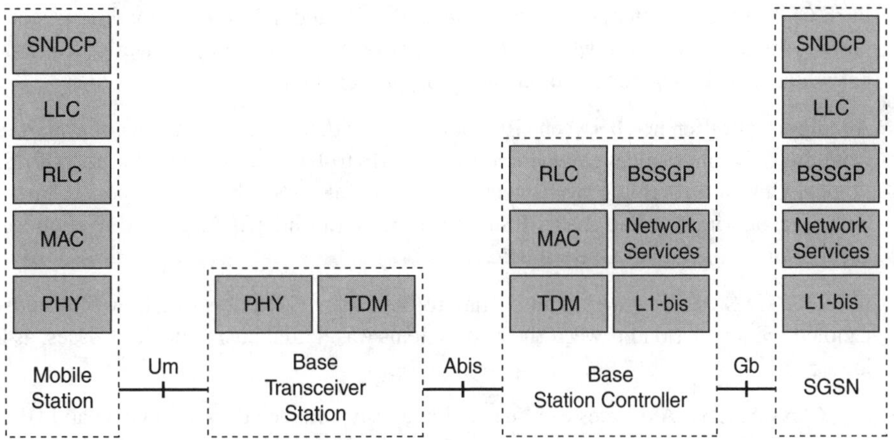

Figure 2-5 *GPRS Access System*

Note Although the Sub-Network Dependent Convergence Protocol (SNDCP) is typically defined as being outside the scope of the GPRS Access System, subsequent sections in this chapter describe how its WCDMA equivalent, the Packet Data Convergence Protocol (PDCP), has migrated into the Access System. Thus, the decision to include SNDCP in the description of the GPRS Access System facilitates comparisons between the two systems.

GPRS Physical Layer

GPRS uses the same basic eight-slot TDMA frame structure as GSM, and a multislot capability where a user may be dynamically allocated several timeslots within a TDMA frame to either transmit or receive in during a TDMA frame. The multislot capability is impacted by the design of the terminal; for example, the peak power able to be dissipated might impact the maximum number of simultaneous transmit slots that can be used within a single TDMA frame, and the use of a shared radio frequency oscillator between transmit and receive functionality might impact the ability of a terminal to support certain multislot configurations.

GPRS also evolves the concepts of different FEC coding rates specified with HSCSD. Whereas CS data has defined two FEC schemes supporting transmission at 9.6 kbps and 14.4 kbps, GPRS defines four FEC Coding Schemes, as shown in Table 2-2.

Table 2-2 *GPRS FEC Coding Schemes*

Coding Scheme	Coding Rate	Throughput in One Timeslot
CS-1	1/2	9.05 kbps
CS-2	2/3	13.4 kbps
CS-3	3/4	15.6 kbps
CS-4	1/1	21.4 kbps

Both CS-1 and CS-2 offer good performance in noise and interference conditions, compared with CS-3 and CS-4, which offer high performance in good propagation conditions but which quickly degrade in non-ideal propagation conditions.

An important difference between GPRS and GSM is that the ciphering layer has moved from the GSM physical layer (where it protects MS to BTS transmissions) to the GPRS Logical Link Control (LLC) layer (where it protects MS to SGSN transmissions). A new ciphering algorithm, called the GPRS Encryption Algorithm (GEA), is used to support encryption of the bursty GPRS traffic.

Because GPRS was designed as an overlay to the legacy GSM network, how the handset handled the interaction between the two systems was defined using device classes, as follows:

- **Class A:** Class A devices can be simultaneously connected to both GSM and GPRS systems, meaning that a user can be transferring packets over GPRS while engaged in a speech conversation.
- **Class B:** Class B devices can be attached to the GSM and GPRS system at the same time but can only operate in one mode at a particular instant. For example, a Class B device transferring packets over GPRS that receives an indication for an incoming CS call will be forced to suspend the GPRS data session while the call proceeds. The GPRS session is then automatically resumed when the call terminates.
- **Class C:** Class C devices can only be attached to one network at a time either GSM or GPRS, and a manual switch will need to be performed to switch between the two.

GPRS RLC/MAC and LLC

Whereas the Radio Link Control (RLC) layer provides reliable data link between the MS and the BSC, the Medium Access Control (MAC) layer controls the access to GSM physical resources, multiplexing RLC blocks from different users onto the shared physical channel together with their associated signaling channels, as shown in Figure 2-6.

As with GSM-RLP, GPRS-RLC can operate in two modes, as follows:

- **RLC Acknowledged Mode:** Provides a non-transparent service using ARQ procedures to trigger the selective re-transmission of data blocks received in error.
- **RLC Unacknowledged Mode:** Does not provide for re-transmission of data frames received in error and instead assumes that the upper layers can accommodate such errors.

Typically, RLC Acknowledged mode is used for transporting TCP sessions, and RLC Unacknowledged mode is used for transporting UDP-based protocols, such as audio or video streaming.

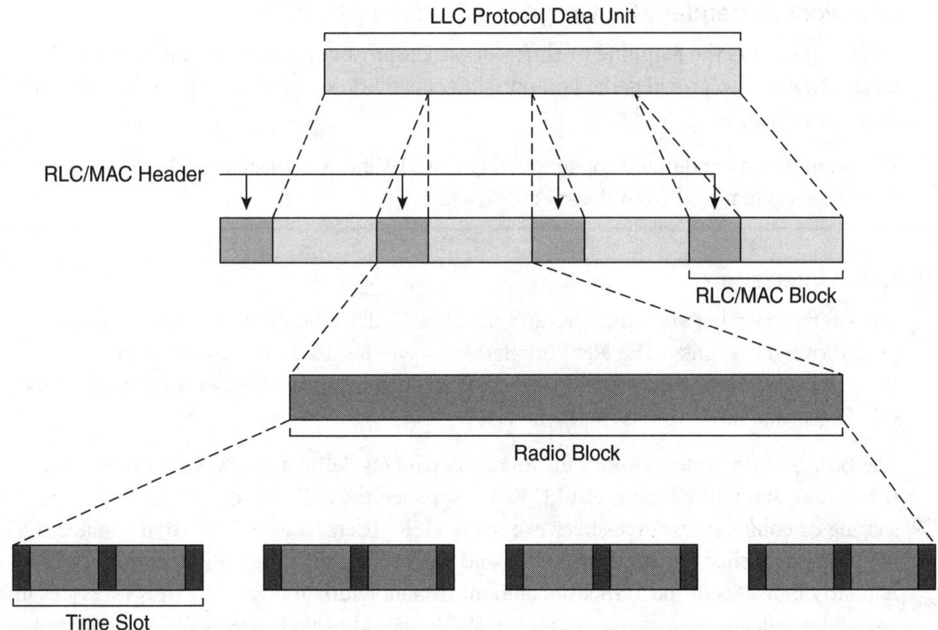

Figure 2-6 *GPRS LLC and RLC/MAC Functions*

The Logical Link Control (LLC) layer (as defined in GSM 04.64) is analogous to the LAPDm procedures used in GSM. In addition to the error detection and possible correction by the RLC layer, as described in the preceding section, the LLC layer also includes optional error recovery and re-ordering functionality.

Other functionality includes the following:

- **The exchange of Exchange Identification (XID) messages:** This is used for LLC-acknowledged mode configuration and ciphering support.
- **Data multiplexing capability:** This is used to allow several logical links to share an LLC instance. This allows signaling, SMS, as well as packet transfer services to be multiplexed onto a common LLC connection.

Because Acknowledged Mode (AM) of operation is implemented at both the RLC and LLC layers, the question arises as to where best to perform re-transmissions. The interaction between ARQ operation at the RLC and LLC layers has been investigated;[4] the results indicate that when Acknowledged Mode of operation is required, it is preferable to perform error recovery at the lower layer by allowing the RLC layer more opportunity for data retransmissions rather than performing such functions at the higher LLC layer.

Sub-Network Dependent Convergence Protocol (SNDCP)

SNDCP supports the mapping of different packet protocols onto the underlying LLC layer. SNDCP also provides the compression capability, supporting the V42bis compression algorithm.

Although originally defined for supporting both IP and X.25 services,[5] X.25 has been subsequently removed from the specifications.

GPRS Gb Interface

The Gb interface between the BSC and the SGSN is based on Frame Relay (FR) transported over TDM links. The Network Services layer is based on the Link Access Procedure for Frame Relay (LAPF), which is an enhancement of the conventional ISDN LAPD protocol used across the A-interface.

The Base Station Systems GPRS Protocol (BSSGP) (as defined in GSM 08.18) supports the routing and multiplexing of LLC PDUs between the SGSN and the BSS, including the sharing of common resources between many GPRS users. A BSSGP Virtual Connection (BVC) is established between the SGSN and each cell supporting GPRS service. The BSS regularly indicates to the SGSN the amount of bandwidth allocated to GPRS services in a particular cell, and so as a minimum, the SGSN should provide a per-BVC queuing function.

Note Although FR-over-TDM is defined in the original Gb specifications, this has not prevented leading operators from distributing out their IP network to the BSC site by using FR-over-GRE or FR-over-MPLS for transporting legacy Gb traffic over a converged IP network. Chapter 7 provides more information on transporting legacy interfaces over IP/MPLS.

GPRS Access Quality of Service (QoS)

The introduction of the GPRS overlay might not be accompanied by an increase in radio resources. In such circumstances, the cellular operator has to determine how to allocate the scarce radio resources between circuit and packet users; the more timeslots reserved for GPRS, the higher the likelihood of good packet throughput but lower the number of speech channels that can be supported. In order to limit the impacts on speech users, GPRS radio resource allocation mechanisms typically define a minimum number of timeslots to allocate to packet services in a cell and then define the ability to dynamically allocate the number of additional timeslots according to the instantaneous circuit-switched traffic load.

Other than issues with allocating sufficient resource to GPRS users, another key QoS attribute for GPRS is its elongated Round Trip Time (RTT). The RTT comprises delays due to radio resource assignment; time for packets to be transferred across the various elements, including the BTS, BSC, PCU, and SGSN, as well as other core network elements; the queuing time associated with the BVC in the SGSN and PCU; and the transmission delay of sending the packets over the RLC/MAC (using, for example, Acknowledged Mode operation), which will be a function of the FEC coding set employed over the physical layer. The ping delay distribution has been measured on GPRS networks supporting CS-2 FEC coding,[6] and the results indicate that the *minimum* ping delay varies between 430 and 510 milliseconds.

A key challenge with early GPRS implementations was the connection interruption when the user changed cells. Whereas GSM handover typically has an interruption of less than 200 ms (with the voice codec being responsible for substituting and then muting the lost speech codec frames to ensure limited impact on the ongoing conversation), estimates of simple GPRS cell reselection interruptions average between 2.2 to 3.4 seconds for a cell update procedure[7] and 4 to 5 seconds if the mobile has moved to a new routing area.[8]

With the requirement to support GPRS service to fast-moving mobiles, a technique for decreasing the interruption time was subsequently specified in 2001, termed Network Assisted Cell Change[9] (NACC). NACC provides additional information to a mobile device by sending detailed neighboring cell information, allowing the service outage around cell reselection to decrease to between 300 to 700 milliseconds. This is still considered insufficient for supporting conversational-type services over GPRS bearers, and so finally in 2004, the specification of the Packet-Switched (PS) handover for GPRS[10] was defined. The specification mimics the procedures used in CS handovers, where resources are allocated in a new cell before the mobile moves to this cell. Simulations[11] estimate that by using PS handover techniques, the service outage can be decreased to below 200 milliseconds for simple cell reselection operations.

Enhanced Data Rates

GSM and GPRS are both based on GMSK, which is a binary modulation type, capable of transmitting one bit of information per symbol. The adoption of different coding schemes and multislot classes might lead to the conclusion that GPRS can support 171.2 kbps services, corresponding to allocating the full eight timeslots in a TDMA frame to a single user and no FEC while operating in CS-4 mode. In fact, a more realistic limit to GPRS is a four-slot device operating with CS-2 coding, which would then support a peak throughput of 53.6 kbps.

In order to increase the throughput further, Enhanced Data Rates for GSM Evolution (EDGE) introduces a new modulation scheme called 8-ary Phase Shift Keying (8PSK), as shown in Figure 2-7. The higher-order modulation allows the data rates to be increased by moving from 1-bit/symbol with GMSK to 3-bit/symbol with 8PSK, as highlighted in Chapter 1.

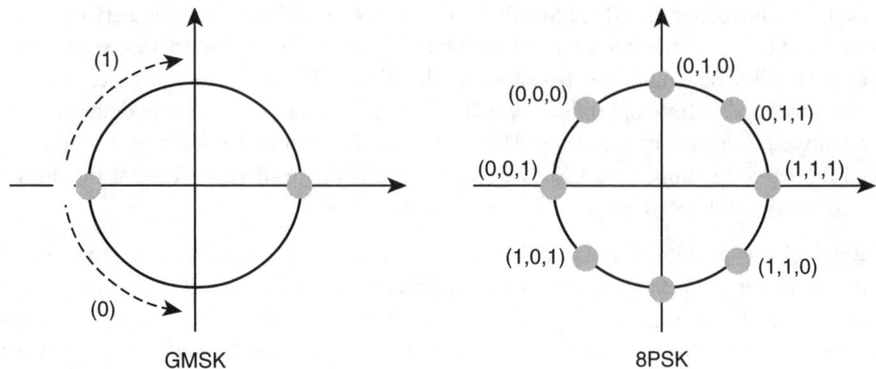

Figure 2-7 *GPRS to EDGE from GMSK to 8PSK*

Note GSM/Edge Radio Access Network (GERAN) is the official term for the access network supporting GSM, GPRS, and EDGE capabilities.

Whereas the original GPRS specification only had the ability to select between four different coding schemes, the option to use GMSK or 8PSK modulation allows EDGE to offer Adaptive Modulation and Coding (AMC) using nine different combinations of Modulation and Coding Schemes (MCS), as shown in Table 2-3.

Table 2-3 *EDGE Adaptive Modulation and Coding*

Modulation and Coding Scheme	Modulation	Throughput in One Timeslot
MCS-1	GMSK	8.80 kbps
MCS-2	GMSK	11.2 kbps
MCS-3	GMSK	14.8 kbps
MCS-4	GMSK	17.6 kbps
MCS-5	8PSK	22.4 kbps
MCS-6	8PSK	29.6 kbps
MCS-7	8PSK	44.8 kbps
MCS-8	8PSK	54.4 kbps
MCS-9	8PSK	59.2 kbps

As outlined in Chapter 1, link adaptation functionality can be used to automatically select the optimum MCS. Figure 2-8 highlights that at the edge of a typical GSM cell, with Carrier-to-Interference Ration (CIR) of around 12 dB, MCS-5 is able to provide a throughput of 16 kbps per timeslot. As the user moves toward the center of the cell (for example, with a cell average CIR of 18 dB), MCS-7 is able to double the effective throughput to 35 kbps per timeslot.

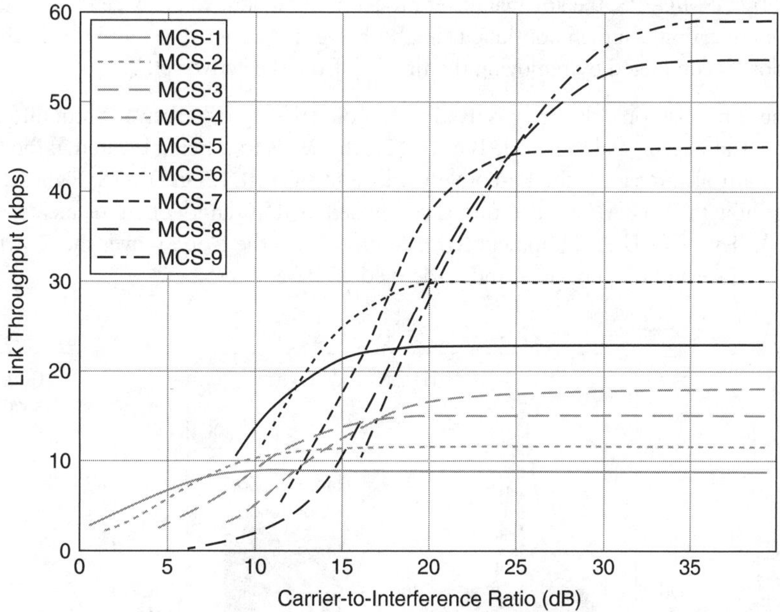

Figure 2-8 *MCS Performance Variations with Carrier-to-Interference Ratio*

The UMTS Terrestrial Access Network

The allocation of spectrum for global mobile communication at WARC '92 triggered the process by which ITU-R would specify IMT-2000 systems. IMT-2000 systems were required to support a maximum data speed of 2 Mbps for indoor office deployments, 384 kbps for pedestrian environments, and 144 kbps for vehicular services. The Universal Mobile Telecommunications System (UMTS) is the evolution of GSM and GPRS, designed to meet the IMT-2000 requirements.

Although the Core Network side evolved only slightly with the introduction of UMTS, the UMTS Terrestrial Access Network (UTRAN) took a revolutionary approach with the shift from TDMA to CDMA-based access technologies.

UTRAN Protocol Architecture of UTRAN

The architecture of the UTRAN has been driven by the capability of CDMA systems to implement "soft-handoff." Soft-handoff refers to the CDMA technique for using multiple sets of active radio links between the terminal and different base stations at any one time, termed the *active set*. Chapter 1 introduced the concept of diversity combining, and soft-handover is a macroscopic diversity technique applicable to CDMA-defined access systems.

Instead of simply switching between cells, implementing a so-called "hard-handover" as used by GSM/GPRS, the soft-handover procedure first adds the new cell to the active set. Communication can then continue using both cells in the active set and finally the soft-handoff is completed by removing the first cell from the active set.

Because macroscopic diversity is used to combine the signals received from different base stations, renamed the Node B in UMTS, this leads to it being located in the base station controller, renamed the Radio Network Controller (RNC) in UMTS. Figure 2-9 illustrates how the UTRAN architecture is composed of RNC and Node B elements, with the mobile device, or User Equipment (UE), connecting to the Node B over the CDMA-based Uu interface and the Iub-, Iur-, and Iu-defined UTRAN interfaces.

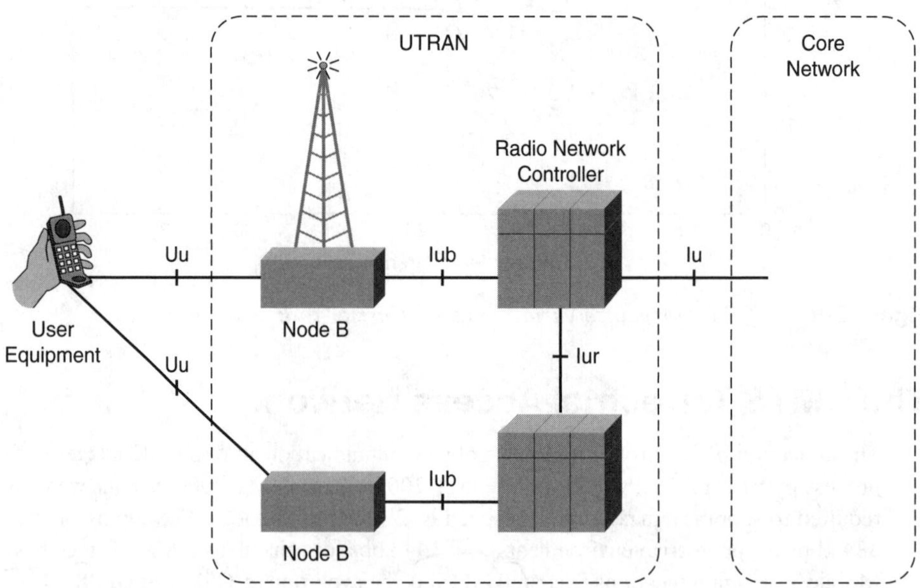

Figure 2-9 *UTRAN Architecture*

The other key departure from GSM/GPRS is that ATM is defined as the transport for the UTRAN interfaces. Figure 2-10 shows the user plane protocols for packet data. The functions included in GPRS SNDCP that were located in the SGSN have been incorporated into the RNC and renamed Packet Data Convergence Protocol (PDCP). In addition, following the example of GPRS, ciphering protection is no longer implemented in the base station, and is instead being integrated into the RLC layer.

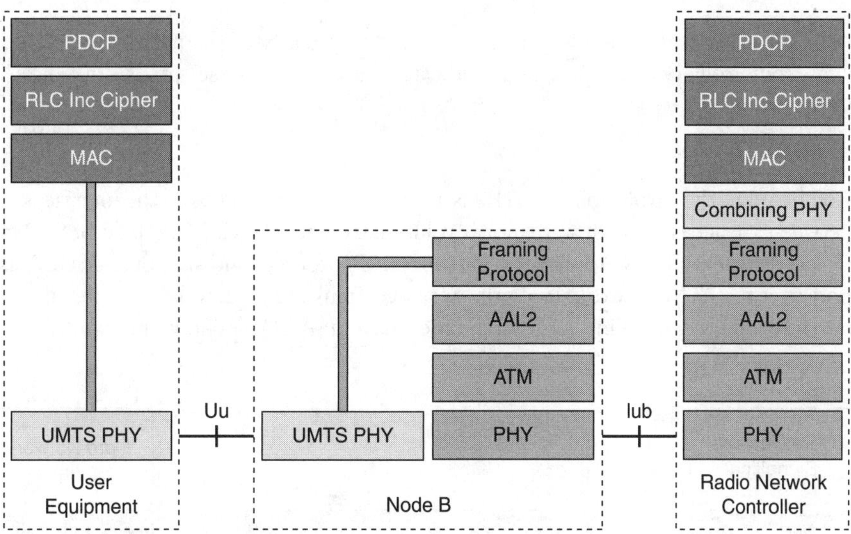

Figure 2-10 *UTRAN User Plane Protocols*

Because base stations are parented to a single RNC (over the Iub interface), the base stations used in an active set might be controlled by different RNCs. Figure 2-9 shows that the UTRAN architecture includes an inter-RNC interface (Iur) to allow serving RNC diversity combining when the Node B is controlled by a different RNC (a drift RNC). Figure 2-11 shows the user plane protocols required to support a mobile with two cells in its active set parented to different RNCs. The Iur interface is used to allow macroscopic diversity combining even when the two cells are controlled by different RNCs. The drift RNC simply switches data transparently between the Iub and Iur interfaces.

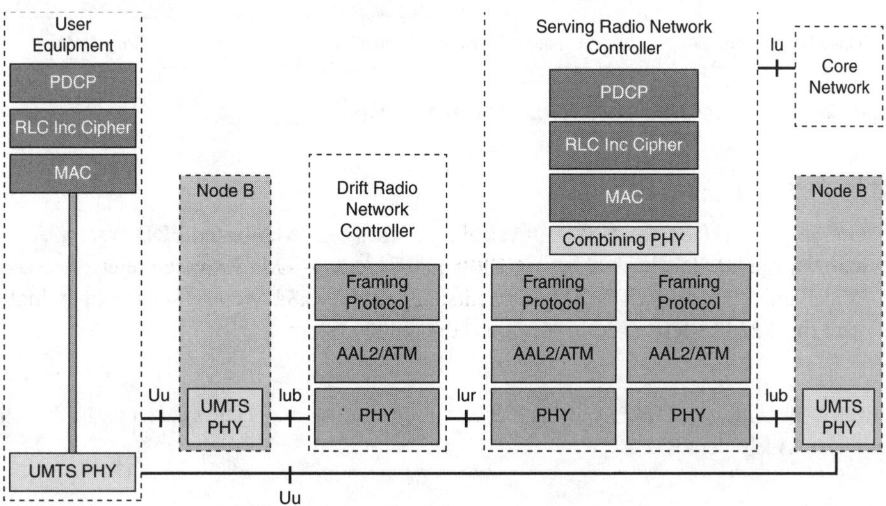

Figure 2-11 *UTRAN Iur Interface*

Note The average active set is directly related to the quality of the network planning. Figures from live network deployments indicate an average active set of 1.38 in a dense urban environment.[12]

Compared to the revolutionary UTRAN architecture, the changes to the interfaces between the access system were more evolutionary, with the GSM-defined BSSAP being replaced with the RAN Application Part (RANAP) protocol and support of SCCP transport over the ATM network, using the Message Transfer Part Level 3 Broadband (MTP3B) and the Signaling ATM Adaptation Layer (SAAL), as shown in Figure 2-12.

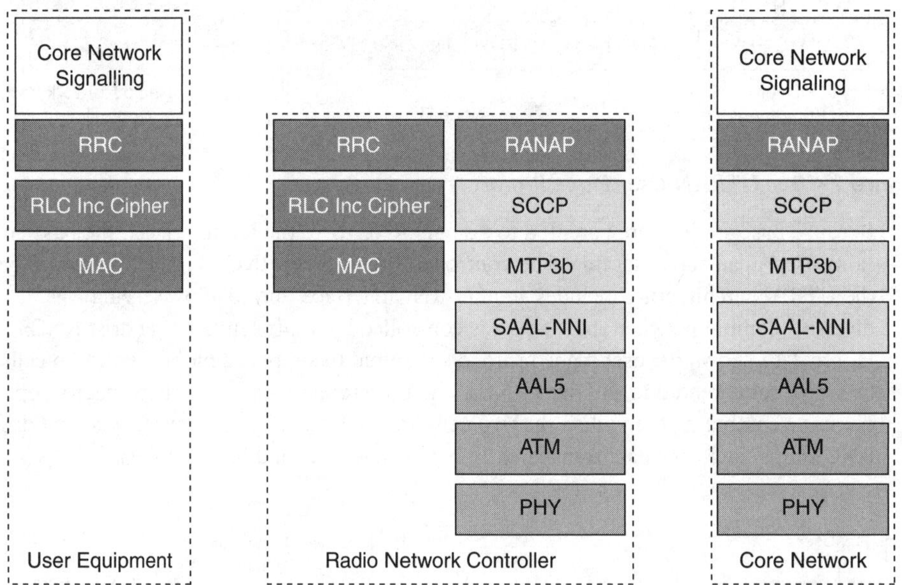

Figure 2-12 *UTRAN to Core Network Control Plane*

UMTS Physical Layer

On the Uu interface, the UMTS physical layer uses a CDMA-based FDD system. A summary of the UMTS physical layer is shown in Table 2-4. UMTS is often referred to as Wideband CDMA (WCDMA) because its chip rate of 3.84 Mcps is substantially higher than the 1.2288 Mcps used in previous cdma2000 systems.

Note A variation of UMTS has been defined for operation in TDD spectrum, but this has not been widely deployed.

Table 2-4 *UMTS Physical Layer Attributes*

Duplex	**FDD**
Channel Bandwidth	5 MHz
Modulation Type	QPSK
Multiple Access Technique	CDMA
Power Control Rate	1500 Hz
Frame Duration	10 ms
Chip Rate	3.84 M chips/sec
Slots per Frame	15 (2,560 chips)
Voice Spreading Factor	128 (AMR 12.2 kbps)
Multipath Mitigation	Rake receiver and macro diversity combining (dedicated channels only)
Voice Source Rate	Adaptive 4.75–12.2 kbps
Maximum User Data Rate	384 kbps
Base Station Synchronization	Frequency only
Forward Error Correction	1/2 and 1/3 rate convolutional coding
1/3 rate turbo coding	

The use of fast power control, operating at 1,500 times per second, prevents uplink-received power imbalances between near- and far-located terminals and allows a lower fading margin by tracking the fast-fading envelope for slow- to medium-speed users.

Table 2-4 shows that UMTS uses Orthogonal Variable Spreading Factor (OVSF) codes of length 128 for voice users (SF=128). Length 32 codes (SF=32) are used for 64-kbps services for both CS and PS bearers, length 16 codes (SF=16) for 128-kbps PS services, and length 8 codes (SF=8) for 384-kbps PS services.

From a code-dimensioning perspective, a 384-kbps IP service is equivalent to the radio resources consumed by 16 AMR voice calls or 4 CS 64 kbps-based video-telephony calls.

Note Because there are one hundred and twenty-eight SF=128 spreading codes available, you might infer that 128 users can be supported per carrier. However, with ten SF=128 codes being required for common channels, this leaves only 118 available for voice users. These must be allocated to each radio link within the active set, and so using an average active set of 1.4, this allows up to 84 voice calls to be supported on a single carrier.

continues

continued

Although up to 84 voice users can be accommodated in simple Additive White Gaussian Noise (AWGN) conditions, downlink power limitations will typically limit the maximum number of voice calls per carrier. Simulations indicate that this figure can fall to around 40 voice users in vehicular conditions.[13]

Whereas conversational voice traffic is deterministic in nature, IP-based packet services are less so and are frequently bursty in nature. Operators could simply allocate a PS 384-kbps radio bearer to a user for optimum user experience, but this would severely restrict the number of users who can access PS services. Instead, the operator will attempt to match the channel-type allocated to a particular user with the instantaneous throughput requirements—in other words, sensing the required bandwidth and switching between 16-, 32-, 64-, 128-, or 384-kbps radio bearers. Although the occupancy of downlink buffers can be used to optimize the downlink radio bearer, the Radio Resource Control procedures need to query the terminal to determine uplink traffic volumes, as highlighted in the subsequent section.

UMTS RLC/MAC

The centralized combining in the RNC for soft-handover requires that UMTS ciphering is implemented in the RLC/MAC layers. This ensures that transmission over the Iub *back-haul* interface are still confidentiality protected.

Just as with GSM, the UMTS RLC protocol provides segmentation and re-assembly, and ARQ services to user plane data and control information. However, contrasting with GPRS, where the overlay approach to adding packet data meant that circuit-switched services were handled separately to GPRS data, in UMTS, the RLC function has been enhanced to operate in Transparent Mode (TM), as well as the more conventional Acknowledged Mode (AM) and Unacknowledged Mode (UM) supported by GPRS. In TM, no overhead is added to the user plane data, ensuring minimum bandwidth expansion for conversational or streaming circuit-switched services. Table 2-5 compares the use of the three RLC modes for different classes of traffic.

Table 2-5 *RLC Transfer Modes*

UMTS QoS Class	Circuit or Packet	RLC Mode
Conversational	CS	TM
	PS	UM
Streaming	CS	TM
	PS	AM or UM

UMTS QoS Class	Circuit or Packet	RLC Mode
Interactive	CS	N/A
	PS	AM
Background	CS	N/A
	PS	AM

The MAC function is responsible for selection of the appropriate transport formats, which determines how data corresponding to different logical channels are mapped to the WCDMA physical layer. Because this mapping determines the QoS received over the radio interface, it is used to prioritize data flows for a single terminal and between flows from different terminals. Figure 2-13 shows the encapsulation of higher-layer Service Data Units (SDU) by UMTS RLC/MAC functions.

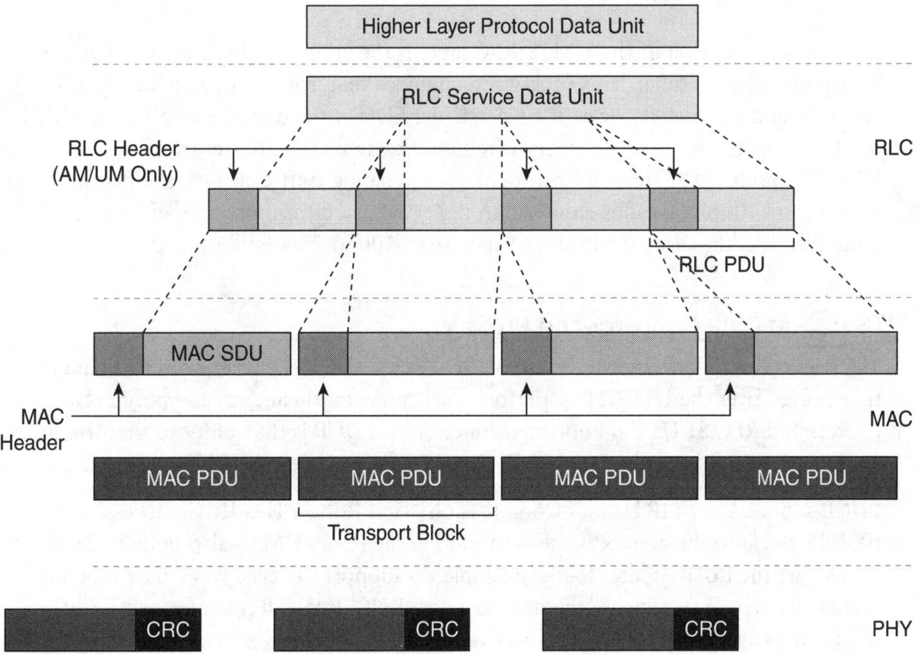

Figure 2-13 *UMTS RLC/MAC Functions*

As described in the previous section, the MAC layer provides the traffic measurement and reporting capability, which is critically important to ensure that the optimum transport channel is selected. The MAC layer monitors the RLC buffer, comparing the level with signaled thresholds. If the level is too low, the Radio Resource Control (RRC) function is signaled to trigger a reconfiguration to a lower throughput transport format/radio bearer, and if the level is too high, a reconfiguration will be triggered to a transport format/radio bearer with higher throughput.

The MAC entity keeps track of the traffic volume information. Three variables are defined in 3GPP 25.321,[14] as shown in Table 2-6.

Table 2-6 *UMTS Traffic Volume Measurements*

Buffer Occupancy	Amount of data in number of bytes that is available for transmission and retransmission at the RLC layer.
Average Buffer Occupancy	Mean of the amount of data available for transmission and retransmission in the RLC buffer averaged over a defined interval duration.
Variance of Buffer Occupancy	Variance of the amount of data available for transmission and retransmission in the RLC buffer over a defined interval duration.

Another key function of the UMTS RLC layer is the ability to discard RLC PDUs on the expiry of a discard timer. This function recognizes that, for certain services, it is beneficial to bound the transfer delay for a particular SDU at the expense of a higher SDU loss, and for other services, functionality is required to avoid RLC buffer overflows. In TM and UM RLC modes used for conversational and streaming traffic classes, the discard timer ranges from 10 to 100 milliseconds.[15] In RLC AM, used for more interactive or background traffic, the discard timer can range from 100 to 7500 milliseconds.

UMTS Packet Data Convergence Protocol

The Packet Data Convergence Protocol (PDCP) layer allows packet-switched data to be transported over the UTRAN by performing segmentation and re-assembly between IP packets and RLC SDUs. An important function of PDCP is the ability to perform header compression and decompression of IP data streams between the RNC and the UE.

PDCP supports both IP Header Compression[16] and Robust Header Compression[17] (RoHC). Because the context state is located in the RNC, UMTS also defines the ability to relocate the RoHC context—for example, to support the case when user mobility causes the system to relocate the user to a new RNC. RoHC has been specifically designed to operate over wireless links where the residual frame error and/or packet loss rates can be significantly higher than those experienced over wireline connections. Chapter 8 provides more detail regarding RoHC operation.

UTRAN Transport Network

Figure 2-10 highlights how the UTRAN Iub interface is conventionally transported using a Framing Protocol over ATM Adaptation Layer (AAL)-2. The Access Link Control Application Protocol (ALCAP), as specified in ITU-Q.2630.1, is used to dynamically set up the AAL-2 transport connections. A single dedicated channel will be conveyed over its own transport connection.

The Framing Protocol (FP) defines a five-byte header, and when conveying AMR 12.2-kbps voice, 31 bytes are required for the payload. Allowing for the three-byte Common Part Sublayer (CPS) AAL-2 header and the five-byte ATM header means there is a substantial overhead in voice transport in the UTRAN, as shown in Figure 2-14.

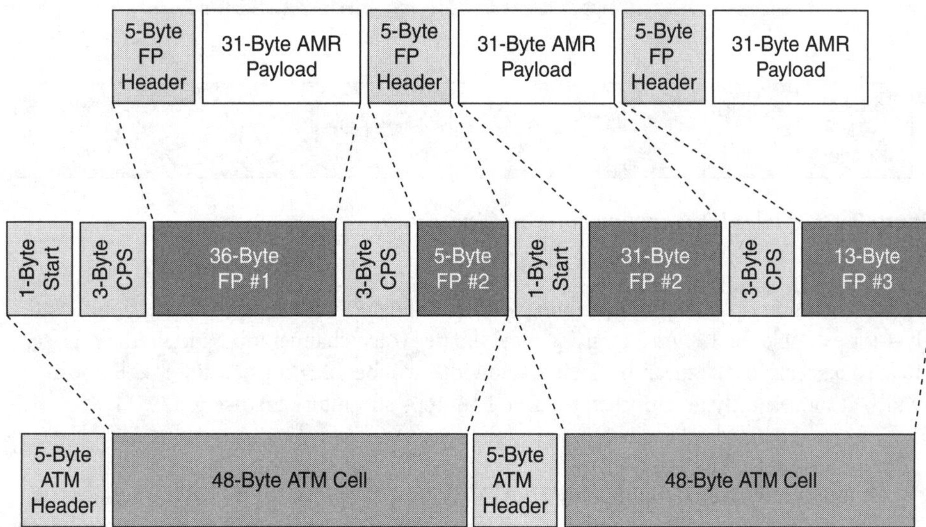

Figure 2-14 *Iub ATM Transport of AMR 12.2*

Figure 2-14 shows that with CPS and FP headers, 39 bytes are required to transport a single voice frame. Compared to the 47 bytes available per ATM cell, it is evident that 39 ATM cells are required to transport 47 AMR voice frames, equivalent to an Iub bandwidth expansion factor for AMR 12.2 kbps of (39 * 53) / (47 * 31) or 42%.

Because the AMR voice codec supports Discontinuous Transmission (DTx), in periods of voice inactivity, Silence Descriptor (SID) frames are sent. AMR has an effective SID data rate of 1.8 kbps, which equates to a frame protocol payload of 5 bytes. Figure 2-15 shows the frame packing of SID frames within an ATM cell and the previous technique used to calculate the Iub bandwidth expansion factor for SID 1.8 kbps of (13 * 53) / (47 * 5) or 192%.

Using this scaling and assuming a Voice Activity Factor (VAF) of 60%, the Iub bandwidth required to support each voice leg in the active set is the following:

12.2 kbps * 1.42 * 0.6 + 1.8 kbps * 2.92 * 0.4 ≈12.5 kbps

Considering a mean active set of 1.38 legs, this means that 12.5 kbps * 1.38, or 17.5 kbps, is required to support each active voice user in a cell. Using the previous figure of a maximum of 88 voice users per WCDMA carrier in AWGN conditions, the maximum Iub bandwidth for the user-plane portion of an all-voice deployment will be of the order of (88 * 17.7 kbps) or 1.54 Mbps per carrier.

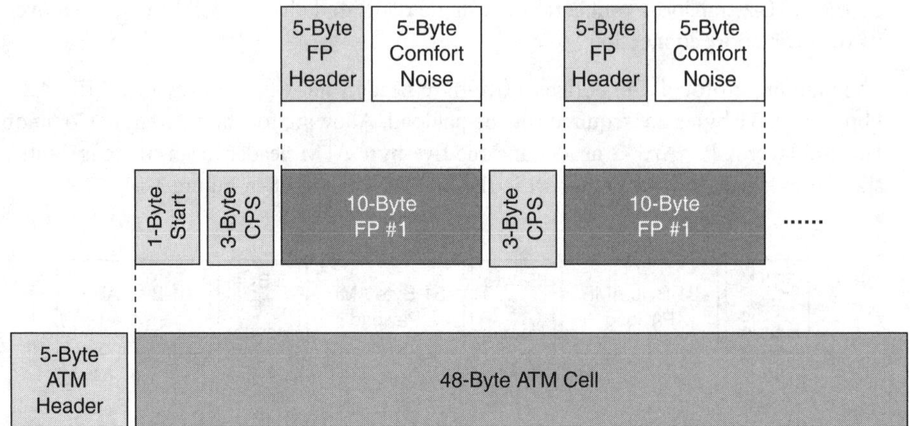

Figure 2-15 *Iub SID Transport for Voice Inactivity*

Note In a non-optimal radio-planning scenario, the mean active set can rise significantly—for example, to 1.8. As a consequence, the per voice channel Iub bandwidth will rise. In such a scenario, the mean backhaul bandwidth will be 12.5 kbps * 1.8, or 22.5 kbps, which is significantly greater than the fixed 16-kbps sub-multiplex used in GSM.

Although originally defining only an ATM transport option for UTRAN interfaces, in 2002 (Release 5) 3GPP enhanced the specification to include an IP transport option; for example, 3GPP 25.426 now includes the option for transporting Iub Framing Protocol over UDP/IP. Chapter 7 provides more detail on the adoption of IP transport in the Access System.

UTRAN Packet-Switched Services

The preceding RLC/MAC section together with the physical layer description describe how the UTRAN can support a wide range of applications with different QoS requirements. The physical layer radio bearers can be configured to use different spreading factors to support a range of throughputs; for example, the Dedicated Transport Channel (DCH) supports rates of 8, 16, 32, 64, 128, and 384 kbps. If throughput requirements are below 8 kbps, small amounts of data can be sent using common (shared) channels to the user on the Forward Access Channel (FACH) and to the network using the Random Access Channel (RACH).

Typically, the access system will be initially configured to operate at the slowest rate using a common channel, corresponding to being in a *Cell_FACH* state. The configuration only changes—for example, reconfiguring the channel to be a DCH and switching to being in a *Cell_DCH* state—when some threshold parameter (for example, related to buffer occupancy) has been passed.

Note This instantaneous switching of access system bandwidth can interact with the congestion control operation defined in TCP. Simulations[18] show that frequent channel switching during a connection degrades the performance of TCP over WCDMA links.

Another key characteristic of packet-switched services is that their always-on nature means that there will frequently be extended periods of time when the packet buffers are empty and no traffic needs to be transmitted over the radio interface. In such situations, the battery life of the terminal can be improved by entering a lower power state where the terminal can be placed in a dormant mode and only activate its receiver periodically to receive incoming pages and/or perform location update procedures. The UTRAN supports two such states; the first is referred to as the Paging, or *PCH*, state. In the *PCH* state, no user data transfer can take place, but the Radio Resource Connection (RRC) is preserved. The second is referred to as the *Idle* state. Just as with the *PCH* state, no data transfer can take place, but in order to free up even more resources, the RRC connection in the network is deleted.

The state transitions between the *Idle*, *PCH*, *Cell_FACH*, and *Cell_DCH* are shown in Figure 2-16.

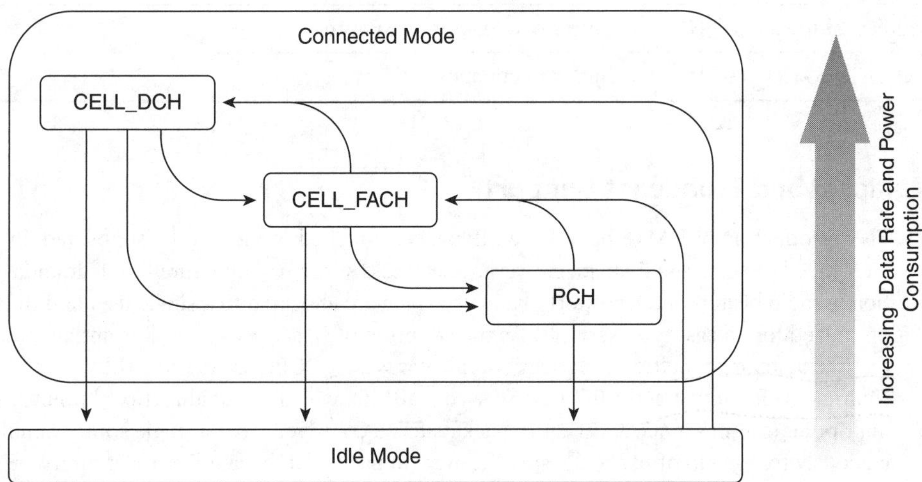

Figure 2-16 *UTRAN RRC State Transitions*

The configuration of the state transition timers and thresholds will be a compromise between the following:

- **Optimizing network resources:** By ensuring that spreading codes are used efficiently to support the required number of users.

- **Optimizing terminal battery life:** By ensuring that periods where the device is required to power its RF components are limited to those times when packets need to be sent.
- **Optimizing the user experience:** By ensuring that TCP throughput and user interaction timing meet expectations.

Importantly, the time to transition from *Idle* to *Cell_FACH/Cell_DCH* is 3 to 5 seconds, whereas the time to transition *PCH* to *Cell_FACH/Cell_DCH* is typically 1 to 2 seconds. Unfortunately, not all networks support the *PCH* state and therefore incur high latencies when transitioning from power-saving states to states where packets can be transferred.

Example trigger values can be tuned to different applications,[19] and typical recommended values are shown in Table 2-7.

Table 2-7 *UTRAN State Transition Thresholds*

Transition	Threshold Parameter
Cell_DCH to Cell_FACH	3-second inactivity
Cell_FACH to PCH	1-second inactivity
PCH to Idle	120-second inactivity
Cell_FACH to Cell_DCH	Buffer occupancy > 256 bytes
Cell_DCH to Cell_FACH	Buffer occupancy < 64 bytes

Multicast and Broadcast Support

The introduction of UMTS has allowed IP packet-switched services to be supported on high speed radio access bearers. However, the access system architecture has its foundation in radio bearers and transport channels, which are allocated to a single user and thus optimized for unicast type services. As the adoption of IP services rises, it is anticipated that the amount of multicast services will increase; thus, 3GPP has defined the Multimedia Broadcast and Multicast Service (MBMS), which is a unidirectional point-to-multipoint (p-t-m) service allowing IP packets to be conveyed from a single source simultaneously to a group of users in a specific area. In particular, because of the scarcity of radio resources, MBMS requirements include the efficient use of scarce radio resources. Compared to a point-to-point (p-t-p) connection where the emitted power is a closed loop controlled at 1,500 times per second, the p-t-m resources need to be able to be received over the complete cell coverage area, thus consuming considerably more power resources than a p-t-p connection to a user located in the vicinity of the cell site.

For example, with a single base station, simulations have shown[20] that providing a 64-kbps multicast bearer with a coverage probability of 95% over a cell requires between 20% and 60% of the complete base station's power budget to be allocated to the 64-kbps p-t-m connection.

Thus, MBMS functionality includes the ability of the RNC to count the number of users with activated MBMS services within a particular cell. When the number of MBMS users is low, the RNC will typically decide to use multiple p-t-p connections for delivering the multicast/broadcast service, triggering a re-configuration to a p-t-m connection only after the number of simultaneous users has passed a threshold.

Clearly, the inefficiencies of the RF system mean that MBMS is not currently commercially viable. This has prompted 3GPP to move to a Single Frequency Network (SFN) architecture, whereby multicast data is simultaneously transmitted from neighboring base stations on the same frequency/scrambling code and combined in the terminal for improved coverage. In Chapter 3 we highlight how SFN adoption will allow the efficiency of the Single Frequency MBMS (SFMBMS) system to be dramatically improved.

Note MBMS support using SFNs is analogous to the approach used by other broadcast systems—for example, the Digital Audio Broadcasting (DAB) and Digital Video Broadcast-Handheld (DVB-H) systems. Chapter 8 describes in detail these vertically integrated broadcast systems.

High-Speed Packet Access

Although the original objective of UMTS was to support data rates of up to 2 Mbps, the preceding UMTS throughput analysis has highlighted that a typical carrier in optimum AWGN conditions only supports a cumulative throughput of 1.54 Mbps, meaning that in reality, the maximum channel that can be allocated is a 384-kbps bearer. Furthermore, the original UMTS system dedicated a radio bearer to a single user and required significant state transition time to switch between different spreading factors and between periods of power-saving "idle mode" and periods when packets were being sent over the radio interface. These deficiencies meant that the original UMTS system was poorly designed to support the increasing adoption of always-on IP applications and services. Consequently, in 2002 (3GPP Release 5), 3GPP augmented the UMTS system to include High-Speed Downlink Packet Access (HSDPA) and in 2006 (3GPP Release 6) to include High-Speed Uplink Packet Access (HSUPA).

High-Speed Downlink Packet Access

HSDPA signals a shift in how radio resources are handled and in some respects away from the fundamentals of CDMA operation. In particular, you will see how soft-handover techniques essential for optimum voice performance are no longer applied to HSDPA bearers. This section looks at HSDPA architecture and HSDPA performance, as well as the key backhaul challenges that become evident once HSDPA is deployed.

HSDPA Architecture

The architecture of HSDPA is driven by the new features. These include the following:

- **ARQ re-transmissions moving to the Node B:** UMTS ARQ functionality was implemented by the RLC function and located at the RNC. Because of the additional transmission and processing delay involved, there was a significant delay in receiving re-transmitted data. In HSDPA, this function is moved to the Node B.
- **Hybrid-ARQ:** UMTS ARQ defined techniques where when operating in RLC-AM mode, if an RLC-PDU was not acknowledged, the complete RLC PDU was re-transmitted. Hybrid-ARQ uses a similar error-detection capability to detect that a PDU was received in error, but now the originally received data, comprising i information bits and r_{orig} redundancy bits, is combined with subsequent re-transmission to provide improved performance. Using such techniques, the subsequent re-transmission may contain the same $(i + r_{orig})$ as the original and be combined by a technique called chase combining; alternatively, the re-transmission may contain only incremental redundancy bits, r_{inc}, such that after each re-transmission, the effective coding rate decreases (for example, being $i/(i+r_{orig}+r_{inc})$ after the first retransmission).
- **Shorter frame duration:** The original 10 millisecond (ms) radio frame is divided into five Transmission Time Intervals (TTI) of 2 ms. The TTI is effectively a TDMA component on top of CDMA, allowing a shared resource to be dedicated to a single user during a TTI and a separate user during a subsequent TTI.
- **Adaptive Modulation and Coding Scheme:** Termed Fast Link adaptation, HSDPA-defined AMC selects the optimum Modulation and Coding Scheme (MCS) that matches the instantaneous radio conditions experienced by a particular user. For example, those users experiencing favorable radio conditions can be allocated 16-QAM radio bearers together with limited coding, resulting in improved throughput. In addition, rather than lengthy procedures being defined to change MCS values, the Node B can select the best scheme every TTI.
- **Fast scheduling:** Instead of the persistent RNC-based scheduling of UMTS, HSDPA uses fast scheduling functionality located in the Node B, which is able to allocate a shared channel to the user that is instantaneously experiencing the optimum radio conditions. In order to accommodate the rapidly changing fading environment, which in UMTS required adaptive power control at 1,500 cycles per second, fast scheduling requires that fast Channel Quality Indication (CQI) information be made available to the scheduler. In HSDPA, each terminal must periodically send its CQI report back to the Node B. The report cycle can range from 2 ms (500 cycles per second) to 160 ms (6.25 cycles per second), with the shorter cycle providing better scheduling performance at the expense of larger CQI reporting overhead.

HSDPA therefore represents a significant departure from the original UMTS architecture, where the Node B was only responsible for physical layer processing and power control operations. In HSDPA, MAC-layer functionality has migrated from the RNC toward the Node B and is termed MAC-HS, as shown in Figure 2-17.

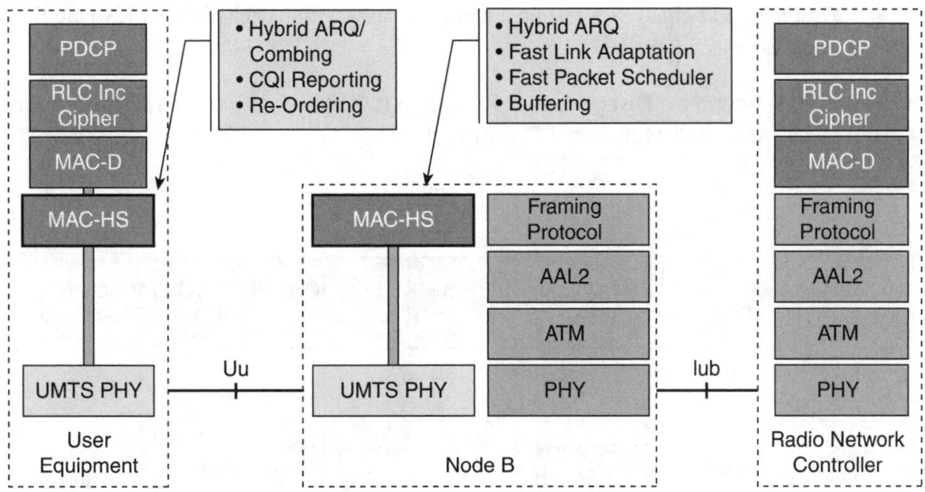

Figure 2-17

Additional HSDPA Functionality

Because such intelligence is distributed to the Node B, the conventional diversity capability centrally located in the RNC can no longer be implemented. Instead, HSDPA needs to operate in hard-handover mode, where the terminal only has one serving HS-DSCH cell at any instant and RRC signaling is used to change the HSDPA serving cell. A key attribute of HSDPA is the interruption in data transmission during such a hard-handover. Observed interruption measurements averaged over different vendor equipment and operator configurations have been performed.[21] These measurements indicate that although the median interruption was 120 ms, over 10% of interruptions during a HSDPA cell change were greater than 480 ms.

HSDPA Performance

Instead of variable spreading factors used in UMTS, the High-Speed Downlink Shared Channel (HS-DSCH) uses a fixed spreading factor of sixteen (SF=16) together with Fast Link Adaptation and Scheduling to offer differentiated throughput between different users. HSDPA defines different classes of User Equipment (UE) depending on how many HS-DSCH codes the device can receive. UEs are defined that can receive up to five, up to ten, and up to fifteen HS-DSCH codes. Another key differentiating characteristic of the terminal is the speed at which it can process HS-DSCH frames. The inter-TTI parameter is used to define the sustained scheduling that a terminal can accommodate, as follows:

- **Minimum TTI equal 1:** A terminal can sustain being scheduled a HS-DSCH for reception every TTI (2 ms).
- **Minimum TTI equal 2:** A terminal can only sustain being scheduled a HS-DSCH for reception every 4 ms.

- **Minimum TTI equal 3:** A terminal can only sustain being scheduled a HS-DSCH for reception every 6 ms.

Figure 2-18 shows how Discontinuous Reception (DRX) is used between TTI reception intervals for UEs with Minimum TTI greater than 1.

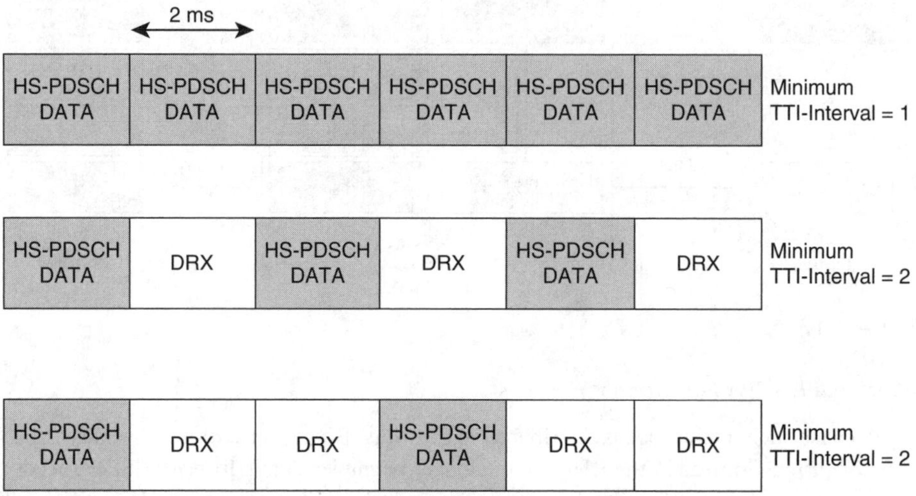

Figure 2-18 *Inter TTI Interval Operation*

HSDPA uses a 1/3 rate Turbo Coding, but Effective Coding Rates (ECR) as low as 0.14 and as high as 0.89 are achieved using repetition coding and puncturing respectively. Table 2-8 shows the nominal data rate achieved using different modulations, different ECR values, and different numbers of HS-DSCH (codes).

Table 2-8 *HSDPA Data Rates for Different Modulation, FEC Rates, and Code Combinations*

		Number of HS-DPCH Codes Allocated			
Modulation	**Effective Coding Rate**	**1**	**5**	**10**	**15**
QPSK	0.14	0.07 Mbps	0.34 Mbps	-	-
QPSK	0.52	0.25 Mbps	1.24 Mbps	-	-
QPSK	0.77	0.37 Mbps	1.84 Mbps		
16 QAM	0.32	0.30 Mbps	1.51 Mbps	3.03 Mbps	4.54 Mbps
16 QAM	0.54	0.52 Mbps	2.59 Mbps	5.18 Mbps	7.77 Mbps
16 QAM	0.77	0.74 Mbps	3.71 Mbps	7.42 Mbps	11.12 Mbps
16 QAM	0.89	0.85 Mbps	4.26 Mbps	8.52 Mbps	12.78 Mbps

Obviously, the more codes allocated to a device, the more complex the device; different HSDPA classes have been defined corresponding to different terminal capabilities in terms of modulation, maximum number of codes supported, and minimum inter-TTI interval, as well as whether sufficient memory is available to support either H-ARQ Incremental Redundancy or whether basic Chase Combining is used. Table 2-9 describes the 12 different terminal categories.

Table 2-9 *HSDPA Terminal Categories*

Category	Max. Number of HS-DSCH Codes	Modulation Supported	Min. TTI Int.	Peak Data Rate
1	5	QPSK and 16 QAM	3	1.2 Mbps
2	5	QPSK and 16 QAM	3	1.2 Mbps
3	5	QPSK and 16 QAM	2	1.8 Mbps
4	5	QPSK and 16 QAM	2	1.8 Mbps
5	5	QPSK and 16 QAM	1	3.6 Mbps
6	5	QPSK and 16 QAM	1	3.6 Mbps
7	10	QPSK and 16 QAM	1	7.2 Mbps
8	10	QPSK and 16 QAM	1	7.2 Mbps
9	15	QPSK and 16 QAM	1	10.1 Mbps
10	15	QPSK and 16 QAM	1	14.0 Mbps
11	5	QPSK ONLY	2	0.9 Mbps
12	5	QPSK ONLY	1	1.8 Mbps

The combination of terminal capabilities, HS-PDCH code allocations, channel quality metrics, and buffer occupancy can be used to adaptively schedule HSDPA transmissions within a cell. For example, Figure 2-19 shows how 5 different terminals with varying capabilities can share 15 spreading codes over different TTI intervals.

Although Figure 2-19 shows 5 terminals adaptively sharing 15 spreading codes, such a configuration is not possible in the first release of HSDPA because of code depletion. If 15 HS-PDSCH codes are dedicated to HSDPA transmissions, this leaves only a single SF-16 branch available for any other transmissions. Typically, the common channels including pilot channels will consume three SF-128 branches. Furthermore, in order to schedule transmissions to the three different users in any TTI, as shown in Figure 2-19, requires three further SF-128 branches.

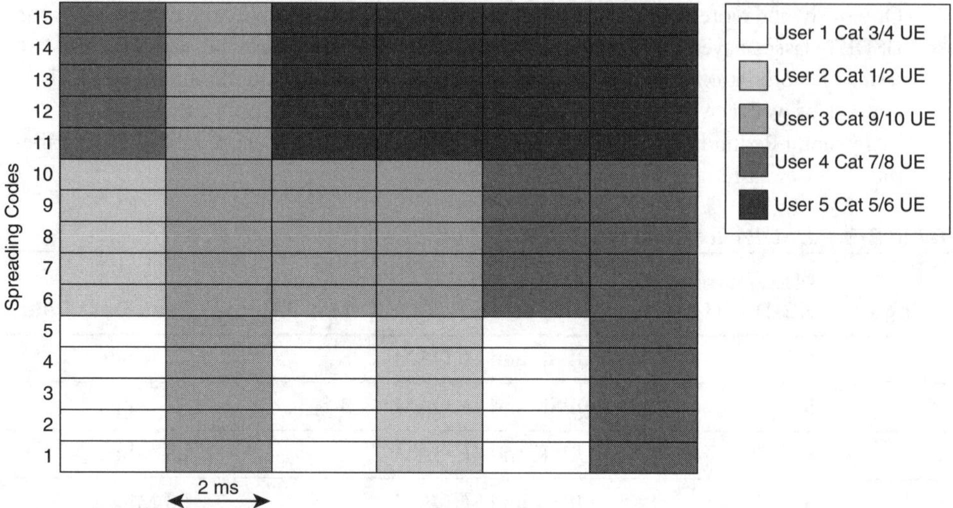

Figure 2-19 *Adaptive Scheduling of HSDPA Transmissions According to UE Capability*

This leaves only four SF-256 codes out of the original SF-16 branch. However, each HSDPA user requires an associated DCH, and so in such a configuration, only four HSDPA users can be supported in the entire cell! This code depletion problem has been addressed in subsequent releases of HSDPA by using a fractional code allocation, allowing ten users to share an associated DCH spreading code.

Note The combination of shorter frame duration and fast ARQ has resulted in a reduction in the Round Trip Time (RTT) for HSDPA. Measured values for a class 6 terminal indicate an RTT between 100–120 ms when in HSDPA mode, compared to 240–260 ms using the slower FACH channel.[22]

HSDPA Transport Network

Even though HSDPA is often marketed as providing 14.4 Mbps peak rates, the preceding analysis demonstrates that this is a purely theoretical number. Simulations have been performed[23] representing a more realistic deployment scenario based on an urban deployment with a mix of pedestrian and vehicular users. Assuming 20% of the base station's power is allocated to overhead channels and all the remaining 80% is allocated to HSDPA, these simulations indicate that the average cell throughputs experienced, even when using 7.2-Mbps capable terminals, will be less than 2.8 Mbps. Even a backhaul network for a HSDPA cell dimensioned below the peak air interface rate may still allow for high peak rates over the air interface due to the additional data buffering available at the base station. However, there is generally a trade-off between radio interface efficiency and the over-provisioning of backhaul bandwidth. Analysis indicates that in order to be able to provide 95% of the available RF capacity—for example, to account for the scenario where a HSDPA user is located in an area of good propagation conditions—requires the backhaul to be over-dimensioned by 20%.[24]

As shown in Figure 2-17, the HSDPA traffic is still transported over AAL2 using a Framing Protocol. Because of the larger payload, the overhead of the transport network is approximately equal to the ATM/AAL2 overhead of 6 bytes out of 53, or 11%. When combined with the over-dimensioning for radio efficiency reasons, this means the transport network should be dimensioned for 1.33 times (1.11 * 1.20) the average cell throughput. This results in a three-sector cell supporting 7.2-Mbps terminals being dimensioned with a minimum backhaul capacity for supporting user plane traffic of at least (2.8 * 1.33 * 3) or 11 Mbps.

Note Using previous scaling figures for voice capacity of 40 vehicular voice calls per sector and backhaul requirements of 17.5 kbps per voice user, the same 3-sector cell configured for supporting purely voice users would require (40 * 0.0175 * 3) or 2.1 Mbps of backhaul capacity for user-plane traffic. This clearly demonstrates why the adoption of mobile broadband data is causing mobile operators to re-assess their backhaul strategies.

Chapter 8 shows how IP can be used to transport the legacy ATM-defined interfaces using pseudo-wire technology, enabling operators to benefit from higher-speed packet-based access technologies in advance of native IP interfaces being supported by base station vendors.

The addition of the HSDPA requires buffers to be configured at the Node B. The utilization of these buffers will be used in deriving the optimum scheduling metrics for the different HSDPA users supported across the cell. Because the size of these buffers is limited, HSDPA implements flow control across the Iub interface in order to prevent data losses at the Node B due to buffer overflow. This rate control is performed on a per-bearer basis to ensure that the effective Iub rate allocated to a particular bearer does not exceed the maximum required rate, which 3GPP terms the Guaranteed Bit Rate (GBR) .

As soon as the RNC detects the necessity to send HSDPA data—for example, due to data arrival at the RNC or a timer expiry that has caused data to be discarded by the RLC entity—the RNC sends a CAPACITY REQUEST control frame to the Node B, including the relative priority of a particular flow. The Node B determines the arrival rate for MAC-PDUs that can be transmitted on the HS-DSCH and reports this information back to the RNC in a CAPACITY ALLOCATION control frame.

HSUPA

The development of HSUPA delayed the corresponding down-link capability by one 3GPP release; whereas HSDPA was first standardized in Release 5 (2002), HSUPA (also known as FDD Enhanced Uplink [EUL]) was included in Release 6 (2005).

HSUPA Architecture

Unlike HSDPA, which introduced a new shared resource for providing improved downlink throughput, the HSUPA architecture is based on the same dedicated channel approach adopted by the earlier UMTS access system. Still, HSUPA has leveraged some other key architectural attributes of HSDPA, including the following:

- **Fast Hybrid ARQ:** As with HSDPA, HSUPA adds an H-ARQ functionality to the base station, with the addition of a MAC-E entity. As with HSDPA, the Node B MAC-E entity can perform combining of retransmitted information with the originally received data.
- **Shorter Transition Time Interval:** To allow latencies to be further reduced, HSUPA supports a 2-ms TTI. However, unlike HSDPA, support of the 2-ms TTI in the uplink is not mandatory in all terminals.
- **Node B-based scheduling:** Whereas HSDPA uses scheduling to multiplex users onto the shared downlink channel, the dedicated channels in HSUPA are allocated continuously and independently of other users. Instead, the uplink scheduling is concerned with controlling the uplink noise rise. The Rise-over-Thermal (RoT) is used to indicate the ratio between the total power received from uplink emissions at the base station compared with the thermal noise. In HSUPA, a single high-peak rate channel can significantly affect the RoT. Thus, the uplink scheduler is used to carefully control the maximum allowed uplink power and hence RoT. Each HSUPA terminal can send a request for transmission indicating its buffer statistics and QoS/Priority and the scheduler decides when and how many terminals can operate and importantly how much power each can be allocated, which effectively limits the uplink data rate.

Because it is a dedicated channel, macroscopic diversity combining is still applied with the E-DCH. Furthermore, as a consequence of the H-ARQ functionality being located in each Base Station within the active set, physical layer re-transmissions can cause packets to be received out of order. Rather than having a single Node B identified for performing packet re-ordering (which would require additional backhaul bandwidth), the RNC (which is already performs diversity combining) is augmented with a new MAC entity, termed MAC-ES, responsible for packet re-ordering. Figure 2-20 shows the new HSUPA functionality at the UE, Node B, and RNC.

> **Note** Unlike HSDPA, Release 6 E-DPDCH does not support adaptive modulation; instead, only BPSK modulation is defined. In Release 7 (standardized in 2007), 16 QAM has been added as a new modulation option in the uplink.

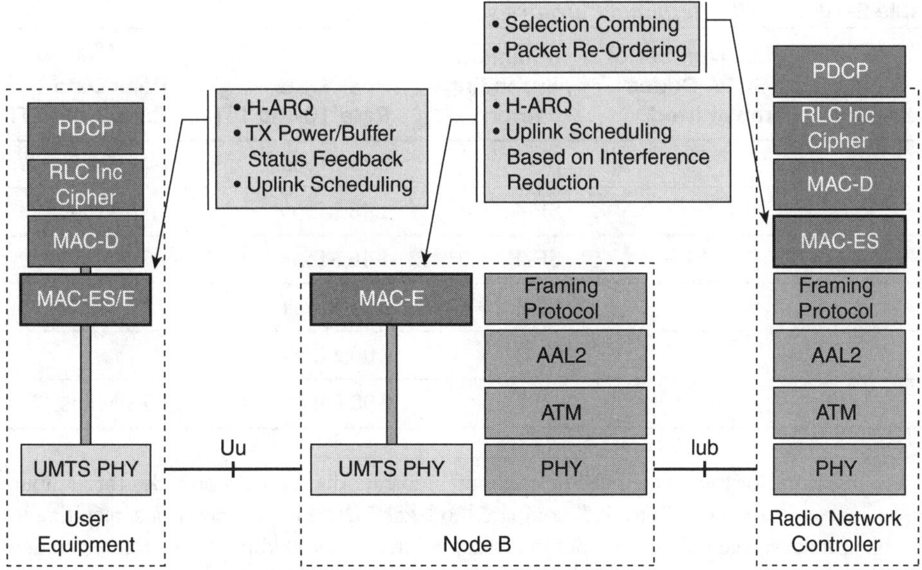

Figure 2-20 *Additional HSUPA Functionality*

HSUPA Performance

HSUPA provides improved performance by allocating shorter spreading factors (including SF=4 and SF=2, for example), compared with SF=8 used for the legacy PS 384-kbps service. HSUPA supports speeds of up to 960 kbps with a single SF=4 OSVF code allocation. In order to support speeds in excess of 960 kbps, HSUPA uses a multi-code architecture—for example, allocating two SF=4 codes in parallel to provide a physical channel rate of 1920 kbps. If speeds in excess of 1920 kbps are required, HSUPA allocates two SF=2 codes for a combined physical channel rate of 3840 kbps. Two SF=2 codes are used instead of four SF=4 codes because of the improved Peak-to-Average-Power Ratio (PAPR) achieved when using only two codes in parallel. Finally, HSUPA defines the use of four codes in parallel, two SF=2 codes and two SF=4 codes, providing a combined physical channel rate of 5760 kbps.

The first release of HSUPA supports six different categories of terminal, as shown in Table 2-10. The terminal categories allow lower-complexity designs by restricting the minimum spreading factor supported or the number of parallel spreading codes that can be transmitted.

Table 2-10 *HSUPA Terminal Categories*

Category	Max. Number of HSUPA Codes Transmitted	Minimum Spreading Factor	Peak Data Rate 10-ms TTI	Peak Data Rate 2-ms TTI
1	1	SF-4	0.73 Mbps	-
2	2	SF-4	1.46 Mbps	1.46 Mbps
3	2	SF-4	1.46 Mbps	-
4	2	SF-2	2.00 Mbps	2.93 Mbps
5	2	SF-2	2.00 Mbps	-
6	4	SF-2	2.00 Mbps	5.76 Mbps

Simulations for the average cell throughput[25] indicate that HSUPA provides throughput gains ranging from 25% to 59% compared to legacy DCH implementations, resulting in an uplink average cell throughput increasing to around 1400 kbps. These figures compare well to laboratory results,[25] which have also analyzed the RTT performance of HSUPA. This data shows that HSUPA provides a further 20% improvement compared to the RTT achievable in HSDPA deployments, so values below 100 ms may be achieved.

Note Note the same experimental analysis[25] indicates that if HSUPA is deployed on the same carrier as legacy voice users, there may be unforeseen interactions between the two systems; for example, the HSUPA terminals may transmit on high power, which can affect the interference experienced by legacy voice users. Experimental data indicates that with 15 voice users in a cell, the HSUPA throughput may drop by up to 75%.

Finally, just as HSDPA had to be enhanced with the introduction of the Fractional-DPCH to allow a high number of HSDPA users to be supported in the active state, a corresponding feature called Continuous Packet Connectivity (CPC) has been defined as part of 3GPP Release 7.[26] CPC is intended to significantly increase the number of E-DCH users that can stay in the *Cell_DCH* state over long periods, allowing transmission to restart with delays less than 50 ms. Because the radio control channel is transmitted continuously in the uplink, even when no data needs to be transmitted, the CPC capability defines the mechanism by which these control channels can be gated (not transmitted) when no data needs to be transmitted on E-DPDCH.

Simulations[27] indicate that compared to the non-gated case, the gating of control channels for cells with a high number of inactive terminals can free up significant radio resources to be allocated to active terminals—doubling the median average cell throughout when 6 active users share the cell with 20 inactive users.

Evolved High-Speed Packet Access

As the need for mobile broadband services increases, the High-Speed Packet Access architecture is continuing to evolve. Termed HSPA+, or evolved HSPA (eHSPA), this IP-centric architecture increases the throughput over the radio interface with the use of Higher-Order Modulation and adaptive antenna techniques. Figure 2-21 shows how HSPA+ used 64 QAM and MIMO to increase the peak throughputs achievable up to 42 Mbps in the downlink (DL) and 11 Mbps in the uplink (UL). Additionally, HSPA+ looks to flatten the access network architecture by re-locating the MAC-D and PDCP functionalities from the centralized RNC to the Node B. Figure 2-22 shows such a re-architecting of the network and demonstrates how HSPA+ can be viewed as an All-IP system with the GPRS Tunneling Protocol (GTP) now originating directly from the Node B.

Note GTP is a UDP protocol for providing network-based mobility in 3GPP networks. Chapter 6 provides more detail on the operation of GTP.

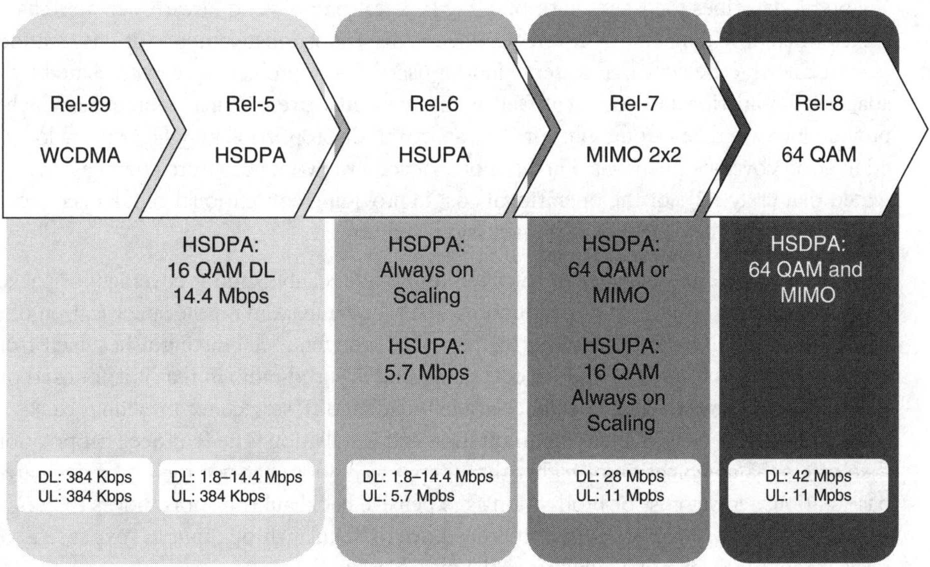

Figure 2-21 *HSPA+ Radio Interface Evolution*

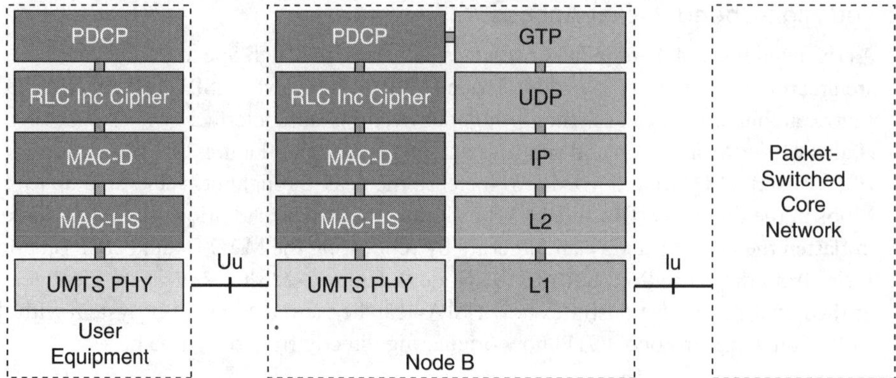

Figure 2-22 *HSPA+ Architectural Evolution*

Home Node B

Chapter 1 describes the issues with Building Penetration Loss and how this creates challenges when providing indoor coverage, where a disproportionate amount of base station resource need to be allocated to serve indoor users. These problems are exacerbated by adaptive modulation and coding as well as the latest adaptive antenna techniques, which provide increase data throughput for IP bearers, but disproportionately favor users located in good coverage positions. Furthermore, Accenture (www.accenture.com) has estimated that up to 52% of the operational cost in providing conventional cellular services is accounted for by cell-site rental, transmission, and power.

As a consequence, and because of the need to provide reliable indoor coverage for packet bearers at an ever lower cost of production, 3GPP has embarked on the specification of a Home Node B (HNB), also known as 3G femtocell. The femtocell distinguishes itself from previous attempts to provide indoor coverage using licensed radio in that it is focused on the residential market, using consumer-grade broadband IP service for providing backhaul connectivity, as well as self-configuration and installation. The femtocell proposition then offers the combination of higher throughput to indoor users via their own dedicated base station, a lower cost of production as expensive backhaul transport moves to consumer broadband IP networks, and improved macro-cellular throughput as "expensive to serve" indoor users are offloaded from the macro network.

Note The Femtoforum (www.femtoforum.org) is an industry body established to promote the deployments of femtocells. The forum has produced a reference architecture that can apply equally to UMTS markets, as well as cdma2000 systems and WiMAX systems. In this chapter, we have decided to focus on the UMTS variant because research indicates that this will likely become the most widely deployed type of femto cell.

Despite the fact that 3GPP had already defined an option for IP transport of the Iub interface, it was decided to not use such an approach when standardizing the HNB architecture. Instead, the legacy RNC functionality has been repartitioned between the HNB and a HNB gateway, as shown in Figure 2-23, with a new Iuh interface defined between the two. In particular, all the user-plane functionality represented by PDCP/RLC/MAC, which had been centrally located in the RNC, has been distributed to the HNB.

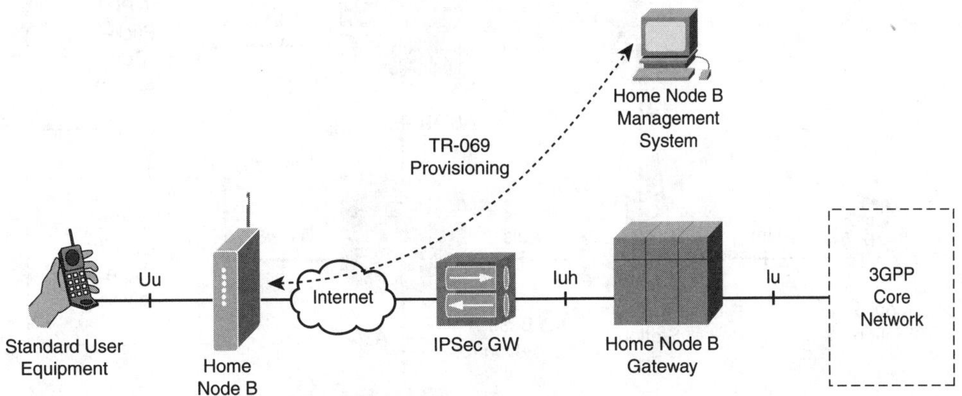

Figure 2-23 *Home Node B PS User Plane Architecture*

Figure 2-23 shows that the Home Node B interfaces to the standard 3GPP Core Network using the Iu interface. This allows standardized hard-handover procedures to be used to support session continuity as users shift between femto and macro-cellular coverage. Finally, Figure 2-23 also demonstrates that femtocell provisioning is achieved using the Broadband Forum TR-069 CPE WAN Management Protocol (CWMP)[28] with a femtocell specific management and provisioning data model. One of the key challenges in femtocell deployments is managing the RF interference. In particular, in UMTS environments, an operator may only have been licensed two or three pairs of 5-MHz channels. In such cases, the femtocell will likely have to share a channel with the macro-area network. Although WCDMA specifies the use of scrambling codes to differentiate emissions from different base stations, the interfering signal will be seen as noise, and if received at a relatively high power, can interfere with the wanted signal. Interference analysis performed by the Femtoforum[29] has shown that defining a HNB with a fixed maximum output power is not satisfactory, and instead the HNB needs to sense its environment and dynamically set its output power, down to a minimum value of 0 dBm.

The cdma2000 Access System

The cdma2000 access system is a CDMA system that has been developed by the 3GPP2 organization (www.3gpp2.org). cdma2000 1xRTT (where 1xRTT refers to the fact that the technology uses a pair of 1.25 MHz channels) has been approved as meeting the IMT-2000 requirements and, like WCDMA, is designated as a 3G system.

Protocol Architecture of cdma2000 Access System

The architecture of the cdma2000 1xRTT access system is shown in Figure 2-24.

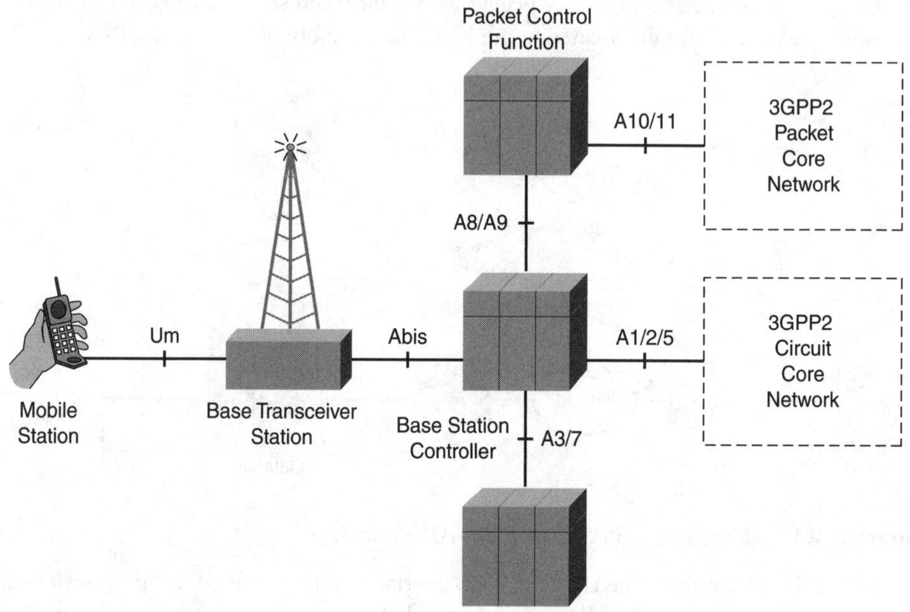

Figure 2-24 *cdma2000 1xRTT Access System Architecture*

The architecture comprises the Base Transceiver Stations (BTS), Base Station Controllers (BSC), and a Packet Control Function (PCF), which is analogous to the PCU in 3GPP's GPRS architecture. The BSC terminates the Layer 2 protocols, including the Signaling Link Access Control (LAC) as well as the MAC protocol for the dedicated logical channels. Diversity combining is also implemented in the BSC in a function called the Selection/Distribution Unit (SDU). In soft-handoff, the SDU selects which uplink frame to be used, and in the downlink, distributes frames to those base stations involved in soft-handoff. Because these cells may be parented to a different logical BSC, the cdma2000 1xRTT access architecture includes inter-BSC connectivity, with the A3 interface used for user traffic and signaling and the A7 interface for signaling only.

Figure 2-24 also shows how the Access System interfaces to the 3GPP2 packet core network across the A8 (user traffic) and A9 (signaling) interfaces to the PCF and to the circuit-switched core network across the A1 (signaling), A2 (voice), and A5 (CS data traffic) interfaces.

A key characteristic of the cdma2000 architecture is the ability to transport the Abis 3G interface over a variety of Layer 1 and Layer 2 technologies. TIA-EIA-828 defines the Abis interface between the BTS and BSC.[30] This specification includes four different options for Abis transport, as shown in Figure 2-25 for signaling and Figure 2-26 for user traffic. For signaling, the Inter-Operability Specification (IOS) application[31] is defined as an IP application that can be transported using TCP, UDP, or SCTP and user traffic that can either be backhauled using AAL2 Service Specific Segmentation and Reassembly (SSAR), UDP, or compressed UDP (cUDP–RFC 2508). cUDP over Multiplexed PPP (RFC 3153) then allows the transport of Abis traffic with lower bandwidth, compared to the traditional AAL2 transport, as shown in Figure 2-27.

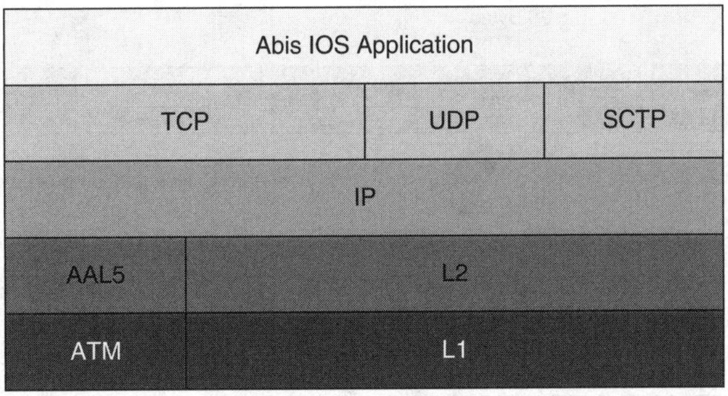

Figure 2-25 *cdma2000 1xRTT Abis Signaling Transport*

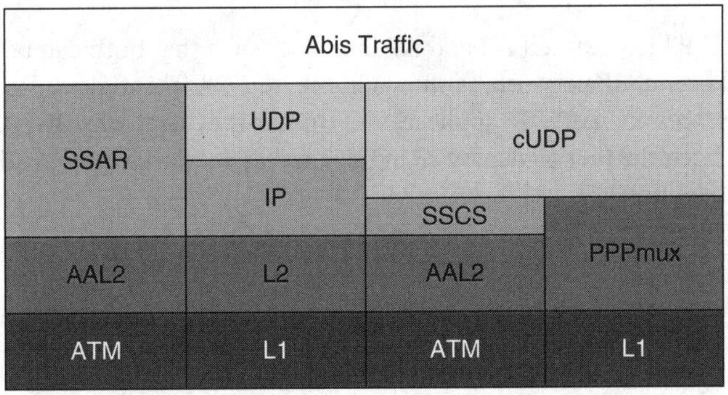

Figure 2-26 *cdma2000 1xRTT Abis Traffic Transport*

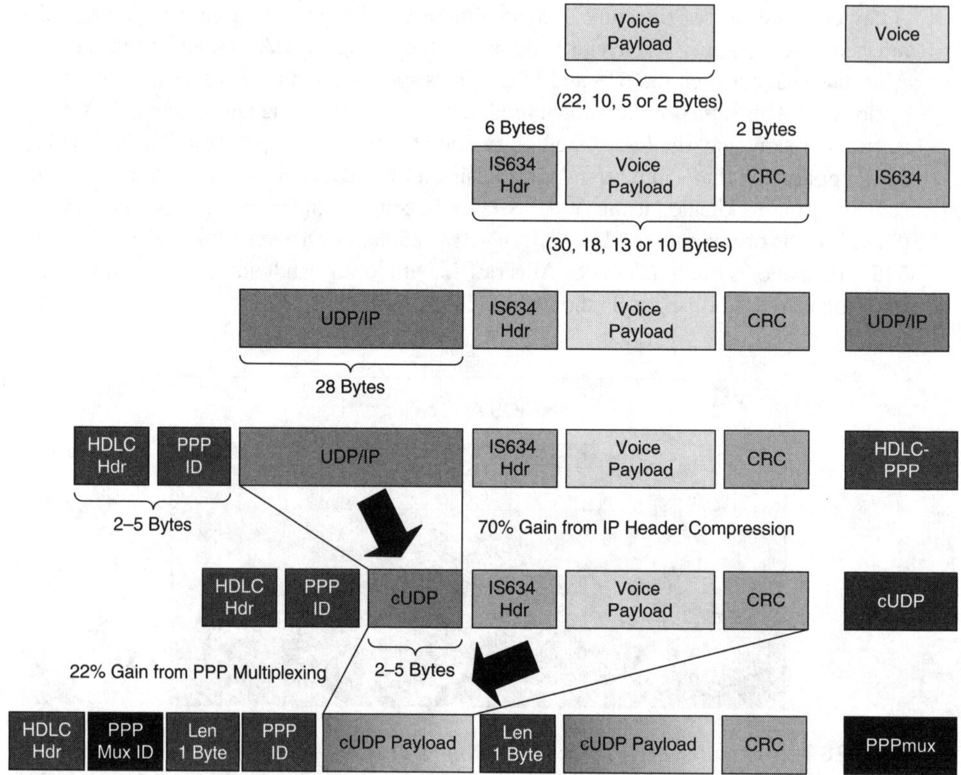

Figure 2-27 *cdma2000 1xRTT Abis Traffic Using PPPmux*

Similarly, 3GPP2 has defined A3 and A7 interfaces such that both can be optionally transported over an IP network, as shown in Figure 2-28. This figure also shows that A8 and A9 interfaces are native IP applications. Thus, it is evident why 3GPP2 cellular networks have been the first to deploy IP in their access networks, well in advance of mobile broadband adoption.

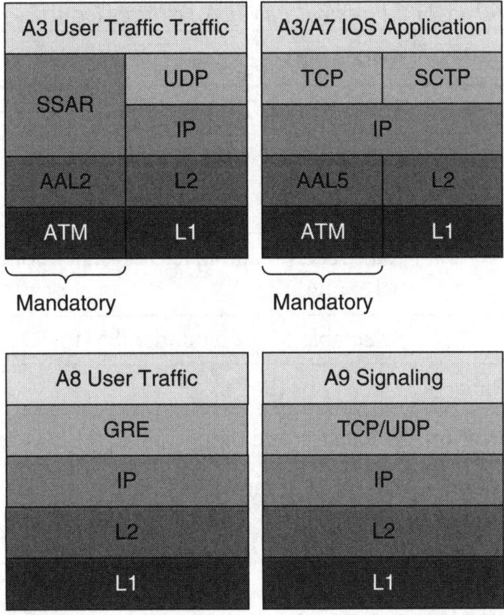

Figure 2-28 *cdma2000 1xRTT A3/A7 and A8/A9 Protocol Transport*

cdma2000 Physical Layer

On the Um interface, the cdma2000 1xRTT physical layer uses a CDMA-based FDD system. A summary of the cdma2000 1xRTT physical layer is shown in Table 2-11. As can be seen, the spreading factor is significantly less than the 3.84 Mcps rate of WCDMA.

The other key difference compared to WCDMA is that cdma2000 1xRTT uses a synchronous mode of operation, meaning that all cell sites need to be time synchronized to a common timing source (GPS is typically used at the cell site). A common Pseudo-Noise (PN) code is used to spread the transmission from all base stations, with each base station using a different time offset so as to enable the mobile to be able to differentiate received waveforms from neighboring cells.

Table 2-11 *cdma2000 1xRTT Physical Layer Attributes*

Duplex	FDD
Channel Bandwidth	1.25 MHz
Modulation Type	QPSK (DL data) BPSK (UL data)
Multiple Access Technique	CDMA
Power Control Rate	800 Hz

continues

Table 2-11 *cdma2000 1xRTT Physical Layer Attributes (continued)*

Duplex	FDD
Frame Duration	5, 20, 40, and 80 milliseconds
Chip Rate	1.2288 M chips/sec
Slots per Frame	16
Multipath Mitigation	Rake receiver and macro diversity combining (dedicated channels only)
Voice Source Rate	Selectable Mode Vocoder (SMV): 8.55, 4.0, 2.0, and 0.8 kbps
Maximum User Data Rate	153.2 kbps (Rel. 0)
Base Station Synchronization	Frequency and time
Forward Error Correction	1/2, 1/3, 1/4 rate Convolution and turbo coding

Although peak voice capacity supports up to 40 simultaneous voice calls, estimates indicate that a typical cdma2000 1xRTT sector can support between 20 and 25 voice channels, depending upon the percentage of pedestrian and vehicular users.[32] The average payload can be calculated using Figure 2-27. Using eight bytes for the IS-638 header, three bytes for cUDP, one byte of PPPmux, and a common four-byte PPP/HDLC header, the average bandwidth expansion due to Abis encapsulation can be calculated to be 12 +4/N bytes, where N is the number of voice frames per PPPmux frame.

Obviously, the efficiency can be increased by simply increasing the number of voice frames per PPPmux payload, but this will lead to increased delay and thus degraded voice quality. Using a typical value of N=10, the average overhead is 12.4 bytes. Then, considering a distribution of voice source rates as shown in Table 2-12, the average voice packet is 8.33 bytes, meaning that the average bandwidth required to support a voice user is (8.33+12.4)*8*50 or 8.3 kbps.

Note This value of 8.3 kbps per cdma2000 voice channel using IP-based backhaul can be compared to the value calculated in the previous section for the overhead of Framing Protocol/AAL2, which resulted in an estimated 12.5 kbps of backhaul being required per WCDMA voice channel.

Table 2-12 *cdma2000 SMV Voice Model*

Voice Rate (kbps)	Voice Frame Size (Bytes)	Probability
8.55	22	29%
4.0	10	4%
2.0	5	7%
0.8	2	60%
Average	8.33 Bytes	

cdma2000 MAC and Signaling Link Access Control Layers

cdma2000 Layer 2 comprises the Signaling Link Access Control (Signaling LAC) and Medium Access Control (MAC). As its name suggests, the signaling LAC is used to provide reliable transmission of upper-layer signaling messages. Figure 2-29 shows the various functionalities of the LAC sublayer, including the following:

- **Authentication:** In cdma2000, authentication is considered to be an access network function (compared to GSM/WCDMA, where authentication is considered a core network function).
- **Integrity:** A Message Authentication Code (MAC) is appended to messages, which is calculated based on the message itself and an integrity key established using Layer 3 procedures.
- **ARQ:** Link control functionality is used to ensure the reliable delivery of upper-layer messages using a selective repeat ARQ process.
- **Addressing:** The addressing sublayer is used to tag PDUs with the identity of the mobile station. The addressing sublayer is only required on common channels—on dedicated channels, the cdma spreading codes uniquely identify the mobile station.
- **Utility:** The utility sublayer is responsible for validating the received PDUs and also for tagging the PDU with radio environment reports, which can be used by upper-layer procedures—for example, handoff and power control.
- **Segmentation and re-assembly:** Upper-layer messages are segmented into sizes that can be transported by the MAC layer, and corresponding re-assembly functionality is defined at the receiving end.

The MAC layer is responsible for multiplexing logical signaling and data channels onto physical channels, allowing signaling and data PDUs to share a common physical dedicated channel. The multiplexing options characterize the QoS requirements (for example, determining the service data rate). One particular multiplexing format is dedicated to the support of the SMV voice codec, supporting 171-, 80-, 40-, and 16-bit options corresponding to the full, half, quarter, and eighth rate vocoded frames produced by the SMV codec.

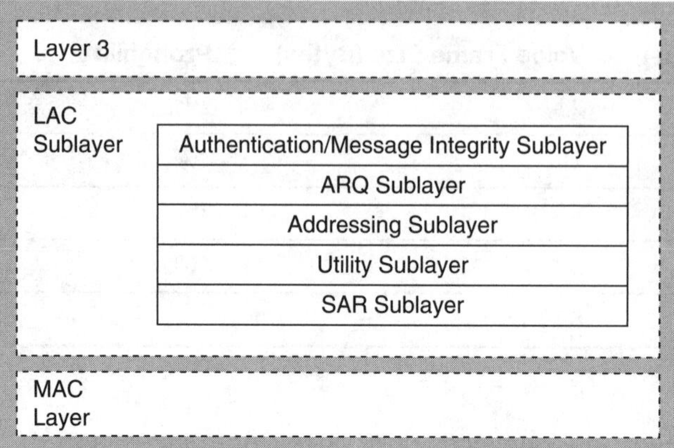

Figure 2-29 *cdma2000 1xRTT Signaling LAC Sublayer*

The MAC layer is also responsible for implementing the RLP, which is used to ensure the delivery of user packet data, sending a Negative Acknowledgment (NAK) if packets are received in error, which are then scheduled for re-transmission. The original RLP format[33] allows two rounds of re-transmission, with the first round comprising two NAKs and the second round comprising three NAKs, before the data is discarded.

cdma2000 Packet Data Operation

In addition to circuit-switched services, cdma2000 1xRTT provide packet-switched services. Data rates up to 153.6 kbps are supported using 1/4 rate coding. For non-real-time services, the channel can be operated with an active set of one; in other words, no soft-handover is supported and instead a cell-switching operation is defined, which can lead to periods of increased instantaneous Frame Error Rates (FER).

For non-real-time services, the packet data channel is operated in burst mode where resources are allocated when required. This allows the channel to be assigned, re-assigned, and de-assigned throughout the duration of a packet data session. The base station can then use smart scheduling in order to increase the utilization of resources when shared between a number of contending packet data users.

In order to share resources and conserve terminal battery power, the cdma2000 MAC defines different MAC states, as shown in Figure 2-30. In the *Active State*, a dedicated traffic channel and dedicated MAC control channel are maintained; in the *Control Hold State*, the traffic channels are de-activated but the dedicated MAC channel is maintained to allow very fast re-establishment of the traffic channel; in the *Suspended State*, there are no logical channels but RLP variables are saved; and in the *Dormant State*, all layer 1 and layer 2 resources are released.

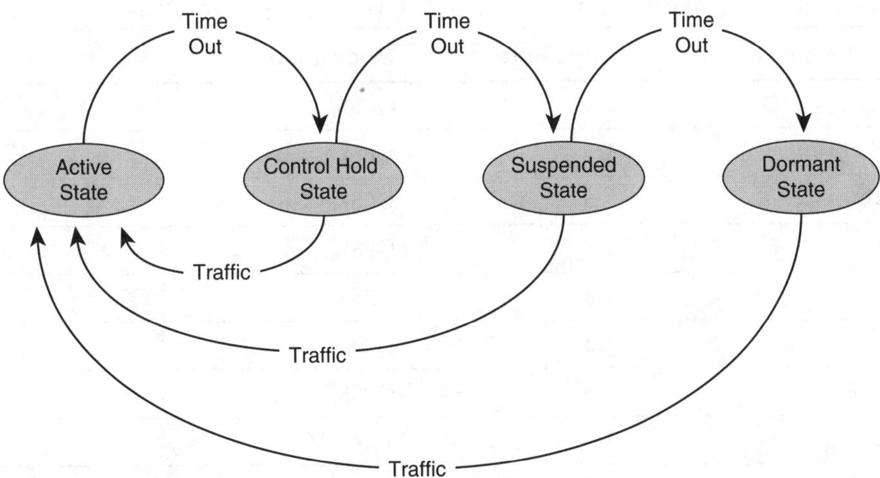

Figure 2-30 *cdma2000 MAC Power-Saving States*

Simulations[34] indicate that the typical average throughput per sector for cdma2000 1xRTT packet data is between 350 kbps and 450 kbps, depending upon whether the propagation conditions correspond to either vehicular or pedestrian environments.

Evolution Data Only

Because cdma2000 1xRTT only supports modest IP data rates, an evolutionary path termed EV-DO (where EV-DO stands for EVolution-Data Only) has been defined. Three revisions of EV-DO have been defined: EV-DO Revision (Rev.) 0, EV-DO Rev. A, and EV-DO Rev. B. The next sections describe these enhancements for packet data transport in more detail.

EV-DO Rev. 0

EV-DO Rev. 0 has added new functionalities to the forward link MAC and physical layers, including support for higher-order modulation (8PSK and 16-QAM), adaptive coding up to 2/3 rate, H-ARQ, and a TDM scheduling capability that allows the system to benefit from multiuser diversity gains. Peak downlink throughput of 2.4576 Mbps is supported, as shown in Table 2-13, but the maximum speed for the uplink remains unchanged from cdma2000 1xRTT at 153.2 kbps. Because this release is suitable for latency tolerant high-bandwidth downlink applications (for example, web browsing), no soft-handover is supported and IP connectivity will be interrupted during handover.

Table 2-13 *cdma2000 EV-DO Rev. 0 Downlink Modulation and Coding*

Data Rate (in kbps)	Code Rate	Modulation
38.4	1/5	QPSK
76.8	1/5	QPSk
153.6	1/5	QPSK
307.2	1/5	QPSK
614.4	1/3	QPSK
921.6	1/3	8PSK
1228.8	2/3	QPSK
1228.8	1/3	16-QAM
1843.2	2/3	8PSK
2457.6	2/3	16-QAM

Simulations[35] have been used to predict the average sector throughput of an EV-DO Rev. 0 sector. These indicate that assuming a proportionally fair scheduler and a mix of pedestrian and vehicular users, the average sector throughput is around 1 Mbps with per user perceived throughput of up to 500 kbps. Typical latency figures of around 110 ms are to be expected.

EV-DO Rev. A

Whereas EV-DO Rev. 0 provides IP connectivity for interactive and best-effort services, EV-DO Rev. A offers further enhancements for supporting QoS-enabled conversational IP services. Because conversational IP services can be bi-directional, EV-DO Rev. A adds new uplink capability, including H-ARQ together with higher-order modulation (QPSK and 8PSK) to offer peak uplink transmission rates of up to 1843.2 kbps, equivalent to the 8PSK configurations available in Rev. 0, as shown in Table 2-13. (The EV-DO Rev. A downlink has also been enhanced with an option for 16-QAM configuration with 5/6 rate coding, which provides an increased downlink peak rate of 3072 kbps.)

In order to support conversational QoS services over IP bearers, the MAC layer has been enhanced with capabilities to differentiate between different flows to a single user. A separate RLP instance is assigned per QoS priority/flow, allowing differentiated packet handling according to the class of traffic transported in a particular flow, as shown in Figure 2-31. Another key enhancement to the MAC layer is the addition of Robust Header Compression (RoHC) functionality, which is essential for efficient Voice over IP (VoIP) transport over EV-DO networks.

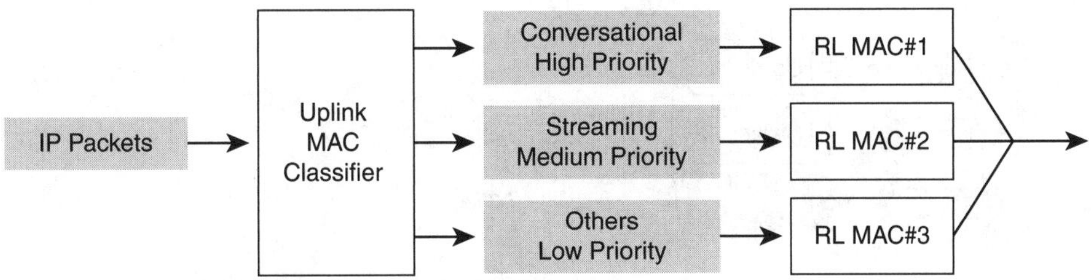

Figure 2-31 *EV-DO Rev. A QoS Differentiation*

Finally, in order to support conversational services to fully mobile users, enhancements have been made to further decrease the RTT experienced by conversational packet services and to improve the handover procedures. Fast-forward sector-switching capabilities allow the mobile to indicate to the network that a handoff is imminent. A *virtual* soft-handoff is implemented by the BSC sending traffic to the current and target cells simultaneously in order to minimize any disruption to ongoing VoIP calls.

The overall result of these enhancements is the ability of EV-DO Rev. A to efficiently support mass adoption of conversational IP services, specifically VoIP. Simulations[36] have shown that, assuming a mix of pedestrian and vehicular users, a 1.25 MHz EV-DO Rev. A sector can support up to 35 VoIP flows, a significant improvement over the 25–30 circuit-switched voice calls that can be supported over a cdma2000 1xRTT sector.

Note This validates that the adoption of H-ARQ, higher-order modulation, multiuser diversity, and Robust Header Compression techniques for enhancing the performance and efficiency of transporting IP bearers over the mobile radio interface, resulting in a superior VoIP capacity compared to legacy circuit-switched radio transport of traditional mobile voice services.

EV-DO Rev. B

Most recently, EV-DO Rev. B, finalized in 2006, introduces 64-QAM modulation together with multicarrier support, which allows the bonding of multiple 1.25 MHz radio channels into an aggregate channel, as shown in Figure 2-32. Although the standard allows up to 17 Rev. A carriers to be aggregated, a more typical deployment may be to use a 5-MHz allocation corresponding to three carriers plus guard bands. In such a scenario, the use of 64 QAM on a single carrier supports peak downlink rates of up to 4.9 Mbps, allowing peak downlink speeds of up to 14.745 Mbps and peak uplink speeds of 5.4 Mbps.

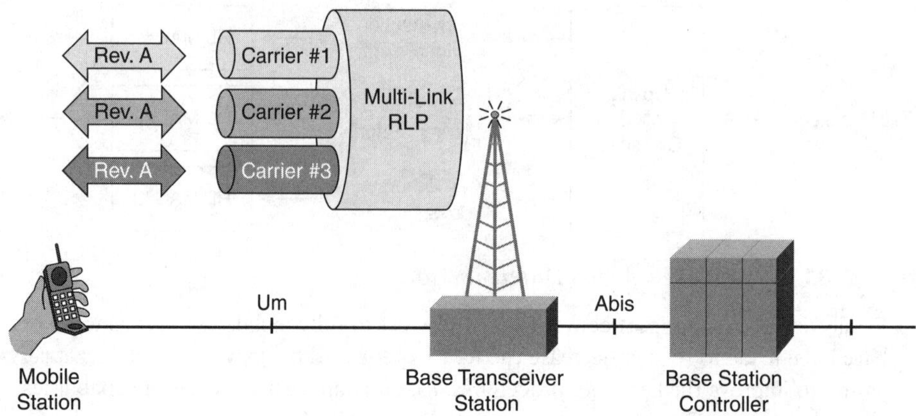

Figure 2-32 *EV-DO Rev. B Multicarrier Support*

Summary

The evolution of the cellular access system has certainly seen dramatic changes since the first voice-centric GSM systems were deployed in the early 1990s with native capability for sending 140-bit SMS messages at an aggregate throughput of less than 800 bps. The adoption of wireless IP-based services has followed—first using a circuit-switched dial-up model and then quickly followed by an overlay approach to supporting always-on packet-switched services. Increasingly complex radio techniques have been applied to these systems, allowing peak IP throughput to increase in excess of 40 Mbps.

The era of delivering IP data services via an overlay architecture is now over, and instead, as the volumes of IP traffic surpasses legacy circuit-switched voice, mobile access system architectures can be optimized for IP service delivery, moving functionality toward the edge of the network, where real-time intelligence can be used to optimally schedule packets for delivery of the time-variant mobile radio propagation environment.

Endnotes

[1]GSM 04.22, Radio Link Protocol (RLP) for data and telematic services on the Mobile Station–Base Station System (MS–BSS) interface and the Base Station System–Mobile-services Switching Center (BSS–MSC) interface.

[2]B.W. Marsden, "A Performance Assessment of the GSM Radio Link Protocol (RLP)," Technical Report UMCS-91-4-2, Dept. of Comp. Science, Univ. of Manchester, http://intranet.cs.man.ac.uk/Intranet_subweb/library/cstechrep/Abstracts/scannedreps/UMCS_91_4_2.pdf.

[3]J. Korhonen, et al., "Measured Performance of GSM HSCSD and GPRS," www.cs.helsinki.fi/u/gurtov/papers/icc01.pdf.

[4]K. Premkumar and A. Chockalingam, “Performance Analysis of RLC/<AC and LLC Layers in a GPRS Protocol Stack,” IEEE Trans. Veh. Tech., Vol. 53, No. 5, Sept. 2004.

[5]3GPP TS 04.65, “Sub-Network Dependent Convergence Protocol (SNDCP).”

[6]C.F. Ball, et al., “Introducing 3G-Like Conversational Services in GERAN Packet Data Networks,” IEEE Veh. Tech. Conf., VTC 2005, Vol. 4, Issue 30, 2005.

[7]M. Lundan and I.D.D. Curcio, “3GPP Streaming Over GPRS Rel. ‘97,” Proc. 12th Int. Conf. on Computer Communications and Networks, ICCCN, 2003.

[8]A. Gurtov, et al., “Multi-layer Protocol Tracing in a GPRS Network,” Proc. IEEE 56th Veh. Tech. Conf., VTC-2002.

[9]3GPP TS 44.091, “External Network Assisted Cell Change (NACC).”

[10]3GPP TS 43.129, “Packet-Switched Handover for GERAN A/Gb mode.”

[11]V. Rexhepi, et al., “Handover of Packet-Switched Services in GERAN A/Gb Mode,” IEEE Global Telecomms. Conf., 2005.

[12]H. Holma and A. Toskala, “WCDMA for UMTS—HSPA Evolution and LTE,” Wiley, 2007.

[13]C. Chevalier, et al., “WCDMA Deployment Handbook, Planning and Optimization Aspects,” Wiley, 2006.

[14]3GPP 25.321, Medium Access Control (MAC) Protocol Specification.

[15]3GPP 25.331, Radio Resource Control (RRC) Protocol Specification.

[16]RFC 2507: IP Header Compression.

[17]RFC 3095: Robust Header Compression (RoHC): Framework and Four Profiles: RTP, UDP, ESP, and Uncompressed.

[18]P.M. Garrosa, “Interactions Between TCP and Channel Type Switching in WCDMA,” Chalmers University of Technology, Master of Science thesis, January 2002.

[19]www.qualcomm.com/common/documents/white_papers/ESG_Optimizing_PS_Data_User_Experience_RevB.pdf.

[20]3GPP 25.803, “S-CCPCH Performance for MBMS.”

[21]Qualcomm Engineering Services, “HSDPA Indoor Deployment Aspects,” 80-W0976-1 Rev. A, www.qualcomm.com/common/documents/white_papers/HSDPA_IndoorDeploymentAspects.pdf

[22]mobilesociety.typepad.com/mobile_life/2008/11/hspa-state-change-measurements.html.

[23]Qualcomm Engineering Services, "UMTS/HSDPA Backhaul Bandwidth Dimensioning," 80-W1193-1 Rev. A, www.qualcomm.com/esg/media/pdf/UMTS_HSDPA_Bandwidth_Backhaul_Dimensioning_Rev%20A.pdf

[24]H. Holma and A. Toskala, "HSDPA/HSUPA for UMTS," Wiley, 2006.

[25]J. Liu, et al., "Performance and Capacity of HSUPA in Lab Environment," IEEE Veh. Tech. Conf., pp. 1906–1909, May 2008.

[26]3GPP 25.903, "Continuous Connectivity for Packet Data Users."

[27]T. Chen, et al., "Uplink DPCCH Gating of Inactive UEs in Continuous Packet Connectivity Mode for HSUPA," IEEE Wireless Comms. and Networking Conf., WCNC 2007, pp. 1684–1689.

[28]www.broadband-forum.org/technical/download/TR-069Amendment2.pdf.

[29]"Interference Management in UMTS Femtocells," www.femtoforum.org/femto/Files/File/Interference%20Management%20in%20UMTS%20Femtocells.pdf.

[30]TIA-EIA-828, "BTS-BSC Interoperability (AbisInterface)," www.tiaonline.org/standards/technology/cdma2000/documents/TIA-EIA-828.pdf.

[31]TIA-2001-C, "Interoperability Specification (IOS) for cdma2000® Access Network Interfaces, Release C," www.tiaonline.org/standards/technology/cdma2000/documents/TIA-2001-C_000.pdf.

[32]J.D. Lim, "Air Interface Capacity and Area Coverage Analysis for cdma2000 Voice and Packet Data Services," IEEE Veh. Tech. Conf., VTC 2001, pp. 1770–1774.

[33]TIA/EIA/IS-707-A-I, "Data Service Options for Spread Spectrum Systems: Radio Link Protocol Type 3."

[34]Qualcomm, "The Economics of Mobile Data," www.wirelessdevnet.com/library/WirelessMobileData.pdf.

[35]www.cdg.org/resources/white_papers/files/Lucent%201xEV-DO%20Rev%20O%20Mar%2004.pdf.

[36]www.cdg.org/news/events/cdmaseminar/050208_voip_summit/9-Mike%20Recchione-Lucent.pdf.

Chapter 3

All-IP Access Systems

While the original adoption of IP data services by the legacy cellular systems as an overlay architecture has been superseded by mobile broadband specific systems, these access systems have evolved from systems which were originally designed and deployed in an era when circuit switched services (that is, primarily targeted for voice) still dominated cellular operator revenue. In the future, the growth of mobile broadband consumption means that IP based services will predominate and access systems designed from an all-IP perspective will be widely adopted.

This chapter describes different approaches to delivering an all-IP access system, in particular, those defined using IEEE technology, including:

- **IEEE 802.11-2007:** As WiFi adoption has increased, legacy cellular systems have been augmented with the ability to integrate IEEE 802.11 based access systems.
- **IEEE 802.16-2005:** Also known as 802.16e, this OFDMA technology is used in the Worldwide Interoperability for Microwave Access (WiMAX) system, an end-to-end all-IP system for providing mobile broadband services.

This chapter will then describe the very latest evolution of cellular systems for supporting all-IP mobile broadband:

- **Long Term Evolution (LTE):** An end-to-end all-IP system standardized by the Third generation Partnership Project, 3GPP (http://www.3gpp.org).

Finally, the chapter will conclude with a view of the future; looking at those systems which are still at the time of writing (2009) yet to complete standardization:

- **IMT-Advanced:** The term the International Telecommunications Union (ITU) has defined to be applied to *4G systems* that are targeted to support capabilities of up to 1 Gbps for low mobility users and 100 Mbps for high mobility users.

Wireless Local Area Networks Access System

The rapid growth of Wireless Local Area Network (WLAN) technologies in both the enterprise and home networking market segments has created the opportunity for service providers to position WLAN based technologies in so-called hotspot deployments in advance of mobile broadband installations. In July 2003, the IEEE approved the 802.11g standard[1] which offered maximum bit rates of up to 54 Mbps, when equivalent cellular services were typically providing wide area GPRS connectivity of 40 kbps. Table 3-1 shows the physical layer characteristics of IEEE 802.11g.

Table 3-1 *IEEE 802.11g Radio Interface*

Duplex	TDD
Channel Bandwidth	20 MHz
Frequency Band	2.4 – 2.497 GHz
Modulation Type	OFDM with BPSK, QPSK, 16-QAM, 64-QAM
Multiple Access Technique	Carrier Sense Multiple Access/Collision Avoidance (CSMA/CA)
Maximum User data rate	54 Mbps
Forward Error Correction Coding Rate	1/2, 2/3, 3/4

For wireless service providers, the emergence of Public WLAN (PWLAN) solutions represented a threat to their establish business model; the economic barrier-to-entry for a PWLAN system can be very low compared to the significant investments required to deploy conventional cellular systems. Conversely, the PWLAN offered wired service providers the possibility to augment their service offerings with nomadic hotspot services.

In order to address these issues, the cellular standardization bodies moved to enhance their systems with the ability to inter-work with WLAN technologies in two distinct ways:

- **Inter-working WLAN (I-WLAN):** I-WLAN viewed WLAN as an all-IP access technology and consequently an architecture was defined which allowed to use the same smart-card based authentication and authorization used by 3GPP cellular operators to authenticate WLAN users. Since 3GPP cellular operators already had an existing customer billing relationship based on smart card credentials, these could be leveraged by those operators looking to deploy public WLAN infrastructure, or sign roaming agreements with public WLAN operators.
- **Generic Access Network (GAN):** The GAN architecture uses WLAN, or more precisely any IP supporting bearer, to replace the lower radio specific layers of GSM, allowing the full range of GSM services to be provided over WLAN bearers, in particular a suitably equipped dual mode cellular phone. Although not strictly an all-IP

technology (2G Circuit Switched voice services are delivered over the IP bearer), it does indicate how IP is disrupting the legacy cellular architecture, in particular for defining in-building propositions.

The following sections describe these access systems in more detail.

Interworking WLAN

While WLAN has been widely adopted in enterprise and residential locations, the cellular operators viewed legacy implementations as being deficient in terms of the security, in particular the original WLAN systems used unencrypted communications which were vulnerable to various attacks. The standardization of the IEEE 802.1X Port Based Authentication specification[2], IEEE 802.11i MAC security enhancements[3] and IETF's Extensible Authentication Protocol[4] (EAP – RFC 3748) offered the foundation for cellular operators to integrate secure Public WLAN into their legacy architectures.

Two different services are defined for I-WLAN[5], one termed "Direct IP access" which simply provides the WLAN device with IP connectivity to a local network, and a second, termed "3GPP IP Access", which uses a Packet Data Gateway (PDG) to allow the WLAN device access to cellular specific services, including secure access to services in the user's home network, as shown in Figure 3-1.

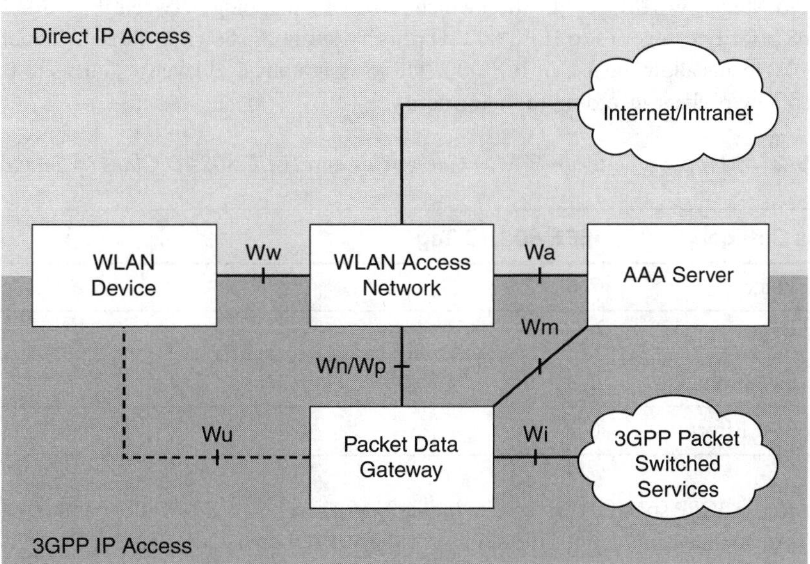

Figure 3-1 *I-WLAN Architecture*

I-WLAN Authentication and Authorization uses EAP together with IEEE 802.1X Port Based Authentication. New EAP methods for EAP-SIM[6] and EAP-AKA[7] have been defined specifically to allow existing smart card based authentication exchanges. These

EAP exchanges allow keying material to be derived for the WLAN radio interface leveraging the same credentials used for cellular access authentication. However, in contrast to legacy cellular networks, which have used SS7 for authentication signaling exchanges, I-WLAN "Direct IP Access" authentication is transported over AAA interfaces, with 3GPP defining both RADIUS and diameter protocol options. Chapter 8, "End-to-End Context Awareness," provides details about the SIM based authentication techniques as well as describing EAP based approaches to authentication and AAA interworking.

Note For the 3GGP community, the adoption of this WLAN architecture triggered the definition of new AAA interfaces for supporting roaming Public WLAN services. The GSMA Association (http://www.gsmworld.com) is the trade body that defines the inter-operator interfaces to support roaming and interworking and it has published guidelines on WLAN roaming in Permanent Reference Document (PRD) IR.61[8].

Other than a requirement to support IEEE 802.1X and IEEE 802.11i capabilities, 3GGP's I-WLAN architecture does not place additional requirements on the WLAN Access Network. However, recognizing that legacy cellular networks differentiate themselves on their ability to support differentiated Quality of Service (QoS), 3GPP additionally defined how the I-WLAN could optionally benefit from the deployment of IEEE 802.11e differentiated QoS capability[9] and the WiFi Alliance's (http://www.wi-fi.org) Wireless Multi Media (WMM) certification which provides a mapping between IEEE 802.11e QoS priority categories to IEEE 802.1D priority levels, as shown in Table 3-2. Such deployments allow the use of IEEE 802.11e to assign physical layer resources to the incoming packets according to their priority.

Table 3-2 *Mapping Between WMM Categories and IEEE 802.1D Class of Service (CoS)*

Access Category	IEEE 802.1D Tag
WMM Voice	7, 6
WMM Video	5, 4
WMM Background	2, 1
WMM Best Effort	0, 3

To access 3GPP specific services, including home based services while roaming, the I-WLAN architecture defines the ability for the WLAN device to establish a secure tunnel to the PDG. Leveraging remote access functionality, the WLAN device establishes an IPSec tunnel using version 2 of the Internet Key Exchange (IKEv2) – RFC 4306. IKEv2 has been selected because it allows the same EAP method used for authenticating WLAN access to be re-used for tunnel authentication.

To provide for QoS when accessing home-based services, the PDG and WLAN device can use Differentiated Services functionality to appropriately color the IP headers. Chapter 4, "An IP Refresher" provides more detail of the Differentiated Services QoS Architecture.

Generic Access Network

The I-WLAN architecture enabled the all-IP services, originally defined for access by cellular subscribers, to be accessible by users with WLAN devices. Unfortunately, with the majority of cellular revenue coming from legacy circuit switched voice services, an operator wanting to offer a full suite of services over an I-WLAN infrastructure would be mandated to deploy a Voice-over-IP (VoIP) solution—for example using the IP Multimedia Subsystem (IMS) together with suitable Telephony Application Servers (TAS), as described in Chapter 9, " Content and Services." Deploying such an infrastructure has proved to be technically complex.

The Generic Access Network (GAN) is the standardized version of Unlicensed Mobile Access (UMA) specified by 3GPP[10]. The GAN architecture leverages the earlier I-WLAN architecture, in particular re-using the SIM based authentication for establishing an IPSec tunnel to a PDG. However, instead of simply using the IPSec tunnel to transport native IP packets from the WLAN enabled device, GAN defines a complete access system. This system includes the use of a new network element, the GAN Controller (GANC), which replaces the functionality of the legacy BSC network element and allows cellular control messages to be sent over TCP instead of LAPD/LAPDm, as shown in Figure 3-2. It also allows circuit switched media to be sent over the Real-time Transport Protocol (RTP) instead of TDM, as shown in Figure 3-3, re-using a common IPSec tunnel for both TCP-based signaling and the RTP-based media.

Note Even though the IPSec function is shown as integrated into the GAN Controller element in Figures 3-2 and 3-3, this is typically delivered as a separate IPSec Gateway network element.

Figure 3-2 shows how legacy core network signaling can be transported over a TCP/IP connection using the newly defined Generic Access Resource Control (GA-RC), Generic Access Circuit Switched Resource Control (GA-CSR) and Generic Access Packet Switched Resource Control (GA-PSR) protocols:

- **GA-RC:** This protocol is used to allow the GAN device to register with GANC as well as providing an application keep-alive in order to enable the GANC to determine when the GAN user has moved outside of WLAN coverage.
- **GA-CSR/GA-PSR:** These protocols are used to set-up the connections used to transport the circuit and packet switched bearers between the GAN device and the GANC. Because the GANC is equivalent to a BSC, GA-CSR/GA-PSR is also able to support handover between GAN and Cellular modes.

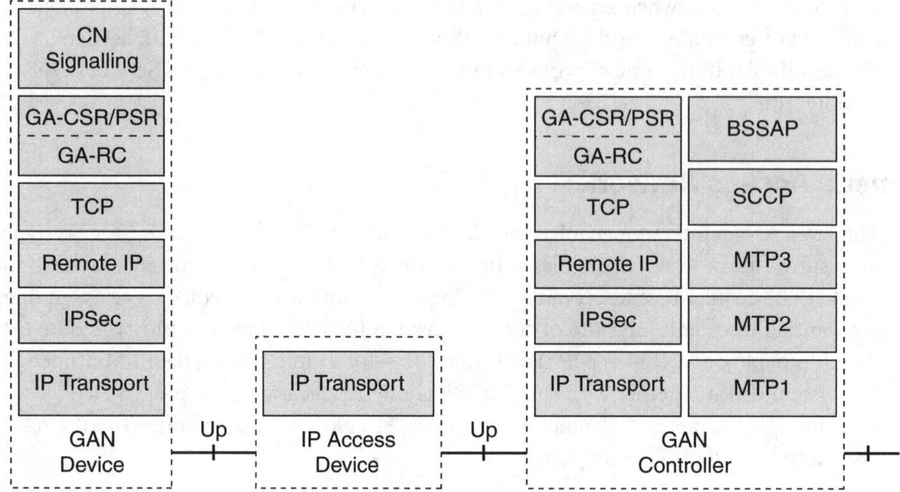

Figure 3-2 *GAN Access System, Signaling Transport*

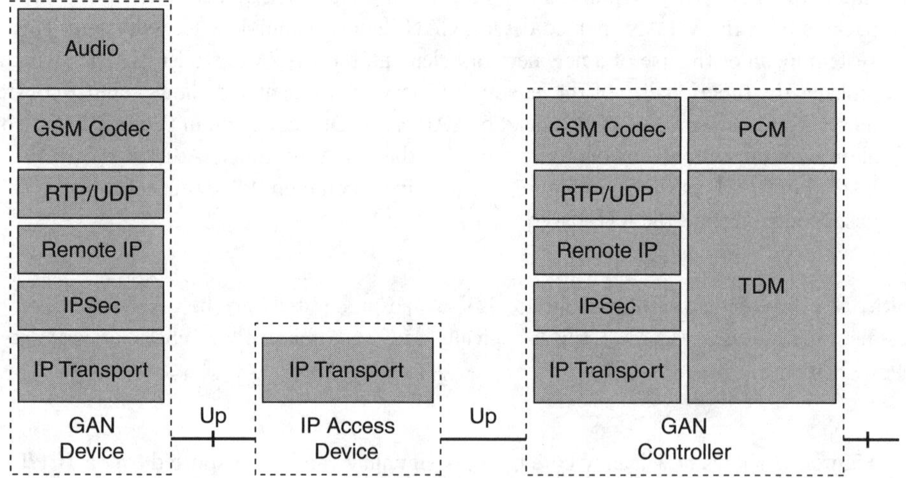

Figure 3-3 *GAN Access System, Voice Transport*

Although originally defined only for GSM and GPRS access, the GAN architecture has recently been enhanced with an Iu-mode of operation, allowing dual mode 3G devices to access legacy services over WLAN access networks.

Since the GANC peers with 2G BSC and 3G RNC elements, conventional handover can be supported if the dual mode phone is able to report "measurements" performed on the WLAN network. Assuming that a dual-mode phone has the ability to support simultaneous communications over cellular and WLAN, the GAN-enabled device will first establish an IPSec tunnel to the security gateway and then register with the GANC, during which it receives system information, including a dummy neighbor cell identity. (A *dummy* neighbor cell may correspond to a GSM frequency that is prohibited from being used in a particular geography.) The cellular network will have been configured to broadcast the same *dummy* cell in its neighbor list. Although native phones will recover this information, they will fail to decode GSM information using the *dummy* cell identity and thus not report any information to the network. However, a GAN device, which prefers WLAN coverage, is provided with the same *dummy* cell information during GANC registration. This will trigger the GAN device to start to report measurements for the *dummy* neighbor cell to the cellular network at an artificially high value. This triggers normal BSC procedures for BSC-to-GANC handover.

In the reverse direction, handover from WLAN to licensed cellular needs to be triggered when the WLAN quality degrades below a certain threshold. The handover is triggered by the GAN device which has visibility of the reception quality of WLAN signals, the packet error rate on the down-link RTP transported Media, possible quality indications in the RTP Control Protocol (RTCP – RFC 3550) messages as well as up-link quality reports sent by the GAN controller.

UMA/GAN has driven new scaling requirements for IPSec implementations (which have been subsequently leveraged by the femto cell community). Traditional IPSec scalability had assumed a small to moderate session count with large throughputs, whereas the GAN model requires massive scale into the hundreds of thousands of IPSec session but with throughput driven by 2G voice usage. Given that IPSec based Up transport should be able to traverse home gateway Network Address Translation (NAT) functionality, the Up interface shown in Figure 3-3 will comprise the following protocols AMR/RTP/UDP/IP/IPSec/UDP/IP.

This expands the bandwidth required for a 12.2 kbps AMR call up to around 64 kbps. Using a typical busy hour voice occupancy of 5% (or 0.05 milliErlangs), the IPSec gateway for a 2.5G GAN Voice subscriber should be dimensioned at around 4 kbps per device.

WiMAX Access System

Whereas previous attempts to leverage IEEE technology in mobile systems have used the IEEE 802.11 family of standards, which were primarily aimed at leveraging Local Area Networking (LAN) functionality for providing hotspot coverage, the Worldwide Interoperability for Microwave Access (WiMAX) communication system is an end-to-end, all-IP wireless system designed to provide *wide area mobile* access to broadband IP services. The WiMAX architecture defines the use of the IEEE 802.16-2005 standard, also known as IEEE 802.16e, for providing the physical and MAC layer support. Whereas IEEE 802.11 technology has been defined for use with un-licensed radio bands, for example the 2.4 GHz unlicensed Industrial Medical and Scientific (ISM) band, WiMAX has been primarily designed for operation in licensed spectrum, for example at 2.3 GHz, 2.5 GHz and 3.5 GHz.

Note IEEE 802.16e has optionally defined the ability to be deployed in unlicensed spectrum. However, the WiMAX MAC layer is based on a Request/Grant access mechanism, which can be termed "aggressive" when compared with WLAN's "polite" contention-based MAC protocol more frequently used in un-licensed deployments. The use of incompatible medium access mechanisms mean that these systems perform poorly when spectrum is shared.

The WiMAX Access System comprises the Subscriber Station (SS), the Base Station (BS) and the Access Service Node Gateway (ASN-GW), as shown in figure 3-4. The various access system interfaces are:

- **R1 interface:** between the SS and the BS corresponds to the IEEE 802.16-2005 specifications.
- **R8 interface:** between BS and BS to support inter-BS communications in order to support fast/seamless handovers.
- **R6 interface:** between the BS and the ASN GW providing control and bearer plane connectivity. The control plane provides tunnel management including the ability to establish, modify and release Generic Routing Encapsulation (GRE) tunnels between the BS and the ASN-GW.
- **R4 interface:** between ASN-GW and ASN-GW in order to support mobility between different ASN-GW.

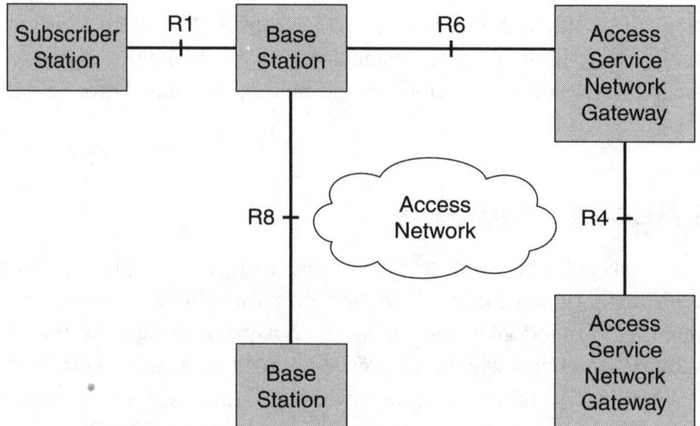

Figure 3-4 *WiMAX Access System Architecture*

The WiMAX Forum (http://www.wimaxforum.org) defined a number of ASN profiles which were intended to manage the various implementation options selected by manufacturers and to assist in multi-vendor interoperability. The Forum defined three different profiles:

- **Profile A:** This represents a centralized ASN-GW with separate BS and ASN-GW equipment. The Radio Resource Management was implemented in both the BS and ASN-GW, with the former including a Radio Resource Agent (RRA) which collects radio resource information from the base station and Radio Resource Control (RRC) function in the ASN-GW.
- **Profile B:** Represents a distributed ASN-GW deployment option whereby the ASN-GW was co-located with the BS.
- **Profile C:** Is a centralized model similar to Profile A but now with all Radio Resource Management functionality being located in the BS.

The decomposition between RRA and RRC functionality in Profile A meant that multi-vendor interoperability is more challenging compared with the other profiles. Hence, Profile A was subsequently deprecated. Furthermore, since Profile B represents a co-location of functionalities defined in Profile C, no further development is seen as necessary. This leads Profile C as being the standards track approach for the WiMAX architecture.

Protocol Architecture of WiMAX Access System

The detailed protocols used in the WiMAX Access System are shown in Figure 3-5.

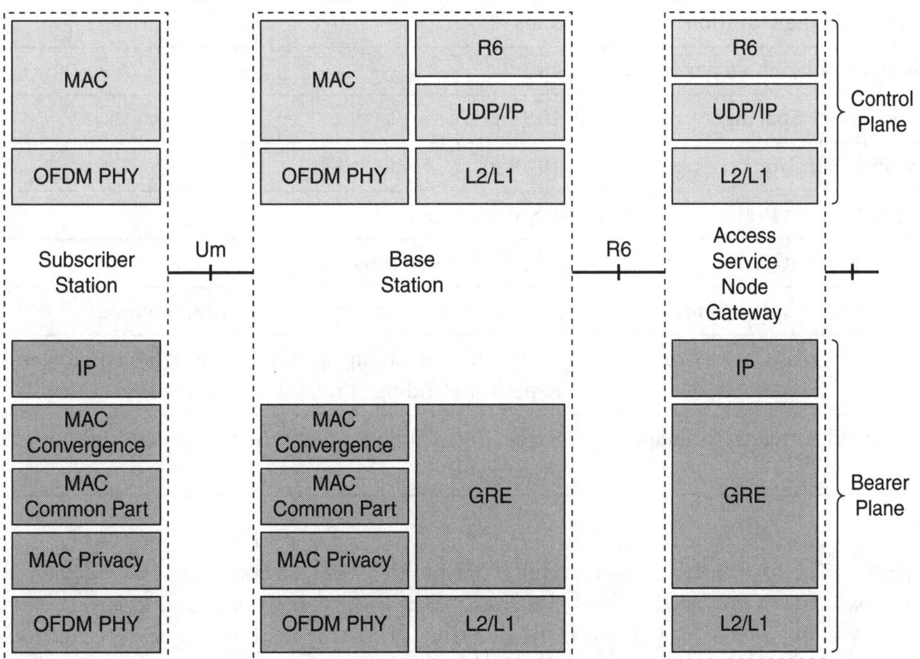

Figure 3-5 *WiMAX Access System Protocol Architecture*

Unlike cellular systems, the WiMAX system is defined as collaboration between two different organizations. The IEEE 802.16 group is responsible for defining the signaling between the SS and the BS and the WiMAX Forum is responsible for defining the signaling between the BS and the ASN-GW across the R6 interface as shown in Figure 3-5. Consequently, unlike cellular systems where Non-Access Stratum (NAS) messages are defined, which allows the wireless terminal to exchange signaling messages with core network elements, no such direct signaling is defined in the WiMAX system.

WiMAX Physical Layer

The WiMAX physical layer is a scalable OFDM-based system which, in contrast to previously defined cellular systems, can be used in a variety of channel bandwidths. Table 3-3 provides the key physical layer attributes of the mobile WiMAX parameters.

Table 3-3 *WiMAX Physical Layer*

Duplex	Primarily TDD
Channel Bandwidth	From 1.25 MHz to 10 M Hz
Modulation Type	QPSK, 16 QAM, 64 QAM (down-link only)
Multiple Access Technique	OFDMA
TDMA Frame Duration	5 ms
Number of symbols per frame	48
Sub-Carrier Spacing	10.94 kHz
Symbol Duration	102.9 μs
Typical Cyclic Prefix	1/8 symbol period
MultiPath Mitigation	OFDM/Cyclic Prefix
Base Station Synchronization	Frequency and Time synchronization required
Forward Error Correction	Convolutional Coding at rates 1/2, 2/4, 3/4 and 5/6 and Repetition Coding at rates 1/2, 1/3 and 1/6
Advanced Antenna Techniques	Space Time Coding (Matrix-A) and Spatial Multiplexing (Matrix-B)

Note The first Mobile System Profile (1.0) from the WiMAX Forum only included an option for TDD operation. However, with the vast majority of spectrum allocated to mobile systems being paired into FDD bands, the WiMAX Forum subsequently decided to add an FDD variant in Mobile System Profile 1.5.

With an OFDMA based physical layer, both up-link and down-link resources can be shared between users; different users can be allocated subsets of OFDM sub-carriers in both the time and, when the optional advanced antenna capabilities are used, in the spatial domain. These subsets, or subchannels, represent the minimum frequency resource which can be allocated to a user.

Subchannels can either be defined as contiguous subcarriers, termed Adaptive Modulation and Coding (AMC), in WiMAX, or pseudo randomly distributed across the channel bandwidth, termed Partial Usage of Subcarriers (PUSC). Whereas the distribution of carriers in PUSC provides additional frequency diversity, AMC allows Multi-User Diversity (MUD) gains, allocating subchannels to users based on the instantaneous channel frequency response.

The TDD WiMAX frame structure, as shown in Figure 3-6, illustrates how the time resources are distributed between users. As with the subchannel allocation, time resources, or slots, are allocated to users depending on propagation conditions, data rate requirements and traffic type. One of the advantages of TDD systems is that the amount of resources allocated to up-link and down-link resources can be altered according to demand and Figure 3-6 shows the TDD frame is divided into a downlink subframe and an up-link subframe.

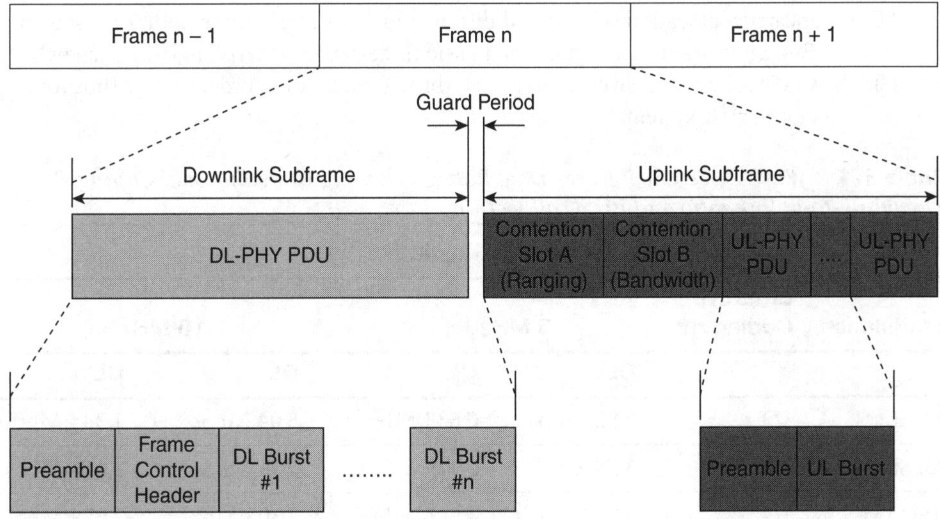

Figure 3-6 *WiMAX Frame Structure*

In WiMAX, the ratio between the sub-frames can vary by a factor of 3-to-1; in other words, up to 75% of the spectrum resources can be allocated to either the up-link or, more likely, the down-link, according to traffic demand. Unfortunately, this flexibility is typically only system-wide, with neighboring base stations having to be time synchronized to ensure that the downlink subframes are synchronously transmitted. Otherwise, the system will suffer from significant self-interference as one base station, potentially placed in an elevated position, is transmitting and has a line-of-sight path to another base station which is scheduled to be receiving the weak signals from the WiMAX devices in its coverage area.

Note All wide area TDD systems typically require time synchronized emissions in order to reduce self-interference. Time synchronization can be delivered using a GPS enabled timing unit at the base station or using adaptive clock recovery, for example, using the IEEE 1588-2008 Precision Timing Protocol version 2 (PTPv2).

The Frame Control Header (FCH) which is transmitted immediately following the preamble includes the mapping information in the Medium Access Protocol (MAP) (DL-MAP and UL-MAP) which indicates how resources in the frame are allocated to each user together with which modulation and coding scheme to apply. The FCH is followed by a number of down-link bursts. After a short guard interval, the initial portion of the uplink subframe is used for ranging purposes, including time and frequency synchronization as well as open loop power control. A second contention slot is also available for subscriber stations (SS) to perform bandwidth requests.

Using a 3:1 downlink-to-uplink ratio, the physical layer data rates are achievable using a PUSC subcarrier allocation scheme and different rates of convolution coding, as shown in Table 3-4. Simulations[11] indicate that a basic three-sector 5MHz Single-In-Single-Out (SISO) WiMAX system delivers average cell throughputs of the order of 17 Mbps for a three-sector 5 MHz system.

Table 3-4 *WiMAX Physical Layer Data Rates, assuming Convolutional Coding, 3:1 Downlink-to-uplink ratio and PUSC allocation*

		Channel Bandwidth			
Modulation	**Effective Coding rate**	**5 MHz**		**10 MHz**	
		DL	**UL**	**DL**	**UL**
QPSK	1/2	2.52 Mbps	0.633 Mbps	5.04 Mbps	1.344 Mbps
QPSK	3/4	3.78 Mbps	0.979 Mbps	7.56 Mbps	2.016 Mbps
16QAM	1/2	5.05 Mbps	1.306 Mbps	10.08 Mbps	2.688 Mbps
16 QAM	3/4	7.56 Mbps	1.958 Mbps	15.12 Mbps	4.032 Mbps
64QAM	1/2	7.56 Mbps	1.958 Mbps	15.12 Mbps	4.032 Mbps
64QAM	2/3	10.08 Mbps	2.611 Mbps	20.160 Mbps	5.376 Mbps
64 QAM	3/4	11.34 Mbps	2.938 Mbps	22.68 Mbps	6.048 Mbps
64QAM	5/6	12.6 Mbps	3.264 Mbps	25.2 Mbps	6.72 Mbps

WiMAX Adaptive Antenna System

One of the key advantages of TDD/OFDMA systems is their suitability to Adaptive Antenna Systems (AAS). The TDD system produces a reciprocal channel which then avoids the complexity of channel feedback mechanisms—the channel response sensed on the up-link by the base station can be assumed to apply to the down-link (assuming the channel is stationary between up-link and down-link subframes). The OFDMA system then allows the transmitted pilot sub-carriers to be shared between the two antennas, avoiding interference between the channel estimation processes. Figure 3-7 shows a down-link resource over two symbols where the pilot sub-carriers are time multiplexed between the two antennas to ensure independent channel estimation.

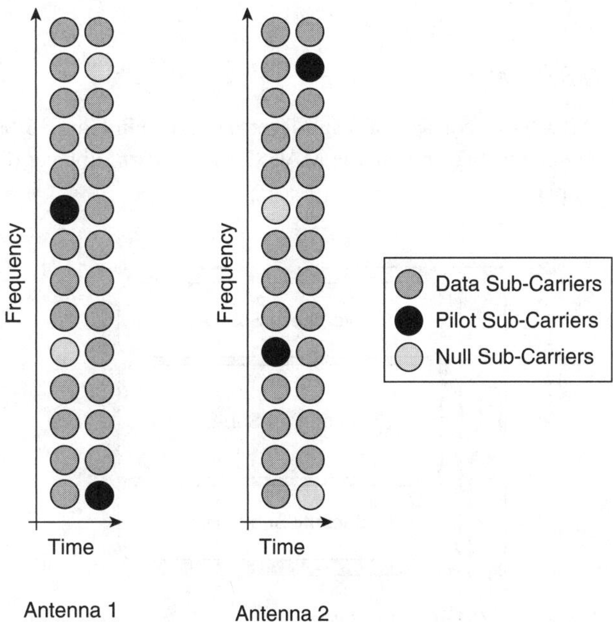

Figure 3-7 *WiMAX MIMO Subchannelization*

Chapter 1 introduced both Spatial Multiplexing (SM) and Space Time Coding (STC) as AAS techniques. Whereas the diversity gains of STC provides improved throughput at low Carrier-to-Interference-and-Noise Ratios (CINRs), SM techniques can be used to provide additional data throughput when the CINR is large enough for supporting the multiple spatially diverse links. At sufficiently high CINR values, MIMO 2x2 spatial multiplexing techniques can be used to double the peak achievable data rates.

Compared with the basis SISO operation, simulations[12] have shown that the use of STC in WiMAX can provide 5 to 10 dB of performance gain depending upon the selected modulation and coding scheme; for example, the CINR required to achieve a 15 Mbps throughput using 64 QAM and 1/2 rate coding is reduced from 20 dB without STC to around 10 dB when STC is used. The same simulations have demonstrated the effective throughput doubling derived from spatial multiplexing. However, these gains come at a significant cost of higher CINR requirements; for example, 7.5dB more CINR is required to achieve the doubling of the highest throughput. This leads to the observation that the AAS system should be configured to operate in STC below a certain CINR threshold and operate in SM mode above that threshold. When looking at the performance of the WiMAX AMC, the CINR threshold should be set to around 15 dB.

Studies on the Cumulative Distribution of CINR values[12] indicate that in certain deployments, less than 20% of subscribers experience CINR greater than 15dB and therefore the majority of users may be challenged to benefit from the gains achievable by Spatial Multiplexing. Beamforming is one technology specifically aimed at increasing the CINR and can hence be used as a technique to increase the proportion of users able to benefit from Spatial Multiplexing.

WiMAX RLC/MAC Layer

The WiMAX MAC layer consists of 3 sub-layers as shown in Figure 3-8; the Service Specific Convergence Sublayer (CS), the MAC Common Part Sublayer (CPS) and the MAC Privacy sublayer.

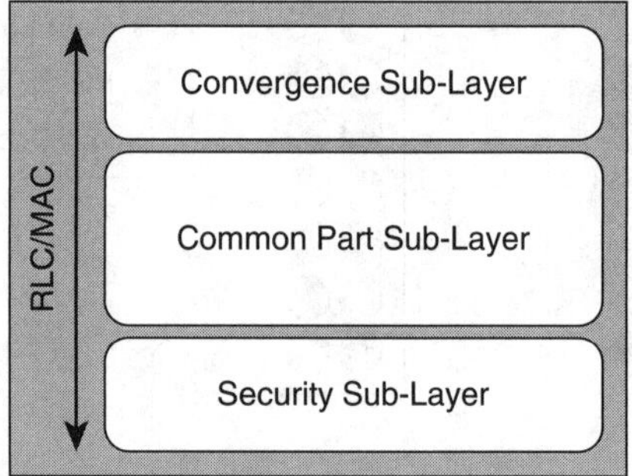

Figure 3-8 *WiMAX RLC/MAC Sub-layers*

IEEE 802.16 does not provide native access to the MAC layer. Instead of exposing the Common Part Sublayer to upper layers, WiMAX defines a logical Convergence Sublayer (CS) to allow interfacing to different higher layers. While a range of different CS types are defined, for the purpose of IP transport, the two relevant CS types are the IEEE 802.3/Ethernet Convergence Sublayer(ETH-CS) and the IPv4/IPv6 Convergence Sublayer (IP-CS), allowing the WiMAX architecture to support both IP and Ethernet packets.

The MAC CPS provides the RLC/ARQ process as well as H-ARQ functionality. The MAC CPS is also responsible for implementing a flexible QoS capability which supports a range of different scheduling options for handling different classes of service. Table 3-5 describes the service flow descriptions associated with different scheduling options for supporting differentiated QoS across the WiMAX access system.

Table 3-5 *WiMAX Service Flows*

Service Flow Description	Example Application	QoS Parameters
Unsolicited Grant Service (UGS)	Voice over IP (VoIP) without silence suppression	Sustained rate Latency tolerance Jitter tolerance Grant interval
Real-Time Polling Service (rtPS)	Streaming audio and video	Minimum rate Maximum rate Latency tolerance Priority
Non-Real-Time Polling Service (nrtPS)	File Transfer Protocol	Minimum rate Maximum rate Priority
Best-Effort Service (BE)	Web browsing	Maximum rate Priority
Extended Real-Time Polling Service (ErtPS)	VoIP with silence suppression	Minimum rate Maximum rate Latency tolerance Jitter tolerance Priority

The service flow types shown in Table 3-5 are the central concept to the MAC protocol, representing a unidirectional flow of packets with particular traffic handling characteristics. The Convergence Sublayer is responsible for classifying incoming packets into service flows and allocating a unique Connection ID (CID) to the flow.

The WIMAX security sub-layer supports strong encryption using the Advanced Encryption Standard (AES) together with privacy and key management techniques. The authentication architecture takes advantage of the Extensible Authentication Protocol (EAP), allowing a variety of different user credentials and authentication methods to be used, including:

- Certificate based authentication with EAP-TLS (RFC 5216)
- Smart card based authentication with EAP-AKA (RFC 4187)
- MS-CHAPv2 based authentication with EAP-TTLS (RFC 5281)

WiMAX Evolution

IEEE 802.16 Task Group 16m is set to enhance current WiMAX air interface capabilities. The 802.16m System Requirement Document (SRD)[13] specifies that the future evolution of WiMAX should be able to support:

- **Increase peak spectral efficiencies:** Up to 8 Bps/Hz for a baseline 2x2 down-link configuration and 15 Bps/Hz in 4x4 configuration.
- **Decreased user plane latency:** Down to 10ms in unloaded systems.
- **Decreased handover interruptions:** Below 60ms for inter-frequency handovers between different spectrum bands.
- **Enhanced multicast and broadcast support:** Spectral efficiency above 4Bps/Hz with a 500m Inter Site Distance (ISD) deployment.

It is currently anticipated that the IEEE 802.16m amendment will be completed by the first half of 2010[14].

Long Term Evolution Access System

Even with advanced mobile broadband capabilities of HSPA, in 2005 3GPP embarked on a study to identify the optimum all-IP architecture and in particular react to the threat that the alternative WiMAX architecture and ecosystem posed to the traditional cellular operators. This original study has lead to the specification of a new all-IP access system, termed Long Term Evolution (LTE), or Evolved UMTS Terrestrial Radio Access Network (EUTRAN). EUTRAN is part of 3GPP Release 8 and the specifications were completed in early 2009.

The requirements for the EUTRAN are listed in 3GPP 25.913[15] and include the following:

- Instantaneous peak data rates of up to 100Mb/s in the downlink and 50 Mbps in the uplink (assuming a 20 MHz channel bandwidth)
- Reduced state transition time between power saving mode and active states to less than 100 milliseconds
- The ability to support a large number of always on users, up to 200 users for 5 MHz spectrum allocations
- Reduced EUTRAN user plane latency of less than 5 ms in unloaded conditions
- Average user throughput being three to four times the rates achievable with HSDPA previously specified in 3GPP Release 6
- The ability to be deployed with flexible spectrum allocations from 1.25 MHz to 20 MHz

The requirements have led to the definition of a new EUTRAN architecture together with a new, flatter, all-IP network, termed the Evolved Packet Core (EPC).

EUTRAN Architecture

The EUTRAN architecture broadly aligns with that of HSPA+ (as described in chapter 2) whereby all radio specific user plane functionality is collapsed into an Enhanced Node B

(ENB), including PDCP, RLC, MAC and PHY protocols as well as Radio Resource Control functionality as shown in Figure 3-9. As with HSPA+, distributing such functions into the ENB means that soft handover is not supported in the EUTRAN.

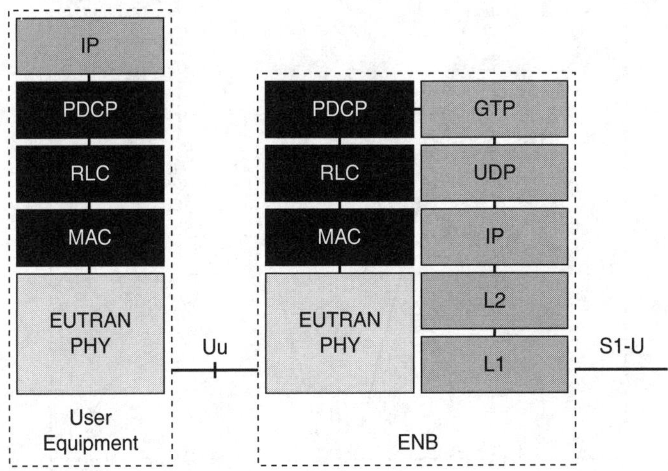

Figure 3-9 *EUTRAN User Plane Protocol*

ENBs are connected to the EPC using the S1 interface, with control plane functionality being communicated across the S1-MME interface and user plane data across the S1-U interface as shown in Figure 3-10. As can be seen, the EUTRAN include multi-homing whereby a single ENB can be parented to multiple Mobility Management Entities (MME) and and Serving Gateways (SGW). The S1-MME interface is based on IP transport with the Stream Control Transmission Protocol (SCTP–RFC 2960) used to provide guaranteed delivery of S1-AP Application layer messages.

Although not currently specified by 3GPP, it is likely that the EPC and ENB will need to perform continuity checks with each other. While the SCTP heartbeat mechanism could be used for such purposes, such techniques can only be used across the S1-MME interface. Hence, it is anticipated that ENB and EPC network elements will implement Bidirectional Forwarding Detection (BFD) over multihop paths[16] in order to provide a generic continuity check mechanisms that can operate over any type of IP transport network.

Taking the lead from the WiMAX R8 approach, ENBs are interconnected to each other by the X2 interface. The X2 interface is used to co-ordinate handovers between different ENBs. During hard handover the X2 interface allows transient tunneling of packets between base stations, in order to be able to handle packets delivered to an old base station after a user has moved to a new one. The X2-AP control plane application is transported over SCTP and user-plane packets are tunneled over GPRS Tunneling Protocol (GTP). Chapter 6, "Mobile Core Evolution," provides details of GTP operation.

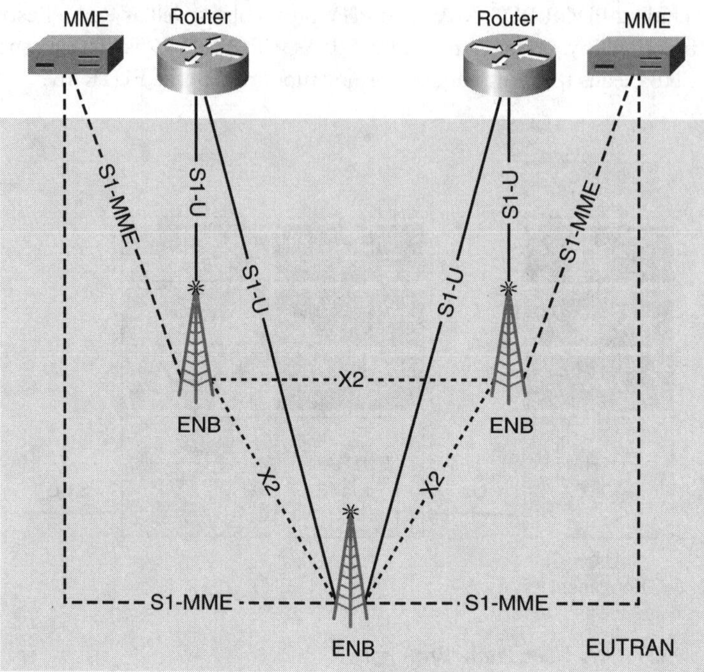

Figure 3-10 *EUTRAN Architecture*

EUTRAN Security

Because EUTRAN user-plane specific radio interface ciphering is terminated at the ENB, the S1 and X2 EUTRAN interfaces are vulnerable to attack if transported over an untrusted IP transport network used for RAN backhaul. Consequently, an option for using IPSec has been defined on both the X2 interface between ENBs, and the S1 interface, between the ENB and a Security Gateway at the perimeter of the trusted transport network. This fragmented approach to security may require the use of multiple IP addresses on the ENB, to allow separation of X2, S1 and Operations and Maintenance (OAM) based IP traffic.

EUTRAN Physical Layer

Similar to WiMAX, LTE physical layer has adopted a multi-carrier approach using OFDMA in the downlink with channel bandwidths ranging from 1.25MHz to 20 MHz. However, in contrast to WiMAX, LTE uses Single Carrier Frequency Division Multiple Access (SC-FDMA) in the up-link. SC-FDMA has been selected because, when compared to native OFDMA, SC-FDMA has improved PAPR characteristics. As has been described in Chapter 1, the PAPR characteristics are important in determining the linearity requirements of the mobile's power amplifier (PA). The adoption of SC-FDMA and its corresponding lower PAPR should allow LTE users at the edge of the cell to operate with a higher PA efficiency. The other key attributes of the LTE physical layer are shown in Table 3-6.

Table 3-6 *LTE Physical Layer*

Duplex	FDD and TDD
Channel Bandwidth	From 1.25 MHz to 20 MHz
Modulation Type	QPSK, 16 QAM, 64 QAM (optional in UL)
Multiple Access Technique	Downlink: OFDMA, Uplink: SCFDMA
TDMA Frame Duration	10 ms with 1 ms subframe
Number of symbols per frame	140
Sub-Carrier Spacing	15 kHz
Symbol Duration	66.7 µs
Cyclic Prefix	4.69 µs (short) 16.67 µs (long)
MultiPath Mitigation	OFDM/Cyclic Prefix
Base Station Synchronization	Frequency synchronization required (FDD and TDD), Time synchronization (TDD and MBSFN)
Forward Error Correction	1/3 rate Convolutional and Turbo Coding
Advanced Antenna Techniques	MIMO 2x2, 4x4

Another key attribute of the LTE physical layer is the ability to operate with either a short or long cyclic prefix (CP). The long CP is particularly useful when combined with another attribute of the LTE physical layer which is its support of a Multicast/Broadcast over a Single frequency network (MBSFN). In an MBSFN, a time-synchronized common waveform is transmitted from multiple cells, allowing the terminal to combine the emissions from multiple cells, and the longer CP allows larger differential delays between those cells involved in the multi-cell transmission. Simulations[17] indicate that in three out of four deployment scenarios, the adoption of SFN techniques is able to increase the MBMS throughput to scale in excess of 1 bps/Hz.

Because of the unique requirements for handling multi-cast transmissions, the MBSFN architecture shown in Figure 3-11 is overlaid on the EUTRAN architecture with IP multicast being used for the point-to-multipoint transport of the multicast traffic.

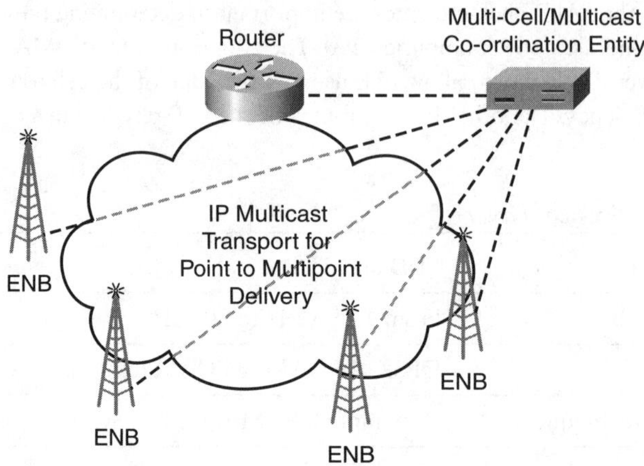

Figure 3-11 *MBSFN Architecture*

Although LTE operating in 2x2 MIMO configuration can support high peak rates of the order of 5 bps/Hz, the average cell throughput is expected to be of the order of 1.7 bps/Hz[18]. Using these figures, the typical down-link speeds will vary with channel bandwidth as shown in Table 3-7.

Table 3-7 *LTE Down-link Speeds with 2x2 MIMO*

Channel Bandwidth, MHz	1.25	2.5	5	10	20
Average fully loaded DL, Mbps	2.1	4.2	8.5	17.0	34.0
Peak Rate DL, Mbps	9.0	18.0	36.0	72.0	144.0

Considering a typical 10 MHz, three sector deployment, this indicates that a cell site may be able to support 51 Mbps of user traffic. The actual dimensioning of the S1 links needs to accommodate the S1 over-dimensioning to allow for radio efficiencies (for example, assuming the same 20 percent value used for Iub over-dimensioning with HSDPA) as well as the GTP/UDP/IP/E header which, for an average size IMIX packet, will add on an additional 15 percent, increasing to 30 percent if the S1 link is transported using an untrusted network and additional IPSec encapsulation is required.

Adding a further 10 percent for signaling traffic means that a typical 3-sector 10 MHz LTE cell should be dimensioned with around 77 MBps of S1 backhaul capacity when using a trusted backhaul network and around 87 Mbps of backhaul from an untrusted third party provider.

EUTRAN PDCP/RLC/MAC

Figure 3-12 shows the decomposition of functions between PDCP, RLC and MAC layers. The ciphering layer has been integrated into the PDCP layer which is also responsible for integrity protection of control plane data. In addition, timer based discard which was, as described in Chapter 2, "Cellular Access Systems", functionally incorporated into RLC protocol for HSPA networks has been moved up to reside in the PDCP layer.

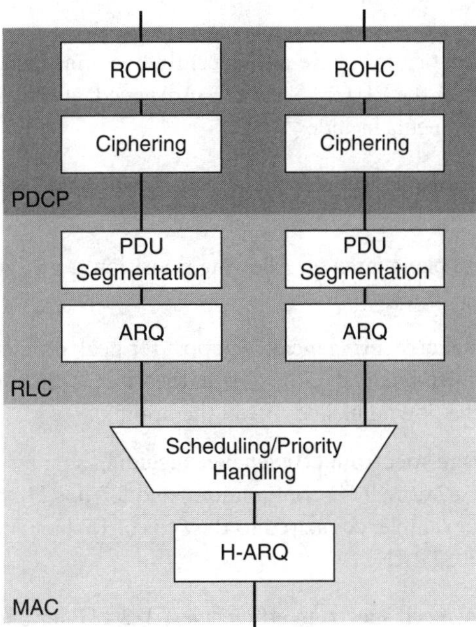

Figure 3-12 *EUTRAN*

In terms of QoS, LTE specifies the concept of an Evolved Packet System (EPS) Bearer. Service data flows which are mapped to a common EPS bearer will have a common MAC/RLC configuration ensuring that they will receive the same scheduling policy, queue management, shaping policy and RLC configuration.

In contrast to earlier HSPA and WCDMA architectures that allowed devices to attach to the network without allocating resources to those devices, in LTE a default bearer is established when an LTE devices attached to the network and remains throughout the duration of the session. Subsequent bearers can be established, including Guaranteed Bit Rate (GBR) bearers. As their name indicates, GBR bearers indicate that dedicated network resources are permanently associated with the bearer and so the EUTRAN access system will typically be required to implement admission control capability.

EUTRAN Sharing

LTE supports functionality, termed S1-flex, for network redundancy whereby a single EUTRAN Access System can be parented to multiple Evolved Packet Core (EPC) networks. This functionality can be used for load sharing of traffic across network elements, for example when the network elements involved belong to the same EPC operator, or support network sharing where the EPC elements belong to independent core network operators. When a device attaches to the EUTRAN, it is directed to the appropriate core network element based on the identity of the service provider sent by the device.

LTE Advanced

Even though LTE specifications have only recently been finalized, requirements for the further advancement of the EUTRAN, or LTE-Advanced, are already being defined[19]. LTE-Advanced requirements include:

- **Increase peak rates:** Downlink peak rates of 1 Gbps, and up-link peak rates of 500 Mbps.
- **Reduced control plane latency:** Allowing transition from a dormant power saving state in less than 10 ms.
- **Increase peak spectral efficiencies:** Support for peak efficiencies of up to 30 bps/Hz in the down-link and 15 bps/Hz in the up-link (assuming a MIMO configuration of 8x8 in the down-link and 4x4 in the up-link).
- **Increased average spectrum efficiencies:** Including a target of 2.4 bps/Hz in the down-link with a 2x2 MIMO configuration and 3.7 bps/Hz with a 4x4 MIMO configuration – for example, compared to the typical 1.7 bps/Hz achievable with the first release of EUTRAN.

Comparing the average cell spectrum efficiencies, 2x2 LTE advanced will likely increase throughput by a factor of (2.4/1.7) or around 40 percent and 4x4 LTE advanced by a factor of (3.7/1.7) or around 120 percent compared to initial LTE 2x2 deployments. This will mean that a 3-sector 10 MHz LTE-advanced cell when operating in 4x4 MIMO configuration will be required to be provisioned with nearly 200 Mbps of backhaul capacity!

ITU-Advanced

Just as ITU-R triggered the definition of third generation systems meeting the defined IMT requirements, ITU-R has commenced the process for developing new recommendations for what is being termed IMT-Advanced and some are calling 4G radio systems. IMT-Advanced systems are targeted to support[20]:

- Enhanced peak data rates of up to 100 Mbps for high mobility deployments and 1 Gbps for low mobility environments
- Peak down-link spectral efficiency of 15 bps/Hz
- Peak up-link spectral efficiency of 6.75 bps/Hz
- Scalable bandwidth up to 40 MHz
- High Speed vehicular, up to 350 kmph

As is evident by the previous sections on WiMAX and LTE evolution, both communities are already evolving their current radio systems in order to meet the IMT-advanced requirements. It is expected that candidate IMT advanced radio systems will be evaluated during 2009, and specifications are anticipated to be complete during the second half of 2010.

Summary

This chapter has described different approaches to delivering an all-IP access system. The reaction of the cellular ecosystem to the widespread adoption to IEEE 802.11 WLAN technology has been introduced, first as a generic all-IP access system and then more specifically for delivering IP bearers on top of which legacy traffic can be tunneled to predominantly in-door users with GAN.

This has been followed with a description of two mobile broadband systems designed for purely packet bearer support, the WiMAX Access Service Network and 3GPP's EUTRAN architecture, both of which have been shown to share common OFDMA/MIMO down-link characteristics as well as scalable channelization approaches to allow operation in various channel bandwidths. With WiMAX and LTE we have two true all-IP systems which define IP interfaces between base stations, requiring IP transport networks to scale to 100 Mbps per cell site and pushing the opportunity to route packets far out in the transport network, a far cry from the n * 64 kbps SDH networks of GSM.

And with ITU-R already dreaming of all-IP systems capable of delivering speeds in excess of 1Gbps, IP looks set to have a fundamental role in the mobile access system long into the future.

Endnotes

[1]http://standards.ieee.org/getieee802/download/802.11g-2003.pdf

[2]IEEE 802.1X, "IEEE standard for Local and metropolitan access networks, Port Based Network Access Control" http://standards.ieee.org/getieee802/download/802.1X-2004.pdf

[3]IEEE 802.11i, "Medium Access Control (MAC) Security Enhancements, Wireless Medium Access Control (MAC) and Physical Layer (PHY) Specifications"

[4]RFC 3748, "Extensible Authentication Protocol (EAP)"

[5]3GPP TS 23.234, "3GPP to Wireless Local Area Network (WLAN) interworking"

[6]RFC 4186, "Extensible Authentication Protocol Method for Global System for Mobile Communications (GSM) Subscriber Identity Modules (EAP-SIM)"

[7]RFC 4187, "Extensible Authentication Protocol Method for 3rd Generation Authentication and Key Agreement (EAP-AKA)"

[8]GSMA IR.61, "WLAN Roaming Guidelines", http://gsmworld.com/documents/ir61.pdf

[9]IEEE 802.11e, "Wireless LAN MAC and PHY specifications: MAC Quality of Service Enhancements", http://standards.ieee.org/getieee802/download/802.11e-2005.pdf

[10]3GPP TS 43.318, "Generic Access Network (GAN); Stage 2"

[11]http://navini.com/assets/pdfs/White_Papers/2006_11_06_Smart_WiMAX.pdf

[12]C. F. Ball, et al, "WiMAX Capacity Enhancements introducing MIMO 2x2 Diversity and Spatial Multiplexing", Mobile and Wireless Comms. Summit, July 2007

[13]IEEE 802.16m System Requirements http://www.ieee802.org/16/tgm/docs/80216m-07_002r6.pdf

[14] Work Plan for IEEE 802.16m Standard, http://www.ieee802.org/16/tgm/docs/80216m-07_001r2.pdf

[15] 3GPP 25.913, "Requirements for Evolved UTRA (E-UTRA) and Evolved UTRAN (E-UTRAN)"

[16]draft-ietf-bfd-multihop

[17]3GPP 25.912, "Feasibility study for evolved Universal Terrestrial Radio Access (UTRA) and Universal Terrestrial Radio Access Network (UTRAN)",

[18]http://www.ericsson.com/ericsson/corpinfo/publications/review/2007_03/files/5_LTE_SAE.pdf

[19]3GPP 36.913, "Requirements for further advancements for E-UTRA (LTE-Advanced)"

[20]http://www.itu.int/md/dologin_md.asp?lang=en&id=R07-SG05-C-0060!!MSW-E

Chapter 4

An IP Refresher

The transition of wireless infrastructures to an IP-based packet transport requires a basic understanding of the IP protocols. The goal of this chapter is to provide the wireless network architect with a framework for making decisions about how to leverage IP to enhance mobile wireless connectivity. The chapter covers the basics of IP routing protocols, switching methods associated with IP, and transport protocols provided by IP. The relationship between the IP protocols and the wireless protocols is emphasized to demonstrate the benefits of transitioning to an IP-based infrastructure.

Routing Protocols

One of the fundamental drivers behind the development of IP was reliability for a massively scalable network. One of the most important elements for achieving that goal is the relationship between the endpoint addresses and the routing processes used to connect the two endpoints. The two are intrinsically associated. The introduction of more endpoints (that is, addresses) increases requirements for route state management. Clearly, the goal is to establish a non-linear relationship between the number of addresses used to represent endpoints and the number of route states that need to be managed. Remarkably, with an estimated 1.6 billion users connected to the Internet, the core routing tables only require 300,000 to 400,000 routes to facilitate packet forwarding. [1] This is accomplished through a well-known principle of address aggregation.

The growth in wireless services and the transition to data-enabled endpoints has dramatically increased the requirements for endpoint address management. The initial deployments for endpoint address assignment assumed that the location of a data endpoint would be fixed and the connectivity would be persistent. Certainly, no one would make that assumption today; therefore, the addressing and routing management have evolved to accommodate the mobility of data endpoints and their temporal nature of connectivity. A brief review of the IP addressing principles sets the foundation for explaining the relevance of routing protocols in the IP-enabled mobile network.

IP Addressing

The general practice for IP network communications is to assign an IP address to each endpoint in the network. The IP protocols are designed to establish an end-to-end communication context between the two endpoints. This means that every node in the network needs to have a viable route to forward traffic between the endpoints. Historically, this meant that the routing nodes in the middle needed to have a route for each and every endpoint. Over time, the concepts of network hierarchy were introduced where groups of addresses could be represented by a single route in the core. Only as traffic transitioned to the periphery of the network were the more specific routes required to reach the endpoint. A corollary exists where the endpoints on the network don't need to know about all the other potential endpoint routes; the endpoints only need to know the nearest aggregation point. This principle has been leveraged for years in classic Internet, service provider, and enterprise network deployments. Figure 4-1 demonstrates how an IP address range can be broken up into subsets in a hierarchical manner. The assignment of an address range can be scoped according to the actual number of hosts needing addresses, thus preserving addresses. The efficient assignment of addresses coupled with the hierarchical representation of macro sets of addresses allows the Internet to scale to massive numbers of subnets and hosts associated with those subnets.

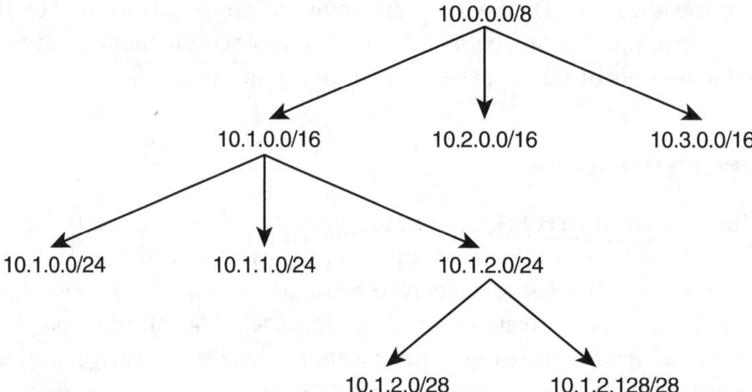

Figure 4-1 *IP Address Aggregation*

The mobile IP network is no different in that route aggregation is required in order to scale to the millions of mobile IP endpoints connected to the mobile service provider. Architecturally, the endpoint aggregation for most mobile IP networks is located at a handful of data centers. The subscriber's IP connection is tunneled to one of these data centers. The tunneling mechanisms will be highlighted later in the chapter; nevertheless, the unique IP addresses are present at the aggregation point. A provider with 50 million endpoints, of which 20 percent are active data subscribers, must provide 10 million connections. If we assume that each endpoint is represented by a unique IP address, we need 10 million addresses. The 10 million connections might be distributed over 20 data service centers, where each service center hosts 500,000 connections. Clearly, the 500,000 unique addresses should not be advertised into the provider's core network; thus, address aggregation is used to minimize the amount of state required in the core. By assigning addresses in blocks associated with each aggregation point, the amount of route state can be minimized in the network core. Figure 4-2 shows how addresses assigned to mobile subscribers can be aggregated at the HA/GGSN, such that only route aggregates are presented to the core network.

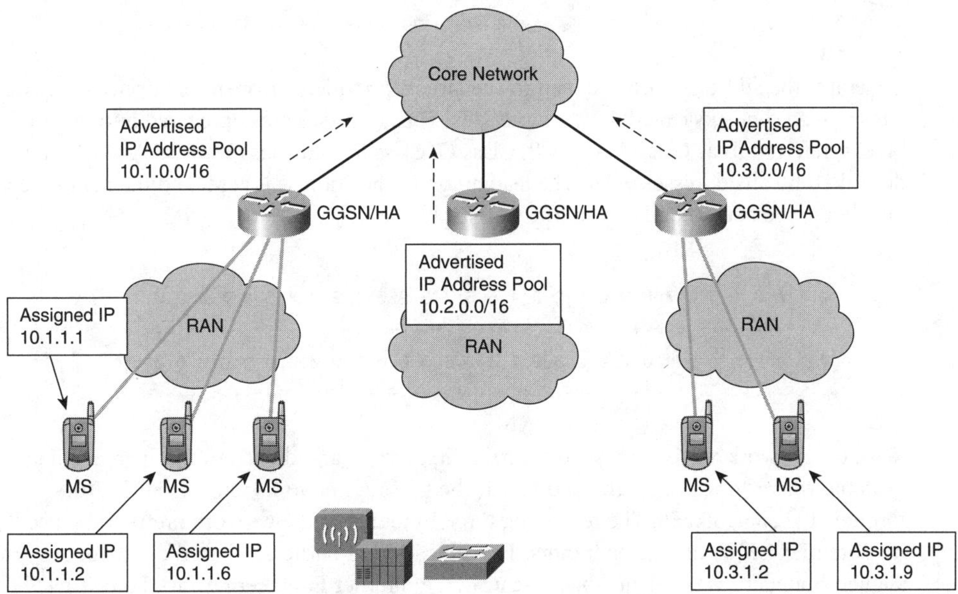

Figure 4-2 *Address Anchor Points in IP Mobile Networks*

The operator has the choice of using IPv4, IPv6, or both addressing mechanisms on the mobile endpoint. Today, almost all operators have chosen to use the IPv4 addresses for assignment to mobile endpoints despite the limited availability of registered addresses. The choice is primarily attributed to the fact that almost all the Internet servers use IPv4 addresses to provide services. IPv6 is beginning to play a role in the next-generation of mobile endpoint connectivity; however, the adoption has been slow. Part of the problem is the caveats inherently created when trying to establish connections between IPv4 and IPv6 endpoints. Next, we look at the two IP addressing mechanisms, IPv4 and IPv6, and describe their relevance in the mobile IP architecture and how routing state is managed in those networks.

IP Version 4 (IPv4)

The IPv4 address is structured as four bytes generally separated by a decimal point on 8-bit boundaries. [2]

```
                    1                   2                   3
0 1 2 3 4 5 6 7 8 9 0 1 2 3 4 5 6 7 8 9 0 1 2 3 4 5 6 7 8 9 0 1
+-+-+-+-+-+-+-+-+-+-+-+-+-+-+-+-+-+-+-+-+-+-+-+-+-+-+-+-+-+-+-+-+
|0|    NETWORK  |      SUBNET   |               Host number     |
+-+-+-+-+-+-+-+-+-+-+-+-+-+-+-+-+-+-+-+-+-+-+-+-+-+-+-+-+-+-+-+-+
```

A

Generally, the addresses are assigned to the largest providers or operators of network systems in macro blocks called network prefixes. The addresses are segregated into macro blocks, referred to as Class A, Class B, Class C, Class D, and Class E. Class A blocks are described by all addresses where the leading bit in the address is zero, and the next seven bits define the network address in the Class A block:

```
                    1                   2                   3
0 1 2 3 4 5 6 7 8 9 0 1 2 3 4 5 6 7 8 9 0 1 2 3 4 5 6 7 8 9 0 1
+-+-+-+-+-+-+-+-+-+-+-+-+-+-+-+-+-+-+-+-+-+-+-+-+-+-+-+-+-+-+-+-+
|0|n n n n n n n|0 0 0 0 0 0 0 0|0 0 0 0 0 0 0 0|0 0 0 0 0 0 0 0|
+-+-+-+-+-+-+-+-+-+-+-+-+-+-+-+-+-+-+-+-+-+-+-+-+-+-+-+-+-+-+-+-+
```

With the network prefix represented by the first byte marked with "n" in the preceding example where "n" can be either a 0 or a 1, the Class A networks range from 0.0.0.0 through 127.255.255.255. The remaining three bytes allow the network prefix to be used by potentially 2^24 unique endpoints. The allocation of addresses based on the byte-aligned boundary was deemed inefficient by the Internet Engineering Task Force (IETF), and that led to the use of a classless Internet Domain Routing (CIDR). [3,4,5] As opposed to allocating address by classes, pieces of a class could be allocated to a provider or operator that reflected a more realistic usage of the host addresses. This more granular allocation requires the use of a network mask to determine the network prefix. The network mask for a Class A network is defined as 255.0.0.0, which emphasizes the fact that the first byte defines the network and the remaining three bytes define the usable space for host addresses. The network mask can also be represented as /8, meaning the first eight bits represent the network prefix. The CIDR model allows the network mask to be extended to non-byte boundaries. The remaining IP network class ranges are described in Table 4-1.

CLASS A

Table 4-1 *IPv4 Address Classes*

Class	Leading Bits	Start	End	CIDR	Subnet Mask
Class A	0	0.0.0.0	127.255.255.255	/8	255.0.0.0
Class B	10	128.0.0.0	191.255.255.255	/16	255.255.0.0
Class C	110	192.0.0.0	223.255.255.255	/24	255.255.255.0

Class	Leading Bits	Start	End	CIDR	Subnet Mask
Class D	1110	224.0.0.0	239.255.255.255	/4	Not defined
Class E	1111	240.0.0.0	255.255.255.255	/4	Not defined

The efficient allocation of addresses becomes more problematic as networks grow. There is a fundamental trade-off between assigning a network range based on the largest possible number of endpoints versus assigning a network range based on the immediate needs. The former approach ensures that only a single network prefix is needed to represent all the endpoints. The latter approach may lead to non-contiguous blocks of addresses, where each block requires a unique network prefix. Typically, a trade-off is made when assigning network prefixes and addresses by allocating addresses in a binary tree and using only a branch of the tree at a time. Figure 4-3 shows how the IP address range is segmented into branches in the binary tree such that smaller and smaller ranges of address may be assigned, yet still be represented by an aggregate IP address range.

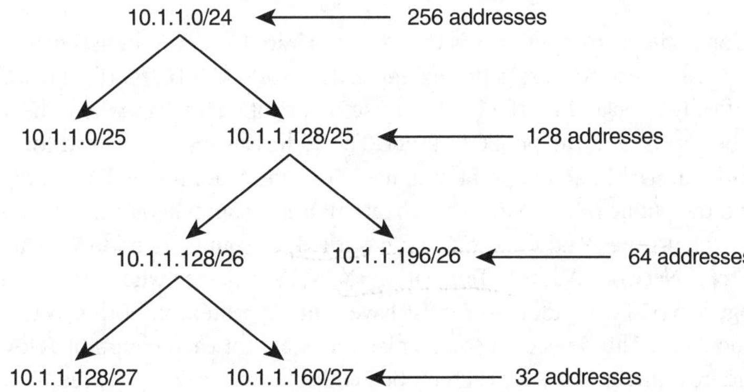

Figure 4-3 *Address Assignment Using Binary Tree*

This allows growth in the address space and expansion of the network prefix range by simply changing the network mask that represents all the endpoints.

If we consider our previous example of 500,000 subscribers connected simultaneously to the gateway in the data center, the number of IP addresses required to service these subscribers would be the same. Assuming a binary assignment of address allocations, a range of 2^19 addresses (524,288) is required to ensure that each subscriber received an IP address. Such a large pool of addresses could be represented by a network prefix with a mask of 255.248.0.0, where the lower 19 bits are used to assign host addresses to the subscriber's endpoint device.

```
                    1                   2                   3
0 1 2 3 4 5 6 7 8 9 0 1 2 3 4 5 6 7 8 9 0 1 2 3 4 5 6 7 8 9 0 1
+-+-+-+-+-+-+-+-+-+-+-+-+-+-+-+-+-+-+-+-+-+-+-+-+-+-+-+-+-+-+-+-+
|0|n n n n n n n|n n n n n 0 0 0|0 0 0 0 0 0 0 0|0 0 0 0 0 0 0 0|
+-+-+-+-+-+-+-+-+-+-+-+-+-+-+-+-+-+-+-+-+-+-+-+-+-+-+-+-+-+-+-+-+
```

With the adoption of mobile IP applications and growth in the subscriber accounts, it is easy to see that the address assignment will be insufficient, and another bit will need to be allocated for subscriber endpoint addresses. In order to grow the network range with minimal impact on the core, the ideal scenario is to move the network mask one bit to the left such that the network prefix 225.240.0.0 is now represented by the following:

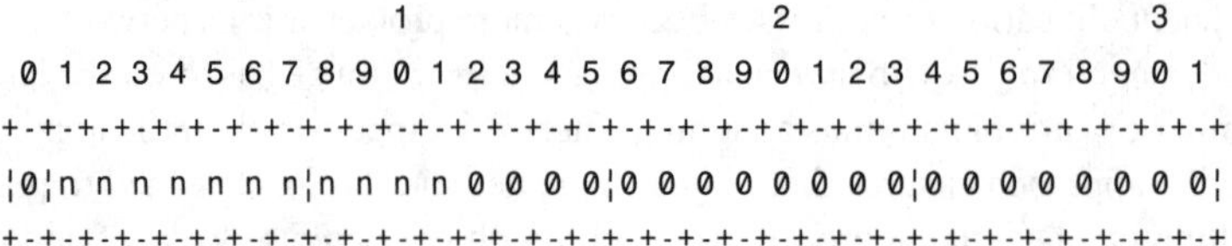
```
                    1                   2                   3
0 1 2 3 4 5 6 7 8 9 0 1 2 3 4 5 6 7 8 9 0 1 2 3 4 5 6 7 8 9 0 1
+-+-+-+-+-+-+-+-+-+-+-+-+-+-+-+-+-+-+-+-+-+-+-+-+-+-+-+-+-+-+-+-+
¦0¦n n n n n n n¦n n n n 0 0 0 0¦0 0 0 0 0 0 0 0¦0 0 0 0 0 0 0 0¦
+-+-+-+-+-+-+-+-+-+-+-+-+-+-+-+-+-+-+-+-+-+-+-+-+-+-+-+-+-+-+-+-+
```

This network prefix represents 1,048,576 endpoints. Clearly, the operator that underestimated the number of endpoints could have assigned hundreds of non-contiguous network prefixes to accommodate the growth, but that comes at the expense of flooding the core with numerous network prefixes. The operator that anticipated the growth would have assigned an extremely large and contiguous range of addresses despite the fact that most of those addresses may not be used for years to come.

One option available to operators is the use of private IP addresses assigned according to the RFC-1918. These addresses (for example, 10.0.0.0/8, 172.16.0.0/16, and 192.168.0.0/16) are specifically allocated by the IETF for use on private networks where the addresses will not be exposed to the public Internet. The addresses may be reused for each private IP network. Invariably, an endpoint assigned a private IP address will need to connect to a service on the public IP network. The private IP is not routable on the public IP network; therefore, the private IP address must be modified to a public IP address. This process is referred to as Network Address Translation (NAT). The device where private IP addresses are changed to public IP addresses must have routing context in both private and public routing domains. This device must also maintain state for each endpoint's flow. The private IP address might allow for each mobile endpoint to receive a unique IP address, but a single NAT device may not scale to handle the number of active mobile subscribers. Clearly, a tradeoff is made between aggregating state in the NAT devices versus efficient use of public IP addresses on mobile endpoints.

Unicast IPv4

The assignment of a unique IP address to each endpoint allows mobile subscribers to establish a direct communication channel between themselves and the remote endpoint. This very important attribute of IP communications offloads end-user connection state from the core routing nodes; the core routing nodes only need to know the path to the destination IP address. One of the implications of this model is that the forward and reverse paths are independent of each other. This model has some fairly significant implications when building services to support IP flows in the provider network. Many IP applications operate in a client/server model, where the client initiates a connection to the server and the server responds. The path the IP packets take from the client to the server may be different from the path the packets take from the server returning to the client. In most cases, the applications don't care which path the flow of packets take. However, enhanced IP services often require establishing some context based on the forward path (from client to server), which becomes relevant for the packet flow in the return path. The implications of this asymmetric routing property of IP unicast packets are emphasized in Chapter 8, "End-to-End Context Awareness," where services such as charging, deep packet inspection, and policy control are applied. In most mobile IP designs, the packet flow converges at the Home Agent for CDMA architectures, the GGSN for GSM architectures, and PDN GW for LTE architectures. The method of routing mobile sessions between mobile endpoint and the gateway is evolving as IP becomes more prevalent in the RAN.

Broadcast IPv4

The IPv4 address model also supports a broadcast communication method that supports communication from an endpoint to all nodes connected to the network prefix. This communication method is commonly used for discovery and network adjacency management between nodes on the same network. The broadcast address is defined by the network prefix, followed by asserting all ones in the host portion of the address. For example, the broadcast address for the network prefix 206.32.0.0 with network mask 255.255.0.0 is 206.32.255.255, which is represented in binary form as follows:

11001110.0010000.11111111.11111111

Packets sent to this destination would be delivered to all nodes on the network with the 206.32.0.0 prefix.

Broadcast traffic does not use the IP broadcast mechanisms because it is inefficient when traversing the tunneling mechanisms between the client and the gateway. Alternative technologies such as DVB-H and MediaFLO have been deployed to bypass the inefficient radio access network aggregation mechanisms.

Multicast IPv4

The IPv4 addressing model supports multicast using the well-known range of addresses, as defined in Table 4-1. The multicast method supports the delivery of IPv4 packets to one or more destinations referred to as *receivers*. The multicast processes create a distribution tree that facilitates replication of multicast packets at the lowest point in the tree. The use of multicast is common in video and file distribution systems, where the number of recipients can be quite large. The distributed replication model conserves bandwidth by minimizing the number of packets that must be transmitted near the source. The core routing nodes use the IPv4 unicast routing tables to determine the path toward the source. The reverse path represents the most efficient path from the source to the recipients. The core routers are able to replicate the multicast packets at each of the branch join locations. Figure 4-4 shows the topology of a multicast distribution tree.

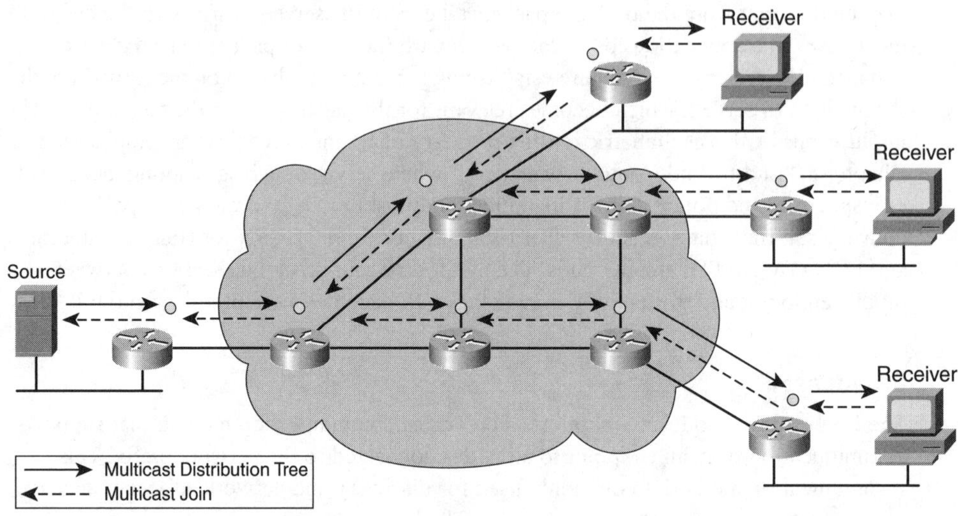

Figure 4-4 *Multicast Distribution Tree*

An important limitation for multicast in the design of IP mobile networks is the extensive use of IP tunnels in the RAN aggregation architecture. The IP tunnels hide the visibility of the original source IP and multicast destination IP from the core routing nodes by encapsulating the multicast in a unicast tunnel packet. The implication is that the multicast packet must be replicated at the head-end of each tunnel. The tunnel architecture may lead to a very inefficient distribution model for multicast. Figure 4-5 shows how the use of tunnels to backhaul mobile IP traffic eliminates the potential points of replication in the aggregation network.

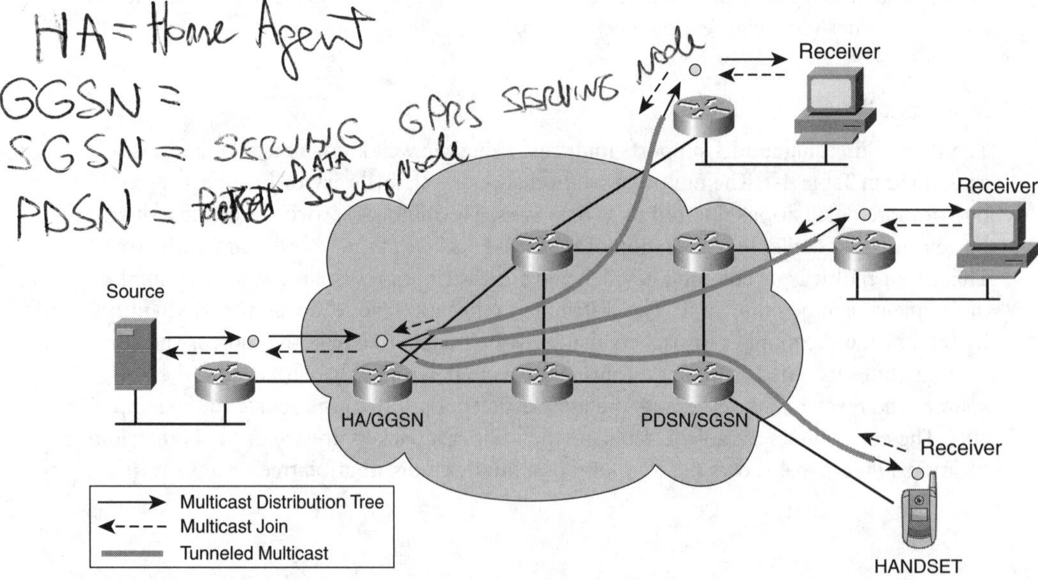

Figure 4-5 *Tunneled Multicast Distribution Tree*

The traditional 3G mobile IP architectures make extensive use of tunnels (for example, GTP and Mobile IP), which mitigates the value of multicast particularly in the RAN. Although the core nodes can certainly facilitate efficient distribution of multicast traffic, the gateways aggregating the mobile subscribers must replicate the multicast for each intended recipient (also known as the *subscriber*). Such replication can be quite detrimental to the RAN network if the number of subscribers interested in receipt of the multicast application is large.

A counter argument is that the likelihood that two subscribers attached to the same cell site are interested in receiving the same content is very small; therefore, enabling multicast in the RAN infrastructure may not provide the intended efficiency gains. Enabling multicast distribution in the RAN is only relevant if the content to be distributed is extremely popular.

IP Version 6 (IPv6) RFC-4291

The deficiencies of IPv4 (most notably lack of available addresses given the growth of the Internet) led to the development of IPv6—the next generation of IP addressing for global communications. The IPv6 protocol increases the address size from 32 bits to 128 bits, and the expanded address field facilitates the assignment of far more networks and systems on those networks. The address field is segmented into two macro components: the network prefix and the end-system address, as shown in Figure 4-6. The exponential growth rate in IP-enabled mobile subscribers makes the use case for IPv6 very compelling. Many of these mobile subscribers will not only need a uniquely assigned IP address for bi-directional session establishment, but the sessions will be persistently active.

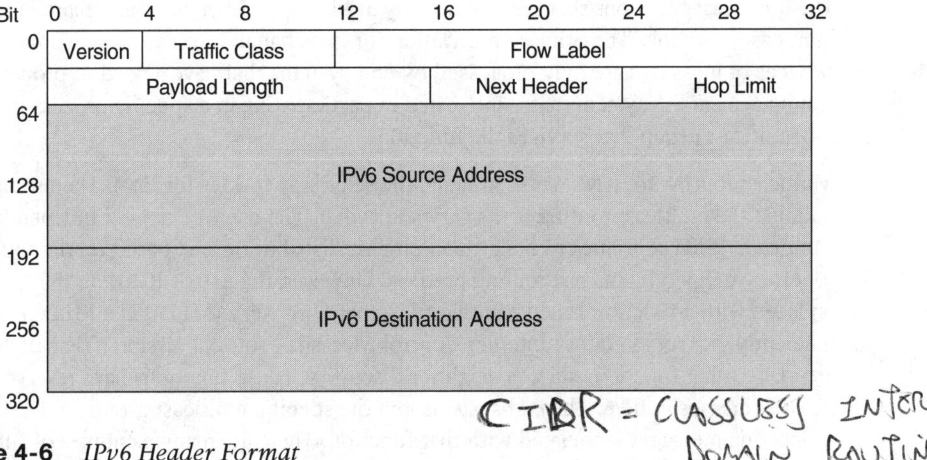

Figure 4-6 *IPv6 Header Format*

The notion of "address classes" is not relevant because the IPv6 address is supported by Classless Internet Domain Routing (CIDR) mechanisms just as IPv4 networks. The network can route the IPv6 address based on aggregates using a variable-length bit mask.

The IPv6 address can be represented in various ways for efficiency; however, the most complete representation is shown as eight sets of hexadecimal characters separated by colons, as follows:

nnnn:nnnn:nnnn:nnnn:hhhh:hhhh:hhhh:hhhh

<——-Network——->|<———Host———->

The IPv6 address can represent three different types of addresses: unicast, multicast, and anycast. Note that there is no explicit broadcast address for IPv6.

Unicast

The unicast address is assigned to a defined interface on the end-system. The unicast address is intended to be globally unique; therefore, it is routable through the entire Internet routing domain should the operator choose to advertise that system's network prefix to the IP network. The IP routing domain operates on IPv6 unicast in much the same way that it does with IPv4, except that the routing table space is adapted to handle the longer network prefixes.

Figure 4-7 highlights a number of important variances that exist between IPv4 and IPv6. Of particular note is the use of IPv6 header extensions and the removal of the checksum in the header.

The removal of the checksum allows the routing nodes to forward the packet with minimal processing. However, the extensions in the IPv6 header facilitate the ability of an IPv6 packet to call out certain processing requirements at intermediate and end-nodes.

Multicast

The broadcast functions that were previously available for IPv4 were assimilated into IPv6 multicast protocols. The primary motivation for this change is to ensure that announce services or messages are only processed by end-systems that have a need to process the announcements. A system that is interested in participating in a specific process must join the multicast group that services the function.

Multicast routing for IPv6 works in much the same way it does for IPv4. The means of building the multicast routing paths vary somewhat. The use of Protocol Independent Multicast (PIM) continues to build the multicast distribution tree based on the routing topology defined by unicast routing prefixes. However, the use of IGMP in the LAN is replaced with a function called Multicast Listener Discovery (MLD). The MLD process is inherently incorporated into Internet Control Message Protocol version 6 (ICMPv6), as are many other functions such as neighbor discovery. These functions have reserved multicast addresses in IPv6. The end-systems join the specific multicast groups to facilitate processing messages associated with that function. There are many examples of functions using specific multicast groups, such as routing protocols, address assignment, neighbor discovery, and so on.

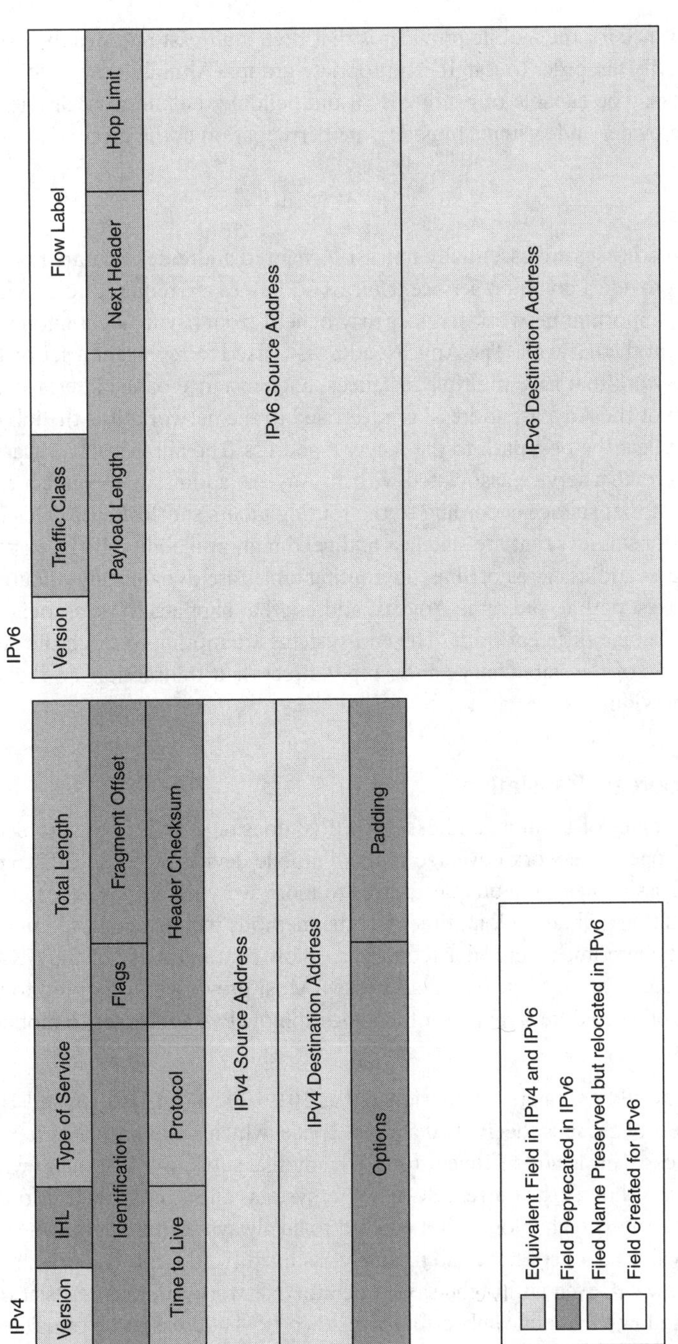

Figure 4-7 *IPv4 and IPv6 Comparison*

The relevance for the mobile provider is that IPv6 multicast requires the end-systems to execute MLD in order to join the appropriate groups. Although the mobile provider core network may be capable of routing IPv6 and building the multicast distribution trees, the mobile provider end-systems must initiate participation in the groups.

Anycast

Anycast addresses are essentially unicast-formatted addresses that are reused in the network to provide a common service. Unicast addresses are required to be globally unique; however, important network services may benefit from having a common identity throughout the network. The Anycast address is used to represent a set of IPv6 interfaces in the network that have multiple instances. Each instance of the interface (and its representation of the Anycast address) is advertised to the network. It is the job of the network to select the best path to the Anycast address. The implication is that end-systems trying to reach a service associated with an Anycast address will connect to the nearest instance of that service according to the routing table's shortest path. This is particularly valuable for services that are stateless and need high-availability. If the system advertising the Anycast address goes offline, the routing tables are dynamically updated with the next shortest path to the same Anycast address that happens to be associated with another interface on a different node. The end-systems attempting to reach the Anycast address are unaware of the state change and simply direct their transactions to the next nearest system providing the service.

Network Address Translation

The availability of far more addresses for IPv6 does not solve all the problems of increasing the scope of network coverage to more mobile devices. Certainly, IPv6 does allow the potential assignment of a unique address to most every network-connected device, but that transition will take a long time, and the methods will be addressed in the next section. In the interim, a method is required to allow continued use of the IPv4 address space in the absence of sufficient addresses. Most providers have opted to use the IETF assigned private address range for the allocation of IPv4 addresses to mobile subscriber handsets.

The private address ranges are designated as 10.0.0.0/8, 172.16.0.0/16, and 192.168.0.0/16. The largest of these is the 10.0.0.0 address space, which accommodates more than 16 million devices. This is not sufficient for all the mobile subscribers of many wireless providers. Although the current 3G wireless systems allow reuse of IP addresses, the next generation of 4G technologies has evolved to an always-on paradigm, where each subscriber will need a persistent and uniquely assigned IP address. The private address space must be reused, even within the same operator. Network Address Translation (NAT) methods allow the mobile subscriber's assigned IPv4 address to be translated to a unique public IPv4 address. NAT by itself doesn't solve the address exhaustion problem because a public IP address is required for each private IP address. An extension to the NAT process, called Network Address Translation-Port Translation (NAT-PT), is to also translate the source port address while reusing the same public IP address. [6] NAT-PT allows transactions from thousands of unique subscribers to apparently originate from the same IPv4 address. Each subscriber's transaction is mapped to a unique transport source port while using the same share IPv4 source address. The NAT-PT translation is determined on-the-fly, usually by a firewall system that separates the provider IP routing domain and the public IP routing domain. Figure 4-8 shows the results of a 10.0.0.0 address translated to a designated IPv4 address on a managed network.

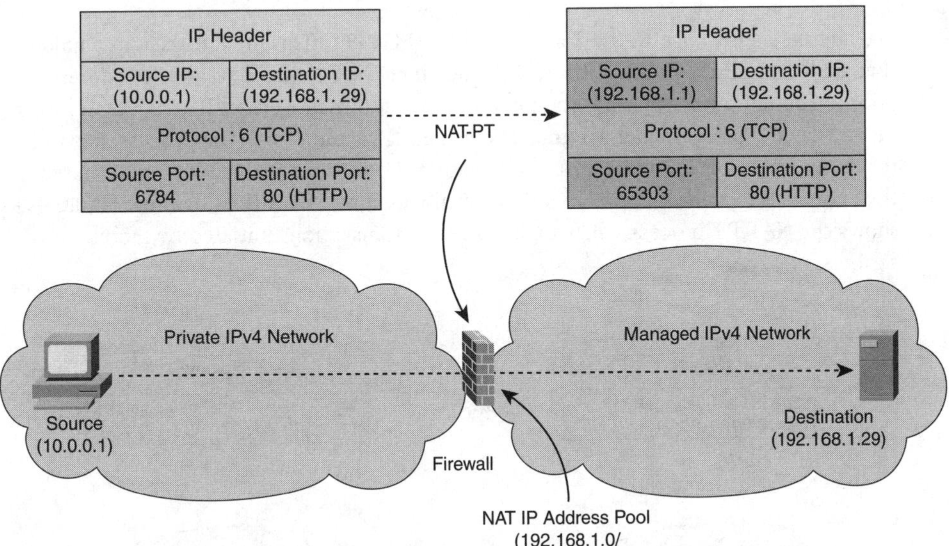

Figure 4-8 *Network Address Translation—Port Translation*

The NAT-PT technique enables the operator to reuse the address space, but it makes server-initiated transactions toward the mobile subscriber client very difficult. In addition, the firewall must maintain the state of the translation, which means that routing, both forward and reverse, must be pinned down on the firewall or another high-availability component that has the exact same state. NAT-PT interferes with the inherent routing paradigms commonly used for IP routing, and that makes resiliency designs more challenging.

Interoperability of IPv4 and IPv6

Clearly, the mobile operators have a challenge on their hands as they try to conserve IPv4 addresses while increasing services and mobility. A number of techniques have been proposed to facilitate a migration from IPv4 to IPv6. Unfortunately, none of them have experienced widespread adoption. The biggest challenge is that increasingly large numbers of handsets require unique IPv6 addresses, whereas the majority of servers of interest use IPv4 with no support for IPv6. Two of the most promising techniques include dual-stack and NAT-PT.

The dual-stack method assigns an IPv6 and an IPv4 address to every handset and requires additional functionality from both the handset and the gateway (for example, PDP context in GPRS for each IPv4 and IPv6 assignment). The IPv6 address is used when transactions are initiated to an IPv6 server; otherwise, IPv4 addresses are used. Unfortunately, this doesn't solve the immediate problem of address exhaustion. It simply gives the provider a means of migrating to IPv6, but the rate of migration is dependent upon all the other organizations on the Internet that manage popular content and their transition to IPv6.

The alternative is to use NAT-PT as defined in RFC 2766. This method assigns a unique IPv6 address to each mobile subscriber, which must be translated to an IPv4 address prior to routing the traffic onto the Internet. The mobile subscriber IPv6 addresses must be translated into a provider assigned and shared IPv4 address. In the process, most of the communication context is lost in translation. There is no means for a server-initiated IPv4 connection to be mapped to a dynamically assigned IPv6-IPv4 binding. Figure 4-9 shows the NAT-PT process when applied to IPv6 transactions initiated by mobile subscribers.

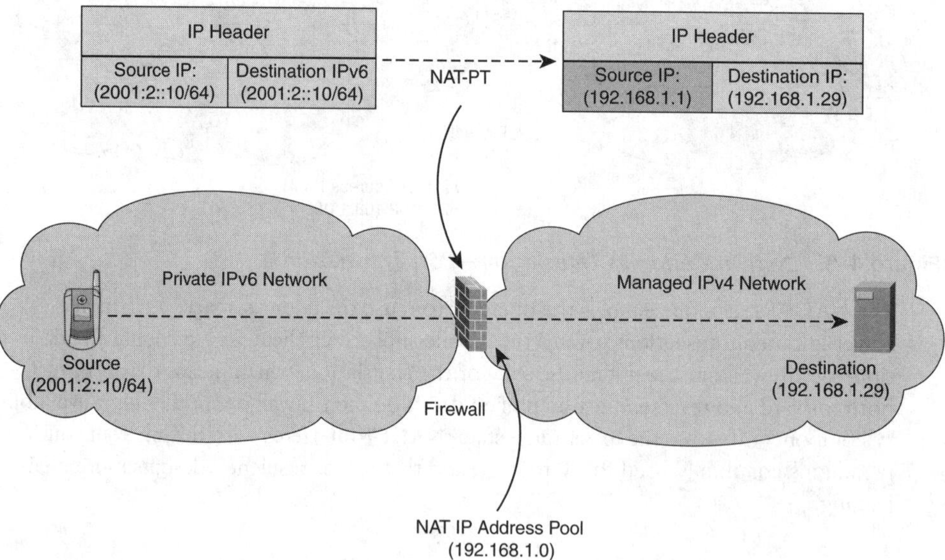

Figure 4-9 *IPv6 Network Address Port Translation—Protocol Translation*

Media Access Control (MAC) Association

Thus far, the discussion has focused on the Layer 3 address assignment. Equally as important is the assignment of Layer 2 addresses that allow endpoints to direct traffic between themselves on the same sub-network. Historically, Ethernet used a broadcast media where all the endpoints could receive and assess the relevance of a packet for local processing. The Layer 2 transmission mediums have changed dramatically over the years and frequently use point-to-point connections. Nevertheless, the endpoints still use a Layer 2 broadcast method to discover other peers and gateways on the same subnet. The endpoints then map and cache IP addresses to medium access control addresses (MAC). These mappings are cached for the duration of the transaction to allow communications between two endpoints to be unicast-directed in the Layer 2 medium.

The relevance of MAC caching is significant in the design of fault-tolerant IP networks. The devices routing packets between endpoints need to have a current view of the bindings (IP to MAC) in order to efficiently direct packets on the shortest available and most efficient path. Of particular interest in mobile networks is the association of tens of thousands of mobile subscriber IP address to a single MAC on the HA or GGSN. Anytime information is cached, such as the IP-to-MAC binding, the information can become stale. There are a couple of approaches to keeping cache information fresh, such as aging and updates. The aging approach simply puts a lifetime on the cache entry. When the entry reaches its lifetime, it is cleared from the cache, and the IP-to-MAC binding must be relearned. To avoid churn in the cache, one option is to reset the lifetime for each observed use of the binding. The assumption is made that the cache is still valid because it is being used. The problem with the aging model is that a failure in the network can take a long time for the binding to flush from the cache. Layer 2 link failures can be used to force a cache flush. This causes the system to revert back to the broadcast model of rediscovering the best IP-to-MAC adjacency associated with the best path. Chapter 7, "Offloading Traditional Networks with IP," highlights the importance of synchronizing failure characteristics of Layer 2, Layer 3, and application layer services.

Routing State

The packet-switched network (PSN) model made a significant deviation from classic (FR/ATM, TDM, and so on) circuit-switched connection-oriented models. The latter used a method where an intermediate switch only needed to know the context for an ingress connection bound to an egress connection. The amount of state required for the switch was minimal. In contrast, the packet-switched network routing model required each intermediate component to maintain routing state for any given packet's destination, irrespective of the ingress interface. The advantage for a PSN is that resiliency can be distributed throughout the network by allowing each routing device to build its routing state based on its view of the network. The disadvantage is that control protocols are required to manage that routing state, and the amount of routing state can be excessive for very large networks. Over the years, many optimizations have been made for both circuit-switching and packet-switching models. In fact, the two domains have been blended through technologies such as Multi-Protocol Label Switching (MPLS). First, a review is provided for the basic packet-switching methods and how these models are relevant for mobile IP infrastructures.

Unicast Routing

The dominant method in use in packet-switched networks is unicast routing. Unicast means that the packet is directed to a single endpoint. This method allows each routing device to look at the packet header and make a routing decision to forward the packet out a particular egress interface leading to that endpoint destination based solely on the router's routing table state. The validity of the router's routing table state is critical for ensuring that the packet is delivered to the right endpoint and not re-circulated or misdirected.

Typically, the mobile IP endpoint has one connection to the packet-switched network; therefore, the context of services provided to that flow is easily identified at the service connection point. Typically, that connection point is bound to the GGSN for 3GPP architectures and to the PDSN or HA for 3GPP2 architectures. These service gateways need to maintain state for each connected mobile IP endpoint. Likewise, the service gateway needs to know a path for the application servers. As a corollary, adjacent nodes need to have a return path for mobile IP endpoints connected to the service gateway. Careful planning is required to ensure that these paths are consistent and reliable. Several techniques are employed to ensure the routing state is managed properly.

Static Routing

The simplest method is the use of static routes. Their advantage is that they are persistent regardless of any perturbations in the network, the state required is minimal, and the absence of a control plane makes the device more scalable. Of course, these advantages are also disadvantages. The persistent state doesn't adapt to changes in the network topology, potentially leading to dropped packets for incomplete paths. Therefore, the static route is typically used on endpoints where a single connection is available to the packet-switched network. As soon as a second interface is added, some dynamic means of managing the state of the routing table on the device is required.

Distance-Vector Routing Algorithms

The initial attempts at implementing a dynamic routing protocol where derived from what is now called distance-vector routing. This method requires the periodic flooding of routes from one routing node to another. In the process, the distance (which is merely a weighted value) between the nodes is added cumulatively to each prefix. The recipient of the flooded route prefix can see the best path by comparison (lowest cumulative distance) for each prefix and choose the shortest path based on distance. The Routing Information Protocol (RIP) became a dominate distance-vector routing protocol and is still widely deployed on many mobile systems. The RIP protocol used a periodic broadcast of all the known routes to a router's neighbors. The routers simply compared all the received updates and picked the path with the shortest cumulative distance.

The problem with distance-vector routing protocols is that they consume a lot of route processing cycles (periodic flooding), take time to detect path failures (wait period for absence of received flooding update), and slow to converge (waiting for an alternate best path). Nevertheless, protocols such as RIP are still in use today. Typically, they are reserved for LAN environments where the scope of the flooding is contained and the path permutations are small.

The distant vector protocols are simple to implement; therefore, vendors frequently implement these protocols on end-systems in mobile IP networks. Sometimes hosts use RIP updates to identify alternate egress paths rather than use static routes. This is especially true for wireless systems that have very specific mobile transmission capabilities, and IP processing is simply not at the top of the priority list.

Link-State Routing Algorithms

The second class of routing protocols, referred to as link-state routing protocols, are designed to compensate for the deficiencies of the distance-vector routing protocols. Link-state routing protocols dynamically manage a routing table based on updates. Similar to distant-vector routing protocols, routes are flooded across the network incrementing their cost based on distance. However, link-state routing protocols build a topology database. The routing node has a complete understanding of the topology of the network. Independently, each routing node can then calculate the shortest path through the network to each routing node and associate a set of flooded prefixes to each path. Once this process is complete, the nodes only need to notify one another of changes in the topology state. As soon as a link fails, the fault is flooded throughout the network. Each routing node can independently build a new topology view and associate prefixes to the new set of paths to each routing node.

The primary advantages of link-state routing protocols is that they are very efficient in terms of bandwidth (initial flood only) and converge quickly to faults in the network (link state change with distribute route calculation). This makes link-state routing protocols ideally suited for WAN infrastructures where bandwidth may be more constrained, the complexity of the topology is increased, and the volume of traffic impacted by a fault can be enormous.

The primary disadvantage to link-state routing protocols is that the route processing is more complex. Each routing node must maintain a complete database of the topology, and the state of the elements in the database must be synchronized with all the other nodes in the network. The implication is that few mobile systems involved in IP transport implement the link-state routing protocols, and those that do usually only implement the basic functions. Ironically, it is the esoteric elements of link-state routing protocols that are most likely needed on mobile systems due to the unique nature of wireless transport of IP.

The core of mobile IP networks will typically use a link-state routing protocol. The data traffic leaving a 3G GGSN or HA toward the network is IP; therefore, traditional routing nodes are used to forward traffic efficiently through the core.

Mobile radio systems, session context-switching systems, and session aggregators (for example, BSC, SGSN, GGSN, HA, and PDSN) with IP interfaces benefit the most from having link-state routing protocols when transitioning to an IP infrastructure. These components are placed throughout the RAN (a wide area network) and need intelligent IP processing to optimally transition to IP transactions. Historically, these components used Layer 2 protocols (for example, TDM, ATM, and FR) where path diversity was limited to the switching systems between the wireless components. The first step in migrating to an IP-based RAN aggregation is to use methods where the Layer 2 context (that is, TDM using Circuit Emulation, ATM, or FR using Layer 2 virtual circuits) is tunneled through IP pseudowire connections. As the wireless switching components such as LTE and WiMAX begin to participate in the IP infrastructure, they too need the more sophisticated capabilities of link-state IP routing protocols.

Open Shortest Path First (OSPF) The Open Shortest Path First (OSPF) protocol was the first widely used link-state routing protocol. OSPF uses a hierarchical routing model where a centralized routing domain is defined within an autonomous system. The autonomous system defines the boundary of administrative routing control. The centralized routing domain is referred to as Area 0. Attached to the Area 0 are sub-networks that may use Area numbers 1 through 255.255.255.255. Figure 4-10 shows the typical hierarchy of an OSPF network.

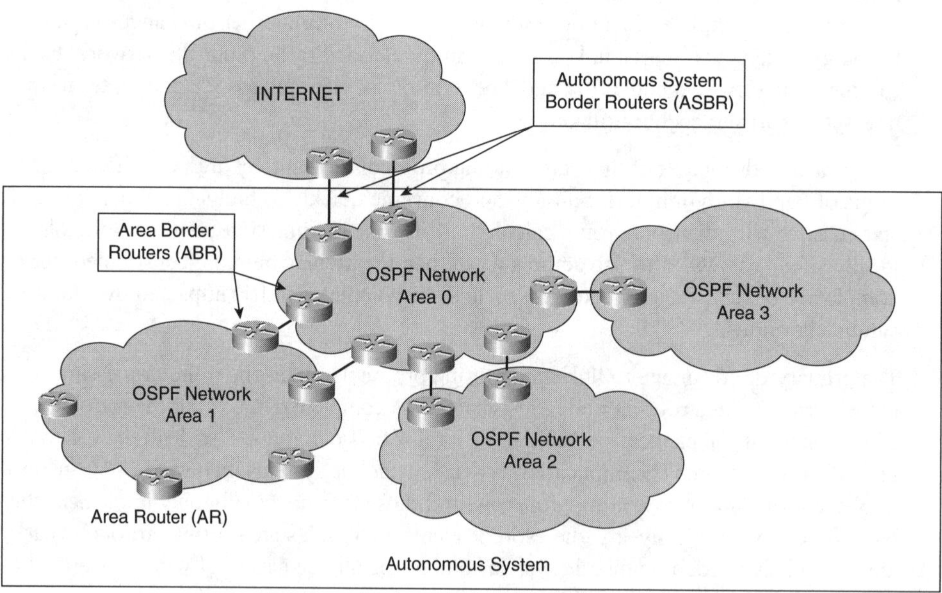

Figure 4-10 *OSPF Network Architecture*

The use of sub-networks is optional; however, large networks with thousands of devices and complex WAN topologies benefit from leveraging the hierarchy of OSPF. Recall that OSPF is a link-state routing protocol, which means that changes in the topology are flooded. One goal of OSPF is to minimize the flooding of changes by aggregating IP route prefixes between the areas and only advertising route aggregate summaries. The OSPF sub-networks contain the flooding of link-state changes in the periphery of the network, as opposed to propagating across link-state changes into Area 0 and into other sub-networks. Typically, the Area 0 routing domain is reserved for the core IP routing devices with highly reliable links, routing nodes, and where few provisioning modifications are necessary. End-nodes are typically connected in one of the sub-network areas where changes occur more frequently. An Area Border Router (ABR) is configured to provide routing between Area 0 and an associated sub-network area.

The implication for using OSPF is that traffic between sub-network areas must travel through Area 0. Forcing traffic through Area 0 usually has minimal consequence because the physical topology is likely to be hierarchical in nature. In contrast, forcing high volumes of inter sub-network area traffic to pass through Area 0 adds expense, delay, and more components in the critical path. Operators tend to limit the geographic coverage of OSPF autonomous systems, such that it conforms to the natural hierarchy of the physical network. For traffic that must flow outside the autonomous system, OSPF uses an Autonomous System Border Router (ASBR) to provide routing paths directly leaving the Area 0 or sub-network areas. The ASBR exchanges IP routing prefixes from the OSPF autonomous system to external routing systems.

OSPF is able to distinguish the types of route prefixes in the autonomous system as either internal or external. Internal prefixes originate from within the autonomous system, whereas external prefixes originate from outside the autonomous system. OSPF policies are used to control the distribution of these prefixes throughout the sub-network area, Area 0, or the entire autonomous system.

OSPF Applicability to Mobile Providers OSPF is applicable to mobile IP providers in several contexts. The first and foremost is the use of OSPF for the mobile provider's IP core network. The IP core network provides routing services between data centers and aggregation centers. A variety of applications may use the core. Smaller mobile providers may choose to use a single OSPF Area 0 for connectivity throughout their core network. The single area allows the operator to connect aggregation sites anywhere in the autonomous system and facilitate the most direct path between two end-systems. Figure 4-11 shows the use of a single OSPF Area 0 for a small mobile provider.

Larger providers are likely to segregate the IP core into multiple sub-networks in order to mitigate the flooding of state information, facilitate distributed administration, and reduce the volume of routing information in the core network. Common services are attached to the OSPF Area 0 to mitigate traffic traversing multiple sub-network areas. Figure 4-12 shows the distributed nature of OSPF in the large provider's IP core WAN.

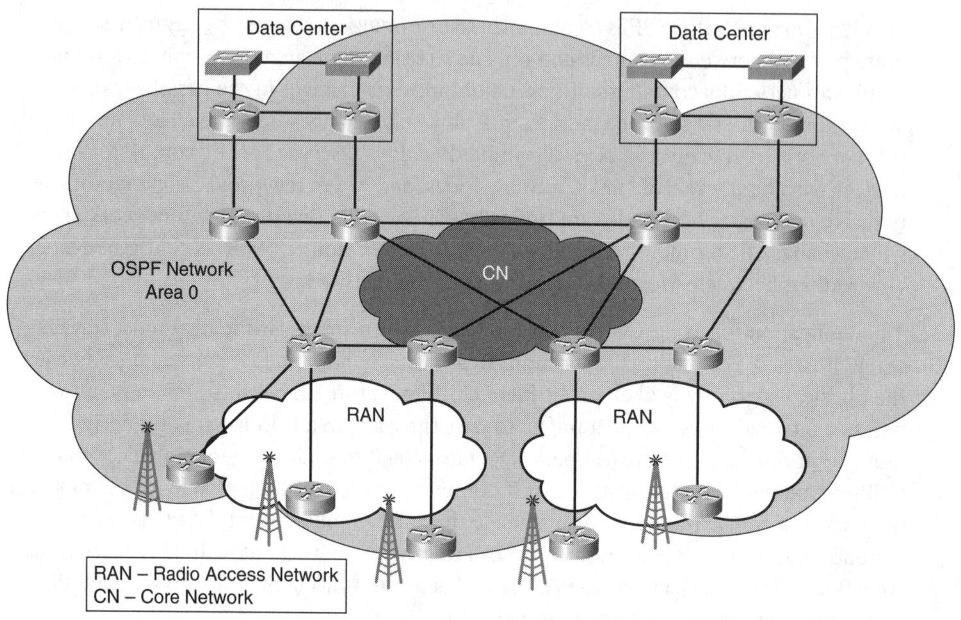

Figure 4-11 *Mobile Provider Single Area IP Core*

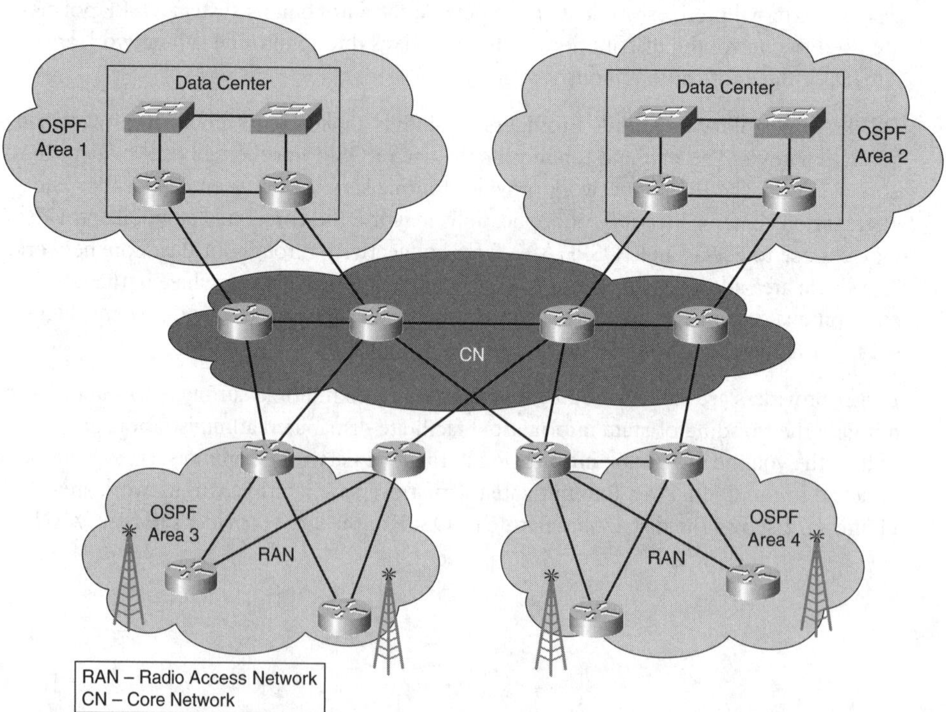

Figure 4-12 *Mobile Provider Multi-Area IP Core*

OSPF is also applicable to a mobile provider's RAN architecture. The RAN typically conforms to a hierarchical topological model; however, the traditional RAN components rarely used IP as the transport protocol of choice. The 4G specifications offer more opportunities to leverage IP RAN networks for resiliency, backhaul efficiency, and services. The choice of routing protocol will become more relevant as providers transition from Layer 2 backhaul technologies such as TDM and ATM to IP or Ethernet. The current 3G architectures merely use a packet-based RAN to backhaul traffic via IP tunnels (for example, Mobile IP, GPRS Tunneling Protocol). The use of tunnels mitigates the requirement to distribute all the network prefixes throughout the RAN and WAN. The 4G models suggest moving the service context establishment closer to the user. This means that subscriber addresses and services addresses will need to be distributed throughout the RAN. The operator must carefully consider how widely distributed the OSPF areas cover when network prefixes need to be distributed to tens of thousands of sites. Figure 4-13 shows the increased scope of IGP coverage required for next-generation IP mobile providers.

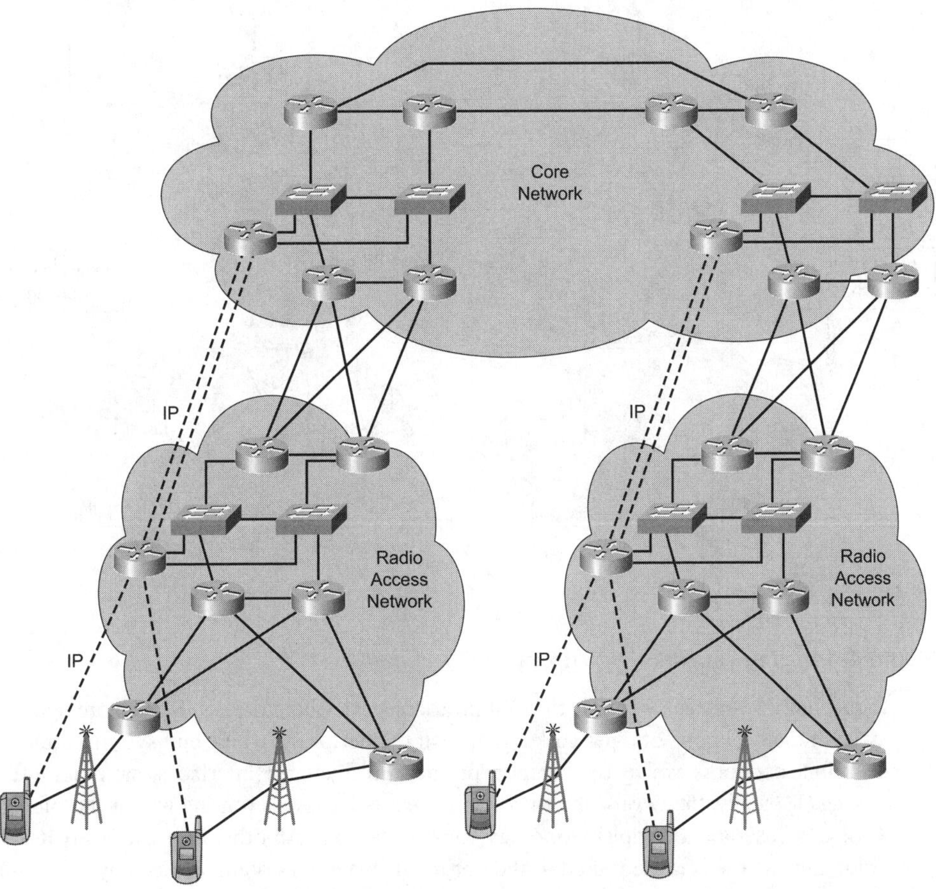

Figure 4-13 *Mobile Provider IP Routing Architectures*

Integrated Intermediate System to Intermediate System (IS-IS) The alternative to OSPF is Integrated Intermediate System to Intermediate System (IS-IS). Integrated IS-IS was derived from the Open Systems Interconnect (OSI) standards but adapted to handle routing for IP as it became clear that end systems would not support the OSI protocol stack. IS-IS is very flexible in describing the routing database, which makes it easy to transport both IPv4 and IPv6 network elements. IS-IS has proven to be a very scalable IGP and is commonly used in Tier 1 Internet service provider backbones. Much like OSPF, IS-IS uses a hierarchical model where the core is referred to as Level-2 area and the sub-networks are referred to as Level-1 area. A router configured with IS-IS resides in a Level-1 sub-network, a Level-2 backbone network, or connects to both a Level-1 sub-network and the Level-2 backbone network. Figure 4-14 shows the architecture of an IS-IS routed network.

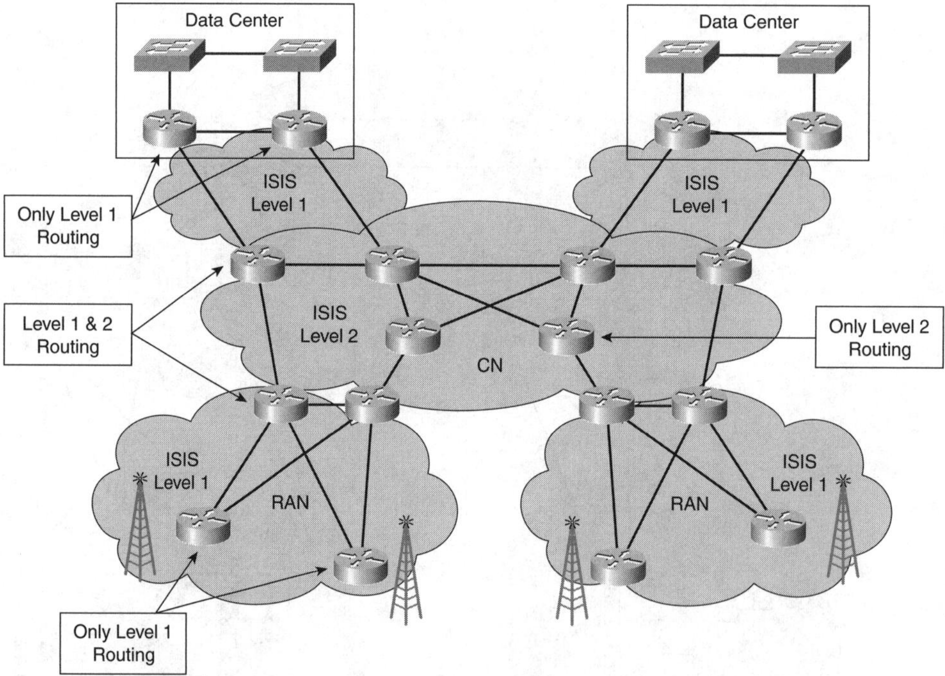

Figure 4-14 *Integrated IS-IS Network Architecture*

Today, few end-systems support the OSI protocol stack; therefore, IS-IS has more relevance in the backbone of a network rather than the periphery where end-systems attach. As mobile networks evolve, the components are introducing IP interfaces that require IP routing. Typically, the Level-1 intermediate system will provide routing within the subnetwork area based on a complete topology view of the area. All other destinations that reside outside the area are routed to the optimum area egress point serviced by a Level-2 router. The Level-2 routers have a complete routing table of the backbone area; however, they only have aggregate routes to network prefixes within the Level-1 areas. The Level-2 routers will forward the packet to the optimum entry point of the destination Level-1 area.

Integrated IS-IS Applicability to Mobile Providers Many vendors' mobile end-systems have very rudimentary IP routing and forwarding capabilities. IS-IS requires the use of OSI network addressing (in addition to IP addressing) for the IS-IS protocol to identify the intermediate system-routing nodes. The protocol uses Connection-Less Network Services (CLNS) to build adjacencies amongst end-systems and intermediate-systems. After the intermediate systems have established their adjacencies using the CLNS protocol, a topology is established. The associated IP network prefixes are populated in the IS-IS routing database, and the shortest IP routes are built. Few mobile end-systems have the ability to build neighbor adjacencies using CLNS. Therefore, an alternative routing mechanism (for example, static route, RIP, OSPF, and so on) is usually required between the mobile end-system and the first IS-IS routing system. After the IP packets reach the first IS-IS-enabled router, the IS-IS routing protocols are capable of forwarding the packet to the destination network prefix.

As noted previously, Internet service providers have been the strongest advocates of IS-IS. Most mobile providers are exploring network convergence (that is, running multiple services on a common IP core network) as a means to conserve costs. The boundary of the IS-IS routing area is likely defined by the edge of the converged IP core. Sub-networks connected to the backbone are likely to use routing protocols other than IS-IS, such as the Border Gateway Protocol (BGP), described in the next section.

Path Vector Routing

The exchange of IP network prefixes across the boundaries of an administrative routing domain requires a much more sophisticated method of control. Many other considerations become relevant besides defining the "shortest path." The IGP typically defines the optimal path for packets flowing across a network managed by a single organizational entity. After the packet leaves the boundaries of the network, another organizational entity becomes responsible for the optimal delivery of the network. The criteria for "optimal" may be quite different between the organizational entities. Attributes such as least cost, fastest links, policies, and agreements with other organizations become relevant. The Border Gateway Protocol addresses these issues through the use of policy control mechanisms in the protocol.

BGP provides a means of advertising route prefixes outside the organizational boundary without revealing the internal routing characteristics handled by the IGP. Figure 4-15 shows the relationship between BGP and the IGP. A best practice for route management is to avoid redistributing external BGP routes into the IGP. The IGP routing table can be sparsely populated with routes to the internal routing nodes only. Meanwhile, internal BGP sessions can distribute the external routes throughout the core network such that every node in the core network has a complete set of both internal and external routes. Alternatively, the internal BGP sessions can be established between the edge nodes only and the traffic switched from edge to edge. Details of various switching methods, such as ATM and MPLS, are addressed in subsequent sections in this chapter.

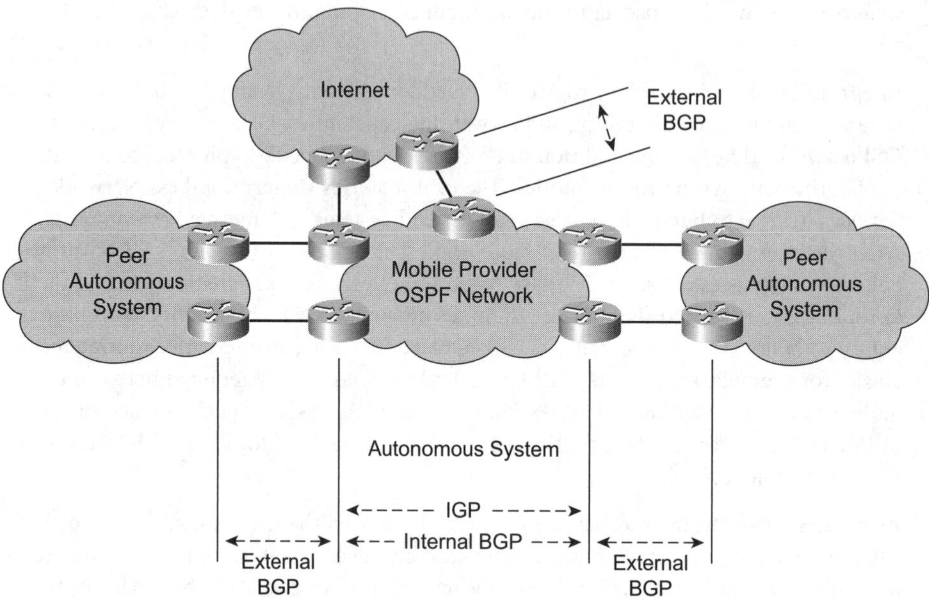

Figure 4-15 *BGP and IGP Relationship*

External routes learned at the organizational boundaries and IP routed through the core network need routing paths defined within the core network nodes; however, those routes are maintained in BGP routing databases that are separate from the IGP routing processes. The two processes can operate independently, whereas the routing node can build a composite routing table called the Forwarding Information Base (FIB) from the two processes based on an order-priority list. The relationship of the routing processes is shown in Figure 4-16.

BGP uses a method of finding the best exit from the administrative domain and using the IGP routing table to forward packets to that best exit. Again, the criteria for "best exit" is based on policies of the provider. The BGP protocol uses the attributes to relay representation of the policy to the BGP neighbors. There are two kinds of neighbors: internal and external. The internal neighbors are the routing nodes of the same administrative routing domain; therefore, the policy will usually remain consistent. The external neighbors are the routing nodes of a different administrative domain, and the policy will likely change as routes are propagated between the organizational entities. The other organizational entities may have links to other providers, creating a partially connected mesh of organizational entities. Each administrative domain will be represented by an Autonomous System Number (ASN). The BGP protocol builds an ordered list of ASN for each routing prefix and builds an IP routing path through the set of administrative domains. The next few sections highlight the use of BGP in various roles within the mobile provider network.

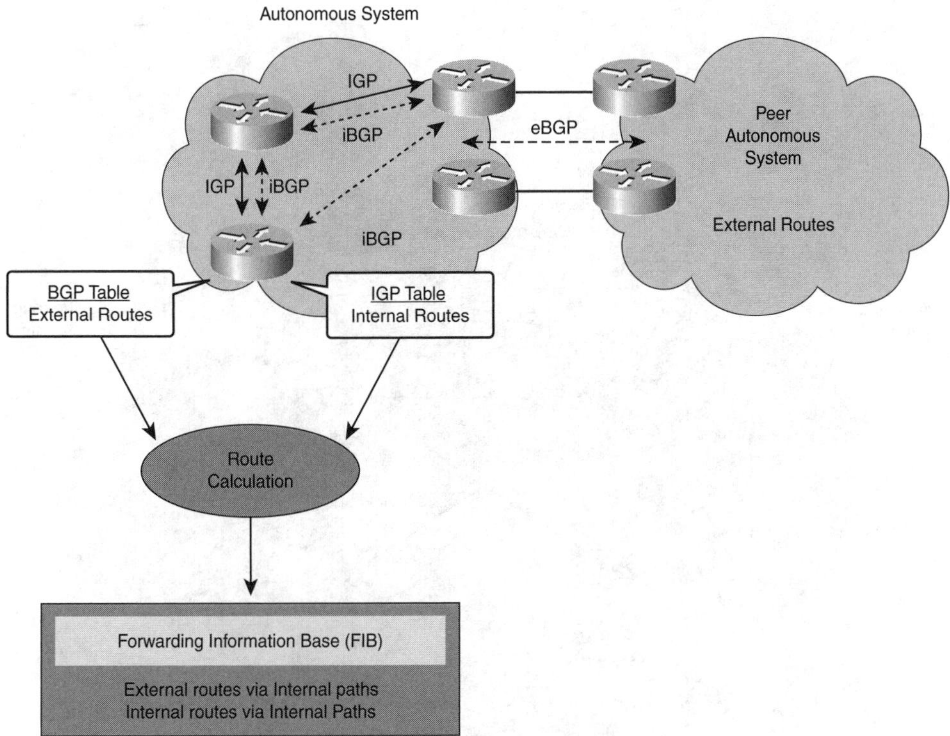

Figure 4-16 *IGP and BGP Route Processes*

Mobile Provider Internet Access The mobile provider needs to propagate the IP prefixes assigned to their mobile subscribers to the provider's Internet peers. Likewise, the mobile provider needs to receive Internet routes from their peers. BGP is commonly used to exchange these prefixes. The mobile provider usually aggregates their mobile subscriber traffic into a few service centers. From here, Internet access is provided. For redundancy, the provider may have the subscribers connect to one or more alternate service centers. The service centers are diversely located, requiring the use of BGP to provide more than one path for access into and out of the mobile provider's administrative domain. Figure 4-17 shows the typical mobile provider network architecture used for Internet access.

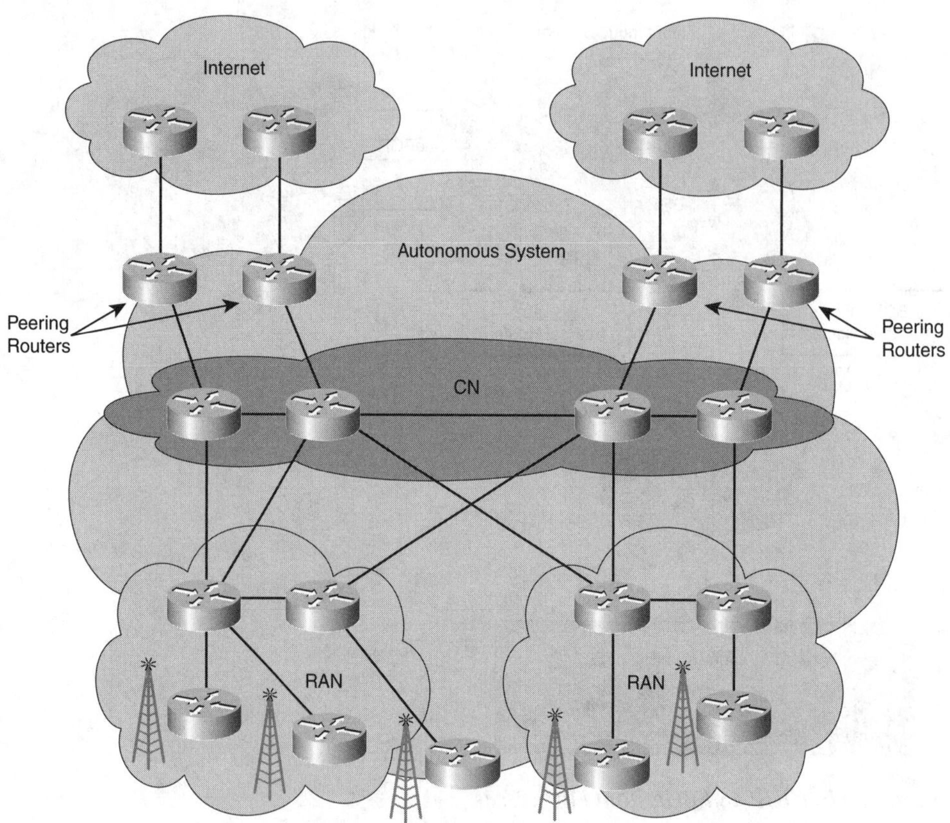

Figure 4-17 *Mobile Provider Internet Access*

The provider may use more than one ASN in order to bias routes; however, the principle of reciprocity comes into play when peering is used. Internet peering methods commonly use the principle of reciprocity as a policy. Routes are exchanged such that the traffic passed between the two peers is "fair." The use of multiple ASNs affects the path vector built by BGP, which is why most mobile providers will use a single ASN for their network. Some mobile providers like to use multiple private ASNs to manage routes internally using policies while hiding the private ASN structure and presenting a single ASN to the peers. Figure 4-18 shows the use of multiple private ASN within a single provider.

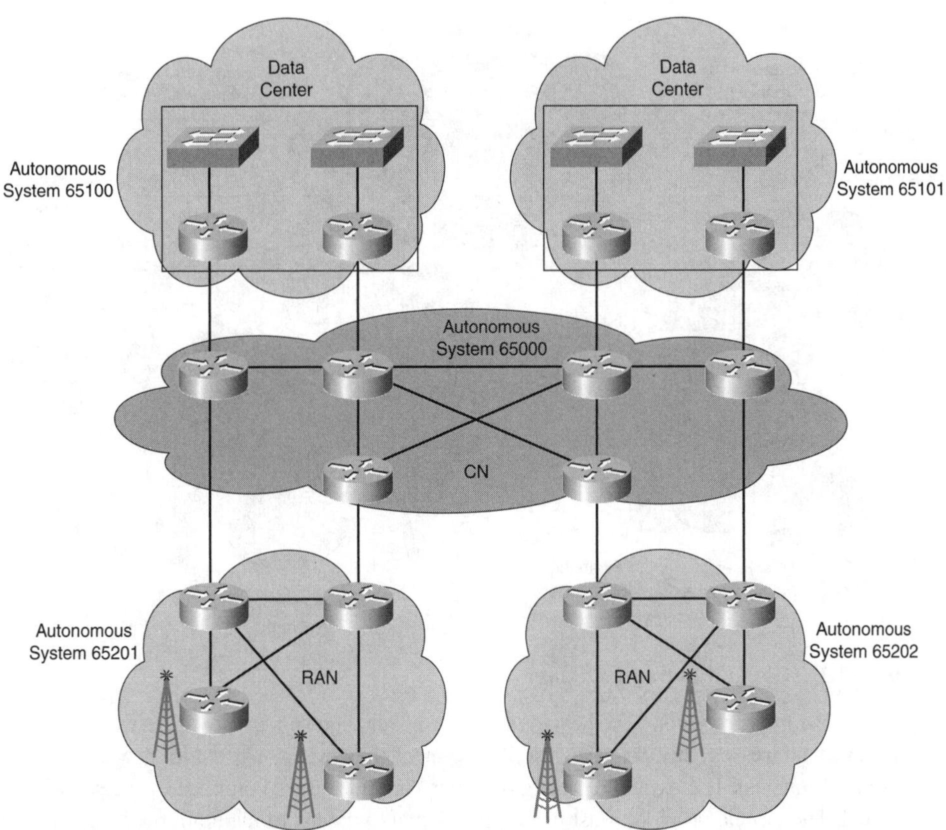

Figure 4-18 *Mobile Provider Private AS*

Global Routing Exchange Peering The mobile provider will also need to establish mobile peering relationships with other providers, such as the GPRS Roaming Exchange (GRX), which allow roaming across diverse networks. These peering relationships are designed specifically for the handoff of mobile traffic. It allows the provider to expand their service coverage geographically through partner networks while presenting to the subscriber a consistent service regardless of the network to which the subscriber is connected. The subscriber establishes a contract with their provider that authorizes roaming across partner networks. The contract between the subscriber and the provider establishes the "home" network. The home network provider establishes peering contracts with its partners. Any time a subscriber roams onto a partner network, the "visiting" network provider serves as a proxy to authenticate and authorize the subscriber. Once connected, the subscriber is provided services similar to the services provided by their home network. Figure 4-19 shows the relationship of the mobile providers and the exchange IP network infrastructure addresses.

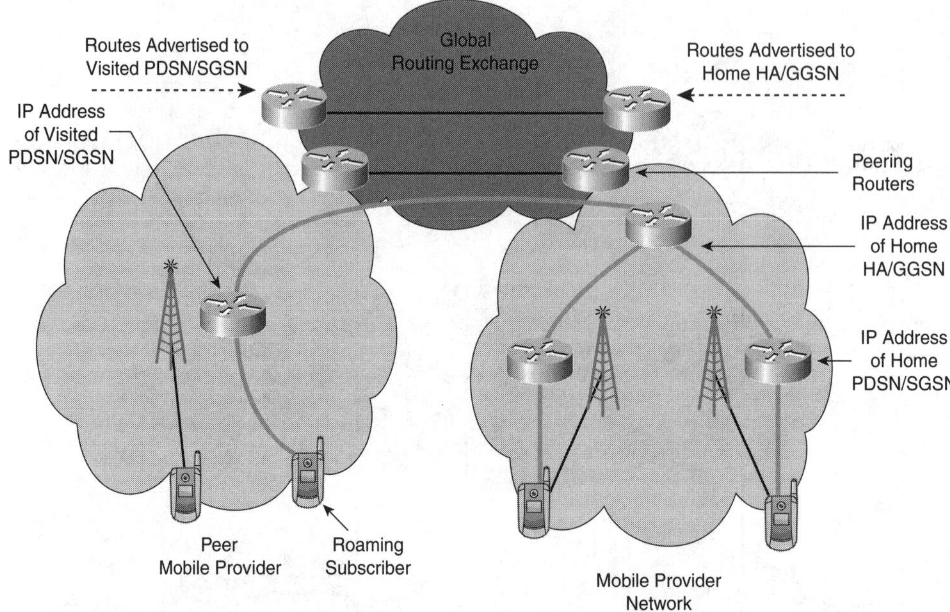

Figure 4-19 *Global Routing Exchange*

Unlike the Internet access, the providers need to exchange some of their network infrastructure addresses (the addresses used to connect the wireless aggregation systems using IP tunnels). The exposure of provider network addresses complicates the security model. The mobile provider must use BGP policy as a means to maintain the security of the provider's core network. The provider augments the security afforded by BGP policy routing policy with many other security mechanisms.

Unicast Routing Summary

The transition of mobile provider RAN and WAN networks to IP networks will enable more opportunities for optimization of traffic, diversity of redundancy, and flexibility to introduce new services. The provider will need to use a combination of unicast routing methods to provide end-to-end connectivity. One of the challenges is to maintain continuity of the routing plane when multiple protocols are used. The network operator must consider various failure scenarios at each routing node and assess the relationship between the routing processes. Frequently, routes from one routing process must be redistributed into another routing process. The redistribution process usually causes some information to be lost in the mapping of routing attributes between different protocols. Careful planning will ensure that failure modes do not preclude end-to-end connectivity.

Multicast Routing

Multicast is complementary to unicast routing. Initially, a special multicast routing protocol was designed that operated independently from the unicast routing protocol. Subsequently, multicast routing was modified to leverage the basic topology information determined by unicast routing protocols. Multicast routing relies on the unicast routing table to determine the best path to the multicast source. The process of building a multicast tree rooted at the source allows the branches to join the tree at the most efficient location in the topology—the farthest point from the root. The process ensures that multicast traffic is replicated as far away from the source as possible, thus conserving bandwidth. Figure 4-20 shows the primary motivation for using multicast.

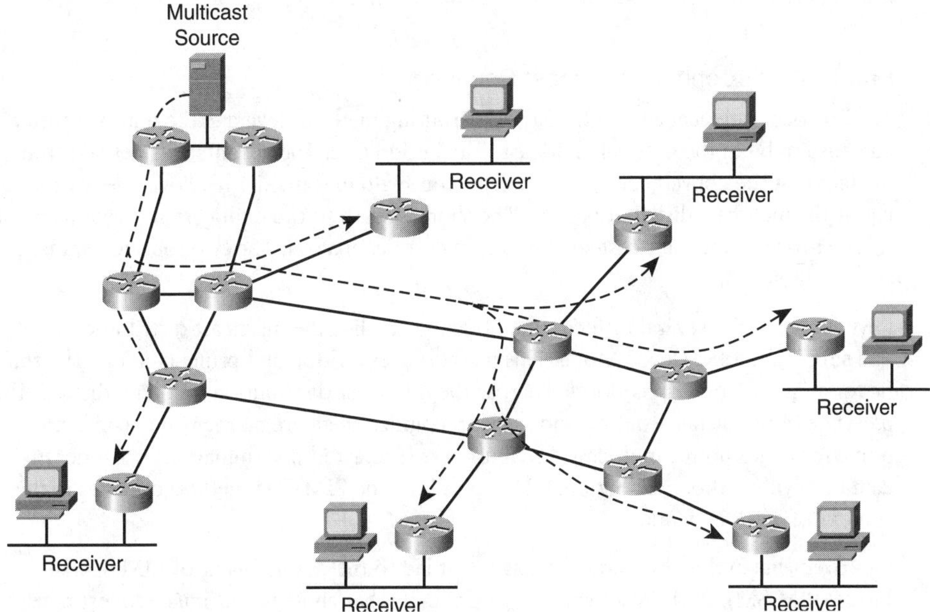

Figure 4-20 *Multicast Traffic Distribution*

There are a number of methods used to maintain the multicast tree topology. Initial multicast routing attempts used a multicast-specific routing protocol called Distance Vector Multicast Routing Protocol (DVMRP). Subsequently, more efficient multicast routing methods were devised based on unicast routing and a technique referred to as Reverse Path Forwarding (RPF). The unicast RPF method relies on the premise that the unicast routing path to the source represents the optimal topology for the multicast distribution tree.

Distance Vector Multicast Routing Protocol

DVMRP establishes a separate multicast routing process independent from the unicast routing processes. Most providers have transitioned to one of the unicast RPF methods; however, some providers still use DMVRP on older systems and as a means of exchanging multicast routes. Very few multicast applications exist that require a transition across provider boundaries and even fewer that are relevant for mobile providers. DMVPN advertises the use of a multicast group between systems. As reachability of the multicast group is propagated across routing nodes, the distance to the source is added cumulatively to the advertisement. Routing nodes build the multicast distribution tree in much the same way distance-vector routing mechanisms build unicast routing paths. The unicast and multicast routing processes are not able to correlate their databases, consolidate routing information, and conserve processing resources.

Protocol Independent Multicast Routing

The Protocol Independent Multicast (PIM) routing methods leverage the unicast routing database to build the optimal multicast distribution tree. The advantage is derived from the fact that the convergence of the unicast routing tables implicitly allows the restructuring of the multicast distribution tree. The shortest path to the multicast source is also the shortest path to the multicast source as a unicast destination. The two routing paradigms are synchronized.

PIM encompasses several different methods to establish the multicast distribution tree. The simplest is PIM Dense Mode. This method uses a flood and prune method. The traffic for a multicast group is flooded across the multicast distribution tree regardless of the presence of recipients. Routing nodes that recognize there are no recipients will send prune messages up the multicast distribution tree to avoid dissemination of multicast data that will be dropped. Figure 4-21 shows how the PIM-DM method operates in the context of an IP network.

Improvements in the PIM traffic management led to the development of PIM Sparse Mode (PIM-SM). PIM-SM operates on a principle that end-systems must request receipt of multicast traffic for a specific multicast group. The absence of a request from one or more end-systems causes the multicast tree to automatically prune itself. The pruning process conserves network bandwidth resources by only flooding multicast traffic to those branches of the tree where receivers have requested access to the multicast stream. Figure 4-22 shows how the PIM-SM method operates in the context of an IP network.

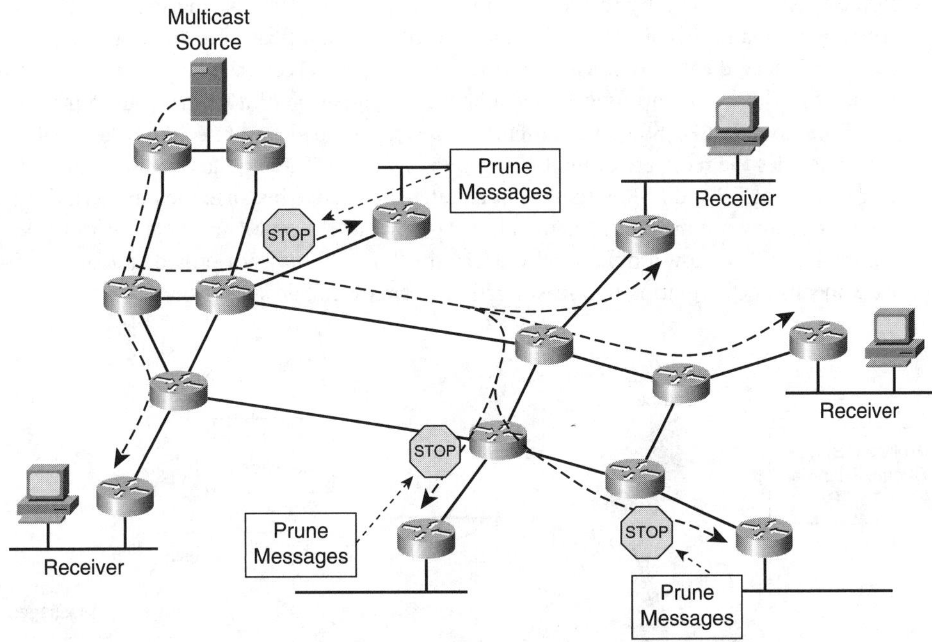

Figure 4-21 *PIM-DM Traffic Distribution*

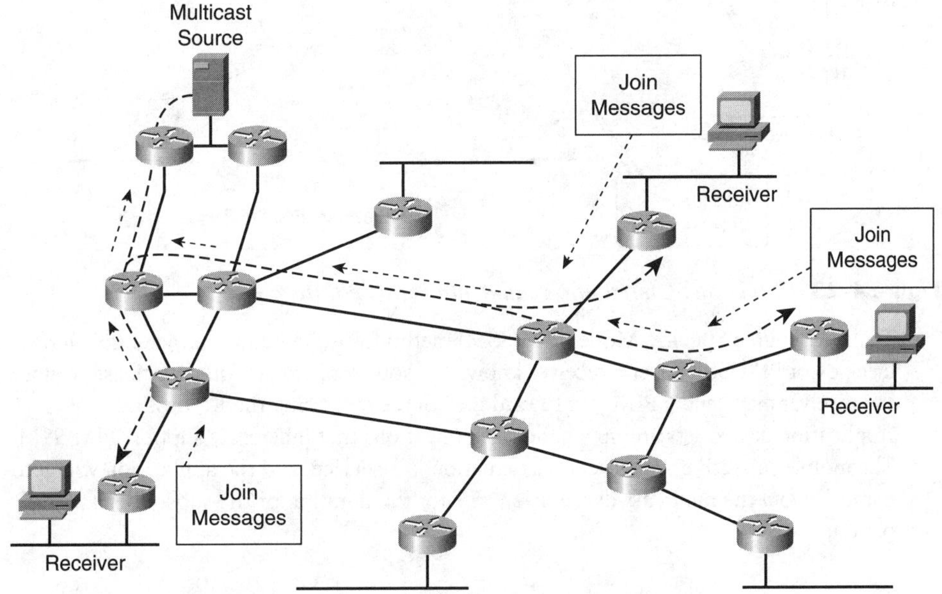

Figure 4-22 *PIM-SM Traffic Distribution*

PIM-SM is complicated by the need to bootstrap the multicast distribution tree. The receivers need a means of discovering the presence of a multicast stream; however, they are not connected to the multicast distribution tree. Several techniques have been created to facilitate this bootstrap process, including the designation of a Rendezvous Point (RP) or a Bootstrap Router (BSR). The potential receivers are made aware of the RP or BSR, which notifies the receivers of multicast groups available. The mobile operator will find that the use of RP and BSR is somewhat counter-productive because the multicast distribution tree may not match the hierarchical topology of the mobile provider network. Figure 4-23 shows how a dynamically selected RP or BSR may not provide the most efficient means of distributing multicast traffic to a set of mobile subscribers.

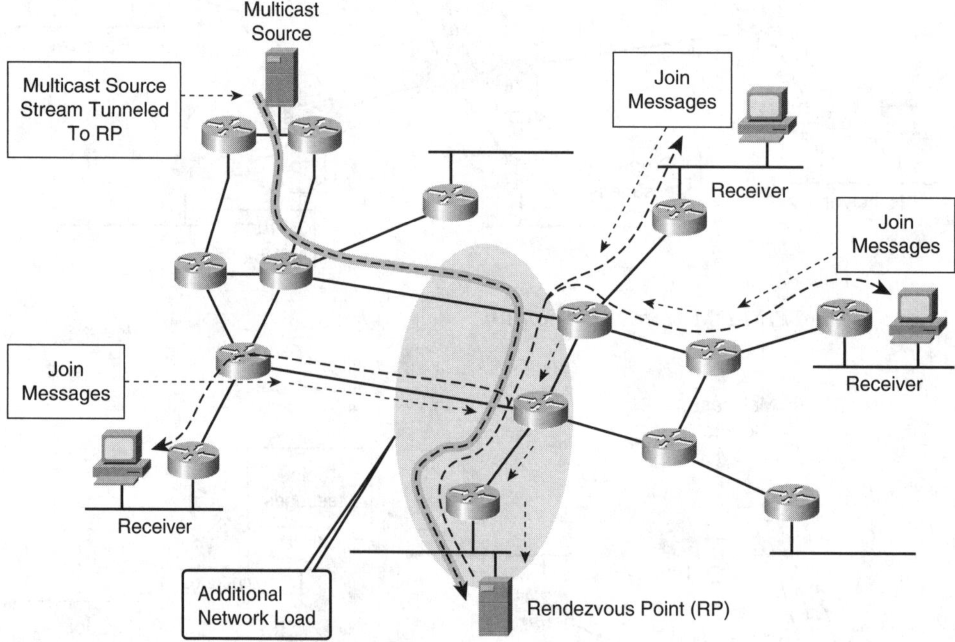

Figure 4-23 *Multicast Distribution via Rendezvous Point*

The PIM Source Specific Mode (PIM-SSM) method was created to mitigate the inefficiencies of PIM-SM. After a receiver knows the source of traffic for a multicast group, the receiver may send a PIM join toward the source bypassing the RP or BSR. Application developers are now building applications that inherently support PIM-SSM. The mobile subscriber can select participation in a service, and the application will automatically join the multicast distribution tree for the duration of the subscriber's participation.

One of the biggest impediments to deployment of multicast on a mobile provider's network is the tunneling architecture used for subscriber aggregation. The absence of a multicast-enabled provider infrastructure requires replication of each subscriber's multicast stream prior to tunneling the traffic to the subscriber. Figure 4-24 shows the legacy mobile provider IP topology and highlights the inefficiency of replicating multicast traffic at the subscriber session manager.

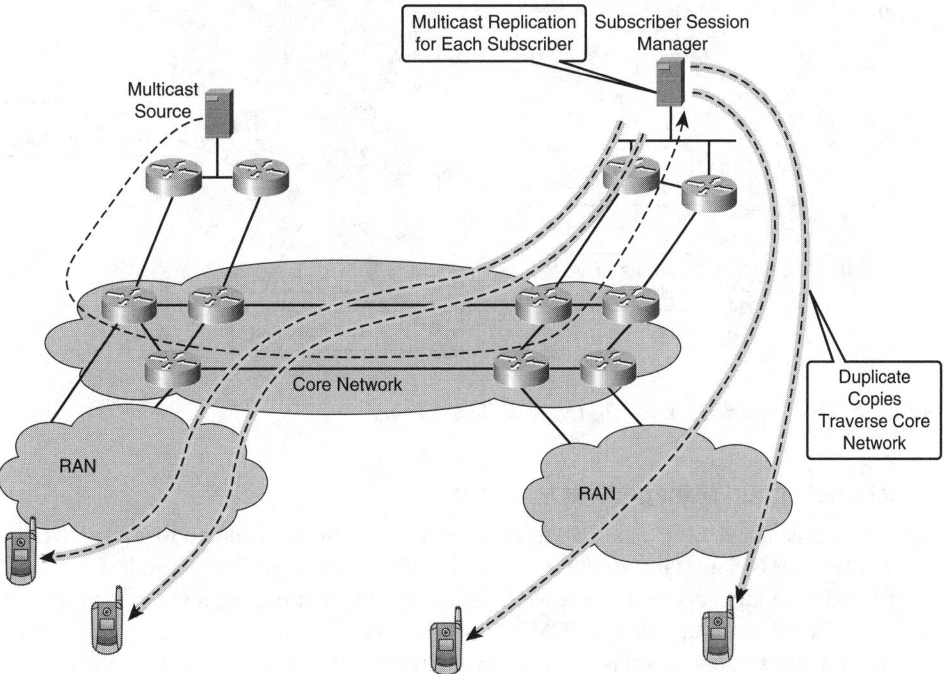

Figure 4-24 *Multicast Distribution on Aggregated Mobile Sessions*

Next-generation mobile IP architectures facilitate more efficient use of multicast where the provider's RAN and WAN execute the replication of multicast traffic. The UMTS architecture leverages the Multimedia Broadcast Multicast Service to replicate traffic at the GGSN, SGSN, and RNC. [7] The multicast-enabled RAN minimizes the number of broadcast/multicast streams that need to be distributed to the periphery of the network. Architecturally, the subscriber session management must be distributed to the periphery of the network in order to manage multicast more efficiently. Figure 4-25 shows the use of distributed subscriber session management where some services are broadcast for all subscribers, whereas others provide two-way multicast services.

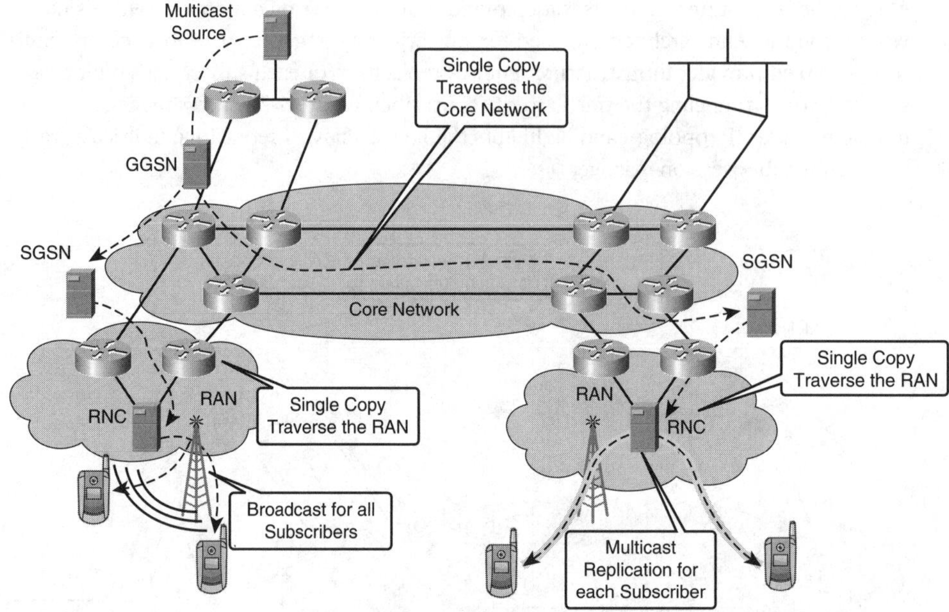

Figure 4-25 *Multicast Distributed Mobile Sessions*

Internet Group Management Protocol

The routing nodes need a method to discover multicast sources and multicast receivers. The Internet Group Management Protocol (IGMP) protocol handles the exchange of group information between the receiver/source and the first routing node participating in the DVMRP or PIM processes. IGMP allows a multicast sender to notify adjacent routers that a multicast application is transmitting multicast traffic to a specific group. The first routing node may then forward the stream on the multicast distribution tree. Likewise, a receiver may notify an adjacent router that access to a multicast stream is required. The router will subsequently join the multicast distribution tree for that group and forward the multicast steam to the local receivers. IGMP uses reports between end-system senders/receivers and the adjacent routers. The reports identify the groups of interest.

IGMP is relevant for the mobile provider in the data center environment. Any multicast applications in the data center will need to make their presence known on the providers' WAN routing infrastructure. The interesting challenge is how to provide multicast services to the mobile subscriber. It is unreasonable for a mobile subscriber to issue an IGMP report requesting to join a multicast group. Architecturally, the multicast stream would have to be replicated on each subscriber's session attachment. Fundamentally, the model of replicating IP multicast on each subscriber session does not scale. The next-generation wireless networks have design broadcast capabilities into the radio access network that operates in parallel to the existing unicast distribution architecture. Figure 4-26 shows the generic architecture used for distribution of multicast traffic to mobile subscribers.

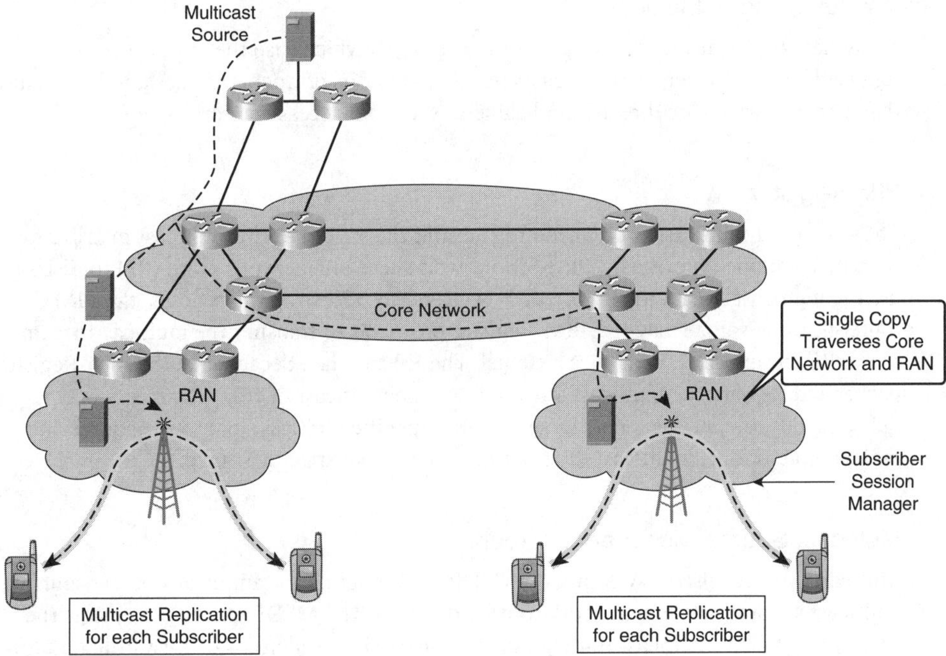

Figure 4-26 *Multicast Wireless Delivery Architecture*

Numerous organizations created variants of this generic architecture, and they primarily focus on where the IP multicast terminates and when the mobile wireless broadcast/multicast begins. Clearly, the goal is to move the IP multicast processes as close to the edge as possible. These wireless edge systems require IGMP functions to join the IP multicast architecture. The edge systems have to convert the IP multicast into a radio multicast architecture that is dependent on the radio systems.

Multicast Listener Discovery

The next generation of IPv6 uses a new method within the IPv6 protocol, as opposed to creating a separate protocol, as IGMP was for IPv4. Multicast Listener Discovery (MLD) is inherently built into the IPv6 protocol stack and performs similar functionality as IGMP in IPv4. The IPv6 protocol has defined several multicast addresses for link-local and interface-local and uses the multicast report and queries to participate in specific multicast groups.

The use of MLD has not become prevalent in the mobile wireless space; however, it too will most likely play a role in the distribution of content via multicast in the data center and on the mobile provider's core network.

Unicast Tunneling of Multicast

Many network elements do not support multicast, in which case the multicast must be tunneled via unicast across those elements. A number of protocols are designed to do just that, some of which are directly applicable to the radio access network.

PIM-Register

The sources of multicast traffic need to transmit the stream to the multicast distribution tree. As mentioned previously, PIM-SM networks use a rendezvous point (RP) to distribute the multicast stream to all potential receivers. To bootstrap the process, the PIM router near the source may use PIM-Register protocols to transmit the multicast stream to the RP encapsulated in a unicast tunnel. The RP can then decapsulate the PIM-Register packet and forward the multicast stream down the multicast distribution tree. Subsequently, the receivers may issue a source-specific multicast join to the source and build a more optimal multicast distribution tree for that specific source.

Multicast Source Discovery Protocol

Multicast Source Discovery Protocol (MSDP) is another important means of transmitting multicast streams between network routing domains. The MSDP protocol connects the RPs from different multicast routing domains and provides a means of forwarding multicast data between them. A multicast stream in one domain can be replicated into the MSDP protocol, which tunnels the multicast stream in a unicast packet. This facilitates linking the multicast domains without having to actually run multicast at the border of the inter-domain routing entities.

The relevance of MSDP for mobile providers will likely between data centers and content providers. The content providers may provide a multicast feed via the Internet; however, subscription services will likely be specifically established between the content sources and the mobile provider as a distributor. MSDP may be the best choice for the mobile provider to obtain multicast streams from various content sources without having to open up their border gateways to multicast.

IP Packet-Switching Protocols

Mobile wireless networks have gradually migrated from a voice-centric infrastructure to a packet-centric infrastructure to accommodate the growth in data services. Although the majority of the data services are based on IP, many of the underlying transport mechanisms continued to use infrastructure based on voice transport. This section looks at the properties of transitioning voice infrastructures to packet infrastructures that are optimized to handle IP traffic.

Connection-Oriented Switching Methods

The dominant service for years in the mobile network has been voice. Voice requires a connection-oriented (CO) switching method for the duration of the call. The initial introduction of data services such as Short Messaging Service (SMS) was defined on top of the existing infrastructure (that is, reusing a signaling channel), and as such was not adapted to truly handle data traffic. Gradually, new data services appeared that required IP processing on the mobile subscriber handset. New methods were devised to allocate channels in the voice infrastructure specifically for data. Chapter 2, "Cellular Access Systems," provided the various means of transporting data service through the signaling plane. The growth of IP data services quickly overwhelmed the voice transport and signaling mechanisms. New mobile provider architectures were introduced that specifically handled data using a Connectionless (CL) switching method. The next few sections address how the traditional voice infrastructures relate to IP packet switching.

Time Division Multiplexing

Time Division Multiplexing (TDM) uses a method of allocating time-slots for transmission of information. The classic voice services allocated time-slots predicated on the digital encoding of voice at 64 kbps. The voice channel is allocated for the duration of the call, and the data stream is continuous. The 64-kbps channel is 100% utilized for the duration of the call. When the voice call terminates, the channel is returned to the pool of resources made available for new calls. The wireless networks adapted the coding rate using various voice compression schemes such as Enhanced Full Rate and Adaptive Multi-Rate (AMR) compression, which optimizes voice delivery over the air-link. The compressed voice data inefficiently used the 64-kbps channels; therefore, the wireless radio networks modified the TDM structure to accommodate these lower bit rate codecs. Voice services typically present a synchronous stream of data. The TDM switching models are inefficient when allocating channels for data services that typically do not result in continuous data streams. For example, most voice codecs use a 20-msec sampling interval where the TDM structure is optimized to receive the voice-encoded data stream at that periodic interval. Data services are asynchronous; therefore, assigning TDM time-slots for data that doesn't show up is wasteful of the frequency spectrum and backhaul capacity. Radio networks adapted the TDM infrastructure to dynamically assign channels for data transactions on an as-needed bases. Figure 4-27 shows how the data transactions are interleaved into the TDM infrastructure.

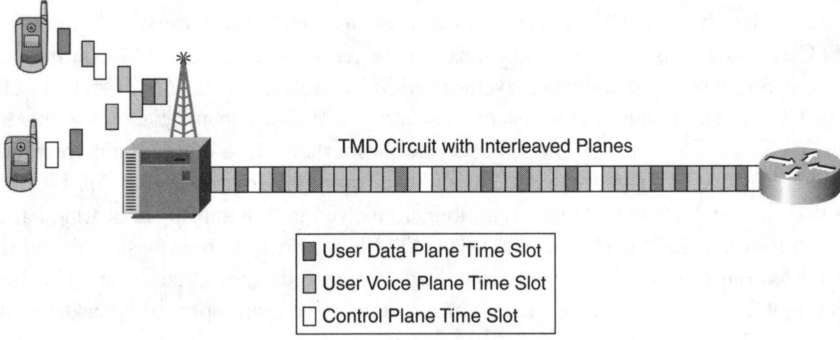

Figure 4-27 *Interleaved Data Services in TDM*

The model presented in Figure 4-27 shows how the data services traffic is interleaved with the voice channels in a general sense. The various radio access network systems (CDMA, GSM, and so on) use different packet encapsulation methods, but the principle is the same.

Frame Relay Switching

Initial releases of 3G architectures (Release 97) introduced the Frame Relay interface between the BSC and SGSN. Subsequent releases (Release 99) allowed the BTS to present a dedicated Frame Relay (FR) interface for data services backhaul. The primary advantage of FR over ATM is that the encapsulation of IP in FR is more efficient than in ATM. The FR service also provided a dedicated channel for data services backhaul; however, it did not provide transport for any voice services. The advantage of converged data and voice in the backhaul trunk is mitigated; however, the transition has an inflection point where it makes more economical sense to dedicate capacity to data services. The removal of data services from the traditional TDM wireless allocation mechanisms allowed the operator to separate the growth of data from voice, as the rate of growth for data is far exceeding the rate of group for voice. The operator is able to reclaim TDM capacity previously used for data and dedicate it for voice for which the transport is optimized. Likewise, the operator is able to scale the FR transport of data bearer services at an appropriate rate and avoid the use of expensive TDM backhaul resources for data transport. FR transport is provisioned in much the same way that ATM is pre-provisioned; a FR Permanent Virtual Circuit (PVC) is established to transport the IP-encapsulated data services.

Asynchronous Transfer Mode

Many of the radio architectures recognized the inefficiency of using TDM for integrated voice and data services and migrated to Asynchronous Transfer Mode (ATM) backhaul mechanisms using a cell-switching model. The ATM switching method preserved the pseudosynchronous capabilities for voice-switched services while allowing data services to be more efficiently interleaved in the trunks leaving the cell site. The 3GPP and 3GPP2 architectures leveraged ATM backhaul in Release 99 and CDMA2000, respectively. In fact, the voice and data can be split into separate ATM Virtual Path Identifiers/Virtual Circuit Identifiers (VPI/VCI) bearer and control channels at the Base Station Controller (BSC). As such, it is possible to optimize the bearer for voice using ATM Continuous Bit Rate (CBR), whereas data bearer leverages ATM Variable Bit Rate non-real-time (VBRnrt). The CBR service simulates to present a pseudosynchronous channel, allowing guaranteed quality of service to voice. The VBR service allows the data to more efficiently interleave in the ATM trunk on an as-needed basis. The primary differentiator with ATM backhaul is that the wireless control plane is no longer involved in dynamically allocating bandwidth for the voice and data services. The ATM bandwidth is pre-provisioned, and the wireless control simply directs the voice and data into the appropriate bearer channels. Figure 4-28 shows the divergence of voice and data in a more optimized backhaul trunk.

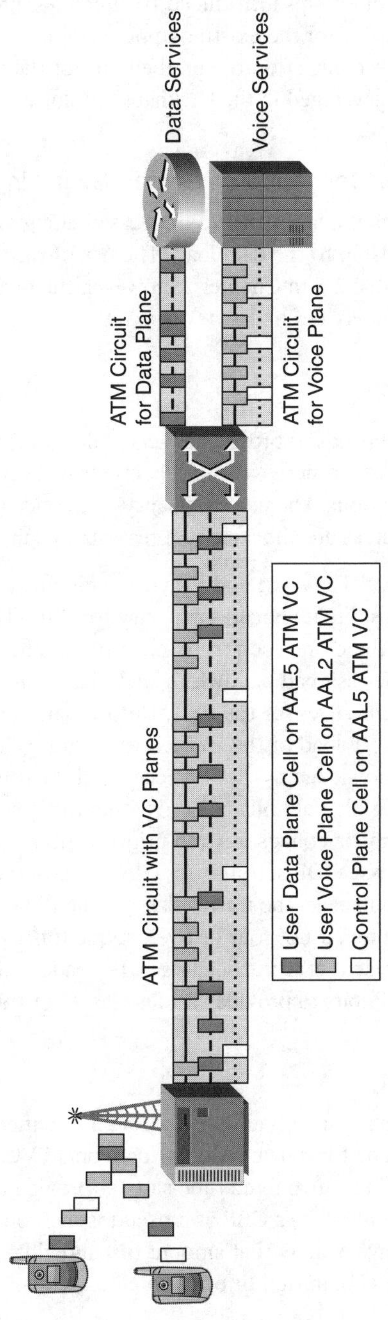

Figure 4-28 *ATM RAN Backhaul*

The 3GPP Release 5 architectures introduced IP interfaces into the BTS/BSC; however, IP simply provided a transport for the existing upper layer protocols, whereas the ATM infrastructure provided a connection-oriented circuit for the transport of IP. The utility of IP routing is still not leveraged in the backhaul topology.

Bandwidth Allocation for Connection-Oriented Switching Methods

One of the most important characteristics of CO switching methods is the virtual circuit capacity and its relationship to the data load. The use of different classes of services was introduced briefly in Table 2-5 in Chapter 2; however, the relationship to voice and data needs to be more adequately defined.

Quality of Service

The RAN infrastructure needs to provide an acceptable level of service quality for both the voice and data services; otherwise, the subscriber will suffer by experiencing interrupted or stalled transactions. The use of Quality of Service (QoS) mechanisms ensures that the transport resources are allocated in a reasonably fair manner.

Frame Rate Scheduling The ATM and FR virtual circuit -witching methods use a frame rate scheduling mechanism that allocates capacity for PVC. The PVC will build a path across multiple trunks; therefore, each trunk must be able to honor the bandwidth request. The PVC can be assigned bandwidth such that each switch scheduler allocates a certain percentage of time slices for the PVC. Unfortunately, the FR and ATM switches have no visibility to the payload of the PVC. The FR and ATM switches only have QoS context based on the knowledge of the PVC class and the use of Cell Loss Priority (CLP) in ATM and Discard Eligible (DE) bits in FR. Neither of these mechanisms is sufficient to adequately manage IP traffic congestion and prioritization. The FR and ATM binary representation of traffic classes (DE set/unset or CLP set/unset) doesn't provide the granularity of QoS needed to manage the traffic classes. The IP network services typically require a minimum of three, if not four or five, unique traffic classes. At a minimum, two bits are required to represent four traffic classes. IP headers take advantage of six Diff-Serv Code Points (DSCP) bits to provide various classes of traffic and drop priorities.

Queue Management

An ATM or FR switching system is able to allocate a specified percentage of an interface's queue schedule time for transmission of data on a PVC. Depending on the PVC class, the schedule time may guarantee time-slots or provide time-slots as available and needed. The ATM scheduler views CBR as a pseudosynchronous circuit; therefore, the trunk interfaces must have exactly that amount of bandwidth available on the scheduler. The same is true for the Committed Information Rate (CIR) on FR PVCs.

The challenge the operator faces when migrating to IP services while using FR/ATM transport is that the class and priority of IP traffic does not correlate directly to the class and QoS models used in FR/ATM switching. One of the advantages of using IP packet-switching methods is that the QoS attributes applied at the IP endpoints may directly correlate to the queue management methods used throughout the transport infrastructure. The next section focuses on the Connection-Less (CL) switching methods that empower the operator with more sophisticated queue management techniques.

Connectionless Switching Methods

The transition to IP packet switching is predicated on a new model where there is no longer state of a particular flow managed in the core of the network. The FR/ATM core node requires state management for each PVC transiting through the node. The CL packet-switching methods only maintain state on how to reach the destination. The packet-switched core allows much greater scale and distributes the routing intelligence to the periphery of network. The core only needs to know generalized route paths referred to as route aggregates, while the edge needs to know how to route to the core and to the locally attached devices. A brief review of the packet-switching methods highlights the importance each technology plays in the transport of IP in mobile wireless networks.

Ethernet Packet Switching

The Ethernet-switching model provides a low cost means of transporting IP packets between end-systems. Historically reserved for use in the LAN environment, it now has relevance in the mobile provider's RAN and potentially the WAN. Ethernet uses a Media Access Control address to identify the end-systems on the Ethernet medium. The MAC is a 48-bit address assigned to each system's interface attached to a LAN. The IP address assigned to the end-system must be correlated with the MAC address, such that adjacent systems on the Ethernet know how to direct IP packets toward the target end-system. The IP address assignment can be statically configured or dynamically assigned with methods such as IP Configuration Protocol (IPCP) or Dynamic Host Control Protocol (DHCP). Subsequently, the Address Resolution Protocol (ARP) is used for the adjacent systems to discover and build the IP-to-MAC association for all end-systems on the LAN.

Binding the IP address to a MAC address is particularly important where fail-over is concerned. Usually, the IP-to-MAC address mapping is dynamically created or statically configured but persistent for the duration the end-system's processing of data. Some end-systems have two or more interfaces that inherently have unique MAC addresses; however, other systems in the network need to forward traffic to end-system's persistent IP address. If the IP address changes, the associated sessions must be torn down and re-established. To mitigate the loading on the control plane, an end-system might clone an interface such that a different interface uses the same IP and MAC address. This eliminates the need to update the binding in neighbor IP systems; however, it does require the switch serving the Ethernet to dynamically re-associate the end-system on a new switch port. Figure 4-29 shows an example of a wireless end-system cloning an interface in various manners.

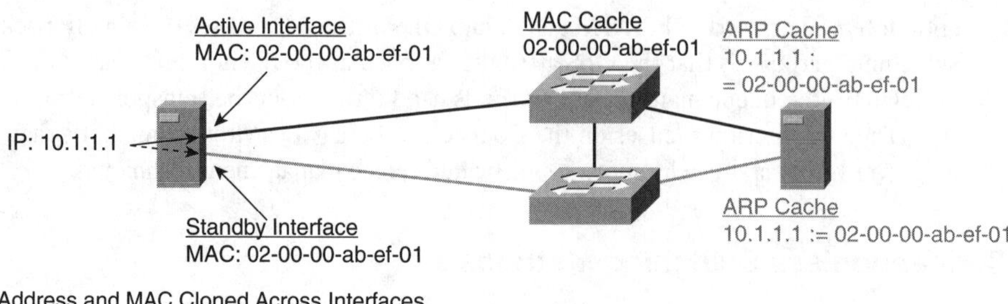

a) IP Address and MAC Cloned Across Interfaces

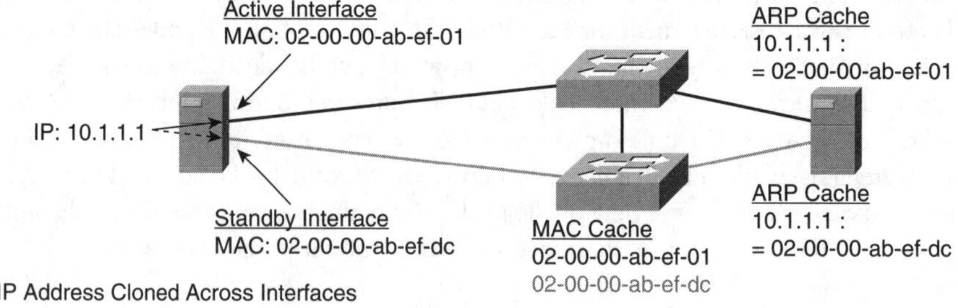

b) IP Address Cloned Across Interfaces

Figure 4-29 *End-System with Cloned Interfaces*

The figure in 4-29a shows an end-system architecture that uses the same IP and same MAC addresses on the cloned interface. Conversely, the figure in 4-29b shows an end-system architecture that uses the same IP, but different MAC address for connectivity. Emphasis in the first example is place of the fact that the Ethernet-switching system must refresh the bridge-forwarding tables for the MAC address from the primary switch to the secondary switch during failure. Conversely, the second example allows the bridge-forwarding tables to be persistent, whereas the end-systems must modify their ARP entries.

The end-system using a cloned interface needs to ensure that only one of the interfaces is active at any given time; otherwise, the network will experience dropped packets due to blocked ports or applications binding to a dormant interface. The Ethernet network generally only accepts one path for forwarding unless several physical interfaces are bundled as a single logical interface. The switched Ethernet environment uses the Spanning Tree Protocol (STP) to determine a loop-free topology in the switched Ethernet environment. Figure 4-30 shows a redundantly connected Ethernet-switched network where ports are blocked by STP to create a loop-free topology.

Most wireless network elements represent a single entity on the Ethernet-switched topology. Many wireless systems have more than one IP address associated with a network element for different functions such as control plane, data plane, and management plane. Managing these interfaces in a separate switching plane is often required. The Ethernet-switching environment must maintain that segmentation. Virtual LAN (VLAN) switching is commonly used for this purpose. The end-system can present a single physical interface to the Ethernet switch where two or more logical interfaces are defined. The logical interfaces are distinguished in the LAN by VLAN tags, as shown in Figure 4-31.

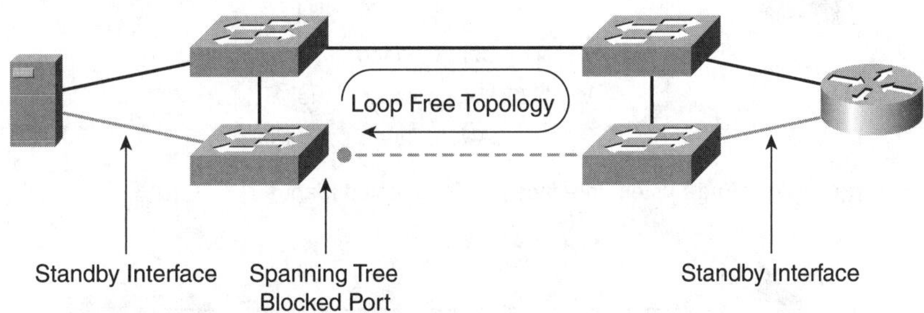

Figure 4-30 *Spanning Tree Loop-Free Ethernet Topology*

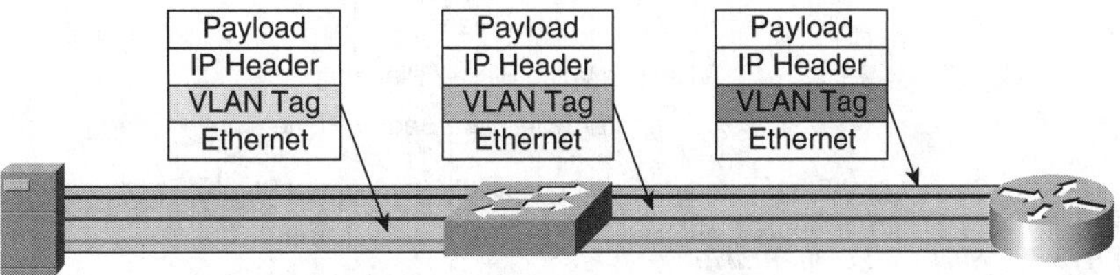

Figure 4-31 *VLAN Tagged Ethernet Encapsulation*

Each logical interface may be assigned a function with a unique IP, MAC, and VLAN configured. Some wireless end-systems use separate interfaces to distinguish between voice and data services, whereas others use separate logical interfaces to distinguish between control, bearer, and management planes. Figure 4-32 shows two different models that end-systems might use to provide delineation of services. The first example shows a network element with a unique physical interface for each service plane. Each physical interface is mapped to a unique VLAN segment on the Ethernet switch. The second example in Figure 4-32 shows a network element with a shared physical interface with logically separate interface descriptors for each service plane. The logical interface descriptors are associated with a unique VLAN instance.

Different wireless standards may dictate which method is used or if all the services are aggregated on a single logical interface. Regardless, deploying flexible network architecture facilitates evolution from one wireless specification to a new specification without a fork-lift upgrade.

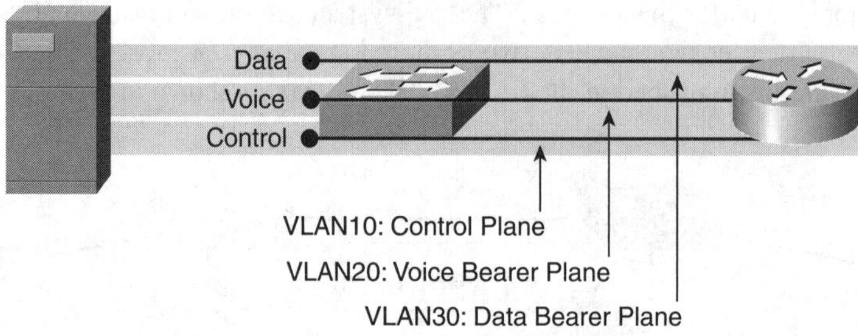

(a) Distinct End-System Interfaces for Segmented Planes

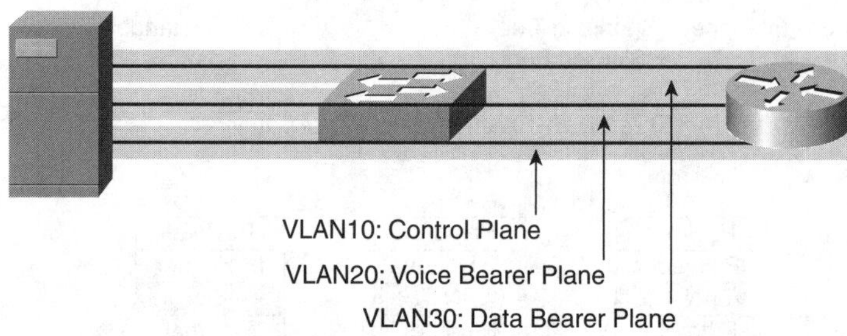

(b) Shared End-System Interface with Logically Segmented Planes

Figure 4-32 *Service Segmentation*

Multi-Protocol Label Switching (MPLS)

The deployment of IP services over ATM networks was always been plagued by the inherent inefficiencies. The IP packet requires multiple ATM cells for transport, and that led to encapsulation inefficiencies. Each cell introduced a minimum of five bytes of overhead in addition to the IP overhead. The fixed-length header of the ATM cell supported high-speed switching in ASICs; however, ATM required the segmentation of IP packets that didn't quite fit naturally into ATM cells. In addition, ATM's rigorously defined QoS models didn't accommodate the elasticity requirements of IP transactions. Nevertheless, operators appreciated the point-to-point characteristics of ATM that created well-defined routing topologies and simplified the bandwidth management in the context of a traffic matrix.

MPLS defines an encapsulation method using fixed-length label (much like a cell header); however, the entire IP packet could be transported in a single frame. Figure 4-33 shows the encapsulation of an IP packet in an MPLS-labeled frame.

The MPLS switching architecture facilitated the establishment of a Label Switched Path (LSP) through the network that was conceptually equivalent to an ATM VC path defined by cell switching, as shown in Figure 4-34.

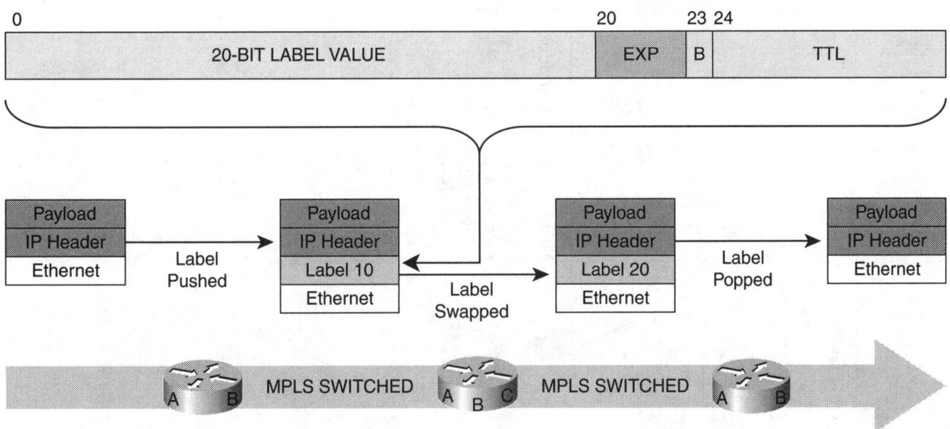

Figure 4-33 *MPLS Encapsulation*

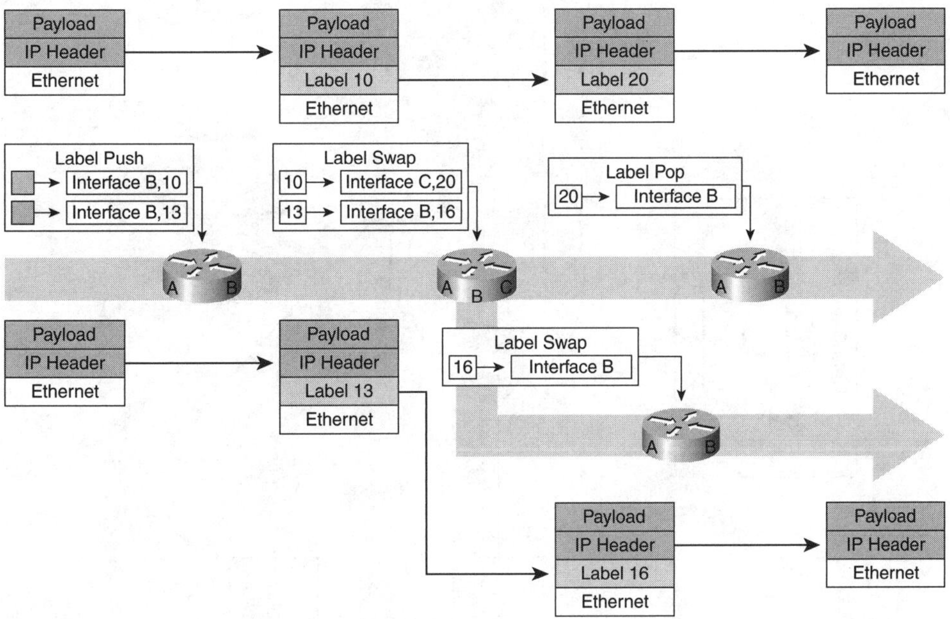

Figure 4-34 *MPLS Label Switched Path*

The correlation was comforting to operators of ATM networks, and the efficiency of MPLS was significant as more applications appeared that used small IP packets such as VoIP. As a result, MPLS effectively replaced ATM as the preferred choice for transporting IP packets in mobile provider core networks. The same principles have become relevant in the mobile provider's backhaul network as well. Figure 4-35 shows where MPLS has initially garnered a role in the mobile provider network.

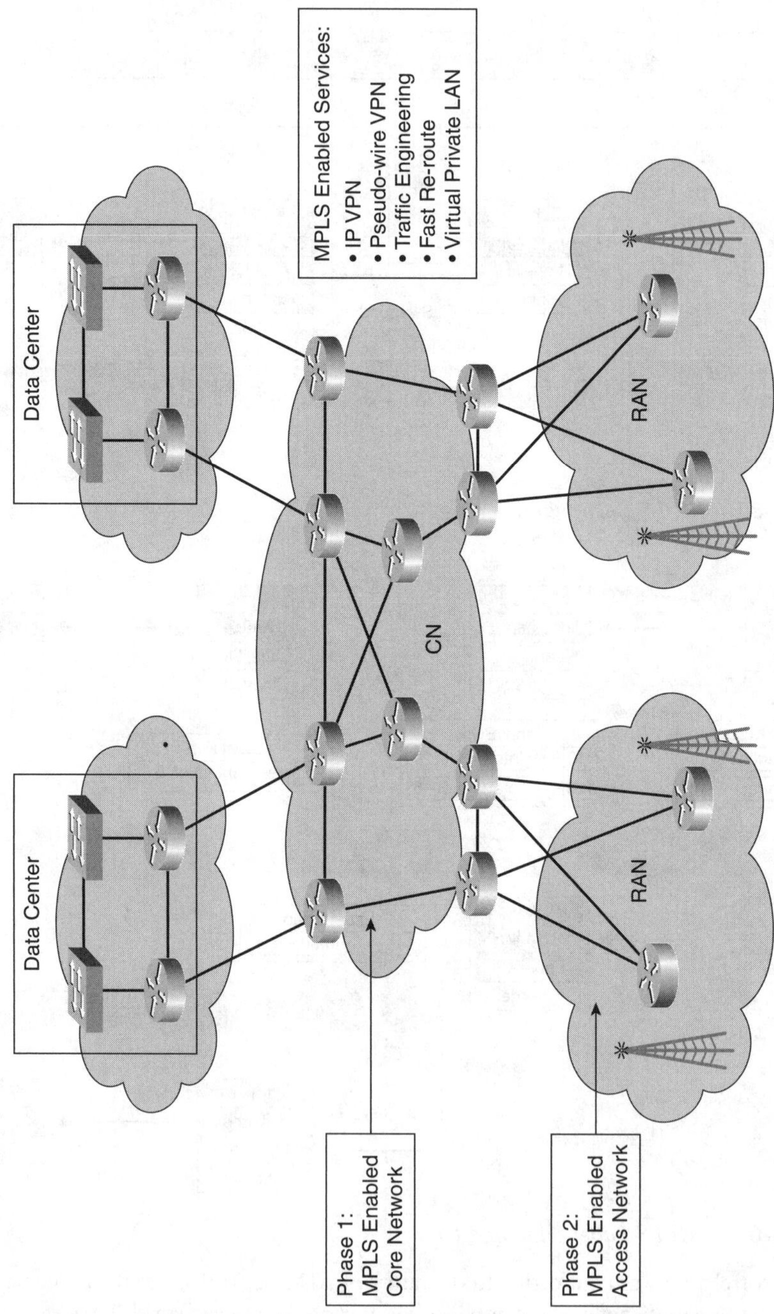

Figure 4-35 *Mobile Provider MPLS Deployments*

Note that MPLS is effectively a shim layer that rides at Layer 2.5 in the OSI layered protocol stack, because MPLS can run over a diverse set of Layer 2 media types, including Ethernet and ATM. The advantage that MPLS offers is a consistent network-switching method edge-to-edge regardless of the Layer 2 media type. Note that MPLS is not an end-to-end protocol; it does not provide addressing for end-systems. That role is reserved for IP and Ethernet. For this reason, MPLS's relevance in the last mile is unlikely. Architecturally, the access networks are migrating to IP over Ethernet, while the backhaul and core networks leverage MPLS to provide a consistent and scalable switching model from edge to edge. Figure 4-36 shows the typical relationship between Ethernet, MPLS, and IP.

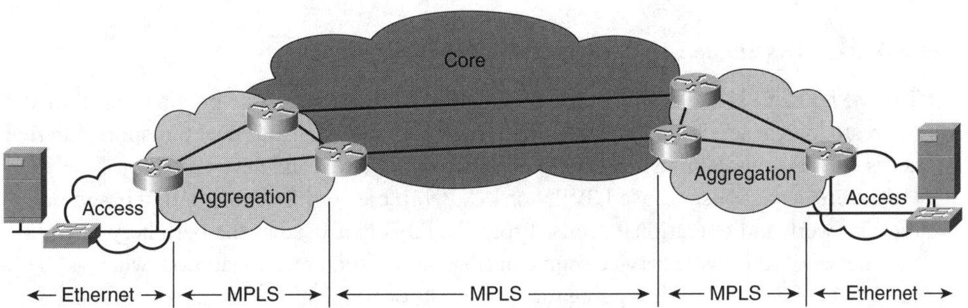

Figure 4-36 *MPLS Architectural Positioning*

The establishment of the edge-to-edge LSP is dependent upon IP. The edge systems use IP as the control plane to establish the Label Switched Path. Numerous IP protocols have evolved to facilitate the establishment of LSPs. The Label Distribution Protocol (LDP) is often used to build a shortest path edge-to-edge LSP in a core network, whereas ReSerVation Protocol-Traffic Engineering (RSVP-TE) is used to control the establishment of an LSP on an operator-defined path. These tools enable the operator to build a scalable core and aggregation network that transports IP packets in an efficient manner. The insertion of an MPLS shim creates an abstraction layer such that the core and aggregation network do not need to be cognizant of all the IP applications. The core only needs to know the context of IP that is needed to build the LSP from edge-to-edge. This advantage significantly improves the scalability of the network by minimizing state management in the core and moving the state management of IP services to the edge. Figure 4-37 highlights the distribution of the state management when using MPLS switching models.

New MPLS services were developed that leveraged the edge-to-edge switching model of the Label Switching Path, including Layer-3 Virtual Private Network (L3VPN) and Layer-2 Virtual Private Networks (L2VPN). The L2VPN service effectively emulated other media-switching types, including FR, ATM, and Ethernet. These methods are used to provide service segmentation or customer segmentation, while leveraging the common MPLS-switching infrastructure.

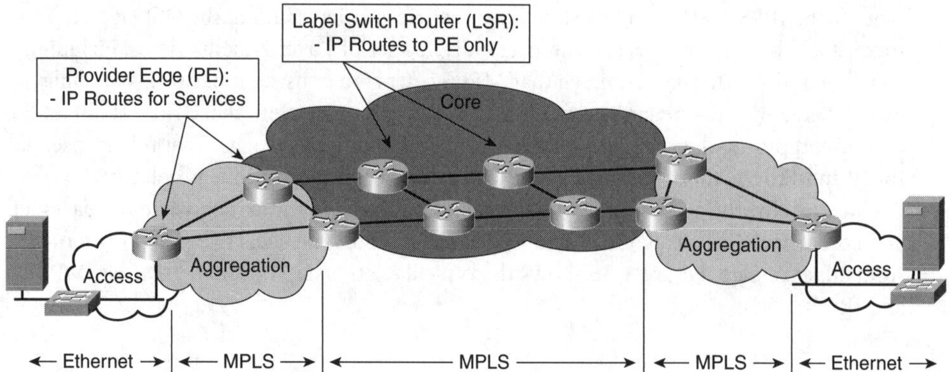

Figure 4-37 *Distributed MPLS Service State Management*

The MPLS L2VPN and L3VPN switching methods offer the mobile provider the ability to create logical service segments for network functions, such as voice transport, Internet access, operations administration and management (OAM), and network control. Operators may choose to use L3VPN or L2VPN to create this segmentation based on their network and operational needs. Typically, L3VPN is used at the periphery of the core network to provide service segmentation and customer segmentation, whereas L2VPN is often used in the aggregation network for backhaul and transport of legacy protocols, while providing a new switching architecture for mobile end-systems that do offer IP-enabled interfaces. The L2VPN and L3VPN are overlay services on the MPLS-switching infrastructure. These services are implemented on the provider's edge network elements. The core network elements have no knowledge of the L2 and L3 services instantiated at the edge; they simply provide a switching path between the provider edge network elements.

The MPLS L2VPN uses Targeted LDP (TLDP) to establish pseudowires (PW) that emulate FR, ATM, Ethernet, or even TDM circuits. The TLDP protocol operates between the provider edge (PE) devices and builds a switching context in the PE that switches the native L2 frames into the PW and vice versa. Architecturally, the Layer 2 switching systems appear to be adjacent to one another, and the core network is transparent. Figure 4-38 shows the architectural model for L2VPN services in relationship to the MPLS switching core network. The L2VPN service provides a means of transitioning the RAN backhaul to an IP-enabled transport without requiring modifications to the mobile wireless network elements.

Mobile providers may use L2VPN as a method of transitioning an ATM core network to MPLS as an overlay or migrating ATM services to the MPLS core. The two approaches are shown in Figure 4-39.

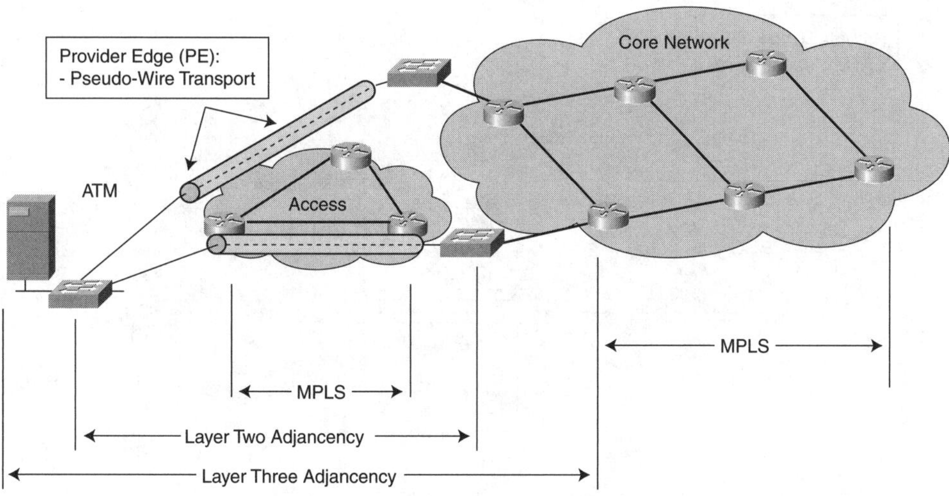

Figure 4-38 *L2VPN Switching Context*

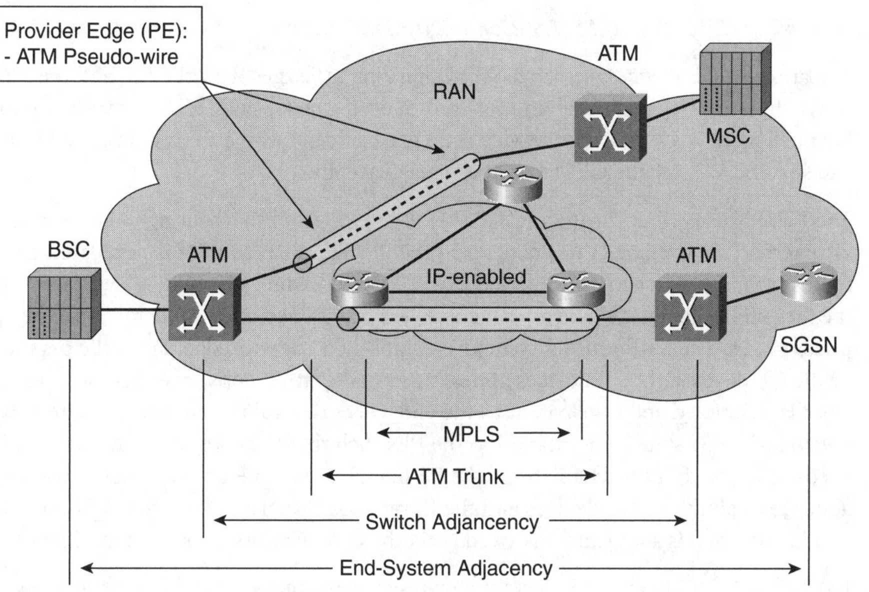

Figure 4-39 *ATM Trunk to MPLS Pseudowire Transition*

Figure 4-39 shows the use of MPLS PW to build a trunk between two ATM switches. The ATM-switched infrastructure simply views the MPLS PW as a circuit. There is minimal signaling exchange between the ATM and the MPLS PE, except for the physical link layer protocols. The ATM control plane is transparently passed through the PW to the remote ATM switch. Conversely, Figure 4-40 shows the use of MPLS PW to emulate an ATM-switched network.

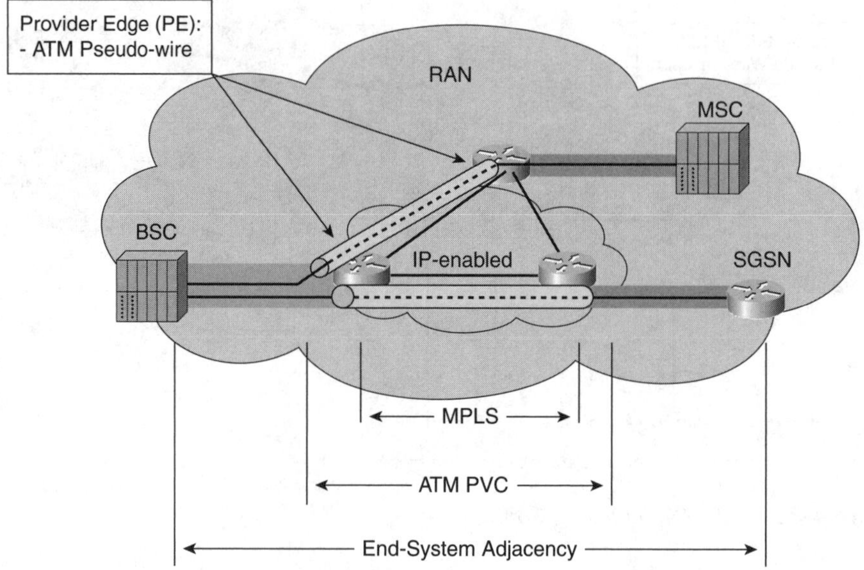

Figure 4-40 *ATM PVC to MPLS Pseudowire Transition*

The attached CE devices exchange ATM signaling messages with the PE, and the PE relays those messages through the PW protocols to the far-end PE. Clearly, the PE must be much more involved in the service state management, as the PE is configured to emulate specific VCs for the CEs to establish an adjacency.

The L3VPN uses Multi-Protocol BGP (MP-BGP) to establish a routing plane that builds virtual route forwarding (VRF) context in the PE. The VRF context is populated with routes from the attached customer edge (CE) devices, while MP-BGP relays the routes to the far-end PE devices, where a VRF context is maintained and populated with the appropriate routes. The VRF routing context is established edge-to-edge. From the perspective of the CE devices, the PE devices appear as virtual routing hops, whereas the core network is abstracted and transparent to the end-systems. Again, the virtual private network (VPN) switching state is distributed to the PEs such that the core MPLS network only needs to know about reachability of the PE devices. The core does not need to know about reachability of CE devices and the IP prefixes associated with that VPN segment. The L3VPN builds a logical VPN overlay on the core network, as shown in Figure 4-41.

L3VPN plays a critical role in maintaining route segmentation for different services and functions. The L3VPN is typically used at the periphery of the core network, where service interfaces are presented. For example, the session manager end-systems (GGSN or HA) may present unique interfaces for each service where MPLS VPN is used to maintain that service segmentation across the core.

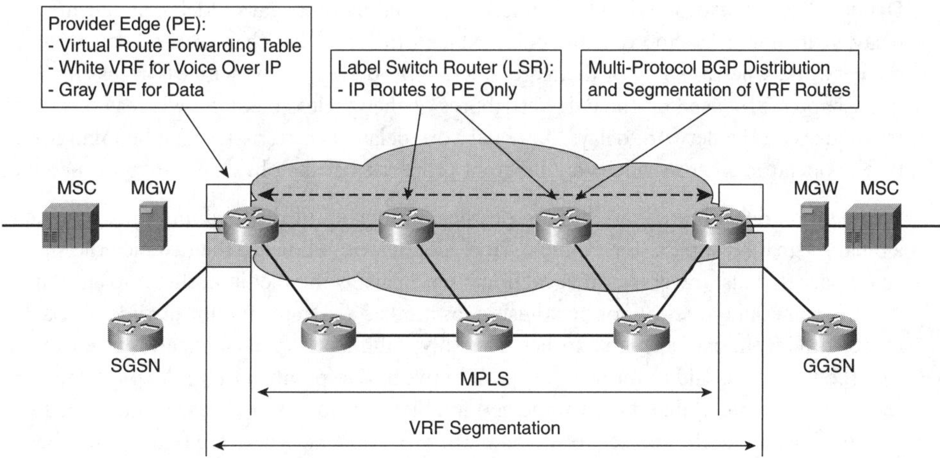

Figure 4-41 *L3VPN Switching Context*

Bandwidth Allocation for Connection-Less Switching Methods

The IP packet-switching models presented require a new model for management of QoS. The early implementation of mobile services was based the assignment of static bandwidth resources. Specific channels were assigned with guaranteed bandwidth for control, management, voice bearer, and data bearer services. The transition to packet switching inherently introduces the statistical multiplexing models. As long as the applications present traffic to the network in a consistent manner, the behavior of the network is predictable and reasonably controlled. The incentive is to exploit the statistical multiplexing properties of packet switching in order to conserve allocation of bandwidth resources. Instead of dedicating capacity for each service or function, the bandwidth is shared amongst many services or functions. To realize efficiency, the peak bandwidth requirements must be statistically multiplexed into a common bandwidth resource. If the aggregate-offered load does not exceed the shared bandwidth resource over a defined period of time, the applications may function without requiring dedicated bandwidth. However, not all applications are created equal. Quality of service is necessary in packet-switching networks to handle the transient behavior of the applications and to ensure that the bandwidth resources are allocated fairly. Fair is a subjective term and is often determined by the operator. Nevertheless, the mobile provider networks have access to a common set of IP QoS tools to define fair allocation of bandwidth according to their own business needs.

Quality of Service

The most common quality of service parameters addressed in the IP network are delay, jitter, loss, and availability. Certainly, there are many other quality of service attributes that are relevant at the application layer, and they are often relevant only to that application. Nevertheless, the application behaviors need to be mapped into the network QoS properties that we have defined.

Delay Delay is attributed to four functions, including propagation delay, serialization delay, switching delay, and queuing delay. Many of these delay characteristics occur in the network, whereas some of them are inherent properties of the wireless access medium. Chapter 2 focused on the delay attributes of the wireless medium, whereas this chapter focuses on the network delay. Many network delay characteristics may be minimized by the operator, whereas others are inherent properties of the physical transport medium.

Propagation delay is attributed to the physical properties of the medium through which a binary signal must pass (for example, fiber, copper, or radio) and the distance the signaled packets must travel over that medium. Given a specific medium, the propagation delay is something that cannot be adjusted, as it takes a certain amount of time for packets to travel from one place to another. The only thing that can be adjusted is to ensure that the medium is laid in the shortest path between two points. Often, the physically shortest path is infeasible due to some geographic obstruction or excessive economic expense to achieve the shortest physical path. Most core networks are built using fiber that runs between major infrastructure junction points (for example, railways, roadways, and so on). The propagation delay is the summation of the delay on each leg of the path. A general guideline for fiber-optic systems is 5 micro seconds of delay per kilometer. [8] Propagation delay across a continent 6000-km wide would lead to a delay of roughly 30 milliseconds.

Serialization is the time required to transmit a packet onto the medium. Serialization delay is minimized by increasing the speed of the medium. Given that most IP packets are bounded by roughly 1,500 bytes, the serialization delay is usually negligible above 2 Mbps. Serialization delay is most pronounced on low-speed circuits that are commonly found in the access and aggregation network. The serialization delay is cumulative across all the interfaces that a packet must traverse. For example, a 1,500-bytes packet that must traverse a 1.5-Mbps circuit will incur an 8-msec delay. If there are multiple 1.5-Mbps circuits the packet must cross, the delay is added for each leg. Most mobile provider RAN backhaul circuits are provisioned on T1 or E1 circuits. The 2G and 3G IP data services are actually provisioned in sub-channels on the backhaul circuit; therefore, the serialization delay can be substantial. After the IP packet reaches the core network with high-speed circuits such as DS3 and above, the serialization delay becomes negligible. The trend is for mobile providers to migrate the IP-enabled end-systems such as base stations to wireless, Ethernet, cable, or DSL backhaul mediums. These high-speed access and aggregation technologies reduce a significant amount of serialization delay for IP packets in the RAN.

Switching is the time required to transfer a packet from an input queue to an output queue on the packet-switching system. The switching delay is usually negligible in most modern packet-switching systems. The TIA/EIA provides a guideline of roughly 3 milliseconds for a set of 5 switches and pair of encoders. [8] Clearly, the delay associated with propagation is more relevant in long-haul circuits and serialization for low-speed circuits.

Queuing delay is the time a packet sits in an output queue waiting to be transmitted onto the link. All the other delay components can be calculated for a system and remain roughly time invariant. Queuing delay is the most difficult delay component accounted for in packet-switching systems. Queuing delay is a function of the offered load on the system and the processing rate. The processing rate of a circuit is known; it is the serialization delay. The offered load for IP applications is often unpredictable and bursty in nature. Of course, some IP applications, such as VoIP, generate a well-behaved stream of packets for a single call; using Erlang analysis, the operator can then estimate the offered load on the system. In contrast, the behavior of end-users' connection to IP-enabled data services, such as web browsing and file transfers, is highly unpredictable. Such applications can quickly fill an output queue, causing significant delays. It is not uncommon for oversubscribed networks to experience delays in the order of 1–2 seconds. However, a properly provisioned network will typically exhibit a much more consistent and acceptable queuing delay. Ideally, each new packet placed on the output queue can immediately begin serialization for transmittal. Any burst in the offered load will cause the queue to fill up with packets, and each packet must wait for the proceeding packets to be serialized in order. Queuing delay is more pronounced in low-speed circuits typically found in the access network, whereas high-speed circuits found in the core rarely exhibit queuing delays. Queuing delays in the core network are generally attributed to exceptions where failures occur in the network and insufficient capacity exists due to improper traffic-capacity planning. In contrast, queuing delays on the low-speed access circuits is common where a single end user can initiate an application that overloads the access circuit. Managing queuing delays in IP-switching networks is an extremely important function when designing a network, and this function will be addressed in a subsequent section on queue management.

Jitter **Jitter** is defined as variability in delay for successive packets relative to a steadily advancing clock reference. Most of the delay components addressed in the previous section are consistent over time. The queuing delay varies over time. As a stream of packets from a single application passes through all the system elements, the queuing delay can increase and decrease according to the burst in offered load at any queue along the way. Many IP applications are quite tolerant of jitter in the network; however, some interactive applications require a steady stream of packets to arrive roughly in order and on time. For example, VoIP codecs typically generate IP packets every 20 msec for a call. The inter-arrival time of the VoIP packets into the network will be consistently 20 msec. However, the egress side of the network may see the VoIP packets arrive well after the expected 20-msec interval due to a transient queuing delay in the network. For example, a burst of three 1,500 byte packets on a T1 access circuit would create roughly 24 msec of queuing delay. Of course, the VoIP application needs to play out the speech on time. A significant jitter delay causes the decoder to run out of packets to process, leaving gaps in the audible output. Most interactive applications and systems that transport streaming content use jitter buffers to absorb the variability of packet arrival on the receiving side such that an unbroken linear play-out is experienced by the user. Network assessments of a well-designed national IP network have demonstrated that less than 2 milliseconds of jitter is easily achieved while commonly operating with less than 100 microseconds of jitter 99.5% of the time.[9] Jitter management is a significant challenge for data services in radio networks where the bearer channel assignments are allocated and revoked according to the transient loads. The initial 2G architectures assigned dedicated bearer channels; however, these resources were not efficiently utilized. The 3G and 4G architectures of mobile provider networks established on-demand bearer channels for data services that significantly improve the efficiency of radio resources; however, the control plane used to dynamically establish the bearer channel cannot react fast enough to handle the bursty nature of IP traffic. Chapter 2 highlighted the fact that 3G bearer setup delays may require 1 to 5 seconds to establish sufficient bearer channel capacity to handle the instantaneous packet load. The bearer setup delays tend to exacerbate the problem of jitter in wireless access networks.

Loss **Loss** occurs anytime a packet is lost in transit between the transmitter and the receiver. Of course, packet loss is likely to occur when a circuit fails or switch fails. These are typically isolated events. Loss is also experienced when an output queue on a circuit becomes completely full, and the next packet destined for the queue has no memory allocated for storage. The switching system has no choice but to drop the packet. The loss can be mitigated by increasing the queue depth; however, the increased queue depth leads to the potential for significant delays as large bursts of packets fill a queue and await transmittal. This is a trade-off that the network operator must consider:

- Bound the delay by limiting the queue depth and increase the potential for packet loss.
- Increase the potential delay by increasing the queue depth and mitigating packet loss.

Applications and transport protocols have different sensitivities to packet loss. Most IP data services, such as web browsing, email, and instant messaging, are tolerant of some packet loss allowing end systems the opportunity to retransmit lost frames. As the packet loss approaches 5%, applications using TCP tend remain in the TCP slow-start phase, thereby dramatically reducing the throughput. Some applications, particularly interactive media such as video conferencing and Voice over IP, require near real-time delivery of the content, and there is no opportunity to retransmit. The encoding format will determine the recoverability of the video and audio stream. The encoders can overcome loss by using techniques such as forward error correction, whereas the decoders can use interpolation as a means of reconstructing the audio or video stream. Voice over IP tends to be more tolerant of loss than video; however, every attempt must be made to avoid packet loss. IP routing and switching equipment typically have large buffers capable of handling transient spikes in data transmission to avoid such loss. Large buffers in networking equipment lead to potential packet arrival jitter experienced at the receivers. A common approach in dealing with interactive applications such as voice and video is providing a jitter buffer at the receiving equipment. The jitter buffer absorbs the early and late packets and plays them out in a synchronized manner to the decoder. The goal is to handle the transient jitter bursts by making the buffer sufficiently large so that the decoder never runs out of data served from the jitter buffer, while also minimizing the delay. Sophisticated algorithms in IP equipment such as media gateways are able to dynamically adjust the jitter buffer to minimize the delay and mitigate buffer losses. Most interactive applications are tolerant of losses not exceeding 0.1% of the packets in the data stream. Table 4-2 highlights the various classes of traffic and their sensitivities to loss.

Table 4-2 *Application Sensitivities*

Application	Traffic Behavior	Loss Sensitivity	Bandwidth Requirement	Class
File transfer services (for example, SMTP, FTP, POP)	Small–large transfer of data	Very tolerant	Low to High	Best Effort
Web browsing (for example, HTTP)	Small parallel set of file transfers	Somewhat tolerant	Low to Moderate	Best Effort
Interactive (for example, Telnet, TN3270)	Series of small two-way transactions	Somewhat sensitive	Low	Reliable
Live audio (for example, VoIP)	Periodic series of small transfers	Sensitive	Low to Moderate	Guaranteed Continuous Rate
Live video (for example, H.323, RTSP)	Periodic series of small and large transfers	Highly sensitive	Moderate to High	Guaranteed with Bursts

The mobile provider's radio link is prone to errors that induce loss, delays, and retransmission. These errors frequently exceed 1% packet loss, which makes interactive media delivery less viable.

Note Excessive jitter that leads to receiver buffer exhaustion or starvation manifests itself as packet loss. There are two choices to reconcile the problem. The first is to increase the receiver jitter buffer size to absorb more variance in packet delay, which inherently increases the playout delay. The second is to shape the bursty traffic in the network such that it conforms to the jitter buffer constraints. Audio traffic is difficult to shape as it is usually a continuous stream with a relative stable bit rate. Video is difficult to shape in the network because synchronization frames must arrive on time to avoid sync loss. Video must generally be shaped at the encoder.

Improvements in the 3G radio transmission technology have improved data delivery performance by allocating sufficient capacity and schedule time to service IP packets. The current methods used in 3G infrastructures such as HSDPA and EVDO Rev. A are adequate for most data services; however, the ability to support interactive media applications is still a bit of challenge. Chapter 1 described the use of the Automatic Repeat Request (ARQ) in RLC, which forces retransmission of lost data in the air-link. ARQ delays approaching 150 milliseconds are extremely disruptive to live-linear application streams, such as interactive voice and video over IP. Next-generation 4G technologies will be better suited to handle the delay and loss requirements of interactive media services by using Hybrid-ARQ, as noted in Chapter 1, "Introduction to Radio Systems." The use of Forward Error Correction (FEC) increases bandwidth consumption, but mitigates the need to retransmit losses on the air-link, which preclude the ability to stream voice and video live.

Note Video delivered as progressive download or download and play may be treated as a file transfer that is less sensitive to loss.

Availability Availability is a measurement of the reliability of the service over time and is commonly measured as the MTTR/(MTTR+MTBF) ratio, where MTTR is the mean-time-to-repair and MTBF is the mean-time-before-failure. Historically, providers have used multiple layers of protection to ensure that the voice and data services are reliable. For example, SONET provided optical protection against fiber cuts and optical switching components. The transport layer might consist of TDM circuits provisioned in the SONET channels, and the provider might use active/standby interfaces on the TDM infrastructure. The transport layer may also use ATM trunks through the TDM circuits where ATM VCs are dynamically rerouted across alternate ATM trunks. The network layer consists of IP packets flowing through the ATM VCs. The network layer uses dynamic IP routing functions to find alternate VC paths through the ATM network. In most providers, different organizations design and operate each layer independently. The result is gross over-provisioning of resources with marginal benefit in overall availability. The convergence of mobile provider core and access networks onto a converged IP infrastructure allows the operators to consolidate the redundancy in each layer into a single IP layer. Improvements in the dynamic routing convergence intervals and alternate path-provisioning techniques identified in MPLS allow the IP network to restore network paths as fast as or faster than SONET (50 msec), TDM, or ATM circuits. The bandwidth saved by eliminating multiple layers of redundancy is tremendous, whereas the operational assessment of components impacting availability is dramatically simplified. The well-managed converged IP networks are capable of operating at 99.999% availability.

Queue Management

Queue management is one of the most important aspects to guaranteeing QoS on an IP network that serves multiple services and applications. The bursty and aggressive nature of certain IP applications can wreck havoc on an IP network if they are not constrained. The queues in the network can quickly fill up and cause loss of packets indiscriminately. The approach to reconciling the quality of service issue is to identify classes of traffic and treat it according to its priority. The general approach is to identify the traffic, classify the traffic based on its priority, mark the traffic accordingly, and then transmit the traffic in a prioritized order. There are a number of tools used to manage the traffic so that important traffic is forwarded in a timelier manner than less-important traffic.

Traffic Classification IP packets use a portion of the IP header to classify the traffic. Six bits are designated in the IP header as the Differentiated Services Code Point (DSCP) field, which is often referred to as DiffServ. Figure 4-42 shows the packet header emphasizing the DSCP bits in the IP header.

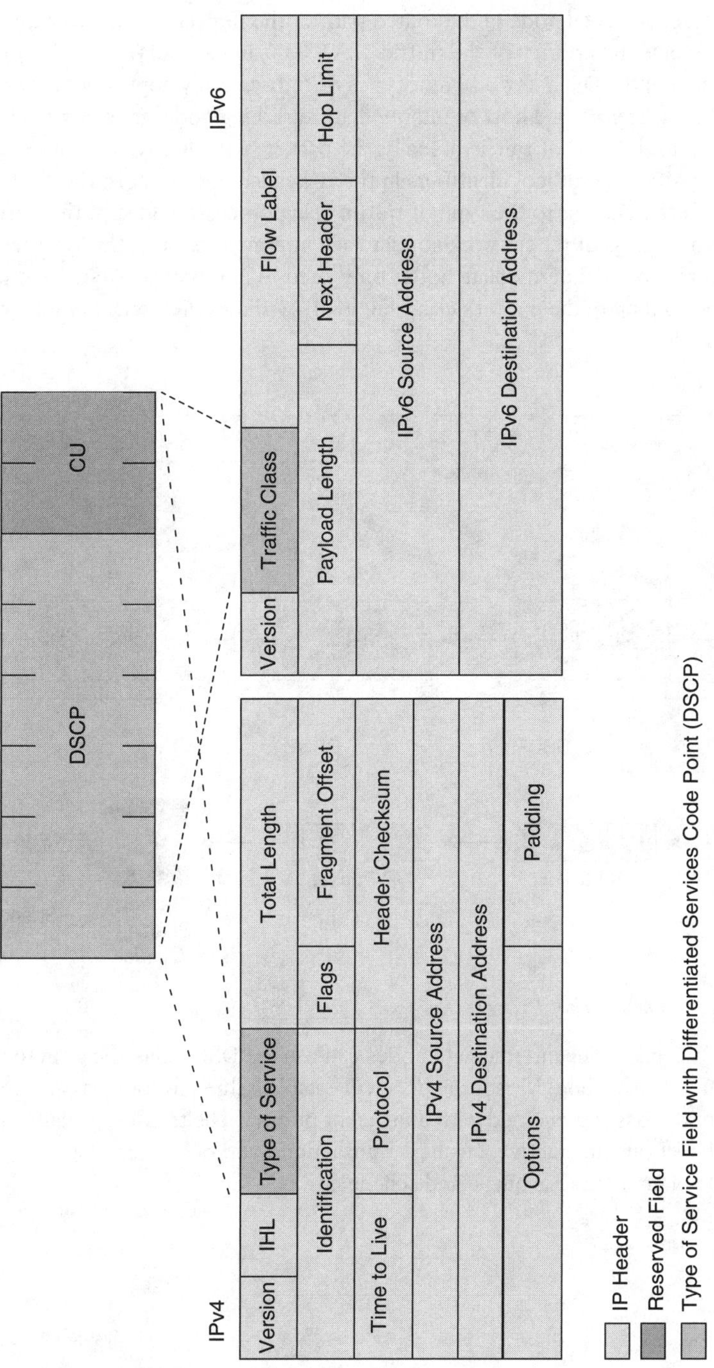

Figure 4-42 *IP Header DSCP Field*

Each packet-switched node in the routed path of the IP packet may evaluate the six bits and determine the priority of the traffic. RFC-3260 and RFC-2475 provide guidelines on how to assign the DSCP for different types of traffic. Many applications do not set the DSCP bits; therefore, the host or intermediate switching nodes must set the DSCP according to the type of traffic. Usually, the packet-switching systems have to infer the type of traffic by protocol identifiers in the IP header. For example, the TCP or UDP port numbers offer clues as to the type of traffic being processed. Ideally, the traffic is classified at the ingress of the network so that each intermediate node does not need to reassess the traffic; intermediate nodes only need to interpret the DSCP and process the packet according to the packet's class. Figure 4-43 shows the typical points of QoS packet processing. [10]

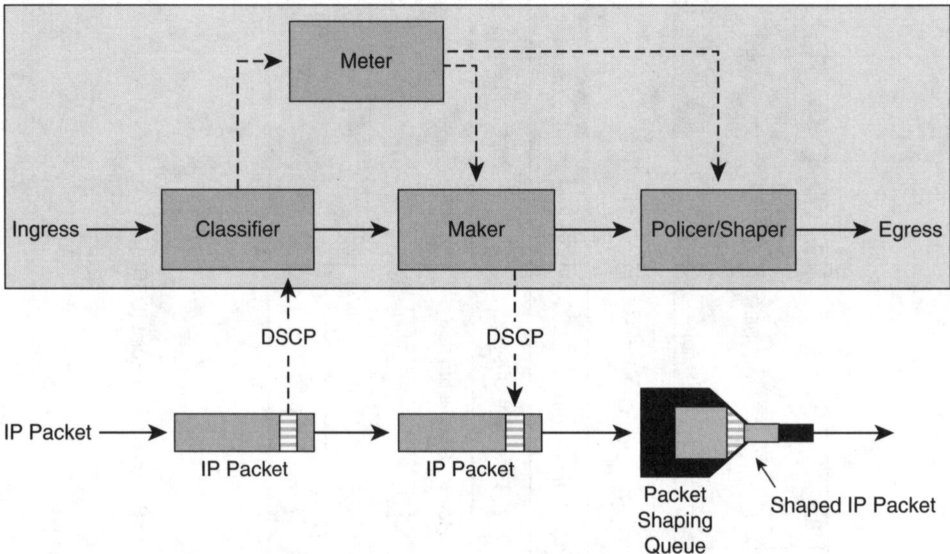

Figure 4-43 *QoS Packet Processing*

Class Queuing The intermediate nodes can use the DSCP classification to treat packets differently at each hop. Most providers will establish three to four classes of traffic, where each class is processed with a different priority. The traffic is usually classified as control, real-time interactive, business transactions, and best effort. Figure 4-44 shows an example of an interface's queue and scheduler.

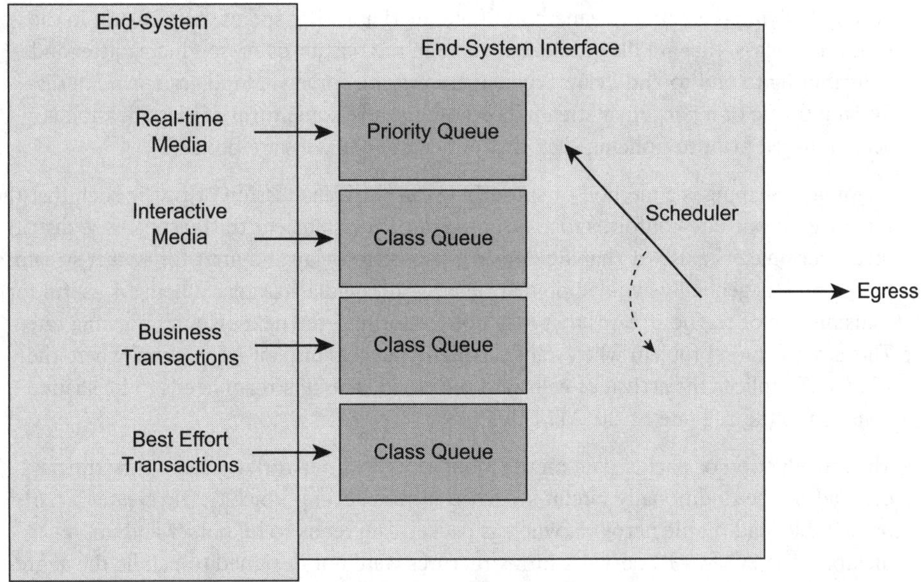

Figure 4-44 *Interface Queue*

The control traffic usually has low-bandwidth requirements; however, it is imperative that the control plane traffic be delivered with low delay. The network usually has several control planes that need to be delivered, including the IP-routing protocols and application-signaling protocols. For example, VoIP may use SIP or H.248 signaling protocols to set up and maintain telephony calls. The real-time interactive traffic usually requires time-bound delivery of the application data. Voice and video packet streams have stringent delivery requirements, where late packets are classified as lost. Real-time interactive packets need to be processed ahead of most other traffic classes to ensure that the packets are not late. A priority queue is usually established with a specified amount of time assigned to schedule transmission of packets on the interface. The operator needs to know roughly how much bandwidth of the interface is required to transmit the real-time interactive traffic with low delay. The scheduler will guarantee that the priority queue is serviced on a regular basis to ensure that packets don't sit in the queue too long. The remaining queues are serviced in order of priority: control, business transactions, and best effort. The goal is to drop traffic from the best-effort queue prior to dropping traffic in the business transaction queue. Likewise, the business traffic queue should be dropped before the control plane traffic.

Policing The provider may determine that certain traffic, particularly in the best-effort class, should not be queued. The use of a policing function enables the operator to discard traffic that exceeds a specified rate, such that it never enters the queue. Ideally, policing is accomplished on the ingress interfaces of a packet switch such that internal switching resources can be preserved for traffic that will be transmitted through the switch. Policing is an effective method of eliminating traffic spikes, particularly in the best effort class, that are likely to accumulate in the output queues inducing jitter and contributing to end-to-end delay. Policing tends to be somewhat indiscriminate in dismissing traffic of a particular stream; however, usually some form of classification is accomplished prior to policing such that only certain classes are policed.

Shaping Shaping is a method of smoothing out the transmission of traffic such that the effective output rate conforms to a specified rate. The transient traffic spikes are distributed over time. The use of shaping does contribute to delay and jitter for packet streams; therefore, it is generally avoided on real-time packet media streams. Shaping is useful for transmission of traffic streams that may not conform to the next switch's policing rate. This is a common problem when transmitting IP packets into an ATM cloud where the ATM PVC polices the arrival of cells into the cloud. The IP stream needs to be shaped to conform to the cell rate of the ATM PVC.

The introduction of packet data on the mobile wireless network creates a new traffic demand on the traditionally circuit-switched infrastructure. Voice traffic creates a fairly predictable load on the network, whereas packet data tends to be bursty and unpredictable. The 2G and 3G network infrastructures were not designed to handle the aggressive nature of data-intensive end-systems; therefore, shaping mechanisms are particularly of value. As 4G systems are introduced, new network infrastructures are built that are more capable of accommodating the transient bursts of packet data.

Ethernet-Switching Methods

IP protocols operate seamlessly over many Layer 2 media types, but Ethernet is commonly used between the mobile media end-systems and the network infrastructure. Ethernet is a cost-effective means of connecting the end-systems to the routing infrastructure. It is prudent to look at the several methods available in Ethernet that are used in conjunction with mobile IP systems. In fact, some of the early 2G and some 3G mobile end-systems used Ethernet as the means of establishing session connections to peers while having very little IP support (routing, dynamic addressing, and so on). The 4G and some 3G end-systems add more IP addressing and routing functions; nevertheless, the Ethernet-switching infrastructure continues to play an important role in providing redundancy and inexpensive aggregation.

Redundancy

Ethernet requires a topology where there are no active alternate paths. The packet-forwarding methods of Ethernet allow the distribution of Ethernet frames on every path during the discovery of end-system MAC addresses. A loop in the Ethernet topology would allow packets to cycle through the network indefinitely, causing a broadcast storm. The loop must be broken either manually or through a control plane that suppresses the loop.

Mobile end-systems that use Ethernet as an access interface are adjacent to routers or connected via an Ethernet switch. Assuming there is only one switch, there is likely no loop in the Ethernet topology. However, some mobile end-systems offer two physical Ethernet access interfaces for redundancy.

Single-Homed Ethernet Attached End-Systems

Most end-systems utilize a single Ethernet interface to connect to adjacent nodes. The single interface represents a single point of failure. The end-system may be directly connected to a routing node; however, the adjacent systems might support redundant routing nodes. Figure 4-45 shows the topology of an end-system connected to redundant routing nodes.

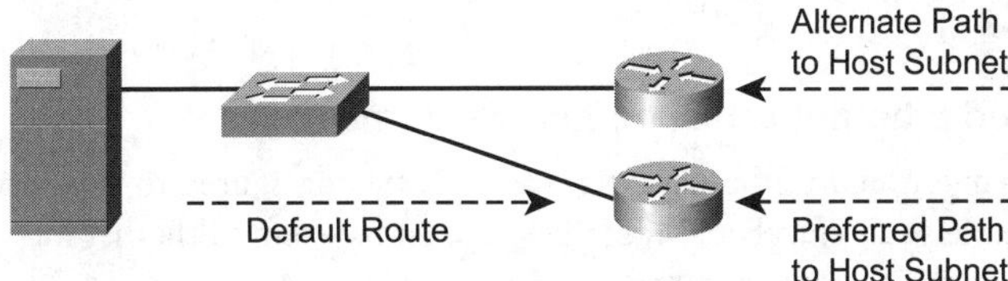

Figure 4-45 *Single-Homed End-System*

Note that the end-system may be connected to a single Ethernet switch that is dual-homed to a routing node. Both routing nodes may advertise a path for the end-system; however, the advertisement into the routing network should be biased to one router or the other. In addition, the routing update should only be sent if the Ethernet interface toward the end-system is operational. If the end-system provides routing updates to the router, the continuity of connectivity is easily maintained. Likewise, the routing nodes may provide routing updates to the end-system such that only one routed node is preferred.

If the end-system does not support routing updates, the adjacent routing nodes will need to manage the continuity of connectivity. Usually a static route is required that reflects the state of the Ethernet interface toward the end-system, and the two are correlated. The end-system also needs to know which routing node to direct traffic to. Unfortunately, the end-system has no visibility to the state of the switch's Ethernet interface connected to the routing nodes. The common technique used to mitigate this issue is Virtual Route Redundancy Protocol (VRRP). The two routing nodes negotiate amongst themselves and present a single virtual interface to the Ethernet switch. If primary routing node fails, the alternate routing node takes over representation of the primary node (that is, IP address and MAC address). The end-system may continue to forward traffic to the alternate routing node because it has taken the role of the primary routing node. Figure 4-46 shows the relationship between the two routing nodes and the end-system when using VRRP.

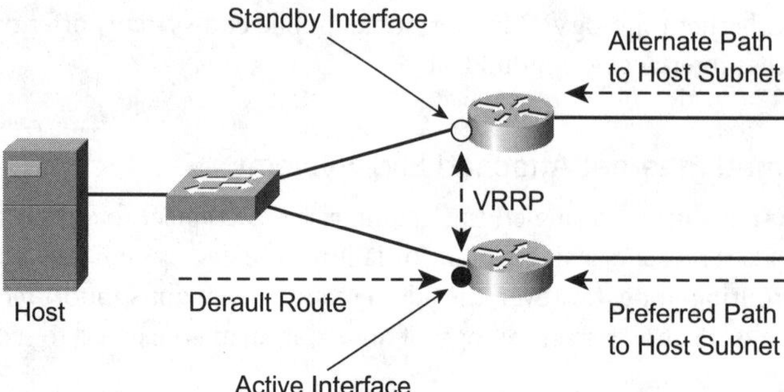

Figure 4-46 *Virtual Route Redundancy Protocol*

Dual-Homed Ethernet Attached End-Systems

An end-system with two Ethernet interfaces may be configured to use either of the interfaces for mobile session traffic. Most likely the end-system's Ethernet interfaces are connected to diverse Ethernet switches, as shown in Figure 4-47.

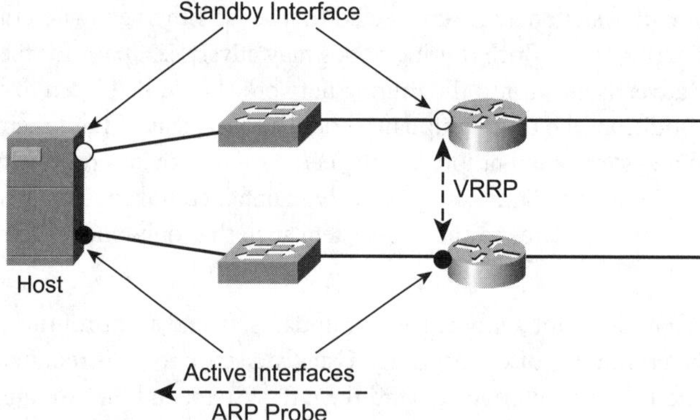

Figure 4-47 *Redundant Ethernet-Switched Interfaces*

If the mobile end-system interfaces or switches fail, the end-system will activate the alternate interface and use the backup path to reach the adjacent routing node. Just as an end-system must route traffic through redundant routers, the adjacent routers need to know which Ethernet interface represents the active end-system interface. The routing nodes have no direct visibility to the state of the end-system interfaces; therefore, some form of state management is required between the end-system interfaces and the routing nodes. A dynamic routing protocol may be used if the end-system uses different IP addresses on the Ethernet-attached interfaces. Alternatively, the end-system may clone the attributes of the active Ethernet interface to the backup interface. The adjacent routing nodes must update their IP to MAC binding in order to take advantage of the end-system's interface state change. Usually, this process is accelerated through the use of gratuitous Address Resolution Protocol (ARP).

Partial Mesh Ethernet Topologies

The end-systems might be connected to Ethernet switches with a much more complex topology. Typically, the data center will support multiple layers of switching hierarchy to maximize scale while minimizing cost of components. Figure 4-48 shows a typical Ethernet-switching aggregation model.

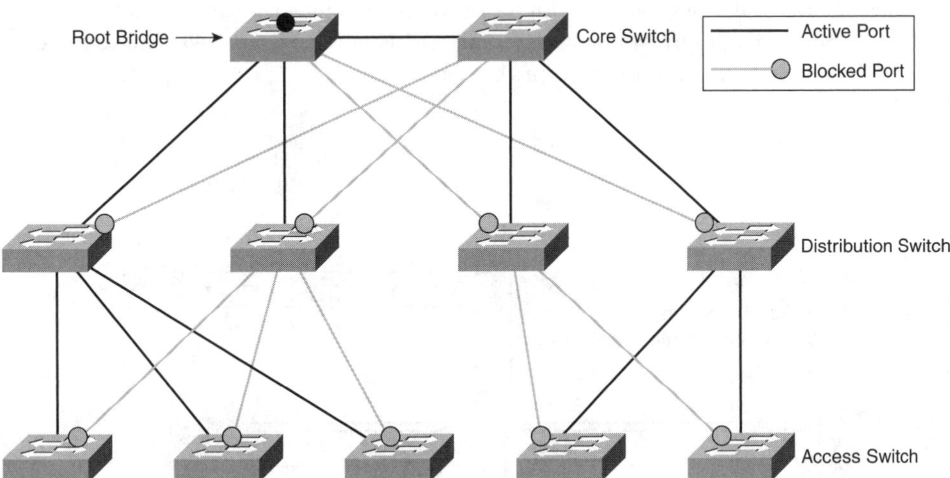

Figure 4-48 *Hierarchical Ethernet Switching*

Note from the diagram that there are many places where the topology creates potential forwarding loops. The Ethernet-switching infrastructure does not tolerate forwarding loops; therefore, the topology must be pruned into a hierarchical tree. Optimally, the root of the tree is co-located with the top of the hierarchy where sufficient capacity is provisioned. The Ethernet system uses Bridge Protocol Data Unit (BPDU) messages to communicate bridge identity, and path costs through the Ethernet environment to the root bridge. The Spanning Tree Protocol (STP) is used to calculate the best paths in the Ethernet environment and to block links that create potential forwarding loops. The network operator can bias which links are blocked in order to induce the traffic to flow over certain links. In the event of a failure, the periodic transmission of BPDUs allow the Ethernet switches to identify alternate paths through blocked interfaces, and the STP can recalculate the next best path through the Ethernet topology.

Most mobile end-systems will not participate in the Ethernet path selection except as noted previously in dual-homed attached systems; however, some switches actually host the mobile end-system functions on a service card. Mobile platforms such as these allow the mobile end-system functions to be tightly coupled to the state of the Ethernet-switching environment.

Virtual LAN Switching

The traditional Ethernet-switching model requires all the application and transport transactions to be aggregated into a shared resource. The segregation of mobile applications is common and in some cases mandatory. For example, the end-system might present unique interfaces for management plane traffic, control plane traffic, and data plane traffic. Virtual LAN switching (Ref. IEEE 802.1p) is used in the Ethernet environment to maintain that traffic segregation until the traffic enters a router where segmentation is maintained through Virtual Route Forwarding (VRF) tables. Figure 4-49 shows a typical segmentation model for different types of transactions.

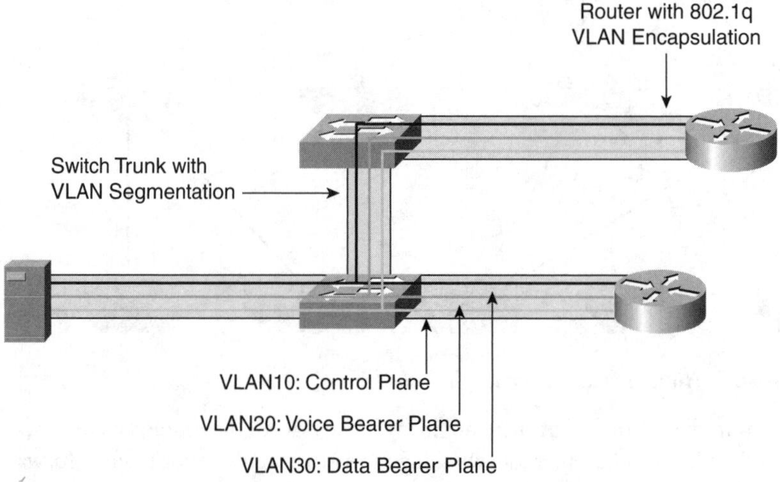

Figure 4-49 *VLAN Segmentation*

Link Segmentation

The VLAN represents a form of encapsulation often referred to as *tagging*. The tagged Ethernet frame allows the transmitting switch to indicate within an Ethernet frame a particular switching context, whereas the receiving switch is able to discern which context the frame should be switched. There are several methods for associating frames to a VLAN.

Trunking The connection between switches is called a *trunk*. The trunk will forward VLAN-tagged Ethernet frames between the switches such that the virtual LAN context is preserved. The operator can define which VLANs should be allowed to extend across the trunk. The use of trunks simplifies the configuration of extending each virtual LAN across a complex mesh of switches. The challenge for the operator is determining if the group of VLANs should all follow the same hierarchical topology. We know that certain wireless applications flow predominately from the handset to the data center or peering exchanges (for example, Internet access or wireless provider services), whereas other wireless applications flow predominately between service centers, such as handset-to-handset communication (for example, voice, push-to-talk). The aggregate flow data and voice traffic may not follow the same topological path. Some paths will be predominately loaded with data, whereas other paths are predominately loaded with voice. When using Ethernet, careful consideration must be applied when determining where the root bridge needs to be established for each virtual LAN. Ethernet will force all the traffic to follow the hierarchical topology determined by spanning tree despite presence of a more optimal path.

The IEEE 802.1s defined a means of building virtual spanning trees using a technique called Multiple Spanning Tree Protocol (MSTP). The switch BPDUs transmitted additional information representing each VLAN such that a unique spanning tree calculation could be performed for each virtual LAN. The MSTP allowed the operator to defined non-congruent virtual LAN topologies using the same physical infrastructure of switches and trunks. This method is particularly important for IP-enabled services where packets are free to follow the most direct path between

Port-Based VLAN The interface on a switched connected to an end-system may be configured as a port-based VLAN. The end-system does not have to transmit VLAN-tagged Ethernet frames; the switch will automatically assign the end-system to the virtual LAN and tag end-system-generated frames with a VLAN tag. Likewise, frames directed to the end-system will have their VLAN tag removed. The port-based VLAN assignment is useful when the mobile end-system needs to be in a single virtual LAN. It will only have access to other end-systems and routers that are also attached to the virtual LAN.

Multiple VLAN Interfaces The interface on an end-system can also be configured with logical interfaces that are treated as an IEEE 802.1q-tagged interface. The end-system may support many logical interfaces, allowing it to interact with more than one virtual LAN where each logical interface is associated with a single virtual LAN. This method of connectivity usually assumes that each logical interface represents an IP endpoint and facilitates segmentation of the virtual LAN all the way into the mobile end-system.

Network Segmentation

The methods described in link segmentation focus specifically in the domain of Ethernet. Segmentation across the network is equally important because LAN environments must be linked across geographic distances. Ideally, the segmentation instantiated in the LAN is preserved across the wide area when connected to a remote LAN. This is a common requirement when connecting mobile wireless data centers. The subscriber session manager functions are able to segment users into different virtual LANs. When geographical redundancy is required, the virtual LAN segmentation must be preserved, as shown in Figure 4-50.

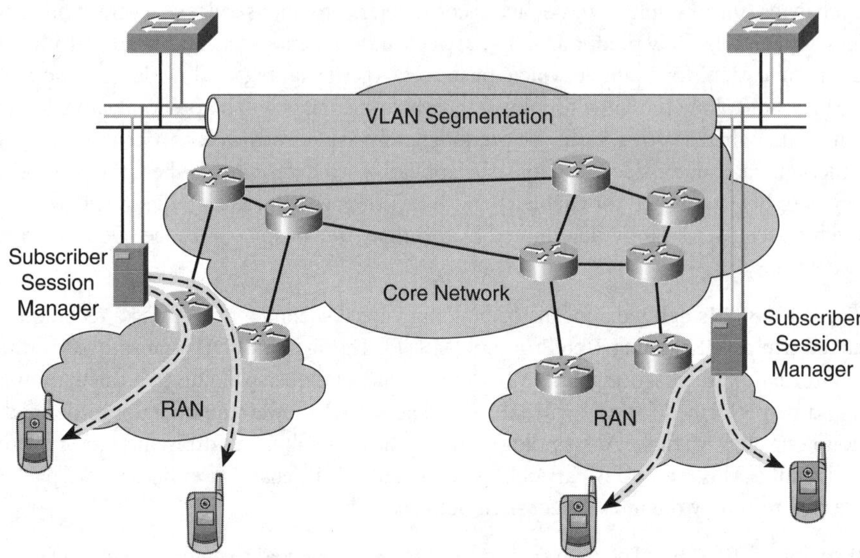

Figure 4-50 *Virtual LAN Network Segmentation*

A number of potential methods are used to maintain that segmentation across the WAN that will be addressed in the next section, "IP Transport Protocols."

IP Transport Protocols

Previous discussions have focused on the basic IP packet-switching methods that are necessary to support mobile IP networks. Attention is now focused on the transport of applications in IP.

Transport of Applications

The fundamental goal of the mobile IP network is to transport applications such as voice calls, download data, interactive multimedia, and many other forms of communication while allowing mobility. Most of these applications must adapt from the wireline environment where certain assumptions are made about the underlying transport. Those assumptions may not hold true in the wireless environment. For example, packet loss and availability may be much more inconsistent in the wireless environment due to radio interference and loss of signal. Delivery of these applications on the wireless infrastructure may require tuning the Layer 2 transport mechanisms along with the IP transport method to ensure that reliable services are maintained.

IP Transport

The IP protocol primarily leverages three transport methods referred to as Transmission Control Protocol (TCP), Stream Control Transmission Protocol (SCTP), and User-Defined

Protocol (UDP). Application developers carefully choose which method they will use as transport based on some fundamental differences in the transport.

Transmission Control Protocol (TCP)

TCP provides a reliable transport method for IP applications. It uses a three-way handshake method for each side to confirm the connection state is present and to disconnect the session. The three-way handshake can generally be described as a request to open a connection by the initiator, an acknowledgment of the open request by the receiver, and a subsequent acknowledgment of the acknowledgment by the sender. The two end-systems may now reliably send application data between themselves while periodically checking the state of the connection. For any data that is lost, corrupted, or excessively late; the TCP protocol takes the responsibility to retransmit the missing data. The application layer is completely unaware of the work accomplished by the TCP layer. In fact, the application assumes that TCP will do its job.

The implication for using TCP is that it successfully delivers data between the endpoints and assures that it is delivered in order to the upper-layer application. The application does not have to manage the state of connection between the two endpoints. TCP is commonly used for data applications where the exact content must be delivered; otherwise, the context is lost. Examples such as web browsing and file transfers commonly use TCP as the means of delivering data.

TCP can be an aggressive protocol as it tries to maximize the delivery rate of the application data. It accelerates delivery of data until loss is incurred; it then backs off and restarts the process. The impact of TCP applications on the mobile IP network is that it will aggressively try to fill the bandwidth available on the most constrained link in the path. Unfortunately, the air-link is likely to be the most bandwidth-constrained link, and it is one of the most precious resources in the path. This is where intelligent bandwidth queuing comes into play. Knowledge of the application type allows the network operator to leverage IP-queuing constructs (that is, DSCP identifiers) to artificially constrain TCP applications through shaping techniques addressed previously. Of course, doing so requires proper classification of the application data at the ingress of the network and queue management of the data at each bandwidth constrained point in the network. Thus, the challenge when coupling together a variety of disparate transport technologies is to ensure that the context is preserved. The Wireless Profiled TCP specification calls out several TCP options that optimize application transport over the wireless air-link. [11] Wireless Application Protocol proxies typically employ Wireless Profiled TCP between the client and proxy while building a corollary TCP session between the proxy and the application origin server. The deployment of WAP proxies in the mobile provider improves the subscriber's access to TCP-based applications despite the lossy environment encountered on the air-link.

User Datagram Protocol (UDP)

UDP makes no assertions about the reliable delivery of data. The application may transmit data via UDP and assume the remote end-system receives the data. There is no handshake process embedded in UDP; therefore, any acknowledgment required by the application is the responsibility of the application. The principal advantage of UDP is that the open feedback loop allows the sender to transmit data in an unregulated manner.

The application using UDP may have no knowledge that data is discarded on a bandwidth-constrained link between the two end-systems. Data may be dropped at any point, and it is likely to be dropped on the queue for the air-link. The data might be dropped on the air-link; however, wireless protocols may recover and retransmit the dropped segment. This poses an interesting dilemma. UDP is ideal for time-sensitive delivery of data. Indeed, UDP is commonly used for the transmission of voice and video media where late of arrival of data is pointless. The linear play-out of voice and video applications requires the application data to be delivered "on time" or dropped. The definition of "on time" is relative because the player may accumulate the application data in a buffer and defer play-out. Doing so allows the jitter in the packet delivery times to be absorbed by the jitter buffer. Of course, the retransmission time of the underlying wireless air-link might cause the UDP payload to be delivered late; thus, the data is treated as lost.

The UDP applications typically allow for some loss of data or they build their own state machine to recover lost data. For example, voice and video codecs tolerate a certain level of loss before the impact becomes apparent to the receiver, either visually or audibly. Too much loss creates visual impairment or audible disruption in the stream. The obvious answer is to increase the jitter buffer such that the application has a longer period of time to accumulate data. This is quite reasonable for one-way transmission of data; however, the extended delay becomes a problem for interactive applications, such as voice. For this reason, different IP transport protocols have been designed to accommodate the various nuances required of the mobile IP applications.

Stream Control Transport Protocol (SCTP)

SCTP deviates somewhat from the services provided by UDP and TCP. [12] Whereas TCP focuses on sequenced delivery of byte-ordered data, UDP and SCTP focus on message delivery. Unlike UDP, SCTP is connection oriented and provides reliable deliver of messages.

The original intent was to use SCTP for the transport of Signaling System 7 (SS7) messages over IP infrastructures. It has expanded its use case to other applications; however, it is particularly important for transitioning the SS7 call-signaling services to an IP transport network. The role of SCTP has expanded in LTE to include transport of signaling traffic in the backhaul, as described in Chapters 2 and 3.

The primary implication for mobile wireless networks is the extensive use of SS7 in the delivery of data services in the form of Short Message Services (SMS). Tremendous growth in the use of SMS has placed a burden on the call control system that was originally intended to be disjointed from the user's data plane in the telephony world. An overloaded SS7 network is subject to user-induced outages in both the control and data plane. The SCTP facilitates offloading the SMS services to an IP network that is optimized for message delivery. The SCTP guarantees the delivery of the messages while ensuring that the SS7 control plane survives.

SCTP is now defined as an integral part of the LTE/SAE architecture for the transport of signaling messages. Specifically, SCTP is used to reliably transport RANAP messages in 3G networks and eRANAP messages on the S1-MME interface between the eNodeB and the MME.

Transport of Common Mobile Applications

The number of IP protocol options is extensive; it would be imprudent to identify and describe them all. Rather, it is recommended that you review the IETF, 3GPP, 3GPP2, and IMS specifications to discern how and when certain protocols should be used. Nevertheless, a few examples are provided in this text to highlight the diverse requirements and differences between the transport methods.

Real-Time Protocol (RTP)

The Real-Time Protocol (Ref. IETF RFC 3550 and 3551) is defined as an IP transport method for applications that require real-time delivery of audio/visual media. As specified, the RTP stream should be carried in UDP. The relevance of RTP in the current mobile IP wireless network is the transition of voice transport from the classic TDM infrastructure to the IP packet-based infrastructure. RTP references various means of encoding voice into packets based on recommendations from various standards bodies, such as the European Telecommunications Standards Institute (ETSI) and the International Telecommunications Union (ITU). The actual format is outside the scope of discussion in this context, but what is relevant is understanding the properties defined by the standards such as the encoded frame size and the time interval between successive frames in an audio stream. These properties become critical when determining the viability of transporting voice over a packet network. The IP network may have sufficient capacity to carry the aggregate set of voice streams; however, it may not. Various methods are required to make bandwidth reservations, manage call control, and monitor the performance of the sessions. The transport of Voice over IP on the air-link is particularly challenging for deployed mobile networks, given the intermittent nature of connectivity and the requirement for consistent delivery of the data stream for voice. This is being addressed in the latest mobile network architectures, such as WiMAX and LTE/SAE. In contrast, transporting Voice over IP in the IP core is much more viable because the bandwidth is usually more than sufficient and the probability of congestion is much lower.

Session Initiation Protocol (SIP)

The establishment of user multimedia sessions is managed through the Session Initiation Protocol (Ref. IETF RFC 3261). From a telephony perspective, SIP replaces SS7 functions that handle call setup and management while providing additional messaging and presence services. SIP is extensible through the use Session Description Protocol (SDP), which describes the type of media that will be transported in the session and identifies the end-systems that transmit and receive the media stream.

SIP sessions are originated from a User Agent (UA) that resides on the user's end-system and terminates on a SIP server. The server may provide several functions, such as SIP proxy, SIP registration, or SIP redirect. When two end-systems are registered in the SIP architecture, they are able to establish media sessions between themselves. The SIP control plane facilitates the establishment of a bearer plane based on the RTP protocol described previously. Figure 4-51 shows the typical relationship between the UA on the end-systems and the SIP server.

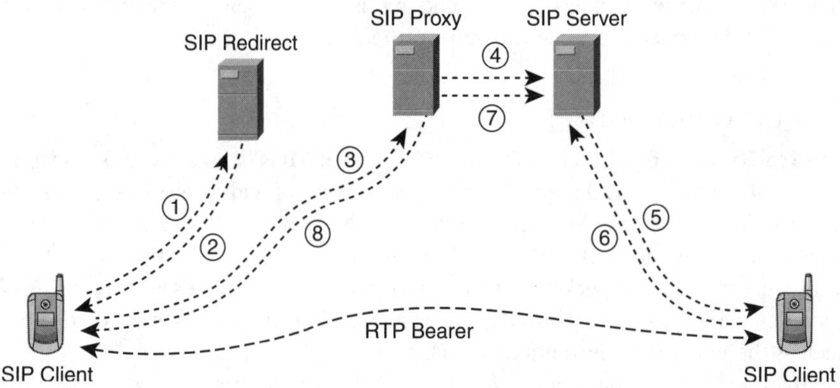

Figure 4-51 *SIP Architecture*

Hyper-Text Transfer Protocol (HTTP)

The Hyper-Text Transfer Protocol (Ref. IETF RFC 2616) is the cornerstone of most Internet data applications in use today. The HTTP methods enabled the use of a simplified user interface referred to as a web browser. The basic primitives in HTTP, such as GET, facilitate the retrieval of data from the server to the client. Likewise, primitives such as POST and PUT facilitate submission of data from the client to the server. The web browser supports references in the displayed data that provide links to other resources. The user's interactions with the web interface facilitate discrete, yet reliable, transactions between the client and server.

The relevance of HTTP to mobile wireless networks is quite important. Subscribers may use micro-browsers embedded in their mobile handset to initiate queries to the network servers. The ability to use micro-browsers in conjunction with an IP-enabled mobile wireless infrastructure opened up a whole new market for providers. Although the bandwidth available to the handset may be rather constrained in early generations of mobile wireless networks, the HTTP protocol can reliably deliver data to the handset using TCP, albeit a bit slowly.

Transport of IP via Tunneling Protocols

Given the subscriber end-systems and the application servers use IP, building an IP-enabled provider infrastructure significantly improves the service capabilities and flexibility of delivering new services. However, there are many network infrastructures that do not natively support IP, or the IP network infrastructure is inappropriate for directly routing subscriber IP traffic. Tunnels are used to encapsulate the subscriber IP protocols described in the previous section. The goal is to provide a scalable, secure architecture that allows the provider to manage subscriber connectivity while providing some level of transparency. Although the provider may provide many services from their data center, many of the interesting subscriber applications will reside on services accessible via the Internet. The provider needs to deliver the subscriber data to the subscriber's end-system without exposing the network core to the Internet. Meanwhile, the provider would like to assert valuable services in the subscriber's application stream. To achieve these goals, the provider will take advantage of the various methods of tunneling IP. The tunneling protocols such as GTP and Mobile IP transfer the subscriber data to the network elements in the wireless architecture that can provide subscriber-based IP services. The tunnels mitigate the requirement for intermediary network elements to have knowledge of every subscriber in the network. The intermediary network elements only need to know how to forward the tunnels.

Mobile IP

The assignment of an IP address to an end-system represents the identity of the system on a global basis. The IP architecture assumes that two end-systems will communicate with an end-to-end context built between their respective IP addresses. If the IP address changes, the higher-level protocols mentioned previously (that is, TCP and UDP) will be terminated. The session context is typically stored as a five-tuple: source IP, destination IP, protocol, source port, and destination port.

The end-systems are represented by the IP addresses, whereas the application is associated with the protocol and ports. Clearly, a change in IP address will disrupt the context of the session. The general guidance is to assign IP address from local resources in order to facilitate route aggregation to minimize state in the network. Of course, the assumption is that the IP end-system would not move. This is not the case with mobile IP hosts. There are several choices to be made when a system moves from one routing domain to a new routing domain, as follows:

- Drop the old IP address and obtain a new IP address from the new routing domain, thus dropping all existing sessions.
- Keep the old IP address and force the routing infrastructure to handle fragments of routes.

- Tunnel traffic through the new routing domain while the end-system retains the original IP address.

Clearly, the first method is disruptive and somewhat defeats the point of mobility. The second method creates a number of problems for network operators by creating network churn and consuming routing memory resources. The most viable approach is the tunneling technique. Mobile IP (Ref. RFCs 3344, 4721, and 3775) is designed to accommodate mobile IP end-systems such that the application sessions are preserved while roaming into new networks and minimizes the impact on the visited network infrastructure. The basic principle is for the end-system to establish a tunneled path to its home network from which its IP address is assigned. If the end-system is within the home network, there is no need for the tunnel because the IP address is inherently routable. In contrast, when the end-system leaves the home network and enters a visited network, it needs to establish a tunnel to the home network. This allows return traffic to the mobile end-system to be directed to the home network, where it is subsequently tunneled through the visited network to the mobile end-system.

This method requires several anchor points for the Mobile IP tunnel. Mobile IP defines two entities as the anchor points: the home agent and the foreign agent. The home agent obviously resides in the home network, whereas the foreign agent resides in the visited network. The mobile end-system is assigned an IP address from its home network, which is not routable in the visited network. When a mobile end-system connects to a visited network, it is assigned a new IP address that is routable in that visited network's routing domain. This address is the Care-of Address (CoA). The foreign agent will establish a Mobile IP tunnel from the visited network using this CoA to the end-system's home agent. To achieve this, the end-system needs to register with the foreign agent and inform the foreign agent of its home agent IP address. The foreign agent will establish a tunneled session to the home agent, where the end-system's home IP address is linked to the CoA address in a binding table. Now the home agent knows that return traffic for the mobile IP end-system should not be directed to the local network but should be tunneled to the CoA associated with the foreign agent. The foreign agent decapsulates the tunneled packet and delivers the IP packet to the targeted end-system using its home IP address.

An alternative architecture is for the client to assume the role of the foreign agent and assimilate the FA functions. In doing so, the client must present the Care-of Address, and the tunnel must be established from the client CoA to the Home Agent. In many cases, the client's network protocol stack must be updated to serve as the co-located foreign agent. Legacy clients will need a separate FA to serve as the CoA.

The need for a foreign agent in the visited network creates a bit of a challenge. There are two approaches to resolving this problem, as follows:

- **A co-located CoA** requires the end-system to perform both roles of Mobile Node and foreign agent. The foreign agent function can use a viable means of receiving a locally relevant IP address in the visited network (for example, DHCP or IPCP), and this address will represent the Mobile Node's CoA. The end-system must then perform the Mobile Node routing function and the foreign agent tunneling function.

The obvious disadvantage is that the end-system must have the ability to perform the foreign agent tunneling function, and the home agent is likely to have a CoA for each end-system roaming as a Mobile Node. The advantage is that the end-system can visit networks where no foreign agent exists.

- **A foreign agent CoA** requires the end-system to discover a visited network foreign agent on the local link. Through a discovery process using agent advertisements and agent solicitation, the Mobile Node is able to identify the CoA of the foreign agent, register, and update the foreign agent and home agent of its state in the visited network. The first step is to determine if the visited network even has a foreign agent and where it is located. This is accomplished through multicast targeted to 224.0.0.11 for IPv4. Secondly, the decapsulated packet directed to the Mobile Node via the CoA must be delivered by the foreign agent to the end-system without IP routing the internal packet. The foreign agent must maintain a mapping of the end-system's link-layer address (for example, the Mobile Node MAC address) to the home agent-assigned IP address. The packets must be unicast directed to the Mobile Node's MAC address because the home agent-assigned IP address is outside the prefix range assigned to the visited network.

Mobile IP has started to play a more important role as end-systems have increasingly become more mobile. Mobile providers use Mobile IP to maintain session state for applications that can't tolerate changing IP addresses. Simple applications such as web browsing using HTTP are more tolerant of IP address changes because the HTTP session is very short lived (on the order of seconds). In contrast, interactive media sessions such as voice and video cannot tolerate IP address changes, and the sessions tend to be much longer in duration (minutes or hours). Mobile IP will become more relevant as mobility increase and the duration of subscriber sessions become extended. The 4G standards for WiMAX and LTE have standardized on the use of Mobile IP (MIP). Proxy Mobile IP (PMIP) is most commonly used for IPv4 deployments because there are few clients with an embedded MIP protocol stack.

The 4G architectures specify the use of IPv6 for client communications; thus, a requirement for Mobile IPv6 is also needed. Mobile IPv6 uses many of the same principles of MIPv4 while taking advantage of some of IPv6's inherent capabilities. Specifically, the Neighbor Discovery method is used to advertise the Home Agent, and the ICMPv6 methods are modified to execute HA Address Discovery and to solicit and advertise Mobile Prefix attributes. Mobile IPv6 supports two modes of operation; one of which optimizes routing by informing the Corresponding Node (CN) that the Mobile Node (MN) is using Mobile IPv6 and providing the CoA to the Corresponding Node. This method requires MIPv6 protocol implementations on the Corresponding Nodes, such as web servers, voice gateways, and messaging servers. Most services are unlikely to use MIPv6; therefore, route optimization will not be viable. The second mode of operation requires the MN to tunnel the traffic via IPv6 encapsulation to the Home Agent in a similar manner used for MIPv4. The primary advantage to using MIPv6 is that the mobility protocol options are extensions to the IPv6 protocol using the options header, and they operate over any link-layer media. In contrast, MIPv4 requires an adjunct set of protocols such as proxy ARP that are link-layer dependent.

GPRS Tunneling Protocol (GTP)

The GTP protocol is defined for use in the GSM architecture for GPRS and subsequently in the 3GPP architecture facilitating transport of GPRS signaling and bearer traffic via an IP tunnel. [13] The principal use of the protocol is to transport data between the SGSN and GGSN on the Gn interface. In the latest version of GTP, two variants are defined—one for signaling, GTP-C, and one for user traffic, GTP-U. The GTP-C allows the SGSN and GGSN to manage the state of user PDP context on the GGSN including setup, teardown, and updates. One of the evolutions of 3GPP was to extend the GTP-U tunnels carrying the subscriber IP addresses across the RAN into the GGSN. Figure 4-52 shows the tunneled connection from the mobile subscriber through the SGSN to the GGSN.

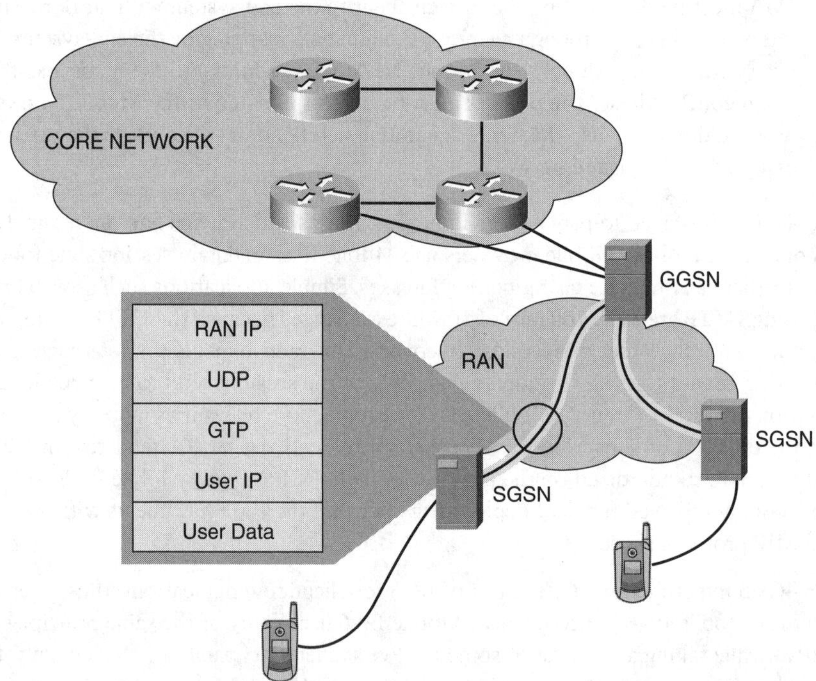

Figure 4-52 *GPRS Tunneling Protocol*

> **Note** The UMTS network architecture only uses GTP-U on the IuPS interface because RANAP serves the role of GTP-C.

As noted previously, the IP addresses assigned to the mobile subscriber's end-system may not be routable in the core network. In fact, the mobile subscriber's IP address is assigned by the GGSN predicated on the fact that the SGSN will tunnel the traffic to the GGSN. This allows the GGSN to aggregate hundreds of thousands of subscriber IP addresses and present them to the IP core network as a single CIDR block. Meanwhile, the RAN routing network only needs to be aware of routing for the GTP tunnel IP addresses.

Tunneling between the SGSN and GGSN is imperative when the mobile subscriber roams off the primary provider's mobile network. As opposed to the mobile subscriber re-registering and being assigned an IP address from the visited network, the mobile subscriber obtains an IP address from their home network, and they retain all the services associated with the service plan. The RAN networks of the two providers are linked through a GPRS Roaming Exchange (GRX) peering interface. The only routes that need to be exchanged are the prefixes associated with the two mobile provider peer's SGSN and GGSN components. The GTP tunnel facilitates bidirectional flow of traffic between the MS and the network via the tunnel. The MS will forward the native IP traffic on the link-layer session established to the SGSN, where the packet is encapsulated in GTP. The GTP is directed to the GGSN, where the packet is decapsulated and routed accordingly within the home provider's network. Return traffic is directed to the GGSN; a binding table associates the mobile subscriber's IP address to a GTP tunnel toward the SGSN to which the mobile subscriber is attached. When using GSM, the packet is GTP encapsulated by the GGSN, routed to the SGSN, decapsulated by the SGSN, and directed on the link-layer radio protocols to the mobile subscriber. The UMTS architecture allows the extension of the GTP-U tunnel down to the RNC where subscriber traffic is encapsulated and decapsulated for tunneling to the GGSN.

The GTP protocol maintains a level of transparency and mobility as the mobile subscriber roams around the visited network. The mobile subscriber might change radio towers many times while retaining the binding to the same SGSN. From the perspective of the GGSN, the mobile subscriber appears to be stationary, whereas in fact it is not. When the mobile subscriber leaves the visited network, the GTP tunnel between the visited SGSN and home GGSN is torn down. The mobile subscriber will need to reestablish a connection to a new SGSN, which will bind a new GTP tunnel to the home GGSN. This process is likely to cause disruption to the subscriber's IP application session.

IP Security Encapsulating Security Payload (IPSec ESP)

IPSec tunnel mode provides a means of tunneling subscriber IP traffic across an unsecured IP network. The original IP packet is encapsulated, encrypted, and authenticated by an originating gateway. The terminating gateway will check the authentication credentials, decrypt and decapsulate the packet, and forward the original packet in the secured routing domain.

IPSec ESP is commonly used to extend the provider's reach across untrusted networks, to hide private IP addresses while routing across a core, or to provide confidentiality of the traffic. The first use case allows providers to attach a remote private network to their core network while leveraging third-party networks, such as peers or even the Internet. In many cases, the private networks use IP addresses assigned from RFC 1918, which are not routable across third-party networks. The ESP process encapsulates the private IP addresses into an IP tunnel that uses registered and routable addresses. The Internet Key Exchange (IKE) is used to associate the private IP address ranges and security policies to

IPSec ESP session. This method mitigates the requirement to assign registered address to every end-system and to share routes with every third-party network.

Note The UMA and LTE standards actually mandate the use of IPSec Tunnel Mode connections established using IKE Version 2.

Until IPv6 becomes widely deployed, the use of private IP addresses will continue to play a prominent role given the number of mobile devices. Lastly, the encryption secures the traffic such that sensitive information such as login identifiers and passwords cannot be easily observed in the packets.

Mobile Internet Key Exchange (MOBIKE)

The MOBIKE protocol (Ref. RFC 4555) was developed as an extension to the IKE/IPSec protocols based on limitations of IPSec to handle mobility and, in particular, the changes to the IP addresses used for IPSec ESP encapsulation. The IPSec ESP assumed that the encapsulating source and destination address would be persistent for the life of the security association (SA). That is not the case for a Mobile Node that is assigned IP addresses dynamically based on the point of attachment on the network. As the Mobile Node roams across various radio access infrastructures, it may need to reestablish the IP connectivity. In doing so, it may also receive a new IP address determined by the subscriber session manager (for example, HA or GGSN). The change of Mobile Node IP address would invalidate any existing IPSec SA. MOBIKE was designed to handle these changes while preserving the context of the SA. The requirement for MOBIKE is to minimize the duration of connectivity loss and minimize the work load on the IPSec concentrator that is serving thousands of Mobile Nodes.

MOBIKE assumes that the Mobile Node will be the initiator because it is the end-system that is mostly likely subject to a change in the IP address, and it has context as to the state of the air-link. The server acting as responder will rarely change its public IP address, which is used for IPSec encapsulation. The goal is to use the existing IKE SA as a means of notifying the responder of the IP address change. This conserves resources on the responder, because establishment of a completely new IKE SA is avoided.

The Mobile Node initiates the process by notifying the responder of the changes in IP address options. The Mobile Node may pick any of the local addresses that it deems most useful and source the update from the preferred IP address. In the secured MOBIKE update, the new IP address is presented, which the responder can validate. Now the responder knows the IPSec encapsulate packets directed to the Mobile Node's new public IP address. The context of the SA is preserved, and the subscriber IP connectivity is restored much faster.

MOBIKE is most useful for Mobile Nodes that need to establish secure connections across the mobile networks to a private complex. Many corporate security policies do not allow exposure of the subscriber traffic from the time it leaves the Mobile Node until it reaches the corporate premises. MOBIKE allows the corporation's Mobile Node to roam across various wireless and wired infrastructures while maintaining the IPSec session to the corporate VPN gateway. The subscriber's application sessions (for example, TCP) are preserved, even though the Mobile Node is occasionally dropping network attachments for short periods of time.

Transport of Layer 2 Frames via IP Tunneling Protocols

Mobile provider network networks have used Layer 2 switching technologies extensively throughout the infrastructure. Although the end-systems have transitioned to packet-switched technologies leveraging IP and Ethernet, the access and core transport networks are largely based on TDM, ATM, and FR. The challenge of managing an increasingly complex mesh of Layer 2 connections increases dramatically as the number of nodes increases. Mobile operators must transition to a packet-based switching model in order to scale.

One approach is to build a native IP network for all the IP-enabled end-systems. This is, of course, the goal of the next-generation mobile wireless specifications. In the mean time, the operator must continue to manage numerous Layer 2 connections because legacy end-systems only offer Layer 2 switching interfaces. The mobile operator may leverage both virtual private wire services (VPWS) and virtual private LAN services (VPLS) to transport the Layer 2 connections over an IP-enabled access and core network. Doing so allows the operator to transition portions of the network to IP without having to completely replace many of the end-systems at the same time.

The VPWS method allows the provide edge (PE) systems to establish a pseudowire between themselves such that Layer 2 frames can be switched across an IP packet network. The pseudowire appears to the two switching endpoints as a native Layer 2 connection. For example, two ATM switches connected via a pseudowire appear to each other as directly connected by a trunk. The ATM switches are not aware of the fact that their cells are being encapsulated in an IP frame and routed across an IP network. The goal of the IP network is to emulate the Layer 2 connection attributes via the pseudowire. The IETF defined several methods for establishing pseudowire; however, the following two protocols have received the most attention:

- Layer 2 Tunnel Protocol Version 3 (L2TPv3)
- Targeted Label Distribution Protocol (T-LDP)

L2TPv3

L2TPv3, defined in RFC 3931, is derived from L2TP tunneling methods that facilitated connection of PPP over an IP tunnel (Ref. RFC 2621). The L2TP method defined a method of connecting a L2TP Access Server (LAC) to an L2TP Network Server (LNS), such that an end-system could establish a point-to-point protocol (PPP) session via a LAC to the LNS. L2TPv3 extended the concept by allowing two LAC devices to be connected such that other Layer 2 protocols could be transported besides PPP.

L2TPv3 facilitated the connection of an attachment circuit (AC) representing the Layer 2 interface in a provider edge router to a pseudowire. The pseudowire is encapsulated in an IP tunnel and routed via the IP core network to the remote provider edge where pseudowire decapsulation occurs and the frame handed off to the remote attachment circuit. The effect is to allow two switches to be connected at Layer 2 via the pseudowire. The L2TPv3 protocol defines the methods for session establishment and negotiating the encapsulation. Additional RFCs are defined for the specific encapsulation of a Layer 2 frame on L2TPv3. For example, RFC 4454 defines the methods of transporting ATM cells across an L2TPv3 pseudowire.

The principal advantage of using L2TPv3 in the mobile provider network is the ability to use a generic IP cloud to transport Layer 2 connections. In fact, the pseudowire can cross autonomous system boundaries by simply following the best IP path to the remote provider edge without having to build context at any of the intermediate IP-switching points. If the two provider-edge devices can reach each other via IP, the L2TPv3 pseudowire can be established to transparently transport Layer 2 frames. This property makes L2TPv3 suitable for a variety of L2 transport services, provided the IP path can meet the performance requirements expected of the Layer 2 switching systems connected by the pseudowire.

Targeted Label Distribution Protocol

The alternative to L2TPv3 is Targeted Label Distribution Protocol (T-LDP) on an MPLS packet-switched network. Similar to L2TPv3, the T-LDP method establishes a pseudowire connection between two provider-edge devices that transport Layer 2 frames. The primary difference is that the Layer 2 frame is encapsulated in an MPLS label as opposed to an IP header. The implication is the core network must support contiguous MPLS label switching between the two provider edges.

An MPLS-enabled switching network facilitates the establishment of Label Switched Paths (LSP) that transports the label-encapsulated pseudowire. The T-LDP control plane operates between the provider-edge devices to establish and maintain the state of the pseudowire. The MPLS packet switch core only needs context of an LSP between the provider-edge devices and does not need packet-switching context of the pseudowire label.

The mobile provider may leverage the MPLS network to establish pseudowire within and between autonomous systems; however, the LSP must be established end-to-end. The provider cannot take advantage of T-LDP until the MPLS path exists. The primary advantage of T-LDP is the ability to exploit the LSP characteristics. The LSP can be traffic engineered (RSVP-TE) or protected (FRR) to provide a specific quality of service needed to support the pseudowire. This is particularly important when transporting TDM frames or ATM cells associated with Continuous Bit Rate (CBR) services. The latency, jitter, and loss of the pseudowire must be minimized to sustain the Layer 2 connection context. Guaranteeing a baseline level of performance across an IP network may be a challenge without some form of end-to-end context between the provider edges.

Transitioning Mobile Provider Networks via Pseudowires

Many mobile providers are aggressively moving data services to new architectures due to the demand growth. These data services are excellent candidates for transitioning their Layer 2 transport mechanisms to an IP-enabled network. The baseline performance requirements between the IP-enabled end-systems and the IP-enabled core are consistent. Transitioning voice services across the IP-enabled core via pseudowires is a bit more of a challenge. Nevertheless, doing so is quite feasible with a well-designed network that is properly managed. Of course, transitioning voice to VoIP dramatically simplifies the evolution to IP-enabled core networks; however, the transition now becomes dependent upon the voice application server's adoption of IP interfaces. The 4G architectures based on WiMAX and LTE inherently assume that the client implements Voice over IP along with all the data services using IP transport. Until 4G architectures are widely deployed, service providers will need to use pseudowires to enable the transition to IP. Many mobile operators are focusing their attention on leveraging pseudowires to transport 2G, 2.5G, and 3G ATM and TDM connections across the RAN. The expectation is that the legacy infrastructure will be in place for an extended period of time. The transition of the ATM and TDM connections to IP-based transport mechanisms allows the mobile operator to deploy a common IP infrastructure servicing both the legacy and next-generation wireless architectures. Combining all the wireless access technologies onto a common infrastructure reduces the costs and positions the network to take advantage of IP interfaces as they become available.

Summary

This chapter has covered the basic tenets of IP network protocols and their associated switching and routing techniques. The intent is to provide a foundation upon which subsequent chapters can build. In addition, the implications of wireless access are highlighted and specific attention is focused on modifications to the basic IP routing and switching architectures necessary to support mobile IP connectivity. The next chapter builds upon this content to emphasize where IP is used in each of the architectural standards associated with 3GPP and 3GPP2.

Endnotes

1. www.internetworldstats.com/stats.htm: Internet World Stats Usage and Population Statistics.

2. IETF RFC-917: Internet Subnets.

3. IETF RFC-1517: Applicability Statement for the Implementation of Classless Inter-Domain Routing (CIDR).

4. IETF RFC-1518: An Architecture for IP Address Allocation with CIDR.

5. IETF RFC-1519: Classless Inter-Domain Routing (CIDR): an Address Assignment and Aggregation Strategy.

6. IETF RFC-2766: Network Address Translation – Protocol Translation (NAT-PT).

7. 3GPP TS 23.246: Multimedia Broadcast/Multicast Service (MBMS); Architecture and functional description.

8. TIA/EIA/TSB116: Telecommunication IP Telephony Equipment Voice Quality Recommendations for IP Telephony.

9. www.ripe.net/projects/ttm/Plots: RIPE NCC Test Traffic Measurements.

10. IETF RFC 2475: An Architecture for Differentiated Services.

11. WAP-225-TCP-20010331-a: Wireless Profiled TCP.

12. IETF RFC 4960: Stream Control transmission Protocol.

13. 3GPP TS 23.060: General Packet Radio Service (GPRS); Service description.

14. 3GPP TS 29.060 Section 6: General Packet Radio Service (GPRS); GPRS Tunnelling Protocol (GTP) across the Gn and Gp interface.

Chapter 5

Connectivity and Transport

The objective of this chapter is to provide options and guidance on the use of IP connectivity in both the Radio Access Network (RAN) and the core network (CN). First, a review is conducted on the various transport modes and their relevance in the architecture. Requirements are examined to address the feasibility of making the transition to IP connectivity for both environments. We first focus on the core network transmission requirements and follow with a discussion on the Radio Access Network transmission requirements.

Transmission Systems

We segregate the transport modes into synchronous and asynchronous methods with wireless and wireline connection types. Each transport mode has unique properties that potentially facilitate cost-savings for the mobile operator. Likewise, each method requires compromises that the operator must assess. The objective of this section is to highlight those compromises and show how the various methods are applied to the CN and RAN environments.

Synchronous Wire-Line

The first transport method is the traditional synchronous wireline connection. The system uses stratum one clocking infrastructure that assures the two endpoints remain synchronous. The switching systems use the synchronous nature of the transport to identify protocol elements associated with different services such as management, control, and data plane. A clocking network that allows timing drift will induce line slips and disrupt communications. End-systems using time division multiplexing assign structured channels to transport certain applications and functions. The transmitter encodes the data stream into the structured channels, whereas the receiver needs to synch up with the transmitter and decode each of the structured channels. If the time alignment of the data stream is off, the structured channels can't be decoded at the receiver. It is imperative that the end-systems maintain synchronous clocking in order to maintain the integrity of the data stream.

Clocking is typically derived near the core of the network, where clock sources are most abundant and reliable. The clock is relayed through switching systems to the periphery of the network. The principal advantage of the synchronous network is the ability to transport data streams through midpoint switching systems that have no need to decode, interpret, or evaluate the payload. The channels can be passed transparently between the TDM switching systems to the end-system that has the ability and need to interpret a specific channel. In this manner, structured channels can be aggregated and disaggregated at various switching points in the network. The principal disadvantage is that end-systems may only need to use the structured channel for a short period of time, thus yielding a low duty cycle and inefficient use of bandwidth. Intelligent end-systems can reuse structured channels. Voice-switching systems do this by assigning a conversation to a structured channel for the duration of the call. The structured channel is relinquished to the pool of available channels when the call ends. Channel resource allocation is the principal responsibility of the mobile-switching systems. Unfortunately, the channel resources allocated for voice are inefficiently utilized when the application is transactional data with short-lived transactions. Assigning a voice channel to a sporadically used data transaction is extremely inefficient.

Early implementations of the mobile data services used a shared channel to aggregate multiple data transactions. This improved the efficiency of the structured channel; however, it did not accommodate the wide variance in bandwidth required for data applications. Where a voice call requires a fairly consistent amount of bandwidth based on the codec chosen (for example, 12.2 kbps for AMR), data requires either very little or a lot of bandwidth depending on the state of the transaction (that is, query, acknowledgment, download or data transfer, and so on). Of course, additional structured channels can be assigned to accommodate the temporary bandwidth requirement; however, those channels will likely be reclaimed. The overhead and complexity of the control plane necessary to manage the allocation and de-allocation of structured channels overwhelms the end-systems trying to transfer the data. As the volume of data transactions increase, the system needs to transition to an asynchronous model to match the inherently asynchronous nature of the data stream.

Asynchronous Wire-Line

One of the principal advantages of migrating to packet transport (IP being the most notable) is that packet switching is inherently asynchronous. The packet-switching model more closely matches the nature of data transactions. Packet-switching systems may still use synchronous circuits; however, that requirement is no longer necessary when considering pure data transactions. The packet-switching systems still need to use the same reference clock for individual circuits; however, all the circuits may have their clock uniquely derived. The packet-switching system absorbs clocking differences between circuits when packets are clocked into input buffers, routed, and subsequently queued on output buffers. Packet-switching systems use packet-queuing mechanisms that make synchronous circuits behave as asynchronous transport methods. Instead of assigning structured channels in the synchronous circuit, the entire circuit is used as an unstructured transport, and packets are clocked into and out of the circuit. The two packet-switching systems still need to use a common clock reference for that circuit; however, one end can be the source, whereas the other derives clocking from the adjacent packet-switching system via the circuit. The packet-switching device absorbs differences in clocks when packets are queued on the input queue. The input queue and output queue are decoupled from a clocking perspective. This provides a great deal of flexibility in the choice of media.

The most notable asynchronously clocked media is Ethernet. The genesis of this method was the Carrier Detection Multiple Access/Collision Avoidance (CDMA/CA) methods. The packet-switching systems monitor the link and determine independently when to transmit while attempting to avoid collision. The receiver's clock recovery mechanism uses a preamble on the Ethernet frame so that the receiver may dynamically align its timing on that interface for receipt of the packet. Each packet is independently clocked into the input queue of the receiver.

Ethernet is a very efficient means of transferring data transactions, as each end-system asynchronously loads the circuit independently based on its need to transfer data. The Ethernet bandwidth may be immediately allocated to accommodate sporadic data transactions even when the volume of data to transfer is high. In fact, a single system can monopolize the bandwidth. An exponential back-off mechanism is used to grant two end-systems a reasonably fair chance of transmitting data.

Clearly, the asynchronous nature of packet switching contradicts the synchronous nature of real-time voice and video data streams (that is, users have a very low tolerance for choppy voice or video services). The initial steps taken to more efficiently utilize bandwidth on the mobile network are focusing on transitioning data services to the packet-switching infrastructure. A closer look at transitioning synchronous applications such as voice and video to the packet core is addressed in subsequent sections.

Synchronous Wireless

The use of wireless frequency assets to provide transport is of paramount importance, particularly at the periphery of the network. The access network may have limited or no synchronous wireline capacity due to the cost of the cable plant. With a radio tower already deployed at the periphery of the radio access network, the addition of fixed radios specifically for backhaul connections toward mobile-switching center is much more feasible. The relatively low bandwidth aggregation requirements at the network periphery make wireless transport viable. For this reason, synchronous wireless transport is very valuable for the mobile operator to improve coverage in a cost-effective manner.

Synchronous wireless transport introduces a unique challenge. Where wireline transport may distribute the reference clock on the L1 circuit to the adjacent switching systems, the wireless transport offers no inherent capabilities. The remote wireless switching systems must either derive clock from a stratum one source such as Global Positioning System

(GPS) clock recovery systems or use the radio waves to recover clocking. Using over-the-air clock recovery mechanisms such as IEEE 1588v2 allows the remote radio systems to synchronize with the wireline network. The section, "Pseudowires for Time Division Multiplexing (TDM)," in Chapter 7, "Offloading Traditional Networks with IP," addresses methods for clock distribution and recovery mechanisms. Interestingly, interference in the spectrum not only disrupts the data transfer, but potentially disrupts the reference clock as well. The impact of a lost clock is substantially more disruptive because no data transfer can occur until the clock is recovered. The use of a GPS clock at the remote tower mitigates the loss attributed to clock recovery when spectrum interface occurs. Clearly, systems and applications that do not require synchronous transport provide many more opportunities to take advantage of wireless transport media. Chapter 6 has a section on bearer-switched independent circuit-switched architecture that describes in more detail how inherently synchronous applications such as voice can be transported over asynchronous packet-switched systems. These mechanisms make the asynchronous wireless environments much more viable.

Asynchronous Wireless

Asynchronous wireless transport facilitates data transfer under the presumption that there is no synchronous clock source for the two wireless terminals. These transport protocols are inherently packet-based and assume the terminals will synchronize the input clock on a packet-by-packet basis. This is the basis of data transfer between the BTS radio and the mobile terminal. A similar property exists between WiFi access points and WiFi clients. The mobile terminal uses its own reference clock with a dynamically discovered offset to sync up to the base station transmitter. The Base Transceiver Station (BTS) or Access Point (AP) must do the same as the mobile terminal may move or experience divergent fading patterns of multipath radio signals. Certainly, a mobile terminal with a GPS receiver may use this as its clock source; however, it will still be out of phase relative to the BTS or AP, and that phase shift is expected to occur frequently due to the mobile nature of the terminal.

The very nature of the radio link means that we must solve the problem of transporting synchronous applications across an inherently asynchronous medium for mobile communications. Adapting synchronous applications to work in a packet-based environment is not only mandatory, but the architectural direction should make the packet-based transport mechanisms consistent and ubiquitous. The importance of IP as a transport mechanism throughout the mobile architecture becomes more relevant. Rather than solve the synchronous clocking problem on a link-by-link basis for transport between each functional component, attention may be focused on facilitating transport of applications via IP end-to-end. Indeed, we expect that voice over IP will eventually be the means with which the voice application is transported across the infrastructure. Now the entire network infrastructure can be IP-based, enabling rapid introduction of many new asynchronous applications—as long as the packet-switched infrastructure meets the minimum requirements for reconstructing any application's synchronous requirements.

Core Network Requirements

The core network provides transport between the mobile-switching centers, data gateways, voice gateways, and data centers. The voice and data traffic is aggregated through the RAN to a service-switching center where traffic is directed to the appropriate voice or data gateways. The challenge with defining the core network requirements is to understand the characteristics of the traffic entering the core network. From a functional perspective, we can break the traffic into generic classes. The principal load on the wireless network has historically been voice; however, user interest in data applications has dramatically changed the architecture.

The core generally must be capable of carrying streamed media and transactional data. Streamed media can be broken into two sub-classes: live-linear and progressive-linear. Live-linear streamed media includes voice and video conferencing, which is sensitive to delay, jitter, and loss. Progressive-linear streamed media includes broadcast audio or video content that is not delay-sensitive; however, it is jitter- and loss-sensitive traffic. Finally, transactional data is not nearly as sensitive to delay, jitter, or loss as the end-systems can leverage recovery mechanisms. In many cases, the progressive-linear streamed content may manifest itself as transactional data where the terminal has sufficient buffer space to queue the application payload for play-out and/or rendering.

The live-linear streamed media has traditionally been carried via structured TDM circuits in the core network. Voice trunks connecting mobile-switching centers facilitate transport of PCM encoded live-linear streamed media. TDM introduced virtually no jitter and incurred very little loss. Delay tends to be a function of the path's propagation delay, which is generally unavoidable. Initially, structured TDM trunks were used to carry the live-linear media, as shown in Figure 5-1.

The structured TDM trunks were terribly inefficient at transporting transactional data. The wireless radio networks were not initially designed to carry broadcast media and high volumes of transactional data; therefore, the core network elements bifurcated into two functional elements: the voice-switching components and the data-switching components. The transactional data is efficiently transported in the data network, whereas the interactive media is efficiently transported in the structured TDM transport elements. Now two networks are needed to handle both voice and data, as shown in Figure 5-2.

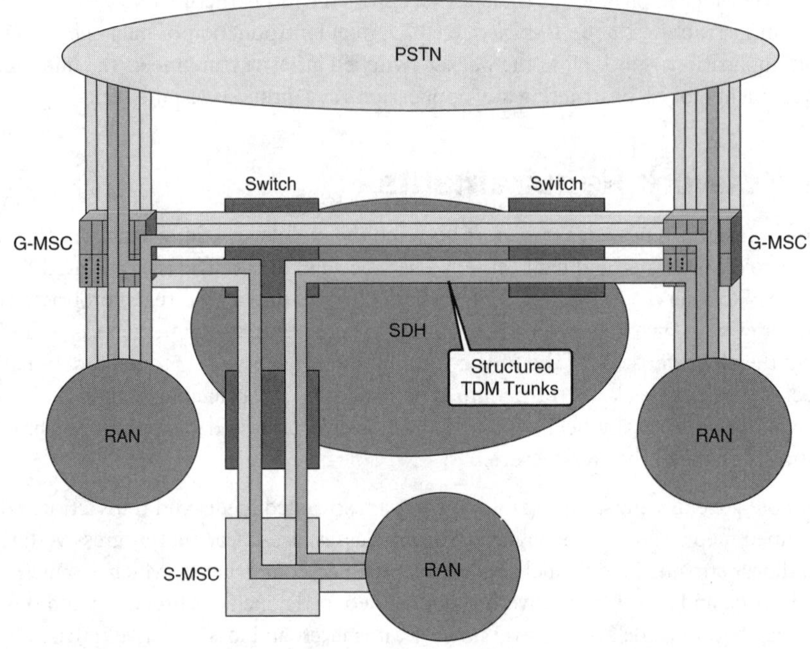

Figure 5-1 *Core Network Transport with Structured TDM*

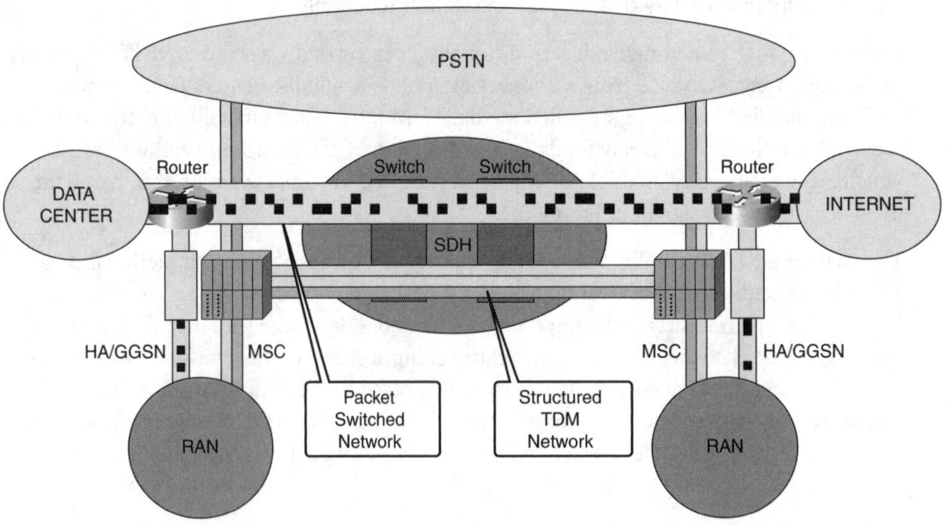

Figure 5-2 *Bifurcated Core Network Transport*

The voice is transported as PCM on a structured TDM network, whereas the transactional data is transported on a packet-switched network using unstructured TDM circuits for connectivity.

Combining the two networks can reduce capital cost and, potentially, operational costs. The goal of the IP Core Network is to efficiently mix the two classes of applications (live-linear and transactional) into a common transport while preserving the characteristics of the transport for the specific live-linear media and transactional data. The feasibility of transporting voice as data (that is, Voice over IP, circuit emulation, and so on) improves as the ratio of data to voice increases. The core network must still meet the constraints of voice (jitter, delay, loss); however, it is easier to design the core network so that data doesn't interfere with the voice traffic. Figure 5-3 shows the combined core network servicing both interactive media and transactional data.

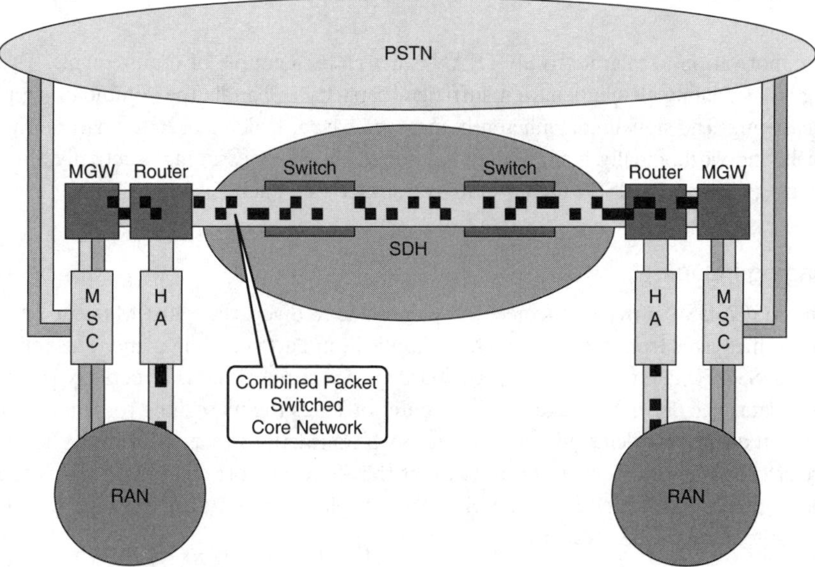

Figure 5-3 *Combined Core Network Transport*

Note that the core network aggregates the bifurcated traffic at the service-switching center into a common transport. The network elements that provide the bifurcated inputs to the core network are different for the various wireless network architectures. These methods are explored in more detail in the "Radio Access Network Requirements" section.

Core Network Communication Planes

The mobile-switching center (MSC) presents several unique interfaces to the core network depending on the type of traffic. We can segregate the traffic into various planes, including signaling, messaging, data bearer, voice bearer, and management. Each of these planes has unique requirements applicable to the core network.

Signaling Plane

The signaling plane leverages SS7 messaging to direct voice calls between MSC and to PSTN gateways. SS7 messaging has traditionally been carried in TDM circuits; however, SIGTRAN defines new methods for extracting the SS7 messages and transporting them in IP packets. [1] The core network must transport the SS7 at TDM prior to the conversion to SIGTRAN. Transitioning SS7 to IP allows the signaling messages to be transported across the IP Core Network.

Note More details on how SS7 signaling is transitioned to SIGTRAN are found in Chapter 9, "Content and Services."

The motivation to migrate to SIGTRAN is driven by a couple of requirements. The existing SS7 signaling elements have insufficient capacity to handle the volume of signaling messaging. The signaling is inherently message-based, which makes it a natural fit for a packet network. Finally, a significant volume of the SS7 messaging is actually Short Message Service (SMS), which is akin to transactional data.

Messaging Plane

The MSC/SGSN provides the necessary interface to divert the Short Message Service (SMS) messages from the SS7 Message Application Part signaling plane. This relieves the classic SS7 TDM infrastructure of the burden of carrying what is effectively transactional user data. The Short Message Service Center offloads the messaging to handle transactions in queues for deferred delivery. The SMS transactions that occur in the SS7 realm are afforded reliable delivery (a function of the SS7 transport on TDM). After the SMS messages are transferred to the SMS-C, the reliable delivery of the message is no longer guaranteed by the SS7 transport. [2]

The introduction of IP transport of SS7 using SIGTRAN allows the SMS messaging to be diverted from the classic TDM infrastructure. The operator now has a choice of using a "cap and grow" strategy—the existing SS7 on the TDM structured network is used exclusively for voice signaling, whereas the SIGTRAN network is used for transport of SMS messaging. The final transition is to make all the SS7 messages IP-enabled such that the entire signaling plane can be transported over the packet core network.

Voice Bearer Plane

The voice bearer has stringent requirements to minimize delay, jitter, and loss. This traffic has historically been transported via 64-kbps channels in structured TDM circuits referred to as trunks. The bandwidth constraints of the air-link and RAN network use more efficient coding schemes between the mobile subscriber and the Transcoder and Adaption Unit (TRAU), which is commonly located next to the MSC. The more efficient coding schemes used on the air-link are carried through the backhaul infrastructure and transcoded to 64-kbps circuits for handoff to the MSC. The initial architecture assumes the use of structured TDM circuits in the core network, leading to an inefficient voice transport across the core network architecture, as shown in Figure 5-4, where transcoding is applied at the TRAU. [3]

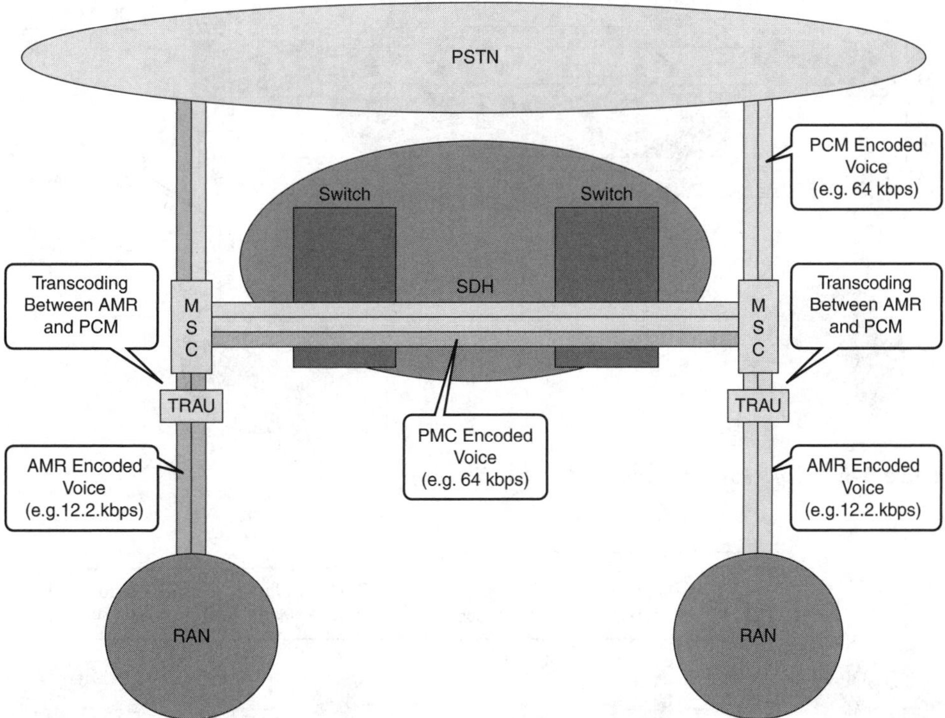

Figure 5-4 *Voice Bearer Switching on the Mobile Wireless Architecture*

The next interim step specified in the 3GPP R4 architecture is to provide encoding techniques on Media Gateways (MGW) that packetize voice bearer traffic for transport between MSCs using a packet-switched infrastructure. This can be accomplished using Circuit Emulation Services (CES) or VoIP. The media gateways require their own control plane to manage the establishment of voice bearer connections. Figure 5-5 shows the use of VoIP media gateways during this transition.

The additional packet encoding of Voice over IP consumes valuable time in the end-to-end delay budget that generally needs to be less than 150 msec. In addition, each instance of encoding and decoding degrades the voice quality and exacerbates bit errors. Several traditional voice-switch vendors are now building the VoIP encoders into the mobile-switching center as a packet control function. This mitigates the requirement of deploying specialized voice gateways; however, it doesn't eliminate the need to transcode the voice bearer at the MSC. The transcoding function translates the voice stream encoded using codecs based on the Radio Access Network architecture to a core network architecture using G.711 PCM-encoded streams. Figure 5-6 shows the use of transcoders in or near the MSC and how they effect the bandwidth consumption.

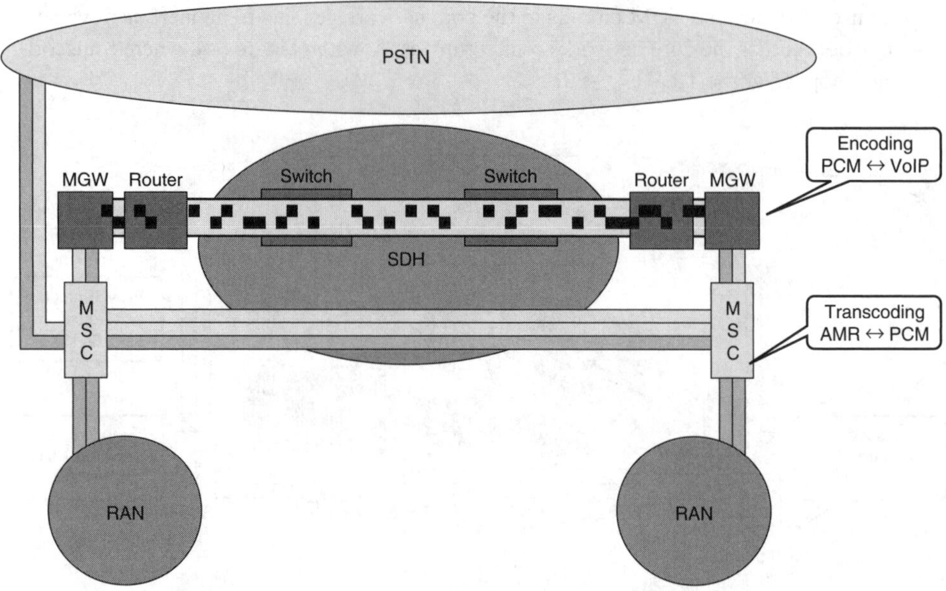

Figure 5-5 *VoIP Packet Transport*

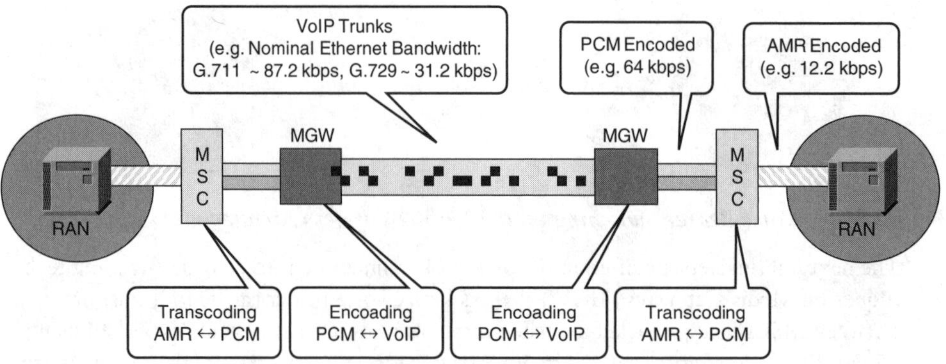

Figure 5-6 *Transcoded Voice Transport*

The transcoded call may now be switched to the PSTN via a Gateway MSC (GMSC). In the case of mobile-to-mobile calls, the remote MSC must transcode the voice bearer stream back to a codec used on the RAN. The back-to-back transcoding adds to the delay characteristics and further constrains the delay budget.

The next step is to introduce tandem-free operations (TFO) to the architecture as introduced in GSM systems. [4,5] The two TRAU handling the transcoding of AMR to PCM negotiate through the voice bearer using in-band signaling the option to remove the transcoding functions. The encoding implemented on the voice stream in the RAN is retained for voice traffic traversing the core network to another mobile subscriber. The elimination of the transcoder functions at both of the TRAU recovers some of the delay budget and minimizes errors introduced through repeated transcoding operations at both TRAU; however, the original low-bit rate voice-encoded stream is still transported in 64-kbps PCM trunks across the core network. TFO doesn't conserve available bandwidth. The AMR voice-encoded stream is effectively tunneled through the core network. Figure 5-7 shows the encoded stream inefficiently carried in the 64-kbps PCM trunk.

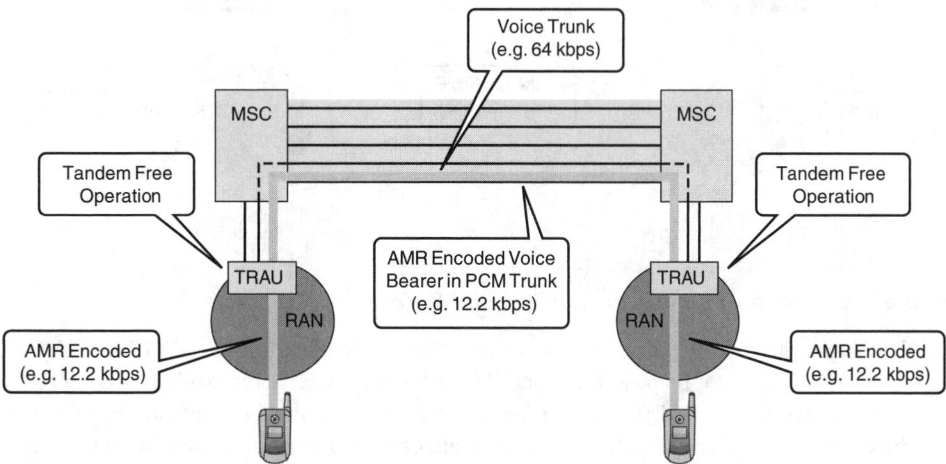

Figure 5-7 *Tunneling-Encoded Voice Bearer*

The TFO functions certainly improved voice quality; however, in many circumstances, such insertion of DTMF tones by the MSC and mobile handoffs required the TRAU to reinstate the transcoder. The TRAU is then required to reassess the viability of removing the transcoder as quickly as possible to improve the voice quality.

The TFO functions were maintained for use in the 3G networks; however, a more robust method called Transcoder Free Operation (TrFO) was developed using out-of-band signaling methods. [6] The TrFO method signals the call with codec options where the end-systems select the most appropriate codec. The MSC handles the signaling, while a media gateway packetizes the AMR encoded bearer for transport across the core network. The TrFO method is not backward compatible with GSM; therefore, the UMTS environment must revert to PCM-encoded bearers or TFO if possible.

Figure 5-8 shows the transport of TrFO traffic efficiently across the core network.

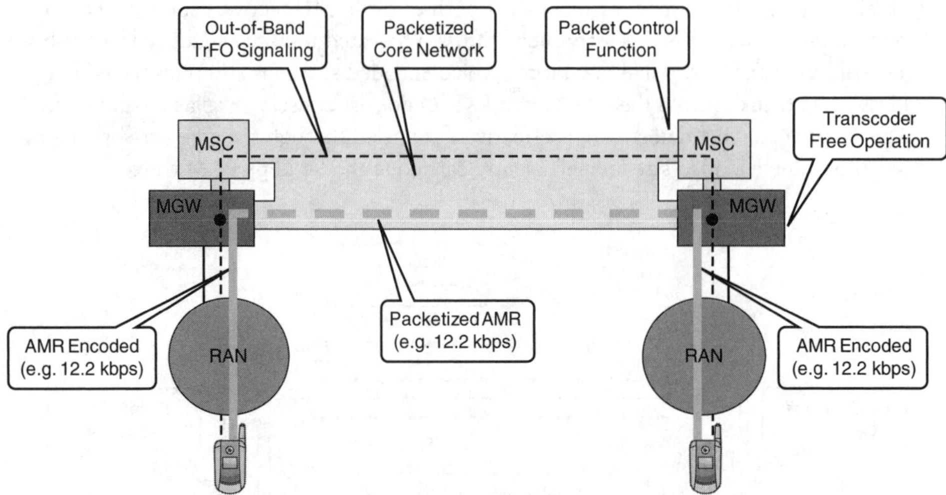

Figure 5-8 *Efficient Transport of TrFO Voice Bearer*

It is important to note that with more efficient encoding mechanisms, DTMF and FAX transmissions cannot be passed in-band. These services were traditionally passed in the audio stream using PCM. The use of low bit-rate codecs in the RAN require the DTMF be carried in the signaling path. The voice media gateway must be capable of detecting the presence of DTMF in the PCM-encoded voice bearer for inbound calls received from the PSTN. Upon detection, the DTMF tones are interpreted and passed as signaling messages out-of-band. The signaling messages are relayed to the mobile terminal. Alternatively, the signaling messages may be transmitted to a remote media gateway. The remote media gateway must transcode the voice bearer and embed the DTMF tones in the PCM stream.

Data Bearer Plane

Each of the mobile architectures uses a similar aggregation approach and Chapter 6 demonstrates how different protocols are used to carry the subscriber sessions up to a subscriber management platform. The mobile data services are switched or tunneled through the RAN and terminated on the subscriber management platform where IP packets are processed. The GSM architecture uses the Gateway GPRS Support Node (GGSN) as the session aggregation platform, whereas the CDMA-2000 architecture uses the Packet Data Serving Node/Home Agent (PDSN/HA). Newer architectures such as LTE and WiMAX have similar platforms referred to as Packet Data Network Gateway (PDN-GW) and Home Agent (HA), respectively.The subscriber sessions are aggregated at the subscriber management platform where each subscriber IP flow is presented to the core network. This interface is typically the first point where the subscriber IP packets are routed natively over L2 media, as shown in Figure 5-9.

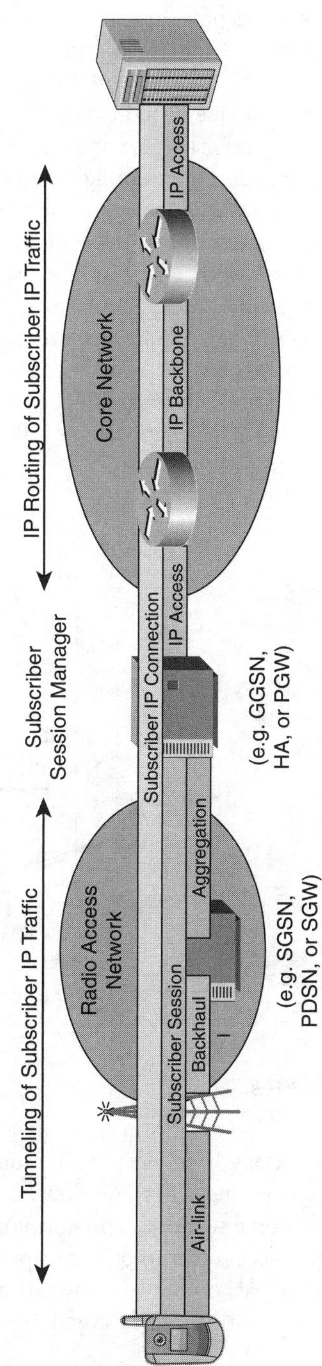

Figure 5-9 *Subscriber Session Management*

IP routing protocols take over at this point and direct the subscriber data to the target IP server. Meanwhile, the subscriber's IP address (or the range of addresses incorporating the subscriber IP) is advertised to the core network for return traffic flows. Each subscriber must be represented by a unique IP address in order to return IP packets from the application. Generally, the subscriber management platform is responsible for dynamically assigning the IP address to the subscriber during session initialization. This approach allows the subscriber manager to advertise an aggregate IP address block to the core network, which represents a pool of subscribers. The aggregated address pool minimizes routing transactions in the core network, whereas the subscriber IP addresses may be allocated and de-allocated frequently. Next-generation architectures are likely to assign persistent IP addresses to clients in order to enable bi-directionally initiated application transactions. Protocols based on Mobile IP allow the application to use a persistent IP address, whereas the network dynamically assigns a client address at the point of network attachment. Figure 5-10 shows the relationship of the subscriber IP assignment and the pool of addresses assigned to the core network.

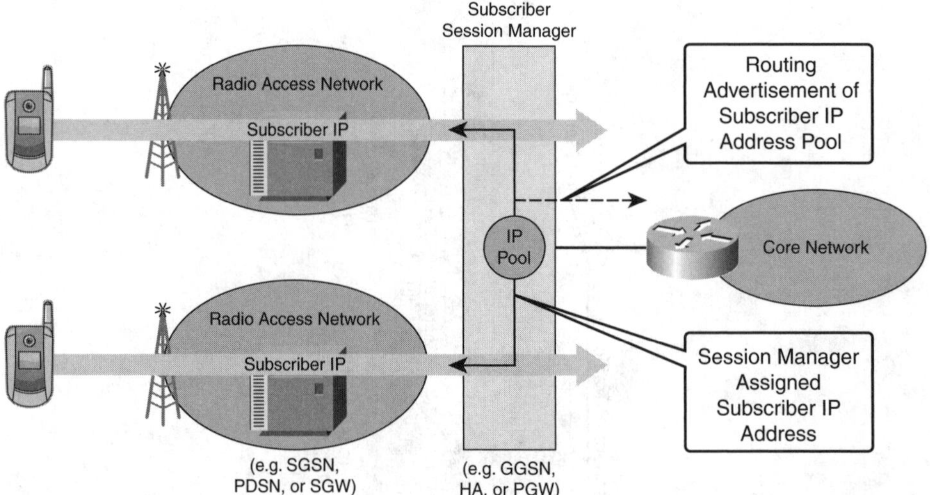

Figure 5-10 *Subscriber IP Routing*

Note that the subscriber management platform serves as an anchor point for the application of subscriber IP services. Many IP services require stateful management of the IP flow (for example, firewall, accounting, and so on). Traffic moving toward the services environment and returning from the services environment usually must pass through the same set of IP processing systems in order to preserve application context. Figure 5-11 shows the flow of subscriber IP packets between the subscriber management platform and the core network where application state is stored.

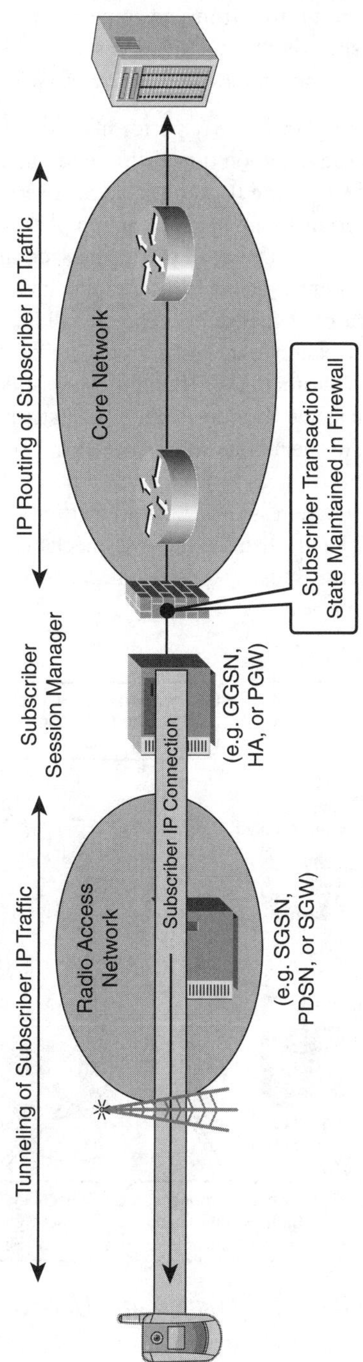

Figure 5-11 *IP Application Flow State*

The core network must return traffic from the application servers back through the chain of IP processing systems such that the application state can be managed properly. The resiliency of the data plane is accommodated in one of two ways: stateful or stateless.

The subscriber management platform may perform a stateful transition to an alternate platform. This requires the aggregation tunnels to be rerouted to the alternate subscriber management platform. Likewise, the IP address block advertised by the subscriber management platform must be transitioned to the backup platform. If the alternate subscriber management platform is not co-located, all the IP transaction states must also be transitioned to back up IP processing systems in a stateful manner. Making all these stateful transitions seamless is a bit of challenge because the failure detection and recovery methods are inconsistent. As an example, the Subscriber Session Manager might be using Virtual Route Redundancy Protocol (VRRP) on the LAN side interface toward the core network. VRRP presents a single IP address that the upstream network element uses for downstream transmission to the mobile subscriber. If the primary Subscriber Session Manager fails, the back-up system assumes responsibility for the subscriber state and also takes the previously used IP address. This backup method commonly used in LAN environments is completely different than the fail-over mechanism used in the RAN between the mobile subscriber and the Subscriber Session Manager. Figure 5-12 shows the stateful transition of the data bearer plane.

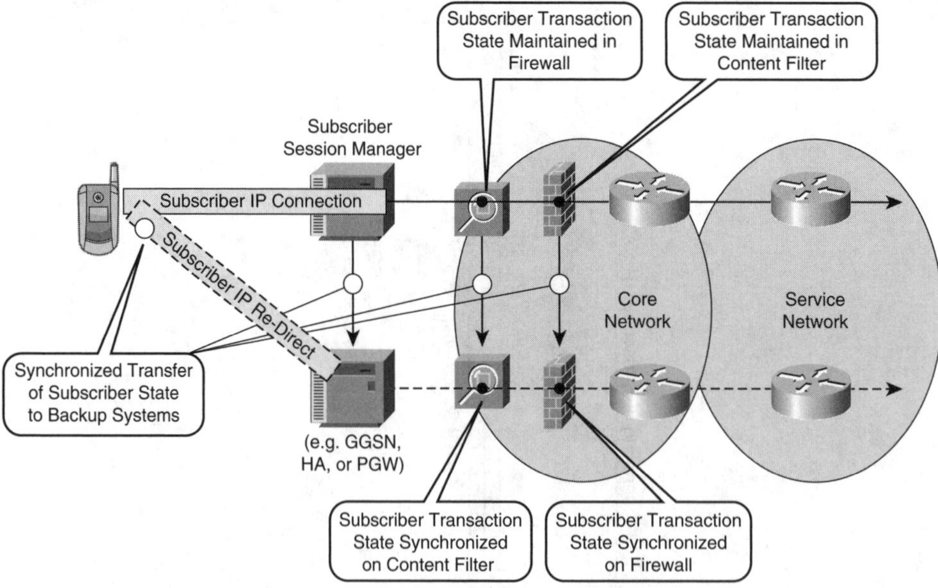

Figure 5-12 *Stateful Transition of the Data Bearer Plane*

The alternative is for the subscriber session to be stateless, where the subscriber session is terminated and re-established on an alternate subscriber management platform. The tunnel initiator in the RAN is required to redirect the session to the backup platform, and the subscriber state is rebuilt as well as the transaction state in subsequent IP processing systems. Figure 5-13 shows the stateless transition of the subscriber data bearer plane. Most mobile operators initially deployed Subscriber Session Manager's using stateless backup services; however, most providers now insist on using a stateful fail-over system.

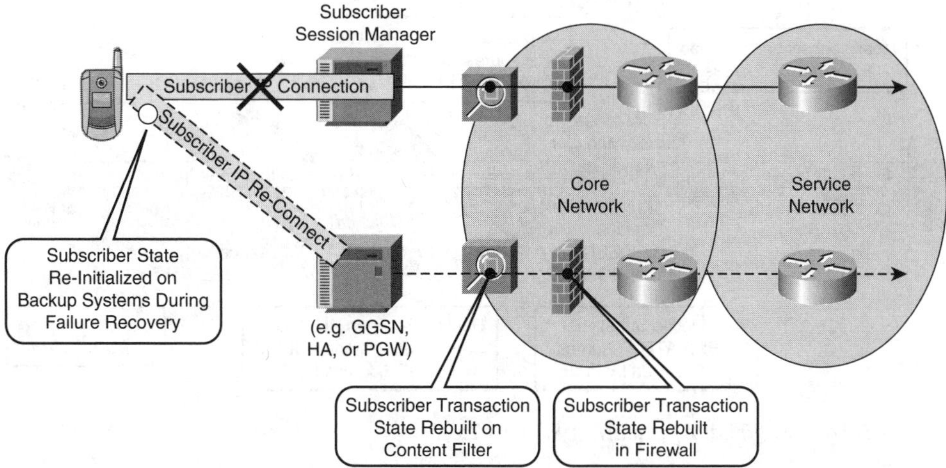

Figure 5-13 *Stateless Transition of the Data Bearer Plane*

The stateless transition is much easier to accomplish; however, the subscriber's applications must reconnect. The process of stateless transition usually disrupts applications that use persistent state, whereas transactional applications are merely delayed while the subscriber state is rebuilt. If the Subscriber Session Manager is able to transfer state to a backup system, the subscriber applications are likely to survive the transition to the backup system.

The core network must provide routing between the subscriber management platforms and the application servers regardless of their location. The application servers may be located within the provider, on a third-party network, or on the Internet at-large. The application servers that are located off-net may require translation of the mobile subscriber's assigned IP address if the address is assigned from a private IP address range. Network Address Translation is a common function of a firewall service, and usually the firewall function is positioned to protect the core network from exterior environments. Mobile subscriber IP addresses may be translated to a public representation of an IP address, which builds state on the firewall on a per-flow basis. The return traffic from the third-party or Internet needs to flow through the same firewall function in order to reverse the translation. The core network simply needs to provide IP routed connectivity between the subscriber management platform and the NAT function, as shown in Figure 5-14.

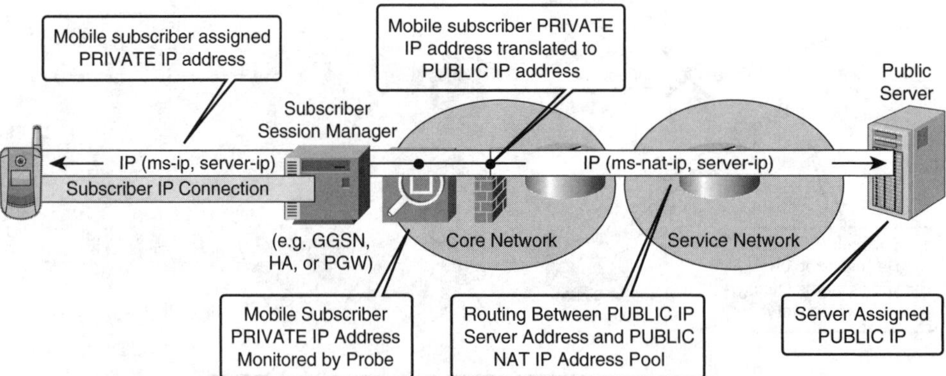

Figure 5-14 *External Application Server Access*

Some applications need to initiate a connection to the mobile client. In such cases, the mobile client needs an assigned address that is addressable by the application server. This address might be a publicly routable address or static NAT address representing the client. Managing subscriber-assigned addresses can be quite a challenge. In most cases, the client is required to initiate the connection to an application server where application state is managed on behalf of the client. The application server, which has an IP address assigned from a publicly routable address block, may act as a proxy communication point for traffic directed to a specific client that needs to traverse the core network. Figure 5-15 shows the proxy application server relationship with the external networks and the mobile subscriber.

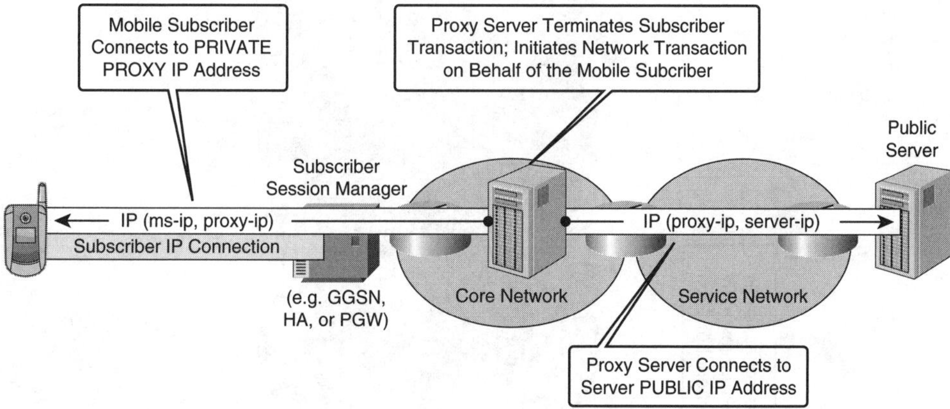

Figure 5-15 *Proxy Application Server*

The data bearer plane may be considered orthogonal to the voice bearer plane. Voice tends to be local in nature from a network architecture perspective. This means there is a high degree of lateral connectivity between mobile-switching centers, where the subscriber is likely to call someone local or in the neighboring mobile-switching center. Conversely, the data bearer plane tends to be external, whereas the subscriber tends to connect to national services in the data center or on the Internet. Of course, the network architecture can be adapted to make the voice and data bearer plane congruent by distributing external data network access for the bearer plane. The mobile operators will trade-off costs for backhauling data bearer to a national data center versus the costs of distributing the data access services to the periphery of the network. Figure 5-16 shows how the access to data services is not congruent with the voice transport. The traffic profiles vary for different mobile operators; therefore, the capacity planners need to perform statistical analysis of the provider's own network to determine the optimal network architecture.

The advantage of making the voice and data congruent is that bandwidth can be shared between the two bearer planes in a more efficient manner. This sharing of bandwidth between the two bearer planes is maximized when voice is transported as data. The mobile operator must pay careful attention to the possibility of overloading the network with user data that might impact the voice bearer traffic.

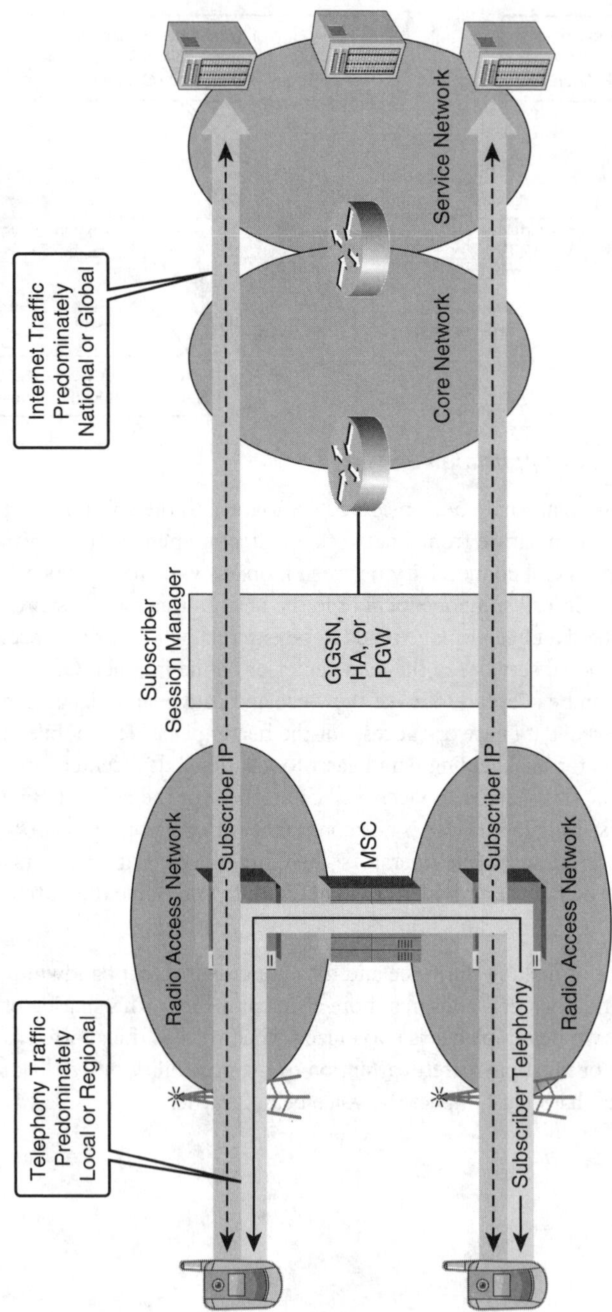

Figure 5-16 *Bearer Plane Traffic Profile Analysis*

Management Plane

A lot of emphasis is placed on the signaling, voice, and data planes of the mobile operator. The management plane is just as important, if not more important. The management plane is used to sustain the systems, monitor the resources, and diagnose problems in the network. Most mobile systems now provide remote terminal access through an IP interface while preserving the viability of the console interface. The console interface may be remotely accessible by using IP-enabled terminal servers. Figure 5-17 shows the redundant access modes to the mobile systems equipment.

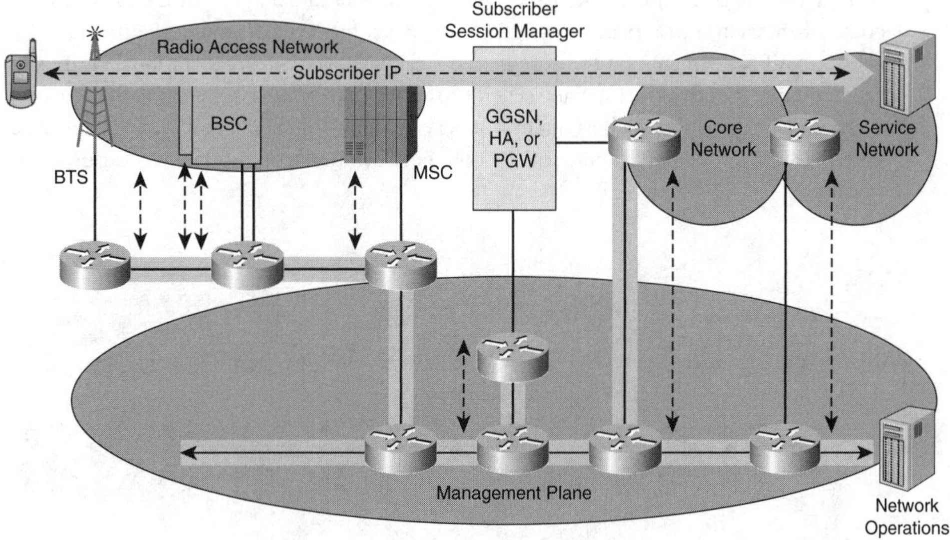

Figure 5-17 *Management Plane Access*

The management plane may traverse the same core network resources as the voice and data bearer plane; however, an out-of-band data communications network (DCN) is always recommended as a backup should impairment occur in the core network. The DCN should use network resources (fiber and switches) that are not shared with the core network. Ideally, both the core network and the DCN may be used for the management plane. However, the cost of building a separate high-speed DCN may be prohibitive; therefore, the operator may chose to bifurcate the management traffic. High-volume traffic may be transmitted in-band via the core network, whereas low-volume, disaster-recovery traffic is transmitted via the DCN. In the event of core network failure, the bearer plane is disrupted, and the primary goal is to restore the core network. The out-of-band DCN facilitates console access to the mobile systems during core network outages such that diagnostics and analysis may be performed.

Converged Core Network

The core network provides transport for several traffic planes that may have different requirements for redundancy, speed of convergence, and efficiency. The core network may be partitioned to accommodate the requirements of each traffic plane.

> **Note** Chapter 7 focuses on various methods using pseudowires to transport different traffic planes across the core network.

Alternatively, the different traffic planes may be segmented using an MPLS VPN architecture where each traffic plane is assigned a VPN segment. Partitioning the traffic planes into VPN segments on the core network allows different organizational entities to manage their respective traffic plane. Each traffic plane may be assigned specific performance characteristics, such as quality of service, fault-tolerance, and security profiles. Figure 5-18 shows the partitioning of the core network to accommodate the various traffic planes.

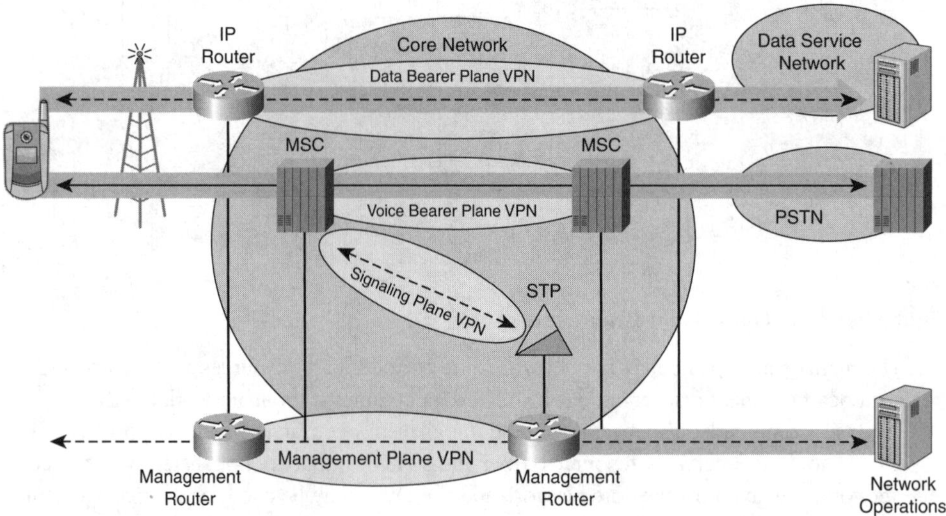

Figure 5-18 *Traffic Planes on Partitioned Core Network*

Data Center Access

The Data Center (DC) houses many of the most critical functions in the mobile wireless network. Not only does the DC support the operator's application servers, but it also hosts many of the signaling services, subscriber management, and network management functions. The DC must preserve the context of each traffic plane, as described in the previous section covering the converged core network (see Figure 5-19).

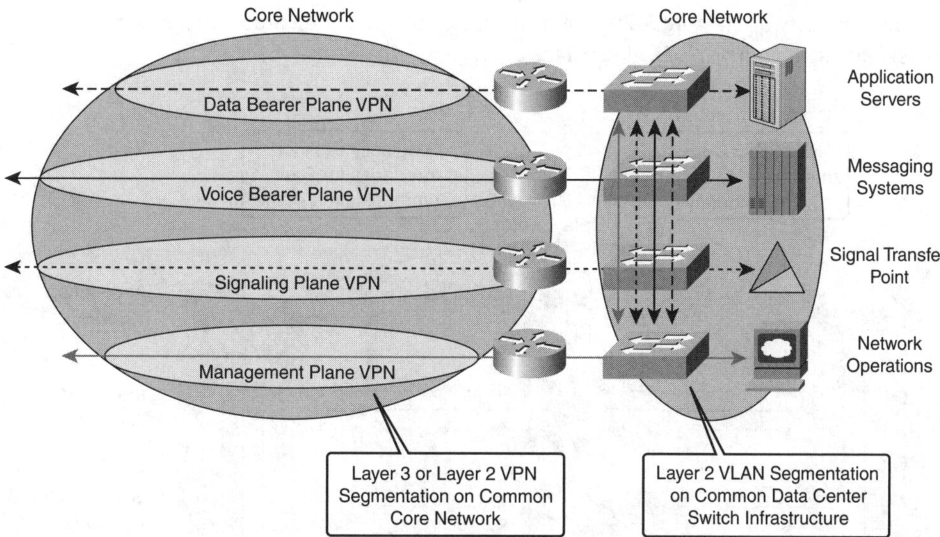

Figure 5-19 *Traffic Plane Extension into Data Center*

The DC typically uses VLAN segments to maintain the partitioning of the core network. The relevant application servers are positioned in the appropriate VLAN according to the traffic plane that it serves. In most cases, the application server must interface with two or more traffic planes. As an example, the Home Location Registrar (HLR) or Home Subscriber Services (HSS) will certainly need a routed IP path to the subscriber management platform. At the same time, the server will need to be accessible by the management plane. Two approaches may be used to connect the server with the multiple traffic planes. The first is to use multiple interfaces where each interface is dedicated to the traffic plane. The second approach is to use a single interface and associate it with the primary traffic plane.

Multihomed Application Servers

The multihomed application server may have a unique interface for each traffic plane. Each interface is assigned a unique Ethernet MAC address and associated IP address. The application server is directly accessible to the systems within each traffic plane. The multihomed system enables the operator to optimize access to the application without the application flow having to traverse another traffic plane.

The capacity planning and traffic engineering configuration remains distinct for each traffic plane. Any quality of service or performance analysis requirements can be isolated by traffic plane, and a unique configuration can be applied. The downside is that multiple interfaces must be managed on the server, and each traffic plane must be designed for the appropriate redundancy. Ideally, the application server can use VLAN sub-interface on a common Ethernet interface to minimize the amount of hardware required. The adjacent Ethernet switches maintain traffic plane separation as the application flows transition into the core network. Figure 5-20 shows the use of physically dual-homed application servers with multiple logical interfaces.

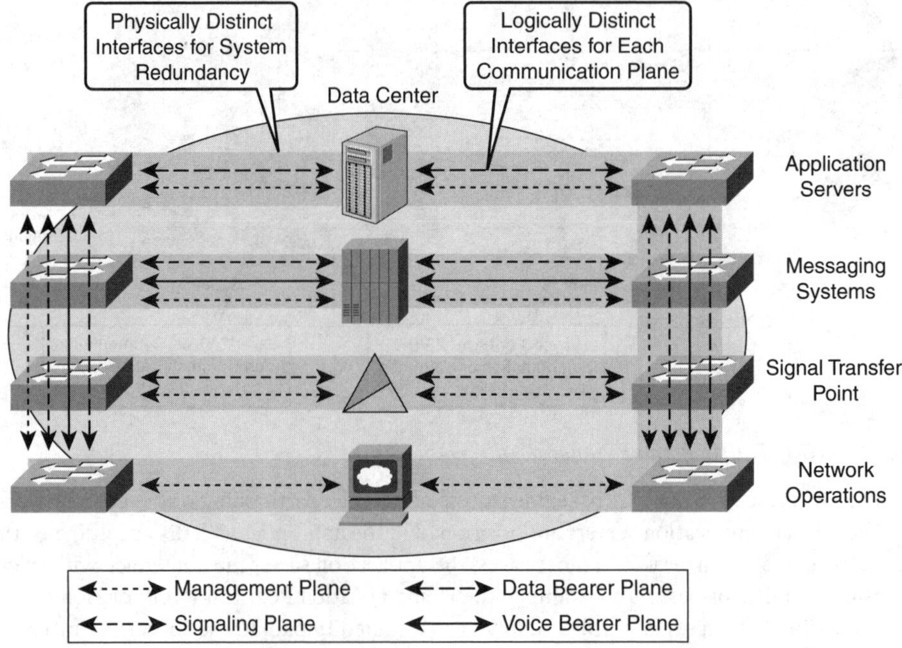

Figure 5-20 *Multi-Homed Application Servers*

The survivability of the multihomed application server is much higher as any of the interfaces may be used to access the system. In fact, the management plane may have two in-band interfaces for remote access in addition to an out-of-band console interface to the DCN. Each of the traffic planes may use a unique fault redundancy model depending on the needs for convergence, reliability, and availability.

The security model for the multihomed application server is fairly simple. Each traffic plane has a set of policy requirements that are unique; a security gateway, such as a firewall or router-based access control list, can be positioned between the application server and the external network. The segmentation allows a traffic plane-specific policy to be applied to the sub-interface of the application server, switch, or router.

Single-Homed Application Servers

The single-homed application server has a single physical interface that connects to one of the traffic planes on the adjacent switch. The switch needs to be aware of application traffic types in order to treat application flows appropriately. The application server is generally connected to the primary traffic plane. For example, a VoIP gateway would most likely connect to the voice bearer plane because the volume of traffic is predominately encoded voice traffic. Nevertheless, the application server also needs access to the signaling plane and the management plane.

The application flows need to transition into the appropriate traffic plane, which requires a gateway function. The gateway function may be hosted in the switch or be a dedicated appliance. The gateway function needs to have fairly strict security policies to protect each traffic plane; therefore, a firewall is commonly used between the traffic planes. For example, a firewall might reside in the switch between the voice bearer plane, management plane, and signaling plane. This allows the voice bearer to bypass the firewall functions, because the application server already resides in the voice traffic plane. Only signaling and management traffic must transition through the firewall. These application flows are much lower in volume; therefore, the firewall processing is appropriately allocated to the most traffic plane that needs the additional security. There is little value in implementing firewall functions between the voice application server and the voice bearer plane. Figure 5-21 shows the relationship of the single-homed application server and the associated traffic planes.

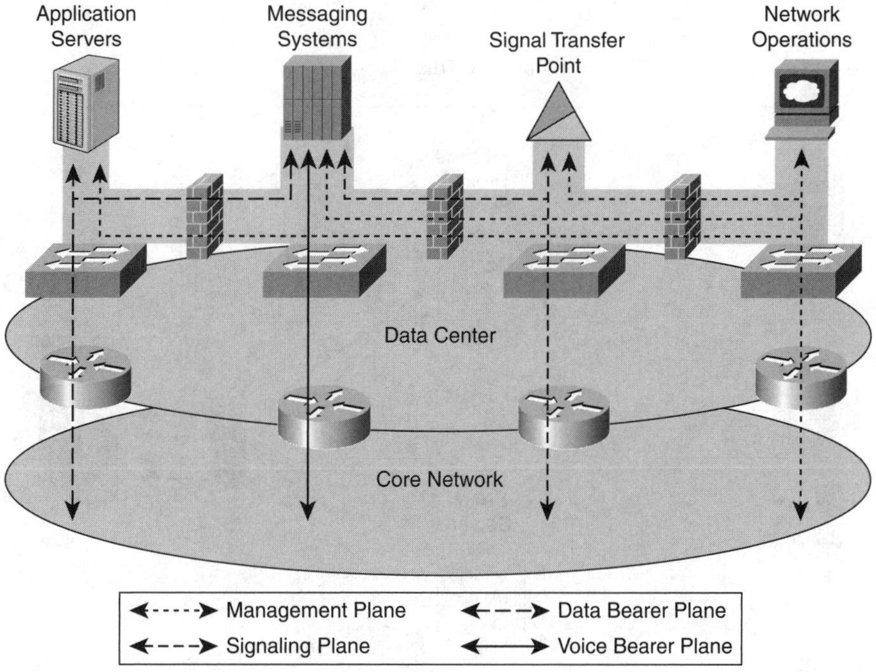

Figure 5-21 *Single-Homed Application Servers*

Survivability of the application server is more challenging as the failure of the server interface or the switch causes loss of connectivity in all traffic planes. Because the in-band management plane is also affected, an out-of-band management plane is required to diagnose and monitor the status of the application server. The fault tolerance model must be designed to handle the traffic plane with the most stringent requirements for convergence, reliability, and availability.

Application Proxy Servers

The DC may host application proxy servers that break subscriber transactions into two segments. Proxy servers may be used to relay application state between two traffic planes or serve as a midpoint between the subscriber and the application server within the same traffic plane. The proxy may serve several purposes. One use is to create a layer of abstraction, where the subscriber identity is masked by the proxy such that the application servers or third-party network is only aware of the proxy identity. That way, the proxy improves the security model by minimizing the exposure of the subscriber to third-party networks. The proxy server may also simplify configuration by segmenting provisioning activities. The subscriber relationship to the proxy server may be decoupled from the application server. The application server may not need to be aware of all the subscribers and provisioned with their credentials; the application server only needs to know that a transaction originated from the proxy server is valid because the proxy server has sufficient knowledge of the subscriber to authorize the transaction. This transitive security model is less secure; however, it allows better scale in the provisioning of application services. Figure 5-22 shows the relationship of the subscriber, the proxy server, and the application server.

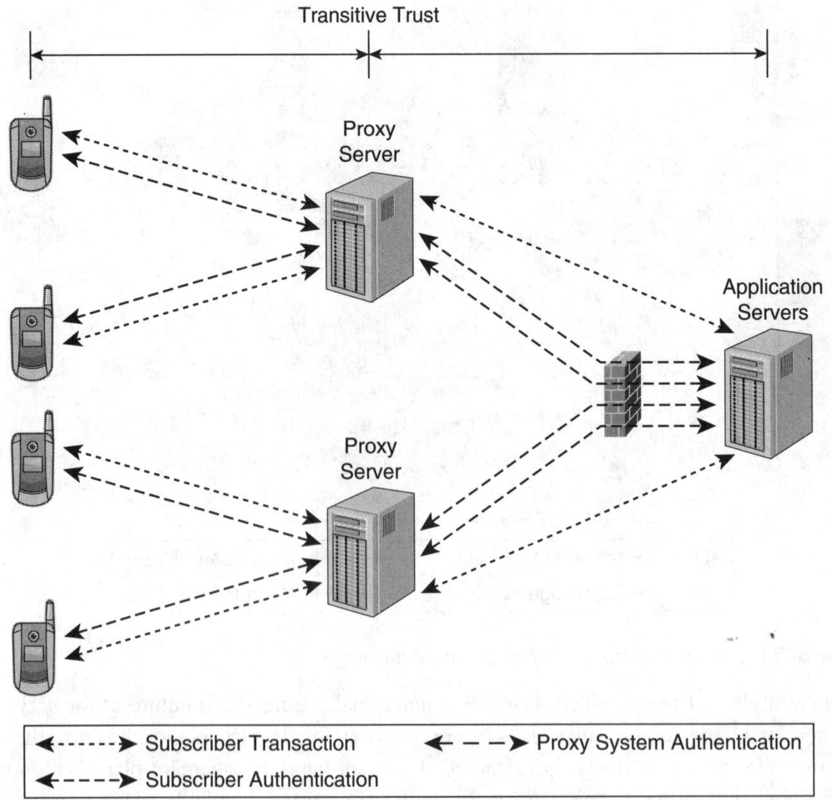

Figure 5-22 *Application Proxy Servers*

Summary of Data Center Requirements

A variety of applications are made available to the subscriber. These applications have a wide range of requirements regarding reliability, scalability, and efficiency. Most newly introduced applications are initially used by early adopters of technology, and the application servers may be centralized in a few data centers such that the transactions between the subscriber and the data center traverse the core network. The growth of the service may require the applications to be co-located with the MSC or subscriber session manager in order to scale and maintain efficiency. The subscriber-application transaction no longer traverses the core network; however, the application content may still traverse core network predicated on the requirement to populate the application server with this content. A content distribution network may be established to efficiently replicate or distribute the application content between data centers in order to make the content readily available to the subscribers. In the next section, the requirements of the RAN are addressed because many applications must be distributed much closer to the subscriber.

Radio Access Network Requirements

The Radio Access Network (RAN) has significantly different requirements from the core network; however, the communication planes that were discussed previously are still applicable. One of the primary differences on the RAN is the traffic matrix model used. Whereas the core network addresses the requirement to move content horizontally across the WAN in a mesh traffic matrix (for example, national calling, distributed Internet services, and so on), the RAN primarily moves content in a vertical manner from the subscriber, through the access infrastructure, toward the mobile core network. The majority of telephony traffic will be local; nevertheless, the traffic must be switched in the MSC. Conversely, the majority of data traffic is not local; therefore, it is aggregated across the WAN toward the subscriber management system.

The discrepancy between the two traffic domains—voice and data—leads to different aggregation models. The method of aggregation varies in relationship to the standards for mobility architectures. In general, the evolution of RAN aggregation has migrated from a converged architecture based on TDM to a bifurcated architecture—TDM serving voice and PSN serving data. The next evolution of the RAN proposes the convergence of the two domains back into common infrastructure based on packet-switched infrastructures.

Converged TDM Aggregation

The initial mobile wireless reference architecture is dominated by traffic from the voice domain. The voice bearer from the mobile subscriber is efficiently encoded for transmittal across the air-link and allocated time slots in the TDM aggregation infrastructure from the cell-site. The management plane, data bearer plane, and signaling plane must be transmitted through the access infrastructure as well; however, the volume of traffic is dominated by voice.

The architecture required to aggregate the cell sites into the MSC is hierarchical in nature, leading to increasing density of interfaces at the aggregation sites. Figure 5-23 shows the network providing the interface connectivity between the cell site and the MSC. Note that the BTS end-systems must be aggregated into the BSC, and the BSC end-systems must be aggregated into the MSC in both the GSM and CDMA architectures.

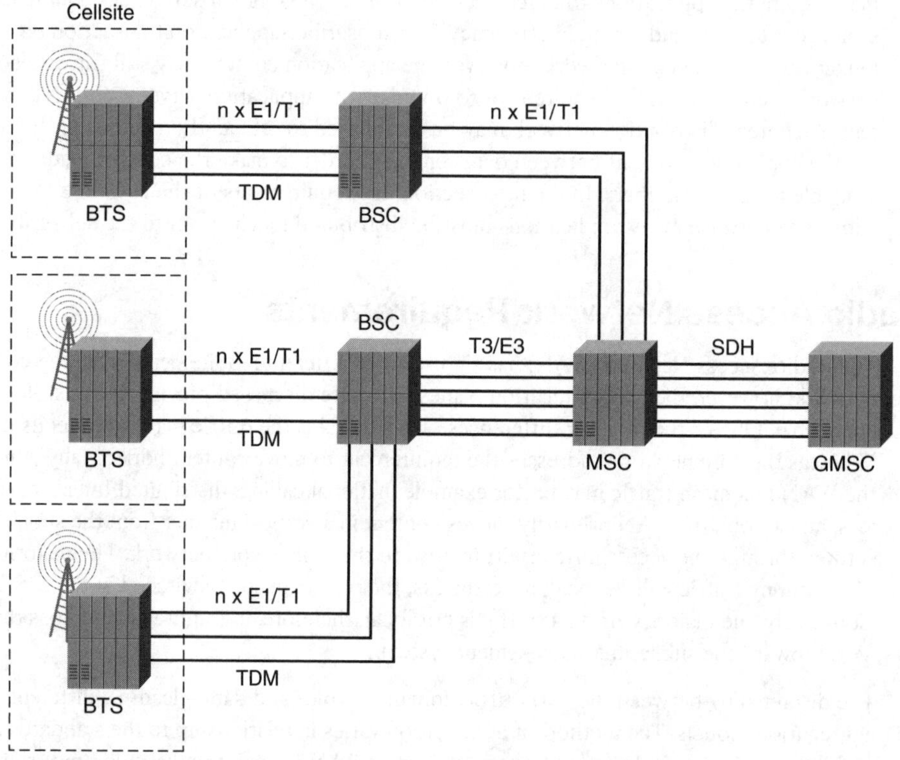

Figure 5-23 *TDM Network Aggregation of Mobile Wireless Traffic*

As described in Chapter 3, "All-IP Access Systems," a load of traffic from a cell site handling predominately voice bearer services requires roughly 2–3 Mbps. Therefore, the TDM infrastructure typically requires two T1 or two E1 interfaces for transmittal of the traffic back to the BSC. The number of cell sites is a function of the coverage area, obstructions within that coverage area, frequency reuse, and many other parameters. Large cities may require upwards of 1,000 cell sites that must be aggregated into BSC, whereas a single BSC serves 50–100 cell sites. The network topology needs to support roughly 200 circuits aggregated at the BSC. Subsequently, the 10–20 BSC need aggregation into the MSC that serves the region. All the voice bearer traffic must be relayed upstream toward the MSC for switching. The voice bearer traffic cannot be hair-pinned at the BSC; therefore, roughly 200 circuits must be aggregated from each BSC into the MSC, yielding 2,000 to 4,000 T1/E1 equivalent circuits.

Divergent Aggregation

The substantial increase in "data" traffic started with the rapid growth in Short Message Services. Although the service used the signaling plane for transport, it quickly overwhelmed the signaling plane capacity and switching systems. The operators quickly focused on off-loading the SMS "data" traffic from the signaling transport plane. The introduction of IP data services on the mobile client caused a dramatic shift in the data traffic profile for a given mobile subscriber when CDMA 1xRTT and GSM GPRS were made available. Very quickly, the bearer loading started shifting from predominately voice bearer to data bearer, and the structured TDM circuits were no longer economically viable as a means of backhaul in the RAN. First, the TDM channel allocation methods were cumbersome for bursty data, and secondly, the bandwidth available was insufficient to provide a meaningful web-browsing experience. The 2G systems evolved to 2.5G and 3G systems, where more efficient methods of data backhaul were provided in the CDMA and UMTS architectures.

The 2.5G systems architecturally evolved to a model where voice bearer and data bearer are split. The two most prevalent architectures have the voice bearer handled by the MSC, whereas the data bearer is handled by the subscriber session manager infrastructure (SGSN/GGSN in the case of UMTS and PDSN/HA in the case of CDMA). The rapid growth of the data bearer traffic requires a more efficient packet-switched infrastructure in the RAN. Initially, Frame Relay was specified for transport of data bearer between the BSC and the SGSN. Subsequently, ATM was specified as the appropriate switching technology to transport both the data and voice bearer. Both architectures provide divergent interfaces for voice and data that are highlighted in subsequent sections, as shown in Figure 5-24.

An interesting inflection point occurs where the volume of data bearer traffic exceeds the volume of voice bearer traffic. When this occurs, the natural next step is to transport voice as data on the packet-switched infrastructure. Indeed, the mobile operator's focus transitions to more efficient transport of data while embedding the voice bearer in the data transport. The 3G Release 4 architecture took advantage of the different ATM Adaptation Layers (AAL2 for voice bearer, AAL5 for voice and data signaling, and AAL5 for data bearer) to aggregate traffic onto a shared switching platform while maintaining distinct signaling and bearer planes. Release 5 further emphasized the aggregation of voice, bearer, and signaling onto a common transport based on IP. The RAN still maintains two distinct interfaces for voice and data; however, the infrastructure is now optimized for data—not voice. The goal is to ensure that the voice service quality is sustained while reducing costs of transporting the data, which is growing exponentially.

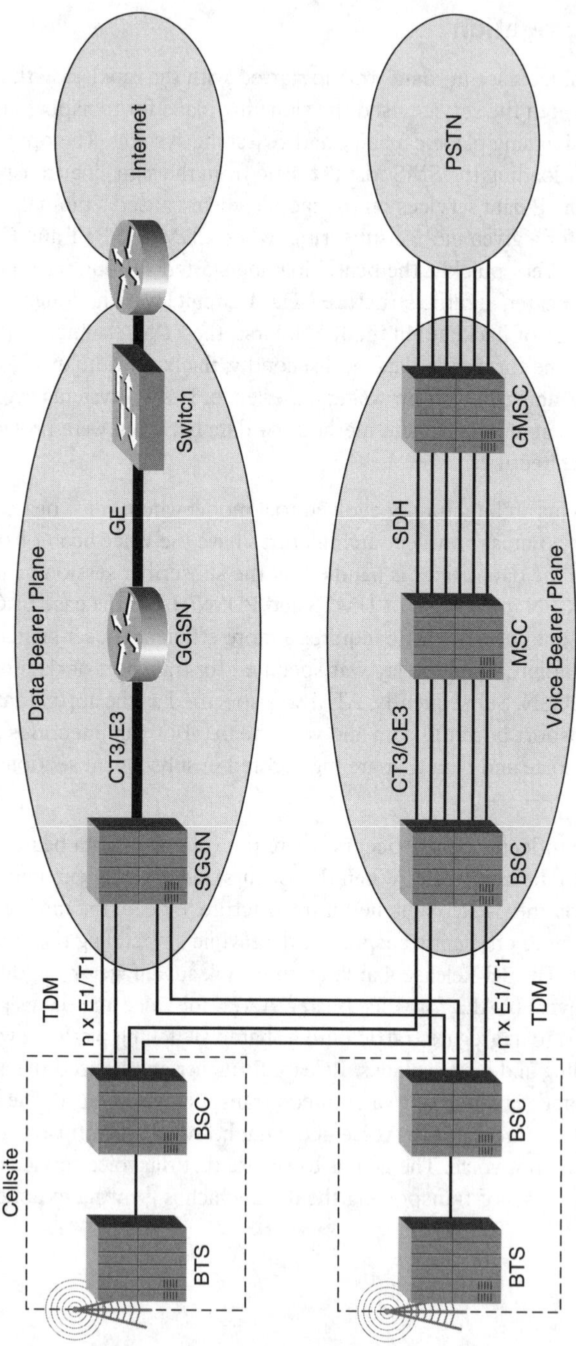

Figure 5-24 *Divergent Voice and Data Bearer*

The requirements of the RAN in this stage of the transition are to provide distinct interfaces for voice and data bearer traffic. Subsequent sections highlight these interfaces and how they correlate with the end-systems in the core network.

Converged PSN Aggregation

Chapter 7, "Offloading Traditional Networks with IP," addresses the means of transporting the ATM via pseudowires on the packet-switched infrastructure where the ATM services both the voice and data planesThis is the first step in convergence of voice bearer and data bearer on the common IP packet-switched infrastructure. The long-term future for convergence on the packet-switched network is to facilitate transport of voice application traffic as data. The RAN will no longer distinguish voice bearer and data bearer except to ensure that the streams are serviced with the appropriate quality of service controls. Next-generation architectures such as WiMAX and LTE use this approach, where the voice application is encoded as VoIP on the user equipment. The VoIP is transmitted alongside any other data application, such as web traffic and mail traffic. The RAN is simply a packet-switched infrastructure facilitating transport of the bearer traffic, regardless of the application. The operator may choose to use Circuit Emulation Services (CES) pseudowires to provide backhaul of TDM circuits carrying. Figure 5-25 shows the converged architecture serving control, management, and bearer traffic.

The requirement for the RAN in this stage of the deployment architecture is to have a consistent means of distinguishing the quality of service requirements for each class of traffic. A class of traffic might be defined as streamed live-linear, streamed progressive-linear, or transactional, as defined previously in this chapter, where each class has different performance characteristics in the packet-switched network.

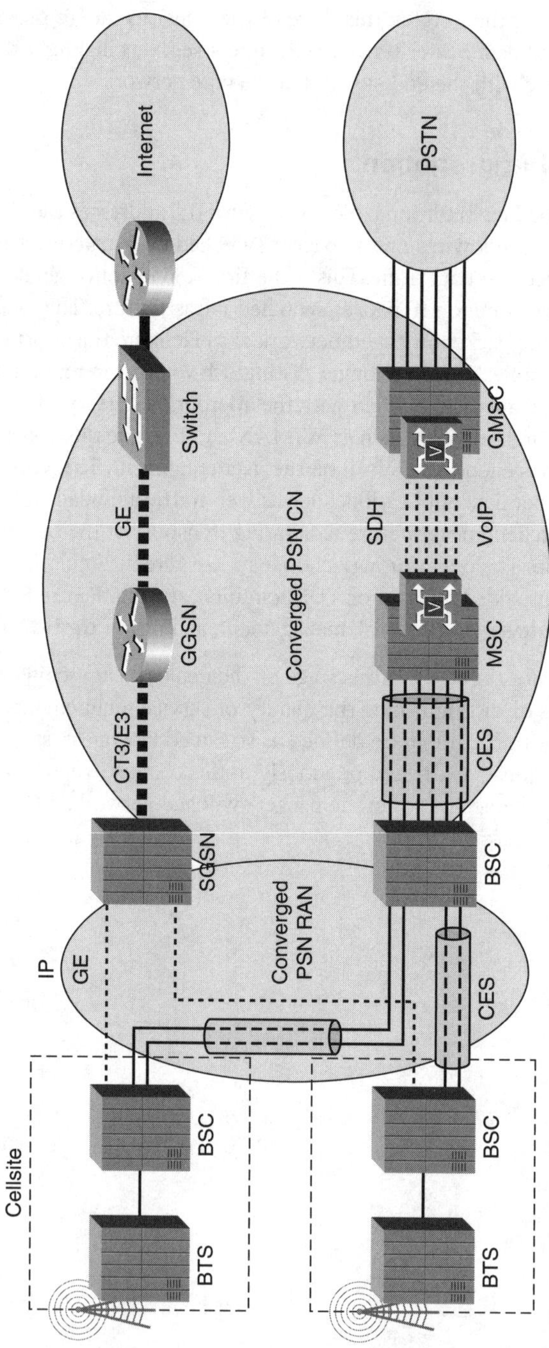

Figure 5-25 *Converged PSN Network*

Summary of Core Network and RAN Transport Requirements

The core network and the Radio Access Network must transport the same classes of traffic; however, the cost models needed for the two infrastructures are quite different. The core network transports high volumes of aggregated voice and data bearers, where economies of scale reduce the cost due to statistical multiplexing. Conversely, the Radio Access Network must transport small volumes of voice and data, but the transport must be able to support localized traffic spikes. The over-provisioned capacity leads to inefficient use of capacity, whereas constrained capacity forces the data bearer traffic to be throttled back, thus impacting the subscriber experience. The previous two sections highlighted the general requirements of the domains in the mobile network architecture. The subsequent sections detail the interfaces used and the network architecture required to facilitate the transition from converged TDM access infrastructure, to divergent voice and data aggregation, and finally to a converged PSN aggregation architecture.

Mobility Network Transport Architecture

A variety of mobile network transport architectures have been defined. In many cases, these architectures are associated with specific radio access technologies. The first section focuses on 3G radio access technologies, whereas the second section focuses on 4G radio access technologies. Each of the sections describes the various mobility protocols and their methods of transport using IP packet-switching methods.

3GPP Mobility Protocols

We first focus on the 3GPP radio access technologies, starting with GSM and UMTS, and follow up with a discussion on the 3GPP2 technologies based on CDMA. Each section describes the protocol stacks associated with the protocol and highlights where IP packet switching becomes relevant in the transport of the voice bearer, data bearer, signaling, and control planes.

Global System for Mobilization (GSM)

The GSM/Edge Radio Access Network (GERAN) architecture was designed to handle both voice and data. Whereas the EDGE architecture was optimized for voice-bearer services, the GSM infrastructure optimized transport for each respective bearer planes. The Radio Access Network shares a common backhaul infrastructure for connectivity of the Base Station Subsystem (BSS). The BSC splits the traffic into the two domains: voice and data. The architecture is divergent at this point where the data is handled by the GSM Packet Radio Support (GPRS) Core Network, whereas the voice is handled by the Network Subsystem (NSS). The GSM reference architecture is shown in Figure 5-26.[7]

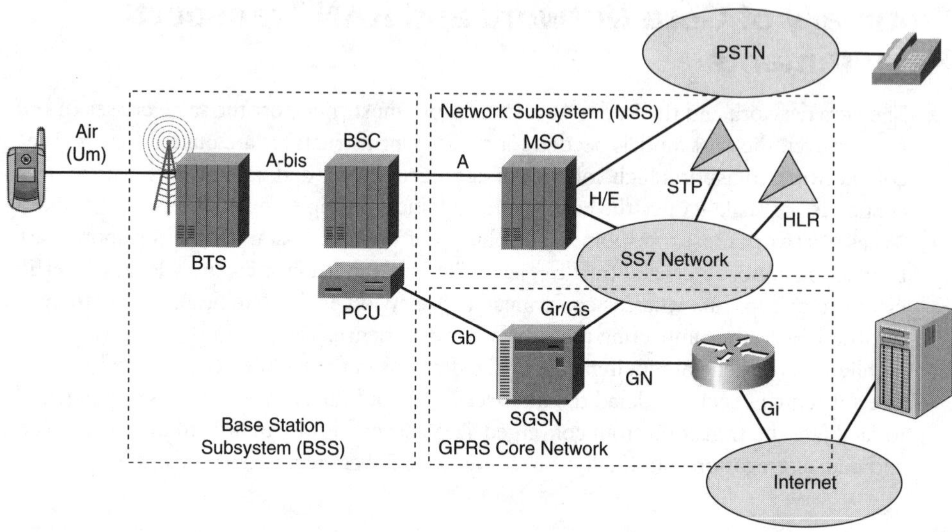

Figure 5-26 *GSM Reference Network Architecture*

The RAN focuses on the Abis, A, and Gb interfaces as part of the wireless aggregation that terminates at the SGSN. The SGSN then presents the Gn interface to the core network for aggregation of GPRS bearer data toward the GGSN. [8]

GSM A Interface Reference

The GSM architecture provides two distinct interfaces from the Base Station Subsystem (BSS). The first is the A interface on the BSC, which is directed to the MSC and serves the voice bearer traffic as well as signaling. The protocol stack SCCP/MTP is carried on a structured T1 or E1 channelized interface. The RAN backhaul for the A interface simply consists of a hierarchical aggregation of TDM circuits from multiple BSC to the MSC, as shown in Figure 5-27.

GSM Gb Interface Reference

The second important interface is the Gb interface connecting the BSC and SGSN. From the BSC, the interface is commonly provided by a Packet Control Unit (PCU) that handles the data bearer. The PCU typically presents the Base Station Subsystem GPRS Protocol (BSSGP) data bearer to the backhaul network in the form of Frame Relay-encapsulated IP packets. The FR interface has a PVC associated with the data bearer service necessary to transport the user data to the SGSN. The backhaul infrastructure may consist of a FR network used to aggregate multiple BSC into a common SGSN, as shown in Figure 5-28.

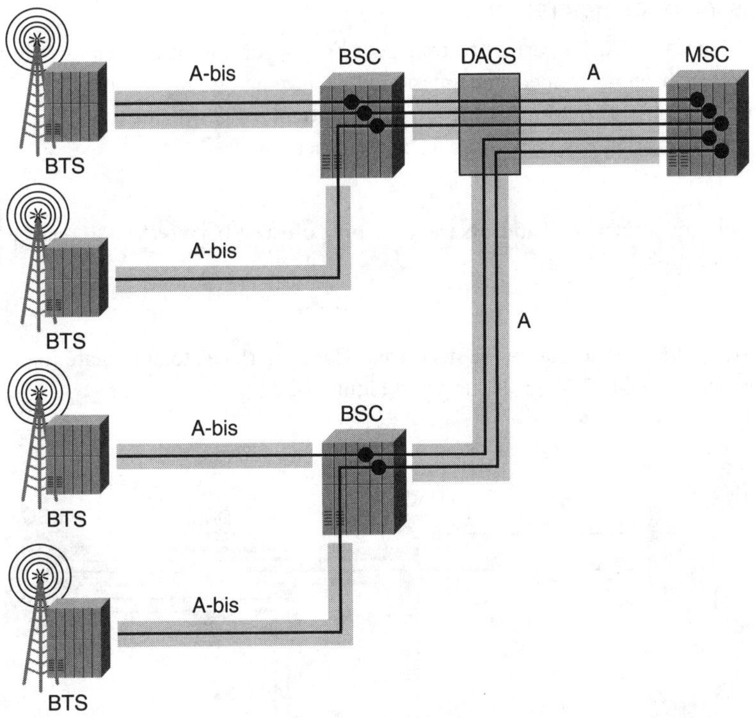

Figure 5-27 *TDM RAN Aggregation of A Interface*

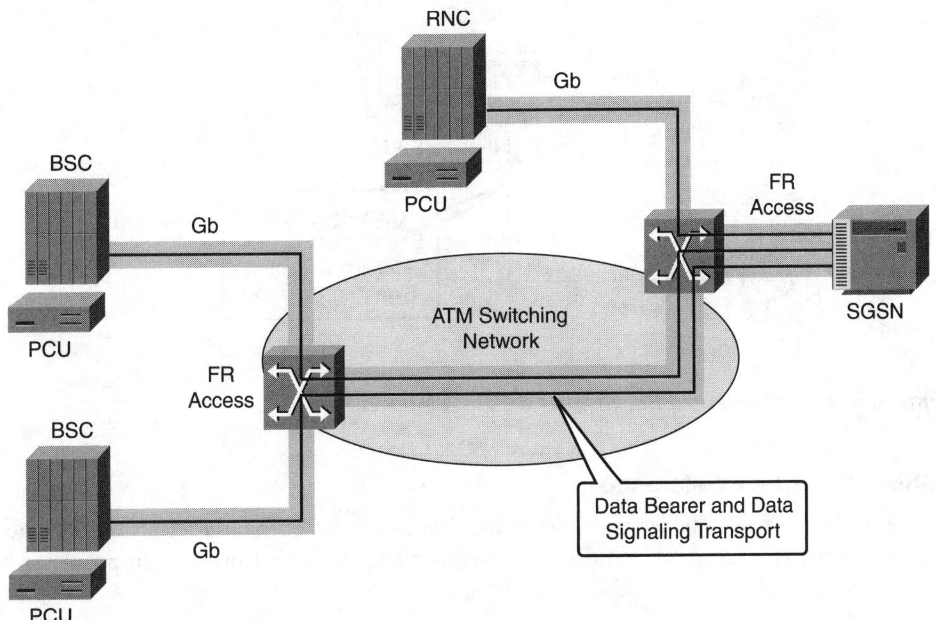

Figure 5-28 *FR RAN Aggregation of Gb Interface*

GSM Abis Interface Reference

The BSC uses the Abis interface to transport both voice and bearer data to the BTS using clocked synchronous framed transmission while leveraging Link Access Protocol–Channel D (LAPD) as the framing protocol for GSM signaling. The voice and data are transported in a structured TDM interface.

> **Note** Subsequent chapters address the transport of the Abis interface in packet format using pseudowires.

The BTS and BSC still require the necessary TDM interfaces to aggregate the converged bearers and signaling traffic, as shown in Figure 5-29.

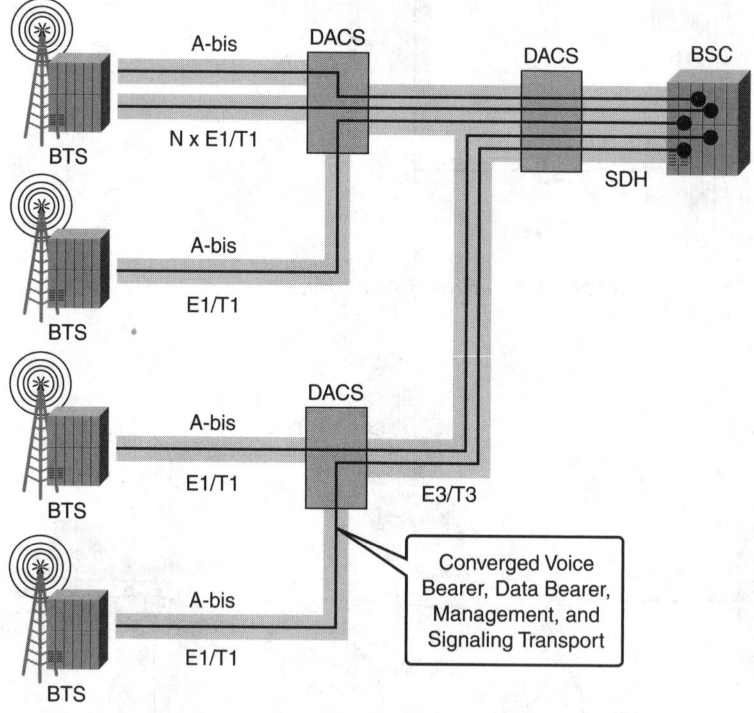

Figure 5-29 *Converged Backhaul of the Abis Interface*

GSM Gn Interface Reference

The Gn interface provides transport of the data bearer plane from the SGSN via the core network to the GGSN. The traffic is inherently packet-based because it is encapsulated in

GTP-U and transported in UDP/IP-encapsulated frames. The GTP packets can be aggregated from multiple SGSN to the GGSN by leveraging an existing packet-switched infrastructure. In many cases, the aggregation may be accomplished using an ATM network that services both FR UNI for the Gb interface and IP over ATM using RFC-1483 for the Gn traffic. Figure 5-30 shows the aggregation of SGSN to GGSN using a packet-switched network infrastructure.

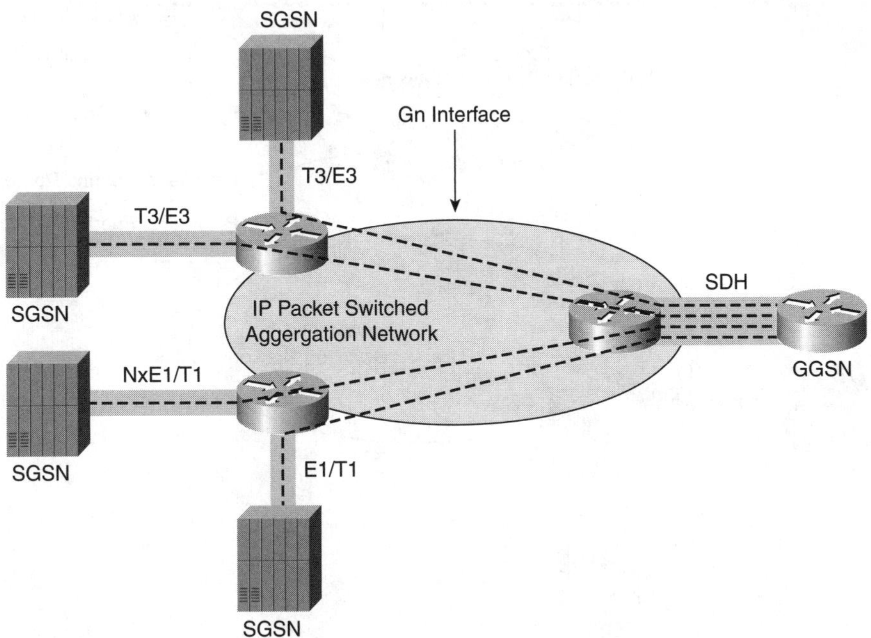

Figure 5-30 *Aggregation of SGSN to GGSN*

The packet-switched infrastructure transporting the Gn interface may use private IP addressing between SGSN and GGSN that are owned and operated by the same entity. In case the user is roaming, the SGSN resides in a partner network (also known as a *visited network*), in which case the Gn traffic must traverse a global routing exchange (GRX). The GRX is an inter-carrier IP transport network defined by the GSM Association that simplifies the roaming interconnection from one provider network to another. A service provider simply needs to connect to one GRX, which provides them the ability to route traffic to multiple GPRS networks. The 2G nomenclature changes the name of the interface of Gp because it refers to inter-provider services between the SGSN and GGSN. The packet-switched infrastructure must now accommodate IP routing paths between organizations; therefore, registered IP addresses are required, as shown in Figure 5-31.

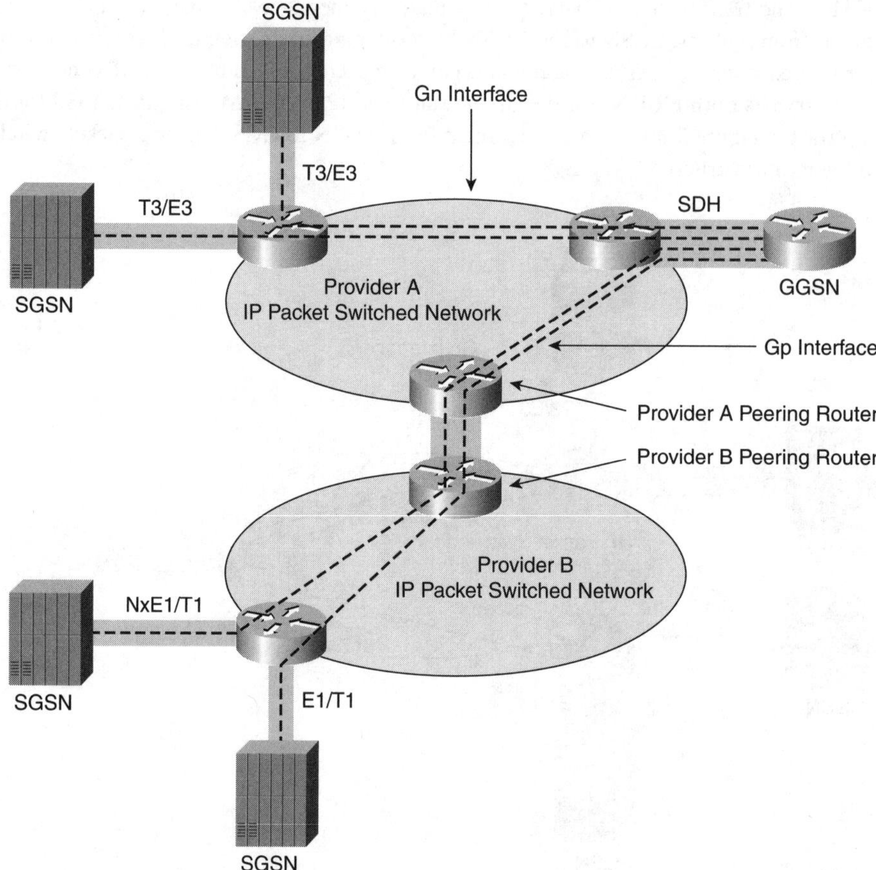

Figure 5-31 *Inter-Provider SGSN to GGSN Connectivity*

GSM Gi Interface Reference

The last interface that needs to be addressed is the Gi interface. This interface is on the GGSN, and it is the point where subscriber IP packets are handed off to the core network for routing and processing. This is the first point of exposure of the subscriber-assigned IP addresses where per-subscriber IP services may be applied. These services might include content filters, protocol filters, encryption services, and so on. The GGSN may have multiple Gi interfaces that are used to associate subscribers to particular services. The obvious service is access to the Internet; however, the provider may offer private

VPN interfaces to enterprises or third-party providers. The Gi interface is usually handed off to an Ethernet switch, where unique VLANs may be assigned to partition the services according to the subscriptions offered by the provider. Figure 5-32 shows the relationship of the GGSN to various partitioned segments that couple to the core network for transport.

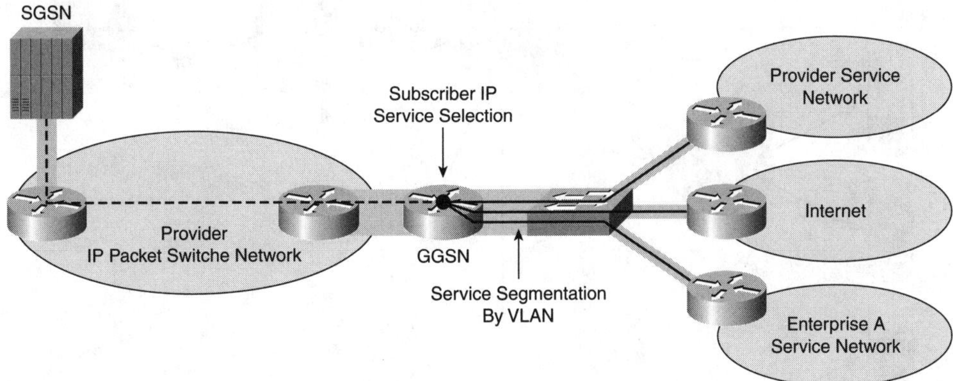

Figure 5-32 *IP Handoff of Subscriber IP Traffic*

Universal Mobile Transport Service—3G

The GSM architecture evolved to a more packet-aware infrastructure referred to as Universal Mobile Transport Service (UMTS). UMTS reuses many of the GSM elements to simplify the migration. Nevertheless, a whole new set of network elements are added that optimize data transport. The next section steps through the architecture and each of the protocol interfaces.

Architecture

The architecture of the UMTS service is modified somewhat from the GSM architecture described previously specifically in the RAN. The architecture improves support of data communication making the end-systems packet aware. The architecture shown in Figure 5-33 highlights the transition of the GSM architecture where the NodeB and RNC replace the functionality of the BTS and BSC, respectively, whereas the MGW is introduced to handle the circuit-switched voice traffic in a packet-oriented manner.

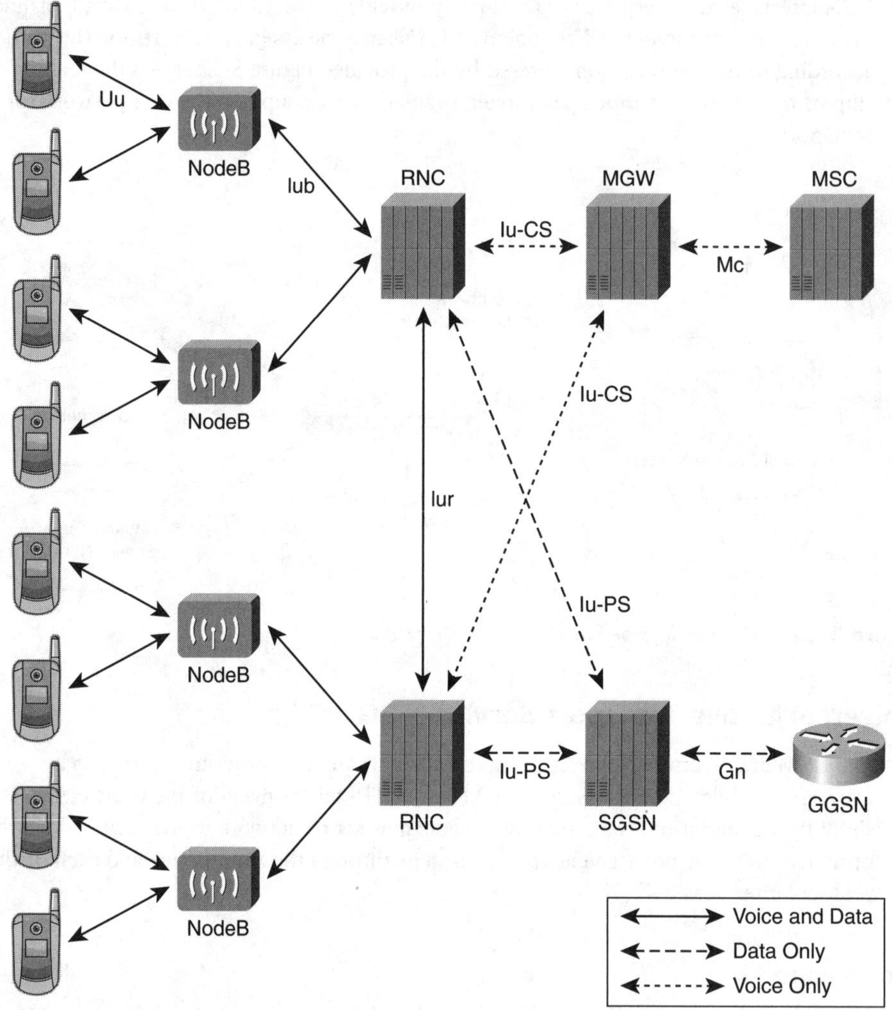

Figure 5-33 *UMTS Architecture*

UMTS Iub and Iur Interface

The NodeB receives the converged voice and data on the Uu interface from the mobile subscriber's user equipment (UE). The traffic is then aggregated via the Iub interface toward the RNC. The Iub interface is based on an ATM transport model where the ATM carries the radio network control plane protocol NodeB Application Part (NBAP) via AAL5 connection, the transport network control plane protocol ALCAP is carried via AAL5, and each user plane voice and data is carried in an assigned AAL2 virtual circuit.[9] All the control and user plane traffic (which includes voice and data) are multiplexed in that ATM circuit between the NodeB and the RNC. The AAL2 transport service ensures that the voice quality is maintained while multiplexing the user data plane into the common physical transmission layer. Figure 5-34 shows the transport model of an ATM network aggregating traffic from multiple NodeB into the RNC.

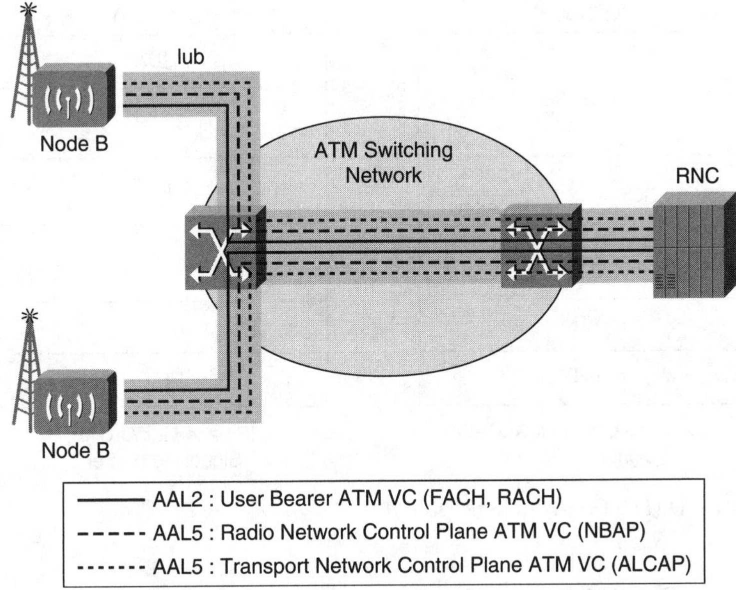

Figure 5-34 *Aggregation of NodeB Traffic into RNC*

The Iur interface between RNC provides a similar method of transport. The logical connection between RNC implies direct connectivity; however, the physical topology may use ATM in a hierarchical manner for switching of traffic, as depicted in Figure 5-34.

The 3GPP Release 5 introduced the option of carrying the Iub data transport and signaling traffic between the NodeB and RNC via the UDP/IP protocol stack. Likewise, the Iur data can be transported between RNC using IP. The absence of specific channels assigned in the transport layer mitigated the requirement for the ALCAP protocol layer used to manage ATM AAL2 channel assignments in the ATM transport model. The signaling protocol can be transported as shown in Figure 5-35. [10]

The IP backhaul mode of Iub allows transport of the IP stack via a variety of media, including PPP over HDLC, Ethernet, or PPPoA. The aggregation network can be modified to accommodate the rise in bandwidth requirements attributed to HSDPA sessions established on the Iub interface. Ideally, the sessions requesting 2.048-Mbps channels are distinguished from those channels carrying voice services in order to mitigate the impact of bursty data transactions on the voice transport. Figure 5-36 illustrates the user plane transport.

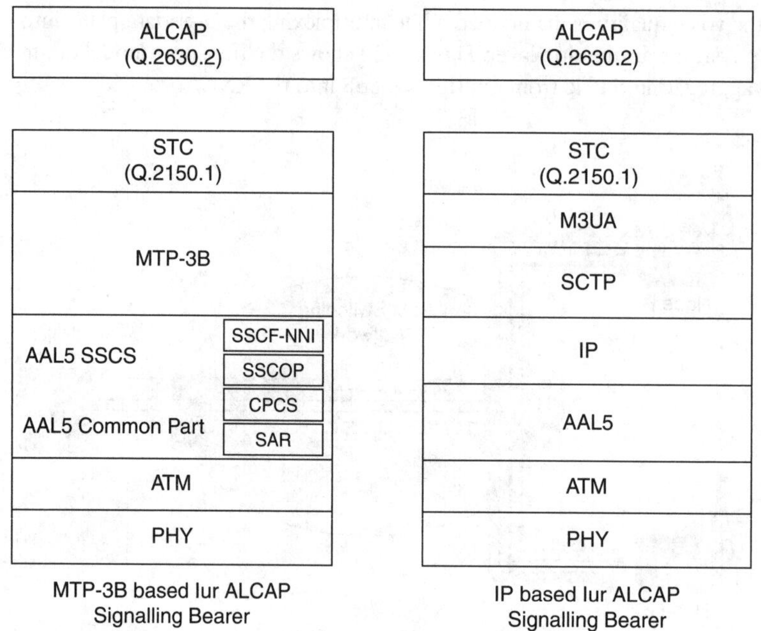

Figure 5-35 *UMTS Control Plane Transport*

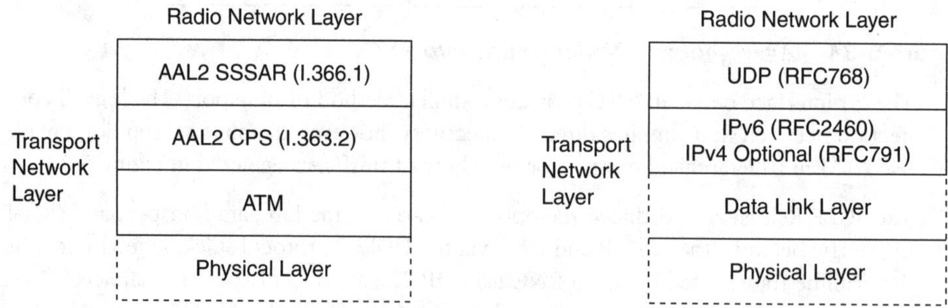

Figure 5-36 *UMTS User Plane Transport*

The RNC to RNC interface must support both signaling and user plane traffic. The 3GPP Release 5 allows the signaling to be transported via several options. [11] The support of ATM is mandatory, as is the use of IPv6; however, this doesn't preclude the use of IPv4, which was introduced in 3GPP Release 8.0. Figure 5-37 shows the encapsulation methods used for Iur signaling.

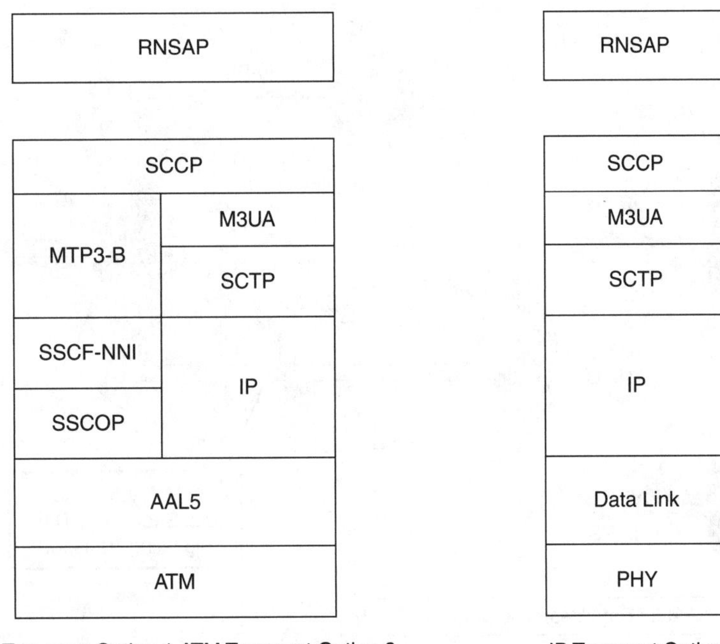

Figure 5-37 *UMTS Iur Signaling Plane Transport*

UMTS IuPS Reference Interface

The IuPS interface provides connectivity between the RNC and the SGSN such that packet-switched data may be transported between the subscriber and the core network. The IuPS interface is based on ATM AAL5, which facilitates efficient transport of IP data traffic on a common ATM infrastructure.

Release 5 introduced the option of transporting the IuPS traffic via IP protocols across PPP/HDLC circuits in order to improve the framing efficiency compared to ATM backhaul. Figure 5-38 shows the network topology used to aggregate the RNC into the SGSN.

UMTS IuCS Reference Interface

The IuCS interface provides connectivity between the RNC and the MSC such that voice bearer, management, and signaling traffic can be relayed efficiently between the RAN and CN. The signaling and management traffic is carried in an AAL5 VC, whereas the voice bearer is carried in an AAL2 VC. The AAL2 VC allows reliable delivery of the voice-bearer traffic. Figure 5-39 shows the network transport model used to aggregate the IuCS traffic carried from the RNC to the MSC.

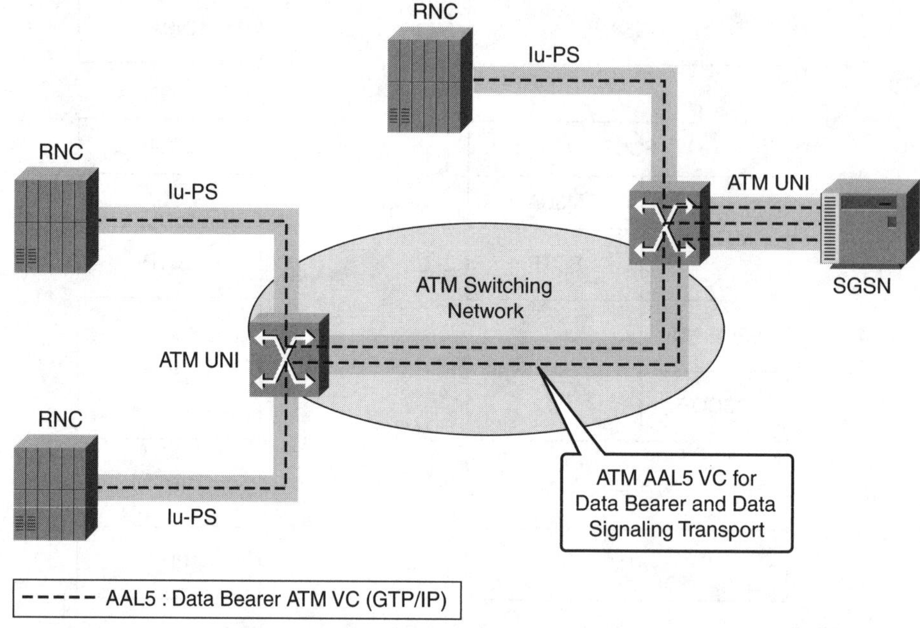

Figure 5-38 *Aggregation of IuPS Traffic*

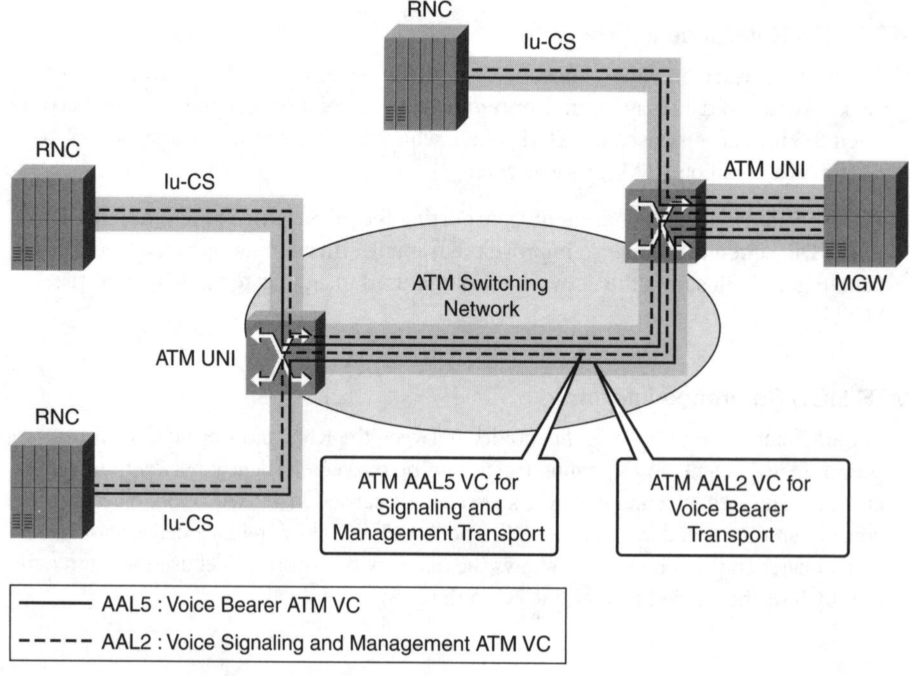

Figure 5-39 *Aggregation of IuCS Traffic*

Release 5 introduced the option of transporting the circuit-switched domain traffic over IP using RTP/UDP encapsulation. The migration to IP as an IuCS transport allows the circuit-switched and packet-switched domain to be converged onto a common backhaul infrastructure that is shared. Figure 5-40 shows the aggregation of traffic of IuCS and IuPS on a common packet-switched infrastructure.

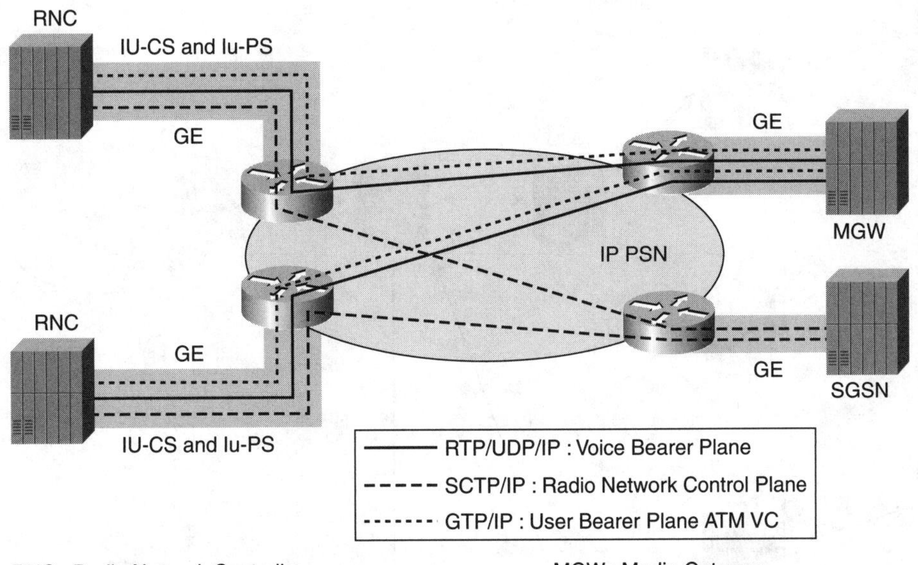

Figure 5-40 *Aggregation of IuCS Traffic on PSN*

3GPP2 Mobility Protocols

The establishment of an alternative radio access technology based on Code Division Multiplexing Access (CDMA) led to the formation of a separate standards development body referred to as 3GPP2. The 3GPP2 organization took on the task of defining the necessary network element functions and protocol interfaces in much the same manner as 3GPP handled the GERAN evolution.

Code-Division Multiplexing Access (CDMA)

Architecture

The 3GPP2 standards leverage a similar architecture to 3GPP.[12] The relationship between the BTS, BSC, and MSC are fairly consistent, as is the use of the PDSN and HA, which correlate to the GSM architecture's SGSN and GGSN. The 2G implementation (now referred to as cdmaOne) focused on the transport of voice and its associated signaling.[13]

The option of providing limited data services through an Inter-Working Function (IWF) is reflected in the architecture shown in Figure 5-41.

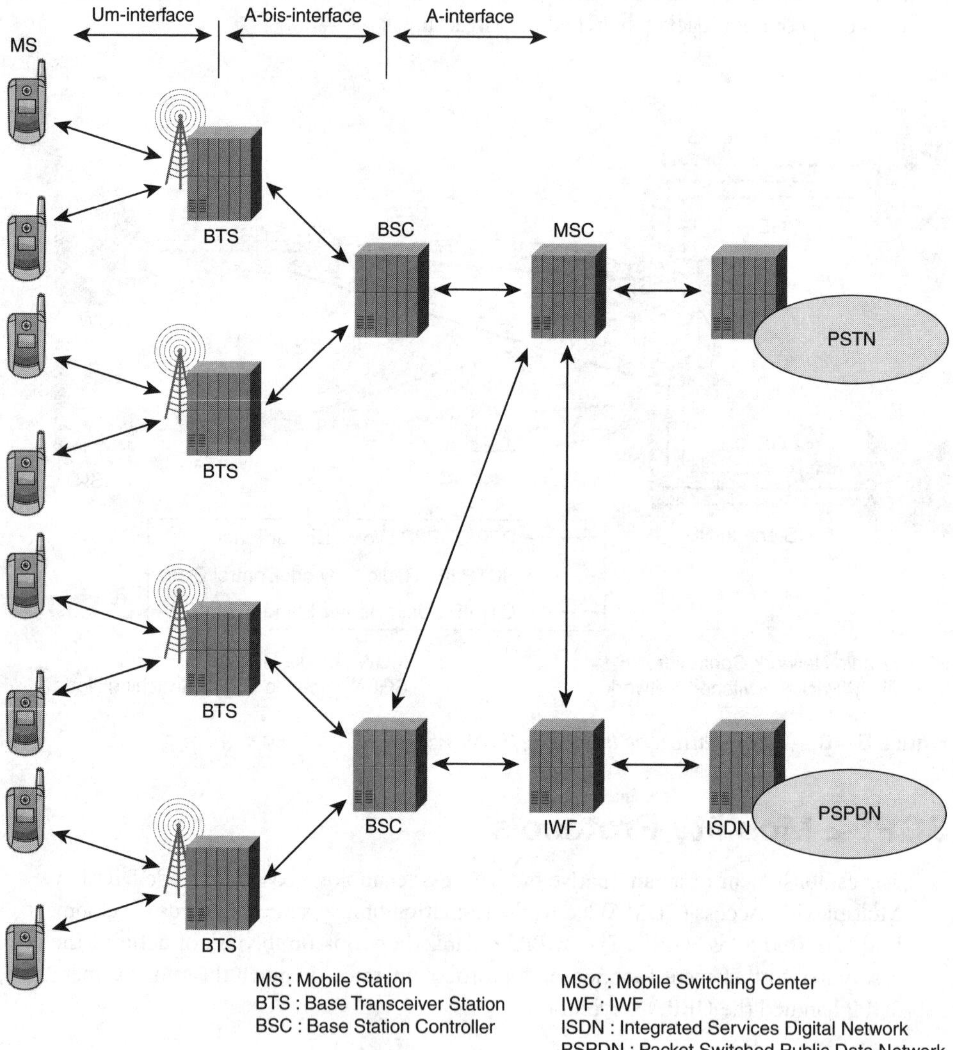

Figure 5-41 *cdmaOne Architecture Based on IS-95*

The cdmaOne implementation relies heavily on T1 and E1 facilities between the BTS and BSC, and between the BSC and the MSC. The cdmaOne architecture uses a converged backhaul model where voice and data bearer as well as signaling use the same transport infrastructure.

The CDMA standards evolved with the release of cdma2000, which provided a dedicated packet-switching infrastructure for handling packet data. Similar to the GSM architecture, the voice and data bearer are assigned distinct transport layer sessions. Specifically, voice bearer is transported by ATM AAL2, while data bearer and signaling is transported by ATM AAL5 sessions. Each of the planes is assigned a unique ATM VC for transport in a common Layer 1 circuit. Voice bearer is handled by the MSC, whereas data bearer is handled by the PDSN. The transport infrastructure may share a common T1 or E1 physical link. Increasing bandwidth requirements are met by aggregating multiple E1 and T1 circuits into an Inverse Multiplexing ATM (IMA) bundle. Higher-speed physical layer circuits, such as T3, E1, and SDH1, may be used as bandwidth requirements increase especially between the BSC and the MSC or between the BSC and PDSN. Figure 5-42 shows the typical transport infrastructure using ATM as the transport method for cdma2000.

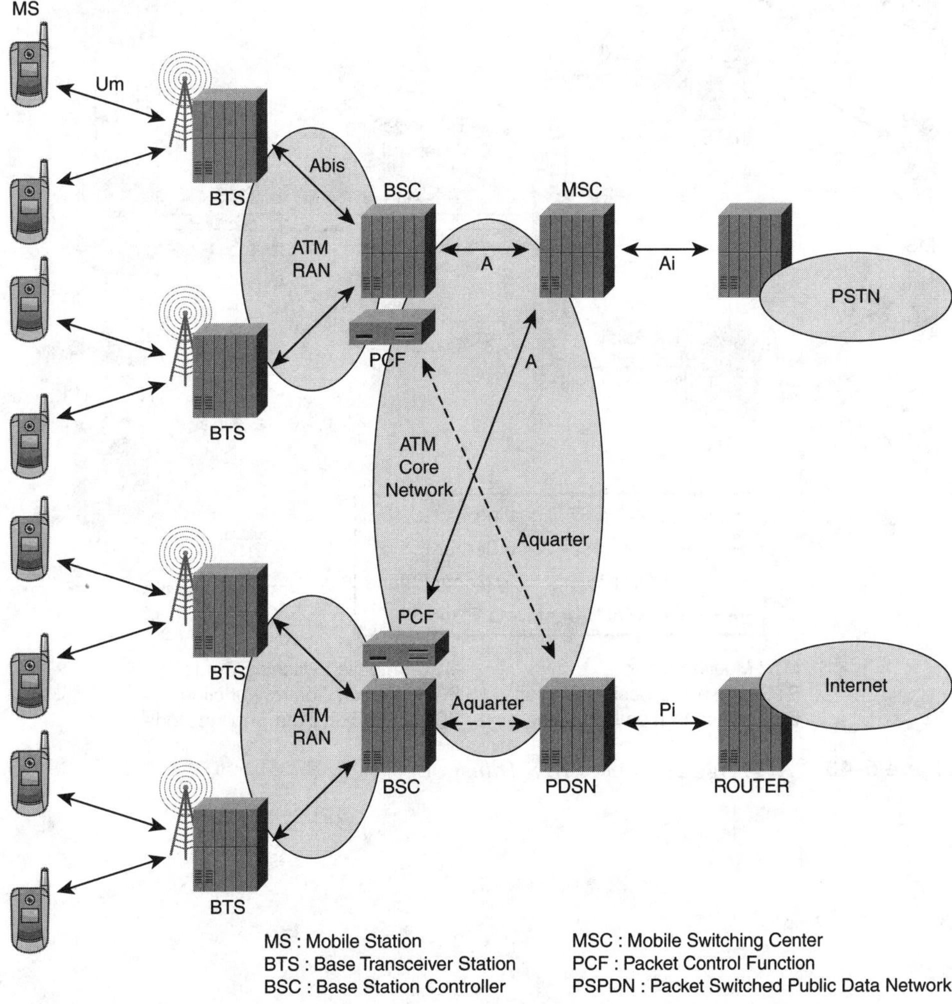

Figure 5-42 *ATM-Switching Infrastructure for CDMA*

Transport Between BTS to BSC

The Abis interface facilitates transport of the signaling and bearer traffic (both voice and data). [14] The signaling traffic is carried via an ATM AAL5 PVC established between the BTS and the BSC. The user (both voice and data) are transported via ATM AAL2 PVC. The specification of Layer 1 is flexible in the 3GPP2 architecture, although ATM transport is mandatory and is commonly used as the backhaul. The BTS and BSC take responsibility for interleaving voice and data in the Abis user interface in an efficient manner that protects the voice bearer services. Figure 5-43 shows the aggregation of BTS sites into a common BSC using ATM-switching infrastructure.

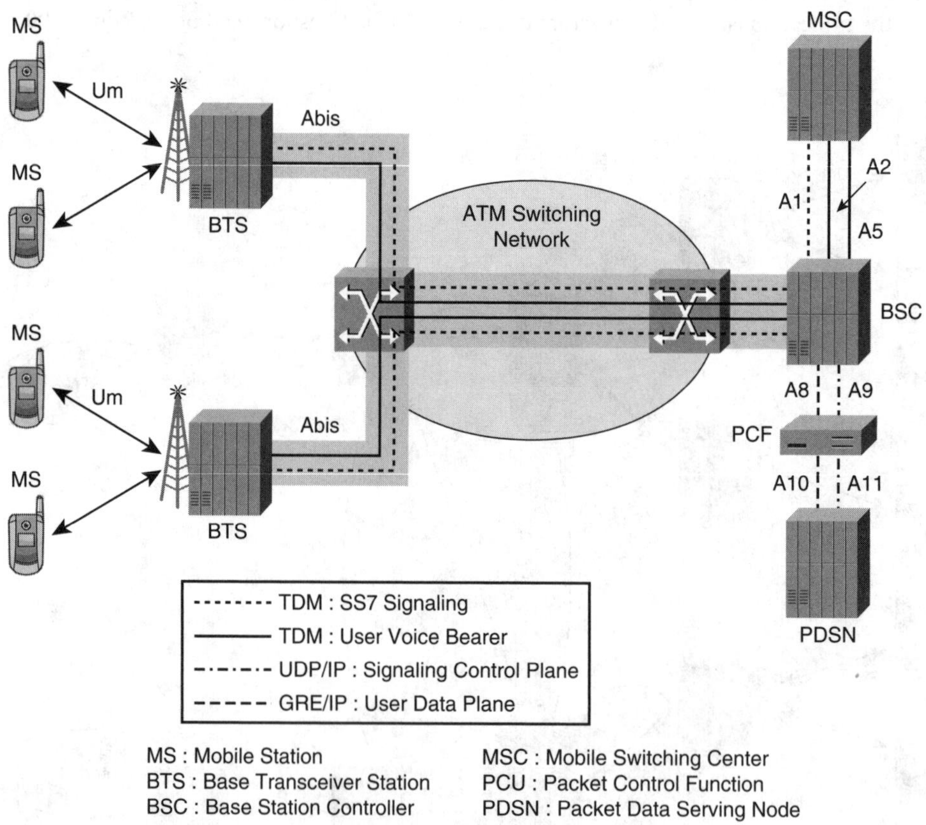

Figure 5-43 *ATM Aggregation of BTS Transport*

Transport Between BSC to MSC

The transport between the BSC and MSC must carry three classes of traffic, as follows:

- Signaling
- Circuit-oriented voice calls
- Circuit-oriented data calls

The signaling is carried via the A1 interface, whereas the user voice and data calls are carried by the A2 and A5 interface respectively. The signaling application layer is handled by the classic SS7 protocols, specifically SCCP carried in message transfer part (MTP). MTP has traditionally used TDM infrastructure as the transport infrastructure. The next-generation architecture leveraging IP infrastructure allows the transport of the signaling application layer using Session Control Transport Protocol (SCTP), as described in Chapter 4, "An IP Refresher." The A2 and A5 transport must carry PCM user data and streaming data, which requires a synchronous transport as well. The architecture usually relies on high-speed TDM circuits, such as T3, E3, and SDH facilities, to transport the set of interfaces between the BSC and MSC.

Transport Between BSC to PDSN

The transport between the BSC and PDSN is inherently data oriented; therefore, a variety of transport options may be used for backhaul. The cdma2000 specifications require the ability to use ATM as the method of transport while allowing alternatives that are more bandwidth efficient. Two options exist: one where the packet control function (PCF) resides in the BSC, and one where the PCF is decoupled from the BSC. Typically, the PCF is commonly co-located with the BSC. The A8 interface between the BSC and PCF handles user data traffic where the PCF relays the information up to the PDSN on the A10 interface. The BSC uses the A9 interface to the PCF for signaling, which relays the signaling to the PDSN using the A11 interface. The A9/A11 interfaces use UDP/IP as the packet transport, whereas the A8/A10 interfaces transport the user data in Generic Route Encapsulation (GRE) tunneled packets carried in IP. The IP traffic may use a variety of L2 transport facilities and commonly share the SDH or ATM facilities that are likely to exist based on the legacy 2G architecture. The higher data rates on the air-link drive increased capacity requirements in the backhaul transport for user data. In many cases, new transport facilities are needed to handle the growth in data that outstrips the capabilities of the legacy transport network. Fortunately, the IP protocols may leverage a variety of layer 2 facilities.

Transport Between the PDSN and the HA

The PDSN may interface directly with the core network where subscriber IP packets are decapsulated from the GRE and routed according to the subscriber's target address. This method, referred to as Simple IP, uses a handoff of the user IP data traffic to the core network. Alternatively, the PDSN may tunnel the subscriber IP traffic via an assigned Home

Agent (HA) using the protocol referred to as Mobile IP. The handoff of the subscriber IP into the Mobile IP tunnels still allows a variety of transport facilities to aggregate user traffic. The HA is then responsible for presenting the subscriber IP traffic to the core network and returning IP traffic to the subscriber. Figure 5-44 highlights the difference between Simple IP and Mobile IP.

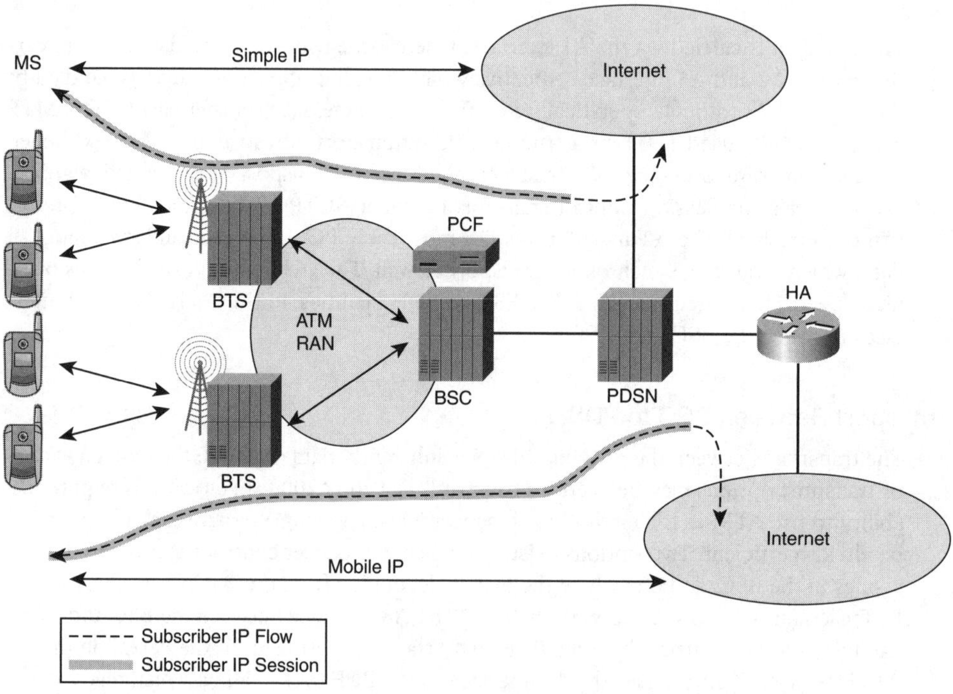

Figure 5-44 *Simple IP and Mobile IP Interfaces*

IP Transport of CDMA 3G Interfaces

The transition of CDMA to High-Rate Packet Data (HRPD) services leads to much higher bandwidth consumption on the access network. ATM transport becomes inefficient when handling bursty data and requires expensive ATM transport facilities. The migration to native IP packet interfaces on the BTS, BSC, and PDSN allows the data transactions to be accommodated by more efficient L1 transport facilities such as Ethernet. Each of the interfaces described previously have been provided the option of using transport technologies other than ATM.

Abis IP-Enabled Transport

The Abis interface carries both user traffic (both voice and data) as well as signaling as referenced in 3GPP2 A.S0003-Av2.0. The TIA/EIA-828-A specification provides alternatives for the transport of signaling and user traffic that may be more efficient than ATM. [15] The consistency of these transport interfaces (particularly on the Abis interface) is somewhat subject to vendor's choice; therefore, the operator is likely to be constrained to a single vendor to support the optional interfaces. The signaling transport has several options, as shown in Figure 5-45.

Mandatory	Optional	Optional	Optional
IOS Application	IOS Application	IOS Application	IOS Application
TCP	TCP	UDP	SCTP
IP	IP	IP	IP
AAL5	Link Layer	Link Layer	Link Layer
ATM	Physical Layer	Physical Layer	Physical Layer
Physical Layer			

Figure 5-45 *Abis Signaling Transport*

The use of IP as the transport means allows the operator to select from a wide variety of link layer protocols, including TDM, Ethernet, ATM, and POS. The general requirements of the higher-layer application must still be met from a performance perspective (specifically reliable transport); therefore, many operators attempt to emulate the ATM model using IP through various pseudowire techniques referred to as RAN Optimization, as described in the Chapter 7.

The user transport is slightly different and can be described as follows (see Figure 5-46).

Mandatory	Optional	Optional	Optional
Abis Traffic	Abis Traffic	Abis Traffic	Abis Traffic
	UDP	cUDP	cUDP
SSSAR	IP	SSCS	PPPmux
AAL2	Link Layer	AAL2	Link Layer
ATM	Physical Layer	ATM	Physical Layer
Physical Layer		Physical Layer	

Figure 5-46 *Abis User Plane Transport*

The user data consists of both voice and data; therefore, the alternative transport methods must ensure that the performance bounds are maintained. Specifically, the transport of voice in the Abis interface is bounded by the delay budget and jitter buffers associated with the end-systems that recover the voice bearer. The use of alternative transports must ensure that the limits of the delay budget and jitter buffers are not exceeded; otherwise, voice bearer services are adversely affected. Data bearer services may be more tolerant because they inherently afford more elasticity in the delay and jitter attributed to network buffering.

Signaling Transport

The signaling interfaces characterized as A1, A3, A7, A9, and A11 all require reliable transport.

The A1 interface connects the BSC to the MSC and provides signaling of circuit-switched data and voice services and relies on a protocol stack, illustrated in Figure 5-47.

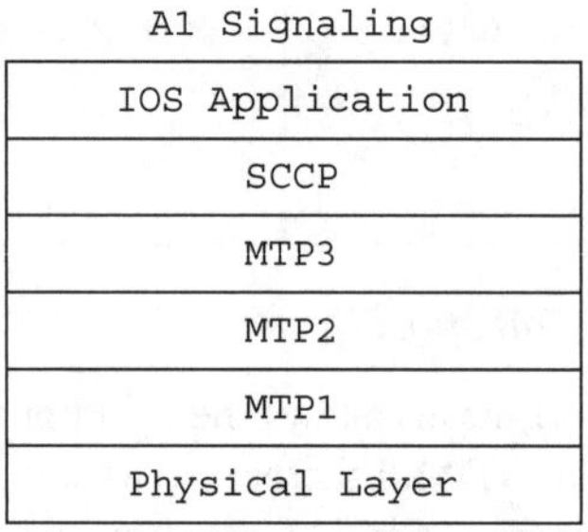

A1 Signaling
IOS Application
SCCP
MTP3
MTP2
MTP1
Physical Layer

Figure 5-47 *Signaling Protocol Transport*

The MTP is commonly transported via TDM circuits, such as T1 or E1, and may be included in channel-structured T3 or E3 circuits.

The A3 and A7 interface connects a BSC to another BSC for inter-BSC handoff of traffic. The protocol stack is illustrated in Figure 5-48.

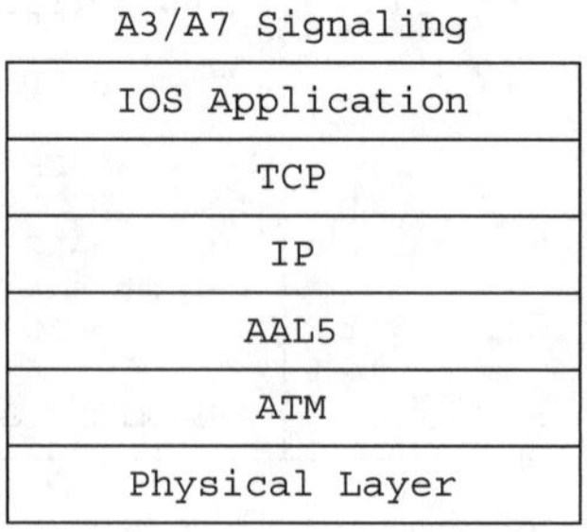

A3/A7 Signaling
IOS Application
TCP
IP
AAL5
ATM
Physical Layer

Figure 5-48 *BSC to BSC Protocol Transport*

The ATM-switching infrastructure may be used to provide interconnectivity between the BSC in a hierarchical manner in order to minimize the transmission and interfaces costs of meshing the BSC together. The transport architecture may be described as illustrated in Figure 5-49.

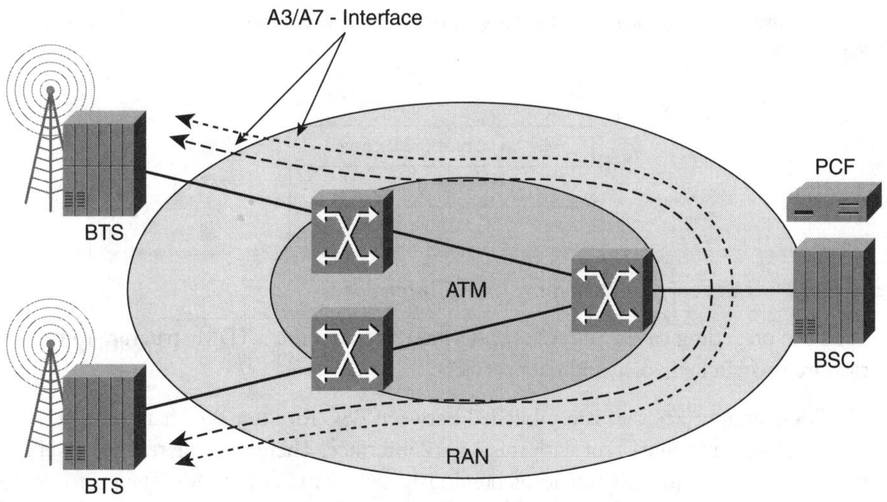

Figure 5-49 *Hierarchical ATM Switching of A3/A7 Interface*

The A9 and A11 protocol stack are implemented as IP applications, as shown in Figure 5-50.

A9 Signaling	A11 Signaling
TCP/UDP	UDP
IP	IP
Link Layer	Link Layer
Physical Layer	Physical Layer

Figure 5-50 *Signaling Transport of A9/A11 Interface*

The A9/A11 protocols may be transported in the existing ATM infrastructure or use alternative link layer transport technologies for improved efficiency.

User Transport

The A2 interface must use a channel-structured TDM circuit to transport the voice bearer. The voice bearer may be carried in the protocol stack, as shown in Figure 5-51.

56/64 kbps PCM		64 kbps UDI
DS0	or	DS0

Figure 5-51 *Voice Bearer Transport on A2 Interface*

The A5 interface that carries data streams between the BSC and the MSC is shown in Figure 5-52.

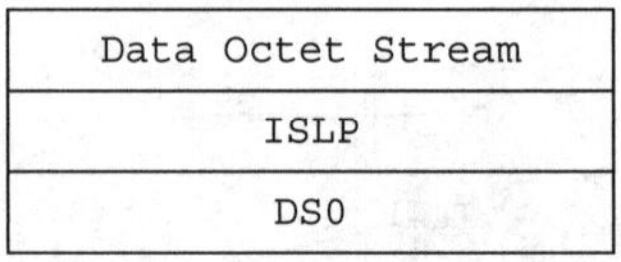

Data Octet Stream
ISLP
DS0

Figure 5-52 *Data Stream Transport on A5 Interface*

In all the preceding cases, the A2 and A5 interfaces require a TDM structure to transport the circuit-switched voice and data services.

The A3 user interface that is established between BSC for inter-BSC handoff also relies on ATM, which is consistent with the A3/A7 interface. Therefore, the transport services may be consistent for this traffic, as previously shown in Figure 5-46. The protocol stack is modified accordingly as the traffic consists of circuit-switched voice and requires a more reliable transport, as shown in Figure 5-53.

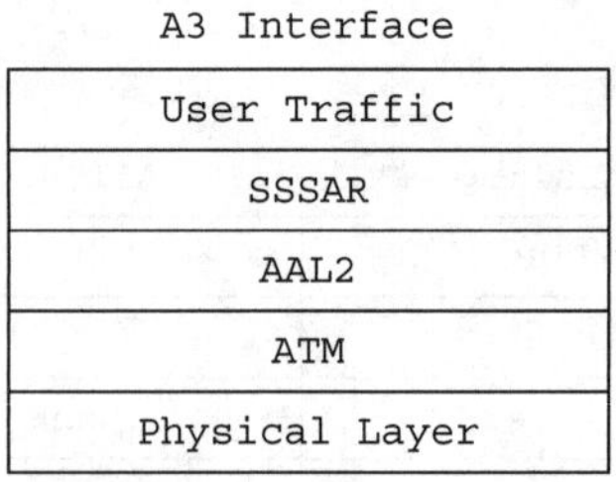

A3 Interface
User Traffic
SSSAR
AAL2
ATM
Physical Layer

Figure 5-53 *Voice Transport on A3 Interface*

The user data services are much more amenable to using packet-switched technologies. The inherent encapsulation in IP affords the operator more flexibility in selection of the link layer, as shown in Figure 5-54.

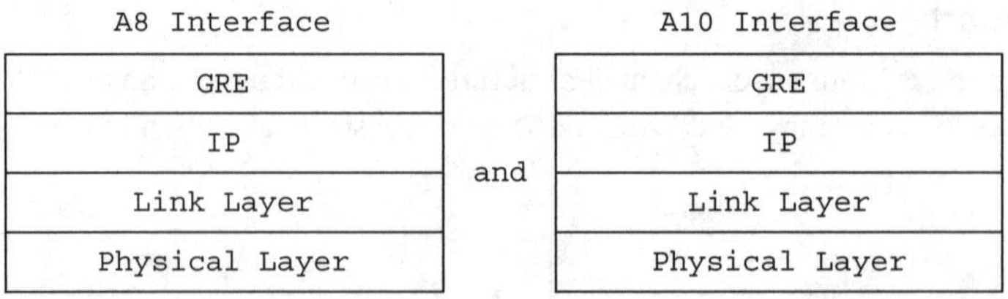

A8 Interface		A10 Interface
GRE		GRE
IP	and	IP
Link Layer		Link Layer
Physical Layer		Physical Layer

Figure 5-54 *Data Transport on A8/A10 Interface*

The operator is at liberty to select the link layer necessary to transport the A10 interface between the PCF and the PDSN such that efficient use of data services is provided. Initial deployments may have used ATM as originally specified; however, more efficient means of packet transport such as PPP have been used to aggregate the user data.

3GPP2 Mobility Protocols Summary

The CDMA architecture defined by the 3GPP2 organization provides a framework for transitioning the wireless services to IP infrastructures in an evolutionary manner. The existing 2G and 3G services are likely to co-exist for an extended period of time. The wireless operator needs to provide an efficient means of transporting both the 2G services described previously, along with the 3G service described in this section.

Long-Term Evolution/System Architecture Evolution: 4G

The growth in data usage has stressed the 2G, 2.5G, and 3G systems to the point where a new architectural model is required. Whereas previous architectures provided facilities for establishing and assigning voice bearer channels, the Long-Term Evolution/System Architecture Evolution (LTE/SAE) is focused on optimizing data transport. There is an implicit assumption that voice will be presented to the network as data. This evolution is consistent with the architectural evolution on wireline networks. The basic premise is that designing a network that transports high volumes of data inherently allows the transport of low bandwidth voice that is encoded as packet data. Instead of optimizing the air-link and transport for a small percentage of traffic (voice) at much greater costs, the operators optimize the air-link and transport for data and accommodate voice. The absence of voice bearer channels means that voice packets must be readily identified and differentiated in their treatment in the transport and air-link. Queue management based on traffic classes, as described in Chapter 3, becomes of paramount importance. The next few sections describe the protocols used in LTE/SAE and highlight the relevance of IP in the transport infrastructure.

LTE/SAE Architecture

The LTE/SAE architecture evolved from the 3GPP standards—specifically, the UTRA architecture deployed for UMTS. LTE provides a transition to All-IP Network (AIPN) architecture, as illustrated in Figure 5-55. [16]

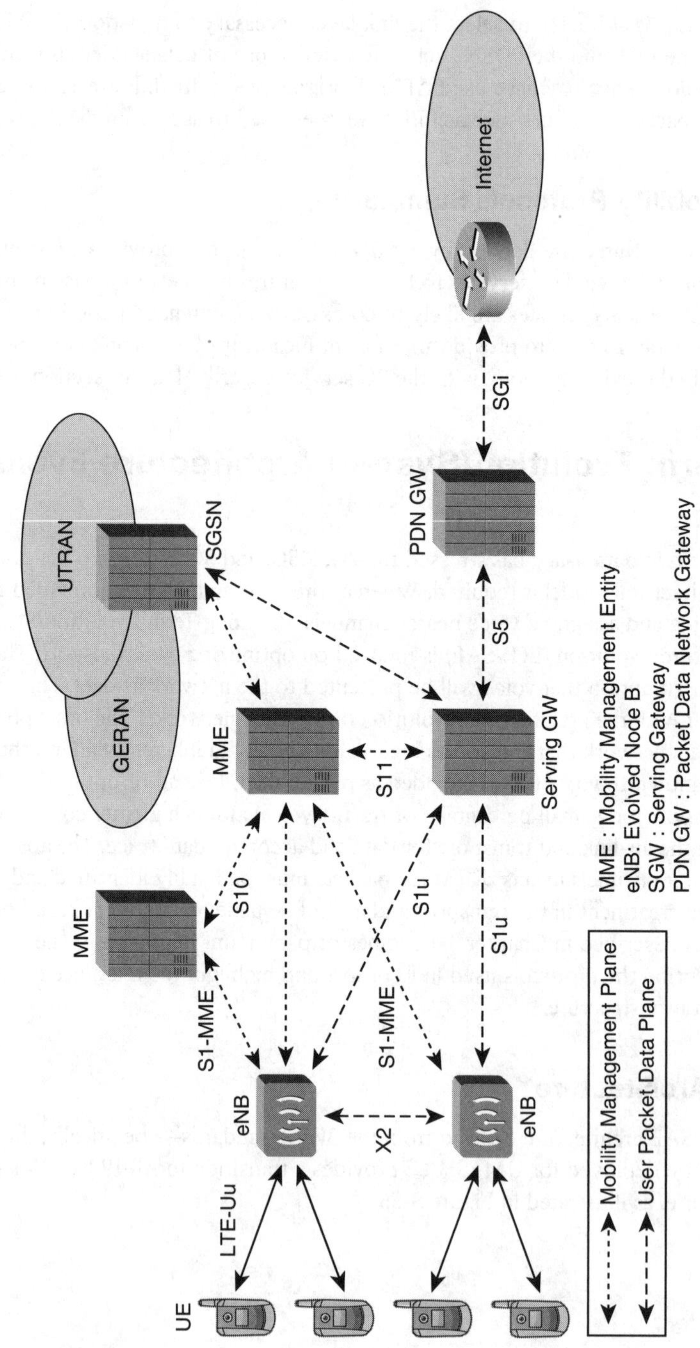

Figure 5-55 *LTE/SAE Architecture*

The eNodeB serves as the radio access system providing the management of the air-link to the User Equipment (UE). The eNodeB uses the S1-MME control plane interface to communicate with a Mobility Management Entity (MME). The eNodeB may connect to one or more MME for control plane management. The eNodeB uses the S1-u interface as the user plane interface to transport both voice and data to the Serving Gateway (S-GW), whereas the X2 interface is used between the eNodeB systems. The LTE architecture provides native IP interfaces for transport of the control plane and user plane between all three entities; therefore, the All-IP Network infrastructure provides a flattened infrastructure in the RAN. The control plane is decoupled from the user plane by separating the functions in the MME and S-GW, respectively. They effectively replace the RNC and SGSN from a 3G architecture. The eNodeB, MME, and S-GW provide a lot more flexibility in handling mobility of the UE while maintaining user plane connectivity.

eNodeB S1-MME RAN Transport Interfaces

The eNodeB uses the S1-MME interface to transport the control plane to the MME. The transport must be reliable; therefore, the protocol stack leverages SCTP for the signaling data and control data. The eNodeB may be connected to several MME to accommodate handoff, provide for reliable connectivity, and improve control plane scalability. The divergent control plane may co-exist in the same transport as the user plane, while appropriate QoS mechanisms are employed to ensure reliable delivery.

Figure 5-56 shows the relationship of connectivity between the eNodeB and the MME. [17]

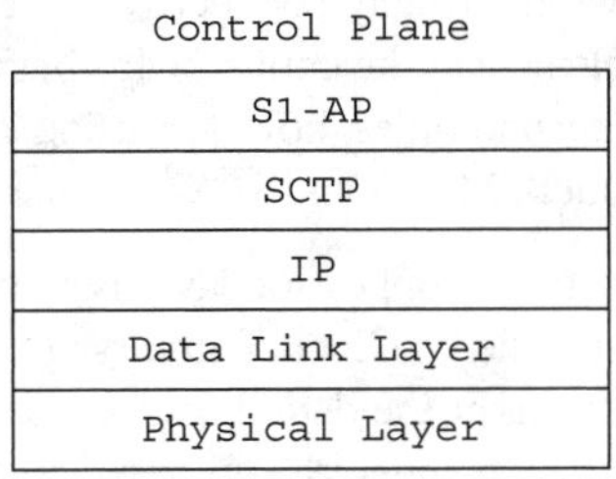

Control Plane
S1-AP
SCTP
IP
Data Link Layer
Physical Layer

Figure 5-56 *S1-MME Transport*

eNodeB S1 Transport Interfaces

The eNBs are also connected by means of the S1 interface to the Evolved Packet Core (EPC). The eNBs support a many-to-many relation between SGWs and eNBs by using multiple S1 interfaces. The S1 interface transports the data plane for both voice and data bearer services using an encapsulation method, as shown in Figure 5-57.

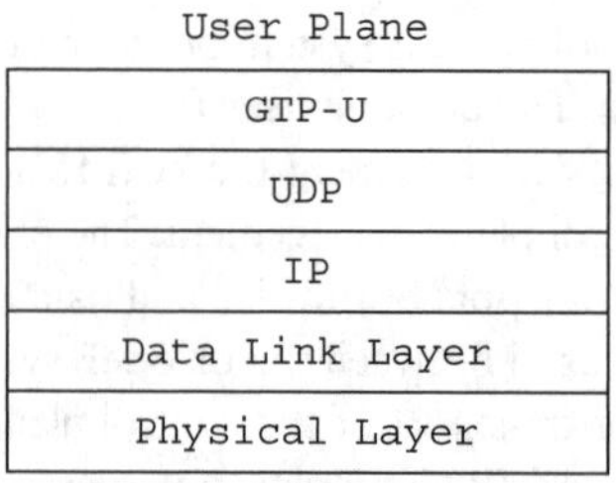

User Plane

GTP-U
UDP
IP
Data Link Layer
Physical Layer

Figure 5-57 *S1 Transport Interface*

The voice bearer and data bearer are carried in the GTP-U encapsulated frame. The distinction between the voice and data must be made by relating the QoS Class Identifier (QCI) to the lower-protocol layers in the form of DSCP on the IP layer. The application layer is responsible for identifying the traffic class and specifying the association of a particular bearer to a class. The DSCP may be correlated to QoS mechanisms enforced in the data link layer to ensure that the voice bearer services are treated appropriately.[18]

eNodeB X2 Transport Interfaces

The eNodeB are connected via the X2 interface to facilitate handoffs between sites. [19] The X2-AP signaling protocols are transported by SCTP to ensure reliable delivery of the control plan. The user plane is transported via GTP-U for transmittal of the bearer traffic between eNB. More importantly, the eNodeB uses IP as the transport for signaling and bearer traffic to the MME and SGW, respectively. An IP-routed network in the RAN aggregation inherently allows any-to-any connectivity between the various eNodeB, MME, and SGW network elements. The connectivity between these network elements could use layer 2 transport technologies; however, using layer 2 transport would mitigate the value of having the eNodeB, MME, and SGW IP-enabled.

Much like the S1 interface set, the application layer is responsible for specifying the QoS Class Identifier (QCI) that sets the DSCP code points in the IP header. The DSCP can be correlated with QoS mechanisms at the data link layer to ensure that the signaling is delivered in a reliable and timely manner, the voice bearer is delivered with priority, and the data bearer is maintained during the handoff between eNB. Figure 5-58 shows the relationship of the signaling and bearer plane as it relates to the X2 transport plane.

Mobility Management Entity (MME) S10, S11, and S3 and S4 Transport Interfaces

The Mobility Management Entity serves as the control plane entity for the E-UTRAN. It facilitates all the Inter-EUTRAN handovers, Inter-RAT handovers, mobility management, and session management. As previously noted, the MME communicates with the eNB via the S1-MME interfaces. The MME also needs to coordinate the session management with peer MME via the S10 interface. The assignment of the termination point of S1-U interface from the eNB toward the SGW is handled by the MME through the S11 interface. The S3 interface coordinates connections from the legacy UTRAN and GERAN

SGSN into the MME, whereas the S4 interface provides the tunneling of user data from the GERAN/UTRAN to the SGW. All three interfaces use the same signaling plane construct as between the eNB and the MME. Specifically, the transport protocol on the S10 and S11 reference interface is defined as shown in Figure 5-59.

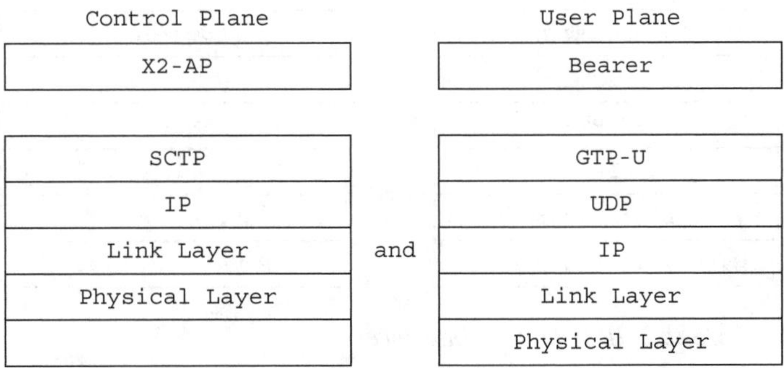

Figure 5-58 *X2 Transport Interface*

Control Plane

GTP-C

UDP

IP

Data Link Layer

Physical Layer

Figure 5-59 *S10 and S11 Transport Interface*

PDN-GW S5 and S8 Interface

The PDN-GW serves as the Local Mobility Anchor (LMA). It assigns the UE an IP address that will be viable for the duration of the session on the AIPA network. This IP address (IPv6 is mandatory or, optionally, IPv4) is assigned to the client for establishing connections to the other IP endpoints accessible via the core network. The Serving Gateway facilitates the relay of the Mobile IP user plane and control plane from the E-UTRAN toward the PDN-GW in the Evolved Packet Core (EPC). The S5/S8b protocol supports two tunneling mechanisms: GTP and PMIP. Use of one tunneling mechanism over the other depends on the inter-operability between the Home PLMN and the Visited PLMN. The PMIP is the assumed method for the S5 interface where the S-GW and P-GW have a trusted relationship. The user plane is aggregated at the SGW, where the GTP-U is terminated and the Proxy Mobile IPv6 is established to the PGW. The SGW serves as the proxy function in the Mobile IP protocols. This function allows the user equipment to operate without knowledge of the MIP protocol stack. The S5/S8b interface uses the PMIPv6 control plane to manage the session state between the SGW and the PGW. Figure 5-60 shows the relationship of Mobile IP on the S5/S8b interface.

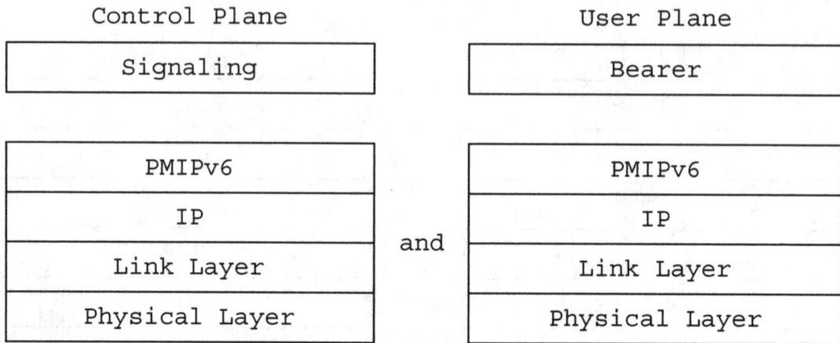

Figure 5-60 *S5/S8b MIP Reference Interface*

Alternatively, the SGW or PGW may prefer to use the GTP-U encapsulation to tunnel the subscriber traffic, in which case the encapsulation between the two entities is reflected as shown in Figure 5-61.

Control Plane		User Plane
Signaling		Bearer
GTP-C		GTP-U
UDP		UDP
IP	and	IP
Link Layer		Link Layer
Physical Layer		Physical Layer

Figure 5-61 *S5/S8b GTP Reference Interface*

The option to use PMIP facilitates a more universal mobility management service for alternative 3GPP access infrastructures. The PMIP enables open access via the S4 interface to the SGSN for GSM and UTRAN mobility. In addition, PMIP facilitates access from non-3GPP. However, the default method for connecting the GERAN and UTRAN is through the use of GTP, as shown in Figure 5-61.

LTE RAN Transport Infrastructure

The transition from L2 transport protocols to IP enables the 4G architecture to leverage IP routing for optimal forwarding of data packets. Voice is still a financially lucrative service for mobile operators; however, the growth of data and the cost of the infrastructure to efficiently handle data driven mobile connections has led operators to invest in packet-switched core networks and Radio Access Networks. Although voice can be encoded into bit streams that are more efficient in TDM than a PSN, the aggregate efficiency of the PSN transport is optimized when voice bearer load is a small fraction of the data bearer load. The mobile operator who is able to transition voice to packet is able to leverage a converged infrastructure that is far more efficient. Figure 5-62 shows a packet-switched architecture serving the RAN where all the traffic flows (control, management, bearer) are served by a common PSN.

The ability to leverage new L2 transport technologies such as Ethernet backhaul allows the operator to find more economical means of aggregating both voice and data. The bandwidth growth of data bearer is more readily accommodated by the packet-switched transport network.

As mentioned at the beginning of this chapter, clocking is of particular importance with CDMA and OFDMA systems. The operator may use several approaches to transition to an All-IP access network, including the following:

- GPS clock synchronization
- TDM clock synchronization
- Clock recovery through packet-timing protocols

The use of GPS clock synchronization requires the investment clock receivers at every tower. The TDM clock synchronization method is easy to use because the legacy 2G and 3G voice services continue to incorporate the previous investment in TDM transport infrastructures, while the operator migrates all the data services to a packet-switched backhaul model. The last approach requires the deployment of packet clock recovery systems based on protocols such as ITU-T Rec. G.8261/Y.1361.

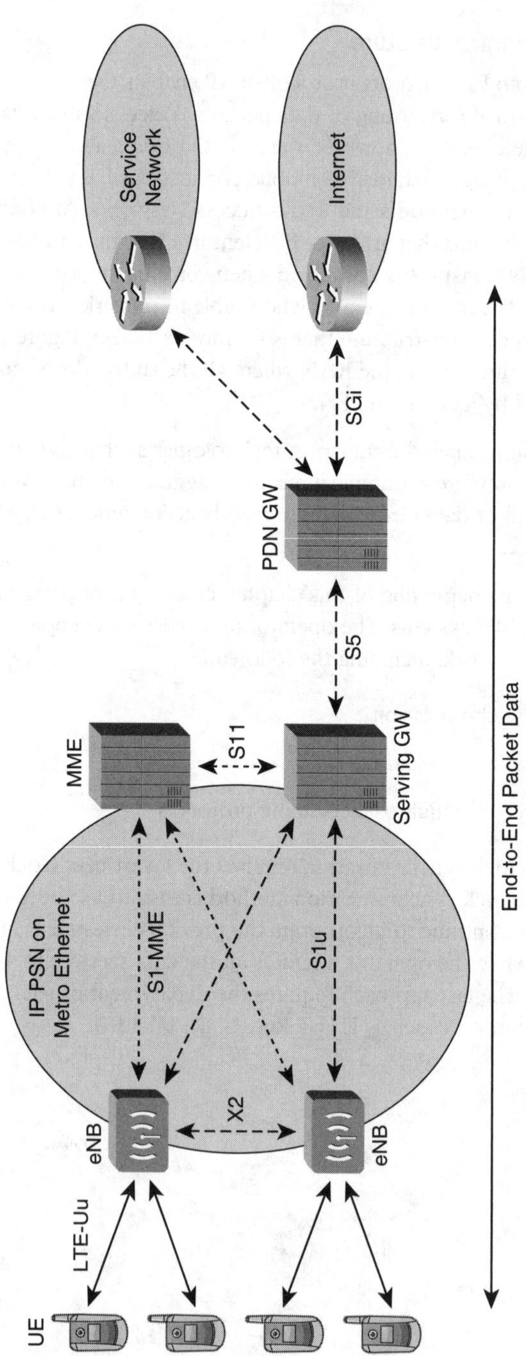

Figure 5-62 *Converged PSN RAN*

Worldwide Interoperability for Mobile Access (WiMAX)

The previous sections focused on LTE/SAE as the evolution from 3G architectures based on CDMA and TDM radio technologies. Independently, the Institution of Electronics and Electrical Engineers (IEEE) began the development of IEEE 802.16. The WiMAX Forum assumed responsibility for defining a network architecture that would allow interoperability amongst network elements using the WiMAX radio access technology.

WiMAX Architecture

The WiMAX Forum defined a network architecture using IEEE 802.16 as an access technique to a network reference model that inherently uses IP networking technologies to deliver both fixed and mobile radio access services. The IEEE 802.16e specification introduces the mobility models, whereas previous specifications only addressed fixed radio access services. [20,21]

The IEEE protocol addresses the radio access link, whereas the WiMAX Forum published specifications to address the Access Service Network (ASN) and the Core Services Network (CSN). The forum's specifications provide a framework to provide fixed IP and Mobile IP access to mobile subscribers. The architecture provides a means of decoupling the ASN from the CSN such that two independent entities can operate as Network Access Provider (NAP) and Network Service Provider (NSP), respectively. The use of standard IP protocols between the network entities assures interoperability when implementing handoffs and roaming agreements.

The ASN functional components in the WiMAX architecture include the Base Station (BS) and the Access Service Node Gateway (ASN-GW). The ASN provides intra-ASN mobility, while also facilitating handoffs to adjacent ASN. The ASN-GW functionally serves as the Foreign Agent (FA) in much the same way that CDMA2000 uses the PDSN to serve as the FA.

The CSN functional components in the WiMAX architecture include the Home Agent (HA), which is also similar to the CDMA reference architecture. The CSN provides subscriber IP connectivity to services either on the Internet or in NSP-provided logical partitions (for example, enterprise, walled garden servers, and so on).

Figure 5-63 shows the WiMAX Forum's architecture defined for WiMAX connectivity. The focus of this section is on the radio access network transport required within the ASN and to the CSN.

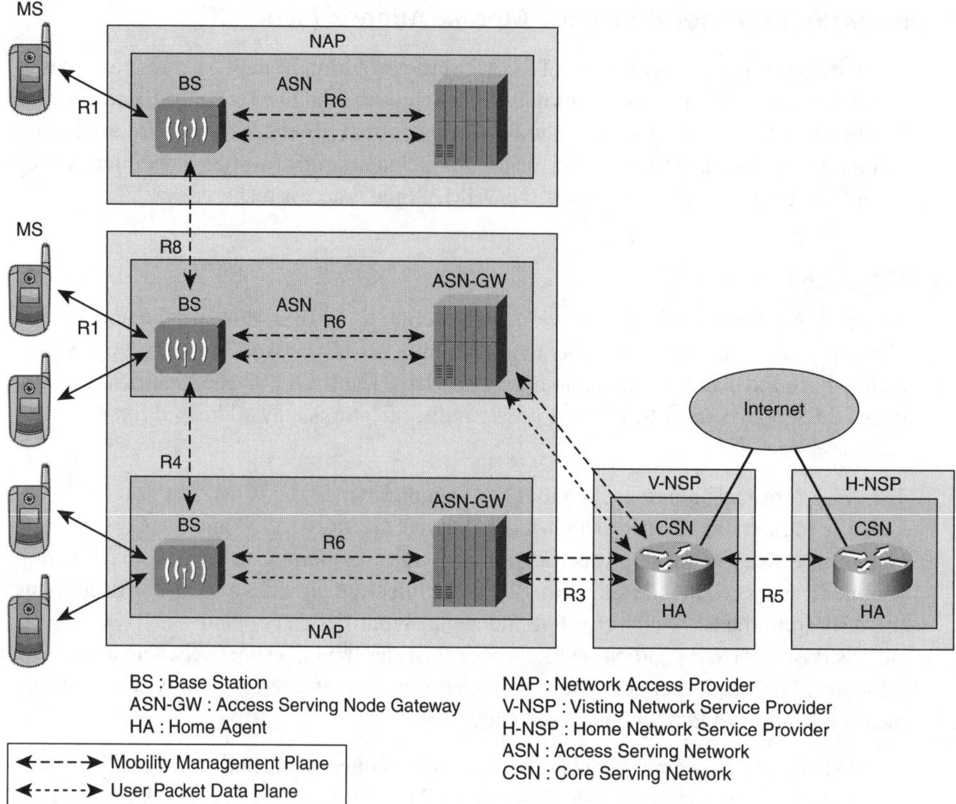

Figure 5-63 *WiMAX Architecture*

Access Service Network Reference Interfaces

The ASN uses several reference points to describe the relationship between functional entities within the NAP. The R1 interface represents the radio interface from the BS toward the mobile subscriber. The transport interfaces include the BS uplink interface, R6, and the ASN-GW uplink interface, R3. These are the primary interfaces that bearer traffic will follow, except during handoff. The R4 interface provides inter-ASN handoff between the ASN-GW, whereas the R8 interface provides handoff between BS within the same ASN. The WiMAX forum established three profiles—Profiles A, B, and C—to describe the distribution of functions within the ASN. Profile A is similar to Profile C, and the forum has adopted Profile C moving forward. Profile C defines the use of a standard protocol exchange on the R6 reference point between the BS and the ASN-GW. Profile B assumes that the BS and ASN-GW are co-resident; therefore, the R6 interface is not exposed and may be proprietary in nature. This section focuses on Profile C because the Profile B uses the same baseline set of interfaces.

The WiMAX Forum also offered several models for subscriber IP connectivity. The fixed wireless service references a Simple IP model, where the subscriber IP is assigned at the ASN-GW and the subscriber is granted network service access at that location. The release of IEEE 802.16e focused on mobility requirements, which relied on either Client Mobile IP (CMIP) or Proxy Mobile IP (PMIP). The PMIP model allowed the mobile subscriber to be agnostic about the use of Mobile IP protocols, whereas the CMIP model required the mobile subscriber to serve as the care-of address for implementing MIP. Figure 5-64 distinguishes between the three architectural models.

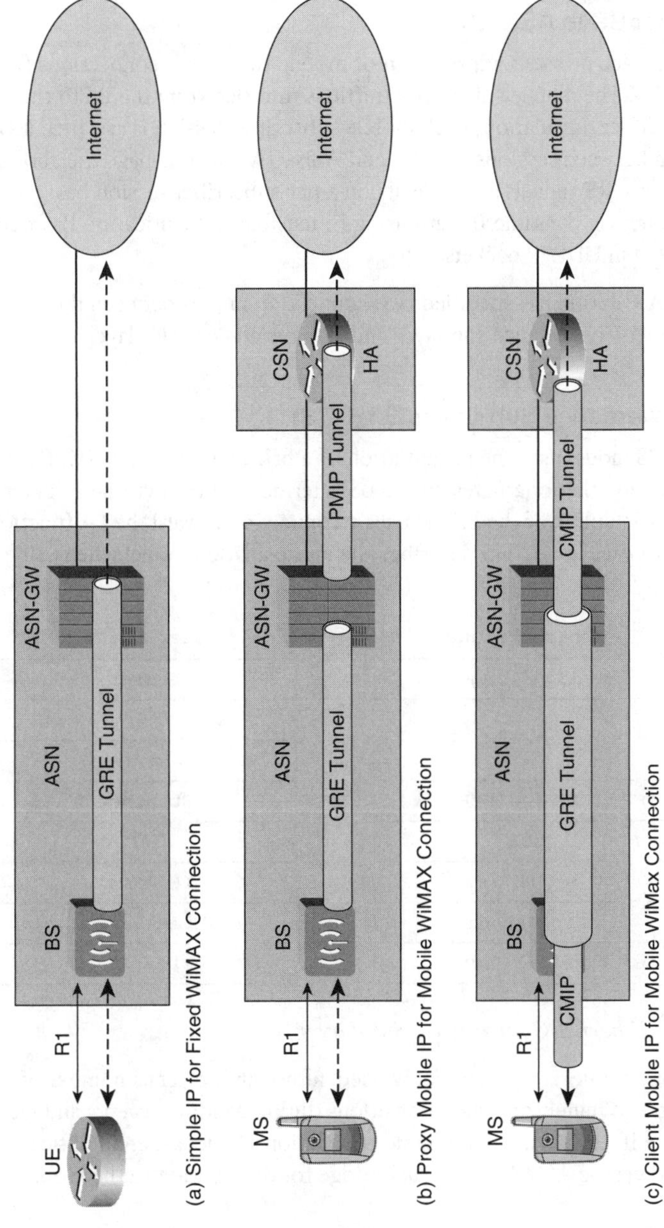

Figure 5-64 *WiMAX IP Connectivity Models*

Note that the ASN-GW serves as the FA for mobility in conjunction with an HA in the CSN. The primary role of the ASN is to handle mobile subscriber authentication, mobility management, and transport to the CSN. One of the principal advantages to WiMAX architecture is the reliance on IP transport protocols defined by the IETF for inter-operability and aggregation.

R6 Protocol for BS to ASN-GW

The R6 interface provides aggregation of mobile subscriber connections from the BS to the ASN-GW. The mobile subscriber traffic is tunneled from the BS to the ASN-GW using GRE/IP encapsulation. Each mobile subscriber session is assigned a GRE key to distinguish between sessions. The BS and ASN-GW must manage the allocation and de-allocation of GRE tunnels assignments on a per-subscriber session basis. The control plane operates on the same IP path using Extensible Authentication Protocols (EAP) encapsulated in UDP/IP packets.

The WiMAX Forum has specified two connection modes between the BS and the ASN-GW: Ethernet-Convergence sub-layer and IP-Convergence sub-layer.

Ethernet-Convergence Sub-Layer (ETH-CS)

The ETH-CS model uses the instantiation of a bridge in the ASN-GW. Each mobile subscriber's session that originates on the BS is terminated on a virtual bridge port in the ASN-GW. The uplink of the bridge uses a connection toward the FA function embedded in the ASN-GW. Figure 5-65 describes the encapsulation model when using ETH-CS.

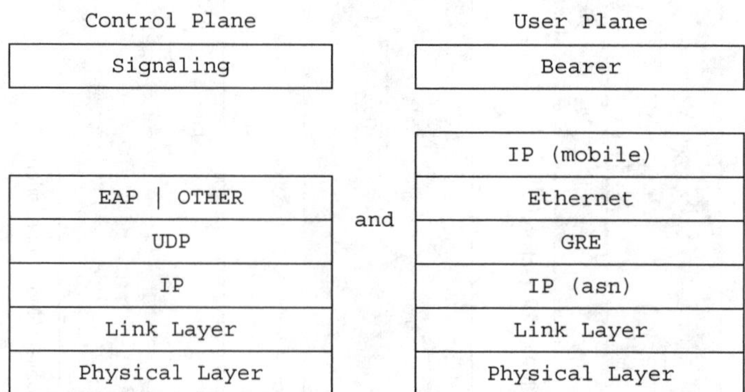

Figure 5-65 *Ethernet-Convergence Sub-Layer*

The ETH-CS model is not commonly used, although it offers a number of advantages with regards to minimizing state transitions during handover events and facilitating access for multiple IP endpoints on the same connection. Broadcast and multicast traffic must be handled via the ASN-GW's virtual bridge for distribution to the mobile subscribers.

IP-Convergence Sub-Layer (IP-CS)

The IP-CS model is more frequently used for WiMAX services where the mobile subscriber operates as an attached station on the FA. As such, the architecture usually supports the assignment of a single IP address associated with the mobile subscriber. Figure 5-66 illustrates the encapsulation model for IP-CS.

Control Plane		User Plane
Signaling		Bearer
EAP		IP (mobile)
UDP	and	GRE
IP (asn)		IP (asn)
Link Layer		Link Layer
Physical Layer		Physical Layer

Figure 5-66 *IP-Convergence Sub-Layer*

R6 Transport

The transport on the R6 link for both control plane and user plane specifies that IP addressing is used between the BS and the ASN-GW. This is true for both IP-CS and ETH-CS; the backhaul infrastructure, specifically the link layer, is unspecified by the WiMAX Forum Network Architecture. The IP transport may use any link-layer transport capable of encapsulating IP. Traditional 3G backhaul infrastructures consisted of TDM and some ATM transport. The timing synchronization requirements between the BS and the ASN-GW are eliminated in WiMAX because it is principally a data service. Although a mobile operator may continue to use TDM and ATM for backhaul, most providers expect to leverage more cost-efficient transport technologies for backhaul, such as Metro-Ethernet services, DSL, cable, and fixed wireless. The advantage of transport technologies that support any-to-any connectivity becomes more relevant when considering the next two interface reference points.

Mobility Handover on R4 and R8 Interfaces

The WiMAX architecture supports macro-mobility and micro-mobility within an ASN and between two ASNs. The default case is for the BS to use the Radio Resource Controller (RRC), which is deployed either in the ASN-GW or a dedicated server. The R4 protocol is used to handle the transfer between ASN. In addition, the R4 protocol may be used to handle transfers between BS in the absence of an R8 interface between the RRC in the BS.

R8 Protocol for BS to BS Handover

The R8 interface reference point facilitates mobility within the ASN. As the mobile subscriber transitions from one BS to another BS, the session needs to be sustained with minimal data loss. The micro-mobility is handled over the R8 interface such that the mobility anchor at the FA is retained. This minimizes the amount of state that must be transferred during the handover. A new tunnel must be established between the new BS and the ASN-GW while data continues to be forwarded by the previous BS. The R8 interface handles that relay of traffic from the new BS to the old BS during the transition. The transport between the BS is also IP; therefore, any link-layer transport capable of encapsulating IP will suffice, as illustrated in Figure 5-67.

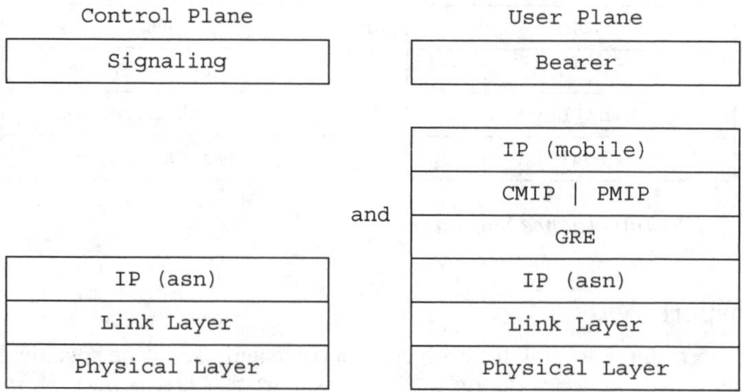

Figure 5-67 *R8 Transport Between BS*

R4 Protocol for ASN-GW to ASN-GW Handover

The mobility within an ASN is handled between ASN-GW on the R4 interface reference point. Unlike the handoff between BS within the same ASN, the anchor FA must be changed. Note that in either case, the mobility between ASN-GW is encapsulated in GRE; therefore, IP transport is used between the ASN-GW, as shown in Figure 5-68.

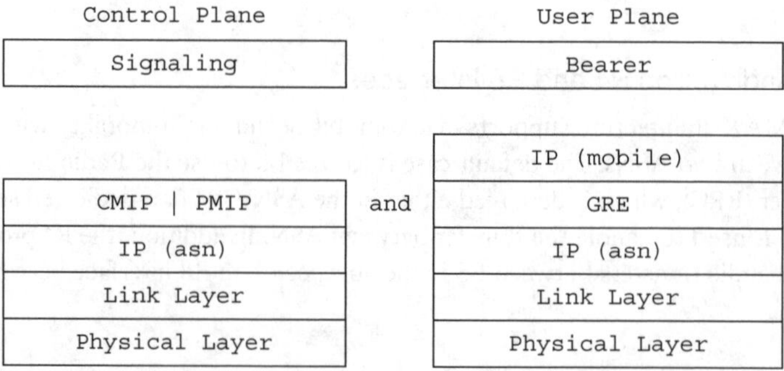

Figure 5-68 *R4 Transport Between ASN-GW*

Transport for the R4 and R8 Reference Interfaces

The ability to directly connect BS via R8 and ASN-GW via R4 using packet transport technologies allows a much more cost-efficient aggregation method. The IP transport does not preclude the use of TDM and ATM, as were commonly used in 3G technologies. However, the use of Metro-Ethernet services allows the systems within an ASN to take advantage of the any-to-any nature of the transport. Figure 5-69 shows how the Metro-E solutions facilitate more efficient connections between ASN systems.

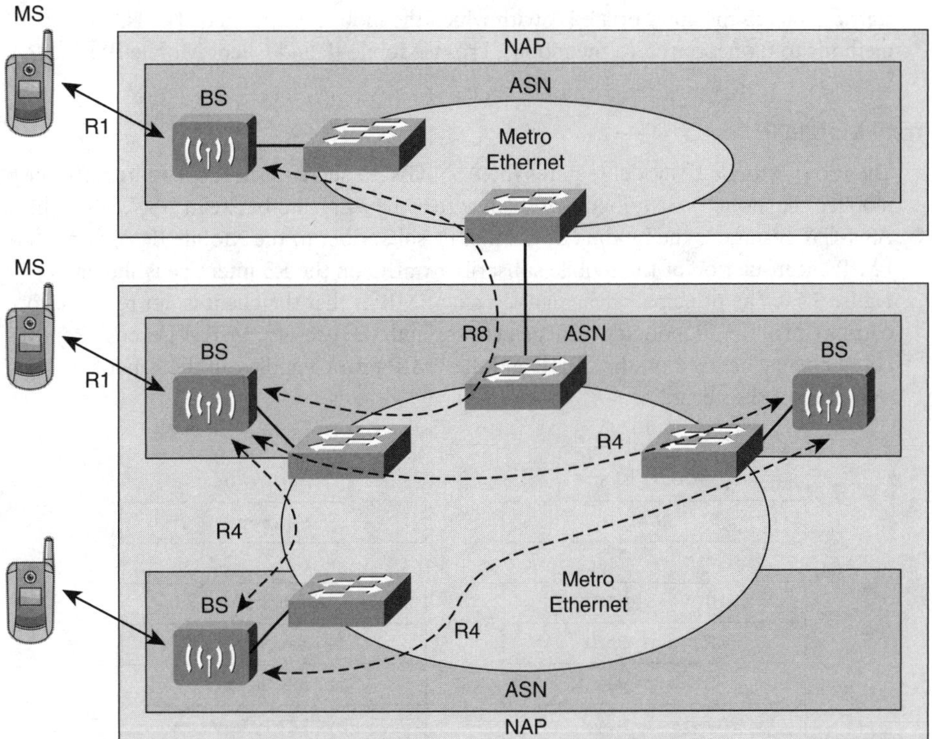

Figure 5-69 *Metro-Ethernet Transport of R4 and R8*

The example in Figure 5-69 highlights how the IP-enabled WiMAX service is able to leverage alternative transport technologies for more efficient mobility. The flattened network architecture can use a variety of transports, and in fact, the transports may consist of a composite of link-layer technologies. One of the advantages of using any-to-any IP transport technologies is that the fail-over mechanisms can be automated in the packet-routing domain through standard IGP routing protocols.

R3 Protocol for ASN-GW to HA

The last interface reference point that will be addressed for radio access network infrastructure is the R3 interface between the ASN-GW and the HA. The relationship between the ASN-GW and the HA is hierarchical in nature. The mobile subscriber's HA serves as the anchor point for communication. The subscriber is assigned an IP address that is bound to the HA and serves as a mobile subscriber's IP for communication to servers accessed through the HA. Regardless of where the mobile subscriber roams, the external networks returns traffic to the HA, which tunnels the traffic down to the mobile subscriber. The HA is responsible for maintaining mobile subscriber state and forwarding the traffic down to the appropriate FA with which the mobile is attached. The HA uses two methods to tunnel traffic to the mobile: Proxy Mobile IP and Client Mobile IP.[22]

Proxy Mobile IP

The Proxy Mobile IP model requires the ASN-GW to serve as the CoA address for the mobile. The mobile subscriber may roam across the ASN and between ASN, while the ASN-GW maintains the binding of the mobile subscriber to the Mobile IP session. The PMIP encapsulation of the mobile subscriber traffic on the R3 interface is shown in Figure 5-70. The principal advantage of using PMIP is that the client is not required to participate in the IP mobility management through the use of CMIP. A generic IP protocol stack may be used on the client, and the PMIP proxy handles all the handoff control on behalf of the client.

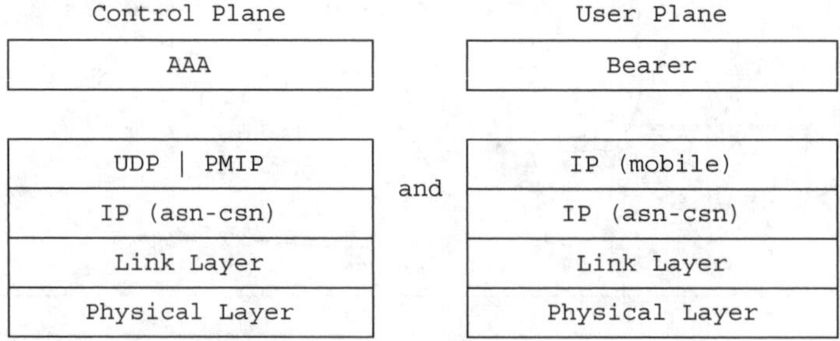

Figure 5-70 *Proxy Mobile IP on R3 Interface*

The PMIP is transported between the ASN-GW and the HA using IP. The Mobile IP protocol is used on the R3 interface between the ASN and the CSN. The transport of subscriber sessions tends to be hierarchical in nature, where many ASN-GW are aggregated onto the HA.

Client Mobile IP

The Client Mobile IP model requires the mobile subscriber to serve as the CoA address for the Mobile IP protocol. The ASN-GW simply relays the MIP protocol between the client on the mobile subscriber and the HA in the CSN. The CMIP model still uses IP transport on the R3 interface between the ASN and the CSN; therefore, any link layer that supports IP can be used, as shown in Figure 5-71.

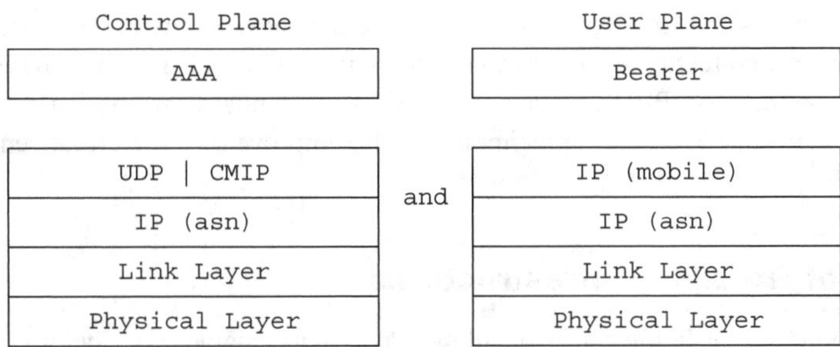

Figure 5-71 *Client Mobile IP on R3 Interface*

The CMIP model is also based on a hierarchical aggregation model, where the HA serves traffic being aggregated at many ASN-GW. The traffic loading is similar to PMIP.

WiMAX Transport Architecture

The use of IP transport for all the ASN interfaces allows the operator to pick and choose the link-layer technology that is most efficient. The ability to use R8 and R4 is just beginning to come into play; therefore, most mobile operators are still using a hierarchical aggregation model where BS are aggregated into ASN-GW and ASN-GW are aggregated into HA. Figure 5-72 illustrates the typical transport architecture that services the ASN.

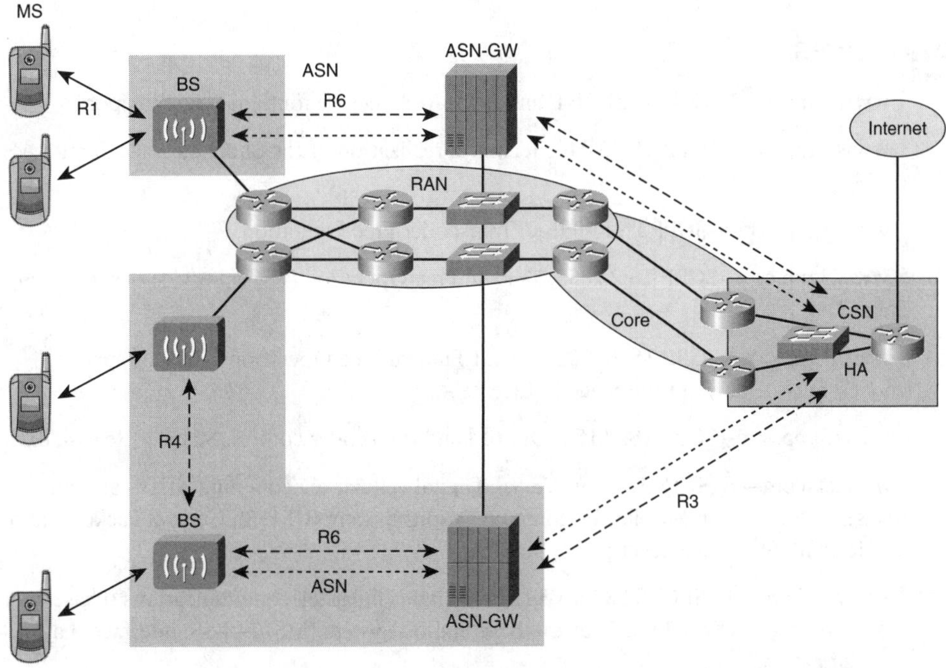

Figure 5-72 *WiMAX ASN Transport Architecture*

Note that the R4 and R8 interfaces may traverse the packet-routed core through hierarchical transport architecture or a flat transport architecture, such as that provided by Metro-Ethernet, Internet, or IPVPN services. The WiMAX standardization of IP transport will allow more diverse aggregation technologies that improve the cost effectiveness of data backhaul.

Evolution of Transport Infrastructures

The introduction of IP interfaces on all mobile systems enables the operator to transition to an All-IP Network (AIPN). The AIPN allows the introduction of services much more rapidly and optimizes the transport based on the rapid growth rate of IP data services. Nevertheless, traditional voice services garner the majority of the revenue at this time. The growth of data services, although not providing an equivalent revenue stream, does allow the operator to transition voice services from TDM-based transport to packet-based transport. The effective cost of voice transport becomes less relevant while the operator attempts to optimize the network to provide cost-effective packet transport to serve voice, video, and data. The use of legacy radio technologies, including 2G and 3G, will continue for an extended period of time. Most operators are focusing on a packet transport network that can serve all three generations of radio access technologies, including 2G, 3G, and 4G. Chapter 7, "Offloading Traditional Networks with IP," addresses various techniques, such as pseudowires, to provide emulated transport of L2VPN services over AIPN transport infrastructure.

Endnotes

1. www.ietf.org—IETF RFC 2719: Framework Architecture for Signaling Transport.

2. www.3gpp.org—3GPP TS 23.040: Technical realization of the Short message Service (SMS).

3. www.3gpp2.org—3GPP2 S.R0096-0: Transcoder Free Operation.

4. www.3gpp.org—3GPP TS 23.053: Tandem Free Operation (TFO); Service description; Stage 2.

5. www.3gpp.org—3GPP TS 28.062: Inband Tandem Free Operation (TFO) of speech codecs; Service description; Stage 3 (Release 4).

6. www.3gpp.org—3GPP TS23.153: Out of band transcoder control; Stage 2 (Release 8).

7. www.etsi.org—ETSI TS 127 060 V3.8.0: Digital cellular telecommunications system (Phase 2 +); Universal Mobile Telecommunications System (UMTS); General Packet Radio Service (GPRS) Service description; Stage 2.

8. www.etsi.org—ETSI GTS 08.08 V5.12.0: Digital cellular telecommunications (Phase 2+) – Mobile-services Switching Centre – Base Station System (MSC – BSS) interface; Layer 3 specification.

9. www.3gpp.org—3GPP TS 25.430: UTRAN Iub Interface: general aspects and principles.

10. www.3gpp.org—3GPP TS 25.426 V5.6.0: UTRAN Iur and Iub interface data transport & transport signaling for DCH data streams.

11. www.3gpp.org—3GPP TS 25.422 V5.1.0: UTRAN Iur Interface Signalling Transport.

12. www.3gpp2.org—3GPP2.A.S0001-0.1: 3GPP2 Access Network Interfaces Interoperability Specification Release A.

13. www.tiaonline.org—TIA/EIA IS-95[a]: Mobile Station – Base Station Compatibility Standard for Dual-Mode Wideband Spread Spectrum Cellular System.

14. www.3gpp2.org—3GPP2 A.S0003-Av2.0: BTS-BSC Inter-operability (Abis Interface).

15. www.tiaonline.org—TIA/EIA-828-A: BTS-BSC Inter-Operability (Abis Interface).

16. www.3gpp.org—3GPP TS 36.300 V8.2.0 Release 8: E-UTRA and E-UTRAN – Overall description.

17. ftp.3gpp.org/Inbox/2008_web_files/LTA_Paper.pdf: UTRA-UTRAN Long Term Evolution (LTE) and 3GPP System Architecture Evolution (SAE).

18. www.3gpp.org — 3GPP TS36.414 V8.2.0 Release 8: Evolved Universal Terrestial Radio Access Network (E-UTRAN); S1 data transport.

19. www.3gpp.org—3GPP TS36.424 V8.2.0 Release 8: E-UTRAN – X2 data transport.

20. www.wimaxforum.com—WiMAX Forum Network Architecture—Stage 2 (Architecture Tenets, Reference Model and Reference Points), Part 2—Release 1, Version 1.3.0.

21. www.wimaxforum.com—WiMAX Forum Network Architecture—Stage 3—Detailed Protocols and Procedures—Release 1, Version 1.2.

22. www.ietf.org—IETF RFC 3344: IP Mobility Support for IPv4.

Chapter 6

Mobile Core Evolution

The role of access networks, as described in Chapters 2 and 3, is to provide simple connectivity to the core network—whether this is a Circuit-Switched Core Network (originally called the Network-Switching Subsystem by GSM) or a Packet-Switched Core Network.

As its name suggests, the Circuit-Switched Core Network provides access to Circuit-Switched (CS) services, including voice, SMS, and CS data. The Circuit-Switched Core is defined for legacy cellular systems, including GSM Edge Radio Access Network (GERAN), UMTS Terrestrial Radio Access Network (UTRAN), and the cdma2000 1xRTT Radio Access Network.

The Packet-Switched Core provides access to IP-based services. The exact composition of the Packet-Switched Core varies according to the Radio Access Network, although each implementation includes common functionality dealing with IP mobility, Quality of Service (QoS), and roaming.

Circuit-Switched Domain

The first cellular systems were conceived in the late 1980s, shortly after the publication of Integrated Services Digital Network (ISDN) recommendations. Chapter 2, "Cellular Access Systems," highlights how the original cellular access network leverages ISDN layer 2 procedures, and this section demonstrates how ISDN layer 3 procedures were leveraged to realize cellular telephony systems. In particular, although the Q.931 protocol[1] has been defined for ISDN call establishment, maintenance, and release, the protocol was missing techniques for handling roaming and mobility.

In order to address these deficiencies, new functional elements were introduced. Figure 6-1 shows the Mobile Switching Center (MSC) as the central component of the CS Core Network, providing access to the Public Switched Telephone Network (PSTN). The MSC is derived from an ISDN switch, implementing Q.931 Call Control, but has been augmented with mobility management capability, enabling it to interact with the new functional entities corresponding to the Home Location Register (HLR) and the Visitor Location Register (VLR). In addition, to support the newly defined Short Message Service (SMS), a Short Message Service Center (SM-SC) is defined for supporting the store-and-forward message service.

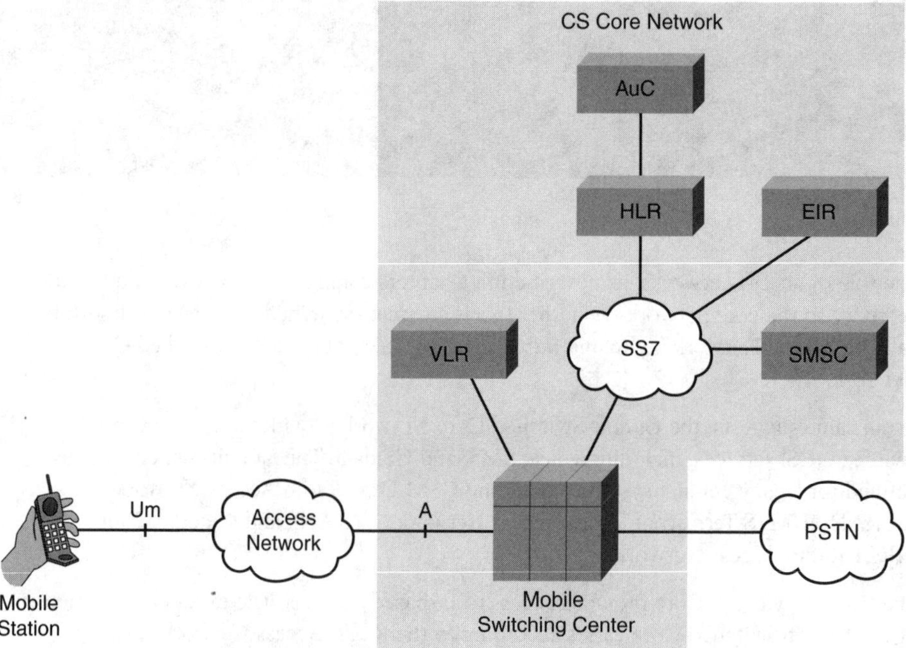

Figure 6-1 *CS Core Network*

As its name suggests, the HLR is located in the subscriber's home network and contains subscriber information related to services, as well as the current location of the user.

Conversely, the VLR is located in the visited network and contains all the information pertaining to those users currently located in the area controlled by a particular VLR. This information includes a subset of the information contained in the HLR that is necessary for providing CS service to the user—for example, information related to voice supplementary services.

Finally, in order to support the store-and-forward SMS service, the SMSC is used for storing and forwarding short messages toward the mobile device.

GSM Mobility Management

Clearly, a conventional ISDN switch has no concept of mobility, so a new layer 3 protocol has been defined that sits below the call control, or Connection Management layer, termed the Mobility Management (MM) sub-layer.[2] The Mobility Management sub-layer is operated between the end-user device and the MSC/VLR and is transparent to the access network, as shown in Figure 6-2.

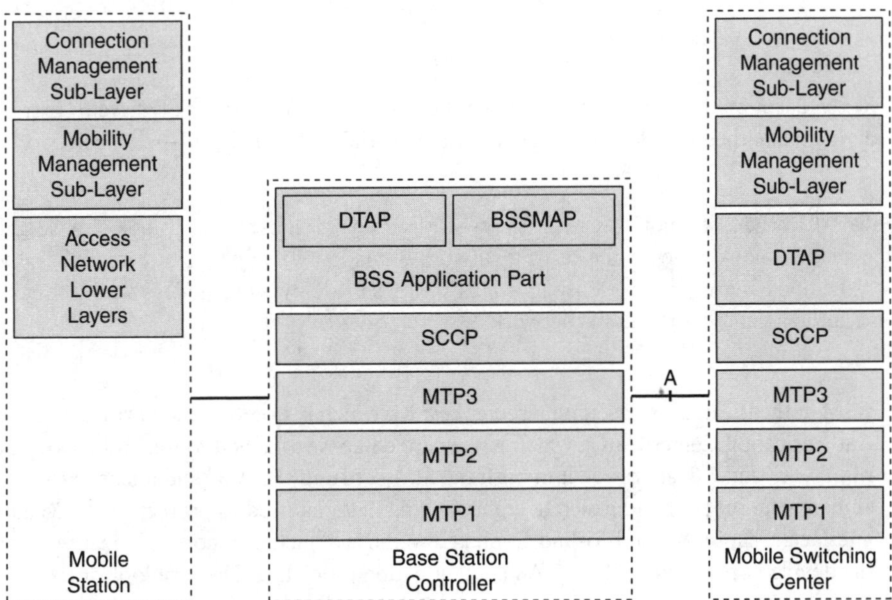

Figure 6-2 *GSM CS Protocol Architecture*

The MM sub-layer is responsible for the following key functionalities:

- Authentication and Key Exchange: Authentication in the GSM system is based on the Subscriber Interface Module (SIM), which includes a secret key together with two algorithms—one for authentication (A3), and a second for generating keying material (A8).
- Location Management: Location management refers to those procedures that allow the core network to contact a particular user—for example, when an incoming call is signaled.
- Temporary Identity Management: In the GSM system, each subscriber is uniquely identified by an International Mobile Subscriber Identity (IMSI). In order to prevent tracking of a particular user, an MSC/VLR can provide the mobile with a Temporary Mobile Subscriber Identity (TMSI), which only has local significance within an MSC/VLR region.

- **Device Identity Request:** The GSM architecture has separated the identity of the user, corresponding to the IMSI, from that of the device, corresponding to the International Mobile Equipment Identity (IMEI). The IMSI is stored in the SIM card, whereas the IMEI is stored in the mobile device and should be stored using tamper-resistant techniques—in other words, the IMEI should not be able to be modified by an unauthorized third party. The Equipment Identity Register (EIR) is a database that contains a black list of all stolen mobile devices, where each device is identified by its IMEI, enabling the MSC/VLR to forbid access from such devices.

Authentication

When users want to receive service from the CS domain, users typically have to first authenticate themselves—or more specifically in GSM, the SIM card—to the network.

Note Clearly, this is not always the case—for example, if a user only wants to make an emergency call. However, if the serving network wants to receive payment for mobile services, the home network may refuse to accept charges made by a user unless that user has been authenticated by the home network.

GSM authentication is based on a secret key, Ki, which is stored in the SIM card, and the Authentication Center (AuC), which is a secure database attached to the HLR. Two algorithms, A3 and A8, are resident in both the SIM card and the AuC and are used to authenticate the user and generate cipher-keying material used to protect the GSM air interface. Chapter 8, "End-to-End Context Awareness," includes more information about the detailed operation of the A3/A8 authentication procedure. Here we look at the Mobility Management procedures that support the operation of device authentication.

Figure 6-3 shows the signaling sequence for the location-updating procedure that, for example, may have been triggered by the user moving into the coverage area of a new MSC/VLR.

The device requests to update its location using a Location Update Request message. The message includes an identity, and in this example, the device provides its temporary identity that was signaled by its previous MSC/VLR. The new MSC/VLR could query the old MSC/VLR for details about the user, including the user's IMSI, but in this example, we assume that isn't the case; instead, the MSC/VLR requests that the user sends his IMSI to the network by using a DTAP Identity Request/Response exchange. The structure of the IMSI conforms to the ITU E.212 numbering standard,[3] and comprises a three-digit Mobile Country Code (MCC), two- or three-digit Mobile Network Code (MNC), and up to ten-digit Mobile Subscriber Identification Number (MSIN).

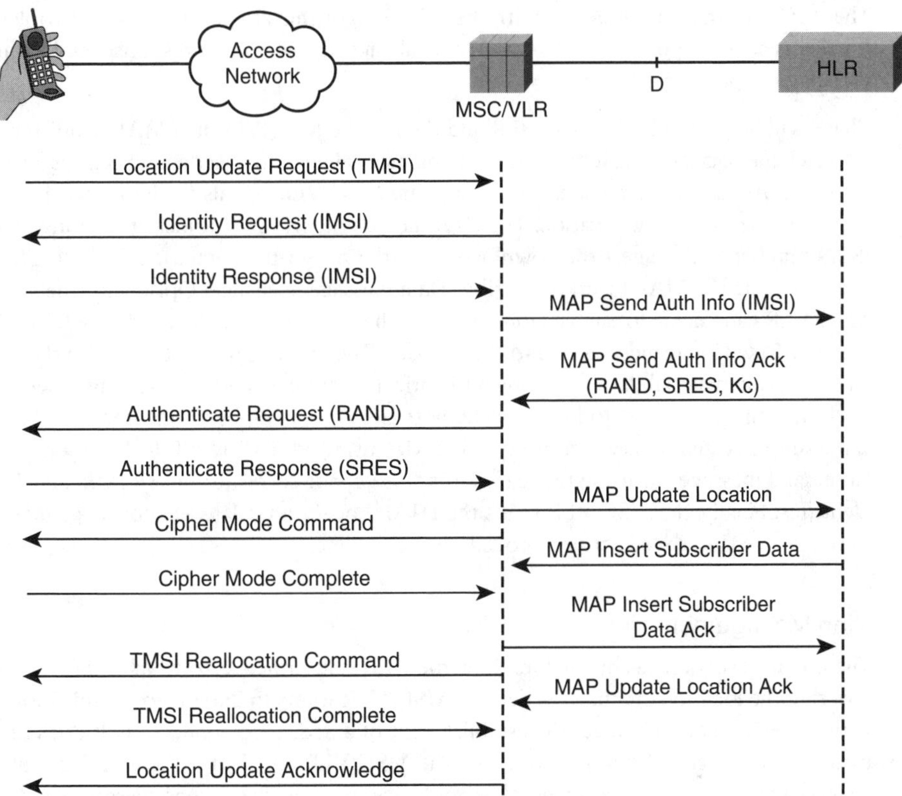

Figure 6-3 *MAP-Based CS Location-Updating Procedure*

The MSC/VLR translates this IMSI into an E.214 Mobile Global Title (MGT), which involves translating the E.212 MCC and MNC into an E.164 Country Code and National Destination Code respectively and appending the E.212 MSIN. The MGT is used as the destination for a message requesting authentication. This is an example of MSC to HLR communications and is defined to use the Mobile Application Part (MAP) Protocol.[4] The MSC/VLR sends a MAP Send Auth Info message, which contains the user's IMSI. The SS7 network routes the MAP message to the HLR, which then passes the user's IMSI to the AuC.

Note The Mobile Application Part (MAP) is a Transactions Capabilities Applications Part (TCAP) user. TCAP in turn uses SCCP connectionless services to support real-time dialogue or exchanges between TCAP end users. Chapter 9, "Content and Services," describes how SIGTRAN techniques can be used to directly interwork between MAP and IP networks.

The AuC uses the IMSI together with the A3/A8 algorithms to generate a set of triplets for the user, corresponding to 1) a random challenge, 2) the correct response, and 3) an associated cipher key.

These will be passed back to the HLR and then to the MSC/VLR in a MAP Send Auth Info Ack message. The MSC/VLR is then able to challenge the user and check for a valid response. Assuming the response is correct, the MSC/VLR signals the HLR that the authentic user has a new location. The HLR records the MSC/VLR identity storing its ISDN number, and triggers the downloading of the subscriber database related to CS services using the MAP Insert Subscriber Data message exchange. Optionally, the MSC/VLR can decide to enable ciphering over the radio interface by sending a BSSMAP Cipher Mode Command message to the mobile.[5] This triggers the mobile to use the cipher-keying material derived during authentication for encrypting the air interface, starting with the Cipher Mode Complete message. Once in cipher mode, the MSC/VLR can issue a new temporary identity to the device using a DTAP TMSI Reallocation Command message, ensuring that eavesdroppers cannot correlate a user's IMSI and TMSI identities. Finally, the MSC VLR sends the DTAP Location Update Acknowledge message to the device, and the structured procedure is complete.

Location Management

The previous section has highlighted how the HLR is informed as to which MSC/VLR is covering the location of a user. When the MSC/VLR wants to initiate communication with a user, it needs to trigger the establishment of a dedicated connection. It does this by a procedure termed *paging*. Although the MSC/VLR could page the user in all the cells to which it provides coverage, this would lead to excessive paging messages and wasted radio resources. Instead of knowing where the subscriber is at the MSC/VLR level, the individual cells are split into separate Location Areas (LA). The Location Area Codes (LAC) are broadcast from each cell, allowing the mobile to determine when it has crossed an LA boundary, triggering a location-update procedure. In this way, the access network configuration can be configured so as to optimally partition resources between paging and location-updating procedures, and of course allow the device to save battery power as individual cell transitions will not necessarily trigger signaling exchanges. Now, when a paging procedure is required, only those cells belonging to a particular LA will be used to page the user.

GSM Mobile Terminated Call

When a Mobile-Terminated (MT) call is made, the call attempt for a particular Mobile Subscriber ISDN (MSISDN) number will be received as an ISDN User Part[6] (ISUP) Initial Address Message (IAM) by the Gateway MSC in the user's home network, as shown in Figure 6-4.

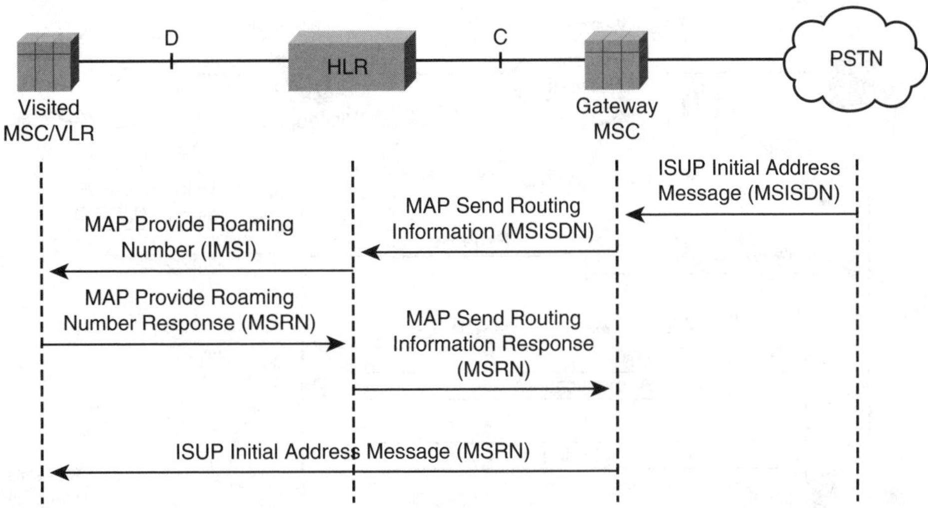

Figure 6-4 *MAP-Based Initial MT Call Exchange*

The Gateway MSC sends a MAP Send Routing Information message to the HLR, including the MSISDN of the user, in order to locate the user in the network. The HLR then performs a mapping between the MSISDN and IMSI. Having previously stored the MSC/VLR currently serving an IMSI, the HLR sends a MAP Provide Roaming Number message to the MSC/VLR, including the user's IMSI. This message effectively requests the MSC/VLR to reserve a temporary roaming number for the incoming call attempt, termed the *Mobile Station Roaming Number (MSRN)*, which identifies both the visited MSC/VLR and the user's IMSI. The MSRN is returned to the HLR in the MAP Provide Roaming Number response message, and the HLR transparently returns the MSRN to the Gateway MSC in the MAP Send Routing Information response message. The Gateway MSC then forwards the ISUP IAM message to the visited MSC, now using the MSRN as the called party address.

The MSC/VLR uses the MSRN to look up the end user's IMSI and identifies in which LA the user is positioned and in particular which Base Station Controller is responsible for that LA. The MSC/VLR sends a BSSMAP Paging Request message to that BSC. This message includes the user's IMSI, which is used by the BSC to determine when to page the user, as well as the LA identifier, and optionally the user's TMSI, as shown in Figure 6-5.

The access network then sends pages to the user in all cells corresponding to the LA. The reception of the page triggers the mobile to establish a dedicated connection in the access network and to send a paging response message, which the access network forwards on to the MSC/VLR, appending the appropriate user's identity. Figure 6-5 highlights that the same authentication, ciphering, and TMSI re-allocation procedures can be used, before the Connection Management Setup message is forwarded to the mobile.

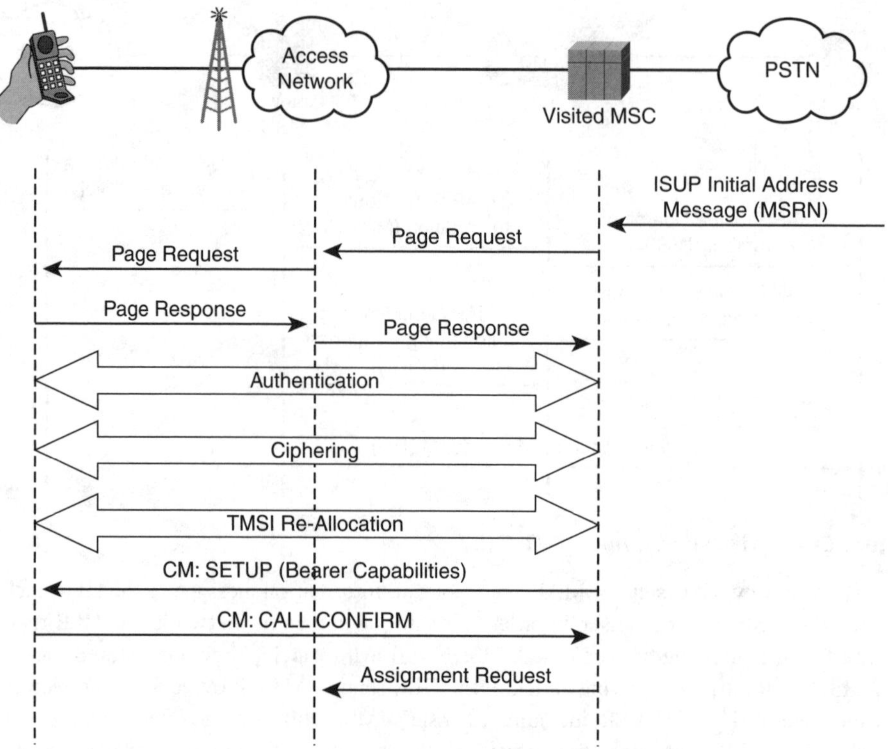

Figure 6-5 *MAP-Based MT Call Setup*

> **Note** The authentication procedure can be skipped if the mobile has provided the MSC/VLR with a cipher key sequence number (CKSN), which matches that in the MSC/VLR and then allows a previous cipher key to be re-used.

The CM SETUP message contains the bearer capabilities that will be required to support the subsequent call—for example, if the SETUP corresponds to a voice call or CS data call, and if data is required, whether the data is preferred to be sent in Transparent or Non-Transparent mode. If the mobile supports the requested bearer capabilities, it replies with a CM CALL CONFIRMED message. Because the previous signaling exchanges will typically have used a Stand-Alone Dedicated Control Channel which is not designed to support the call media (as described in Chapter 2), the MSC/VLR now triggers the assignment of a traffic channel by sending a BSSMAP Assignment message to the access network. This message includes the channel type definition; in this example, this indicates that a speech channel is being requested to be assigned, as well the speech codec type. Conversely, if the ISUP bearer capabilities indicated that the call corresponded to a CS data call, the Assignment message would include information concerning the data rates, indication of service asymmetry, as well as whether the data will be transferred using Transparent or Non-Transparent radio link protocol.

Figure 6-6 shows the signaling exchanges after the mobile has sent the CM CALL CONFIRMED message indicating that it has the capabilities to accept the call. The mobile indicates to the MSC that it has started to alert the user by sending the CM ALERTING message to the MSC. When this message is received by the MSC/VLR, it sends an ISUP: Address Complete message to the Gateway MSC and generates ringing tones for the calling subscriber. Finally, when the user answers the call, the mobile sends the CM CONNECT message to the MSC/VLR, which is acknowledged by the MSC/VLR, and the originating exchange is signaled using the ISUP Answer message.

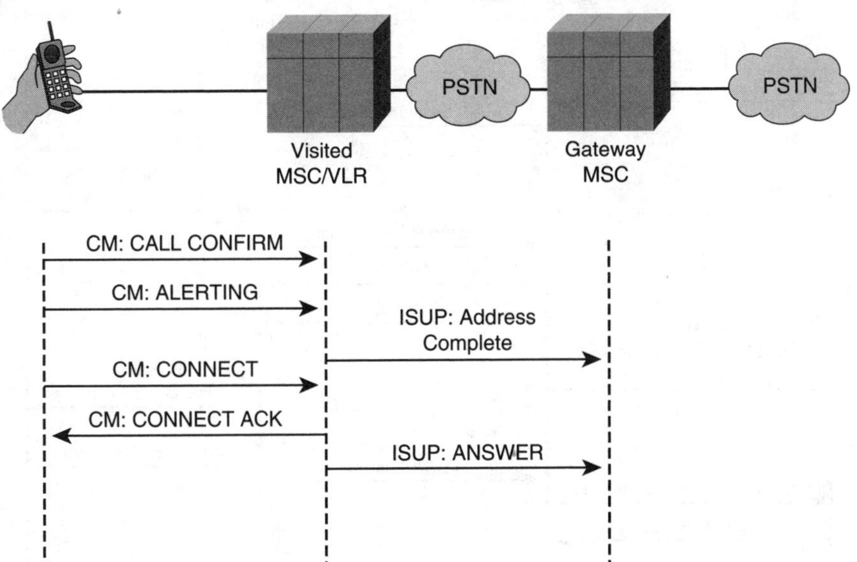

Figure 6-6 *MAP-Based MT Call Accepted*

A combination of ISUP signaling between exchanges, MAP signaling to/from the new registration data bases, and standardized ISDN Connection Management signaling, together with cellular-specific mobility management procedures and BSC signaling, support the origination and termination of mobile calls. The next section details the additional procedures necessary to accommodate cell changes during a call.

GSM Handover

After a mobile call has been established, the mobile may move into another cell. This cell may be under the control of the same BSC, in which case the access network simply informs the core network that the handover has taken place. However, if the new cell is controlled by a different BSC, the MSC is involved because a traffic channel needs to be established to the new BSC before the handover occurs.

An even more-complex scenario arises when the new cell is located in a service area of a different MSC/VLR. In this case, a traffic channel needs to be established between the original MSC/VLR, termed the *anchor MSC*, and the new MSC/VLR, termed the *relay MSC*, over the E-Interface, as shown in Figure 6-7.

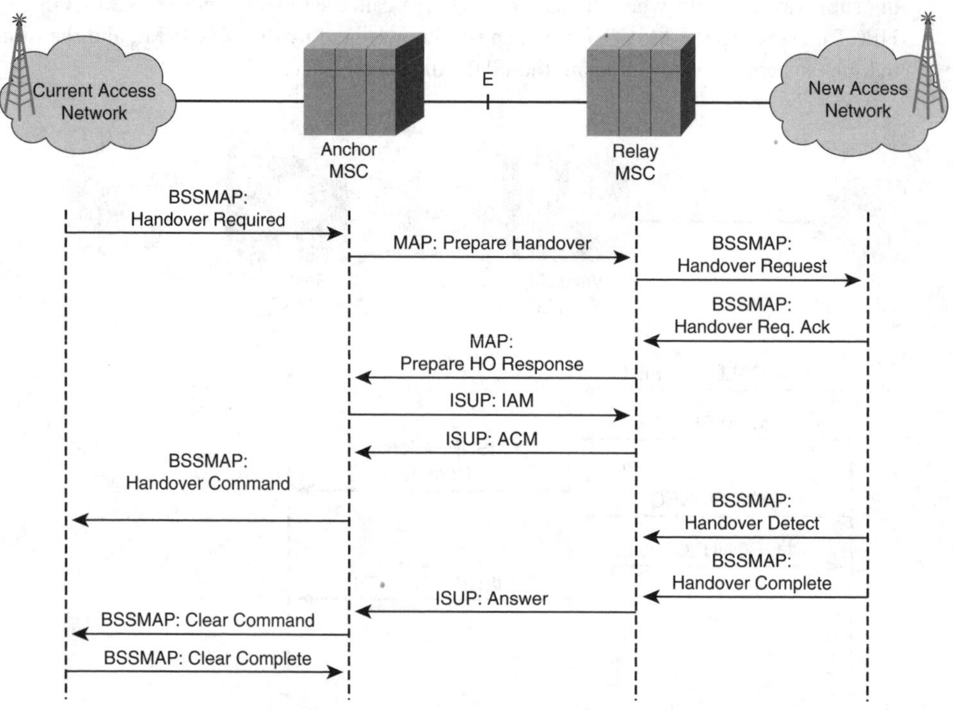

Figure 6-7 *MAP-Based Inter-MSC Handover*

The procedure is initiated by the current access network, which sends a BSSMAP Handover Required message to the MSC/VLR that includes a list of target cells—in this example, including one that is in the service area of another MSC/VLR. The handover request, including the target cell information, is passed to the new MSC/VLR using the MAP Prepare Handover message. The new MSC/VLR determines which BSC controls the target cell and then sends a BSSMAP Handover Request message to that BSC, triggering the new access network to allocate resources for the call. The new access network responds back with a BSSMAP Handover Request Acknowledgment message, which includes the chosen physical channel description together with a handover reference. This information is sent back to the original anchor MSC/VLR using a MAP Prepare Handover Response message, which also includes a handover number used for routing the call between MSCs. The original MSC/VLR then uses this handover number to initiate a call to the relay MSC/VLR using normal ISUP procedures.

After the relay MSC confirms with an ISUP answer message, the Anchor MSC/VLR knows that all resources have been established in the target access network and thus sends a BSSMAP Handover Command to initiate the handover to the channel provided by the new access network using the handover reference to uniquely identify the procedure. After the new access network detects the handover reference on the new channel, it sends a BSSMAP Handover Detected message to the relay MSC/VLR; after the layer 2 signaling connection is re-established, it sends a BSSMAP Handover Complete message to the relay MSC/VLR. This triggers the relay MSC/VLR to send an ISUP Answer message to the Anchor MSC/VLR, which then switches the voice path from the circuit toward the old access network to the new circuit toward the relay MSC/VLR and clears the resources used on the old access network.

The original MSC/VLR stays in the circuit and anchors the call. Any advanced call processing (for example, Intelligent Networking (IN) operations) occurs at the Anchor MSC with the relay MSC/VLR being transparent to user signaling until the call is terminated when it is likely that the user will finally perform a location update in the cell belonging to the relay MSC/VLR.

Note If the mobile device subsequently moves to another cell in the service area of a third MSC/VLR, a subsequent handover occurs. The original anchor MSC/VLR still remains in the circuit, but after the call is established through the third MSC/VLR, the first relay MSC/VLR is dropped.

Short Message Service

The SMS service supports the transfer of short 140-byte messages between an SM-SC and a mobile user. The SM-SC performs store-and-forward operations for both mobile-terminated (MT) and mobile-originated (MO) short messages. Figure 6-8 shows the case of a MT-SMS. The SM-SC sends a MAP Send Routing Info for SM message along with the recipients MSISDN, and the HLR responds with the user's IMSI, as well as the ISDN number of the MSC/VLR serving the location in which the mobile is located. The SM-SC forwards the short message to the MSC/VLR, which then uses the IMSI to attempt to forward the message to the user.

The message may be successfully transferred or alternatively fail to be delivered, perhaps because the user is momentarily out of coverage, or the memory capacity of the terminal's SIM card that is used to store SMS messages is exceeded. In those error scenarios, the SM-SC may register with the HLR to be kept informed when the user is next available to receive a short message. The HLR will then set its message waiting flag for that particular user and be responsible for monitoring when the particular user is ready again for receiving SMS messages—for example, signaling the SM-SC that the user has subsequently performed a location-updating procedure.

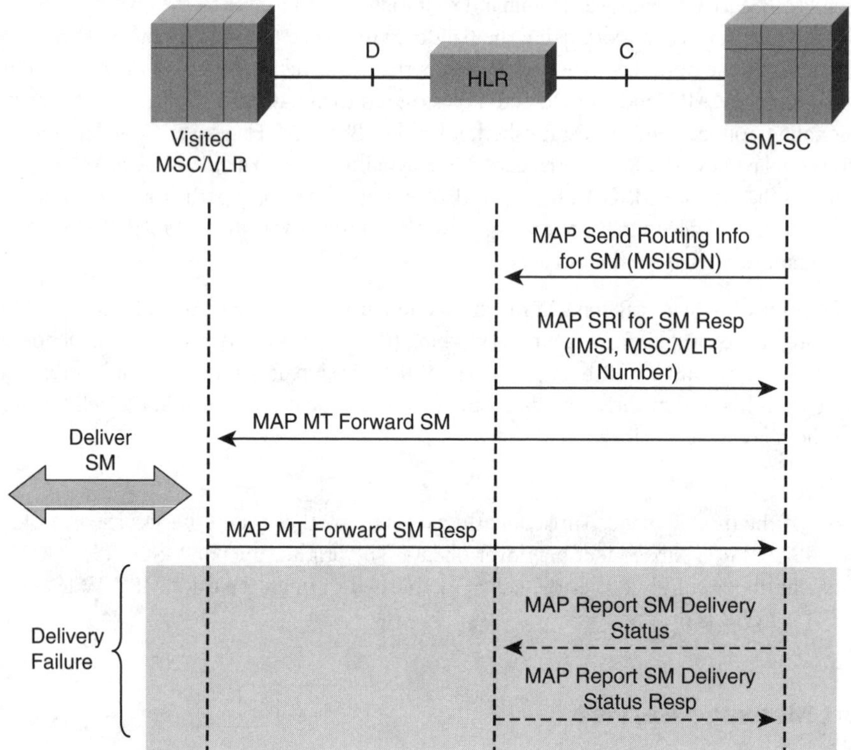

Figure 6-8 *MAP-Based Store-and-Forward SMS-MT Operation*

> **Note** The store-and-forward nature of SMS makes it ill-suited to message delivery where specific service levels are required.
>
> Recent studies by Anacom[7] indicate that in real-world deployments, the delivery success rate for SMS was around 98 percent, with the average SMS requiring nine seconds to be delivered. This compares with an average delay of 54 seconds for the newer Multimedia Messaging Service (MMS), which was been defined to enable the sending of larger multimedia objects, such as audio, video, and images.

Because an SMS message can only carry 140 bytes of data, an extension mechanism called SMS concatenation has been specified to segment longer messages into smaller parts, each of which is sent separately and then combined in the receiver. Each smaller part comprises 134 bytes of information (or 153 characters if the GSM default 7-bit coding is used). Each concatenated SM includes a modulo 256 reference number that is equal for all segments, a maximum number of short messages in the concatenated message, and a sequence number allowing the original long message to be re-assembled. No additional Radio Link Protocol techniques have been defined—for example, to facilitate any retransmission when only one out of a series of message segments has not been received.

cdma2000 Core Network

The GSM System has defined the MAP procedures for supporting mobile voice service delivery to cellular subscribers using the GSM Access Network. The cdma2000 Access Network has defined a corresponding Core Network, which uses American National Standards Institute-41 (ANSI-41[8])-defined SS7 signaling messages between the same common set of functional elements, as shown in Figure 6-1. Comparing Figure 6-9 with Figure 6-4, it is evident that although the nomenclature differs, the procedures are broadly similar. For example, where the GSM-MAP Provide Roaming Number message triggers the MSC/VLR to return an MSRN, an ANSI-41 ROUTREQ message is sent to the MSC/VLR; this responds with a Temporary Local Directory Number (TLDN), which is used to route the ISUP IAM message between the Originating MSC/VLR and the serving MSC/VLR.

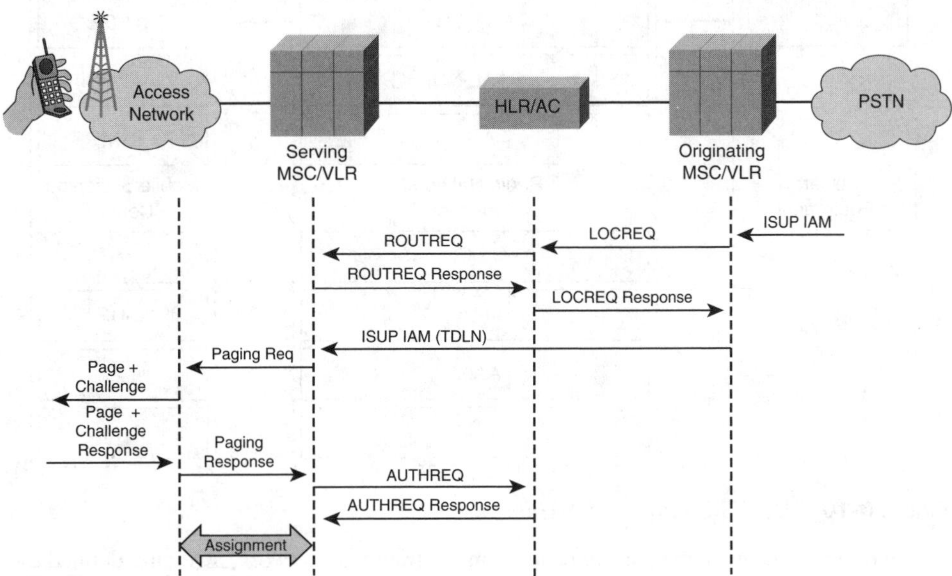

Figure 6-9 *ANSI-41-Based cdma2000 MT Call Setup*

WCDMA Core Network

The move from GSM to WCDMA, which triggered a revolution on the air interface, produced only an evolution on the Circuit-Switched Core Network functionality. The most significant change is related to the adoption of ATM as the transport technology for the Iu-CS interface between the WCDMA-based access network and the core network. Figure 6-10 shows the signaling and user-plane protocol stacks used across the Iu-CS interface. GSM's BSSAP has been replaced with the Radio Access Network Application Part (RANAP), which can be transported using the MTP3 broadband (MTP3-B) protocol, and the Adaptive Multi-Rate (AMR)-encoded voice is encapsulated in the Iu User-Plane (UP) protocol, which is then transported using AAL2.

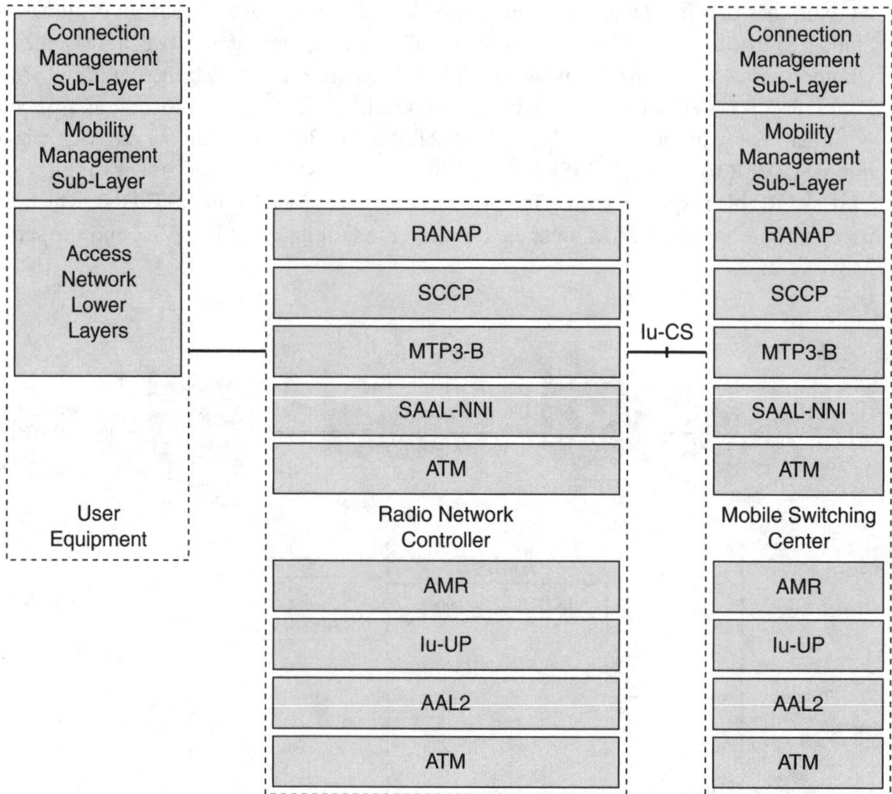

Figure 6-10 *UMTS CS Protocol Architecture*

In order to decouple the control plane from the transport network, 3GPP has defined the use of an Access Link Control Application Protocol (ALCAP)—for example, ITU-T Q.2630.1[9] is defined to automatically establish the AAL2 connections for transporting the Iu-UP bearer traffic. Previous GSM procedures had defined the use of a Circuit Identity Code (CIC) in the BSSAP Assignment Request message sent from the MSC to the access network, as shown in Figure 6-5, where the CIC defines the PCM multiplex and timeslot over which the call will pass. In WCDMA, the sending of the equivalent RANAP RAB Assignment Request message only includes the QoS and transport addresses. On receiving the RAB Assignment Request message, the access network requests the setup of the Iu user-plane transport using the Q.2630.1 protocol, where the request contains the AAL2 binding identity to bind the Iu user-plane transport to the Radio Access Bearer.

Another key change with the WCDMA Core Network is a logical shift of the speech codec from the access network into the core network. Chapter 2 describes how GSM-coded speech is split into three categories, with differing levels of error correction and detection applied to each category of bits. Although this was easy to achieve when the codec was logically integrated into the access network, additional functionality needs to be added to the Iu UP protocol in order to support Unequal Error Protection (UEP) by defining RAB sub-flows. For example, a speech codec with three categories of coded bits define three sub-flows, each with particular Service Data Unit (SDU) size. The Iu UP protocol includes an indicator identifying the sub-flow combination so that each can receive appropriate coding by the access network.

Evolved IP-Based CS Core Network

The changes in the CS Core Network for UTRAN access have been minor compared to the revolution in the access network. Whereas the CS Core Network functionality has been well-defined to support mobile telephony, IP has had a key role in transforming the transport of the CS Core Network, allowing operators to leverage core IP networks to transport legacy CS voice. The CS Core Network is evolving in different ways to accommodate a more IP-centric architecture.

Bearer Independent CS Architecture

In the new architecture proposed in 3GPP Release 4, the monolithic MSC is decomposed into a control-plane element dealing with call control and signaling, termed the MSC-Server (MSS), and a user-plane element for switching traffic, realized by a Multimedia Gateway (MGW).[10] Figure 6-11 shows the evolution from the legacy CS architecture toward the decomposed approach.

The decomposition of conventional MSC into MSC-Server and MGW components allows those operators deploying such an architecture to examine where best to locate those functions. Call control can now be centralized in a data center with the MGW located close to PSTN Points Of Interconnect (POI) and other areas where large amounts of media need to be handled.

Instead of being based on standardized ISUP, the Nc interface has been defined to use an enhanced call control protocol supporting call bearer separation. The original 3GPP architecture specified ITU-T Bearer Independent Call Control (BICC).[11] BICC was developed to allow any type of bearer to be used, including TDM, ATM, and IP transport. Current standardization efforts in 3GPP Release 8 include specifying an alternative Nc protocol based on the SIP-I, which supports the ISDN service set required for MSC server inter-connection.[12]

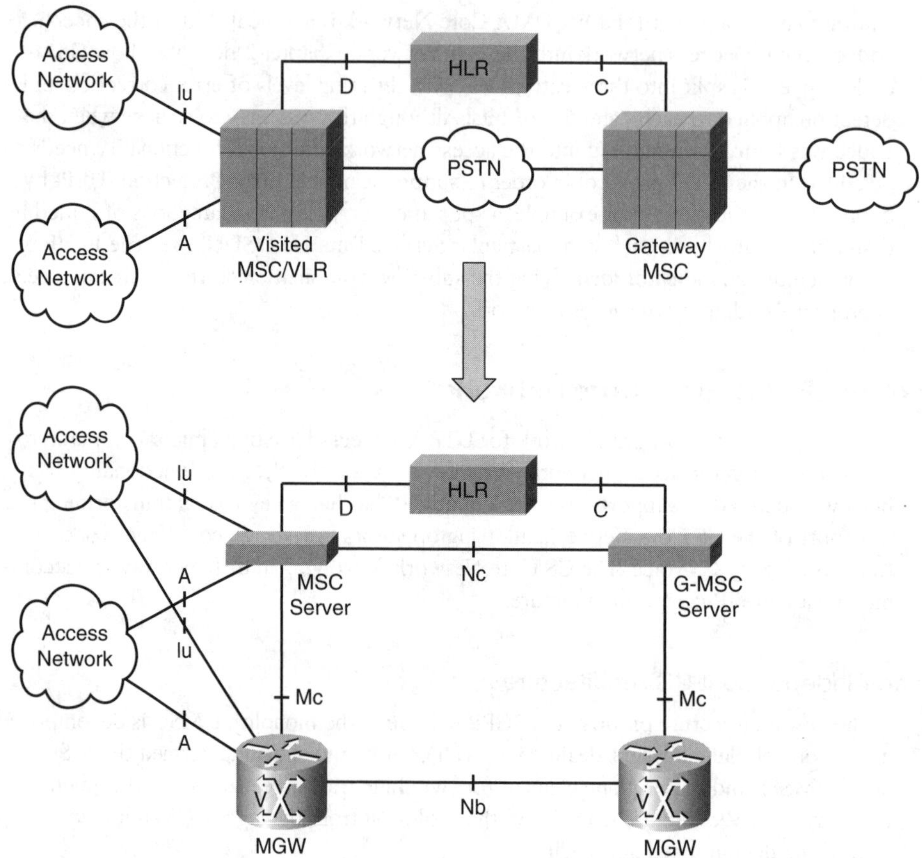

Figure 6-11 *UMTS Release 4 Split MSC*

> **Note** SIP-I has been standardized by the ITU[13] and defines extensions to the standard SIP protocol to transport ISUP messages across a SIP network.

In order to allow the decoupling of control and user plane, the Mc interface is defined between MSC server and MGW. The protocol used over the Mc interface is H.248 together with 3GPP-specific packages.[14] Chapter 9 includes detail of H.248 operation.

> **Note** The original specification of the Mc interface was too loosely defined, hindering multi-vendor interoperability. To address the large number of Mc implementation options, the MultiService Forum (http://www.msforum.org) has defined an Mc Implementation Agreement.[15]

Finally, the Nb interface is used to connect the MGWs, with both ATM and IP options being defined for voice transport. When using the IP option for Nc transport, RTP/UDP/IP is used to carry speech using the Nb User-Plane (UP) protocol; in other words, if Adaptive Multi Rate (AMR) coding is used, AMR/Nb-UP/RTP/UDP/IP is used between MGWs. The Nb-UP protocol is similar to the Iu-UP protocol used between the UTRAN Access Network and conventional MSC and is independent of the speech codec used.

Transcoder Free Operation

The definition of the Nb-UP interface between the MGWs in the split MSC architecture allows to selectively remove the transcoders from the core network with a feature called Transcoder Free Operation (TrFO), as highlighted in Figure 6-12. Prior to such architectural approaches, Tandem Free Operation (TFO) had been used to steal the Least Significant Bits (LSB) from ITU-T G.711 speech samples and use these for transcoder-to-transcoder operation. The LSBs can be used to exchange TFO control frames and, if a common voice codec can be agreed, the LSBs can be used to send the compressed voice between the transcoders, avoiding any loss in quality due to the conversion to/from G.711.

With the TrFO, the Nc interface between MSC servers is used to negotiate Out-of-Band Transcoder Control (OoBTC).[16] Because the framing protocol used over the Iu interface is identical to that over the Nb interface, the architecture then supports the end-to-end transport of speech sub-flows between two access networks. Chapter 5, "Connectivity and Transport," describes the transport of TrFO traffic over the core IP network.

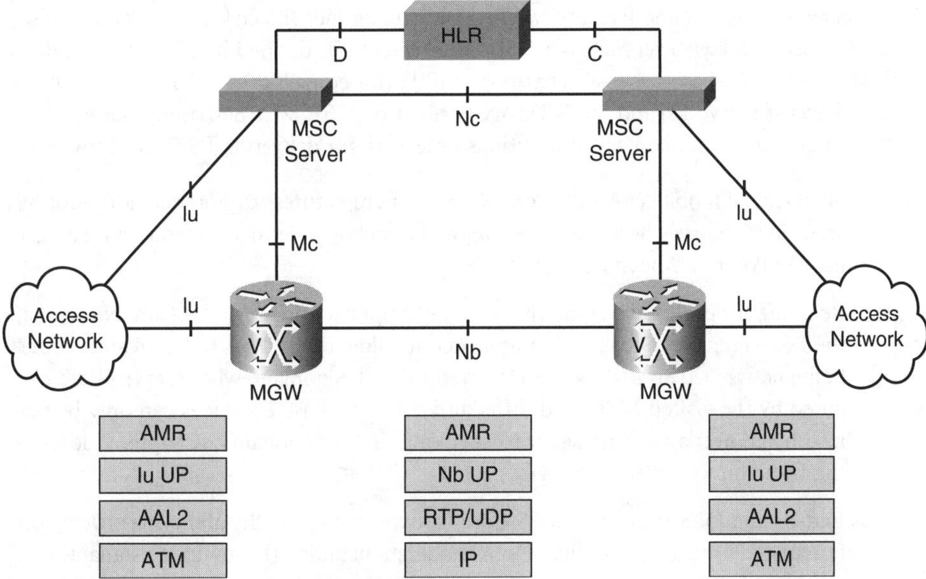

Figure 6-12 *Transcoder Free Operation*

Iucs/IP

The Release 4 split MSC architecture allows operators to deploy a converged IP core for transporting legacy voice traffic. However, the Iu-CS interface between the access network and the core network was still based on legacy ATM or TDM transport technology; thus, an all-IP E2E system was still not realizable. In order to address this shortcoming, 3GPP Release 5 defined IP transport of Iu interfaces, both within the access network, as well as between the access network and the core network.

The same architectural technique that had allowed the decoupling of the control plane from the transport network is re-used to support IP transport of the Iu interfaces, including Iu-cs. Now, instead of using RTP/UDP/IP to transport the Nb UP protocol, it is used for transporting Iu UP protocol across the Iu-CS interface.

A/IP

In order to allow legacy GSM networks to benefit from converged core network architectures supporting both GSM and WCDMA Access Networks, IP has recently been defined as an option for transport of the A interface. 3GPP Release 7 introduces the optional transport of BSSAP over MTP3 User Adaptation Layer (M3UA), enabling the native SS7 protocols to be transported over an IP (SIGTRAN) network. 3GPP Release 8 is targeted to include A interface user-plane transport over IP. 3GPP 43.903[17] describes how RTP/UDP/IP will be specified to transport either G.711, compressed voice, or CS data/fax across the A/IP interface.

Packet-Switched Domain

As its name suggests, the Packet-Switched Domain defines the core network architecture for accessing IP-based services. The various architectures defined by 3GPP (for GERAN-, UMTS-, and LTE-based access networks), 3GPP2 (for cdma2000 1xRTT- and EV-DO-based access networks) and the WiMAX Forum (for IEEE 802.16e-based access networks) provide a common set of functions necessary for delivering PS Core Network:

- Hierarchical mobility: All PS Core Network architectures support the notion of hierarchical mobility, where a transient mobility anchor is defined together with a permanent IP Point of Attachment (PoA).
- Roaming support: Leveraging the roaming support defined for CS Core Networks, the PS roaming architecture is augmented to allow the IP PoA to be located in the home network. This differs from the traditional CS domain, where services are executed by the visited MSC, and differentiated home-based services can only be realized by an overlay of Intelligent Networking (IN) functionality. (Chapter 9 describes the IN architecture for CS services).
- End-to-End QoS Support: All PS Core Networks support the ability to provide differentiated Quality of Service (QoS) handling, including the ability to signal the access network that a particular user, or an IP flow from a particular user, needs to

receive differentiated priority handling in order to be able to realize an End-to-End (E2E) QoS capability.

- **Per Subscriber IP Policy Enforcement:** In order to provide a foundation for delivering differentiated IP services, the IP Core Networks support IP Policy Enforcement on a per-subscriber basis, including defining a framework where IP applications can dynamically change the per-subscriber policy.

Note Chapter 8, defines the generic policy enforcement architectures, including how dynamic control is realized. Chapter 8 also describes in detail the different traffic classes and their associated attributes, which are used in the classification of packet-switched data traffic.

Although delivering a common set of functions, the PS Core Networks differ in the detailed protocols used in realizing the Packet-Switched Core.

In particular, three different approaches for delivering IP mobility have been defined. The following sections describe the issues with providing IP mobility and compare the alternative approaches and architectures.

Core Network Mobility Support

Chapter 4, "An IP Refresher," introduced IP routing concepts, describing how an IP address comprises a subnet portion and a host portion. IP routing is based on a variety of forwarding algorithms that are indexed by subnet value. To enable route aggregation, these subnets are by nature hierarchical and fixed. This means that when a host, such as a mobile device, obtains an IP address from a PoA, IP packets destined toward the host continue to be routed toward the original PoA, even after the mobile has moved to a new subnet. This fundamental characteristic can be used to differentiate between mobility protocol support, as follows:

- **Network-based local mobility:** Where mobility happens below layer 3, making the entire network appear as a single subnet. Consequently, devices can move without encountering changes in their IP addresses, thus hiding mobility from the IP layer and above.
- **Layer 3-based IP mobility:** Where mobile IP functionality is used to accommodate change of subnets during an IP session.

Importantly, both techniques make use of IP tunneling in order to realize mobility functions, allowing both to be realized using IP networks.

The other key to differentiating between mobility protocols is to understand whether they are focused on providing micro-mobility, macro-mobility, or a combination of the two. Micro-mobility is typically limited to scenarios where both the origin and target locations, together with the transient mobility anchor, are administered by the same organization. Conversely, macro-mobility includes those scenarios where different organizations are involved in providing the mobility service—for example, in a roaming deployment where the permanent IP POA is located in the home domain.

Other than the organizations involved, the two types of mobility are typically distinguished based on performance requirements. Micro-mobility is used between locations in close proximity, meaning mobility events will be more frequent, and consequently the performance requirements associated with those events may be more stringent, compared to the infrequent mobility events occurring when a mobile device crosses administrative boundaries. Table 6-1 describes the micro- and macro-mobility protocols defined for different access networks. You can see that there are three core IP mobility protocols: GPRS Tunneling Protocol (GTP), Mobile IP (MIP), and Proxy Mobile IPv6 (PMIPv6) .

Table 6-1 *Access Network and IP Mobility Protocol Definition*

Access Network	Micro-Mobility Protocol	Macro-Mobility Protocol
GERAN	L2 Specific Protocol	GTP/GTP-C
UTRAN	GTP/RANAP	GTP/GTP-C
E-UTRAN	GTP/S1-MME	GTP or PMIPv6
cdma1xRTT	A10/A11	MIP
cdma1xEV-DO	A10/A11	MIP
WiMAX	R6	MIP or PMIPv6
WLAN	L2 Specific Protocol	PMIPv6

The following sections describe these protocols before introducing the PS Core Network architectures for supporting the different access networks.

Note Table 6-1 demonstrates that GTP decouples the user-plane mobility from control-plane aspects, with the GTP control-plane protocol (GTP-C) being used only when supporting macro-mobility use cases. Consequently, discussions of the control plane specifics for supporting GTP-U tunneling are deferred to the sections describing the various PS Core Network architectures.

GPRS Tunneling Protocol

The GPRS Tunneling Protocol (GTP) is a UDP-based tunnel protocol that provides mobility based on a Packet Data Protocol (PDP) context and has been specified by 3GPP in 29.060.[18] GTP-U has been allocated UDP port 2152 by IANA. GTP-U is a network-based mobility protocol, meaning that from the mobile device's perspective, the entire cellular network can be viewed as a simple point-to-point connection.

Before a mobile device can receive services from the PS Core Network, it must first activate a PDP context. GTP tunnels are identified by a Tunnel Endpoint Identifier (TEID) and are used to carry encapsulated Tunneled Protocol Data Units (T-PDU). The T-PDU typically corresponds to an IP packet to/from a mobile user, with the maximum size of a T-PDU being 1,500 bytes.

Figure 6-13 shows the 32-bit TEID in the GTP header fields, which should be a random number, dynamically allocated by the receiving side entity.

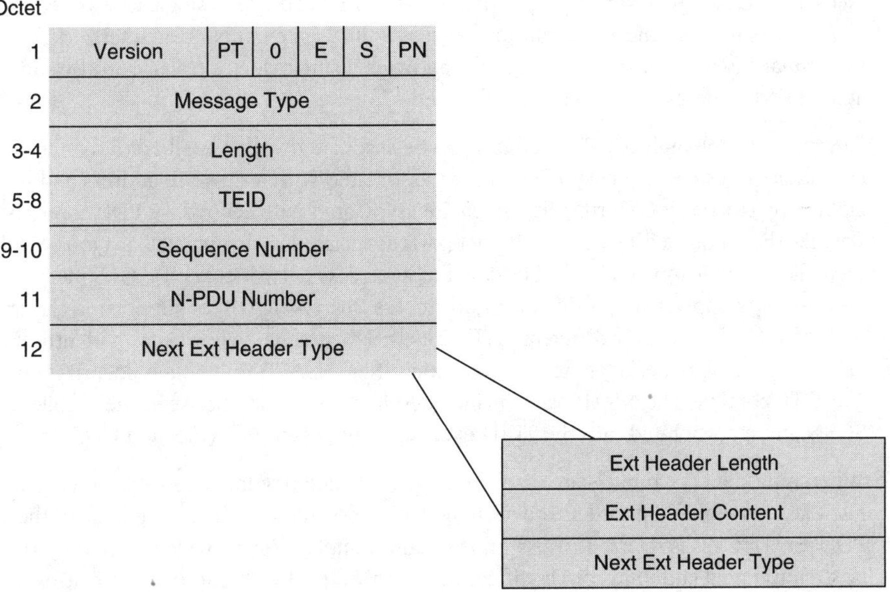

Figure 6-13 *GTP Header Fields*

The other fields are described as follows:

- **Version:** The original version 0 of GTP has been replaced with GTP version 1. GTP version 2 has been defined for use in the Evolved Packet Core (EPC) supporting the EUTRAN, but only for control messages (GTP-C).
- **Protocol Type (PT):** GTP is used to support both mobility procedures and charging record transport. The latter is termed GTP' and is signified by having the PT set to zero.
- **Extension Header Flag (E):** When set to "1," is used to signify the presence of the Next Extension Header field.
- **Sequence Number Flag (S):** When set to "1," is used to signify the presence of the Sequence Number Field. GTP supports the option to guarantee the transmission order of T-PDUs, in which case, the S flag is set to "1" and the Sequence Number field is increased for each T-PDU sent over GTP-U.

- **N-PDU Number Flag (PN):** When set to "1," is used to signify the presence of the N-PDU Number Field. The Network Protocol Data Unit (N-PDU) Number is used to support packet delivery following mobility events when operating in acknowledged mode.
- **Length:** The length of the packet following the mandatory portion of the header.

GTP supports the ability of a user to have multiple GTP tunnels (corresponding to multiple TEIDs) simultaneously active. These GTP tunnels may terminate on different IP PoAs—for example, allowing a mobile device to be multihomed to different Packet Data Networks (PDN) by having multiple IP addresses assigned over a single access network. 3GPP refers to this concept as multiple Access Point Name (APN), characterized as multiple Primary PDP contexts—for example, allowing a single device to have an IPv4 address and an IPv6 address simultaneously allocated.

Alternatively, the multiple GTP tunnels can be associated with a single IP PoA—in which case, there is a single primary PDP context associated with a single IP address and up to eight supplementary GTP tunnels, which are associated with secondary PDP contexts. Besides the unique TEID, each PDP context is associated with a particular QoS, which then allows the mapping from GTP tunnel to an access network-specific QoS mechanism—for example, using different Radio Access Bearers (RAB) for supporting the transport of T-PDUs sent over different GTP tunnels. The mobile device uses an identifier called the Network Services Access Point Identifier (NSAPI) to uniquely identify a particular GTP context. The NSAPI value is included in the signaling between the mobile and SGSN and incorporated into the TEID exchanged between the SGSN and GGSN.

When multiple GTP tunnels are associated with a single IP address, an Access Control List (ACL) is required in order to determine which downlink TEID to use to send the T-PDU. In GTP, this is referred to as a Traffic Flow Template (TFT), which is used by the upstream tunnel endpoint for classification of downlink T-PDUs into Conversational, Streaming, Interactive, and Background traffic classes, as shown in Figure 6-14. The TFT is provided by the mobile device when the secondary PDP context is established. Filtering can be based on the following attributes:

- Remote IPv4/IPv6 address
- Protocol number/next header type
- Destination port or port range
- Source port or port range
- Type of service/traffic class type or IPv6 flow label
- IPSec Security Parameter Index (SPI)

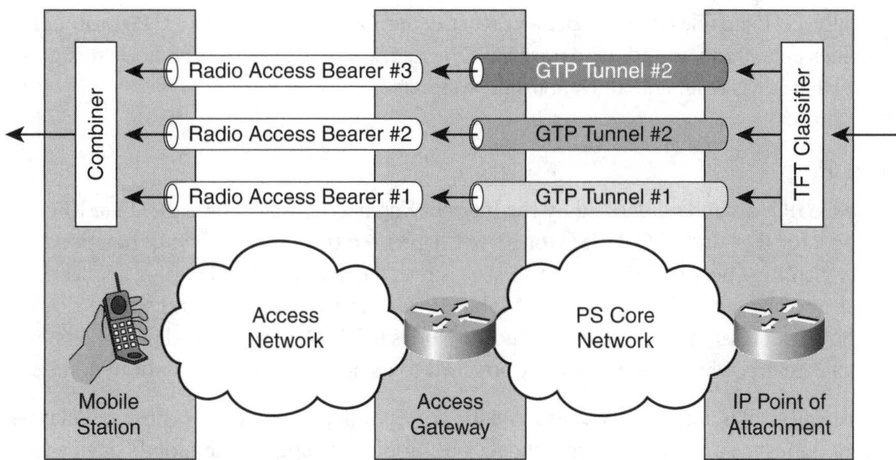

Figure 6-14 *GTP QoS Support*

GTP does not include any inherent security functionality. This section has focused on GTP-U for user-plane data transfer and not the associated control plane described in Table 6-1—for example, RANAP, S1-MME, or GTP-C. When examining the security threats for GTP-U, it has traditionally not been considered necessary to protect the GTP-U interfaces between operators—for example, when supporting roaming scenarios where the IP PoA is in the home network.[19] However, most recently in the definition of the EUTRAN, 3GPP has since recommended applying supplementary integrity and confidentiality protection to the GTP-U user-plane interface to the Enhanced Node B (ENB).[20, 21] This is realized by mandatory implementation of tunnel mode IPSec to protect the GTP-U interface for both S1 and X2 user planes. See Chapter 3, "All-IP Access Systems," for more information on the EUTRAN architecture.

In addition to mobile unicast services, GTP supports the definition of a multicast service tunnel as part of the Multimedia Broadcast and Multicast Service (MBMS). MBMS is a downlink point-to-multipoint service with modes for multicast and broadcast data. The technology transmits a multicast and broadcast stream from a single source, which is then replicated to a group of mobile users.

A single MBMS-GTP tunnel can be used for delivering all packets to those users who have joined a particular multicast service. Two options are defined for delivering the multicast traffic over the GTP tunnels, as follows:

- **IP unicast:** Sending multicast traffic into a unicast GTP tunnel, in which case multiple MBMS-GTP tunnels will need to be established to each access network-serving users who have joined the multicast service.
- **IP multicast:** Sending multicast traffic into a multicast GTP tunnel, in which case a single MBMS-GTP tunnel can be used to serve all users who have joined the multicast service.

Finally, GTP includes its own element reset detection mechanism. The GTP protocol defines echo_request and echo_response messages. These allow a GTP node to signal its peer that it has reset and all established contexts have been lost.

Mobile IP

Mobile IP is a standard defined by the Internet Engineering Task Force (IETF) in RFC 3344[22] for IPv4 and RFC 3775[23] for IPv6. Chapter 4 introduced Mobile IP functionality, demonstrating how it enables users to stay connected and maintain ongoing applications while moving between IP networks. Mobile IP enables the user to keep the same IP address, a "home address," allowing Correspondent Nodes (CN) to continue sending packets to the mobile device, whether it is currently attached to its home link or is away from home.

Whereas GTP is a network-based mobility protocol that can make an entire cellular network appear as a point-to-point connection, Mobile IP exposes the mobile device to subnet transitions, performing mobility at the network layer rather than below it.

Figure 6-15 shows the three components of Mobile IP, as follows:

- **Mobile Node (MN):** A device such as a cell phone, PDA, or laptop whose software enables Mobile IP capabilities.
- **Home Agent (HA):** A router on the home network serving as the anchor point for communication with the Mobile Node; it tunnels packets from devices on the Internet, called Correspondent Nodes, to the Mobile Node. The tunnel termination point toward the Mobile Node is termed the *care-of-address (CoA).*
- **Foreign Agent (FA):** An optional router functionality defined in Mobile IPv4, where the router can function as the care-of-address for the Mobile Node when it roams to a foreign network, delivering packets from the Home Agent to the Mobile Node.

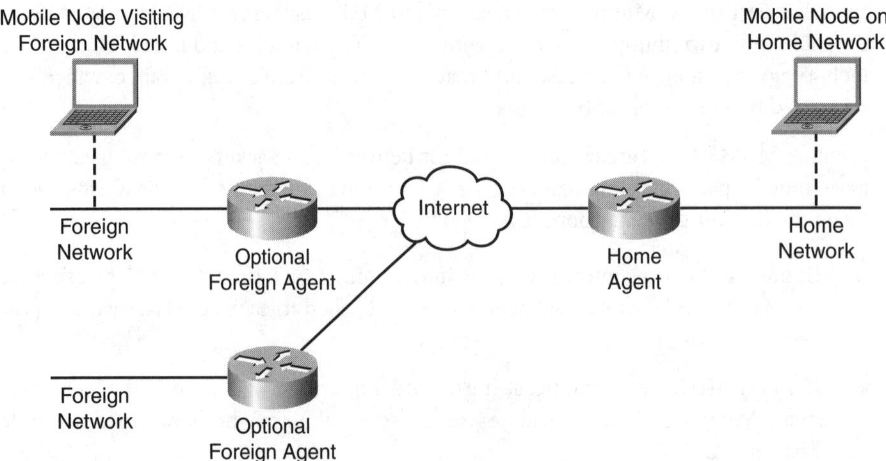

Figure 6-15 *Mobile IP Components*

The Mobile IP process has three main phases, as follows:

- **Agent Discovery:** A Mobile Node discovers its Home Agent and optionally its Foreign Agent during agent discovery.
- **Registration:** The Mobile Node registers its current location with the Home Agent and optionally its Foreign Agent during registration.
- **Tunneling:** A reciprocal tunnel is set up by the Home Agent to the care-of address (current location of the Mobile Node on the foreign network) to route packets to the Mobile Node as it roams.

Agent Discovery

During the agent discovery phase, the Home Agent, and optionally the Foreign Agent, advertises its services on the network by using extensions to the ICMP Router Discovery Protocol (IRDP) or ICMPv6. The Mobile Node listens to these advertisements to determine if it is connected to its home network or foreign network. Rather than waiting for agent advertisements, a Mobile Node can send out an agent solicitation. This solicitation forces any agents on the link to immediately send an agent advertisement.

If a Mobile Node determines that it is connected to a foreign network, it acquires a care-of address (CoA). Two types of care-of addresses exist, as follows:

- In MIPv4, a care-of address may be acquired from a Foreign Agent.
- In either MIPv4 or MIPv6, a collocated care-of address may be acquired.

A Foreign Agent CoA is an IP address of a Foreign Agent that has an interface on the foreign network being visited by a Mobile Node. A Mobile Node that acquires this type of CoA can share the address with other Mobile Nodes.

A Collocated CoA (CCoA) is an IP address temporarily assigned to the interface of the Mobile Node itself. The Mobile Node can acquire this address through conventional mechanisms—for example, stateful auto-configuration using the Dynamic Host Configuration Protocol (DHCP) or stateless auto-configuration when operating with MIPv6. This CoA represents the current position of the Mobile Node on the foreign network and can be used by only one Mobile Node at a time.

Registration and Binding Updates

The Mobile Node is configured with the IP address and mobility security association of its Home Agent. In addition, the Mobile Node is configured with either its home IP address, or another user identifier, such as a Network Access Identifier (NAI).

The Mobile Node uses this information to form a Mobile IP Registration Request message. It sends this message to its Home Agent either through the Foreign Agent or directly if it is using a CCoA. If the registration request message is sent through the Foreign

Agent, the Foreign Agent is responsible for checking the validity of the message. If the registration request is valid, the Foreign Agent relays it to the Home Agent.

The Home Agent checks the validity of the registration request message, which includes authentication of the Mobile Node. If the registration request message is valid, the Home Agent creates a mobility binding (an association between the Mobile Node and its CoA), a tunnel to the CoA, and a routing entry for forwarding packets to the Home Address (HoA) through the tunnel.

The Home Agent then sends a Mobile IP registration reply message to the Mobile Node, through the Foreign Agent (if MIPv4 is being used and the registration request was received via the Foreign Agent) or directly to the Mobile Node. If the registration request message is not valid, the Home Agent rejects the request by sending a registration reply message with an appropriate error code.

The Foreign Agent checks the validity of the registration reply message. If the message is valid, the Foreign Agent adds the Mobile Node to its visitor list, establishes a tunnel back to the Home Agent (if reverse tunnel is enabled), and creates a routing entry for forwarding packets to the home address. It then relays the registration reply message to the Mobile Node.

Finally, the Mobile Node checks the validity of the registration reply message, including proper authentication of the Home Agent. If a valid message specifies that the registration is accepted, the Mobile Node has confirmed that the Home Agent and possibly the Foreign Agent is/are aware of its location. In the CCoA case, it adds a tunnel to the Home Agent.

Thus, a successful Mobile IP registration sets up the routing mechanism for transporting packets to and from the Mobile Node when it is away from its home access network. Now if the Mobile Node moves to a new subnet, it will acquire a new CoA. The MN will then trigger a Binding Update signaling exchange to the Home Agent, which then updates its binding cache, allowing packets to continue to be sent to the MN, even after its CoA address has changed.

Tunneling

Data packets addressed to the Mobile Node are routed to its home network, where the Home Agent now intercepts and tunnels them to the CoA toward the Mobile Node. Tunneling has two primary functions: encapsulation of the data packet to reach the tunnel endpoint, and de-encapsulation when the packet is delivered at that endpoint.

In MIPv4, the default tunnel mode is IP encapsulation within IP encapsulation (RFC 2003). Optionally, GRE and minimal encapsulation within IP (RFC 2004) may be used. Figure 6-16 illustrates MIPv4 encapsulation with Foreign Agent CoA.

As the figure shows, the Home Agent is responsible for encapsulating any downlink packets sent to the Mobile Node's home address into a tunnel, which terminates at the Foreign Agent.

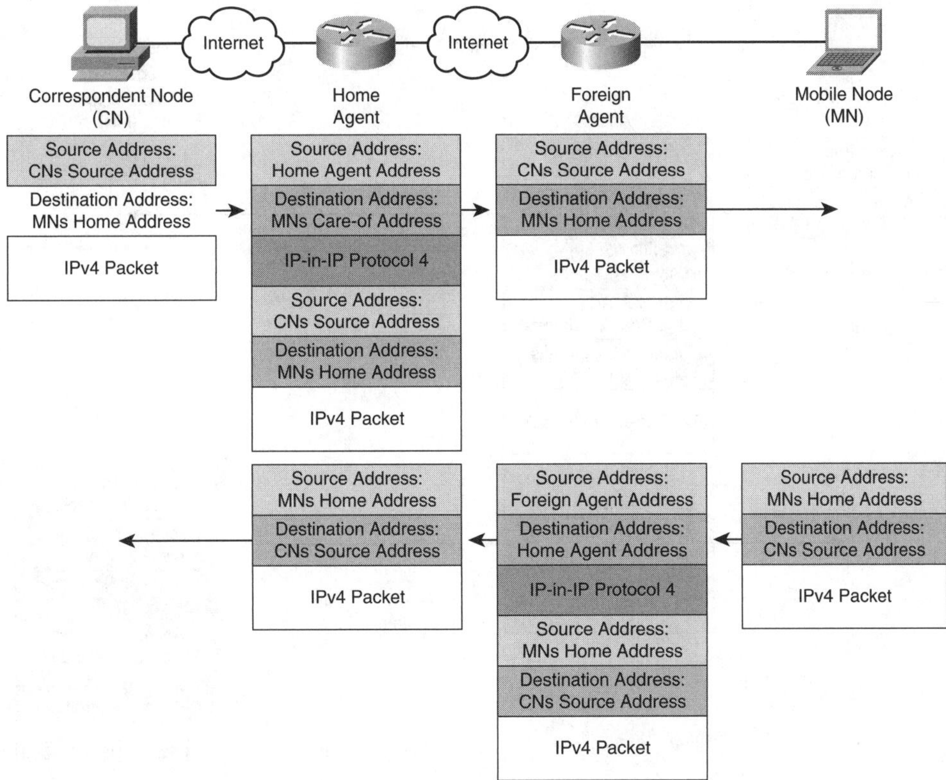

Figure 6-16 *MIPv4 Encapsulation with Foreign Agent Allocated CoA and Reverse Tunneling*

In the return direction, the Mobile Node sends packets using its home IP address, effectively maintaining the appearance that it is always on its home network. In MIPv4, these packets are optionally reverse tunneled back to the Home Agent, and Figure 6-16 shows the encapsulation used when such reverse tunneling is operational. Reverse tunneling is particularly useful because it ensures that topologically correct source IP addresses are visible to the access network, allowing the administrator to implement techniques to limit IP address spoofing—for example, deploying Unicast Reverse Path Forwarding (URPF).

In CCoA mode, the encapsulation is directly between the Home Agent and the Mobile Node, for both MIPv4 and MIPv6. Figure 6-17 illustrates the case of CCoA with reverse tunneling demonstrating the use IPv6 encapsulation (RFC 2473) for the MIPv6 case.

Note Figure 6-17 highlights one of the challenges with MIP CCoA deployments, where all packets sent over the access network will always have an encapsulated payload. This results in both an expansion in the access network bandwidth requirements and degraded performance of any access network IP compression techniques—for example, Robust Header Compression.

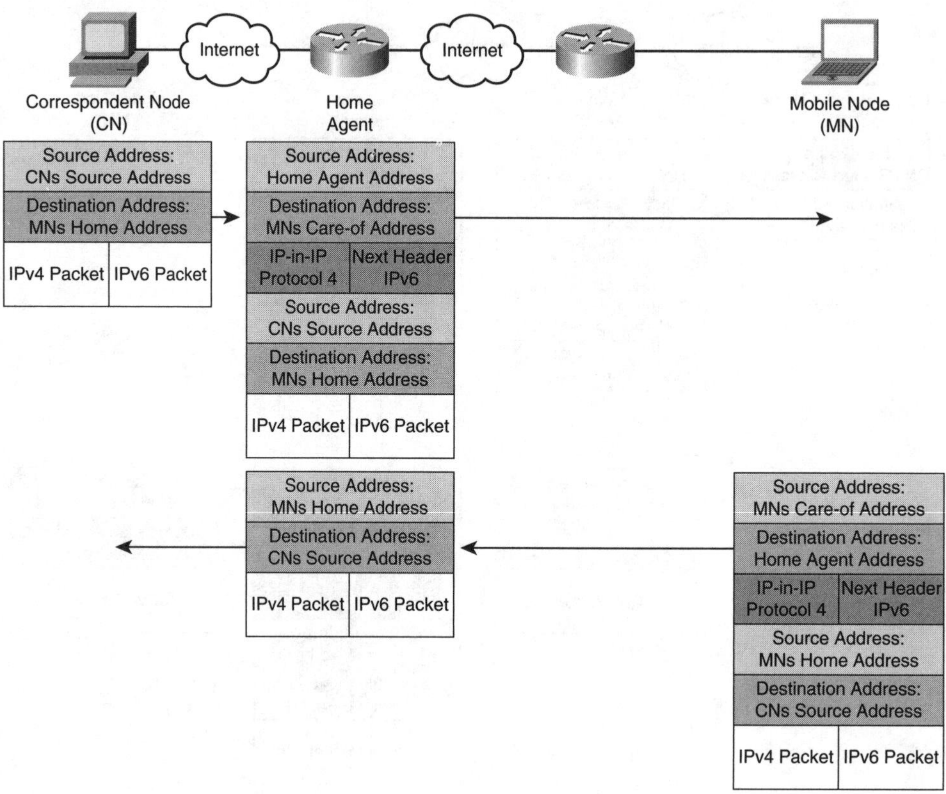

Figure 6-17 *MIP Encapsulation with CCoA and Reverse Tunneling*

Optimal Routing

Bidirectional tunneling can be used with a simple IPv6-enabled CN. When the CN supports MIPv6, packet forwarding may be optimized by the operation of Route Optimization. Route Optimization requires the MN to register its binding association with the CN, including its CoA. This allows the CN to send a packet directly to the MN, using this CoA instead of the home address, as shown in Figure 6-18.

The IP applications in the MN need to be shielded from the operation of Route Optimization, and so MIPv6 defines the use of a routing header for the CN to communicate the home address to the MN. The MN then swaps the CoA in the destination address with the home address in the routing header, shielding the operation from upper-layer applications.

In the return direction, the CN also needs to shield its applications from the Route Optimization operation. Figure 6-18 shows the MN sending packets to the CN using its CoA as the packet's source address. The MN will then use the Destination Options to transport its home address to the CN, allowing the CN to switch the source address from the CoA to the HoA.

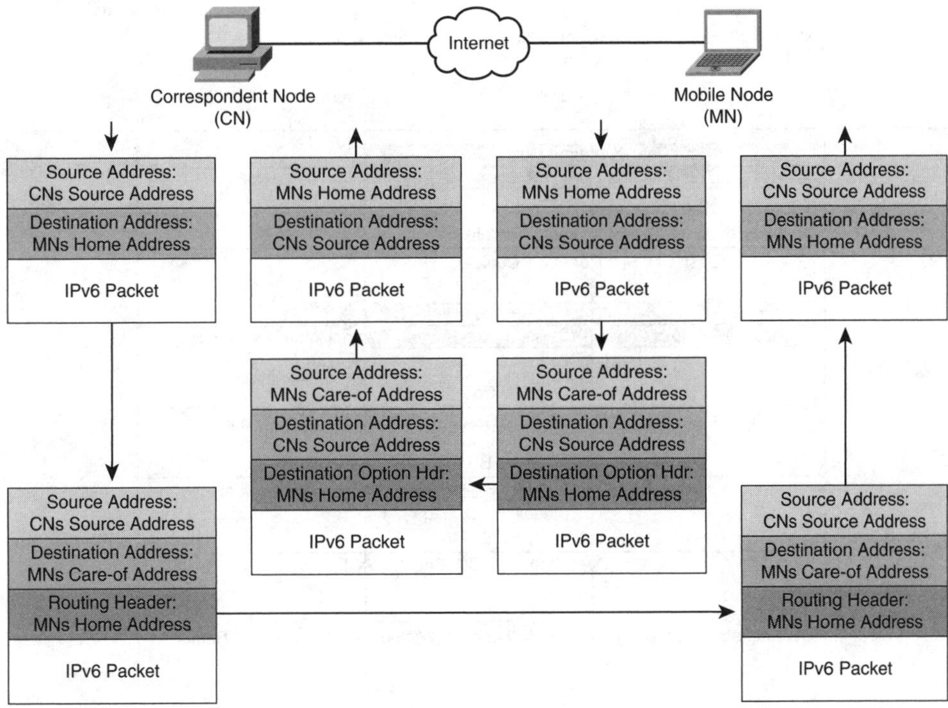

Figure 6-18 *MIPv6 Route Optimization*

MIPv6 defines a Return Routability exchange as a security procedure to achieve route optimization. This is required for the CN to ascertain that packets sent directly from a MNs CoA corresponds to the same entity sending packets from a MNs HoA via bidirectional tunneling through a Home Agent.

Figure 6-19 shows the message exchanges for the Return Routability procedure, which needs to be performed before Route Optimization can occur.

The procedure is initiated by the MN sending a Home Test Init (HoTI) message to the CN via the already established bi-directional tunnel, which will then have the MNs HoA as its source address. The MN sends a second message, the Care-of Test Init (CoTI) message, directly to the CN using the MNs CoA as the packet's source address. Both the HoTI and CoTI message contain random numbers in their cookies.

The CN responds to the HoTI message with a Home Test (HoT) message, which will be tunneled to the MN via the Home Agent. The message includes the random cookie value from the HoTI, a home nonce index, and a home key-generation token, generated by a hash function of the HoA and home nonce.

Similarly, the CN responds to the CoTI message with a Care-of Test (CoT) message, which will be sent directly to the MNs CoA. The message includes the random cookie value from the CoTI, a care-of nonce index, and a care-of key-generation token, generated by a hash function of the CoA and care-of nonce.

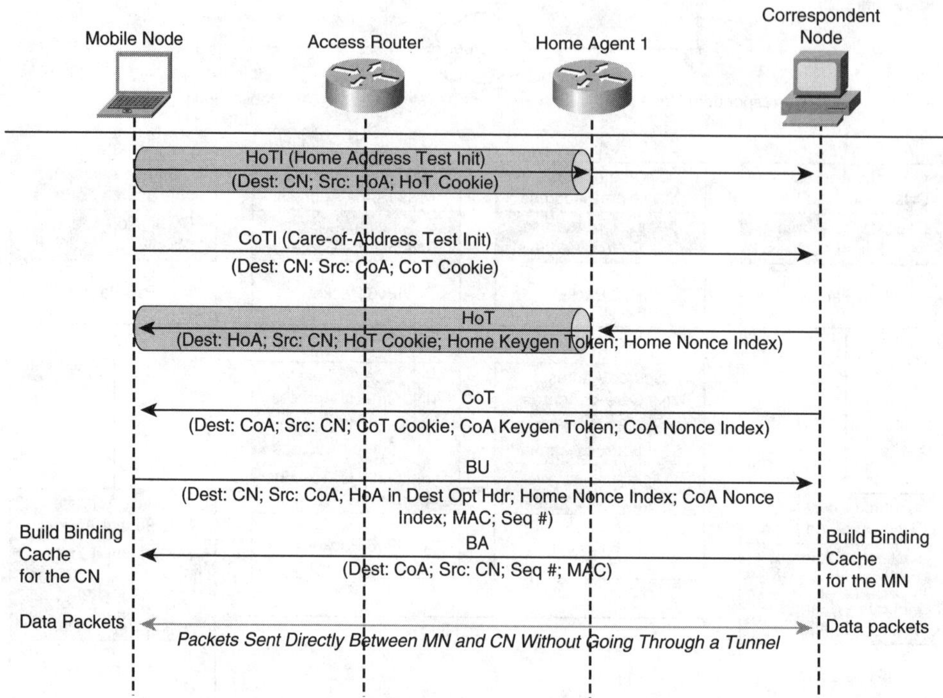

Figure 6-19 *MIPv6 Return Routability Procedure*

After the MN has received both HoT and CoT messages, the Return Routability procedure is complete, and the MN has sufficient information to send a Binding Update (BU) message directly to the CN. The BU message contains the nonce indexes from the HoT and CoT messages, and a Message Authentication Check code derived using a key derived from a combination of both home key and care-of key-generation tokens and a hash function of the BU message, CoA, and CN address.

The CN is then able to confirm that the BU message originated from an entity that has previously received both CoT and HoT messages, creates a binding cache entry, and sends a Binding Acknowledgment back to the MN, which is integrity protected using the same key-generation tokens.

Mobile IP Security

Unlike GTP, where the network entities are assumed to be trusted, the MIP messages originate from mobile devices, over possibly un-protected access links. Therefore, the Mobile IP protocol includes integrated security mechanisms.

MIPv4 uses message authentication to protect messages between MN and HA, with all registration messages between the MN and HA required to contain a Mobile-Home Authentication Extension (MHAE). Optionally, messages to the FA are protected using the Mobile-Foreign Authentication Extension and Foreign-Home Authentication Extension to protect messages between MN and FA, and HA and FA, respectively.

The integrity of the registration messages is protected by a pre-shared key between the MN and HA. Message Digest algorithm 5 (MD5) is used to compute the message authenticator over the message with the value being appended in the MHAE. Replay protection uses the identification field in the registration messages, either an NTP timestamp and sequence number or random nonces.

MIPv6 further enhances the integrated security and RFC 3776 mandates that IPSec Encapsulating Security Payload (ESP) in transport mode is used to protect the Binding Update/Binding Acknowledge messages exchanged between MN and HA, as well as the HoTI/HoT messages used in the Return Routability procedures. Although the Security Association (SA) can be based on a shared secret (similar to MIPv4), MIPv6 supports both version 1 and version 2 of the Internet Key Exchange (IKE) to dynamically create the security associations. (IKEv1 operation is defined in RFC 3776, and IKEv2 operation in RFC 4877.)

Note The "I-WLAN Core Network" section later in this chapter describes how IKEv2/EAP is used to create the IPSec SA for remote IPSec access via WLAN. These same techniques can be used for dynamically generating the SA for MIPv6 operation, including the use of smart card-based credentials using EAP-SIM and EAP-AKA methods.

Proxy Mobile IPv6

Mobile IP, as described previously, ensures that mobility-aware hosts can move across multiple access routers, including moving between different access technologies, while ensuring IP applications are unaffected by the change in care-of address.

The requirement for hosts to be mobility aware coupled with the additional overhead required for CCoA operation prompted the IETF to form a new Working Group (WG) focused on Network-based Local Mobility Management (NetLMM). The NetLMM WG was tasked with defining a protocol where IP mobility is handled without the involvement from the Mobile Node, where mobile functionality in the network is responsible for tracking the user and triggering signaling on its behalf.

Note In many respects, this was a recognition that the majority of mobile subscribers were being supported using network-based mobility via the GTP protocol defined by 3GPP. Although GTP continues to be a network-based mobility protocol applied to 3GPP access networks, the mobile industry was calling for a network-based mobility protocol that could be integrated with non-3GPP access networks.

The network-based mobility protocol selected by the NetLMM WG is based on Proxy Mobile IPv6 (PMIPv6) and specified in RFC 5213.[24] As its name suggests, PMIPv6 uses the MIPv6 concepts, but now instead of a mobile host performing the mobility signaling, a proxy mobility agent performs signaling on behalf of a mobile device attached to the network.

Two new network functions are defined in PMIPv6: the Local Mobility Anchor (LMA) and the Mobile Access Gateway (MAG). The LMA provides the home agent function within a PMIPv6 domain, being the topological anchor point for the Mobile Node's care-of address. The MAG is a function of an access router responsible for triggering the mobility-related signaling on behalf of the attached mobile device.

Figure 6-20 shows the signaling exchanges involved with PMIPv6 network-based mobility.

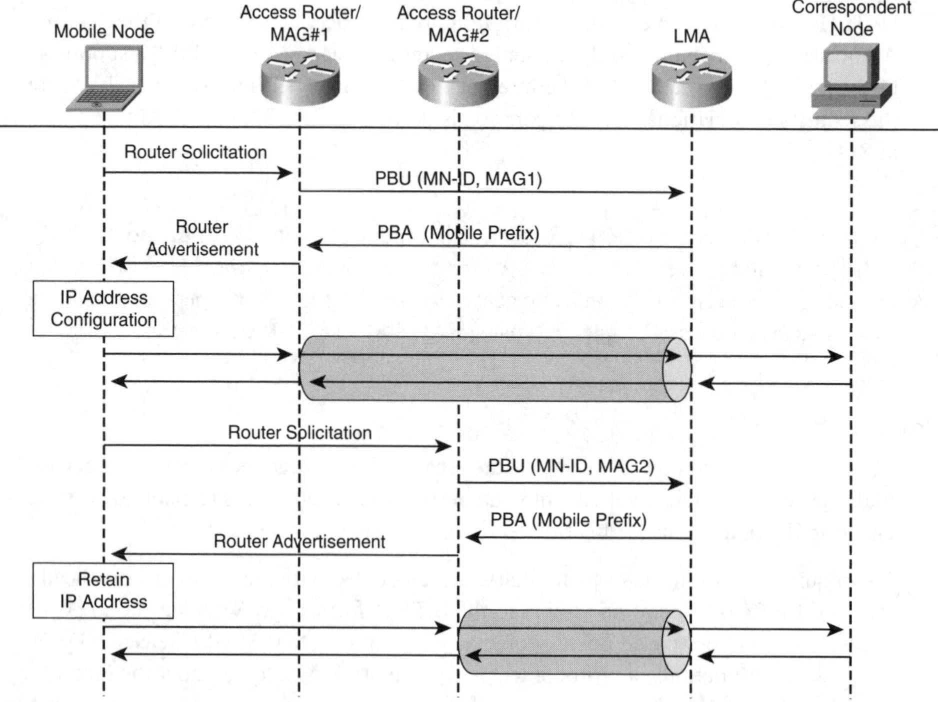

Figure 6-20 *PMIPv6 Network-Based Mobility*

A mobile device enters the network and attempts to configure its IP interface by sending a Router Solicitation message to the Access Router. As part of the network attachment procedure, the MAG will have received a MN identity. For example, a Chargeable User ID (defined in RFC 4372) may have been returned to the Access Router as part of the authentication exchange. The MAG forms a Proxy Binding Update (PBU) message including the MN Identifier Option and sends this to the LMA.

When the LMA accepts this binding, it sends a Proxy Binding Acknowledgment (PBA) message back to the MAG, including the Mobile Node's home network prefixes, and triggers the establishment of a bi-directional tunnel between the LMA and the MAG.

The MAG, on receiving the PBA, confirms the tunnel setup and advertises the home prefixes toward the Mobile Node with a Router Advertisement message. The mobile device then configures its IP address using the home prefixes supplied by the LMA, creating an IP address that topologically belongs to the LMA.

The MAG now acts as the default gateway for the Mobile Node, ensuring that any packet sent by the Mobile Node will be received by the MAG and reverse tunneled toward the LMA. Similarly, when the LMA receives packets destined toward the mobile device, it tunnels these to the MAG, where they are de-encapsulated before forwarding on to the mobile.

If the mobile device now moves areas such that it is covered by a new MAG, the same PBU/PBA signaling exchange occurs; because the home prefix signaled and advertised by the new MAG is identical to the old prefix, the mobile device retains its IP address configuration.

IPv4 Support

Network-based mobility can be used with IPv6-based home addressing while sending PMIPv6 mobility messages over an IPv6 transport network. Clearly such an architecture is restrictive in that the majority of hosts and mobile transport networks are based on IPv4. As a consequence, PMIPv6 network-based mobility has been enhanced to support both IPv4 hosts and IPv4 transport networks.[25]

IPv4 hosts are supported by the MAG inserting an IPv4 Home Address Option in the PBU message. If the IPv4 address value in the option is set to all zeros, this indicates the mobile has just entered the PMIPv6 domain and requires an IPv4 HoA to be allocated. The IPv4 Address Acknowledgment option is used in the PBA to signal the IPv4 HoA, and the MAG can then allocate the host address using conventional techniques—for example, using PPP's IP Control Protocol (IPCP) or Dynamic Host Control Protocol (DHCP).

Finally, because IPv4 packets need to be tunneled between the MAG and LMA, when an IPv6 transport network is used, IPv4-over-IPv6 encapsulation mode is used.

Note DHCP-based IPv4 address allocation requires additional functionality in order to coordinate between the different DHCP servers. For example, when changing access routers, the Mobile Node will typically send a unicast DHSPREQUEST message to its current DHCP server. If that server was co-located with the old MAG/Access Router, the Mobile Node needs to be forced to update its DHCP server address to one that serves the new MAG/Access Router.

Finally, to support PMIPv6 transport by IPv4 networks, the IPv4 or IPv6 payload packet can be encapsulated using the following options:

- **IPv4:** IPv4 or IPv6 payload packet carried in an IPv4 packet.
- **IPv4-UDP:** IPv4 packet carried as a payload in an UDP header of an IPv4 packet.

- **IPv4-UDP-TLV:** IPv4 packet carried as a payload in an IPv4 packet with UDP and TLV headers.
- **IPv4-UDP-ESP:** IPv4 payload packet carried in an IPv4 packet with UDP and ESP headers.

Overlapping IP Address Support

One of the challenges with supporting legacy use cases, including IPv4 deployments, is the possibility that two mobile devices connected to the same MAG will be allocated the same IP address—for example, if a common LMA is configured to support a mobile Virtual Private Network service where the Mobile Nodes are associated with different VPNs, and each VPN is configured to allocate RFC 1918 private addresses to attached mobile devices. Unfortunately, the only identifier used in the PMIPv6 tunnels is the Mobile Node's IP address, which is now insufficient to allow correct forwarding of packets to the VPN-attached Mobile Nodes.

In order to address such issues, a new mobility option allowing the use of GRE encapsulation between the LMA and MAG has been defined.[26] Using such techniques, the uplink and downlink GRE keys can be used to distinguish between packet payloads sent to different Mobile Nodes, or even between different flows to/from the same Mobile Node.

PS Core Network Architectures

The PS Core Network provides access to IP-based services. The PS Core Network needs to provide a similar set of core functionalities compared to the CS Core Network, including user authentication and roaming access. The PS Core Network is also responsible for providing IP specific functionalities, for IP address allocation, including access to the public Internet or a private VPN service, IP mobility management allowing continuous IP access to/from moving devices, and session management, including a framework for supporting end-to-end Quality of Service.

The previous sections have highlighted how different standardization bodies have defined different PS Core Network architectures supported by different IP mobility protocols. The subsequent sections describe how these different PS Core Networks deliver a similar set of core functionalities to the attached mobile devices.

UTRAN PS Core Network

The UTRAN PS CN is shown in Figure 6-21. This figure indicates that the PS CN comprises two elements: the Serving GPRS Support Node (SGSN) and the Gateway GPRS Support Node (GGSN).

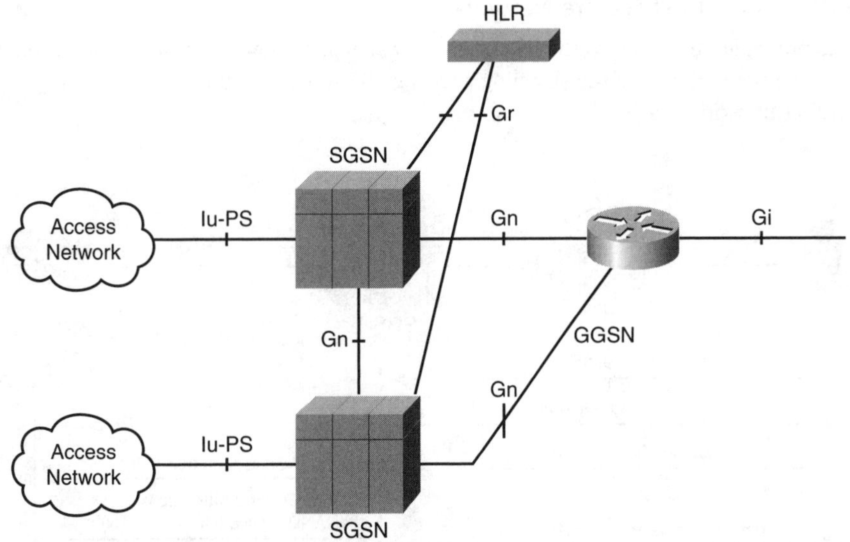

Figure 6-21 *UTRAN PS Core Network*

When 3GPP defined their overlay architecture for supporting IP services, they borrowed many of the concepts already employed in the CS Core Network. The SGSN authenticates the user using the same techniques as the CS Core Network, such that an authentic mobile device can attach to the PS Core Network.

As described in the preceding section, GPRS mobility is based on PDP contexts; after attaching to the network, the mobile device needs to first establish a PDP context. Unlike in the CS world, where a user's context was fixed throughput the duration of a voice session at the Anchor MSC/VLR, the 3GPP PS CN defines the ability to transfer the active contexts of a user between SGSNs using the inter-SGSN Gn interface, as shown in Figure 6-21.

The other key architectural difference between the CS and PS Core Networks is that in the CS Core Network, voice services are executed by the MSC/VLR in the visited network, whereas in the PS Core Network, the GGSN is most likely to be in the home network, even when a subscriber is roaming.

Note The PS Core Network architecture does not preclude GGSN deployment in a visited, roamed-to network. However, operators have been keen to offer differentiated services via service portals in the home network. Deploying the GGSN in the home network ensures that the subscriber's operator has full visibility of all packets and is consequently able to provide differentiated services—for example, pre-paid-based data-roaming services or mobile VPN access, where users packets are tunneled switched at a home GGSN from GTP into a corporate VPN service.

Attaching to the PS Core Network

The procedure to attach to the PS core is very similar to the attach procedure to the CS core. Figure 6-22 shows the signaling exchange between a mobile device, the SGSN, and HLR at network attach.

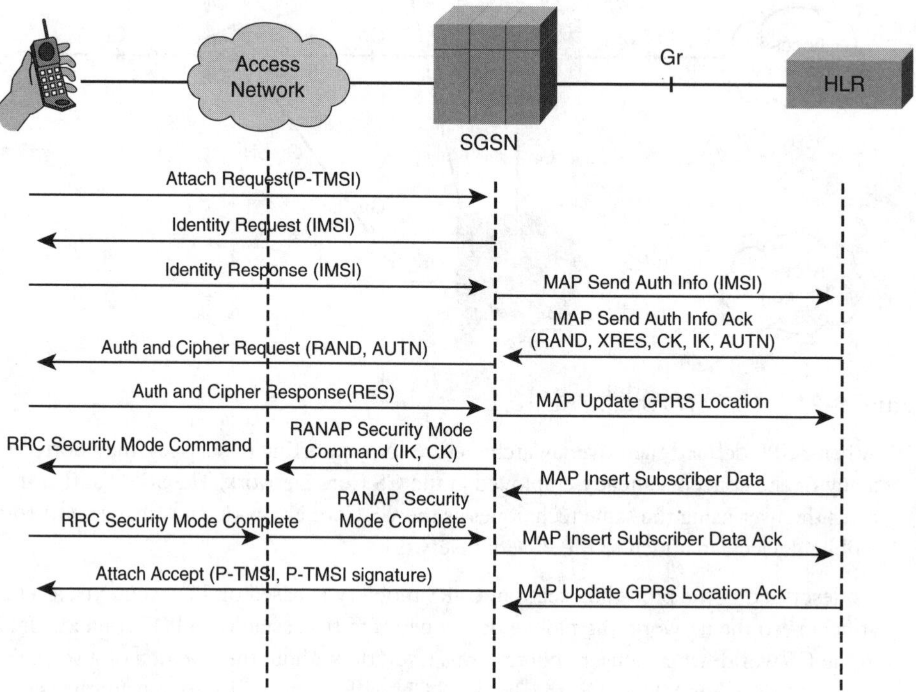

Figure 6-22 *PS Core Network Attach*

The procedure is initiated by the mobile sending an Attach Request message to the SGSN, now using a Packet-TMSI (P-TMSI) for identification. The SGSN is responsible for authentication and thus recovers the IMSI and uses this to request authentication information from the HLR, using the same MAP Send Auth Info message that was used by the MSC/VLR.

In this instance, the HLR knows that the signaled IMSI corresponds to a UMTS subscriber and responds with a set of authentication vectors comprising the quintuplets (RAN, XRES, CK, IK, and AUTN). The UMTS authentication algorithm differs from the GSM one in that separate ciphering and integrity keys are defined (CK and IK, respectively) and authentication is mutual, requiring the additional Authentication Token (AUTN).

The mobile device is provided the AUTN and challenged with the RAND value. The AUTN includes a Message Authentication Code so that the mobile device can check that the challenges were generated by its home HLR, as well as a sequence number to prevent replay attacks. The mobile device uses its SIM card to check the validity of AUTN and responds to the challenge with the result, RES. The SGSN checks that RES and XRES match and then triggers an update of the GPRS location in the HLR. The MAP Insert Subscriber Data exchange is re-used from the CS procedure, but in this case, the subscriber data related to PS services is downloaded from the HLR to the SGSN.

The application of ciphering is triggered by the SGSN sending a RANAP Cipher Mode Command message to the access network, including the necessary keying material for protecting the access network. The SGSN may also allocate a new P-TMSI in the Attach Accept message, in which case the SGSN can also allocate a P-TMSI signature. The P-TMSI signature is a three-octet hash of the allocated P-TMSI. In subsequent exchanges, if the mobile provides both P-TMSI and P-TMSI signature, the SGSN can authenticate the UE by means of the P-TMSI/P-TMSI signature combination, negating the need for lengthy authentication procedures.

Access Point Name

An access point name (APN) identifies a packet data network (PDN) that is configured on and accessible from a GGSN. A PDN corresponds to particular routing domain, and APNs can be configured to use overlapping IP addresses. The APN corresponds to a DNS name of a GGSN and is composed of the following two parts:

- **The APN Network Identifier:** Defines the external PDN to which the GGSN is connected.
- **The APN Operator Identifier:** Defines in which operator PS Core Network the GGSN is located.

For example, the APN used to access a Cisco corporate VPN service may be of the form "cisco.mnc150.mcc310.gprs," where 310 is the Mobile Country Code and 150 is the Mobile Network Code in which the GGSN is located.

The APNs to which a subscriber is authorized to access are downloaded from the HLR as part of the GPRS Attach Procedure. The APN is also provided by the Mobile Node when it activates a PDP context and the SGSN is responsible for checking that the APN is valid; otherwise, the PDP context request will be rejected.

PDP Context Activation

In order to send and receive IP packets, the mobile device must first establish a PDP context. Figure 6-23 shows the signaling procedures involved with context activation, which is initiated by the mobile sending an Activate PDP Context Request message to the network. The message typically includes the APN to which the PDP context should be established, as well as the requested QoS parameters.

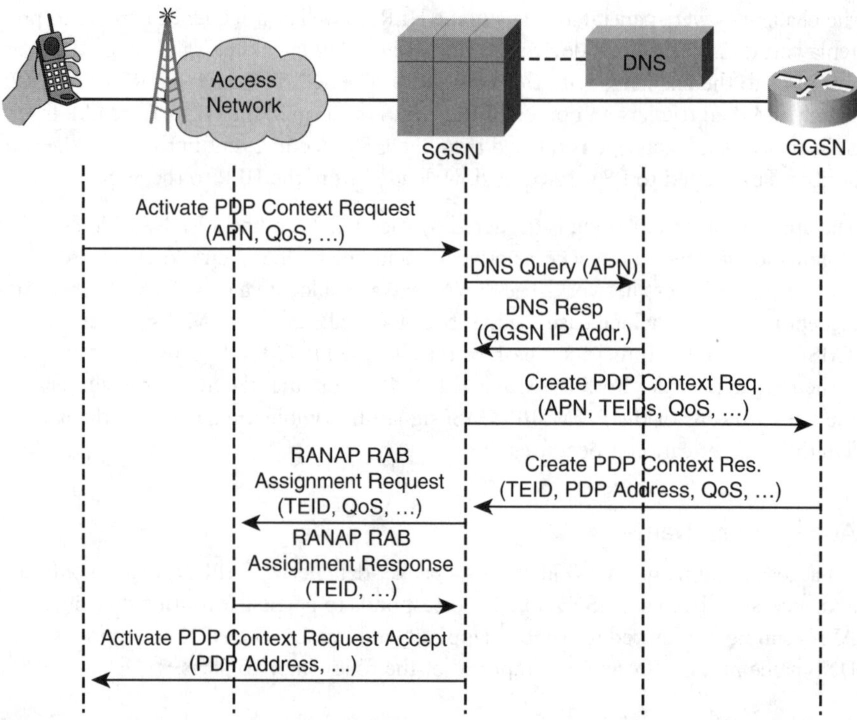

Figure 6-23 *PDP Context Activation*

The SGSN will then use the APN to query its local DNS in order to derive a GGSN IP address, for example using the APN as a Fully Qualified Domain Name in a DNS procedure. The SGSN will then send a GTP-C Create PDP Context Request message to the GGSN. Table 6-2 shows some of the key information elements in this message.

Table 6-2 *Create PDP Context Request Message*

Information Element	Description
TEID Data	TEID that SGSN expects to receive GTP-U messages for this user.
TEID Signaling	TEID that SGSN expects to receive GTP-C messages.
Access Point Name	APN for this PDP context.
SGSN Address for Signaling	IP address for GTP-C messages.
SGSN Address for User Traffic	IP address for GTP-U messages.
QoS Profile	QoS to apply to this PDP context, including traffic class and bit rates.

The GGSN allocates a PDP address to the context, which may be an IPv4 or IPv6 address, and responds with a Create PDP Context Response message including the data and signaling TEID, possibly down-negotiated QoS and GGSN IP addresses for use by the SGSN.

At this stage, the SGSN triggers the establishment of a Radio Access Bearer (RAB) for transporting the PDP context in the access network. This is achieved by an exchange of RANAP RAB Assignment Request/Response messages, including TEIDs for the GTP-U tunnel between the access network and the SGSN. The procedure ends with the SGSN signaling the mobile that the PDP context request has been accepted, including providing the mobile its PDP address for use on this PDP Context.

At the end of this procedure, the PS user plane is established, as shown in Figure 6-24. GTP tunnels are used between the UTRAN and SGSN and between SGSN and GGSN to enable packets to be forwarded to/from the mobile device.

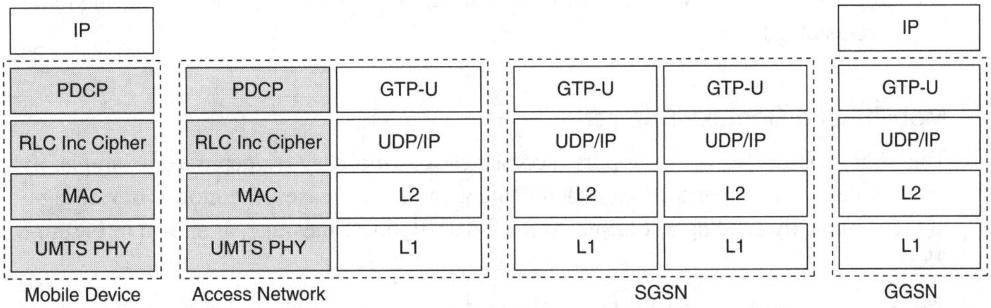

Figure 6-24 *PS User Plane After PDP Context Established*

The same procedure can be used to establish a secondary PDP context using the same PDP address; in this case, the request includes the QoS for the secondary context, as well as the TFT, which allows the GGSN to forward downlink packets into individual GTP-U tunnels.

Established PDP context can subsequently modified—for example, the QoS associated with a PDP can be downgraded and upgraded by either the GGSN, SGSN, access network, or mobile device.

PDP Preservation and Paging

After the PDP context is established and radio bearers configured, packets can be forwarded to and from the attached mobile device. However, during the session, there may be periods of inactivity when access network resources can be reclaimed—for example, to save the device's battery life or allow those resources to be used by other devices. In such instances, the PDP preservation procedure can be used to release RAB resources and the GTP-U tunnel between SGSN and RNC while preserving the PDP context.

However, if any of the PDP context corresponds to streaming or conversational traffic, the SGSN needs to inform the GGSN by sending a PDP context modification message, indicating that the maximum bit rate for those context has been modified to 0 kbps. For other PDP context (in other words, those corresponding to background or interactive traffic classes), the GGSN is not informed.

If a downlink packet arrives at the SGSN after RAB resources have been released, the packet cannot simply be forwarded because the GTP-U tunnel between SGSN and RNC has been torn down. Instead, the SGSN needs to perform a paging procedure by sending a RANAP Paging message to the RNC, which then triggers the mobile device to send a service request back to the SGSN, initiating Radio Access Bearer establishment together with GTP-U resources between the RNC and SGSN.

If the SGSN had previously indicated to the GGSN that streaming or conversational PDP contexts had been modified to 0 kbit/s, it triggers another PDP context modification signaling exchange, indicating to the GGSN that radio resources are again available by changing the bit rates associated with the PDP context to those negotiated during radio bearer re-establishment.

Mobility and Context Transfer

The GTP PS Core Network supports access network mobility triggered, for example, by the mobile device moving into a new routing area. In such cases, the mobile device signals the move by sending a Routing Area Update Request message, as shown in Figure 6-25.

This request includes the P-TMSI and P-TMSI signature, as well as the old Routing Area Identifier (RAI). The new SGSN needs to recover the PDP context information from the old SGSN; thus, it uses the old RAI to determine which SGSN holds the existing contexts. The new SGSN sends an SGSN Context Request message to the old SGSN, which is a GTP-C message, including the P-TMSI and P-TMSI signature provided by the mobile. The old SGSN, which previously allocated these identities, can then authenticate the request. If the old SGSN has established GTP-U tunnels to the access network, it sends a RANAP SRNS Context Request message to the access network, requesting it to stop sending downlink PDUs towards the mobile device and to provide the next GTP sequence numbers to be used on the uplink.

The old SGSN responds to the new SGSN with PDP context information and mobility management information, including cached authentication quintuplet information that the new SGSN acknowledges. The old SGSN then signals the old access network that buffered and unacknowledged downlink PDUs need to be sent back to the old SGSN, which forwards these to the new SGSN for subsequent sending to the mobile. The new SGSN updates its location with the HLR, triggering the PS Subscriber Profile to be downloaded. The new SGSN signals the mobile device that its routing area update has been accepted, providing new P-TMSI and P-TMSI signatures, which the mobile acknowledges with a Routing Area Update Complete message.

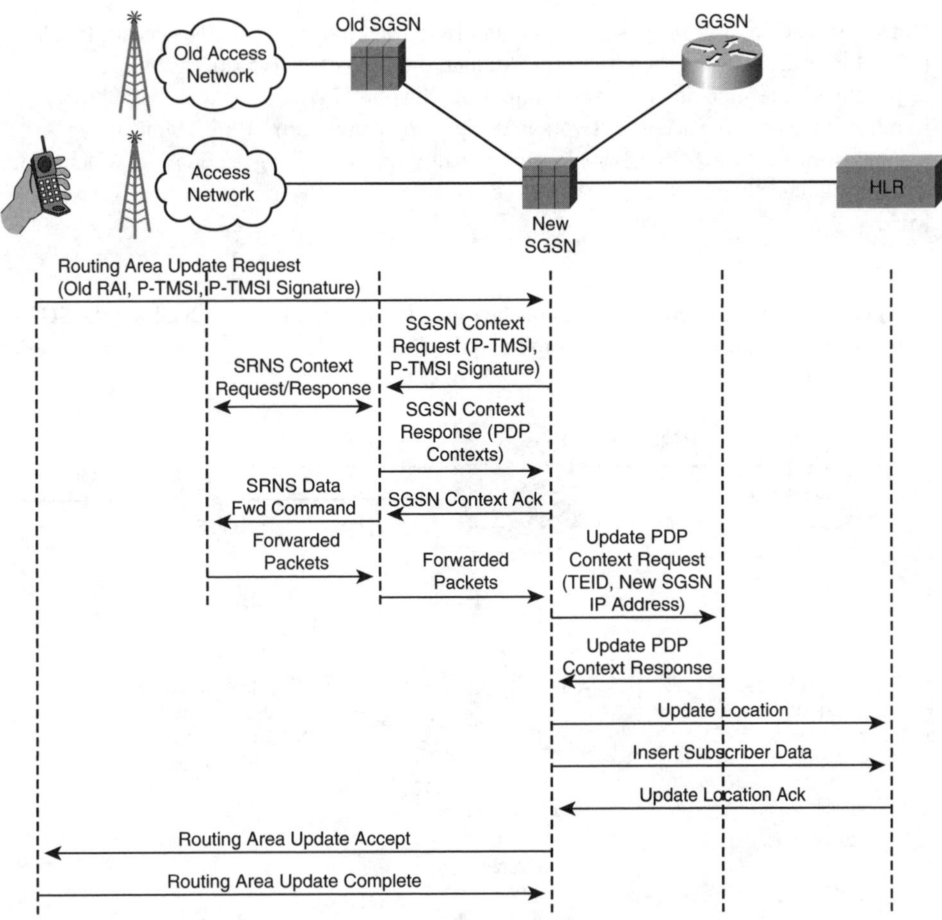

Figure 6-25 *PDP Context Transfer*

Note As is evident, GTP provides more than the simple network-based mobility of the GTP-U protocol, including GTP-C-based context modification and transfer capability.

Direct Tunnel

As data speeds increase from the original UTRAN peak speeds of 384 kbps up to HSPA peak speeds of 14 Mbps and more, the strain on the PS Core Network has triggered a flattening of the PS Core Network with a feature called "direct tunnel." The direct tunnel feature has built on the shift of packet-handling features out of the SGSN toward the GGSN. This left the SGSN in non-roaming, connected mode operation, adding little value from a user-plane perspective by simply switching from one GTP-U tunnel into another.

Note The SGSN user plane still has an important role to play in other scenarios. In idle mode, for instance (when there is no GTP tunnel to the access network), the SGSN is responsible for terminating idle mode, buffering downlink PDUs instead of simply forwarding those onto the access network and triggering paging procedures. Similarly, in roaming scenarios, the SGSN provides functionality for performing accounting, which then enables roaming charges to be levied by the visited access network back to the home network.

Figure 6-26 shows a representation of the direct tunnel function, which allows the SGSN to trigger the removing of itself from the data plane.

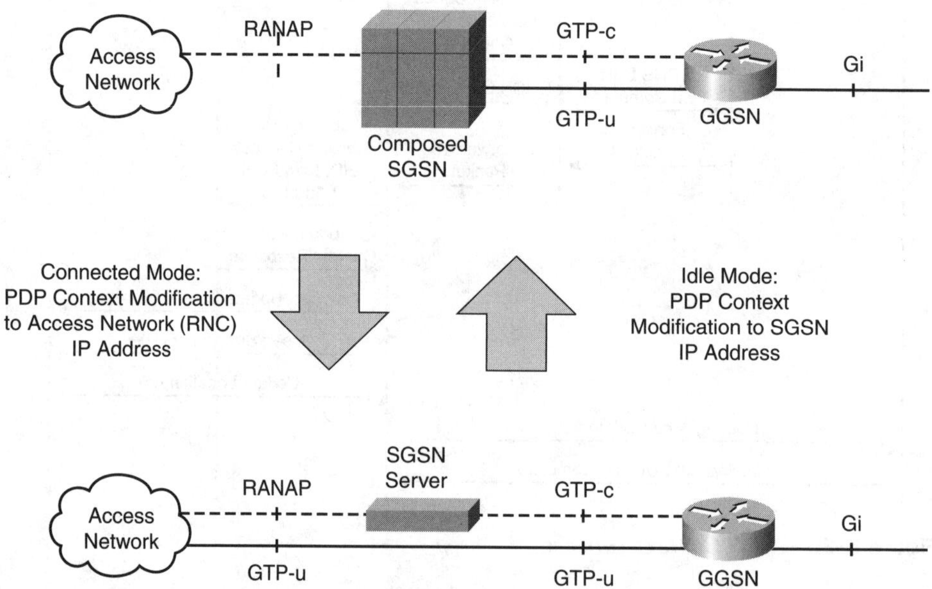

Figure 6-26 *GTP Direct Tunnel Architecture*

In non-roaming scenarios in connected mode, the GTP-U tunnel is able to be transported directly between the GGSN and the RNC in the access network. Conversely, if the access network triggers a PDP preservation procedure to free up resources, the SGSN will, as part of the procedure, trigger a PDP context modification back to a GTP tunnel terminated at the SGSN.

The direct tunnel feature then allows for existing SGSN hardware to scale to support the significantly higher data throughputs experienced with the latest HSPA access networks.

cdma2000 Packet Core Network

The architecture of the cdma2000 Packet Core Network (PCN) is shown in Figure 6-27 and highlights four core elements, as follows:

- **Packet Control Function (PCF):** Responsible for relaying packets between the PDSN and the access network and performing idle mode termination. In EV-DO networks, the PCF is augmented with Session Control and Mobility Management functionality.
- **Packet Data Serving Node (PDSN):** Acts as the access gateway for mobile devices including terminating the Point-to-Point Protocol (PPP) session with the mobile device, authentication, accounting, and address assignment. It supports two modes of operation: Simple IP and Mobile IP. When operating in Mobile IP mode, the Foreign Agent is co-located with the PDSN.
- **Mobile IP Home Agent (HA):** When operating in Mobile IP mode, a MIP HA is used to provide a permanent HoA as the mobile moves between PDSNs and allows roaming mobiles access to home-based services.
- **AAA Server:** Performs authentication for PPP and Mobile IP sessions.

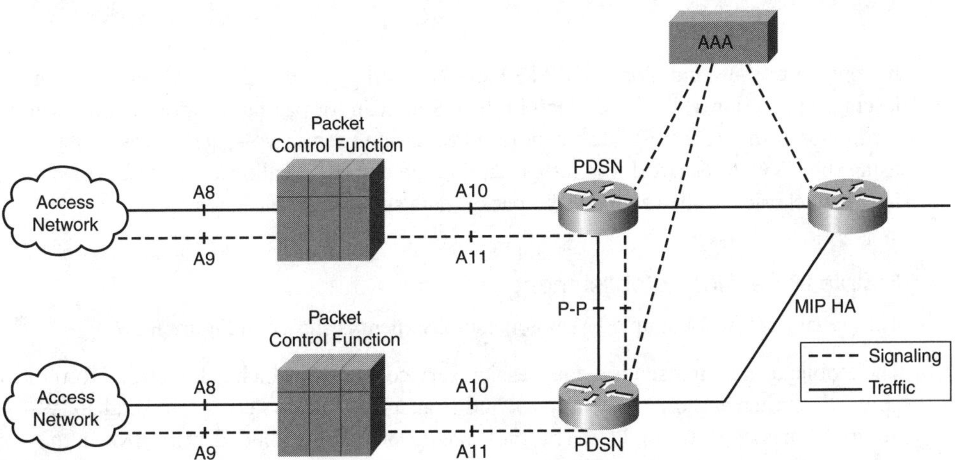

Figure 6-27 *cdma2000 Packet Core Network Architecture*

Table 6-3 provides a description of the different interfaces together with their protocol stacks.

Table 6-3 *cdma2000 PCN Interface Transport*[27]

Interface	Transport	Description
A8	Data/GRE/IP	Transport encapsulated user traffic between access network and PCF.
A9	Signaling/UDP/IP	Signaling used to establish A8 tunnel.
A10	Data/GRE/IP	Transport encapsulated user traffic between PCF and PDSN.
A11	Signaling/UDP/IP	Mobile IP-like signaling to allow the PCF to trigger the establishment of a GRE tunnel to the PDSN.
P-P	Signaling/UDP/IPSec Data/GRE/IPSec	Used for fast inter-PDSN handoff.

Note The A10-A11 interface is also referred to as the R-P interface, indicating that it represents the demarcation between the Radio network specifics of the PCF and access network and the Packet network specifics of the PDSN and MIP HA.

In contrast to the stand-alone 3GPP PS Core Network, the cdma2000 PCN architecture leverages procedures already defined in the CS domain for paging, handover, and session setup. For example, the establishment of a PS session uses a two-stage process, first reusing the CS Core Network for authenticating the device and allocating a low-rate signaling channel prior to the second-stage packet data session establishment.

Simple IP Session Establishment

The signaling flow for simple IP session establishment is shown in Figure 6-28.

The mobile device first sends a data session service request, which is forwarded to the CS core, which then authorizes the request and triggers the access network to send an A9-Setup A8 message[28] to the PCF. This message includes the mobile identity (IMSI), the QoS parameters, and A8 tunnel endpoint description.

The PCF then establishes the A10 connection by sending an A11-Registration Request message[29] to the PDSN, including the mobile identity. The PDSN updates its binding entry for the A10 connection, creating an association between the mobile's IMSI, PCF IP address, and PDSN IP address, and responds with an A11-Registration Response. The PCF and PDSN then use the IP addresses returned in this message as the A10 connection.

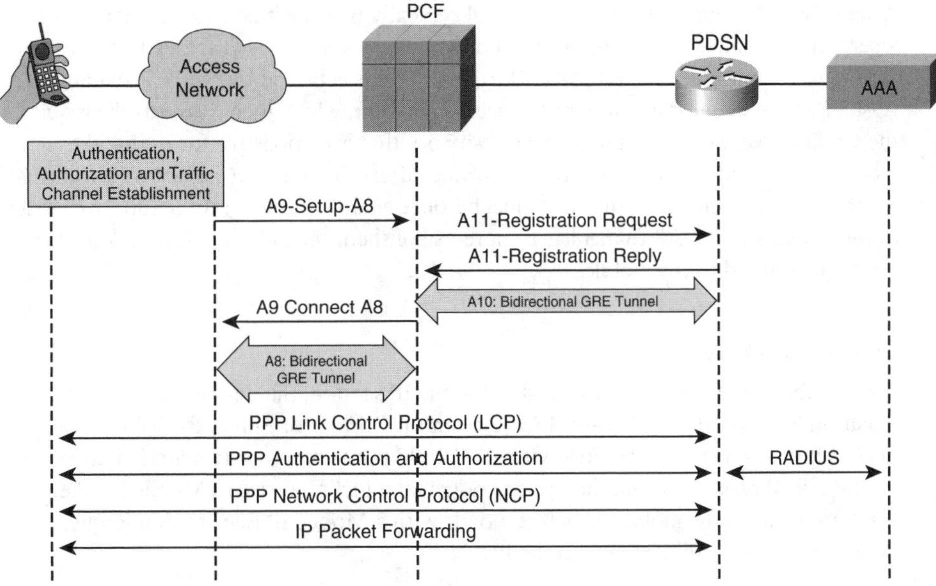

Figure 6-28 *cdma2000 Simple IP Session Establishment*

Note A per-mobile device, A10/GRE tunnel, is used to transport data packets between mobile and PDSN. The single GRE tunnel supports all IP sessions to the mobile—compared to the multiple GTP sessions for the 3GPP PS Core Network. Thus, differentiated QoS handling is signaled based on the IETF Differentiated Services (DiffServ) architecture. Chapter 4 provides detail on DiffServ-based QoS.

After establishing the A10 connection, the PCF sends an A9-Connect A8 message back to the access network with its A8 tunnel endpoint description.

After the A8 and A10 sessions are established, the mobile begins PPP negotiation, as shown in Figure 6-28. For example, during the LCP phase, PPP compression can be negotiated. After LCP, PPP authentication and authorization occurs, during which the PDSN sends a CHAP challenge to the mobile that responds by sending its response to the challenge together with its Network Address Identifier (NAI), which is in the form user@domain. On reception of the response, the PDSN derives the home AAA server from the NAI and then, acting as a RADIUS client, sends a RADIUS Access-Request message containing the mobile IMSI, challenge, and response to the AAA server. The AAA server authenticates the user, responding with a RADIUS Access-Accept message if the user is valid.

Finally, PPP NCP occurs, where the mobile device uses IPCP to request an IP address from the PDSN. Following address allocation, mobile packets can be transferred between mobile device and PDSN.

After a period of inactivity, the mobile will typically be transitioned to the dormant state, where the A8 tunnel is released. When a downlink packet arrives at the PCF, it must trigger the re-establishment of the A8 GRE tunnel. This is achieved by the PCF sending an A9-BS Service Request message to the access network, which then forwards the request the CS Core Network. It is the CS Core Network that is responsible for paging the mobile device and establishing a traffic channel after which the access network will trigger the re-establishment of the A8 tunnel by once again sending an A9-Setup A8 message to the PCF. After the A8 tunnel has been re-established, the buffered downlink packets can be forwarded to the mobile.

Session Mobility

If the mobile device wants to establish a Mobile IP session, the device will signal its intention by using the Mobile-IPv4 Configuration Option for PPP in the NCP phase (RFC 2290); see Figure 6-29. Following RFC 2990 procedures, no IP address is allocated in PPP's NCP phase; instead, the option triggers the PDSN to send a Mobile IP Agent Advertisement to the mobile, which responds with a Mobile IP Registration Request to the Foreign Agent collocated with the PDSN.

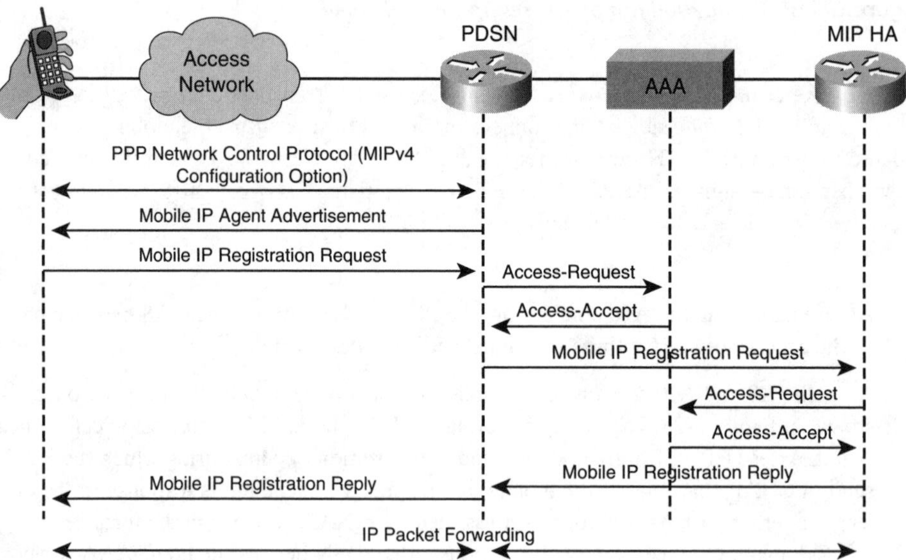

Figure 6-29 *cdma2000 Mobile IP Session Establishment*

Because the mobile does not know in advance whether it will be allocated a private HoA (RFC 1918) or a public HoA, the mobile must request reverse tunneling in its registration request. Normal Mobile IP signaling continues, with the MIP Home Agent allocating a HoA in the Mobile IP Registration Reply message.

Using regular inter-PDSN handoff procedures, when the mobile moves to an area covered by a new PDSN, it will first need to establish a PPP connection, acquire a new care-of address, and register its previous HoA with its Mobile IP Home Agent before IP services can continue. Unfortunately, the multi-phased PPP procedures between the mobile and PDSN are a major source of delay and thus inhibit seamless handover.

Therefore, the cdma2000 PCN also supports fast inter-PDSN handoff, where the mobile's PPP session remains anchored at the old PDSN, and an inter-PDSN connection (the P-P interface) is used to tunnel traffic from the new PDSN to the anchor PDSN. Because the same PPP session is being used, the mobile does not have to obtain a new care-of address or perform Mobile IP signaling to the MIP HA. The anchor PDSN will bi-cast data to and from the old and new PCF while the mobile performs the active handoff.

Figure 6-30 shows the signaling flows for fast inter-PDSN handoff.

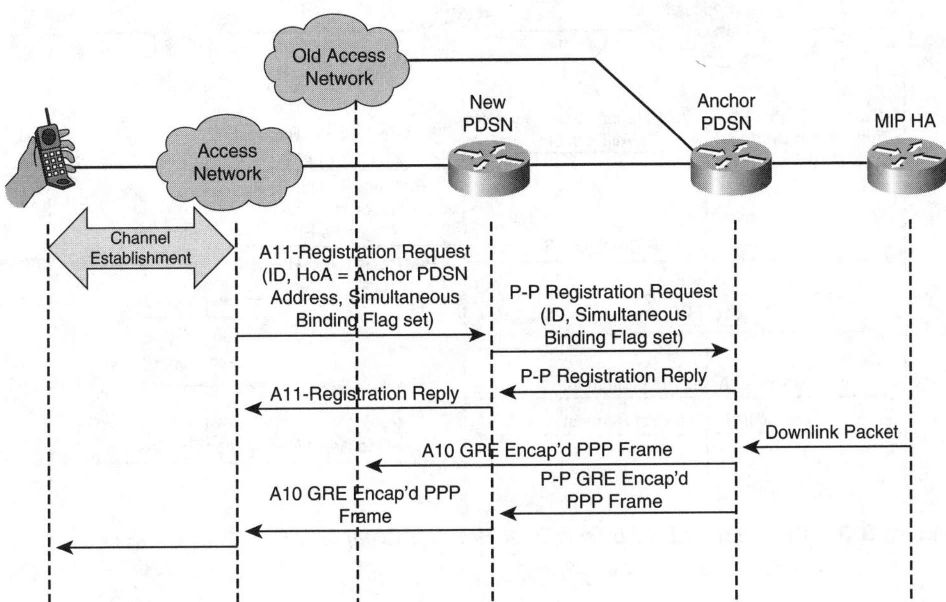

Figure 6-30 *cdma2000 Fast Inter-PDSN Handoff*

The fast handoff is signaled by the PCF in its A11-Registration Request message, which now includes the anchor PDSN address, as well as the simultaneous bindings flag. The new PDSN then signals the anchor PDSN using a P-P Registration Message[30] (the P-P signaling messages use the same format as the A11 messages). This message includes the mobile's IMSI and triggers the anchor PDSN to update its binding cache to simultaneously support the GRE tunnel over the old A10 interface to the old PCF and the GRE tunnel over the P-P interface to the new PDSN.

Now, when the anchor PDSN receives downlink packets for the mobile, it bi-casts the PPP frames over both A10 and P-P connections. The new PDSN is then responsible for transparently switching packets between the A10 and P-P tunnels. Only after the mobile enters the dormant state will it initiate a PPP session to the new PDSN and Mobile IP re-registration to the MIP HA.

Figure 6-31 shows the completion of the fast handoff as the mobile device enters its dormant state. The access network/PCF signals the new PDSN that the mobile is entering the dormant state with an A11-Registration Request message. The new PDSN signals the same to the anchor PDSN, which replies to the request, indicating that PPP should be negotiated. The new PDSN then releases the P-P connection by sending a P-P Registration Request message with lifetime set to zero. The new PDSN sends an LCP Configure-Request to the mobile device, triggering a PPP exchange, following which the device registers with the new PDSN.

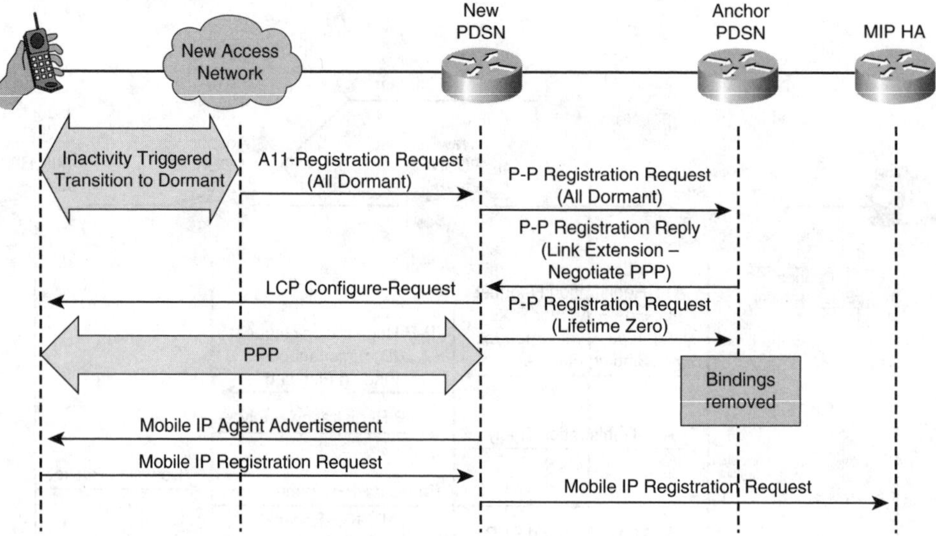

Figure 6-31 *cdma2000 Fast Inter-PDSN Handoff Completion*

I-WLAN Core Network

The Interworking WLAN Core Network allows I-WLAN users access to home operator-defined services using "3GPP IP Access," as described in Chapter 3 . The Packet Data Gateway (PDG) shown in Figure 3-1 can be used by remote users to access home-based services. In particular, because the PDG is required to implement a similar set of per-subscriber functionalities as delivered by a traditional GGSN, an implementation option has been defined that allows the PDG functionality to be partitioned between a Tunnel Termination Gateway (TTG) component and a conventional GGSN component.[31] Such a partitioned PDG is shown in Figure 6-32.

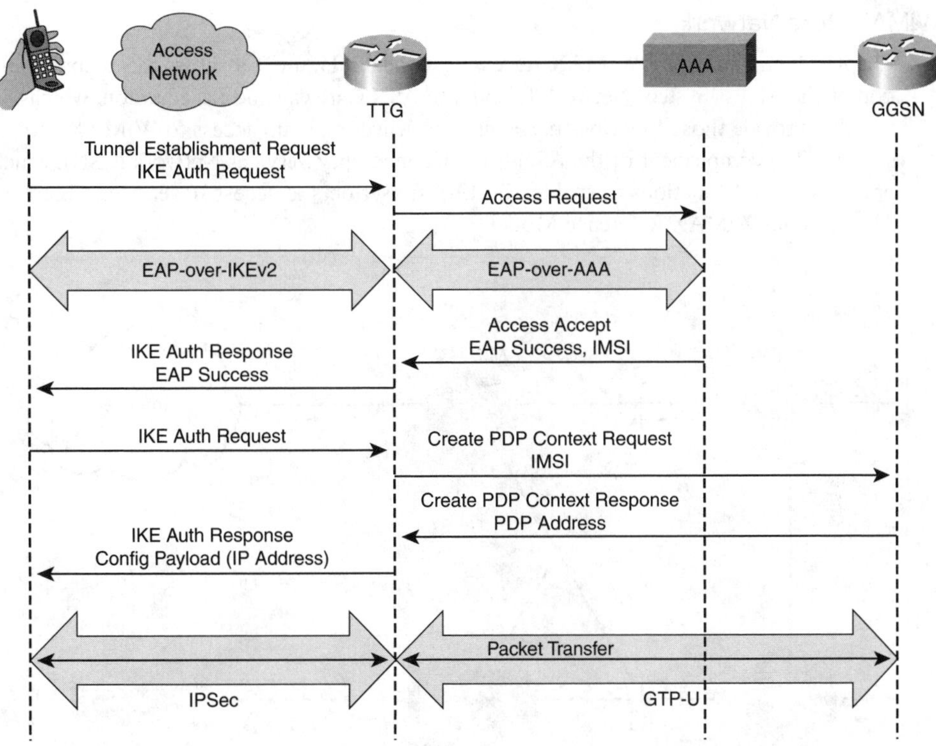

Figure 6-32 *I-WLAN Partitioned PDG*

The mobile uses IKEv2 to negotiate the IPSec security association, authenticating itself using an EAP method—for example, EAP-SIM (RFC 4186) or EAP-AKA (RFC 4187), which are described in greater detail in Chapter 8. The successful authentication and authorization trigger the TTG to send a PDP Context Request message to a conventional GGSN. As with cellular access, the GGSN will allocate an IP address to the mobile using the Create PDP Context Response message.

This IP address is provided back to the requesting mobile in the IKE AUTH response message, and the TTG is then responsible for implementing tunnel switching to/from the IPSec tunnel between the TTG and the mobile and the GTP-U tunnel between the TTG and GGSN.

Note Even though the partitioned PDG architecture allowed integration into GTP, it did not support seamless mobility between WLAN and cellular access. In particular, the I-WLAN has limited support for multiple tunnels—for example, there is no ability to perform a context transfer between an SGSN and a TTG.

WiMAX Core Network

Chapter 3 introduces the WiMAX Access System, and Figure 3-4 shows the decomposition of the Access System Network (ASN) into ASN Gateway and Base Station, which together provide those functions necessary for delivering radio access to WiMAX subscribers. The complement of the ASN is the Connectivity Services Network (CSN), which provides a set of functions to enable WiMAX subscribers to access IP services. Figure 6-33 shows the WiMAX Reference Model.[32]

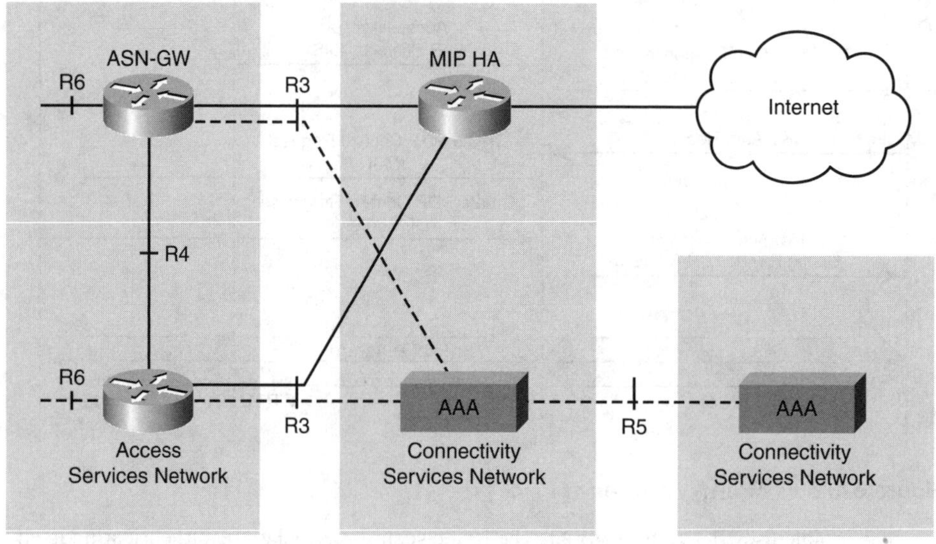

Figure 6-33 *WiMAX Core Network Reference Model*

As illustrated in the figure, two key reference points are defined: R3 and R5 between the ASN and CSN and between two CSNs, respectively. The R3 interfaces is used to support AAA, policy enforcement, and mobility management capabilities, including the tunneling techniques used to transfer data between the ASN and CSN. The inter-CSN R5 interface is defined to be used in a roaming scenario when IP egress occurs in a visited network, but users still need to be authenticated and authorized by their home service provider.

The WiMAX ASN supports inter-ASN mobility using the R4 interface where a user is anchored at a particular ASN GW. In the ASN-anchored case, mobility functionality is limited to the mobile device and ASN. Conversely, the WiMAX Core Network is architected to support macro-mobility, or CSN-anchored mobility. In this case, both ASN and CSN are involved with mobility management. Two different mobility management architectures are supported by the WiMAX Core Network, as follows:

- **Client Mobile IP (CMIP)-based:** Where the Mobile Node is suitably enabled with Mobile IP (IPv4 or IPv6) capability.

- **Simple IP Client with Proxy Mobile IP (PMIP)-based:** The WiMAX architecture defines the use of Proxy MIPv4 (PMIPv4), which is documented as an Informational Internet-Draft.[33]

Note The WiMAX R1.0 architecture was defined prior to the standardization of PMIPv6 by the IETF's NETLMM Working Group—thus the use of a protocol specified in an Informational Internet-Draft. In release R1.5 of the WiMAX architecture, it is anticipated that WiMAX will define an amendment to support PMIPv6-based mobility.

Session Establishment

WiMAX uses EAP Authentication to generate a Mobile IP Root Key, which can then be used to generate mobility keys and the Security Parameter Indices required for MIP security. In addition, during device authentication, keying material is delivered to the ASN-GW to enable it to derive the MN-FA keys/SPI when operating in Client MIPv4 mode and MN-HA keys/SPI when operating in PMIP mode. The FA-HA keys are also piggybacked on top of an authentication exchange for Client MIPv4 access, but these are not session specific.

For CMIP-enabled devices, IP address management uses MIPv4/MIPv6 instead of DHCP, and the HA FQDN or IP address can be appended to the AAA messages by the home network during access authentication. When a new ASN connection is established to the mobile, the FA in the ASN sends a configurable number of agent advertisements toward the mobile. The mobile then performs a MIP Registration toward the HA in order to obtain its home address. The mobile can use vendor-specific MIP extensions (for example, RFC 4332) in order to obtain further host configuration parameters such as DNS Server address.

For non-CMIP-enabled devices, address management and host configuration is performed using DHCP. Typically, the ASN includes a DHCP proxy. PMIPv4-based address allocation may be triggered by the RADIUS Access Accept message including PMIP attributes or by the receipt of a DHCPDISCOVER message, as shown in Figure 6-34. The PMIPv4 client initiates the MIPv4 registration procedure. If the HoA was received in the RADIUS Access Accept message, the PMIPv4 client will use this HoA in its request; otherwise, it will set the HoA field to 0.0.0.0. In either case, the CoA field is set to the FA-CoA address that is configured locally.

The registration request is sent to the FA, which forwards the message to the HA, using the FA-CoA as the source address and the HA address as its destination. If a HoA is 0.0.0.0 in the Mobile IP Registration Request message, the HA assigns a HoA. Otherwise, the HoA in the Mobile IP Registration Request message is used. The HA responds with the Mobile IP Registration Response message. The source address for this Mobile IPv4 message over R3 is the HA address, and the destination address is FA-CoA. The FA forwards the message to the PMIP4 client.

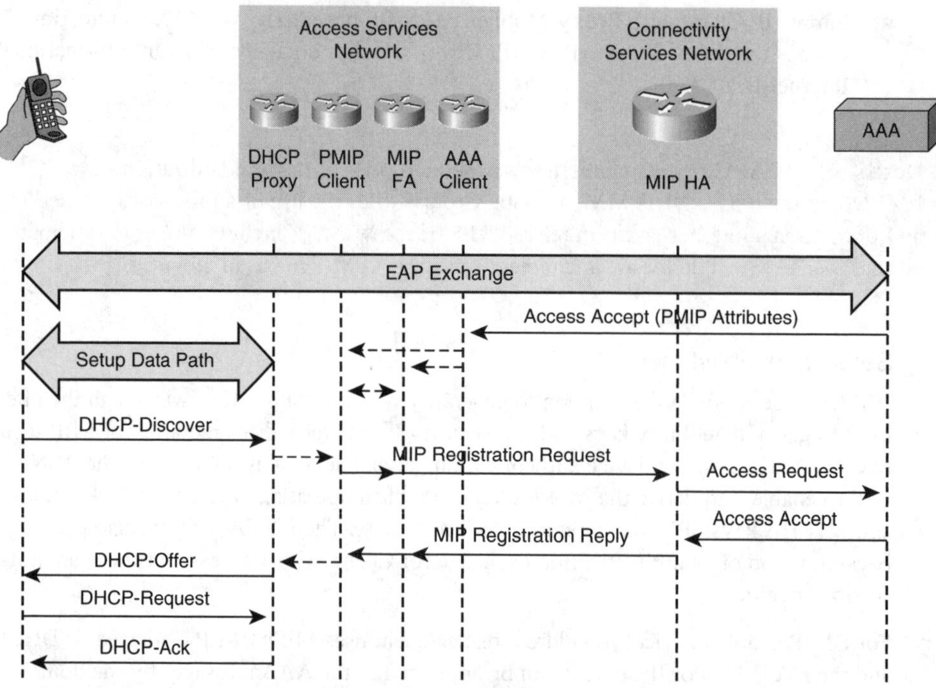

Figure 6-34 *WiMAX Core Network PMIPv4 Connection Setup*

The PMIP client then provides the DHCP proxy with the HoA, and the proxy includes this in the DHCPOFFER message to the MS. The MS sends a DHCPREQUEST to the DHCP proxy with the information received in the DHCPOFFER. The DHCP proxy acknowledges the use of this IP address and other configuration parameters as defined in RFC 2131 (Dynamic Host Configuration Protocol) by sending the DHCPACK message.

Note To allow seamless access across ASN boundaries, WiMAX specifies that a common DHCP server IP address be used across the network.

Once the session is established using either DHCP or MIP signaling, the core network is configured to tunnel packets from the MIP HA toward the mobile, as shown in Figure 6-35.

Session Mobility

The WiMAX Core Network is designed to support macro-mobility, or CSN-anchored mobility, involving both the ASN and CSN in mobility management. The trigger for WiMAX macro-mobility will typically be when the mobile moves to a base station covered by a new FA. If the mobile starts ranging in an ASN that does not contain its context, including keying material, the mobile's context first needs to be retrieved from the old ASN, as shown in Figure 6-36. The Base Station ID included in the Ranging Request message allows the new ASN to recover the Authentication Keying material from the old ASN.

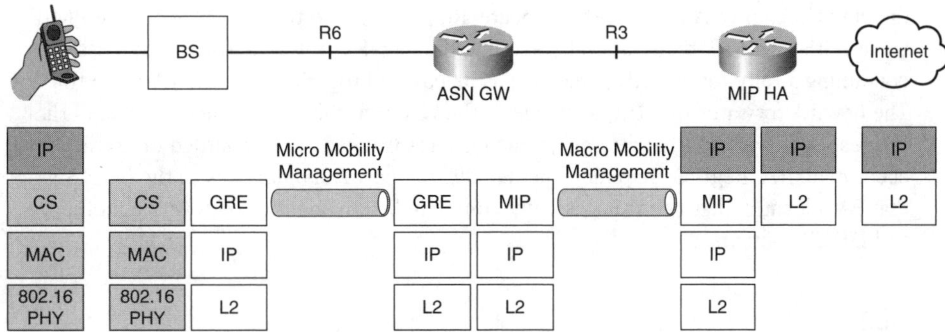

Figure 6-35 *Packet Flow Through WiMAX Core Network*

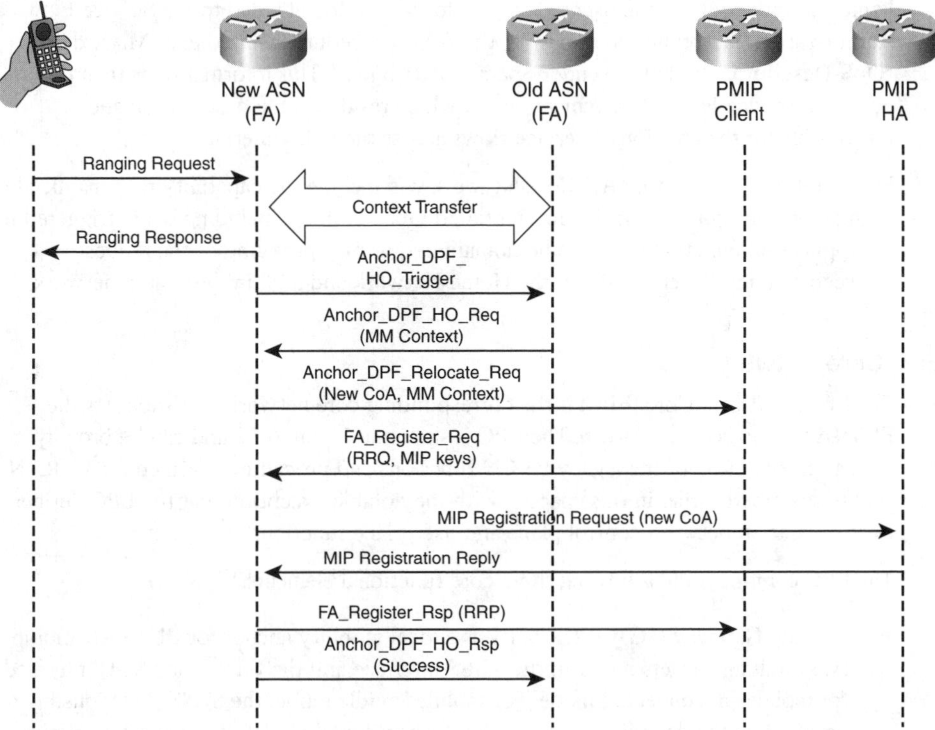

Figure 6-36 *PMIP-Based CSN-Anchored Mobility*

The new FA triggers an FA relocation by sending an Anchor_DPF_HO_Trigger message to the old FA. The old FA responds with the an Anchor_DPF_HO_Req message, including Mobility Management context of the mobile, mobility mode (CMIP or PMIP), MIP4 information, HA IP address, HoA and CoA, and DHCP IP time of lease remaining. The new ASN sends an updated mobility context, including the new FA address together with the new CoA, in an Anchor_DPF_Relocate_Req message to the PMIP client. The PMIP client initiates a MIP registration by sending the new FA an FA_Register_Req message containing a fully formed RRQ message as its payload together with the FA-HA MIP key. The new FA forwards the RRQ message to the HA with the mobile's new CoA, and the HA responds with an RRP message, which is encapsulated and forwarded on to the PMIP client in an RA_Register_Rsp message. Finally, the new ASN indicates to the old ASN that FA relocation has been successfully completed, allowing it to remove the mobility and DHCP contexts.

QoS

The Release 1.0 of the WiMAX Core Network supports the pre-provisioning of differentiated QoS handling. Chapter 3 describes how the IEEE-802.16-2005 specification supports differentiated QoS handling over the air interface. The AAA server in the user's home network contains the user's QoS profile. This is downloaded to the Service Flow Authorization (SFA) function as part of the AAA procedure, using the WiMAX-defined "QoS-Descriptor" RADIUS Vendor-Specific Attribute.[34] This information is then provided to the Service Flow Management entity, which resides in the base station and is responsible for the creation of service flows across the radio interface.

Future releases of the WiMAX Core Network will include the capability to dynamically change the configuration of the differentiated QoS handling, including being triggered by an Application Function in the home domain, requiring a proxying of the request between a Policy Function (PF) in the Home Network and a PF in the visited network.

EPC Core Network

The Evolved Packet Core (EPC) is the corresponding core network that supports the EUTRAN radio access network. The EPC is shown in Figure 6-37 and can be broadly seen as an evolution of the legacy PS CN functions and procedures defined for UTRAN access described earlier in this chapter, with the notable exception that the EPC defines a clear separation between control-plane and user-plane functions.

The EPC comprises the following three core functional elements:[35]

- **Serving Gateway (SGW):** The SGW is a local mobility anchor for EUTRAN mobility, switching packets between the S5/S8 interface and the GTP-based S1-U interface for mobiles in connected mode. For mobiles in idle mode, the SGW is responsible for terminating the downlink data path, and when downlink data is received, buffering the data and triggering a paging procedure by signaling the Mobility Management Entity (MME) over the S11 interface.
- **Mobility Management Entity (MME):** The MME is the control-plane function for EUTRAN access. It is responsible for authentication and key management for mobile devices, as well as performing the tracking and paging procedures for mobiles in idle mode. The MME authorizes bearer activation/deactivation including gateway (SGW and PDN) selection.

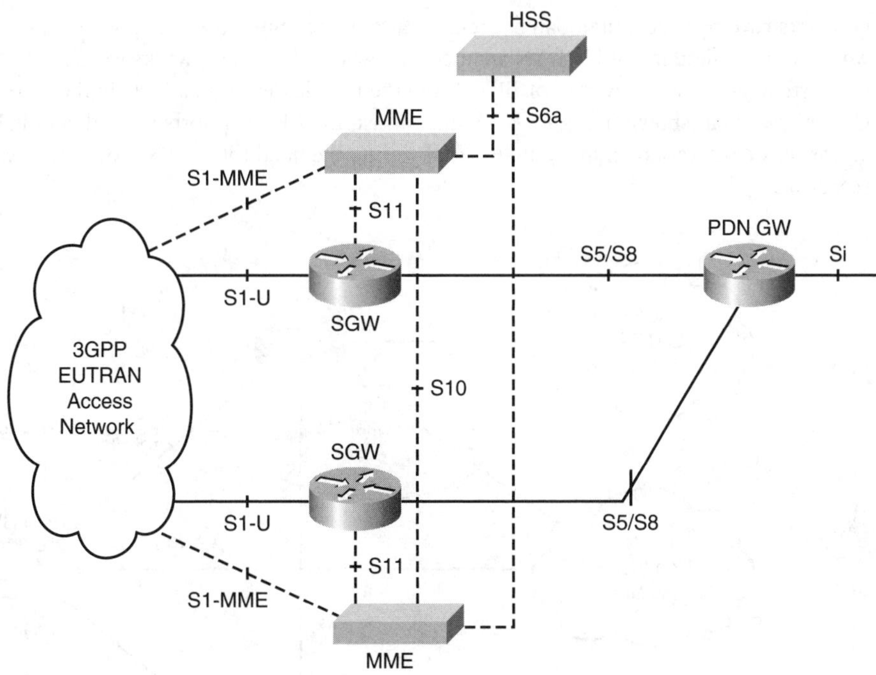

Figure 6-37 *EPC Architecture for EUTRAN Access*

- **Packet Data Network Gateway (PDN GW):** The PDN GW is the permanent IP Point-of-Attachment for access via the EUTRAN. The PDN GW performs IP policy and charging enforcement on packet flows to/from mobiles devices. The same APN concepts from the UTRAN PS Core Network apply, allowing a mobile device to have simultaneous connectivity to multiple PDNs.

Because this is an all-IP system, the legacy MAP/SS7-based authentication and authorization has been replaced with an S6a approach based on the Diameter protocol.[36]

The S11 interface is used to decompose the control- and user-plane functions between the MME and SGW, and the S10 interface is used for context transfer operations, although the frequency of context transfer will be reduced as the multihoming capability of S1-MME should allow a single MME/SGW to handle control and user-plane functions for a mobile device as it moves within the EUTRAN.

Both S10 and S11 are based on GTP-C and require a new set of features compared to legacy GTP-C functionality. Rather than simply extend GTPv1-C, the EPC uses a new version of GTP for the control plane, version 2.

Non-3GPP Access

Although the EPC architecture for EUTRAN access can be broadly seen as an evolution of the current UTRAN PS Core Network with the SGSN being decomposed into MME and SGW elements, the revolutionary aspect of the EPC relates to how non-3GPP access networks have been accommodated. Previous attempts to integrate non-3GPP access networks have resulted in the I-WLAN architecture, where all such networks were deemed un-trusted, requiring an overlay of IPSec from the mobile device to a PDG in the 3GPP Core Network, as shown in Figure 6-32. In contrast, the EPC supports trusted non-3GPP access networks, as shown in Figure 6-38, obviating the need for an IPSec overlay in such scenarios.

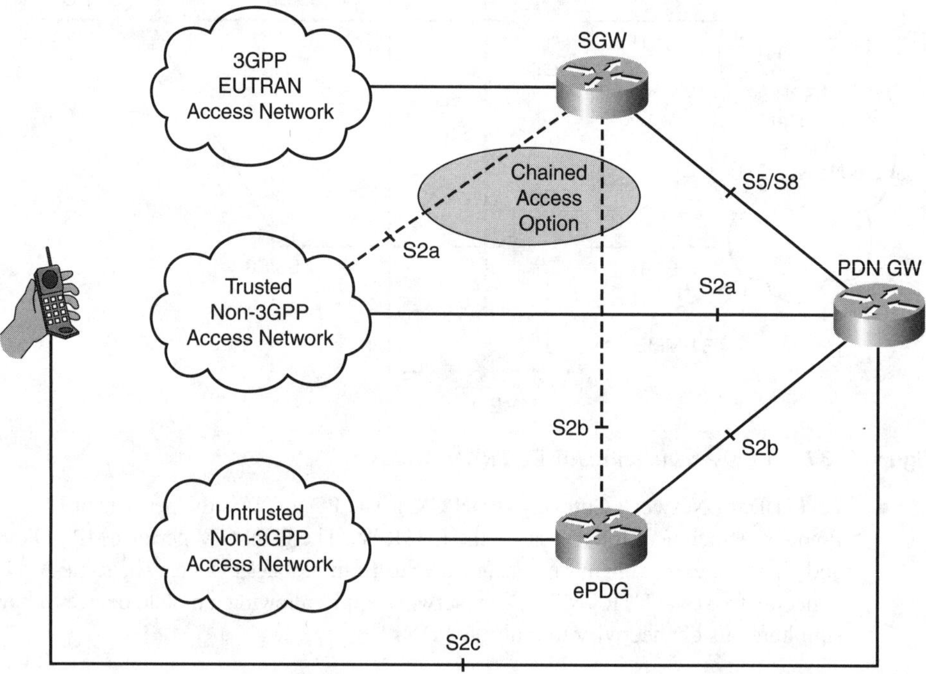

Figure 6-38 *EPC Architecture for Non-3GPP Access*[37]

The S2 mobility interfaces are used to support non-3GPP access networks, where:

- S2a is based on PMIPv6 (RFC 5213). To enable access via legacy trusted non-3GPP access networks (for example, cdma2000-based networks), S2a also supports Client MIPv4 in FA mode.
- S2b is based on PMIPv6 and can be seen as an evolution of the TTG concept. In this case, an evolved PDG (ePDG) tunnel switches packets between IPSec and PMIPv6 tunnels.
- S2c is based on Client Mobile IP using Dual-Stack MIPv6 (DSMIPv6), as specified in RFC 4877.

The definition of the EPC has now provided the cellular industry with the first opportunity to provide a converged packet core network, capable of supporting all-IP EUTRAN access via GTP-based S1, legacy cdma2000 access via MIPv4-based S2a, and WiMAX Release 1.5 access via PMIPv6-based S2a.

EPC Macro-Mobility and E2E QoS

With a legacy of GTP-based roaming interfaces, 3GPP has naturally defined GTP-based S5/S8 interfaces between the SGW and the PDN-GW, using GTPv1 for the user plane and GTPv2 for the control plane. Using the chained access option shown in Figure 6-38, the same GTP-based S5/S8 can be used to support non-3GPP access networks. Instead of such a GTP-based evolution, several companies within 3GPP preferred an architecture where the protocols between its core network elements were based on IETF-defined protocols.[38] As a consequence, 3GPP agreed to define both GTP and PMIPv6 variants for the S5/S8 interfaces.

The next key question concerned the functional decomposition for the GTP- and PMIP-variants. When using a GTP-based core network, the PDN GW acts as the macro-mobility anchor and includes the functionality to support multiple PDP contexts per user, as well as the associated downlink classification capability in order to map downlink packets into different PDP contexts. Although such an architecture could be realized with PMIPv6—for example, using different GRE keys to represent the different secondary tunnels—such an architecture is at odds with both cdma2000 and WiMAX Core Networks, which assume a single mobility tunnel between the macro-mobility and micro-mobility anchors, with downlink traffic classification being implemented at the micro-mobility anchor.

Consequently, when PMIPv6 has been defined by 3GPP for the S8 and S5 interfaces, a different functional decomposition is used between the SGW and PDN GW to allow a single PMIPv6 tunnel between these elements. Figure 6-39 compares GTP- and PMIPv6-based EPC architectures. As the figure illustrates, in order to deliver an end-to-end differentiated QoS architecture for the PMIPv6-based core network, an out-of-band AAA-based policy interface is used to deliver the classification information to the SGW, and the binding of flows to radio bearers is performed by the SGW and not the PDN GW.

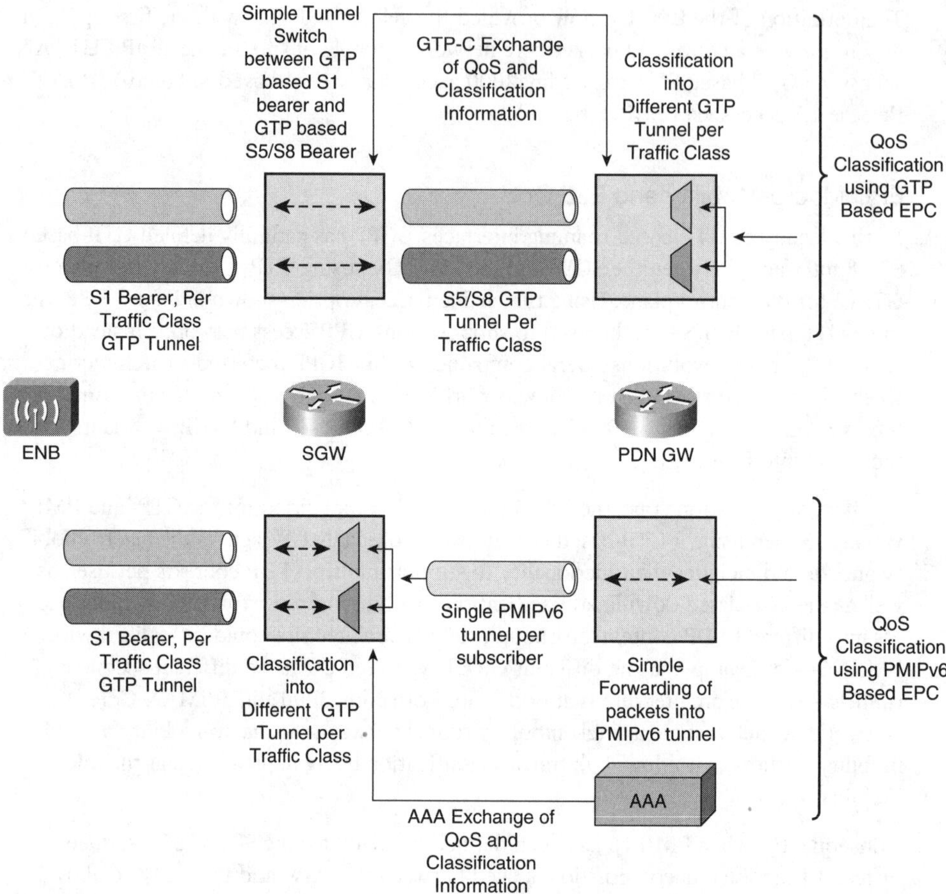

Figure 6-39 *QoS Classification for GTP- and PMIPv6-Based EPC*

Summary

This chapter introduced the Circuit-Switched and Packet-Switched Core Networks, which provide the access to voice-, SMS-, and IP-based services accessible via cellular radio networks.

The core concepts for handling mobility have been introduced together with examples of mobility management and voice call set-up procedures. These concepts have changed little since their original development as part of the GSM Network-Switching Subsystem. What has changed is the increasing use of IP for transporting circuit-switched voice traffic, first with the split MSC Server/MGW architecture for bearer independent call control. This has allowed operators to decommission core TDM links, instead converging voice transport over a common IP/MPLS network. The second phase involves the use of

IP transport of the core interfaces between the access network and the MSC components. This has been defined for UTRAN access networks and is currently undergoing standardization for GERAN networks. These options allow an end-to-end IP network to support all legacy voice traffic.

Whereas the core CS networks are built on a common foundation of ISUP signaling, the core PS networks have taken different approaches to providing mobility, from the GTP-based approach for IP access over UTRAN bearers, client-based MIPv4 approach for IP access over cdma2000 bearers, PMIPv4-based approach for IP access over IEEE 802.16e bearers, and ending with the converged Evolved Packet Core defined by 3GPP, which can accommodate GTP-, CMIPv4-, PMIPv6-, and DSMIPv6-based mobility.

This chapter described the different PS Core Network architectures, highlighting how all support core functionality, such as hierarchical mobility, QoS differentiation, and support for roaming deployments. These architectures highlight that IP mobility is far more than a choice between different protocols, with control-plane context transfer requirements being fundamental for end-to-end system definition.

Endnotes

[1]ITU-T Recommendation Q.321, "ISDN user-network interface layer 3 specification for basic call control."

[2]3GPP 24.008, "Mobile radio interface Layer 3 specification; core network protocols; Stage 3."

[3]ITU-T Recommendation E.212, "The international identification plan for mobile terminals and mobile users."

[4]3GPP 29.002, "Mobile Application Part (MAP) Specification."

[5]3GPP 48.008, "Mobile Switching Center—Base Station System (MSC-BSS) interface; Layer 3 specification."

[6]Integrated Services Digital Network (ISDN); Signaling System No.7 (SS7); ISDN User Part (ISUP).

[7]http://www.anacom.pt.

[8]ANSI/TIA/EIA-41, "Cellular Radiotelecommunications Intersystem Operations."

[9]ITU-T Q.2630.1, "AAL type 2 signaling protocol (Capability Set 1)," Dec. 1999.

[10]3GPP TS 23.205, "Bearer-Independent Circuit-Switched Core Network."

[11]ITU-T Q.1901, "Bearer Independent Call Control."

[12]3GPP TS 23.231, "SIP-I-Based Circuit-Switched Core Network."

[13]ITU-T Q.1912.5, "Interworking between Session Initiation Protocol (SIP) and Bearer Independent Call Control Protocol or ISDN User Part."

[14]3GPP TR 29.232, "Media Gateway Controller (MGC)—Media Gateway (MGW) interface; Stage 3."

[15]http://www.msforum.org/techinfo/approved/MSF-IA-MC.001v2-FINAL.pdf.

[16]3GPP TS 25.153, "Out-of-band transcoder control; Stage 2."

[17]3GPP TS 43.903, "A-interface over IP Study (AINTIP)."

[18]3GPP TS 29.060, "General Packet Radio Service (GPRS); GPRS Tunneling Protocol (GTP) across the Gn and Gp interface."

[19]3GPP TS 33.210, "Network Domain Security; IP network layer security."

[20]3GPP TR 33.821, "Rationale and track of security decisions in Long-Term Evolved (LTE) RAN / 3GPP System Architecture Evolution (SAE)."

[21]3GPP TS 33.401, "3GPP System Architecture Evolution (SAE): Security Architecture."

[22] C. Perkins, RFC 3344, "IP Mobility Support for IPv4," Aug. 2002.

[23] D. Johnson, C. Perkins, and J. Arkko, RFC 3775, "IP Mobility Support in IPv6," June 2004.

[24] S. Gundavelli, K. Leung, V. Devarapalli, K. Chowdhury, B. Patil, RFC 5213, "Proxy Mobile IPv6," Aug. 2008.

[25] R. Wakikawa, S. Gundavelli, draft-ietf-netlmm-pmip6-ipv4-support, (work in progress).

[26] A. Muhanna, M. Khalil, S. Gundavelli, K. Leung , draft-ietf-netlmm-grekey-option, (work in progress).

[27]3GPP2, "Interoperability Specification (IOS) for CDMA 2000 Access Network Interfaces—Part 2 Transport."

[28]3GPP2, "Interoperability Specification (IOS) for CDMA 2000 Access Network Interfaces—Part 6 (A8 and A9 interfaces)."

[29]3GPP2, "Interoperability Specification (IOS) for CDMA 2000 Access Network Interfaces—Part 7 (A10 and A11 interfaces)."

[30]3GPP2, "cdma2000 Wireless IP Network Standard; Packet Data Mobility and Resource Management."

[31]3GPP TS 23.234, "3GPP System for Wireless Local Area Network (WLAN) Interworking; System Description."

[32]WiMAX Forum Network Architecture, "Stage 2: Architecture Tenets, Reference Model, and Reference Points."

[33]K. Leung, G. Dommety, P. Yegani, K. Chowdhury, "WiMAX Forum/3GPP2 Proxy Mobile IPv4," draft-leung-mip4-proxy-mode (work in progress).

[34]WiMAX Forum Network Architecture, "Stage 3: Detailed Protocols and Procedures."

[35]3GPP TS 23.401, "General Packet Radio Service (GPRS) enhancements for Evolved Universal Terrestrial Radio Access Network (E-UTRAN) access."

[36]3GPP TS 29.272, "Evolved Packet System (EPS); Mobility Management Entity (MME) and Serving GPRS Support Node (SGSN)-related interfaces based on Diameter protocol."

[37]3GPP TS 23.402, "Architecture enhancements for non-3GPP accesses."

[38]3GPP Technical Specification Group Services and System Aspects, Plenary Report, Meeting #34, 04–07 December 2006, http://www.3gpp.org/ftp/tsg_sa/TSG_SA/TSGS_34/Report/SP_34_Approved_Rep_v100.zip.

Chapter 7

Offloading Traditional Networks with IP

Traditional mobile networks, such as today's 2G (GSM, CDMA 1x) and 3G (UMTS/HSPA and EVDO) networks, are based on Time Division Multiplexing (TDM) for transmission. These TDM networks comprise the majority of the backhaul networks for transport of voice and data traffic. Figure 7-1 shows backhaul penetration worldwide by technology.[1]

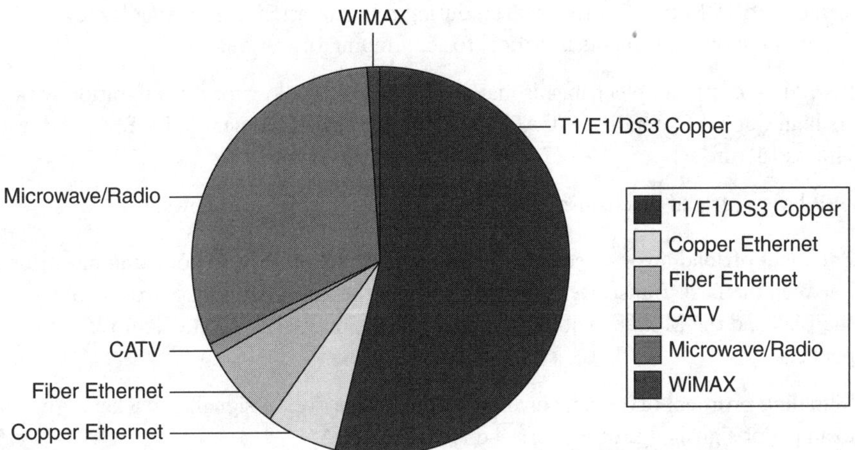

Figure 7-1 *Backhaul Network Penetration*

As mobile network data traffic grows, and user demand and dependency on the mobile operator as a data access provider increases, mobile operators are exploring various offload mechanisms to migrate legacy TDM networks to modern Ethernet and IP. Figure 7-2 demonstrates the increased bandwidth requirements per base station, to support next-generation mobile services.[2]

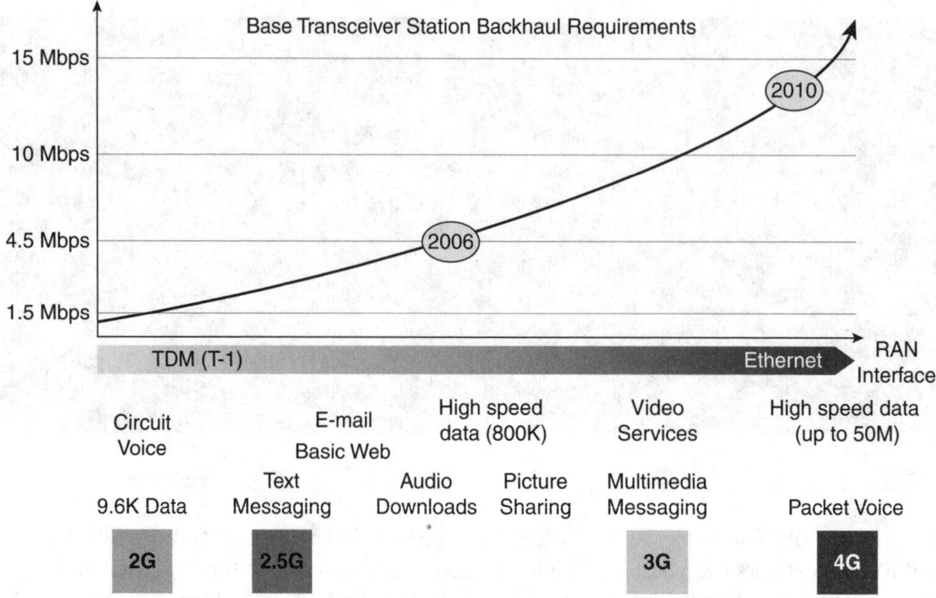

Figure 7-2 *Backhaul Bandwidth Requirements*

This migration allows a mobile operator to shed excess Operating Expenditures (OPEX) associated with TDM transport. However, during this migration, supporting legacy TDM interfaces and network elements is critical for continuing operations.

Various IP-based offload mechanisms may be employed to allow for this migration without the high Capital Expenditure (CAPEX) outlay for new equipment (BTS, BSC, and MSC infrastructure).

These IP-based offload mechanisms can be largely categorized as follows:

- **Backhaul offload** involves encapsulation of standard TDM protocol communications between the Base Transceiver Station (BTS) and the Base Station Controller (BSC), the BSC and the Mobile Switching Center (MSC), or inter-BSC/MSC, into IP packets.
- **Signaling protocol offload** involves protocol conversion of signaling packets. An example of signaling protocol offload is SS7/SIGTRAN.
- **Bearer protocol offload** involves protocol conversion of bearer packets. Examples of bearer protocol offload include Transcoder-Free Operations (TrFO) mechanisms and IP Soft-Handoff mechanisms.

Backhaul Offload with Pseudowires

Pseudowires allow for the emulation of point-to-point or point-to-multipoint links over a Packet-Switched Network (PSN). Pseudowire technology provides a migration path, allowing an operator to deploy packet-switched networks without immediately replacing legacy end-user equipment.

Each pseudowire presents a single, unshared "circuit" for carrying "native" services, such as ATM, SONET/SDH, TDM, Ethernet, or Frame Relay, over the PSN. The PSN may either be Layer 2 Tunneling Protocol Version 3 (L2TPv3), MPLS, or generic IP.

Many standards organizations, including the Internet Engineering Task Force (IETF), the Metro Ethernet Forum (MEF), and the International Telecommunications Union Telecommunications Standards Sector (ITU-T), have defined the encapsulation techniques for transport of the relevant protocols in mobile networks today, as follows:

- **IEEE RFC3985:** Pseudowire Emulation Edge-to-Edge (PWE3).
- **IEEE RFC5087 and ITU-T Y.1453:** Time Division Multiplexing over IP (TDMoIP).
- **IEEE RFC4553:** Structure-Agnostic Time Division Multiplexing over IP.
- **IEEE RFC5086:** Circuit Emulation Services over Packet-Switched Networks (CESoPSN).
- **IEEE RFC4717 and ITU-T Y.1411:** ATM Pseudowires.
- **IEEE RFC4842:** Synchronous Optical Network/Synchronous Digital Hierarchy (SONET/SDH) Circuit Emulation over Packet (CEP).

Pseudowire Use-Cases

Prior to discussing pseudowire technology itself, the following examples should help to clarify various uses for pseudowire technology in mobile networks. The examples discussed may not be applicable to all mobile operators or all mobile infrastructure vendors, but are representative of some of the many deployment scenarios where pseudowires have been successfully deployed as an offload mechanism. The examples cover four scenarios, as follows:

- TDMoIP Pseudowire for CDMA/EVDO or GSM Backhaul Networks
- CESoPSN Pseudowire for Inter-BSC/MSC Connectivity
- ATM Pseudowires for UMTS R4 Connectivity
- Pseudowires for Multi-RAN Environments

Details of each pseudowire technology and implementation follow.

TDMoIP Pseudowires for EVDO or GSM Backhaul Networks

As discussed in Chapter 4, "An IP Refresher," the traditional mobile backhaul network for a CDMA or GSM network consists of TDM interfaces on both the Base Transceiver Station (BTS) and the Base Station Controller (BSC). These TDM interfaces connect to a backhaul provider's T1/E1 circuits for transport. Figure 7-3 illustrates a mobile backhaul network with standard TDM backhaul.

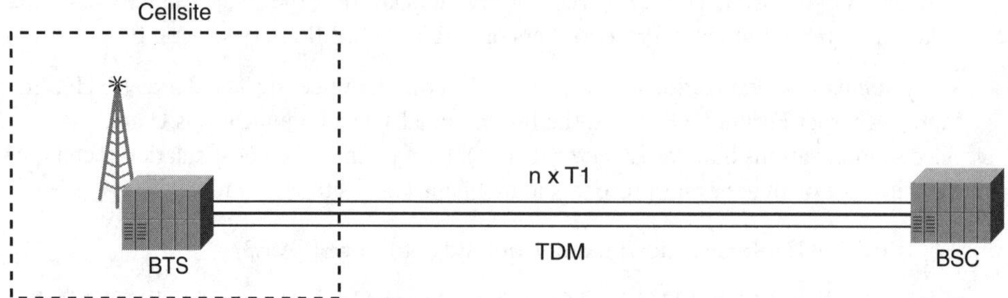

Figure 7-3 *Traditional TDM Mobile Backhaul Network*

TDM pseudowire technology plays a key role in allowing mobile operators to migrate their backhaul networks between the BTS, or cell site, and BSC or MSC location. The pseudowire provides a "transparent wire" between these locations and preserves the integrity of the TDM framing as it is transmitted across the PSN. Figure 7-4 illustrates a mobile backhaul network that uses TDMoIP pseudowires for transport.

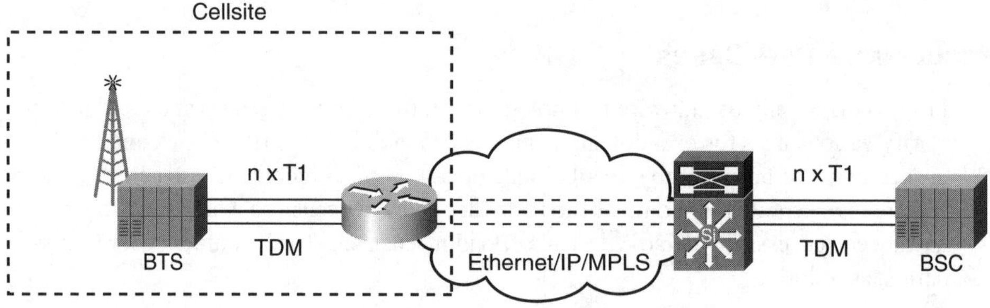

Figure 7-4 *Mobile Backhaul Network with TDM Pseudowires*

CESoPSN Pseudowires for Inter-MSC/BSC Connectivity

As discussed in Chapter 4, the traditional MSC and BSC functionality and connectivity is typically TDM-based. Interconnectivity between all BSCs/MSCs is essential for handling mobility of a voice session in a circuit-switched voice (GSM, CDMA 1x) environment. However, in order to support such an environment, typical mobile deployments rely on a combination of point-to-point TDM circuits between BSC and MSC, and fully-meshed or star configurations of TDM circuits from the MSC toward the core network. Figure 7-5 illustrates one such topology.

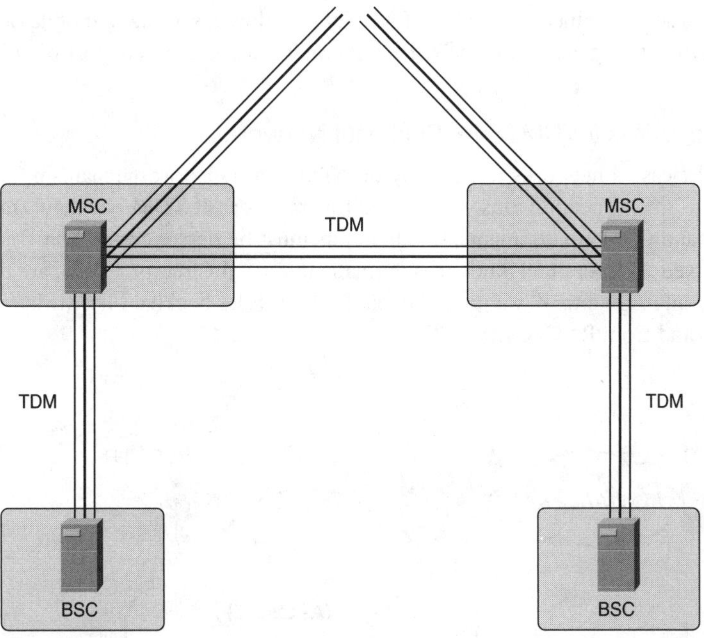

Figure 7-5 *Inter-MSC/BSC Connectivity*

The overall cost of maintaining a fully-meshed, point-to-point TDM architecture is significant from an OPEX perspective. By reducing the number of TDM circuits required from the Local Exchange Carrier (LEC), a mobile operator may immediately see impact to operating margins. One such way to reduce the number of circuits is to leverage CESoPSN pseudowires for interconnecting MSC and BSCs, as illustrated in Figure 7-6.

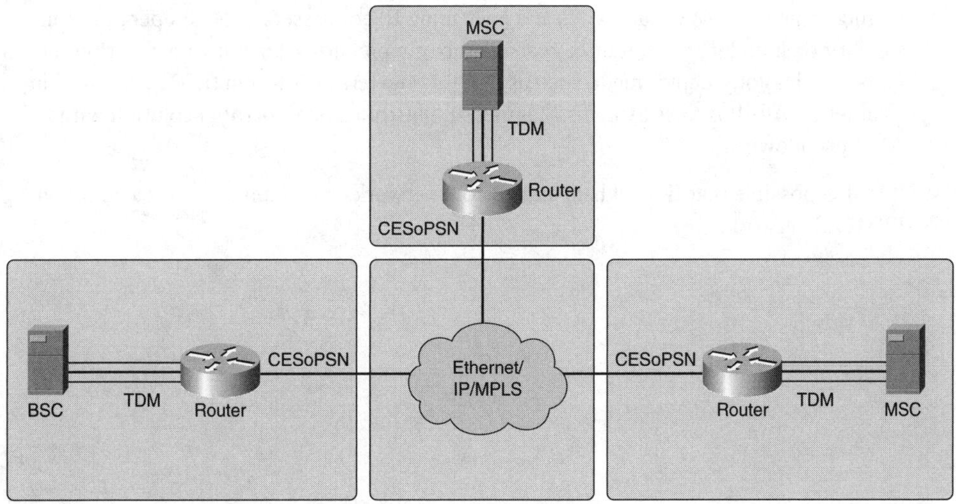

Figure 7-6 *Inter-MSC/BSC Connectivity with CESoPSN Pseudowires*

Inter-MSC/BSC connectivity with CESoPSN pseudowires allows a mobile operator to use existing infrastructure, namely their IP core network, for transport of voice traffic.

ATM Pseudowires for UMTS R4 Backhaul Networks

UMTS Release 4 networks rely heavily on ATM as a transport mechanism for data traffic. Similar to the model previously discussed for transport of TDM backhaul traffic in CDMA and GSM environments, fixed circuits must be deployed to allow for mobility. These fixed ATM circuits, known as Permanent Virtual Circuits (PVCs), are discussed in more detail in Chapter 4. Figure 7-7 depicts a UMTS R4 backhaul network, from Node B to RNC and from RNC to MSC/SGSN.

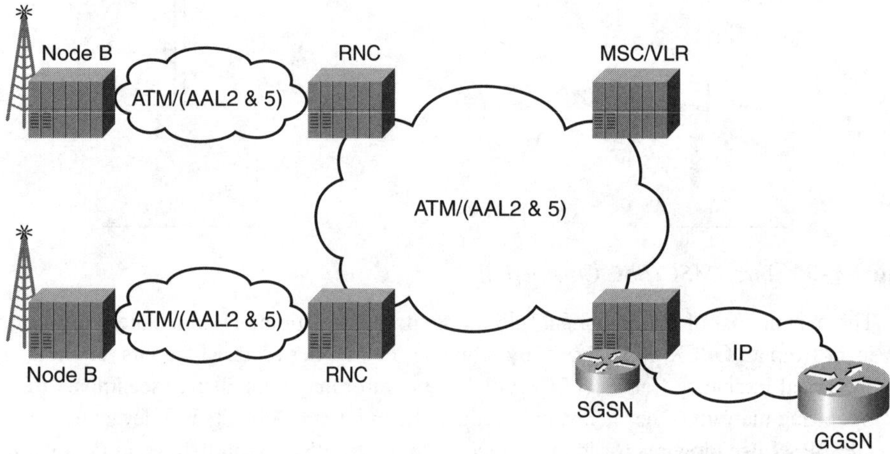

Figure 7-7 *UMTS R4 Backhaul with ATM*

By migrating to ATM pseudowires and leveraging IP core assets, mobile operators can simplify their architecture, reduce costs, and begin preparing for fourth-generation mobile technology deployment, such as 3GPP Long-Term Evolution (LTE), discussed in Chapter 3, "All-IP Access Systems." Figure 7-8 illustrates one potential solution with ATM pseudowires.

It is also possible that IP backhaul and IP core networks may converge over a common IP/MPLS network.

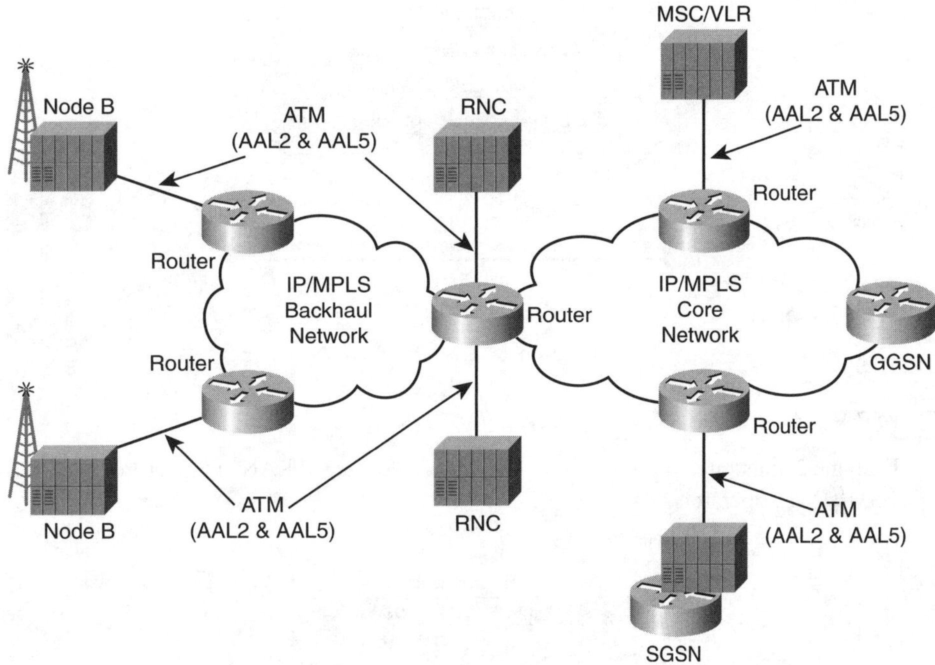

Figure 7-8 *UMTS R4 Backhaul with ATM Pseudowire*

Converging Multiple RAN Technologies over Common Pseudowire

As mobile operators complete their transition from solely circuit-switched voice networks to voice and data networks, mobile networks begin to become an overlay of multiple radio technologies. With all these multiple overlays requiring unique circuits (TDM or ATM), mobile operators incur large OPEX for maintaining multiple different backhaul networks. For instance, a CDMA operator maintains a CDMA 1x voice network and EVDO data network simultaneously. Even if the radio access cards reside in the same physical element, mobile operators use unique circuits for voice and data traffic in order to facilitate troubleshooting and problem isolation.

Pseudowires present an opportunity for mobile operators to deploy a unified backhaul architecture while still managing each circuit individually.

Example 1, illustrated in Figure 7-9, highlights a converged RAN architecture for a CDMA operator.

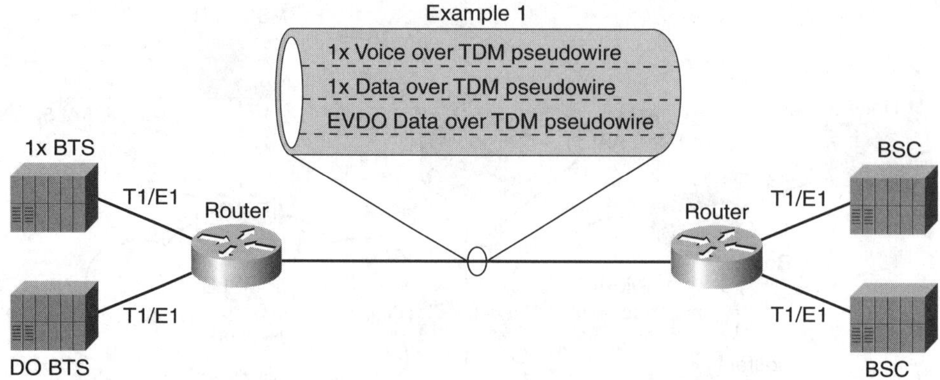

Figure 7-9 *Converged RAN Architecture for CDMA*

Example 2, illustrated in Figure 7-10, highlights a converged RAN architecture for a GSM/UMTS operator.

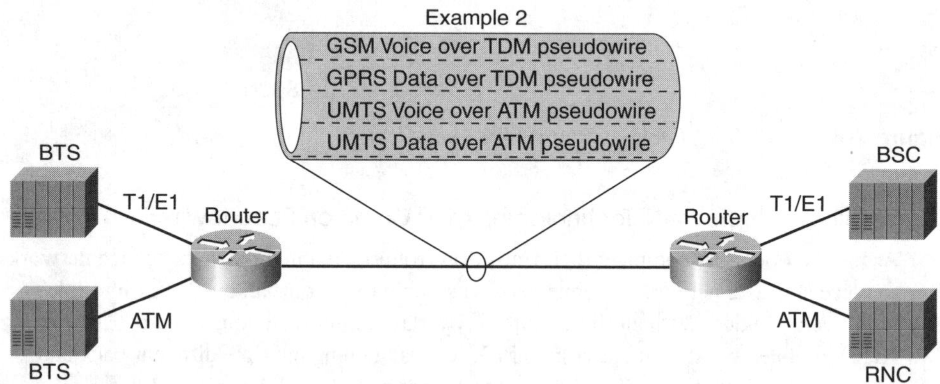

Figure 7-10 *Converged RAN Architecture for UMTS*

Note With the initial 3G release, there is no differentiation between voice and data traffic on the link between the Node B and the RNC (contrary to what is shown in the figure). The whole traffic is encapsulated in a Frame Protocol and send to/from the RNC. The differentiation is done later. This is changed in later releases of UMTS.

Pseudowire Emulation Edge-to-Edge (PWE3)

Pseudowire Emulation Edge-to-Edge RFC 3985 provides the structure and architecture for emulation of Frame Relay, ATM, Ethernet, TDM, and SONET over packet-switched networks using IP or MPLS.

Pseudowires for Time Division Multiplexing (TDM)

At the most basic level, TDMoIP pseudowires segment T1/E1 frames, encapsulate these frames in Ethernet, and fragment the frames into IP packets for transport across the PSN. At the destination, the IP header is stripped, the Ethernet frame is decapsulated, and the original bit stream is reconstructed, including regeneration of clock information. Figure 7-11 illustrates a high-level view of a TDMoIP pseudowire.

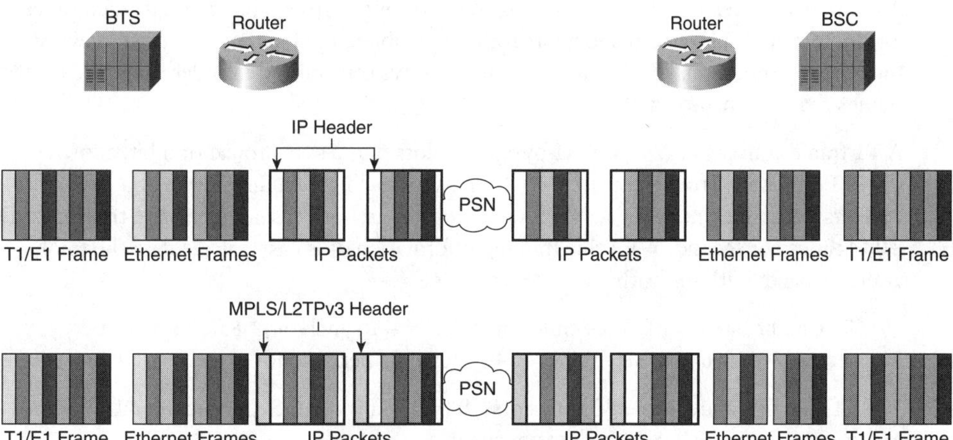

Figure 7-11 *High-Level View of TDMoIP Pseudowire*

Structure-Awareness of TDM Pseudowires

TDM over IP pseudowires can be categorized into two classes, as follows:

- **Structure-Agnostic Transport over Packet (SAToP):** With structure-agnostic transport, the protocol may disregard all structures imposed on TDM signaling or framing. Therefore, this transport method is simply bit-by-bit transport. Structure-agnostic TDM over IP is standardized in RFC4553. The PE devices in SAToP transport network do not participate in TDM signaling and do not interpret the TDM data. This implies that there are no assurances that network degradation does not impact the TDM structure.
- **Structure-Aware Transport over Packet:** With structure-aware transport, such as TDMoIP and CESoPSN, the integrity of the TDM structure is ensured, even in cases of network degradation. Because PE devices have exposure to the TDM signaling, individual channels are exposed, allowing the network to utilize Packet Loss Concealment (PLC) and bandwidth conservation mechanisms on a per-channel basis.

TDM Structures

A frame structure refers to the way a single communications channel is multiplexed in several individual channels. By multiplexing the underlying channel, more than one data stream may be simultaneously transmitted at a time. Because TDM is based on the time domain, a single frame is actually a constant-length time interval. Within this time interval, fixed-length timeslots, each representing a single circuit-switched channel, are transmitted.

A multiplexer is responsible for assigning data, or bytes, from a bitstream to each timeslot, and a demultiplexer is responsible for re-assembling the bitstream. Although every timeslot may not be used, the entire frame is always transmitted in order to ensure that frames remain synchronized.

A T1 frame consists of (24) 8-bit (1-byte) timeslots plus a synchronization bit, allowing for 193 bits. An E1 frame consists of 32 timeslots, each containing 8 bits, or a total of 256 bits per frame, including a synchronization bit. In both cases, frames are transmitted 8,000 times per second. With this framing information, it is easy to calculate the total available bandwidth for both T1 and E1 circuits:

> T1 Circuit Bandwidth = (24 timeslots * 8 bits + 1 synch bit) * 8,000 frames per second / 1*10^6 bits/Megabit = 1.544 Megabits per second

> E1 Circuit Bandwidth = 32 timeslots * 8 bits * 8,000 frames per second / 1*10^6 bits/Megabit = 2.048 Megabits per second

Multiple channels, each containing 8000 8-bit samples per second, are multiplexed together using TDM framing, as illustrated in Figure 7-12.

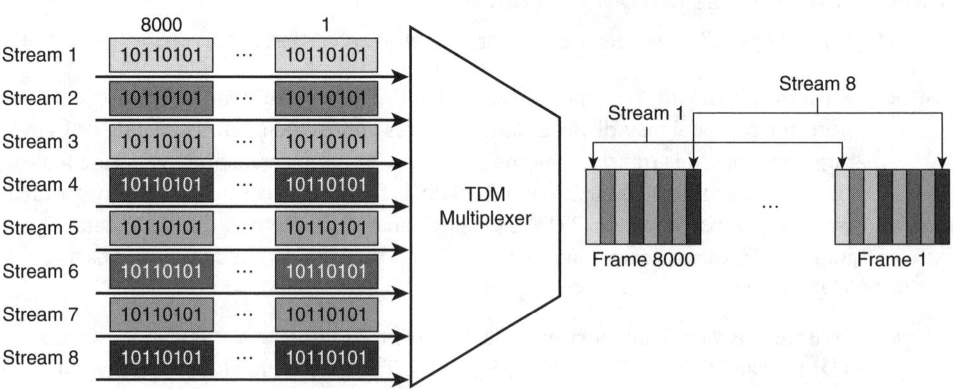

Figure 7-12 *TDM Frame Multiplexing*

Structure-Aware Transport

Structure-aware emulation assumes that the TDM structure itself, including the framing and control information, are available to the pseudowire edge device. With this information available, pseudowire encapsulation can be done in a more intelligent manner, with the edge device selecting specific channel samples from the TDM bitstream. Structure-aware transport may ensure the integrity of the original TDM structure via three distinct adaptation algorithms, as follows:

- **Structure-Locking:** Structure-locking ensures that each packet on the pseudowire contains an entire TDM structure, or multiple/fragments of TDM structures. The exact number of frames included is locked for all packets, in both directions. The order of the frames in the PSN is the same as those within the TDM frame sequence. When a TDM bitstream arrives, consecutive bits from the bitstream, most significant first, fill each payload octet. Structure-locking is not used in TDMoIP.
- **Structure-Indication:** The structure-indication method is derived from ATM Adaptation Layer 1 (AAL1), described in Chapter 4. Unlike structure locking, structure indication allows for pseudowire packets to contain arbitrary-length fragments of the underlying TDM frames. These fragments are taken from the bitstream in-sequence, from the most-significant bit first. The pseudowire packets also include pointers to indicate where a new structure begins. Because the bitstream sequence is identical to the sequence contained in the PSN, this method is commonly known as "circuit emulation."
- **Structure-Reassembly:** The structure-reassembly method allows for specific components of the TDM structure to be extracted and reorganized within the pseudowire packet structure by the ingress pseudowire edge, with enough information such that the other edge of the pseudowire may reassemble the original TDM structure. The structure-reassembly method allows for bandwidth conservation by only transporting frames/timeslots that are active. This method is commonly known as "loop emulation."

TDMoIP uses the structure-indication algorithm for constant-rate, real-time traffic and the structure-reassembly algorithm for variable-rate, real-time traffic. CESoPSN uses the structure-locking algorithm.

Packet Loss Concealment (PLC)

TDM networks are inherently lossless. Because TDM data is always delivered over a dedicated channel at a constant bitrate, TDM bitstreams may arrive with bit errors, but are never out of order and never get lost in transit.

The behavior of a TDM network is not replicable in a cost-efficient manner over an IP network. Implementation of Quality of Service (QoS) and traffic-engineering mechanisms may be used to reduce traffic loss, but there is no guarantee that packets will not arrive out of order, or arrive at all. Packet-Switched Networks are inherently unreliable, and leverage higher-layer protocols to provide for sequencing, retransmission, and reliability.

Because TDM pseudowires carry real-time bitstreams, it is not possible to rely on retransmission mechanisms. Packet Loss Concealment (PLC) masks the impacts of these out-of-order or lost packets. In the case of lost packets, arbitrary packets are inserted into the bitstream to ensure that the timing is preserved. Because a TDM pseudowire packet is considered lost when the next packet arrives, out-of-order packets are not tolerated. TDM pseudowires use different types of arbitrary packets to conceal packet loss, as follows:

- **Zero Insertion:** Insertion of a constant value, or zero, in place of any lost packets. For voice, this may result in some choppiness.
- **Previous Insertion:** Insertion of the previous frame value in place of any lost packets. This method tends to be more beneficial for voice traffic, because voice tends to have a stationarity aspect. This stationarity means that the missing frame should have characteristics similar to the previous frame.
- **Interpolation:** Because a TDM pseudowire is considered lost when the next packet in sequence arrives, the receiver has both the previous and next packets upon which to base the missing frame value. Interpolation algorithms ranging from linear (straight-line interpolation of missing frame value) to more predictive (statistical calculations of missing frame value) may be used; however, there is no standard method for TDM pseudowire frame interpolation.

Time Division Multiplexing over IP (TDMoIP)

TDM over IP was first developed by RAD Data Communications in 1998, and first deployed in 1999 by Utfors, a Swedish broadband communications operator later acquired by Telenor.

Generic Encapsulation

The basic structure of a TDMoIP packet is depicted in Figure 7-13.

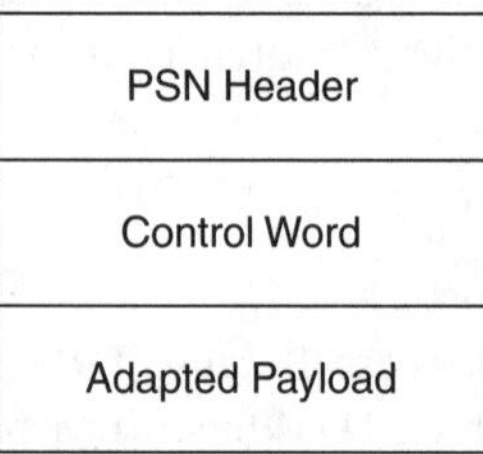

Figure 7-13 *TDMoIP Packet Structure*

TDMoIP packets are composed of three main parts, as follows:

- **PSN Headers:** PSN headers contain IP, MPLS, L2TPv3, or Ethernet information required to send the packet from the pseudowire ingress device toward the destination device, or pseudowire egress device. For example:
  - IP transport requires that the source/destination IP address and port number be included in the header.
  - MPLS transport requires that the MPLS tunnel label be included in the header.
  - L2TPv3 transport requires that the L2TPv3 Session Identifier (pseudowire label) be included in the header.
  - Ethernet transport requires that the Ethernet source/destination MAC address, VLAN header, and Ethertype be included in the header.
- **Control Word:** The Control Word is included in every TDMoIP packet. The Control Word includes information on TDM physical layer failures/defects (local or remote), length of the packet (to indicate if the packet is padded to meet PSN minimum transmission unit size), and sequence number (for detection of lost or misordered packets).
- **Adapted Payload:** The pseudowire ingress device uses either structure-indication or structure-reassembly in order to fill the packet payload.

OAM

Defects in a TDMoIP network may occur in multiple different locations. Depending on the location of the defect, standard TDM OAM mechanisms or TDMoIP mechanisms may be used to alert the TDM peer. Figure 7-14 illustrates the multiple defect locations in a TDMoIP network.

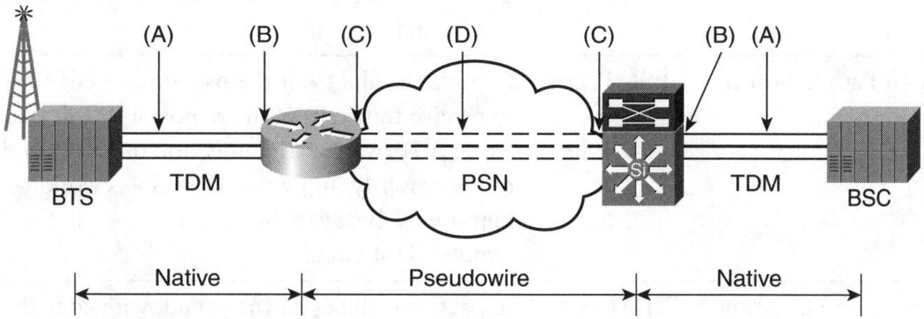

Figure 7-14 *TDMoIP Network Defect Locations*

Table 7-1 includes information about the reference points illustrated in Figure 7-14 and correlated OAM mechanisms, if available.

Table 7-1 *Reference Points and OAM Mechanisms*

Reference Point	Description	OAM Mechanism
(A)	Defect in the L2 TDM network that impacts any number of circuits terminating on the pseudowire edge devices.	The defect is communicated to the pseudowire edge devices and the remote TDM peer via native TDM OAM mechanisms.
(B)	Defect on the pseudowire edge TDM interface.	
(C)	Defect on the pseudowire edge PSN interface.	
(D)	Defect on the PSN that impacts any number of pseudowires terminating on the pseudowire edge devices.	The defect is communicated to the pseudowire edge devices via PSN or pseudowire OAM mechanisms.

Each pseudowire edge device is responsible for maintaining the state of both forward- and reverse-path traffic. Information on the forwarding paths is communicated to the pseudowire edge devices via Forward- or Reverse-Path indication notifications. Table 7-2 discusses the traffic impacts of the received messages.

Table 7-2 *Indication Notifications*

Indication	Source	Impact
Forward-Path Indication	TDM Peer	Impacts ability of the pseudowire edge device to receive traffic over the TDM circuit from the local TDM device. Note: The pseudowire edge device may be able to detect this directly if the failure occurs in the local port or link.
Forward-Path Indication	PSN Peer	Impacts the ability of the pseudowire edge device to receive traffic from the remote TDM device Note: A Forward-Path indication on the PSN does not necessarily imply that the PSN is working improperly, because the defect may be in the remote TDM circuit.
Reverse-Path Indication	TDM Peer	Impacts the ability of the pseudowire edge device to send traffic to the local TDM device.
Reverse-Path Indication	PSN Peer	Impacts the ability of the pseudowire edge device to send traffic to the remote TDM device. Note: This indication may be indicative of either a PSN fault or a remote TDM fault.

TDMoIP includes its own Operations and Maintenance (OAM) signaling path for reporting of bundle status and performance statistics. OAM signaling provides increased reliability to a protocol stack (TDMoIP pseudowires) that is inherently not reliable. The messages are similar to ICMP messages for the IP network.

Connectivity messages are sent periodically from pseudowire edge to pseudowire edge. A response from the remote pseudowire edge device indicates connectivity. Because forward and receive paths may be different, connectivity messages must be sent in both directions.

Performance messages are sent either periodically or on-demand between pseudowire edge devices. Metrics pertinent to pseudowire performance, such as one-way and round-trip delay, jitter, and packet loss, may be measured.

In addition, standard PSN mechanisms, such as Bidirectional Forwarding Detection (BFD) and MPLS Label Switch Path Ping (LSP-Ping), or other protocol-specific detection mechanisms (L2TP mechanisms described in RFC 3931) may be used over each individual pseudowire, as well as the tunnel itself. These mechanisms may be used continually (proactive notification of defects) or on-demand (reactive notification of diagnostics).

Circuit Emulation Services over Packet-Switched Networks (CESoPSN)

Circuit Emulation Services over Packet-Switched Networks (CESoPSN) is defined in RFC 5086, which was first drafted in January 2004.

Packet Structure

Packet structure of CESoPSN is very similar to that of TDMoIP, except for the inclusion of an optional fixed-length RTP header. This packet structure is illustrated in Figure 7-15.

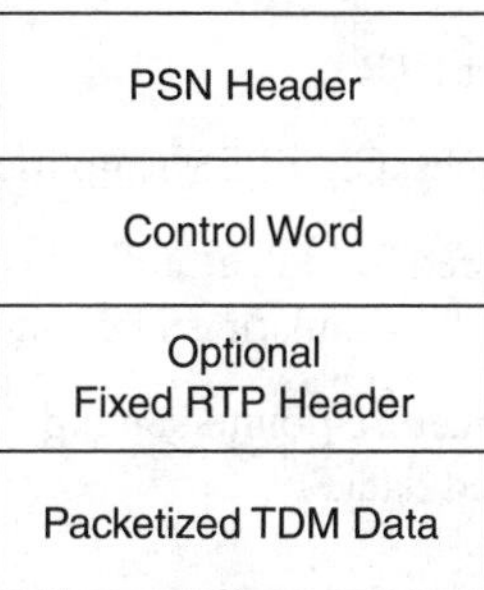

Figure 7-15 *CESoPSN Packet Structure*

RTP

CESoPSN may use an optional RTP header for the transport of timing information. Timing is further discussed later in the chapter in the section, "Timing." The RTP header includes specific timestamp information that can be retrieved in the following two manners:

- **Absolute Mode:** In Absolute Mode, the edge pseudowire device recovers the clock information from the incoming TDM circuit. In this mode, the timestamps are closely correlated with sequence numbers.
- **Differential Mode:** In Differential Mode, the edge pseudowire device has access to a high-quality synchronization source. In this mode, timestamps represent the difference between the synchronization source and the TDM circuit.

CESoPSN Versus TDMoIP

Although both CESoPSN and TDMoIP provide for transport of TDM frames over PSNs using pseudowires, there are numerous differences between the two protocols themselves. These differences include the following:

- TDMoIP uses the structure-indication and structure-reassembly mechanisms, whereas CESoPSN uses the structure-locking algorithm. Therefore, CESoPSN transmits consistent, fixed-length packets, whereas TDMoIP has several payload lengths (minimum of 48 bytes) depending on the type of traffic being transmitted.
  - This allows for CESoPSN to have a lower packetization delay in instances where the pseudowire is carrying multiple timeslots.
  - By the same token, using structure-locking creates inefficiencies when transporting unstructured T1 streams. CESoPSN payload is required to begin at a frame boundary. This means that T1 frames must be padded to create the consistent packet size.
- CESoPSN mandates use of RTP.
- By transporting entire frames, CESoPSN simplifies packet loss compensation.
  - CESoPSN does not need to look at individual timeslots. Instead, CESoPSN inserts a packet of all 1's, simulating TDM fault mechanisms.
- TDMoIP must look for structure pointers, jump to the beginning of the next structure, and insert interpolated data.

ATM Pseudowires

An ATM pseudowire uses an MPLS network for the transport of ATM cells.

Note ATM pseudowires follow the PWE-3 architecture, and therefore only ATM-specific information is included in this section.

Defined in RFC 4717, ATM pseudowires provide many of the same benefits as TDMoIP and CESoPSN:

- Simplification of network architecture and reduction of number of core networks supported
- Preserving existing legacy services during migration to next-generation IP services
- Using a common PSN to provide both legacy and next-generation services

The generic architecture of an ATM pseudowire service is illustrated in Figure 7-16.

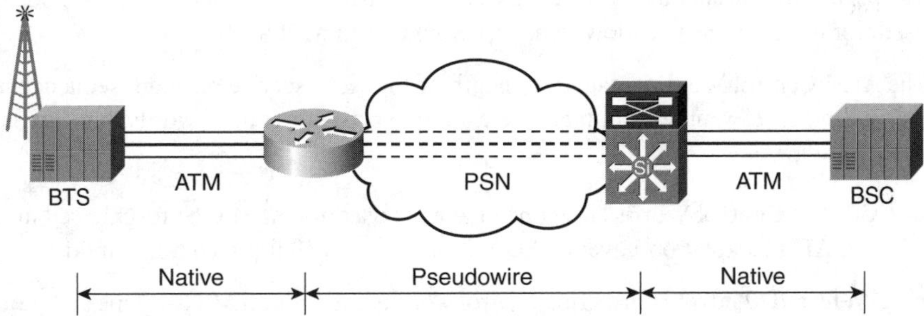

Figure 7-16 *ATM Pseudowire Architecture*

As with all pseudowire services, the intent of an ATM pseudowire is not to perfectly emulate the traditional service, but instead to provide a transport mechanism for the service. This means there are distinct differences between the traditional ATM service and an ATM pseudowire, namely the following:

- ATM cell ordering is optional.
- ATM QoS model can be emulated, but is application-specific in nature.
- ATM flow control mechanisms are not understood by the MPLS network, and therefore cannot reflect the status of the PSN.
- Control plane support for ATM Switched Virtual Circuits (SVCs), Switched Virtual Paths (SVPs), Soft Permanent Virtual Circuits (SPVCs), and Soft Permanent Virtual Paths (SPVPs) are supported only through vendor-proprietary solutions.

Generic Encapsulation

Figure 7-17 illustrates the general encapsulation method for ATM pseudowires.

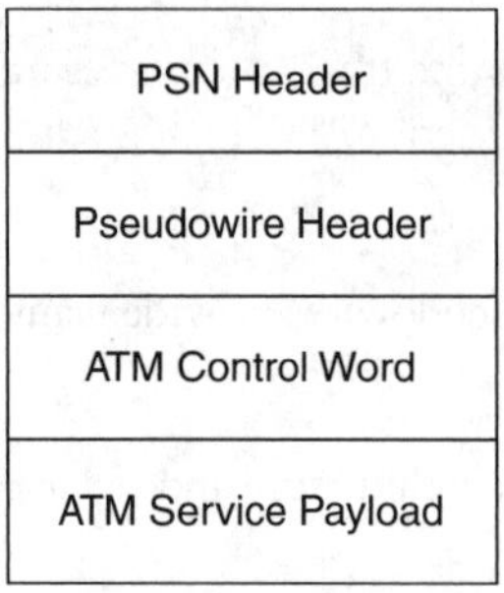

PSN Header
Pseudowire Header
ATM Control Word
ATM Service Payload

Figure 7-17 *ATM Generic Encapsulation Method*

The PSN Transport header is used to transport the encapsulated ATM information across the network. The structure of this header depends on the type of transport protocol being used.

The pseudowire header maps an ATM service to a particular tunnel. If MPLS is being used, for instance, the pseudowire header would be an MPLS label.

The ATM Control Word contains the length of the ATM service payload, sequence number, and other relevant control bits. There are two types of control words that can be used, as follows:

- **Generic Control Word:** This control word is used for ATM One-to-One cell mode and ATM Adaptation Layer (AAL) 5 Protocol Data Unit (PDU) frame mode.
- **Preferred Control Word:** This control word is used for ATM N-to-One cell mode and AAL5 Service Data Unit (SDU) frame mode.

Cell Mode Modes

There are two methods for encapsulation of ATM cells: N-to-One mode and One-to-One mode.

N-to-One Mode

N-to-One mode is the only required mode for ATM pseudowires. This encapsulation method maps one or more ATM Virtual Circuit Connections (VCCs) or Virtual Path Connection (VPC) to a single pseudowire. The N-to-One mode allows a service provider to offer an ATM PVC- or SVC-based service across a PSN.

With N-to-One mode, the ATM header is unaltered during this encapsulation, so ATM Virtual Path Identifier (VPI) and Virtual Circuit Identifier (VCI) are present. This information is required to be preserved since concatenation of cells from multiple VCCs may occur.

N-to-One mode has the following limitations:

- Explicit Forward Congestion Indication (EFCI) cannot be translated to a PSN congestion mechanism. Conversely, PSN congestion mechanisms cannot be translated to EFCI.
- Cell header detection/correction that exists in ATM cannot be replicated in the PSN.
- Cell encapsulation only functions for point-to-point MPLS Label Switched Paths (LSPs). Point-to-multipoint and multipoint-to-point are not supported.

One-to-One Mode

One-to-One mode is an optional encapsulation method that maps a single VCC/VPC to a single pseudowire. Because only one VPI/VCI is transported on a pseudowire, the pseudowire context (MPLS Label, for example) is used to derive the corresponding VPI/VCI value. The One-to-One mode also allows a service provider to offer an ATM PVC- or SVC-based service across a PSN.

The same limitations as N-to-One mode apply for One-to-One mode.

AAL5 Frame Encapsulation

There are different optional encapsulation methods that exist specifically for AAL5—one for SDUs and one for PDUs.

AAL5 SDU frame encapsulation is more efficient than using either N-to-One or One-to-One for AAL5. Because the pseudowire edge needs to understand the AAL5 SDU in order to transport it, the device must support segmentation and reassembly.

AAL5 PDU frame encapsulation allows for the entire AAL5 PDU to be encapsulated and transported. Because of this, all necessary ATM parameters are transported as part of the payload. This simplifies the fragmentation operation because all fragments occur at cell boundaries, and the Cyclical Redundancy Check (CRC) from the AAL5 PDU can be used to verify cell integrity.

Defect Handling

Figure 7-18 illustrates the four possible locations for defects on the ATM pseudowire service. These four locations are as follows:

- **(A):** ATM connection from ATM device to pseudowire edge device.
- **(B):** ATM interface on the pseudowire edge device.
- **(C):** PSN interface on the pseudowire edge device.
- **(D):** PSN network.

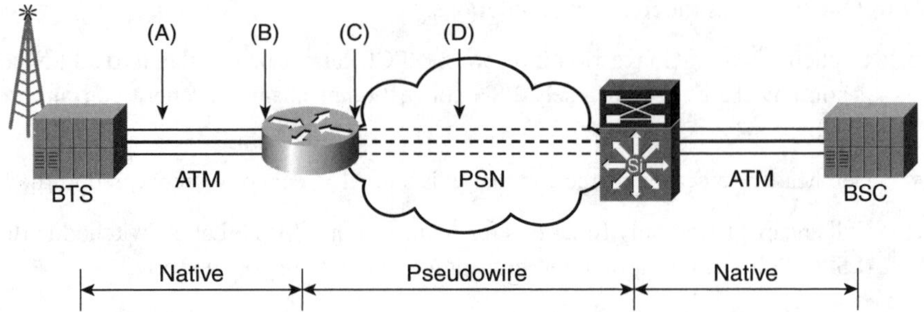

Figure 7-18 *ATM Defect Locations*

In all cases, the pseudowire edge device uses standard ATM signaling methods to notify the receiver of cell loss. This information is transported across the PSN to the receiver.

SONET/SDH Circuit Emulation over Packet

> **Note** SONET/SDH Circuit Emulation over Packet (CEP) follows similar premise and structure to all other PWE3 standards, and therefore only SONET/SDH-specific information is included in this section.

To transport SONET/SDH over packet, the Synchronous Payload Envelope (SPE) or virtual tributary (VT) is fragments, prepended with a pseudowire header, and optionally a RTP header. The basic CEP header is illustrated in Figure 7-19.

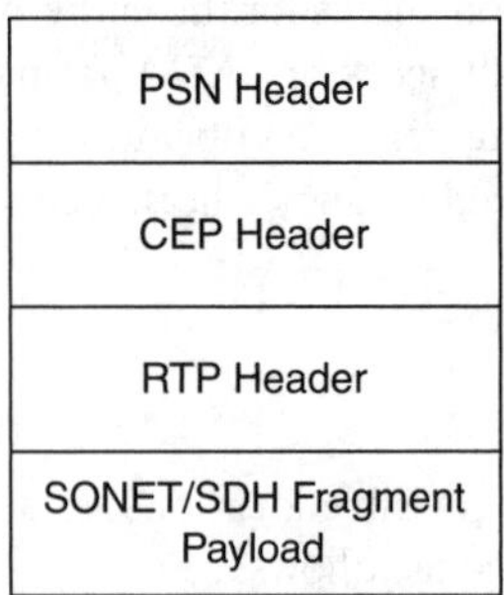

Figure 7-19 *Basic CEP Header*

The CEP header supports both a basic mode, which contains the minimum functionality necessary to perform SONET/SDH CEP, and an extended mode, which contains additional capabilities for some optional SONET/SDH fragment formats. These options fall into two categories, as follows:

- Dynamic Bandwidth Allocation (DBA) is an optional mechanism for SPE transmission suppression on a channel-by-channel basis when one of two trigger conditions are met—that the SONET/SDH path or VT is not transmitting valid end-user data or that the circuit has been de-provisioned, or unequipped.
- Service-Specific Payload Formats are special encapsulations that provide different levels of compression depending on the type and amount of user data traffic. The payload compression options are provided for asynchronous T3/E3 Synchronous Transport Signal 1 (STS-1), fractional VC-4, fractional STS-1, and others.

Fragments

When fragmented, the SONET/SDH fragments must be byte-aligned with the SONET/SDH SPE or VT. That is, the SONET/SDH byte cannot be fragmented, and the first bit in the SONET/SDH must be the most significant bit in the SONET/SDH fragment. In addition, bytes are placed into the fragment in the order in which they are received.

SONET/SDH CEP lies above the physical layer, and assumes that native transport functions, such as physical layer scrambling/unscrambling that SONET/SDH optical interfaces perform as part of their binary coding, occurs as part of the native service. However, CEP does not assume that scrambling has occurred, and fragments are constructed without consideration of this.

Abis/Iub Optimization for GSM Networks

Chapter 2 discusses GSM RAN Abis interface and UMTS RAN Iub interface. GSM RAN Optimization is a method for optimizing and encapsulating structured (NxDS0) TDM signals between the BTS and BSC into IP packets. The optimization is performed by removing nonessential traffic on the GSM Abis interface. Such nonessential traffic includes idle subrates that have a repeating pattern every 20 msec, idle TRAU frames used to keep subrates in-sync for GPRS, and speech TRAU frames with silence used to provide white noise that lets the other party know that the call has not been dropped. In addition, High-Level Data Link Control (HDLC) signaling data flows, which are part of the GSM Radio Link Protocol (RLP), can be optimized by suppressing inter-frame flags.

Note Chapter 2 describes the GSM Abis interface and UMTS Iub interface, including the protocols, functions, and capabilities of these interfaces.

Optimization is done at the bit level, resulting in no impact to voice quality or data throughput. This bit level optimization makes GSM Optimization radio-vendor independent and radio software version independent. Figure 7-20 illustrates GSM Abis optimization.

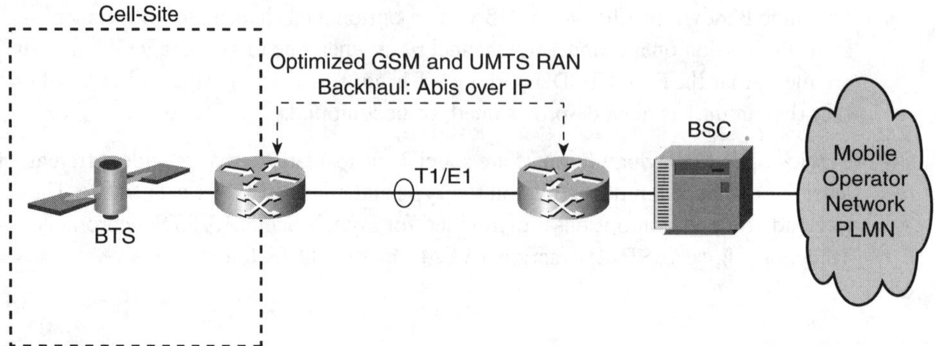

Figure 7-20 *GSM Abis Optimization*

Timing

Today's mobile networks are reliant on accurate timing, or accurate distribution and synchronization of precise clock information, in order to accurately transport voice and data traffic. In existing radio architectures, frequency synchronization is typically achieved through the backhaul network itself. These legacy architectures are based on TDM backhaul. Because TDM carries time inherently, the radio architecture itself was designed with frequency synchronization embedded in the physical layer.

Radio Access Network and Synchronization

The need for synchronization has always been inherent in Radio Access Networks. As discussed in Chapter 1, "Introduction to Radio Systems," radio networks fall into two categories:

- **Frequency Division Duplexing (FDD),** in which two sets of frequencies are used for transmit/receive. These networks require frequency synchronization in order to accurately send and receive traffic.
- **Time Division Duplexing (TDD),** in which a single frequency is used for transmit/receive and a demarcation based on timeslots is identified for both transmission and reception. These networks require time synchronization in order to accurately send and receive traffic.

Table 7-3 provides a reference for today's wireless technologies and their synchronization requirements.

Table 7-3 *Wireless Technologies and Synchronization Requirements*

Application	Service
TDM Support	Frequency/Timing
3GPP (GSM, WCDMA FDD)	Frequency
3GPP (LTE, eMBMS)	Time (TDD Mode) Frequency (FDD Mode)
WiMAX (IEEE 802.16d/e)	Frequency Time
DVB-T/DVB-H	Time
TD-SCDMA 3GPP2 CDMA	Time Frequency

In mobile networks, high-quality frequency and time/phase synchronization are useful and in some cases required. The accuracy of these services differs based on the radio technology and standards organization. The synchronization service accuracy based on application (radio technology) is referenced in Table 7-4.

Table 7-4 *Synchronization Service Requirements*

Synch Service	Application	Expected Quality
Frequency	TDM Support	Primary Reference Source (PRS) Traceable
	3GPP/3GPP2 BS	Frequency assignment shall be less than ± $5x10^{-8}$ (± 0.05 parts-per-million [ppm])
	WiMAX (IEEE 802.16)	.16D: Reference frequency accuracy shall be better than $\pm 8*10^{-6}$ ($\pm 2*10^{-6}$) .16e: Reference Frequency Tolerance at BS: $\leq \pm 1*10^{-6}$
	DVB-T/H/SH/T2	Frequency shall provide a traceable Primary Reference Clock (PRC) source for 10MHz signal
Time	802.16D/e TDD	Better than 5µs
	DVB-T/H	Within 1µs accuracy
	3GPP LTE	Better than or equal to 3µs
	3GPP2 CDMA BS	*Should* be less than 3 µs *Shall* be less than 10 µs
	3GPP eMBMS	TBD

Network Synchronization Options

In order to achieve the stringent quality requirements identified in Table 7-4, there are multiple network synchronization options, as follows:

- **Free-running oscillator:** A free-running oscillator is one that has never been synchronized to a reference clock. This oscillator's accuracy is based on the technology within the oscillator. In this model, each network element would either contain or be connected directly to a free-running oscillator and rely on the local clock for all synchronization. Table 7-5 highlights the different oscillator technologies and accuracy.

Table 7-5 *Oscillator Technology and Accuracy*

Technology	Stratum Level	Accuracy
Hydrogen Maser		$1x10^{-15}$
Cesium	1	$1x10^{-11}$
Rubidium	2	$5x10^{-11}$
Crystal	3/4	$4.6x10^{-6}$

- **Global Positioning System (GPS):** GPS synchronization relies on a GPS satellite to provide the clock source. All GPS satellites contain a Cesium standard clock. Because GPS satellites circle the globe twice per day, any device relying on GPS for synchronization must also calculate geographic location in order to determine from which satellite it can receive signals.
- **Physical layer:** Physical layer synchronization has long been used for transporting clock information. SONET/SDH and T1/E1 are well-known examples of physical layer synchronization. More recently, Synchronous Ethernet (SyncE) uses the Ethernet physical layer interface to pass timing from node to node in much the same way. SyncE is discussed later in this chapter in "Packet-Based Timing."
- **Higher layer:** Higher-layer synchronization relies on a packet-based protocol to distribute clocking information. IEEE 1588v2 and Network Time Protocol (NTP) are discussed later in this chapter in "Packet-Based Timing."

Introduction to Timing

This section provides an overview of timing, including definitions, clock hierarchies, and reference clock architectures. These hierarchies and architectures are leveraged repeatedly in many different circuit-switched and packet-switched timing protocols, and understanding these architectures provides the foundation knowledge for the remainder of this chapter.

Understanding Timing Definitions

Before defining architectures, it is important to understand some of the basic definitions that will be used continually throughout the remainder of this chapter. This section provides some of these basic definitions.

Precision, Accuracy, and Stability

Precision, accuracy, and stability are used to measure the reliability of a clock signal.

- **Precision** is defined as the ability of a measurement to be consistently reproduced. When referencing timing, precision refers to the amount of variation of a set of measurements.
- **Accuracy** is defined as the ability of a set of measurements to consistently match the exact value being measured. In the case of timing, the value being measured is a predefined reference time.
- **Stability** is defined as the amount a measurement changes as a function of time or environment (temperature, shock, and so on).

The goal of every clock is to be highly precise, highly accurate, and highly stable. In practice, however, every clock signal has unique characteristics of precision, accuracy, and stability. These clock signals can fall into six broad categories, as follows:

- **Accurate, precise, stable:** This clock source produces a consistent measurement as a function of time and environment that is representative of the predefined reference time. Figure 7-21 illustrates this type of clock source.

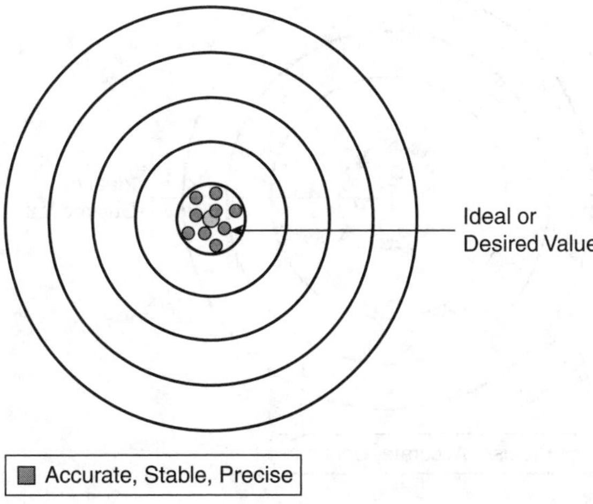

Figure 7-21 *Accurate, Precise, Stable*

- **Accurate, imprecise, stable:** This clock source produces a large variety of measurements, consistent as a function of time and environment, which are representative of the predefined reference time. Figure 7-22 illustrates this type of clock source.

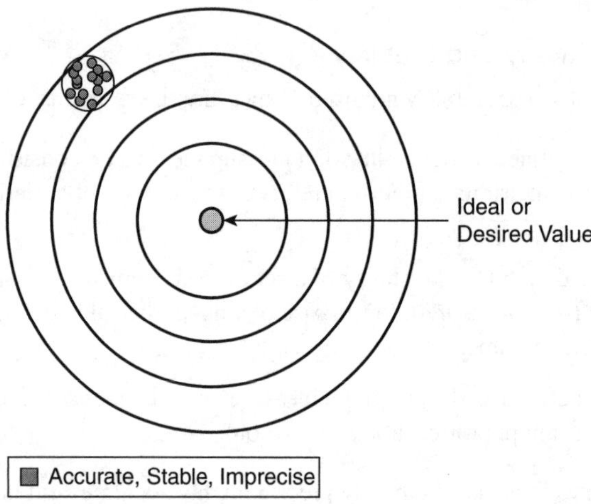

Figure 7-22 *Accurate, Imprecise, Stable*

- **Precise, accurate, unstable:** This clock source produces a small variety of measurement, inconsistent as a function of time and environment, which are representative of the predefined reference time. Figure 7-23 illustrates this type of clock source.

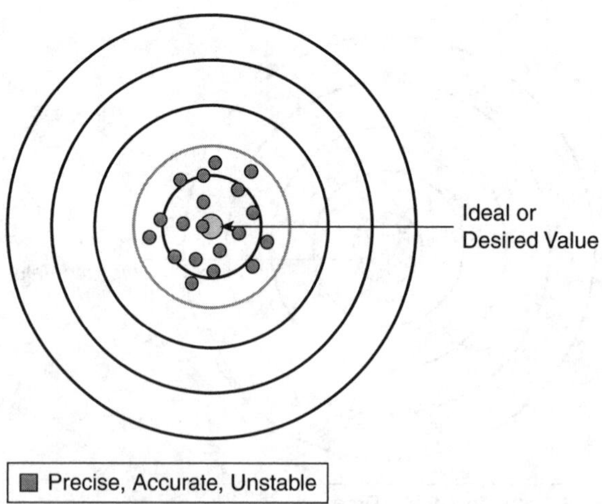

Figure 7-23 *Precise, Accurate, Unstable*

- **Inaccurate, precise, stable:** This clock source produces a small variety of measurements, consistent as a function of time and environment, which are not representative of the predefined reference time. Figure 7-24 illustrates this type of clock source.

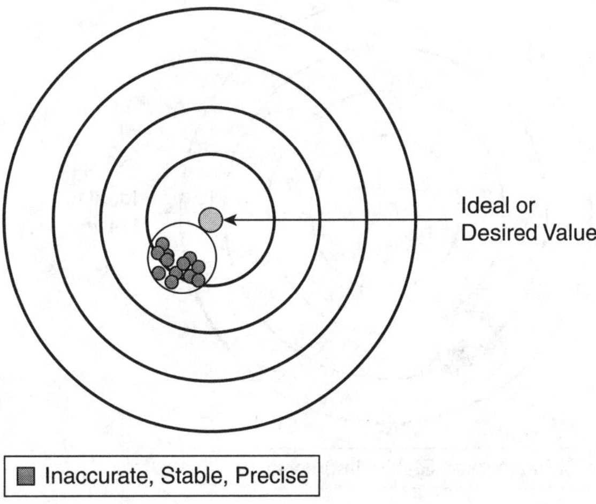

Figure 7-24 *Inaccurate, Precise, Stable*

- **Accurate, imprecise, unstable:** This clock source produces a large variety of measurements, inconsistent as a function of time and environment, which are representative of the predefined reference time. Figure 7-25 illustrates this type of clock source.

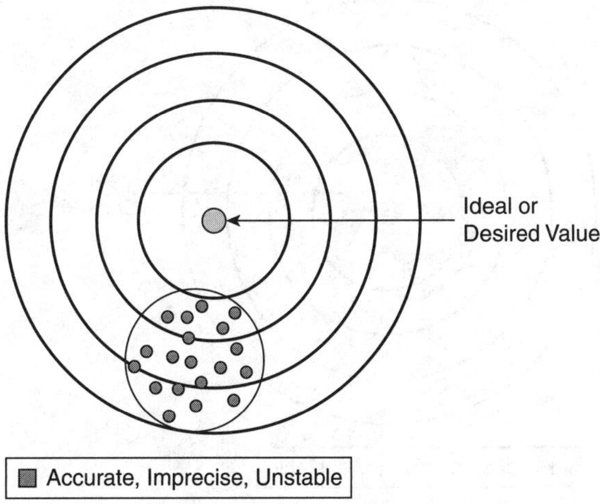

Figure 7-25 *Accurate, Imprecise, Unstable*

- **Inaccurate, imprecise, stable:** This clock source produces a large variety of measurements, consistent as a function of time and environment, which are not representative of the predefined reference time. Figure 7-26 illustrates this type of clock source.

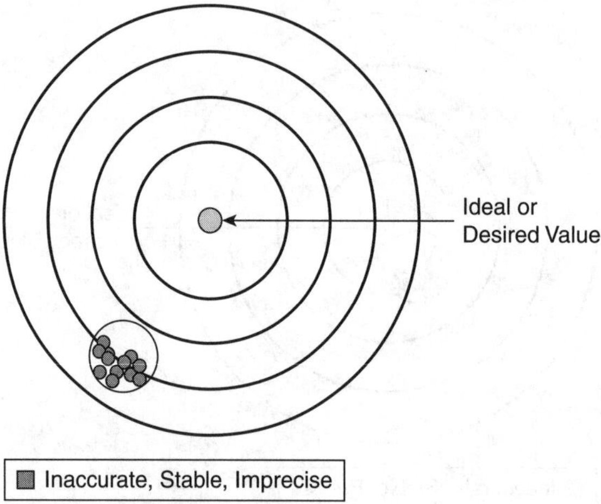

Figure 7-26 *Inaccurate, Imprecise, Stable*

- **Inaccurate, precise, unstable:** This clock source produces a small variety of measurements, inconsistent as a function of time and environment, which are not representative of the predefined reference time. Figure 7-27 illustrates this type of clock source.

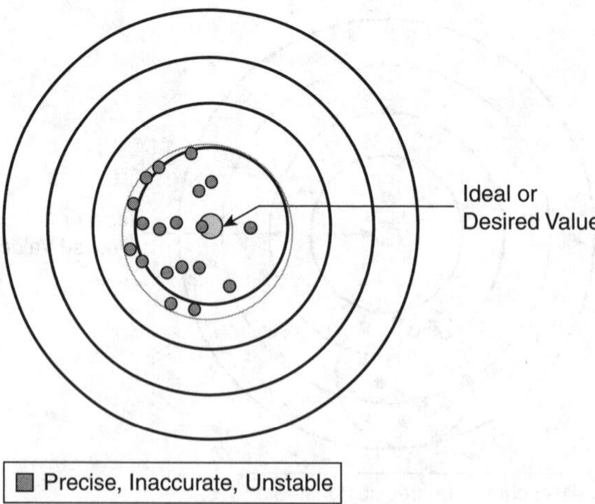

Figure 7-27 *Inaccurate, Precise, Unstable*

- **Inaccurate, imprecise, unstable:** This clock source produces a large variety of measurements, inconsistent as a function of time and environment, which are not representative of the predefined reference time. Figure 7-28 illustrates this type of clock source.

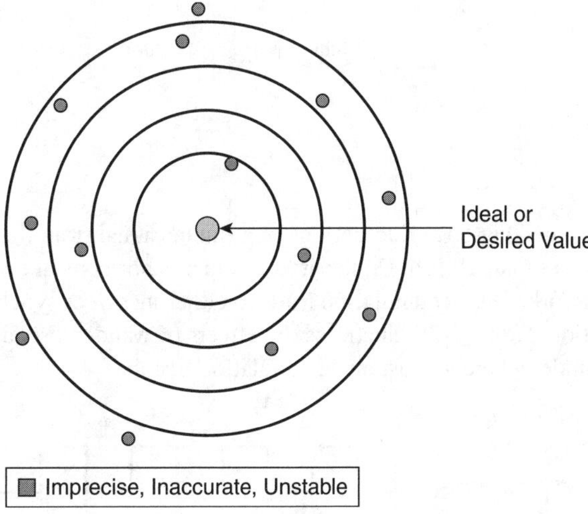

Figure 7-28 *Inaccurate, Imprecise, Instable*

Synchronization

Synchronization refers to timing that requires multiple devices to operate as part of a system at the exact same time. In transporting time-based data traffic, synchronization of all network elements can be achieved in multiple ways. These elements can be synchronized in the following two key ways:

- Frequency synchronization refers to the need for two network elements (transmitter and receiver) to operate at the same rate—that is, both network elements need to operate at the same rate.
- Phase/Time synchronization refers to the need for two network elements to be able to accurately identify the end of a frame or byte. Phase/time synchronization first requires frequency synchronization.

Jitter

Jitter refers to the short-term fluctuations of a timing signal from their ideal positions in time (variations greater than or equal to 10 Hz). Jitter, which is constant over time, makes a clock source unstable. Figure 7-29 illustrates the effects of jitter.

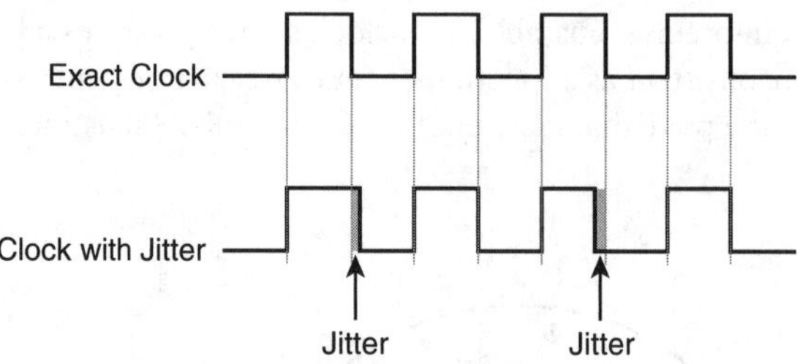

Figure 7-29 *Jitter*

Wander

Wander refers to the long-term fluctuations of a timing signal from their ideal positions in time (variations less than 10 Hz). Unlike jitter, wander is not constant over time, and accumulates in a network. This accumulation leads to either incorrect synchronization or loss of synchronization. Figure 7-30 illustrates the effects of wander. Frequency Drift is a specific type of wander where a constant accumulation occurs.

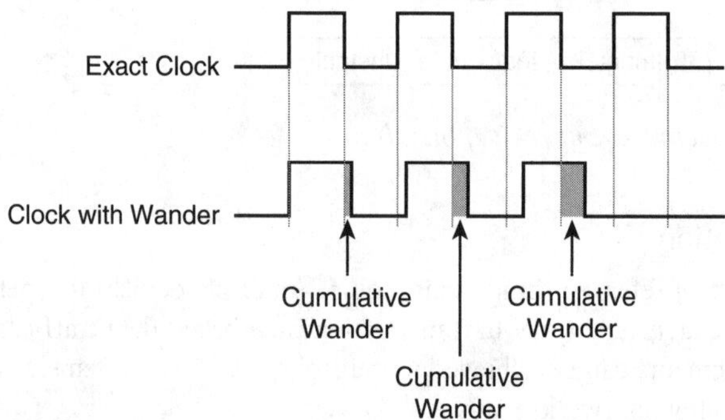

Figure 7-30 *Frequency Drift*

Timing Architectures

Many different timing architectures have been deployed to all accomplish the same end-goal—maximum accuracy, stability, and precision of timing information to all nodes within the network. These timing architectures are dictated by standards-based hierarchies, with each tier of the hierarchy representing a different level of precision. Once the hierarchy is established, operators have varied in their deployment models for distribution and synchronization of this clock information. This section looks at the various clock hierarchy considerations and network architectures that have been deployed.

Clock Hierarchy

Clock standards have a hierarchy defined by the International Telecommunications Union (ITU) Telecommunications Standardization Sector (ITU-T) and the American National Standards Institute (ANSI). For simplicity, ANSI clock hierarchy is used within this chapter. The hierarchy defines the relationship between every clock within a synchronization domain and the model for distribution across the domain. The hierarchy is based on five quality metrics, as follows:

- Accuracy.
- **Holdover Stability**, or the ability to continue to preserve accurate time when a clock's reference signal is lost.
- **Pull-In/Hold-In Range**, or the largest offset/differential between the reference frequency and nominal frequency for which the clock can still acquire "lock."
- Wander.
- **Time to First Frame (193 bits) Slip**, or the length of time that the clock can remain accurate.

The ANSI and ITU-T clock standards are summarized in Table 7-6.

Table 7-6 *ANSI/ITU-T Clock Standards*

ANSI Stratum	ITU-T Clock Level	Accuracy	Holdover Stability	Pull-In Range	Wander	Time to First Frame Slip
1	PRC	$1x10^{-11}$	None	None	None	72 days
2	Type II	+/-0.016 ppm	$+/-1*10^{-10}$/day	0.016 ppm	0.001 Hz	7 days
-	Type I	Not Defined	$+/-2.7*10^{-9}$/day	0.01 ppm	0.003 Hz	
3E	Type III	+/-4.6 ppm	$+/-1.2*10^{-8}$/day	4.6 ppm	0.001 Hz	3.5 hours
3	Type IV	+/-4.6 ppm	$+/-3.9*10^{-7}$/day	4.6 ppm	3 Hz	6 minutes
-	Option I	+/-4.6 ppm	$+/-2*10^{-6}$/day	4.6 ppm	1–10 Hz	
SMC	Option 2	+/-20 ppm	$+/-4.6*10^{-6}$/day	20 ppm	0.1 Hz	
4	4	+/-32 ppm	None	32 ppm	None	

The network is controlled by a Primary Reference Clock (PRC), or Stratum 1 clock, which is accurate to $1x10^{-11}$. Synchronization requires the distribution of the reference signal from the PRC to all network elements. The master-slave method is used for this propagation. The synchronization between hierarchies is unidirectional; that is, synchronization is always transferred from a higher layer to a lower layer. The Stratum 1 clock receives information from any number of Stratum 0 clocks. The Stratum 1 clock provides the reference clock for multiple Stratum 2 clocks, and each Stratum 2 clock provided the reference clock for multiple Stratum 3 clocks. This hierarchy is illustrated in Figure 7-31.

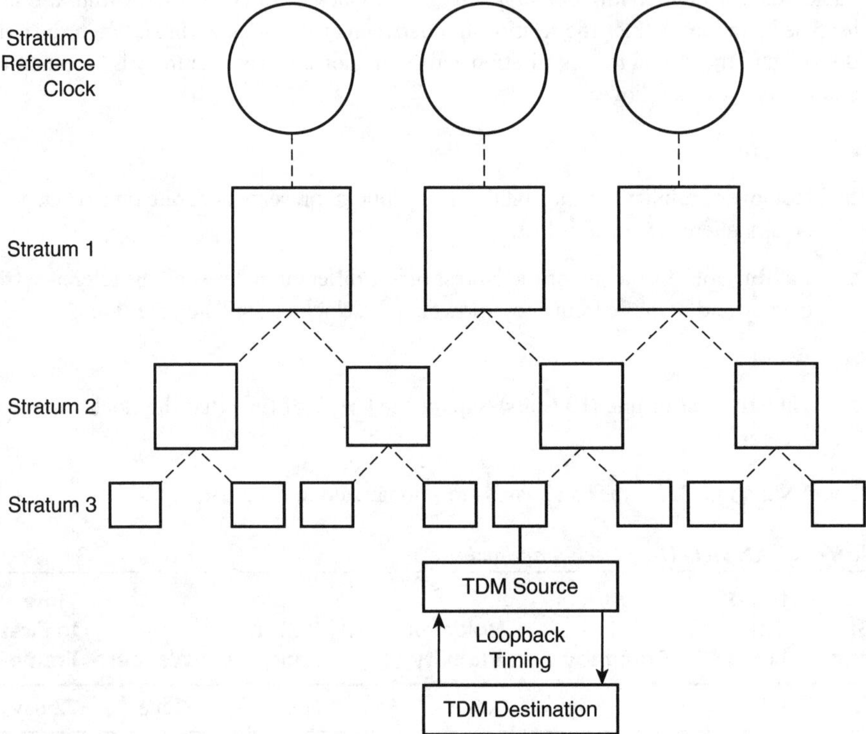

Figure 7-31 *Clock Hierarchy*

PRC Architectures

A PRC is designed to provide highly-accurate time, and therefore tends to rely on more than one Primary Reference Source (PRS). A Cesium-beam tube is always used in the generation of a PRC signal because of their accuracy in ensuring no aging or frequency drift. Three types of PRCs have emerged (and have been identified by The European Telecommunications Standards Institute [ETSI]), as follows:

- Autonomous PRCs with up to three local Cesium tubes incorporated within the PRC and used as the PRS.
- Radio-controlled PRCs, which use remote Cesium tubes in the radio infrastructure (either satellite-based, like GPS, or land-based, like Long Range Aid to Navigation [LORAN]-C) as the PRS.
- PRCs that use a combination of local Cesium tubes and radio-based Cesium tubes.

In the event of a failure of one of the PRS, the PRC can use one of the other PRS as the reference; however, the failover time must be within the Maximum Time Interval Error (MTIE) defined by ITU-T.

Table 7-7 depicts the MTIE defined by ITU-T for each clock level.

Table 7-7 *MTIE by Stratum*

ANSI Stratum	ITU-T Clock Level	Phase Transient
1	PRC	-
2	Type II	MTIE < 150ns
-	Type I	MTIE < 1μs
3E	Type III	MTIE < 150ns
3	Type IV	MTIE < 1μs
-	Option I	MTIE < 1μs
SMC	Option 2	MTIE < 1μs
4	4	No Requirement

Figure 7-32 illustrates these three types of PRC architectures.

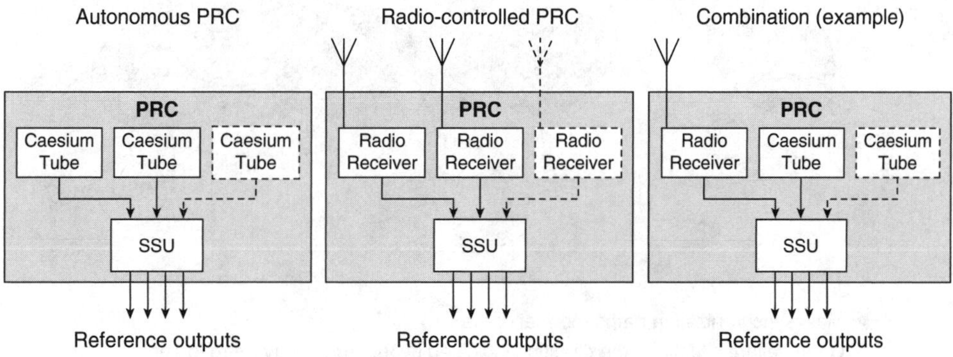

Figure 7-32 *PRS/PRC Architectures*

PRCs can be deployed in multiple different architectures. These architectures provide different levels of resiliency, complexity, and cost. In general, the following principles are adhered to in all PRC architectures:

- The synchronization distribution is tree-shaped.
- The synchronization network can be decomposed into multiple synchronization chains.

- Several stratum of slave clocks with different properties/roles exist.
- A higher-quality level is never slaved to a reference signal of a lower-quality.
- The SSU provides timing to a portion of the network. If the SSU's reference signal is lost, the SSU supplies timing to the network downstream.
- Radio-controlled PRCs use remote Cesium tubes in the radio infrastructure (either satellite-based, like GPS, or land-based, like Long Range Aid to Navigation [LORAN]-C) as the PRS.
- PRCs use a combination of local Cesium tubes and radio-based Cesium tubes.

Figure 7-33 provides an example of a synchronization network, including the Synchronization Supply Unit (SSU).

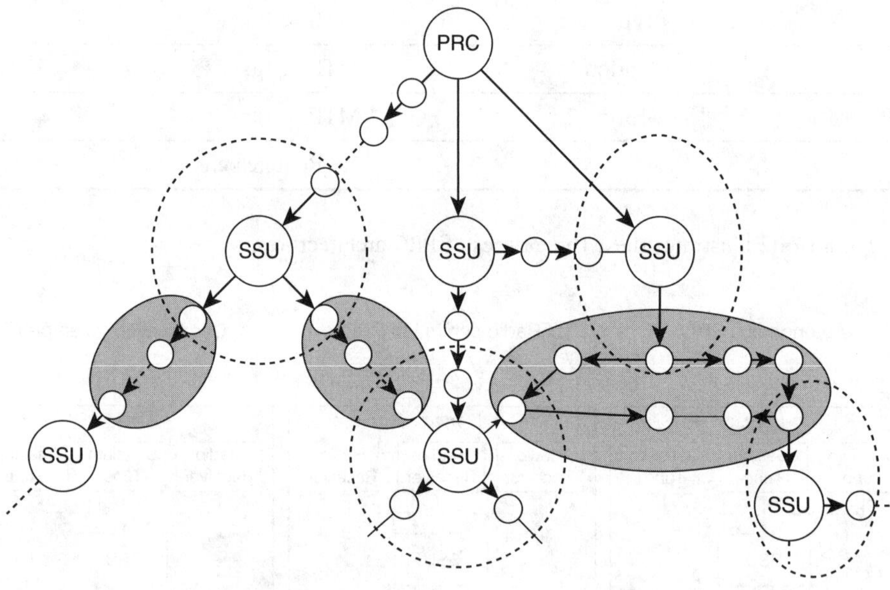
PRC
SSU
SSU
SSU
SSU
SSU
SSU
Main synchronization paths (normal operation).
Under failure situations the direction indicated by the arrow may be reversed.
Standby synchronization paths.
Paths without arrows may be used in either direction, depending on the failure situation.
Network nodes, areas of intra-node synchronization distribution (examples).
Transport network, areas of inter-node synchronization distribution (examples).

Figure 7-33 *Synchronization Network Example*

SSUs are used to provide reliable distribution of clock information. SSUs are part of every synchronization domain, including the PRC. SSUs receive clocking information from higher-layer clocks and distribute the clock information to all local equipment. SSUs also have the ability to provide accurate holdover mode, in the event that their clock source is lost.

The SSU does not belong to the transport network, but only provides the timing for the transport network elements within its synchronization domain.

There are two primary methods for providing clock synchronization, as follows:

- Master-slave synchronization, which has a single PRC from which all other clocks are synchronized. Synchronization in this method is achieved by sending timing signals from one clock to the next, in a hierarchical fashion. Figure 7-34 illustrates this master-slave synchronization network architecture.

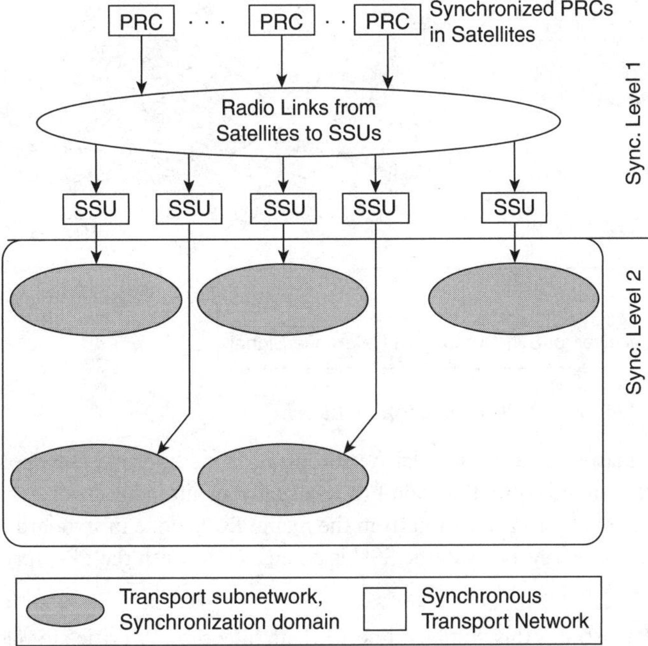

Figure 7-34 *Master-Slave Synchronization Network*

- Mutual synchronization, in which all clocks are interconnected. In this method, there is no unique PRC or hierarchical structure defined. Figure 7-35 illustrates this mutual synchronization network architecture.

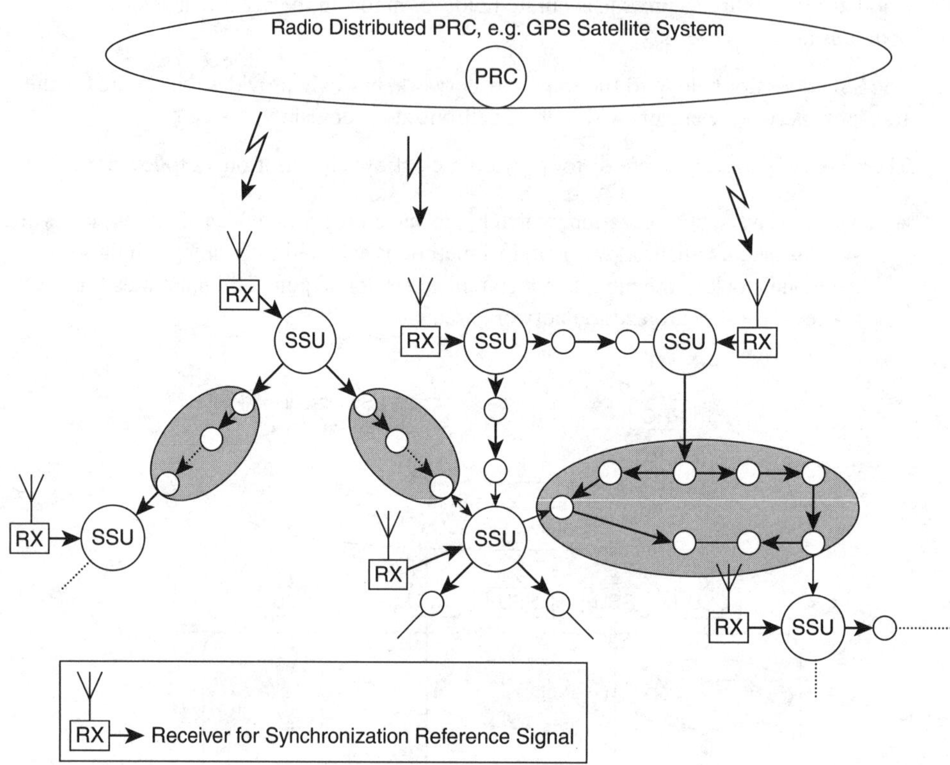

Figure 7-35 *Mutual Synchronization Network*

In practice, master-slave and mutual synchronization methods may be deployed in combination. In this architecture, the main PRC is usually an autonomous or combined PRC (see Figure 7-32). Synchronization from the main PRC is done in standard master-slave hierarchical fashion. At Level 2, the SSU is connected to both the PRC (primary) and an off-air PRC (backup).

Figure 7-36 illustrates this combined network architecture. Priorities for clock source and synchronization are identified in the figure.

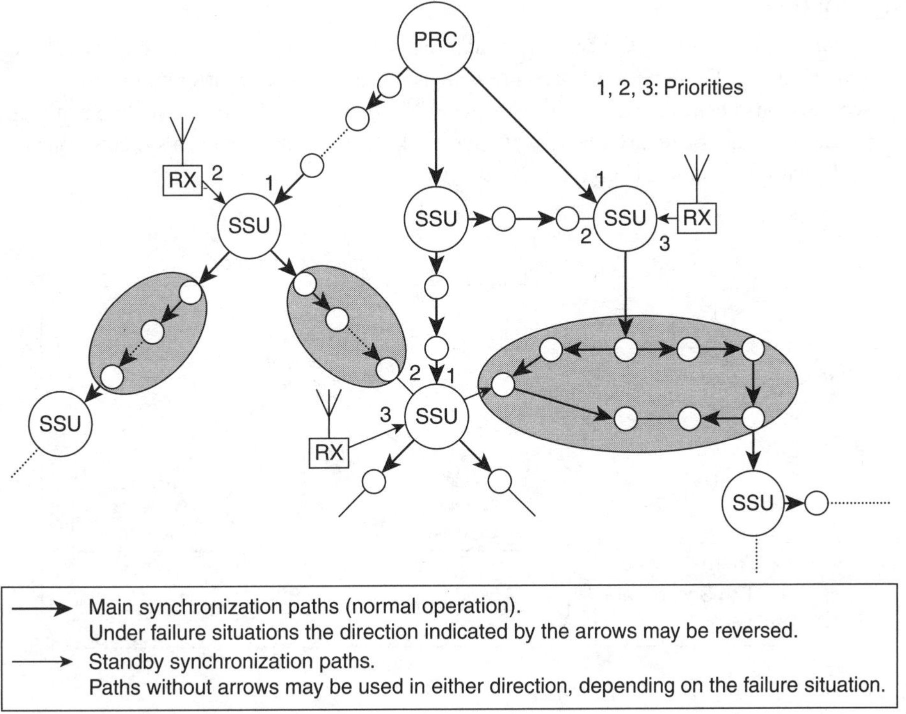
PRC
1, 2, 3: Priorities
RX
SSU
RX
SSU
SSU
RX
SSU
RX
SSU
SSU
Main synchronization paths (normal operation).
Under failure situations the direction indicated by the arrows may be reversed.
Standby synchronization paths.
Paths without arrows may be used in either direction, depending on the failure situation.

Figure 7-36 *Combined Master-Slave and Mutual Synchronization Network*

Timing Modes

Timing modes define what a clock is referenced to. Network elements may operate in four different timing modes, as follows:

- External timing, where the reference source signal is received via a local timing interface directly.
- Line timing, where the reference source signal is received from one or more data interfaces that also carries timing information.
- Loop timing, where the reference source signal is received from only one data interface as part of a ring topology.
- Through timing, where the reference source signal is transported transparently across the network element.

These timing modes map to four network architectures—synchronous networks, asynchronous networks, pseudo-synchronous networks, and plesiochronous networks.

Synchronous

A *synchronous network* is one where all clocks within the network have identical long-term accuracy. These networks require synchronization to avoid jitter and wander. Synchronous networks have a single active PRC source signal and rely on line timing to distribute clock information across the network. Figure 7-37 depicts a synchronous network that relies on line timing for clock source.

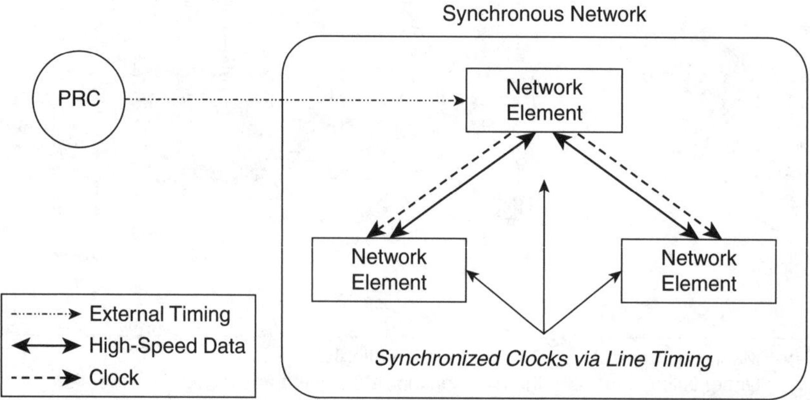

Figure 7-37 *Synchronous Network*

Asynchronous

An *asynchronous network* is one where not all clocks within the network have identical long-term accuracy due to multiple clock sources. In an asynchronous network, clocks are operating in free-running mode. These networks do not require that all clocks be synchronized to operate properly. Figure 7-38 depicts an asynchronous network.

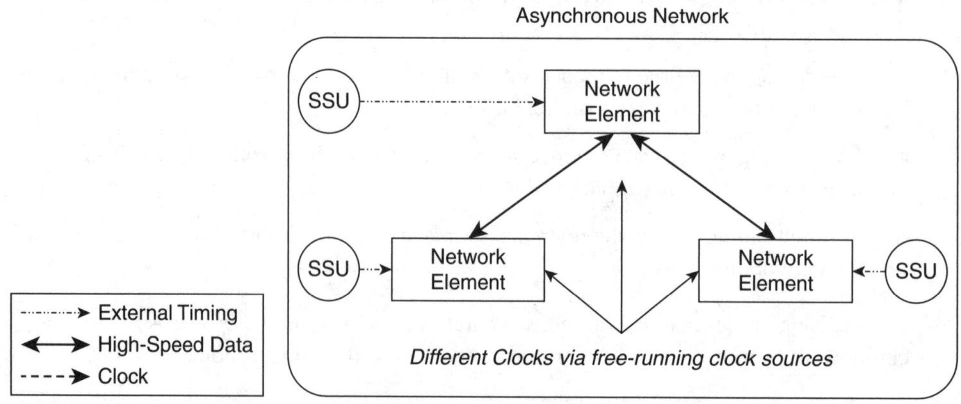

Figure 7-38 *Asynchronous Network*

Pseudo-Synchronous

A *pseudo-synchronous network* is one where not all clocks use the same PRC, but all rely on PRC-level accuracy for their reference source. These networks require synchronization to work properly. Figure 7-39 depicts a pseudo-synchronous network.

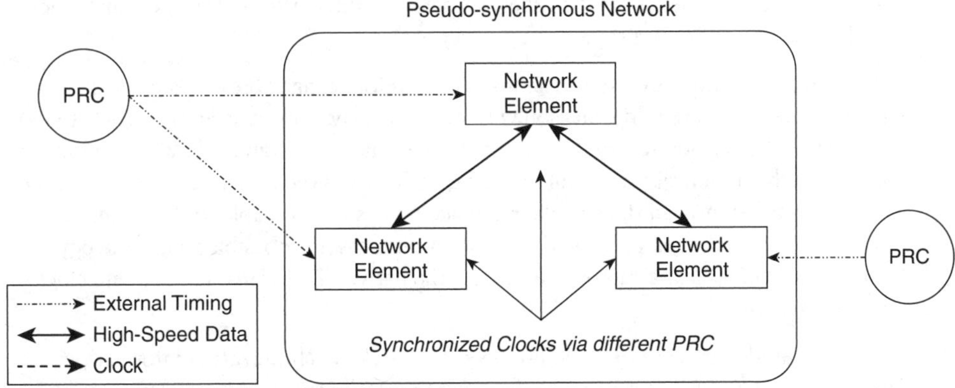

Figure 7-39 *Pseudo-Synchronous Network*

Plesiochronous

A *plesiochronous network* is one where different parts of the network are not perfectly synchronized with each other. Plesiochronous networks operate within a threshold of acceptable asynchronization; that is, two network elements act as if they are synchronized, but must accept and cope with time slips. A plesiochronous network is depicted in Figure 7-40.

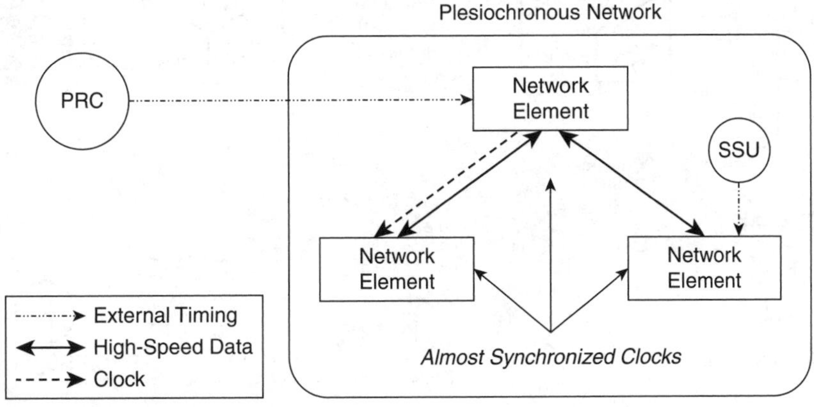

Figure 7-40 *Plesiochronous Network*

Packet-Based Timing

TDM networks are inherently synchronous. All network components must be synchronized with each other to ensure that data is not lost. In a native TDM network, clock synchronization is performed at the physical layer, and clocking information is carried along with data traffic. Clock slips occur when the receiver and transmitter have clocks that either run faster or slower than the other. These clock slips result in frames being either added or lost from the data stream.

IP networks, by nature, are asynchronous, and therefore cannot provide a constant bitrate. Packets reach their destination with random delay, known as jitter or Packet Delay Variation (PDV), already inserted. It is possible to remove random delay with a "jitter buffer," which temporarily stores all incoming packets and then forwards them at evenly spaced intervals; however, the original reference time is not available to determine what those evenly spaced intervals should be. Due to this, it is not possible to use the physical layer clock synchronization information from the native TDM frame for accurate clocking over pseudowires.

Although pseudowire endpoints do not need the clock synchronization information directly to implement the packet-switching functions, the constant bitrate applications that leverage the pseudowire transport must receive accurate timing information. This requires that the packet-switched network—that is, the pseudowire itself—provide this information to the applications. In such architecture, the reference clock may be connected directly to the synchronous network elements on each side of the pseudowire (see Figure 7-41) or to the pseudowire interworking function (see Figure 7-42).

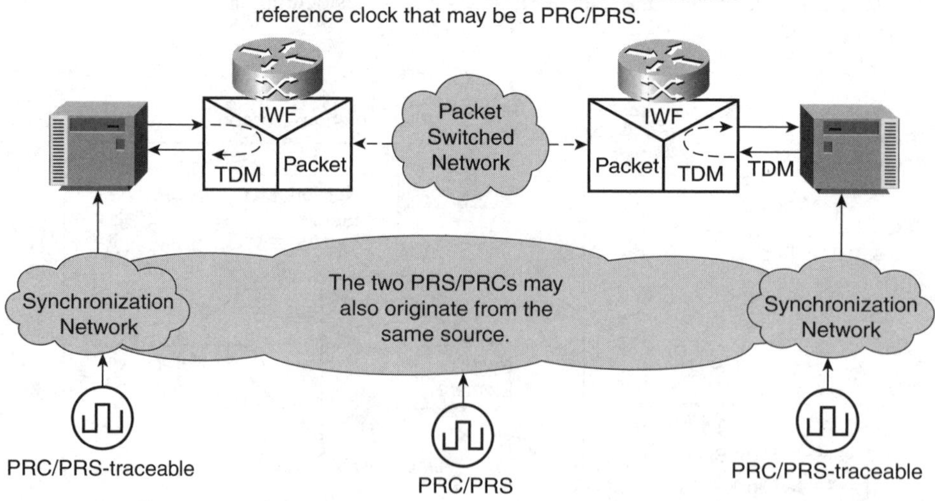

Figure 7-41 *Pseudowire Network Synchronization—Reference Clock Connected to Sync Network Elements*

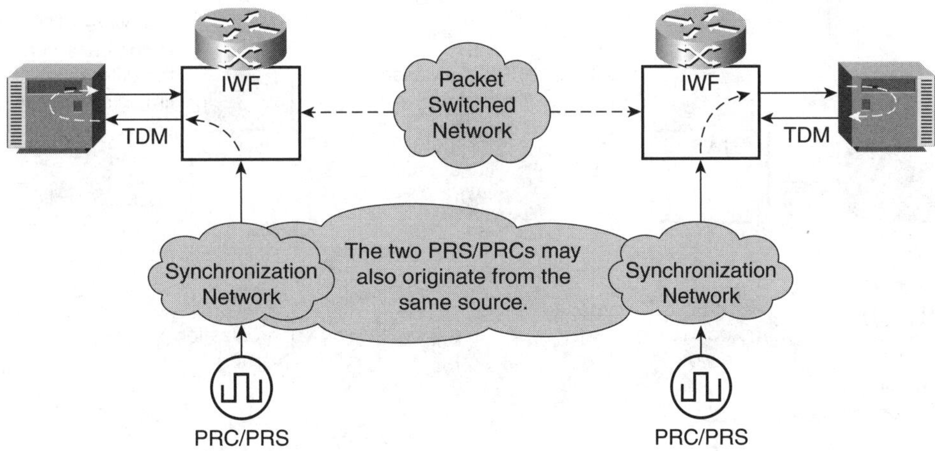

Figure 7-42 *Pseudowire Network Synchronization—Reference Clock Connected to Pseudowire IWF*

Although there are a large number of solutions for providing synchronization information, the same models presented previously in the "Timing Modes" section apply to packet-based networks, namely external timing, line timing, and loop timing.

Clock Recovery over Packet

Clock recovery is an important consideration when providing circuit emulation services over a PSN. The receiving Interworking Functions (IWF) must accurately recover the clock source from the sending IWF. There are two methods to provide clock recovery over packet, as follows:

- **Differential Clock Recovery** involves having a reference clock available at both sides of the pseudowire. Only the difference between the reference clock and the IWF service clock is transmitted across the pseudowire. Although this solution provides accurate frequency information and is tolerant to network delay, delay variation (jitter), and packet loss, the differential clock recovery solutions are expensive because they require multiple reference clocks. CESoPSN optionally may use differential clock recovery. Figure 7-43 illustrates differential clock recovery.
- **Adaptive Clock Recovery** involves having a reference clock available only at one side of the pseudowire. A timestamp is applied to all outbound packets by the sending IWF. The receiving IWF uses the information in the timestamp to recover the original reference clock information. Although this solution is less expensive (only a single reference clock is required), adaptive clock recovery is more susceptible to delay variation. TDMoIP uses adaptive clock recovery. Figure 7-44 illustrates adaptive clock recovery.

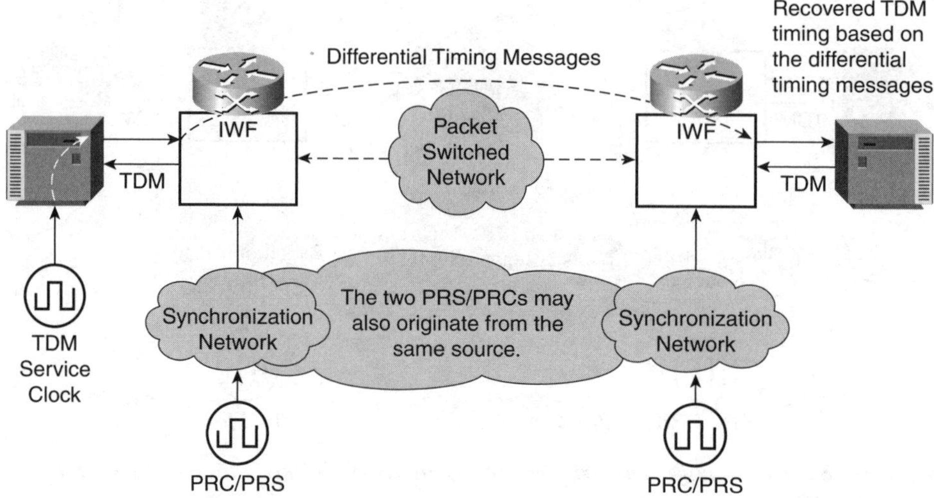

Figure 7-43 *Differential Clock Recovery*

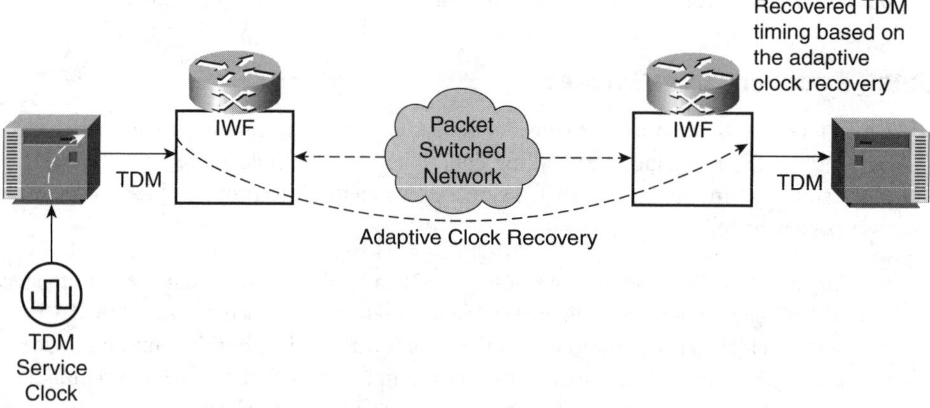

Figure 7-44 *Adaptive Clock Recovery*

Timing over Packet Solutions

There are four technologies for addressing synchronization over a packet network: Synchronous Ethernet (SyncE), Precision Time Protocol (PTP), Network Time Protocol (NTP), and Timing over IP Connection and Transfer of Clock BOF (TICTOC).

Any timing protocol should operate over the generic Internet with little or no intervention or management. Due to the unpredictable nature of the Internet, however, the accuracy of the protocol is greatly diminished. The accuracy of the frequency and time distribution is improved when operated over a managed network.

SyncE

Synchronous Ethernet (SyncE) is a line-timing method for transporting timing information over the Ethernet physical layer. Built on a Layer 1 model similar to SONET/SDH, SyncE provides accurate frequency synchronization, but does not provide time/phase synchronization.

SyncE specifications and requirements rely on four primary standards, as follows:

- **ITU-T G.8261:** Timing and synchronization aspects in packet network
- **ITU-T G.8262:** Timing characteristics of Synchronous Ethernet equipment slave clock
- **ITU-T G.8264:** Distribution of timing through packet networks
- **ITU-T G.781:** Synchronization layer functions

SyncE standards provide additional functionality to the 802.3 Ethernet standards while maintaining interworking between existing asynchronous Ethernet nodes and synchronous Ethernet nodes.

SyncE uses Synchronization Status Messages (SSMs) to transport timing information. Downstream clocks use the SSM for troubleshooting purposes, as the SSM will communicate if the clock source is a synchronized signal or derived from a free-running oscillator. These SSMs are transmitted using the Ethernet OAM protocol (ITU-T Y.1731 standard).

PTP

IEEE 1588v2, Precision Time Protocol, defined a protocol for precise, real-time, network-wide synchronization accuracy in the sub-millisecond range.

Each PTP domain consists of a number of clocks that synchronize with one another using the PTP protocol. Clocks within a PTP domain may not necessarily be synchronized with clocks within a different PTP domain.

Four types of clocks are defined within PTP, as follows:

- **An Ordinary Clock (OC)** has a single interface in a single PTP domain. The OC may be a master or slave, and may be responsible for providing time to an end node or application.
- **A Boundary Clock (BC)** has multiple interfaces in a single PTP domain. These interfaces may consist of multiple master interfaces, but only a single slave interface. The BC transfers all timing on the slave interface to the master interfaces. The BC can only be responsible for providing time to an application, not an end node.
- **A Transparent Clock (TC)** provides information on the time taken for a PTP message to transit the device and provides this information to all clocks receiving the PTP message. There are two types of transparent clocks:

- **A Peer-to-Peer Transparent Clock (P2P TC)** also provides corrections for any propagation delay on the link connected to the port receiving PTP messages.
- **An End-to-End Transparent Clock (E2E TC)** provides only the time taken for a PTP message to transit the device.

The PTP establishes a communications path across the network between all OCs and BCs. TCs may lie within the communications path, but, in general, P2P TCs and E2E TCs cannot be mixed in the same path.

Prior to synchronization, the clocks are organized into a master-slave hierarchy through a series of PTP Announce messages. The hierarchy contains a grandmaster, or PRC, multiple masters, and multiple slaves. This selection process is the Best Master Clock Algorithm (BMCA), which includes a clock class, based on where the clock has synchronized its timing from; clock accuracy, based on maximum accuracy threshold; and time source, based on the type of clock from which the advertising clock has received its timing (Atomic, GPS, Terrestrial Radio, PTP, Internal oscillator, and so on).

Synchronization in PTP

Once the hierarchy is established, each slave then synchronizes with its master using either a Delay Request-Response mechanism or a Peer Delay mechanism. These mechanisms cannot be mixed over the same communications path.

Delay Request-Response Mechanism The Delay Request-Response mechanism consists of four messages: Sync, Follow_Up (optional), Delay_Req, and Delay_Resp. Sync and Follow_Up messages are typically multicast, but may be unicast. Delay_Req and Delay_Resp are typically unicast messages between master and specific slave. Figure 7-45 illustrates this Request-Response mechanism.

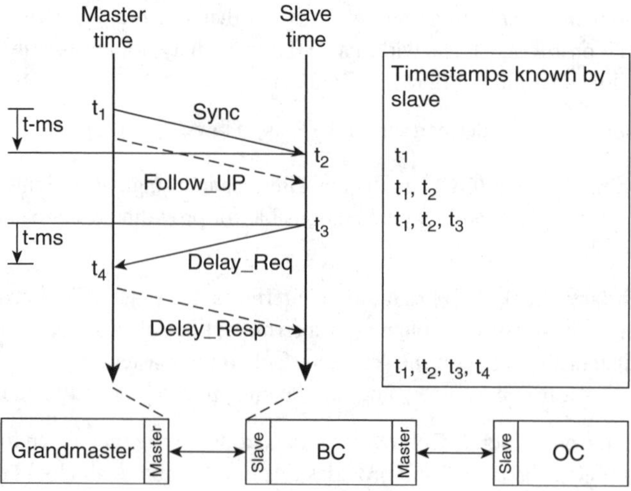

Figure 7-45 *PTP Delay Request-Response Mechanism*

Propagation time, or transit time, and an *offset*, or processing time, are calculated during this process.

Assuming a symmetrical link:

- The propagation time is $[(t_2\text{-}t_1)+(t_4\text{-}t_3)]/2$.
- The offset is $t_2\text{-}t_1-$(propagation time).

Assuming an asymmetrical link:

- The propagation time is the average of the slave-to-master and master-to-slave propagation times.
- The offset is the difference between the actual master-to-slave time and the average propagation times.

Peer Delay Mechanism The Peer Delay mechanism is limited to point-to-point communications paths between two OC, BC, or P2P TC. The Peer Delay mechanism is also symmetric; that is, it operates separately in both directions.

The Peer Delay mechanism consists of five messages: Sync, Follow_Up (optional), Pdelay_Req, Pdelay_Resp, and Pdelay_Resp_Follow_Up (optional). Figure 7-46 illustrates this Request-Response mechanism.

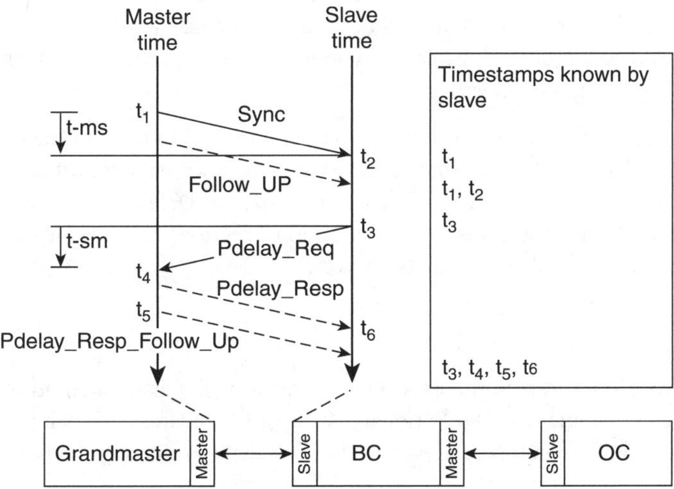

Figure 7-46 *PTP Peer Delay Mechanism*

A propagation time, or the transit time, and an offset, or the processing time, are calculated during this process.

Assuming a symmetrical link:

- The propagation time is $[(t_4-t_3)+(t_6-t_5)]/2$.
- The offset is t2-t1–(propagation time).

Assuming an asymmetrical link:

- The propagation time is the average of the slave-to-master and master-to-slave propagation times.
- The offset is the difference between the actual master-to-slave time and the average propagation times.

When using an E2E TC in the network, the E2E TC is not synchronized at all. Instead, the E2E TC timestamps the Sync message or Follow_Up message on both ingress and egress, and computes the time taken for the message to traverse the node from these timestamps. This time is the residence time, and is included in the message as a Correction field, such that OC and BC may account for this processing time. Each E2E TC in the chain adds its own residence time to the value already contained in the Correction field.

PTP Profiles and Conformance

PTP supports extensible profiles that allow for transport of optional features and attribute values, including interworking and desired performance levels required for a particular application. These profiles are created by numerous third parties, such as standards or industry organizations and vendors.

Network nodes are required to conform to the normative sections of the IEEE 1588 standards and at least one PTP profile. IEEE 1588 defines two default profiles: Delay Request-Response Default PTP Profile and Peer-to-Peer Default PTP Profile. In addition, a network node may comply with certain optional sections of the standards but must implement the optional section in its entirety.

NTP

The Network Transport Protocol (NTP) is the most predominant method of synchronizing clocks on the Internet. The National Institute of Standards and Technology (NIST) estimates over 10 million NTP servers and clients deployed in the Internet.

The most recent version, NTPv4, extends upon previous versions (NTPv3–RFC 1305) by introducing accuracy to the tens of microseconds (with a precision time source, such as a Cesium oscillator or GPS receiver), dynamic discovery of servers, and includes an extensibility mechanism via options.

A NTP node operates as either a Primary (Stratum 1) server, a Secondary (Stratum 2) server, or a client. Primary servers synchronize to national time standards via radio (terrestrial or satellite). A client synchronizes to one or more upstream servers, but does not provide any synchronization services to downstream nodes. A Secondary server synchronizes to one or more Primary servers and also provides synchronization services to one or more downstream servers or clients.

NTP Protocol Modes

There are three NTP protocol modes: client/server, symmetric, and broadcast.

In client/server mode, clients and servers send unicast packets to each other. Servers provide synchronization services to the clients, but do not accept synchronization from them. In client/server mode, clients are responsible for pulling synchronization from the server.

In symmetric mode, a peer functions as both a client and server. Peers provide synchronization services and accept synchronization from other peers. In symmetric mode, peers push and pull synchronization from each other.

In broadcast mode, a server sends periodic broadcast messages to multiple clients simultaneously. On instantiation of communication, unicast messages are sent between client and server such that the client can accurately calculate propagation delay. Following this unicast exchange, the client listens for broadcast messages generated by the server. In broadcast mode, the broadcast server pushes synchronization to clients.

Offset

The basic operation of NTP synchronization involves determining the offset in clock from one network node to another. This works as follows:

1. The NTP client sends a packet to a specified NTP server. In this packet, it stores the time the packet left as defined by its clock (t_1).
2. The NTP server receives the packet and notes the time it received the packet, according to its clock (t_2), and the time the client sent the packet (t_1).
3. The NTP server sends a packet back to the client and includes what time it was sent according to its clock (t_3). The packet sent back contains three timestamps: t_1, t_2, and t_3.
4. The client receives the packet from the server and notes what time it receives the packet according to its clock (t_4).

Figure 7-47 illustrates this synchronization flow.

Assuming a symmetrical link:

- The propagation delay is $(t_4\text{-}t_1)-(t_3\text{-}t_2)$.
- The clock offset is $[(t_2\text{-}t_1)+(t_4\text{-}t_3)]/2$.

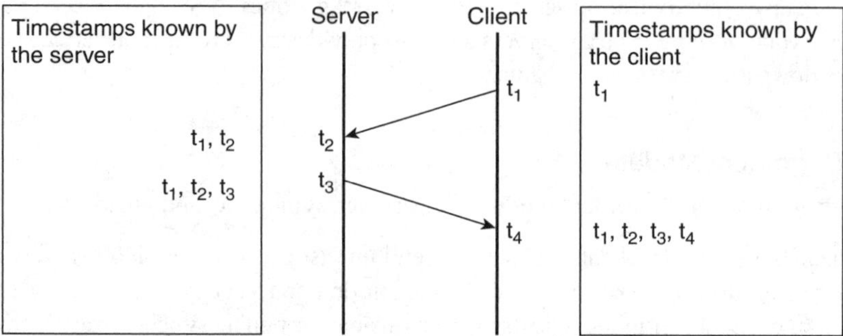

Figure 7-47 *NTP Offset Calculation*

Although the basic algorithm seems simple, the NTP architecture is more complex than expected. Once a server sends information to a client, the client uses a combination of clock/data filter, selection, clustering, and combining algorithms to determine its local offset. Figure 7-48 depicts a typical NTP architecture.

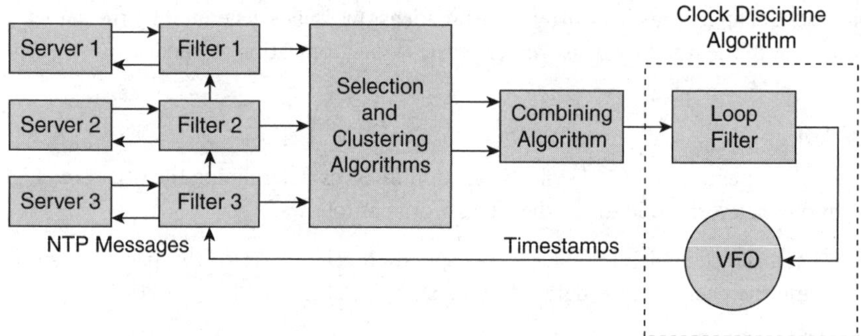

Figure 7-48 *NTP Architecture*

NTP Clock Filter Algorithm

The NTP clock filter algorithm analyzes the stream of NTP data received to determine which samples are most likely to represent accurate time. The algorithm produces the offset, delay, dispersion (maximum error in measurement), jitter, and time of arrival information that is used to calculate the final offset for the system clock. These values are also used to determine if the server is functioning properly and whether it can be used as a reference source. The NTP clock filter algorithm actually consists of four other algorithms, as follows:

- The NTP selection algorithm scans the stream of NTP data and discards samples that are clearly incorrect, known as *falsetickers*, and keeps only those that appear to be accurate, known as *truechimers*. Falsetickers may be caused by the long-tail effect of Packet-Delay Variation (PDV) or network degradations, such as congestion and reroutes caused by node failures.

- The NTP cluster algorithm then discards those samples that are statistically furthest from the mean until a minimum number of samples remain.
- The NTP combine algorithm produces the final values based on a weighted average calculation from the samples remaining.
- The NTP clock discipline algorithm takes the final values output from the combine algorithm and uses these to discipline the local clock.

NTP Poll Interval

The NTP poll interval is the term used to define how often a new calculation of offset should be made. The poll interval is determined dynamically by the clock discipline algorithm based on the observed clock offset measurements. The poll interval will increase if the internal oscillator frequency stays constant. If the oscillator frequency changes, the poll interval will decrease in order to track these changes.

NTP Security Considerations

Because NTP broadcast clients are vulnerable to broadcast storms from spoofed or misbehaving NTP broadcast servers, NTP includes an optional authentication field. This optional authentication field supports MD5 encryption. This encryption can be negotiated between a broadcast client and server during instantiation.

TICTOC

The Timing over IP Connection and Transfer of Clock BOF (TICTOC) draft standard was written to provide a robust IP/MPLS-based time and frequency distribution architecture. TICTOC, like other protocols, can be decomposed into two layers corresponding to time and frequency. Implementations may vary depending on the exact need of the application. For example, if an application or network node only needs time synchronization and not frequency synchronization, only the time layer may be present.

Figure 7-49 illustrates the TICTOC layers.

TICTOC Clients

TICTOC clients are comprised of up to four modules (illustrated in Figure 7-50)—the frequency acquisition module, the frequency presentation module, the time acquisition module, and the time presentation module.

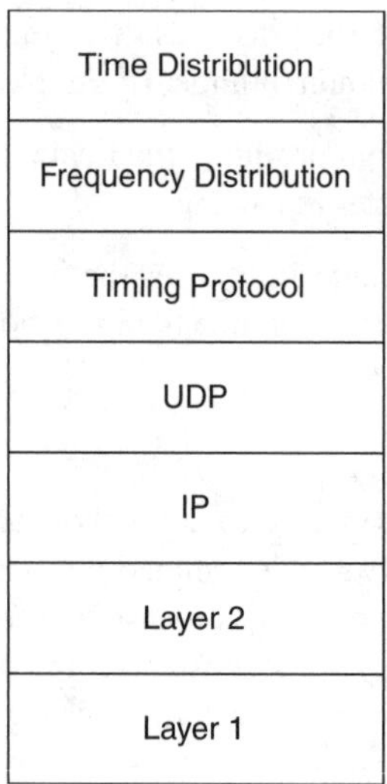

Figure 7-49 *TICTOC Layers*

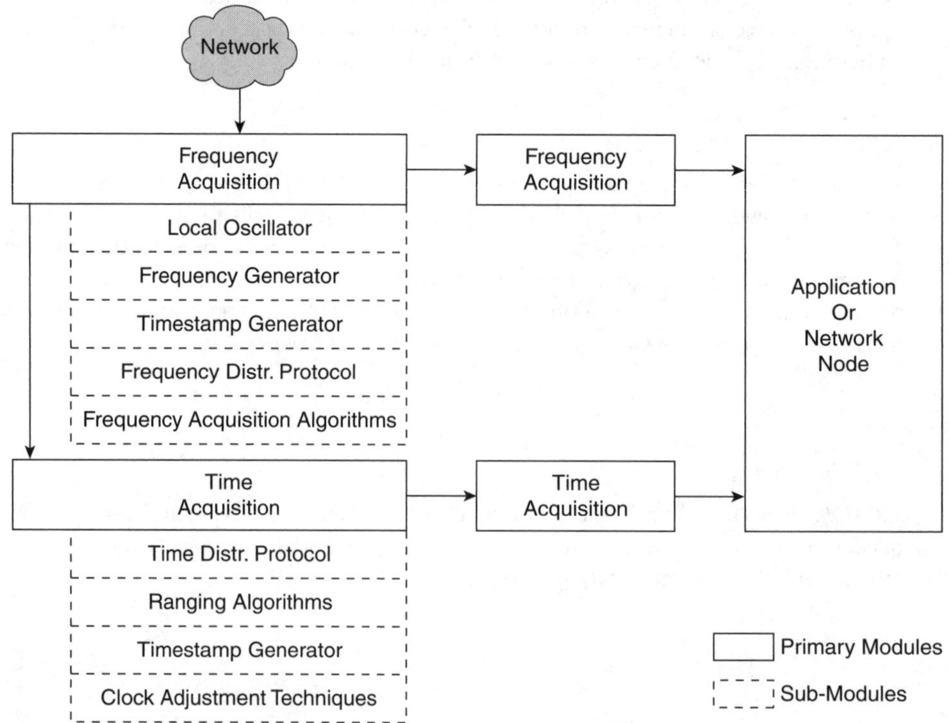

Figure 7-50 *TICTOC Client Modules*

Frequency Acquisition Module

The *frequency acquisition module* retrieves the frequency information distributed over the network. The frequency acquisition module may be divided into the following sub-modules. These sub-modules may not all be present depending on requirements and implementation:

- Local oscillator. Both master and clients in the TICTOC architecture need a local oscillator. The master uses a Cesium clock, whereas the clients may use a lower-accuracy oscillator, such as quartz crystal. The client's local oscillator must be adjusted to match the master's oscillator to ensure synchronization. Disciplining the local oscillator is based on arrival time and information received in packets from the frequency distribution protocol.
- Frequency generator.
- Timestamp generator.
- Frequency distribution protocol. The frequency distribution protocol is used to distribute frequency across the network. This protocol may be the same or different than the protocol used to distribute time. Frequency distribution protocols in TICTOC are one-way, and may be unicast, multicast, or broadcast. Although multicast distribution is supported, there is the inherent risk that a multicast replication operation may add variable delay.
- The frequency acquisition algorithms are used to re-acquire the source time from the received packets. As with all packets in a PSN, the packet distribution protocol packets are subject to Packet Delay Variation (PDV). The frequency acquisition algorithms are used to filter out the PDV through a two-step process, as follows:
    - **Packet Selection and Discard Algorithms:** These algorithms are similar to those used in NTP to eliminate those packets that would lead to accuracy degradation of the recovered frequency. This packet selection algorithm works by selecting a series of packets that are all similar in result, as long as the sample still represents a relatively high percentage of packets.
    - **Filtering and control servos:** With linear averaging, the time to calculate and eliminate frequency drift effects would be so high that the frequency difference calculated would no longer be relevant. "Control loops" are used to accurately model the frequency drift effects on sampled packets in a non-linear manner.

Frequency Presentation Module

If the frequency is needed by the application, the *frequency presentation module* formats this information into the application-specific requirements. Presentation methods may include graphical display, clock discipline, and so on.

Time Acquisition Module

The *time acquisition module* requires a stable frequency reference. Even if frequency is not needed, the time acquisition module may rely on the frequency acquisition module to retrieve information. The time acquisition module may also retrieve information from an external source, such as a GPS receiver. This module allows multiple TICTOC clients to share a common offset. The time acquisition module may be divided into the following sub-modules. These sub-modules may not all be present depending on requirements and implementation:

- **Time distribution protocol:** The time distribution protocol is used to accurately synchronize a clock based on measured offset between client and master oscillators. Ranging algorithms are used to estimate this offset. Time distribution protocol, unlike frequency distribution protocol, is typically bi-directional, requiring both client and master to send and receive packets.
- **Ranging algorithms:** Ranging is the estimation of propagation delay within a network. This is done in a manner similar to PTP, where a packet is sent from the master with a timestamp, followed by a second packet with a timestamp. These timestamps on the packets indicate the time that the master injected the packet into the network. The client then has sufficient timestamp information to calculate the propagation delay.
- Clock adjustment techniques
- Timestamp generator

Time Presentation Module

The *time presentation module* formats information from the time acquisition module into a format that is relevant to the application requiring synchronization.

Generic Modules

TICTOC supports various generic modules that may be applied to frequency distribution, time distribution, or both. These modules include enhanced security (certificate-based), auto-discovery of masters, master clock selection algorithms, OAM, performance monitoring, and network management.

Combining Protocols

SyncE, PTP, NTP, and TICTOC need not be mutually exclusive within a network. A combination of these protocols, along with external means of synchronization, may be leveraged. For instance, because SyncE provides a highly accurate frequency source and TICTOC provides a highly accurate time source, a network may use the SyncE's physical layer frequency synchronization as the source for TICTOC's IP layer time synchronization input.

Summary

This chapter discussed one of the predominant IP migration methods for today's mobile networks. Whether driven by technological or financial decisions, backhaul network evolution to IP-based mechanisms is a clear operator strategy, and pseudowire transport mechanisms provide a bridge between the legacy TDM systems presented in Chapter 2 and the All IP systems presented in Chapter 3. Although not without their share of complexity, including time and frequency synchronization, IP backhaul networks are an obvious value to mobile operators. With such a large number of solutions for both pseudowire transport and synchronization, mobile operators need to understand the technologies themselves and determine which best meets their requirements.

Endnotes

[1]Source: ABI Research

[2]Source: ABI Research

Chapter 8

End-to-End Context Awareness

As networks become increasingly complex and traffic shifts toward IP-based services (see Chapter 9, "Content and Services"), intelligent networks (or those capable of not only routing traffic efficiently, but also recognizing applications and enforcing traffic policies), form the foundation upon which these services ride. With such rapid shifts in network traffic models, industry trends, and subscriber expectations, reactively dimensioning and optimizing IP networks for a specific type of traffic is no longer a feasible approach. Mobile operators must build IP networks that are flexible enough to accommodate today's traffic model, while dynamically adapting to a shifting, often unpredictable, future state of network traffic. This chapter discusses the shift from independent, IP-aware networks to networks that are interdependent, subscriber-aware, device-aware, and application-aware.

Policy

Before defining a target state and future direction for intelligent networking, it is important to first understand the concept of "policy" itself as it exists in today's mobile networks, how it is being leveraged, and what protocols are used to enforce it.

Policy is broadly defined as a set of business functions, or rules, that define how a combination of subscriber, group of subscribers, flow (5-tuple), or application interacts with the network. These business rules are enforced by network elements that directly interact with the subscriber, flow, or application that requires policing. The three key elements involved in all network policies are broadly defined as follows:

- **Policy Decision Point (PDP):** The PDP is responsible for the translation of business rules into actionable network enforcement or response. The PDP consists of two main components:
  - **Correlation function:** The correlation function pieces together information from the subscriber profile, business rules, and network element utilization to build a matrix of all available resources and determine upon which conditions policy should be enforced.

    - **Decision function:** The decision function takes the correlated information, or raw data, and determines the correct network action in order to apply the policy conditions.

  The PDP sits adjacent to the bearer flow, and has no direct interaction with the subscriber or flow itself. Instead, the PDP relies on network elements and applications to provide information on their individual state.

- **Policy Enforcement Point (PEP):** The PEP resides directly in the bearer flow and is responsible for receiving policy conditions from the PDP and applying them. In any given network, there may be many PEPs, each either performing a unique aspect of policy (for instance, a QoS PEP, a charging PEP, and so on), or all working independently to provide a specific aspect of policy (for instance, an MPLS PE providing MPLS-TE and a Network Mobility Anchor providing DSCP enforcement).

  A PEP may receive policies directly from the PDP, may have static policies configured, or may request policies from a PDP.

- **Policy Information Point (PIP):** The PIP is any network element with the capability of sending information to the PDP. Information may be as simple as link/interface utilization or as complex as application-specific requirements for delivery of service.

  A PIP can be co-located within a PEP (that is, the PEP plays a bi-directional role of both sending and receiving information), can be co-located within a PDP (that is, the PDP plays a policy proxy role), or can be any standalone element in the network.

  A PIP can work in two different modes—Push Mode or Pull Mode. In Push Mode, the PIP sends information to a PDP without an explicit request from the PDP. In Pull Mode, the PIP sends information to the PDP only when requested.

Figure 8-1 illustrates the interactions between a PDP, PEP, and PIP. The Network Element (NE) denoted in the illustration may be any network element seeing traffic, or the network as a whole.

The interactions illustrated in Figure 8-1 are described in Table 8-1.

Table 8-1 *Policy Enforcement Interaction Descriptions*

Network Element	Function	Interactions
NE-A	PIP	Provides information on the subscriber, including identity and location, to NE-B.
	PEP	Enforces authentication/authorization parameters, including key challenges and so on, as requested by NE-B.
NE-B	PDP	Determines authentication mechanisms and validating successful authentication from NE-A.

Network Element	Function	Interactions
NE-C	PDP	Correlates information from multiple PIPs and distributes charging rule policy to NE-D.
NE-D	PEP	Enforces charging policy rules as requested by NE-C.
NE-E	PEP	Enforces static policy rules, such as ACLs or rate shaping.
NE-F	PIP	Distributes subscriber balance to NE-C.
NE-G	PIP	Provides application information received from NE-I to NE-C.
	PDP	Correlates application information received from NE-I and link utilization information received from NE-H and distributes QoS rules to NE-H; same as NE-A.
NE-H	PIP	Provides information on link utilization to NE-G.
	PEP	Enforces QoS rules as requested by NE-G; same as NE-A.
NE-I	PIP	Provides information on application requirements to NE-G.

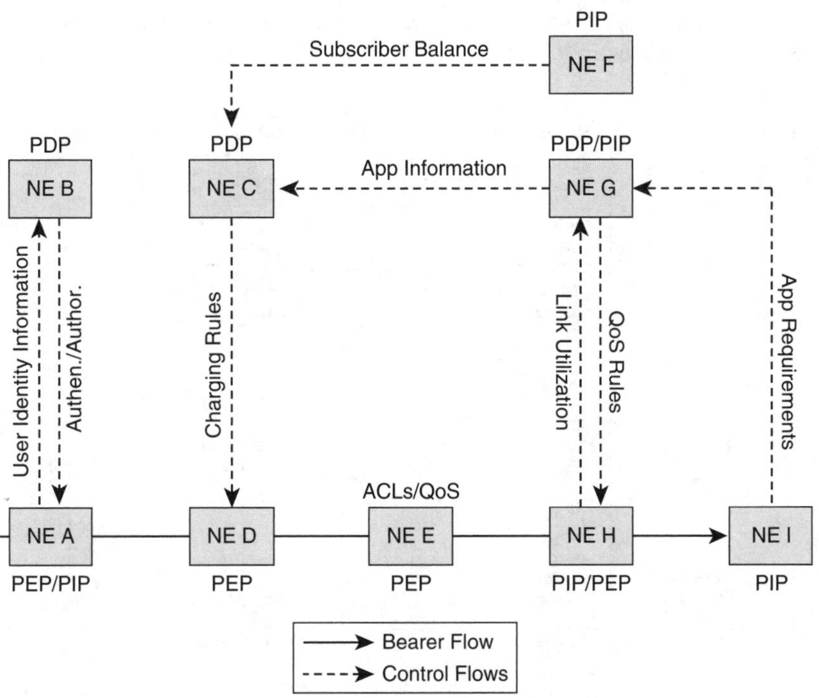

Figure 8-1 *Policy Element Interactions*

PDPs, PEPs, and PIPs work together in a network to enable either proactive or reactive policy control.

Proactive and Reactive Policy Control

Network policies may be either proactive or reactive in nature. Both proactive and reactive policies provide unique values for a mobile operator.

Proactive Policy Control

Proactive policies are those that are in effect 100% of the time, or are dependent on a static set of fixed variables. As networks have "busy hours," or those times when a high percentage of users are active, one important fixed variable in determining proactive policies is time-of-day.

Proactive policies are designed to protect the network infrastructure and allow a fair-use access for all subscribers on the network. For instance, by rate-capping peer-to-peer applications to a maximum percentage of bandwidth, voice and video users will not be impacted by the large amounts of peer-to-peer traffic on the network.

Proactive policies tend to work in either a "push" method, where the PDP sends policies to relevant PEPs without any network intervention, or a "static" method, where the policies are directly configured on network elements.

Figure 8-2 depicts an example of both methods. NE-D is enforcing a proactive prepaid charging rule "pushed" from NE-C, whereas NE-E is enforcing static Quality of Service (QoS) and Access Control Lists (ACLs).

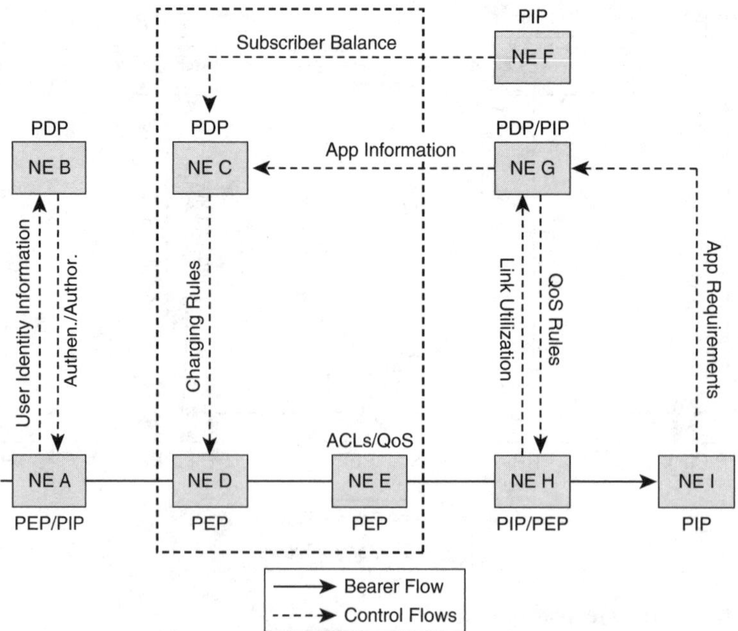

Figure 8-2 *Proactive Policies*

Reactive Policy Control

Reactive policies are those that react to some immediate network condition (for example, bandwidth starvation or security breach) by applying a policy that mitigates, resolves, or in some way alleviates the condition. Reactive policies may be triggered by crossing certain network thresholds, by a new application or subscriber instantiation, or via some predictive algorithm. In all cases, a reactive policy decision is based on receiving some indication from a PIP that requires intervention.

Reactive policies may work in a "pull" method, in that the PDP first requires information from the network prior to determining the course of resolution and sending out policies, or "push" mode, in that policies are pushed to the network and applied to the user session based on information received by the PDP. The PDP may receive this information from a single PIP or multiple PIPs, and a specific policy for enforcement may be pushed to a single or multiple PEPs.

Figure 8-3 depicts the "pull" method. NE-H informs NE-G of link utilization and NE-I informs NE-G of application-specific requirements. With this information, NE-G then pushes specific QoS rules to NE-H.

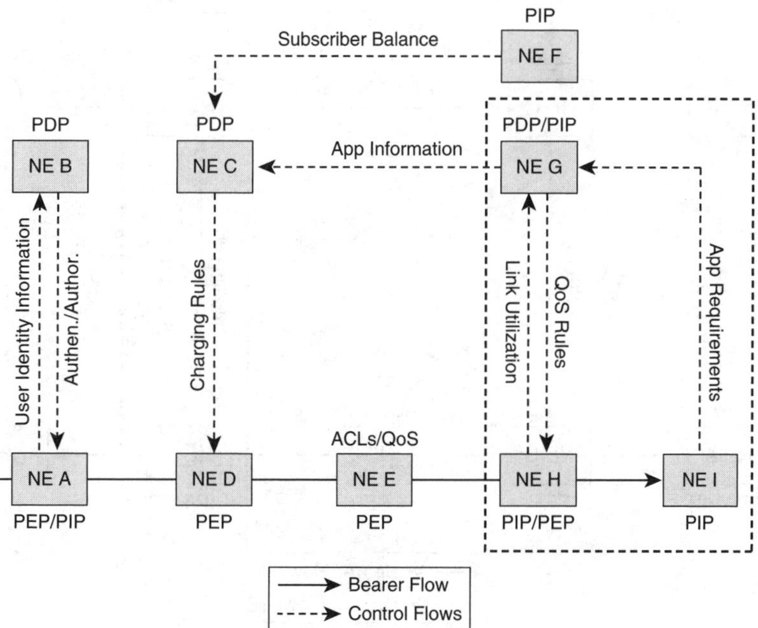

Figure 8-3 *Reactive Policies*

Both proactive and reactive network policies can be broadly categorized as global or subscriber-specific.

Global Policies

Global policies are those defined and applied at a network level, and not tied to specific subscribers. Examples of network-wide policies may include limiting peer-to-peer traffic to a certain percentage of network resources or always prioritizing VoIP and video traffic.

These policies tend to rely on Policy Information Points to provide higher-level statistics, such as network utilization and link utilization, in addition to lower-level statistics, such as percentage of VoIP traffic. The policies are usually pushed to the network at defined intervals determined by the service provider.

Figure 8-4 depicts global policy enforcement. NE-H informs NE-G of link utilization. NE-G then pushes specific QoS rules to NE-H.

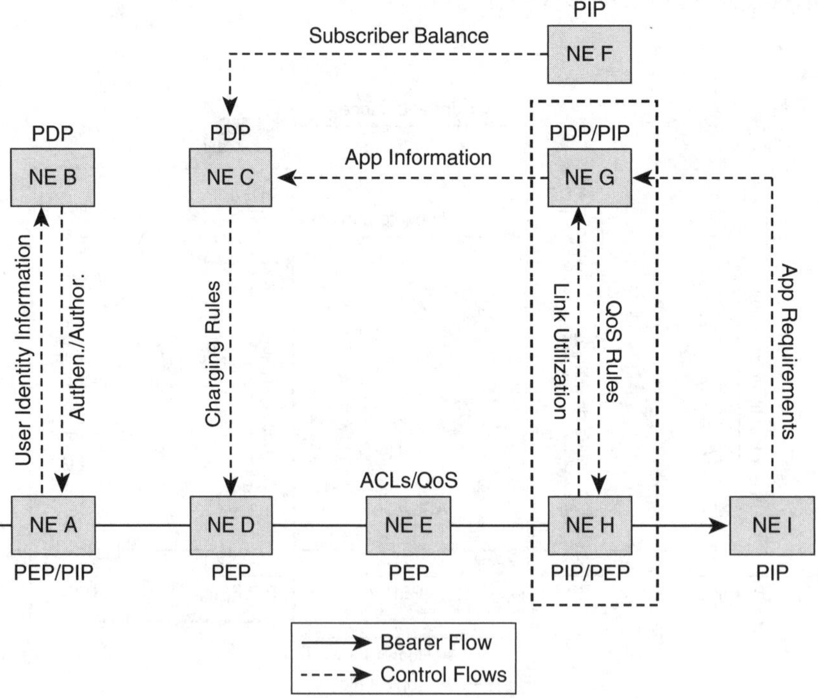

Figure 8-4 *Global Policies*

Subscriber-Specific Policies

Subscriber-specific policies are those defined and applied on a per-subscriber basis. Subscriber-specific policies may be anonymous, grouped, or unique in nature (see Table 8-2).

Table 8-2 *Subscriber-Specific Policies*

Subscriber Type	Definition
Anonymous	Subscriber policy in which all subscribers are treated equally. The network has no information other than the IP address of the subscriber, and applies/enforces policies on a per-IP basis.
Grouped	Subscriber policy in which all subscribers within a specific group are treated equally. The network has either a user ID or group ID, mapped to the subscriber's IP address, and applies/enforces policies on a per-IP basis. In this model, the network may also enforce per-group global policies.
Unique	Subscriber policy in which each subscriber is treated uniquely. The network has a user ID, mapped to the subscriber's IP address, and applies/enforces policies on a per-IP basis.

Figure 8-5 depicts a subscriber-specific policy. NE-C notifies NE-D of a set of charging rules to enforce for a particular subscriber.

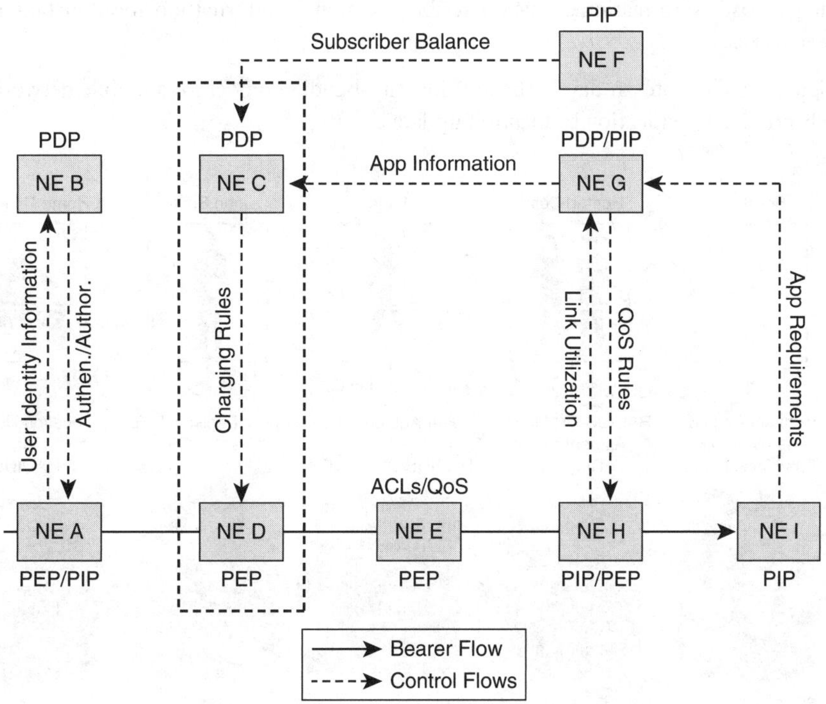

Figure 8-5 *Subscriber-Specific Policies*

In order to provide grouped or unique subscriber-specific policies, the network must be aware of the subscriber. This awareness may come from multiple sources:

- **Authentication:** When a user authenticates to the network, user and device identity may be provided by the mobile terminal. These user/device identification methods are described later in this chapter in the section, "Network Policy Protocols." During authentication, the network can obtain a mapping between subscriber ID and IP address.

  Either RADIUS or Diameter, both described later in this chapter, may be used for authentication of a subscriber in a mobile network.

- **Application-Layer Information:** When a user attempts to use a specific application, the network may become aware of the subscriber information in one of two methods:
  - The application may signal a PDP as to the user-specific information.
  - The application-layer information may contain user-specific information, and the network may rely upon application-layer inspection, or Deep Packet Inspection (DPI). DPI is discussed later in this chapter.

During the life of a user session, information about the subscriber is constantly being updated. These updates may include information about the subscriber's usage for charging purposes, information about subscriber location, or information about instantiated user services.

Figure 8-6 illustrates a "day in the life" identity-building model for a mobile network from subscriber authentication to location updates.

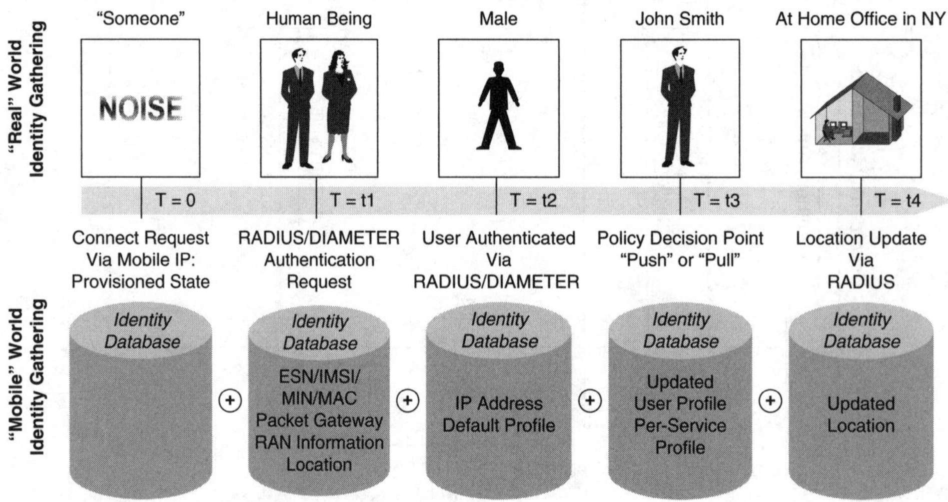

Figure 8-6 *Identifying a Subscriber*

As more information becomes available, the network policy infrastructure may better identify the subscriber, and the network may better apply and enforce specific subscriber policies.

Figure 8-7 illustrates the application of these policies based on different levels of information.

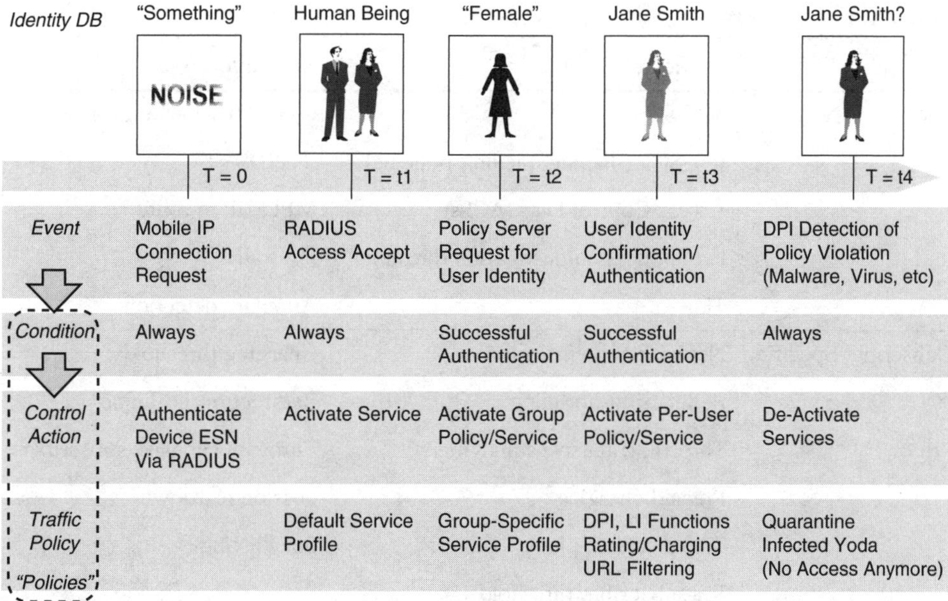

Figure 8-7 *Policy Application Based on Subscriber Information*

For instance, at T=t2, the subscriber can only be identified as part of a specific group, and therefore a group subscriber-specific policy is enforced. However, at T=t3, the subscriber can be uniquely identified, and individual policies are applied. Further, if the network detects that the subscriber is in violation of a policy, a reactive policy may be applied, as seen at T=t4.

The network may simultaneously enforce global and subscriber-specific policies. In addition, a network may also simultaneously enforce anonymous, grouped, and unique subscriber-specific policies. Such determinations are made by network administrators and mobile operator marketing departments together based on both network infrastructure capabilities and desired subscriber perception of network quality.

Policy Examples

Up to this point, we have discussed policy in a very theoretical manner. In order to provide an additional layer of clarity prior to considering mobile network and policy applications itself, Table 8-3 provides examples of commonly-applied network policies and how they are classified, including examples of some policies that can either be classified as proactive or reactive.

Table 8-3 *Policy Example Classification*

	Proactive	Reactive
Global	MPLS-TE	Call admission control
	IP DSCP (shaping/queuing/policing)	IPS/IDS
	Access Control Lists (ACLs)	MPLS/IP re-route
	Per-application/destination threshold	Firewalls
	Time-of-day	Anomaly detection
Subscriber-Specific	Network authentication	Charging thresholds
	Redirection/hotlining	Redirection/hotlining
	Throttling abusive subscribers	Throttling abusive subscribers
	Prepaid charging	Session teardown
	Tiered service plans	Blacklisting
	Per-subscriber threshold	
	Time-of-day	
	Device-specific	

A Network of Networks

Today's mobile networks are really much more than a single, end-to-end design. Instead, they are multiple networks, each relying on unique authentication methods, QoS algorithms, and tunneling protocols. Figure 8-8 illustrates an end-to-end architectural view of a mobile network. These elements are described in more detail in Chapter 2, "Cellular Access Systems."

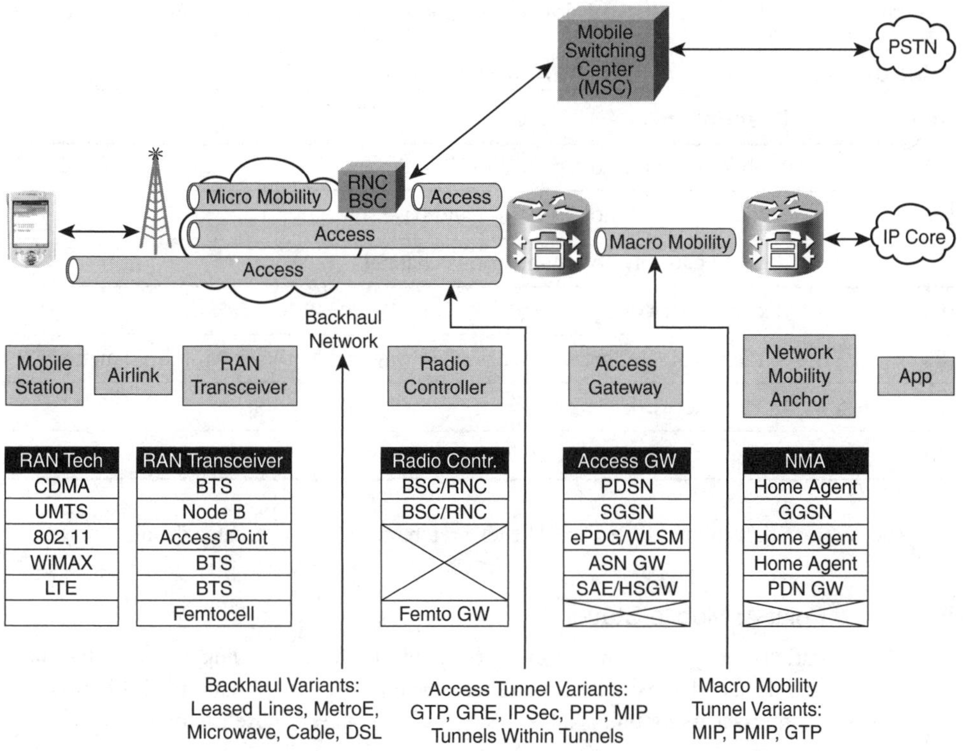

Figure 8-8 *End-to-End Network View*

Network Independence Today

A model for discussion in this chapter is to compartmentalize the mobile network itself into the unique domains that all function independently. Figure 8-9 depicts this compartmentalization, and will be used as a reference model for this chapter.

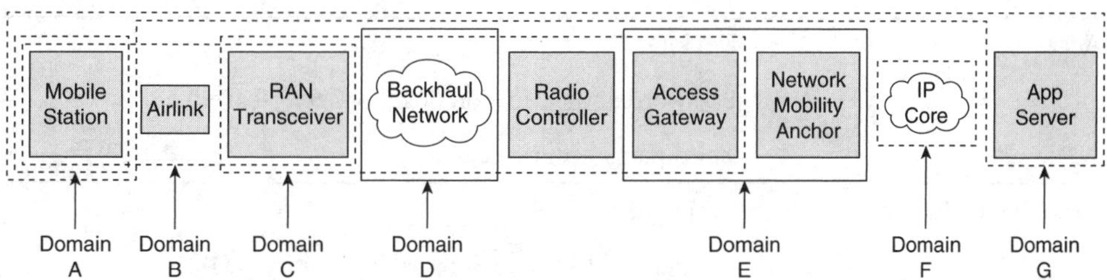

Figure 8-9 *End-to-End Network Reference Model*

Table 8-4 describes the different domains of the reference model illustrated in Figure 8-9.

Table 8-4 *Reference Points and OAM Mechanisms*

Reference	Description
(A)	Mobile station, or the device itself
(B)	Airlink between mobile station and base station
(C)	RAN to gateway communications channel
(D)	Backhaul network
(E)	RAN core, including the Access Gateway and Network Mobility Anchor
(F)	IP Core network
(G)	Transport and Application layer mechanisms

The sections that follow cover each of these reference points in greater detail.

Reference Point A: Mobile Station

Mobile stations today have a wide range of capabilities for controlling access, determining user and device identity, adjusting to network conditions, and handling both intra-access and inter-access mobility. Table 8-5 describes some of these capabilities.

Note Although Reference Point A denotes the mobile station specifically, the handset functions described are actually the result of a joint procedure between the handset and network. Reference Point A may indirectly involve linkage to the Radio Controller and Access Gateway in real-world implementations.

Table 8-5 *Mobile Device Capabilities*

Function	Capabilities
Access Control	Keylock
	Password authentication (local or server-based)
	Third-party security clients
User/Device Identity	SIM card
	International Mobile Subscriber Identity (IMSI)
	Electronic Serial Number (ESN)
	Phone number or Mobile Identification Number (MIN)

Table 8-5 *Mobile Device Capabilities*

Function	Capabilities
	Media Access Control (MAC) address IP address (IPv4 or IPv6, or both) Subscriber ID (username/password)
Mobility	CMIP Dual anchoring Dual-mode (multi-radio)
Network Conditions	Device buffer Retransmissions for lost packets/data Call handoff User notification (that is, "The call was lost")

Reference Point B: Airlink

The airlink provides authentication and encryption mechanisms necessary to secure and protect radio resources, as well as maintain subscriber privacy standards. These mechanisms are summarized in Table 8-6, sorted by radio access technology.

Table 8-6 *Airlink Capabilities*

RAN Technology	Mechanism
GSM/UMTS/HSPA (3GPP)	A3/A8—Mechanism for authentication and key generation of a mobile subscriber. This key is then used for voice and data traffic encryption. The A3/A8 algorithm is only performed in the SIM and GSM AuC (see Chapter 2) to ensure confidentiality. A5—Mechanism for scrambling voice and data calls over the airlink. A5 is performed in the Mobile Terminal and network (SGSN for 2G GPRS; RNC for 3G UMTS).
CDMA/1x/EVDO	Cellular Authentication and Voice Encryption (CAVE)—One-way mechanism for network authentication of a mobile device.
WiMAX	Counter Mode with Cipher Block Chaining Message Authentication Code Protocol (CCMP)—128-bit key mechanism (based on Advanced Encryption Standard [AES]) for providing authentication and data integrity.

The sections that follow provide more detailed information on each of these protocols.

Reference Point C: RAN to Gateway Communication

RAN to Gateway communication is used for registering a subscriber to the IP network for data communications, and signaling micromobility of user data sessions. Each standards organization supports different functiont over this communications channel, as referenced in Table 8-7.

Table 8-7 *RAN to Gateway Communications Protocols*

RAN Technology	Interface	Protocol	Mechanism
GSM/UMTS/HSPA (3GPP)	Gb Iu-ps	FR or IP ATM	Interface for transfer of GPRS Mobility Management (GMM) and Network Management (NM) packets. Gb also adds authentication and confidentiality via ciphering mechanisms, flow control, and a logical tunnel between MS and SGSN/RNC.
CDMA/1x/EVDO	R-P	PPP	A10/A11—Interface for establishment of new data sessions (registration), authentication, intra-PDSN handoffs (mobility), re-registration (keepalives), and accounting.
WiMAX	R6	GRE	Interface for authentication, IP tunnel establishment, security, QoS, and mobility.

Reference Point D: Backhaul Network

Backhaul networks rely on transport QoS mechanisms described in Chapter 3, "All IP Access Systems." Ethernet, TDM, Frame Relay, and ATM all have unique capabilities to perform traffic shaping and policing. Scalability and resiliency in the backhaul may be built via multiple load-shared TDM circuits (see Figure 8-10), mesh or partial mesh wireless circuits that connect into optical rings (see Figure 8-11), or via other IP-based pseudowire mechanisms discussed in Chapter 7, "Offloading Traditional Networks With IP."

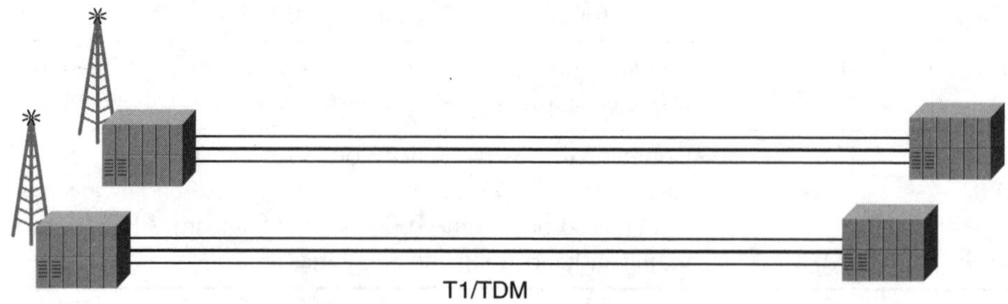

Figure 8-10 *Load-Shared TDM Circuits*

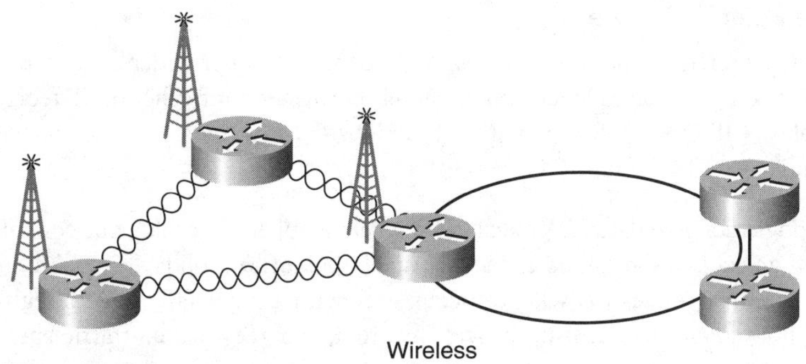

Figure 8-11 *Partial Mesh Microwave Backhaul*

Reference Point E: RAN Core

The RAN Core reference point consists of the Access Gateway and the Network Mobility Anchor. Table 8-8 highlights the different protocols and functions within the RAN Core.

Table 8-8 *Mobile Device Capabilities*

RAN Technology	Interface	Protocol	Mechanism
GSM/UMTS/HSPA (3GPP)	Gn/Gp	GTP over IP	Support for macromobility and charging, with tunnel originating at the Access Gateway (SGSN) and terminating at Network Mobility Anchor (GGSN). Gn interface provides this function for SGSN/GGSN located within the same network operator. Gp interface provides this function between two different operators for roaming scenarios. See Chapter 3 for more information.
CDMA/1x/EVDO	Mobile IP	CMIP	Support for macromobility, with tunnel originating at mobile device and terminating at Network Mobility Anchor (HA). See Chapter 3 for more information.
WiMAX	R3	PMIP	Support for macromobility, with tunnel originating at the Access Gateway (ASN) and terminating at Network Mobility Anchor (HA). See Chapter 3 for more information.

Reference Point F: IP Core

The IP Core reference point consists of all IP devices from provider edge to provider edge, including all core (P) elements. Chapter 3 provides a refresher on IP technology. Examples of IP Core QoS capabilities, from most-basic to most-complex, include the following:

- **Congestion avoidance:** A mechanism where an operator builds out core infrastructure in excess of required capacity (usually link utilization near 50%) in order to ensure that congestion will not occur, even with a single failure. Although congestion-avoidance mechanisms provide greater guarantees that all traffic entering the IP network will be routed successfully, the cost of infrastructure is quite high.
- **Diffserv:** A mechanism to classify, mark, and prioritize traffic on a per-hop basis by embedding a 6-bit Differentiated Services Code Point (DSCP) value in the IP header. Diffserv allows for certain flows (Intserv), such as voice and video, to be given preferential treatment across the core network.
- **MPLS Traffic Engineering (MPLS-TE):** A mechanism to intelligently route traffic and optimize network paths based on the resources that a particular flow requires. MPLS-TE allows for oversubscription of core networks by providing numerous routing paths between two destinations.
- **Call Admission Control (CAC):** A mechanism for ensuring that resources are available within the IP network prior to accepting a new flow. CAC allows for guarantees that new flows routed across the IP network do not negatively affect the performance of existing flows already en-route.

Other mechanisms for controlling traffic, such as Black Hole Routing and Denial of Service (DDoS) techniques, are discussed in Chapter 9, "Content and Services."

Reference Point G: Mobile Transport and Application Layer

There are numerous mechanisms to enforce policy within applications via network resources, in addition to inherent capabilities within the application. Examples of these mechanisms are summarized in Table 8-9.

Table 8-9 *Application Policies*

Function	Capabilities
Access Control	Password authentication
	Charging models (prepaid or postpaid)
	Time-of-day restrictions
Security	Access Control Lists
	Firewalls
	Intrusion Prevention Systems

Function	Capabilities
Data Integrity	Retransmissions (application- or TCP-layer)
	Acknowledgments (application-or TCP-layer)
	Feedback loops
QoS	Subscriber prioritization
	DSCP marking
	Throttling of abusing subscribers
	Resource Reservation Protocol (RSVP)

Network Interdependence Tomorrow

As networks evolve, such independent systems and methods for ensuring policy become difficult to engineer, synchronize, monitor, and maintain. As such, tomorrow's mobile network model will include a more-integrated approach to policy, including a common charging model, QoS model, security model, and mobility model from the mobile terminal to the application. Such mechanisms alleviate the multiple layers of encryption, authentication/authorization, identity, charging, and QoS enforcement and provide a holistic view of end-to-end device, network, and application capabilities. Figure 8-12 illustrates this model.

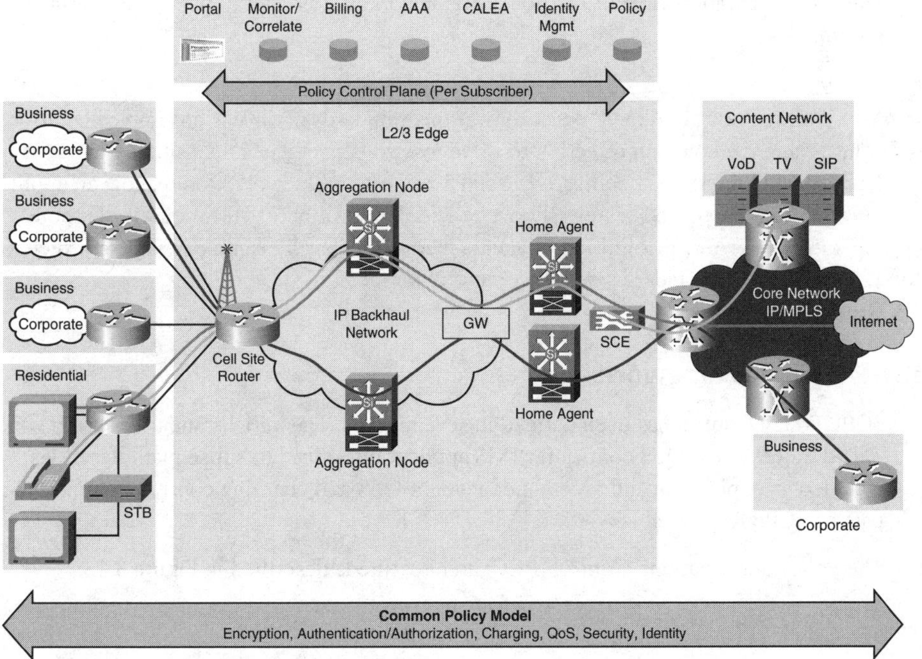

Figure 8-12 *Common Policy Model*

One such model, discussed in Chapter 9, is the IP Multimedia Subsystem (IMS). This model provides for a common policy layer across all SIP-based applications; however, operators need a common model that extends to both SIP-based and non-SIP applications.

In order to understand how to engineer a network with interdependence of elements in mind, it is important to understand the basic framework and architecture of mobile policy control, including conceptual, standards-based, and practical implementations.

Policy in Wireless Standards

Many standards organizations, beginning with 3GPP, have all adopted policy frameworks for controlling network traffic.

Note Policy work actually originated in CableLabs (PacketCable specifications) and IETF. 3GPP specified this policy framework for mobile IMS-based application.

These standards organizations built a policy framework built around operator-delivered services, specifically SIP-based protocols, where the application layer has the ability to notify a PDP of application requirements. In addition, there is an assumption that the PDP always has significant information on the subscriber, attained from a PIP. This PIP, in mobile networks, is either the Access Gateway or AAA server.

This section explores each of the policy frameworks across 3GPP, 3GPP2, and WiMAX Forum.

Note Although this book will cover the various standards organizations implementations of policy, there is a common direction to drive toward convergence on a single policy server definition and interface specification. Such a common framework would allow an application layer to be deployed seamlessly over a wide range of access technologies without any specific changes or recognition of access media. One such example is the convergence of 3GPP and 3GPP2 standards around common interfaces.

3GPP Policy Framework

3GPP Policy Control has been defined in several steps. The initial standards started with pulled mode access QoS control for IMS applications only, but subsequent iterations included an application and access independent QoS and charging control architecture as part of 3GPP Release 7.[1]

The Policy and Charging Control (PCC) architecture is described in Figure 8-13.

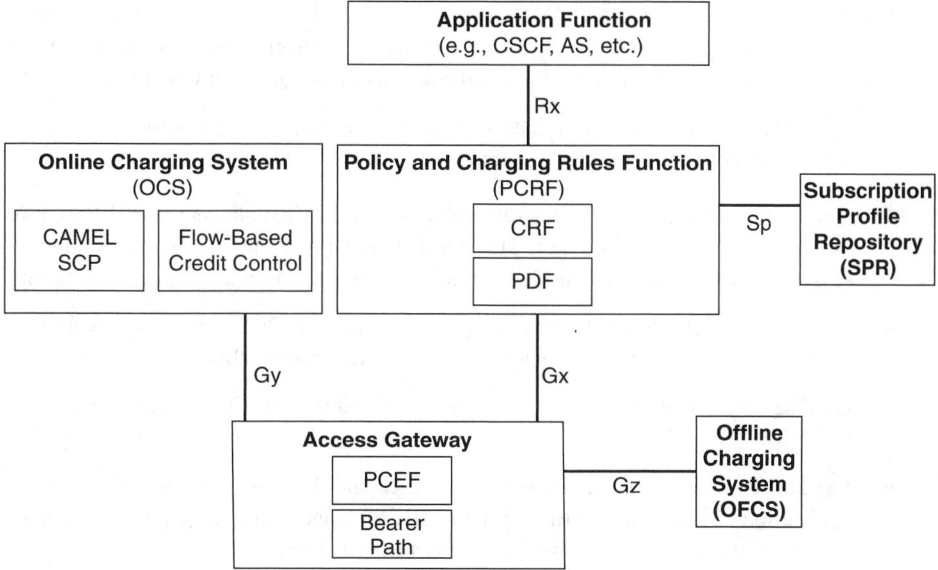

Figure 8-13 *3GPP Policy and Charging Control Model*

This policy model, flow-based in nature, looks at every data session and determines how it needs to be treated. The gateway can be a GPRS Gateway (that is, a GGSN) or any other packet gateway aggregating mobile data traffic.

In addition to subscriber authentication, the 3GPP standards define within the packet gateway a Policy and Charging Enforcement Point (PCEF), which is responsible for identifying service flows and enforcing QoS and charging policy rules.

Other functional elements defined include the following:

- **Policy Control and Charging Rules Function (PCRF):** The PCRF defines how a specific data flow should be handled, including QoS- and charging-specific handling. This decision is based on a number of factors, including subscriber profile, network resource availability, and roaming state.
- **Subscription Policy Repository (SPR):** The SPR contains all relevant subscriber information, including subscriber category (for group-level enforcement), allowed services, specified QoS, and charging rules.
- **Online Charging System (OCS):** The OCS is comprised of two components—a legacy CAMEL SCP (used for voice charging) and a Service Data Flow-Based Credit Control Function. The OCS is used to provide prepaid charging for both voice and data services.
- **Offline Charging System (OFCS):** The OFCS is responsible for receiving Charging Data Records (CDRs) from the PCEF, and feeding this information to the operator's billing platform for postpaid charging.

The Application Function can be IMS or non-IMS. The AF is responsible for communicating application policy requirements to the PCRF. This information is then used by the PCRF to determine both charging rules and bearer control (QoS and CAC) rules.

The 3GPP PCC model is layered in nature, with numerous interlayer interactions. These interactions are defined as reference points, including the following:

- **Gx:** The Gx reference point, between the PCEF and PCRF, allows the PCRF to have direction control over the PCEF. This interface is used for initializing/maintaining sessions, "push" and "pull" models for policy retrieval, and bearer flow information.
- **Gy:** The Gy reference point, between the PCEF and the OCS, allows the OCS to determine credit control and charging mechanisms for the subscriber.
- **Gz:** The Gz reference point, between the PCEF and the OFCS, is used for transmittal of CDRs.
- **Rx:** The Rx reference point, between the PCRF and AF, is used for transmitting application-specific information to the PCRF. Messages from the AF over this interface include application bandwidth requirements, as well.
- **Sp:** The Sp reference point, between the PCRF and the SPR, allows the PCRF to request subscriber-specific information from the database. This information enables the PCRF to make policy decisions based on the subscriber profile.

Figure 8-14 highlights how the elements within the 3GPP framework interact over the different interfaces.

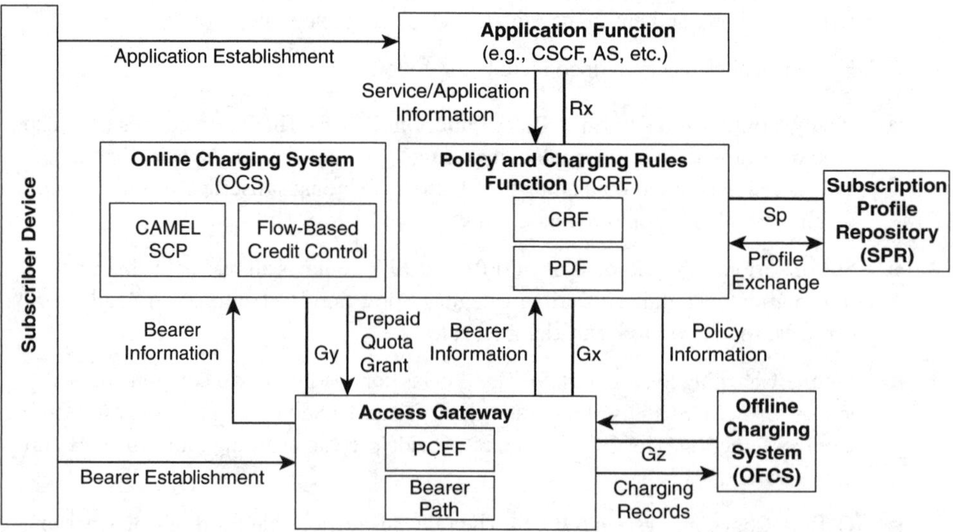

Figure 8-14 *3GPP PCC Interactions*

Edge Policy Admission Control

3GPP standards focus on edge policy admission control. This edge policy control focus, as illustrated in Figure 8-15, performs charging and QoS-related functions only at the edge of the mobile network, but can also be used as a trigger for changes on the access layer.

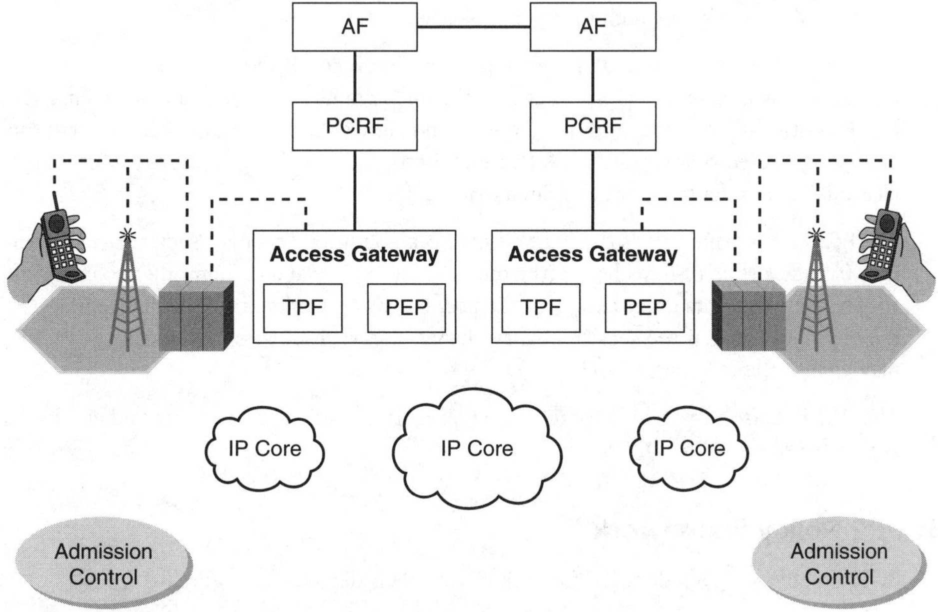

Figure 8-15 *3GPP Edge Policy Control*

This limited scope does not take into account end-to-end resource availability in determining and enforcing policy rules.

3GPP QoS Grants

For QoS control, the AF interacts directly with the PCRF and the PCRF interacts with the gateway, as illustrated in Figure 8-15. 3GPP QoS is comprised of three key functions, as follows:

- **Gating:** The decision to either allow or block traffic for a particular flow.
- **Control:** The QoS enforcement of traffic to a maximum rate. This QoS policy may be authorized by the PCRF or statically configured in the gateway.
- **Reporting:** The capability to report resource utilization information in the gateway to the PCRF. The reporting function also includes the capability to react to application events by modifying the bearer plane.

The PCEF within the gateway is responsible for each of these functions.

3GPP Charging Rules

3GPP standards are explicit on charging use-cases for prepaid subscribers using 4-tuple (Source IP, Destination IP, Source Port, Destination Port) information. The OCS communicates a quota grant and a basis to the PCEF. A *quota grant* is a non-denominational unit of credit that the subscriber may use. A *basis* is the method by which a subscriber will be charged—time, volume, or event—and is determined by the type of application the user is accessing. So, for instance, if the OCS grants four units of quota for a video service, the subscriber may watch four minutes of video.

The PCEF is responsible for all prepaid quota enforcement. If the user has available quota, he may access the service. Because the OCS grants quota in small increments, the PCEF continually requests additional quota, and allows the subscriber session to continue as long as credits are available. A PCEF requests additional quota prior to consuming all available in order to ensure continuity of service.

The PCEF also reauthorizes the quota if network conditions change. Such network events may include a time-of-day change (the quota grant expires at a certain time), roaming status change (the quota grant expires if the user moves networks), or QoS change (the quota grant expires if the service quality changes). In each of these instances, the PCRF may change the charging model.

The PCEF is also responsible for reporting usage information for both prepaid and postpaid subscribers to the OFCS.

3GPP2 Policy Framework

3GPP2 defines a layered model for policy control, as depicted in Figure 8-16.

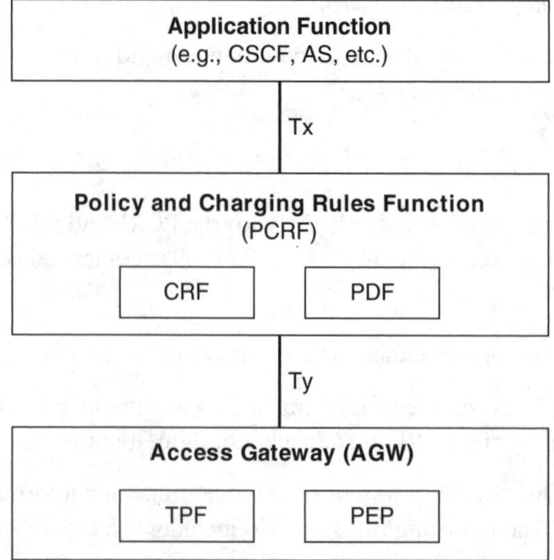

Figure 8-16 *3GPP2 Service-Based Bearer Control*

The policy model acts on all traffic on a per-IP flow basis. This policy model, referred to as Service-Based Bearer Control (SBBC), incorporates two functions into the Packet Gateway, as follows:

- **Traffic Plane Function (TPF):** The TPF is responsible for all bearer plane routing and switching, in addition to enforcement of charging rules.
- **Policy Enforcement Point (PEP):** As the generic name implies, the PEP is responsible for denial of IP bearer flows (Call Admission Control) and QoS policy enforcement. The PEP is also responsible for communicating with the Policy and Charging Rules Function (PCRF).

In addition, the packet gateway is also responsible for authentication of the subscriber during initial connection.

At the signaling layer, the PCRF is divided into two functions:

- **Policy Decision Function (PDF):** The PDF acts as the PDP for all QoS and Call Admission Control functions. The PDF is responsible for determining both if and what level of service the subscriber is entitled to.
- **Charging Rules Function (CRF):** The CRF acts as a PDP for all charging-related functions. The CRF determines how to charge the subscriber—prepaid or postpaid, and at what rate, based on both static and dynamic variables.

At the application layer, the Application Function (AF) is responsible for communicating policy requirements to the PCRF. This information is then used by the PCRF to determine both charging rules and bearer control (QoS and CAC) rules.

While initial definition was focused on defining a SIP-based AF, the AF may be any type of application server that has the ability to communicate directly with the PCRF.

These layers of the policy model are linked via well-defined interfaces, as follows:

- **Ty interface:** The Ty interface, defined as the interface between the Access Gateway and the PCRF, is a Diameter-based interface used for communicating Service-Based Bearer Control (SBBC) information. This interface is responsible for the following three key functions:
  - **Authorize, revoke, or modify the IP flow:** The PCRF either permits or denies establishment of a bearer channel for the particular IP flow. After this is established, the PCRF may modify policy parameters, such as charging basis or QoS requirements.
  - **Receive information from the Access Gateway about available network resources:** During the life of a subscriber session, it is possible that the network resources required to deliver a specific service are no longer available. In this instance, the PCRF may choose to either revoke authorization or modify policy parameters.

- **Bi-directional communication of charging information:** The Access Gateway communicates information that the PCRF may use for charging correlation, whereas the PCRF communicates information on charging rules dynamically.

- **Tx interface:** The Tx interface, defined as the interface between the PCRF and the AF, is a Diameter-based interface used for communicating application-layer information to the PCRF. This information is then used by the PCRF correlation function to determine what policy rules will be sent over the Ty interface. This interface is responsible for the same three key functions:
  - **Establish, revoke, or modify a service flow:** The Application Function notifies the PCRF that the subscriber is authorized to access the particular service requested.
  - **Receive information from the Access Gateway about available network resources:** The PCRF acts as a proxy from the Access Gateway to the AF of available resources. The AF may then determine if the resources are insufficient to deliver the service requested, or if the service flow can be modified in such a way that allows access to the service to continue.
  - **Bi-directional communication of charging information:** The AF provides further information to the PCRF that may be used for charging correlation and establishing charging rules.

Figure 8-17 highlights how the elements within the 3GPP2 framework interact over the different interfaces.

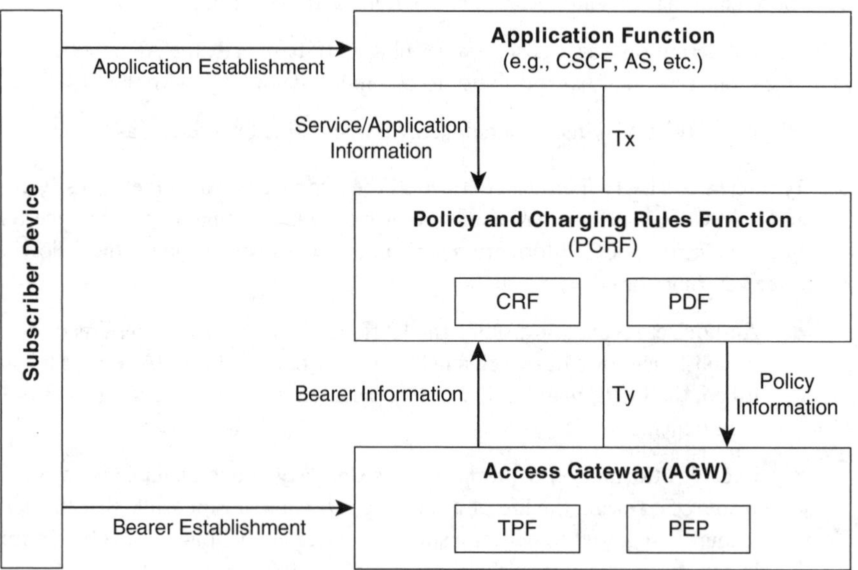

Figure 8-17 *3GPP2 SBBC Interactions*

3GPP2 QoS Grants

3GPP2 has specifically developed a gating function for packet flows. This gating function, which resides as part of the Access Gateway PEP, is responsible for controlling how IP bearer resources are used. 3GPP2 QoS policy control is based on a segmented end-to-end QoS model. These segments are broadly defined as the originating access network, the backbone network, and the terminating access network. Figure 8-18 illustrates the 3GPP2 segmented end-to-end QoS model.

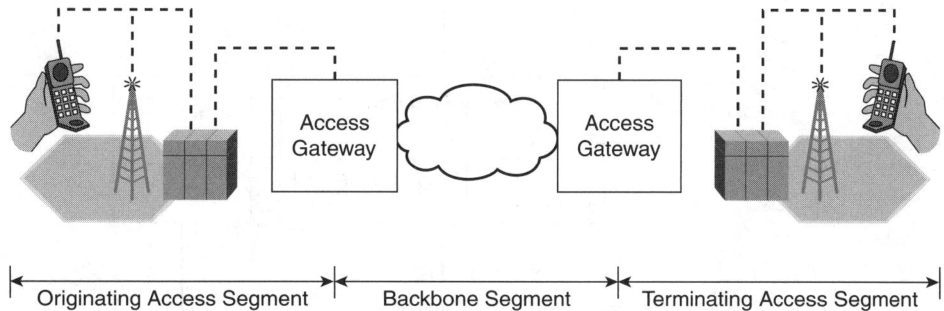

Figure 8-18 *3GPP2 Segmented QoS Model*

The 3GPP2 model includes two phases for QoS establishment:

- **Reserve Phase:** During the Reserve Phase, specific parameters for a packet flow are requested by the mobile terminal. This request is sent to the Access Gateway. The Access Gateway sends information to the PCRF, which determines the Authorized QoS parameters. The Access Gateway then compares the authorized QoS parameters to the Requested QoS parameters to determine proper gating rules. The resources are reserved on the originating and terminating access segments, as required.
- **Commit Phase:** During the Commit Phase, the gates are already established as "opened," allowing bearer traffic to flow under the predetermined QoS policy.

At any time during the life of a specific packet flow, resource reservation parameters may change. A number of different triggers may result in gates being opened, closed, modified, or deleted. If the trigger is generated by the AF, information is sent only to the PCRF, which, in turn, updates the Access Gateway.

3GPP2 Charging Rules

3GPP2 charging rules align closely with work previously done by 3GPP. The charging rules are defined either in the CRF or locally on the Access Gateway. Upon instantiation of a charging rule, the information is installed into the TPF of the Access Gateway, and both online (prepaid) and offline (postpaid) charging are supported. These charging rules are specifically supported for applications that are easily identified (that is, operator-hosted services).

WiMAX Policy Framework

As illustrated in Figure 8-19, WiMAX Forum has also specified a unique framework for QoS and flow-based service management.

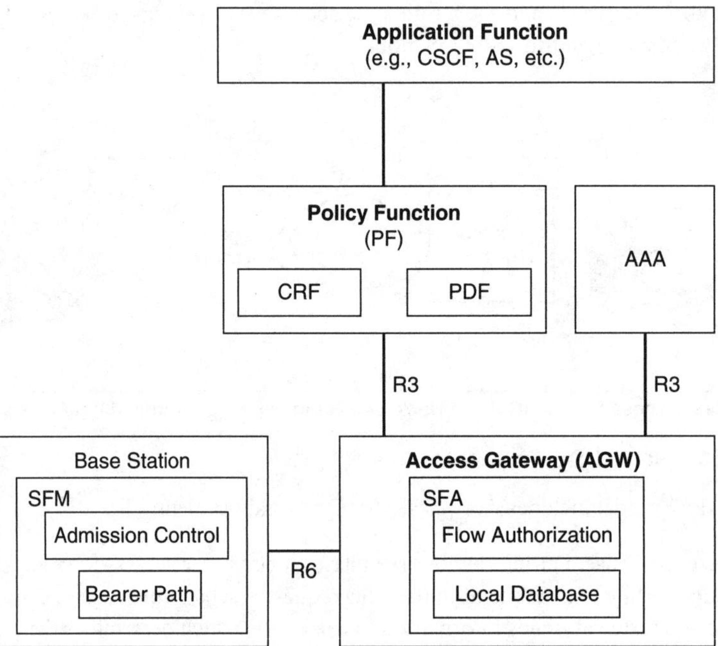

Figure 8-19 *WiMAX Forum Service Management Framework*

The policy model, similar to 3GPP and 3GPP2, acts on all traffic on a per-IP flow basis. However, this architecture deviates further from the 3GPP and 3GPP2 models in that interactions and policy enforcement extend across the entire Access Service Network (see Chapter 2).

The following functions are defined within the WiMAX Policy Framework:

- **Service Flow Manager (SFM):** The SFM resides in the Base Station and acts as a policy enforcement point for all Over the Air (OTA) flow management. The SFM receives policy information from the Service Flow Agent. The SFM is responsible for the following:
  - Creation of service flow
  - Call Admission Control per service flow
  - Activation of service flow
  - Modification of service flow
  - Deletion of service flow

- **Service Flow Agent (SFA):** The SFA resides in the ASN Gateway and is responsible for communicating with the Policy Function to retrieve policies. The SFA validates all policies, and then communicates these policies to the Service Flow Manager (SFM).
- **Policy Function (PF):** The Policy Function is responsible for determining general policy rules and application-specific rules.
- **Authentication, Authorization, and Accounting (AAA):** The AAA is the subscriber policy rules and subscriber QoS profile repository. During initial authentication, the AAA may push a default policy to the Access Gateway.
- **Application Function (AF):** The AF is responsible for communicating policy requirements to the PF. This information is then used by the PF to determine both charging rules and bearer control (QoS and CAC) rules.

The WiMAX service flow management model is similar to both 3GPP and 3GPP2 in its hierarchical nature. The interfaces between these layers are defined as follows:

- **R6:** The R6 interface lies between the Access Gateway and Base Station. This interface carries all policy objects from the SFA to the SFM.
- **R3:** The R3 interface lies between the Access Gateway and the policy decision. The Access Gateway may communicate via the R3 interface to the AAA for subscriber-specific policies or to the PF for general and application-specific policies.

Figure 8-20 highlights how the elements within the WiMAX framework interact over the different interfaces.

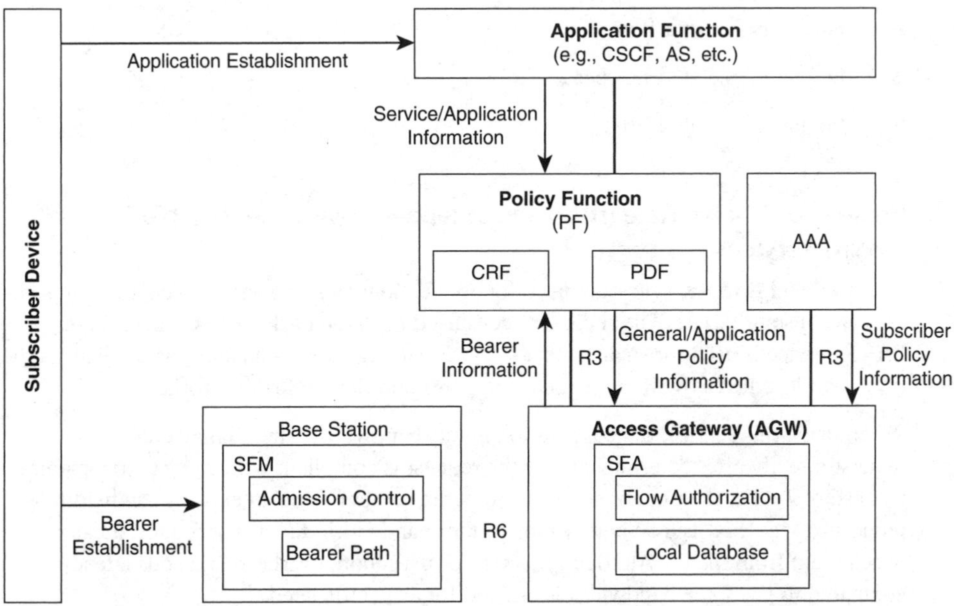

Figure 8-20 *WiMAX Service Flow Management Interactions*

WiMAX QoS Grants

WiMAX Forum defines services flows for providing QoS. These service flows are unidirectional flows of packets and are associated with specific QoS parameters. These service flows are then mapped into grant services. WiMAX Forum defines five grant services, as follows:

- Unsolicited Grant service
- Real-Time Variable Rate services
- Extended Real-Time Variable Rate services
- Non-Real-Time Variable Rate services
- Best-Effort services

The sections that follow describe these services in greater detail.

Unsolicited Grant Service (UGS)

The UGS is used for applications that use fixed-length data packets at a constant bitrate. Examples of such applications include T1/E1 emulation and VoIP without Silence Suppression.

When using this service, the base station grants periodic bandwidth to the application without any explicit bandwidth request to the Access Gateway (ASN). This eliminates the overhead and latency associated with those bandwidth requests.

The UGS enforces the following parameters:

- Maximum Transmit Rate
- Maximum Tolerated Latency
- Maximum Tolerated Jitter

Real-Time Variable Rate (rtVR) and Extended Real-Time Variable Rate (ErtVR) Services

The rtVR and ErtVR services are used for applications that use variable-length data packets at a constant bitrate. The rtVR service is used for large packet sizes, whereas the ErtVR service is used for small packet sizes. Streaming video is an application that fits the rtVR profile, whereas VoIP with Silence Suppression fits the ErtVR profile.

When using this service, the base station grants bandwidth. The BS may grant this request directly after determining that the request is compliant with service flow parameters established at the time of service flow setup, or may issue an explicit bandwidth request to the ASN. The ASN may either grant bandwidth directly or request a bandwidth grant from the PF. Although this service uses more overhead and adds latency compared to UGS, the bandwidth is granted for a specific need.

The rtVR and ErtVR services enforce the following parameters:

- Minimum Reserved Rate
- Maximum Sustained Rate
- Maximum Latency
- Traffic Priority
- Jitter Tolerance (ErtVR only)

Non-Real-Time Variable Rate (nrtVR) Services

The nrtVR services are used for applications that use variable-length data packets at a minimum guaranteed rate. nrtVR applications are also tolerant to delay. An example of an nrtVR application is File Transfer Protocol (FTP).

Similar to rtVR and ErtVR, nrtVR relies on explicit bandwidth grants before authorizing an application.

The rtVR and ErtVR services enforce the following parameters:

- Minimum Reserved Rate
- Maximum Sustained Rate
- Traffic Priority

Jitter and latency are not enforced because the applications requesting this service are delay-tolerant.

Best Effort (BE) Services

BE services are used for applications that do not require any minimum service guarantee. These applications are transported across the RAN with lowest priority, and may be subject to dropped packets. An example of a BE application is web browsing, where TCP retransmits any lost packets. BE service is designed for background traffic on the network, and only Maximum Sustained Traffic Rate is enforced.

Maintaining State in a Mobile Network

State information in a mobile network is critical to supporting any type of policy. Information about the subscriber may be stored in numerous locations, with each element having unique/different information about the subscriber, the subscriber's application, the network conditions, and other aspects of an overall policy framework. By fragmenting this information, a mobile operator lacks complete visibility into all aspects that should be factored into determining network policy.

Table 8-10 defines some of the elements that maintain subscriber state.

Table 8-10 *State Elements in Mobile Network*

Function	State Information
Access Gateway	User location (cell/sector ID)
	Charging information (prepaid or postpaid)
	Amount of data sent/received
	Flow information (5-tuple)
	Airlink QoS parameters
Network Mobility Anchor	User Point-of-Attachment (Access Gateway)
	Charging information (prepaid or postpaid)
	Services instantiated (destination IP address)
	Flow information
HLR/HSS	Subscriber identity (MSISDN, IMEI)
	User location (cell/sector ID) [If subscriber active]
	Last known location (If subscriber inactive)
AAA Server	Initial user policy
	Subscriber identity
	Subscriber IP address
	Billing information
Billing System	Prepaid credit remaining
	Usage statistics/models

Network Policy Protocols

Building on the basics of policy, policy standards, and policy control architecture, we now look at policy protocols, establishment, and signaling across multiple, distinct domains—namely the RAN domain and the IP domain.

RAN Authorization and Encryption

The RAN domain capability for policy enforcement involves authorization of the subscriber session and encryption of the bearer traffic. There are numerous methods for providing session authorization and encryption, and each standards organization may utilize one or more of these methods. There are four main protocols used, as follows:

- A3/A8
- CAVE
- AKA
- CCMP

A3/A8

The A3 and A8 algorithms are used in 3GPP networks for authorization of the subscriber device and to generate a key for encryption of both voice and data bearer traffic.

The A3 algorithm is used for authentication of the subscriber, and the A8 algorithm is used for generating encryption keys. A third algorithm, A5, is used for the encryption itself.

These algorithms are implemented together and are commonly known as the A3/A8 algorithm. The A3/A8 algorithm capabilities are defined in 3GPP TS43-020.

The A3/A8 algorithm is implemented in the Subscriber Identity Module (SIM) and the Authentication Center (AuC). It was designed to provide three key functions for the 3GPP RAN, as follows:

- Confidentiality of the subscriber identity
- Authentication of the subscriber identity
- Confidentiality of the subscriber voice and data traffic

Confidentiality of the Subscriber Identity

To ensure that an intruder listening to the signaling exchanges on the RAN cannot determine a subscriber identity, a pseudo-identity other than the IMSI is used on the airlink. This pseudo-identity is known as the Temporary Mobile Subscriber Identity (TMSI).

The TMSI is location-specific, and has no relevance outside of that specific geographic area. To avoid confusion and overlapping TMSIs, the TMSI is also associated with a specific Location Area Identification (LAI).

The VLR to which the subscriber is registered is responsible for keeping a TMSI/IMSI mapping database. As a user updates location, a new TMSI is assigned by the VLR. This new TMSI is communicated in an encrypted manner.

Authentication of the Subscriber Identity

Every SIM in a 3GPP network is assigned an individual subscriber authentication key that is known only to the SIM and the HLR. This 128-bit key, denoted as Ki, is the unique attribute required for subscriber authentication.

To protect the subscriber identity, the Ki is never transmitted. For GSM voice calls, the A3 algorithm is used to authenticate the subscriber, with the Ki being one of two parameters input into the algorithm. The other parameter is a 128-bit random number generated by the AuC.

This random number is transmitted across the mobile network to the mobile device. Both the AuC and the SIM run the A3 algorithm using the same inputs to produce a 32-bit signed response (SRES). The mobile device then transmits this SRES to the MSC. The MSC compares SRES value received from the mobile device to the computed SRES from the AuC to determine if the user is authenticated.

Figure 8-21 illustrates this process.

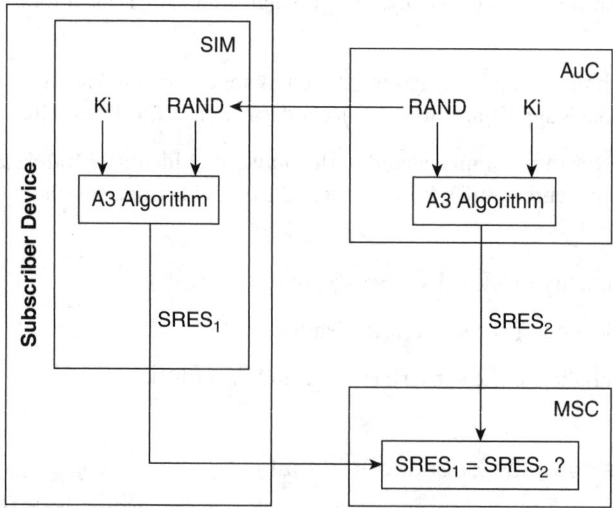

Figure 8-21 *GSM A3 Algorithm*

Confidentiality of the Subscriber Voice and Data Traffic

Confidentiality and encryption of subscriber GSM voice traffic is provided via a combination of the A8 algorithm, which computes a ciphering key based on the same inputs as the A3 algorithm, and the A5 algorithm, which uses the A8 algorithm output and frame sequence numbers to create a 114-bit keystream. The A5 encryption and decryption functions for GSM voice reside on both the mobile terminal SIM and Base Transceiver Station (BTS). Figure 8-22 illustrates this process.

Because the A5 algorithm uses the frame sequence number in computing the keystream, the encryption cipher is resynchronized on every frame. Because the TDM frame sequence number repeats approximately every 3.5 hours, a new cipher key may be established to ensure keystream repeat.

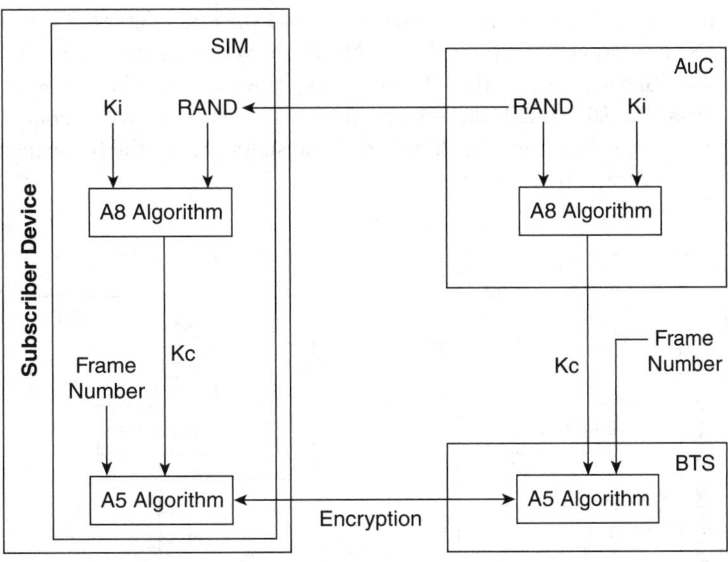

Figure 8-22 *GSM Voice A5/A8 Algorithm*

Confidentiality and encryption of subscriber GPRS data traffic is also provided in a similar manner, except that the A5 algorithm resides further back in the network at the SGSN. The Kc, derived from the A8 algorithm, and a Logical Link Layer (LLC) frame number are used as inputs into the A5 algorithm. This method allows for the cipher to be re-synchronized on every LLC frame. Unlike the TDM frame sequence number, the LLC frame number is large enough that keystream repeat is not a factor. Figure 8-23 illustrates this process.

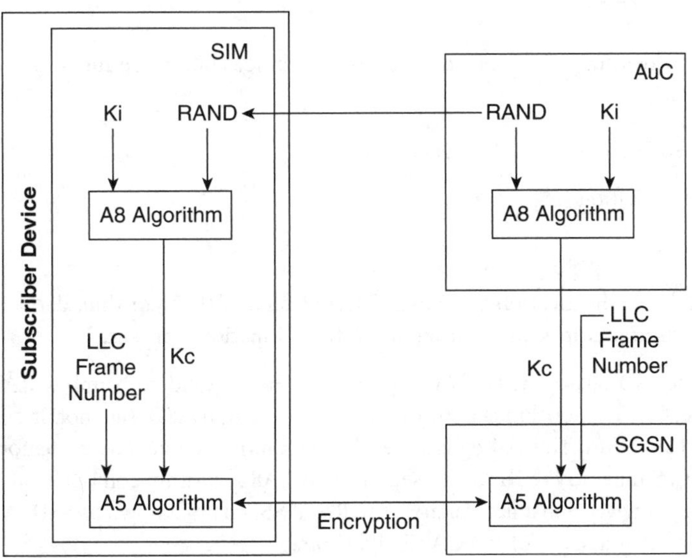

Figure 8-23 *GPRS Data A5/A8 Algorithm*

Confidentiality and encryption of subscriber UMTS voice and data traffic is provided by the UMTS Encryption Algorithm (UEA). The UEA function resides on the mobile terminal (not the USIM!) and either the RNC or SGSN, depending on whether the traffic is voice or data. The UEA builds the keystream as a function of the Kc computed via the A8 algorithm, the bearer identity, the direction of transmission, and the frame number. Figure 8-24 illustrates this process.

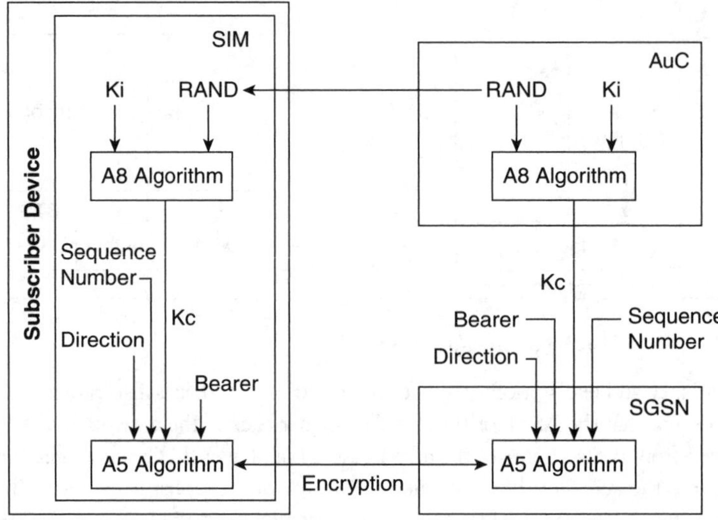

Figure 8-24 *UMTS Voice/Data A5/A8 Algorithm*

CAVE

CDMA divides authentication and encryption services into three function phases, as follows:

- Shared Secret Data (SSD) Generation
- Authentication
- Encryption

The Cellular Authentication and Voice Encryption (CAVE) algorithm, defined in 3GPP2 TR-45, is used multiple times during these three functional phases.

During the SSD phase, the HLR/AuC provides a 56-bit Random Number, RANDSSD, as a challenge. CAVE algorithm is performed using this RANDSSD, the mobile subscriber ESN, and an A-Key. This A-Key is stored locally on the mobile device memory and in the HLR/AuC. Similar to the Ki value used in the A3/A8 algorithm computations for 3GPP, this A-Key is never transmitted across the RAN. SSD pairs, known as SSD_A and SSD_B, are generated as a result of the CAVE algorithm.

During the Authentication phase, a Global Challenge process is conducted. The SSD_A is further run through the CAVE algorithm, along with a Random Number (RAND1) generated by the MSC, the ESN, and Mobile Identity Number (MIN).[2] This process is run both by the mobile terminal and the MSC. The result computed is known as the Authentication Signature (AUTHR), and the MSC compares the AUTHR value received from the mobile terminal with that internally computed.

During the Encryption phase, the SSD_B is further run through the CAVE algorithm, along with a Random Number (RAND2) and ESN to generate a 520-bit Voice Privacy Mask (VPM). The last 40 bits of the VPM, known as the Private Long Code Mask (PLCM), is used to scramble the voice.

The SSD_B, RAND, and ESN are also used to generate the Cellular Message Encryption Algorithm (GMEA) Key for data signaling encryption and the Data key for data encryption.

Figure 8-25 illustrates the three-phase authentication and encryption process.

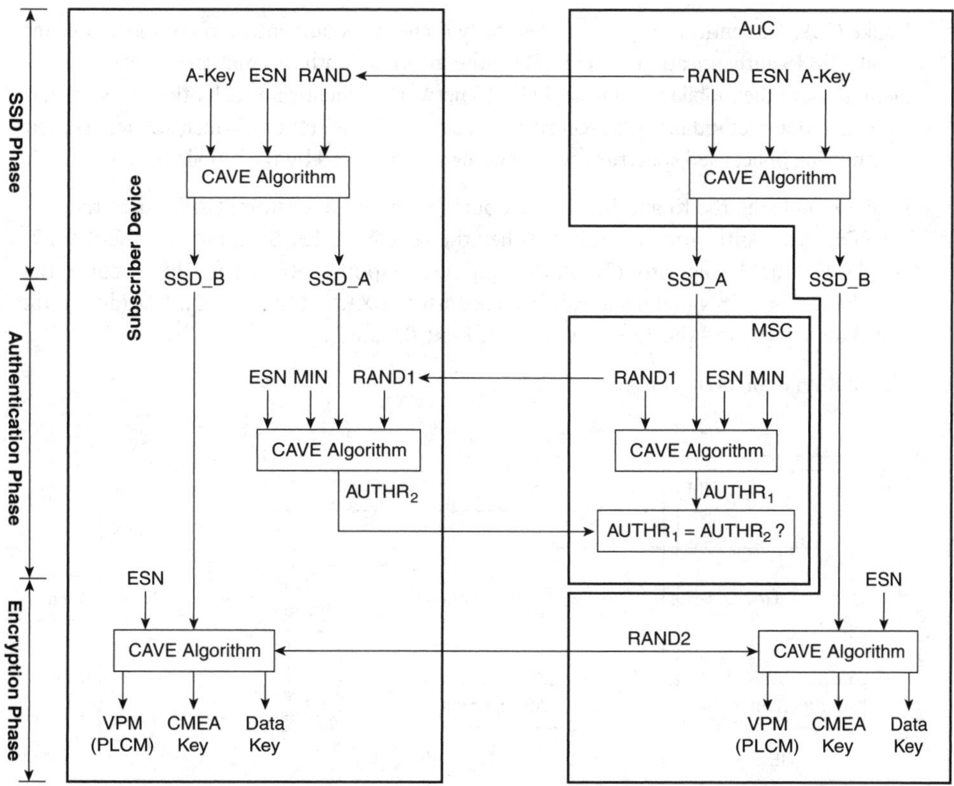

Figure 8-25 *CAVE Authentication and Encryption*

AKA

Authentication and Key Agreement (AKA) is a challenge response-based authentication mechanism that was developed to supplant CAVE. AKA was standardized as part of 3GPP2 X.S0004. At present, there are no CDMA networks using AKA in place of CAVE; however, there are numerous UMTS networks using AKA for authentication and key exchange. AKA divides authentication and encryption services into two functional phases, as follows:

- **Authentication Vector Generation:** During this phase, authentication vectors—each consisting of a random number (RAND), expected response (XRES), Cipher (CK), and Integrity (IK) keys, and an authentication token (AUTN)—are generated by the AuC and sent to either the MSC (voice) or SGSN (data).
- **Authentication and Key Agreement:** During this phase, each side runs an algorithm (A3 in UMTS) and computes a response. The response is sent from the mobile terminal to the authenticating node for comparison. If these values match, the mobile terminal is authenticated.

Unlike GSM authentication, which relies solely on network authentication of the mobile terminal, UMTS authentication uses mutual authentication. With this mutual authentication method, both the mobile terminal and UMTS network authenticate each other. This mutual authentication method provides security against rogue base stations, which are base stations transmitting in licensed spectrum but not owned or operated by the mobile operator.

Rather than using the Ki and RAND as inputs for the A3 algorithm, UMTS uses the RAND and an Authentication token. When the UMTS SIM (USIM) receives the RAND and AUTN, the A3 algorithm is run to compute a response (RES). The RES is sent to the VLR (voice) or SGSN (data) and validated against the XRES for accuracy. In addition, the USIM also computes the 128-bit Ck and 128-bit Ik values.

Figure 8-26 depicts this process.

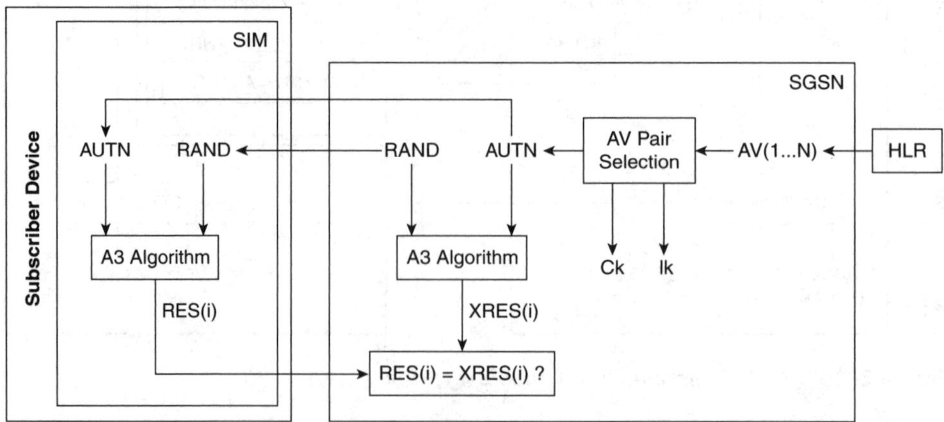

Figure 8-26 *UMTS AKA Using A3 Algorithm*

CCMP

Counter Mode with Cipher Block Chaining Message Authentication Code Protocol (CCMP) was developed as part of 802.11i standards for usage with Wireless LAN networks, but has been leveraged for use within WiMAX standards as a link-layer security protocol. CCMP is defined in RFC 3610.

CCMP uses the Advanced Encryption Standard (AES).[3] AES is a block cipher. During AES encryption, a mathematical algorithm combines a 128-bit data stream with a 128-bit key, producing a 128-bit of encrypted data. This data, as with all encryption algorithms, can only be decrypted if the original key is known.

CCMP uses Counter Mode for link-layer confidentiality and Cipher Block Chaining Message Authentication Code (CBC-MAC) for authentication and message integrity.

Counter Mode

Counter Mode does not use the AES algorithm directly to encrypt data. Instead, an arbitrary counter is selected, and the AES algorithm is applied directly to the counter. This encrypted counter is then run through the binary bitwise operator XOR. This operator returns a 1 when either the first bit of the actual data or the first bit of the encrypted counter is 1, and returns a 0 when neither or both the first bit of the actual data and the first bit of the encrypted counter is 1. Table 8-11 provides an example of the XOR operation.

Table 8-11 *XOR Operation*

Data	Encrypted Counter	XOR Result
0	0	0
0	1	1
1	0	1
1	1	0

For each subsequent block of data, the counter is incremented by an arbitrary value. The same AES key may be used for numerous packets. The maximum number of packets that may be encrypted using the same key is defined by a protocol-selected Nonce value. Figure 8-27 illustrates how Counter Mode operates.

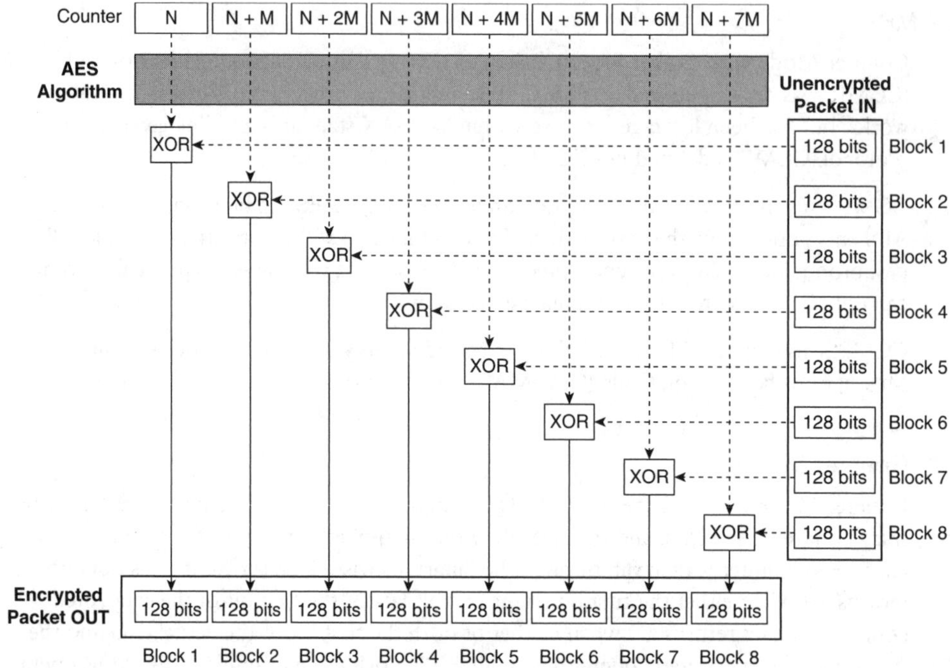

Figure 8-27 *Counter Mode for Link-Layer Confidentiality*

> **Note** Counter Mode has one interesting property worth noting:
>
> When applied twice, the XOR operation produces the original data. For this reason, both the sender (encryptor) and receiver (decryptor) need only understand how to apply the AES algorithm for encryption. After the decryptor runs the AES algorithm on the counter, the XOR algorithm can be used to produce the unencrypted data.

CBC-MAC

CBC-MAC process derives a Message Integrity Code (MIC). This message integrity code is created by a serial process of encryption and XORing of data. The process follows two steps:

1. Encrypt the first block of data with the AES algorithm.
2. XOR the result with the next block and encrypt the result with AES algorithm.

This process is relatively simple, but very powerful. A single bit change in the final MIC can produce a different result when decrypted. Figure 8-28 illustrates how CBC-MAC operates.

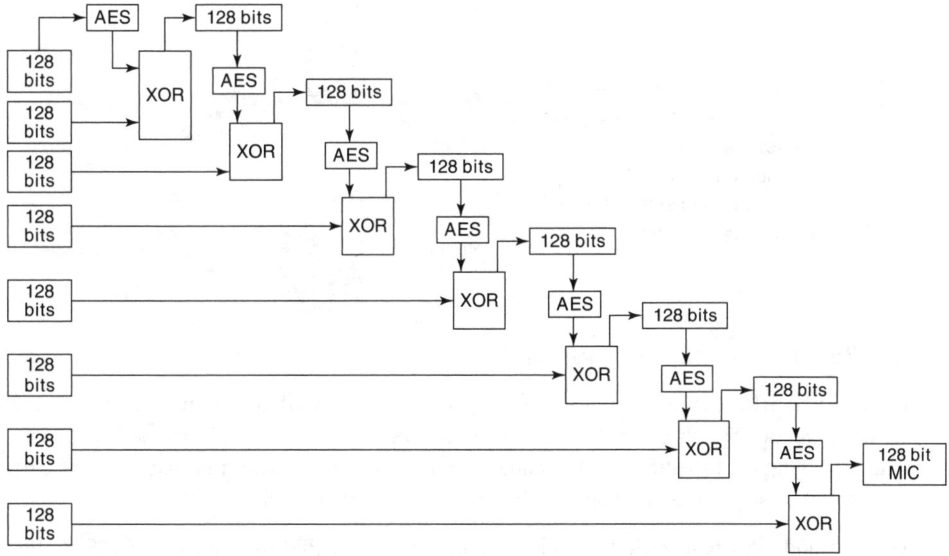

Figure 8-28 *Counter Mode for Link-Layer Confidentiality*

IP Authentication and Authorization

Following successful authentication and encryption in the RAN, voice over IP (VoIP) and other bearer traffic is then authenticated a second time by the IP network. This authentication phase involves the packet gateway interacting with an AAA server to determine if the mobile terminal is allowed access to mobile data services. Two key protocols are used for authenticating a subscriber—Remote Authentication and Dial In User Service (RADIUS) and Diameter.

RADIUS for AAA

RADIUS is an authentication protocol standardized in RFC 2865. Through a client-server model (see Figure 8-29), RADIUS provides a centralized access and authentication system for mobile networks.

RADIUS defines a Network Access Server (NAS) that originates requests to an Access, Authentication, and Accounting (AAA) server. For mobile networks, this NAS device may be any Access Gateway (GGSN, PDSN, ASN) or Mobility anchor (Home Agent).

Within each RADIUS message, specific information is transmitted that is relevant to the NAS client and server for making decisions. This information is carried via RADIUS attributes, which are Type-Length-Values (TLV). Each TLV carries one piece of information (user name, for example). Multiple TLVs are typically carried in the same RADIUS packet.

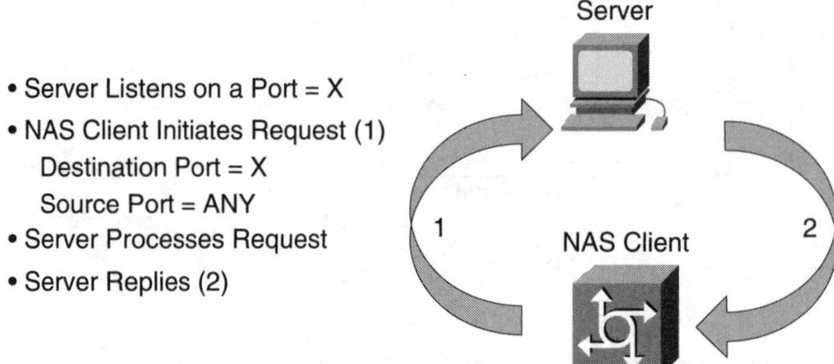

Figure 8-29 *RADIUS Client-Server Model*

The RADIUS RFC defines a number of commonly-used RADIUS attributes, but also defines a Vendor-Specific Attribute (VSA) [RADIUS Attribute 26]. Within the VSA, each vendor is assigned a specific vendor value, and may include information that is specific to that vendor. Cisco has been assigned VSA number 9, represented as 26/9.

Mobile standards organizations also have unique VSAs. 3GPP2 uses VSA 26/5535; 3GPP uses 26/10415; WiMAX uses 26/24757.

RADIUS is a UDP-based protocol that includes application-layer reliability. Each RADIUS message requires a response. This response may include some actionable attributes in response to a query or may simply be an Acknowledgment (ACK).

During the life of a user session, multiple RADIUS messages are communicated between the Access Gateway and AAA server. These message types are defined in RFC 2865. Table 8-12 explains the role of each of these messages in a mobile network.

Table 8-12 *RADIUS Messages in Mobile Networks*

Message	Function
Access Request	The Access Request message is sent from the Access Gateway to the AAA server. This message is used upon session instantiation to request access for a particular mobile subscriber. Information included in this Access Request includes the following: ■ **Subscriber-specific information:** The Access Gateway includes information that uniquely identifies the mobile subscriber in the IP domain (user name, IP address, MAC address, and MSID). ■ **Location-specific information:** The Access Gateway includes information that identifies the mobile subscriber location (that is, cell ID, LAC/RAC, GPS position, and so on). ■ **Standards-specific information:** Each mobile technology includes unique VSAs for technology-specific information. One valuable piece of standards-specific information is a correlation ID. This value is used to correlate all charging records for a particular subscriber.

<table>
<tr><th>Message</th><th>Function</th></tr>
<tr><td>Access Response</td><td>The Access Response message is sent from the AAA server to the Access Gateway in response to the Access Request message. Information included in the Access Response includes the following:
■ Response Type: Either accept or reject.
■ Response Reason (Optional): If rejected, the AAA may provide additional information as to why the session was rejected.
■ IP Address (Optional): The AAA server may provide an IP address for the subscriber. This IP address may be selected from either a generic or a specific pool. The network may use this IP address to determine how to handle the subscriber session (that is, routing rules, QoS rules, and charging rules).
■ Default Policy (Optional): The AAA server may provide a default policy to the Access Gateway. This may either be the set of rules to be enforced by the TPF, or a rule name that is meaningful to the Access Gateway.</td></tr>
<tr><td>Accounting Start</td><td>The Accounting Start message is sent from the Access Gateway to the AAA server. This message notifies the AAA when the session has finished being established, the subscriber is fully connected to the network, and user data traffic begins. This record may be used for charging purposes</td></tr>
<tr><td>Accounting Update</td><td>The Accounting Update message, also commonly known as an Interim Accounting message, is sent from the Access Gateway to the AAA server. This message notifies the AAA of any usage by the subscriber, such as the total amount of time and subscriber data transferred since the last Interim Accounting Message. If the message is the first Interim Accounting Message, the information is since the initial Accounting Start Message.

The Accounting Update message is typically generated at set intervals (for example, 30 seconds). However, if the subscriber's state changes, the Access Gateway may send an immediate Accounting Update to notify the AAA. One such example is a roaming change.</td></tr>
<tr><td>Accounting Stop</td><td>The Accounting Stop message is sent from the Access Gateway to the AAA server. This message notifies the AAA of the termination of the subscriber session. Information about the entire session, including usage, is transmitted for charging purposes.</td></tr>
</table>

Figure 8-30 depicts a call flow of these messages in a mobile network.

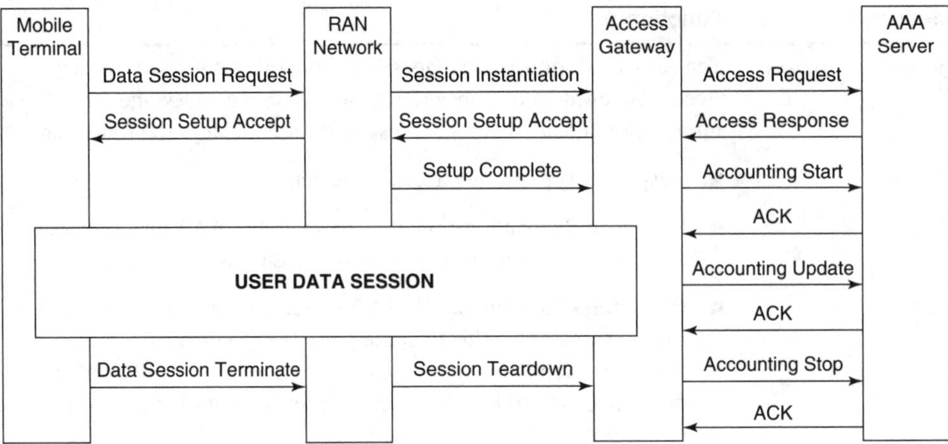

Figure 8-30 *RADIUS Call Flow*

RADIUS Packet of Disconnect

In addition to the preceding standard messages, the RADIUS Packet of Disconnect (PoD) is an important tool for enforcement of subscriber policy. The RADIUS PoD is an Access Request packet that is used when the network wants to revoke previously-accepted authentication.

Note A RADIUS Change of Authorization (CoA) message is another message that may be used to modify session information. Although CoA is not defined in mobile standards, many mobile operators use this function of their RADIUS subsystem to implement session modification.

Any network element or server may send the PoD to the Access Gateway to initiate session teardown. Instances where a PoD may be sent include the following:

- **Detection of fraudulent use:** The network detects either intentionally malicious (DoS) or inadvertent (P2P, virus infection) traffic that is violating operator Terms of Service (ToS).
- **Prepaid balance exhaustion:** The network determines that the subscriber no longer has sufficient balance to continue the session, and there is no way to redirect the session.

EAP

Extensible Authentication Protocol (EAP), defined in RFC5247, provides a universal authentication framework. Rather than providing a specific authentication method, the EAP framework was designed to support both current and future authentication methods. The framework has evolved to support multiple wireless and point-to-point methods, including the following:

- EAP Subscriber Identity Module (EAP-SIM)
- EAP for UMTS Authentication and Key Agreement (EAP-AKA)
- EAP Transport Layer Security (EAP-TLS)
- EAP Tunneled Transport Layer Security (EAP-TTLS)
- EAP Flexible Authentication via Secure Tunneling (EAP-FAST)

The sections that follow describe each of these methods in greater detail.

EAP Basic Framework

The three main components of the EAP framework are as follows:

- **EAP Peer:** The EAP Peer is any device that is attempting to access the network. The EAP Peer has a supplicant that allows EAP to run over a specific transport-layer protocol. This transport-layer protocol may be IPSec, PPP, 802.1X, or various other protocols. In mobile, the subscriber terminal would be the EAP peer.
- **EAP Authenticator:** The EAP Authenticator is the Access Gateway that requires authentication prior to granting access.
- **Authentication Server:** The Authentication Server invokes a particular EAP method for authentication, validates EAP credentials, and grants access to the network.

Logically, EAP authentication and connectivity is between the EAP Peer and Authentication Server. The EAP Authenticator has no specific EAP function other than to proxy EAP messages between these two points. In fact, the authentication-specific information transported in the EAP messages is encrypted, so the EAP Authenticator has very limited role in EAP authentication.

RADIUS Support for EAP

The RADIUS protocol, via RFC3579, was extended to support the transport of EAP messages between a NAS device and RADIUS AAA server. With these extensions, RADIUS has become the de facto standard for transport of EAP messages between the EAP Authenticator and Authentication Server.

Figure 8-31 depicts the end-to-end relationship between EAP Peer, EAP Authenticator, and Authentication Server.

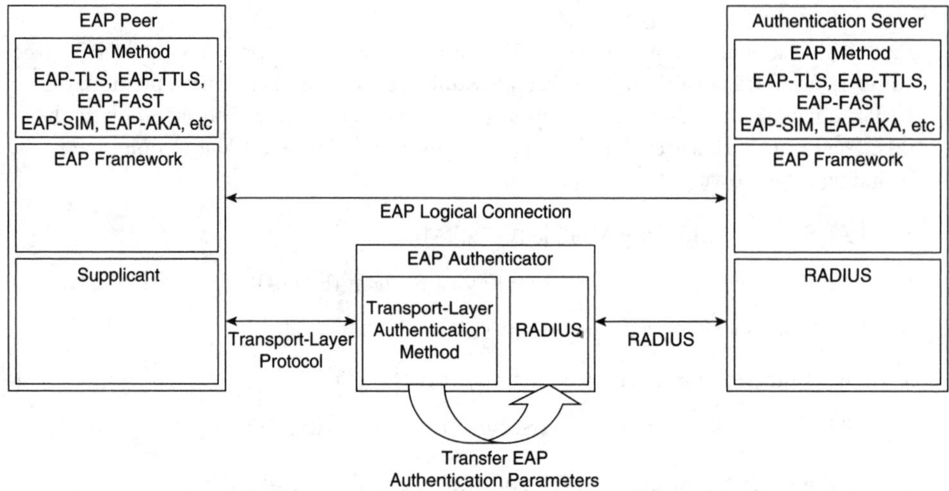

Figure 8-31 *EAP Message Communication*

EAP-SIM

EAP-SIM is defined in RFC 4186. Developed as a method for authenticating subscribers via GSM SIM over an IP network, EAP-SIM provides the same features and functions as standard GSM-based challenge-response authentication using the A3/A8 algorithm. EAP-SIM has been leveraged in building the Generic Access Network (GAN), or Unlicensed Mobile Access (UMA) dual-mode service. GAN/UMA is discussed in greater detail in Chapter 2.

Figure 8-32 provides a functional diagram of EAP-SIM. As with standard GSM authentication, the Ki value used in deriving the Signed Response (SRES) is never transported. Both SIM card and Authentication Center store this value and use a random number (RAND) in generation of the SRES.

The key difference between EAP-SIM and standard SIM-based authentication is that the SIM provides a nonce value. This value is used to derive a Message Authentication Code (MAC) by the AuC. The SIM card receives both the RAND and MAC, and then validates the MAC prior to running the A3 algorithm. This provides an additional layer of authentication over the standard GSM algorithm, as the MAC derivation provides a mutual authentication mechanism.

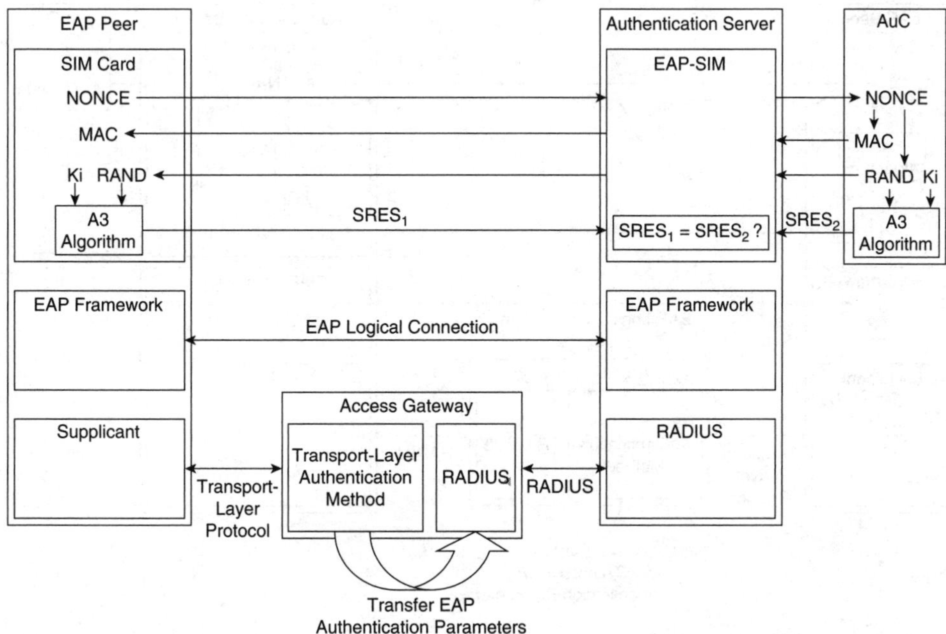

Figure 8-32 *EAP-SIM Message Communication*

EAP-AKA

EAP-AKA is defined in RFC 4187. Developed as a secure authentication mechanism via USIM for devices connected to an IP network, such as WiFi, EAP-AKA provides the same mutual-authentication capabilities as standard SIM authentication.

Figure 8-33 provides a functional diagram of EAP-AKA.

Because AKA is used for both network authentication and IMS authentication in a UMTS environment, EAP-AKA is typically used for offering IMS-based services over non-3GPP access links.

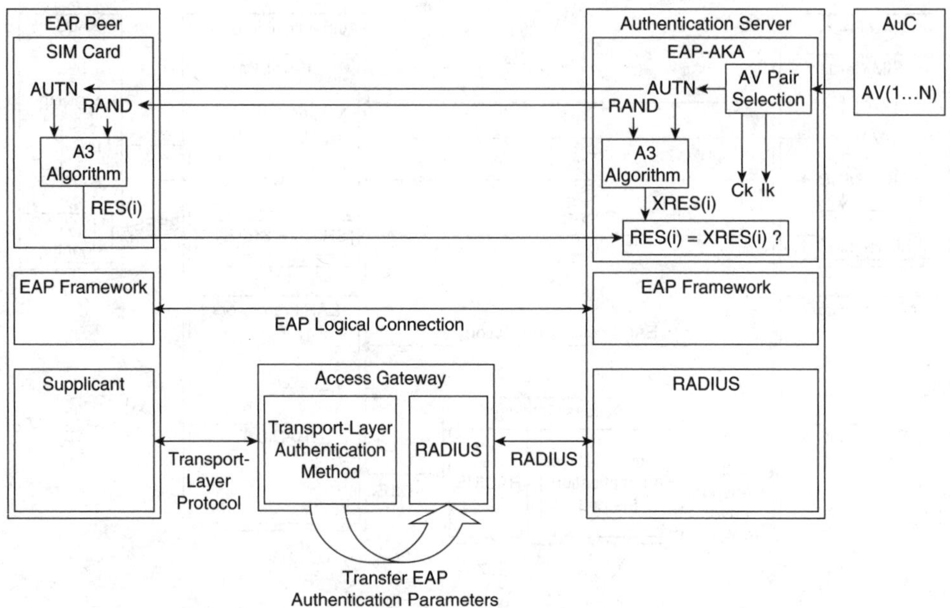

Figure 8-33 *EAP-AKA Message Communication*

EAP-TLS

EAP-TLS is defined in RFC 5216. Based on Public Key Infrastructure (PKI), TLS provides a certificate-based method for mutual authentication and dynamic key generation. EAP-TLS is extensively used in both WiFI and WiMAX networks for authentication and encryption.

EAP-TLS is based on Secure Sockets Layer (SSL) Version 3.0. EAP-TLS performs SSL authentication over EAP instead of over TCP. As EAP-TLS is based on mutual authentication, both the EAP Peer and Authentication Server must have certificates. Each side validates the other via certificate and private key.

Figure 8-34 provides a functional diagram of EAP-TLS.

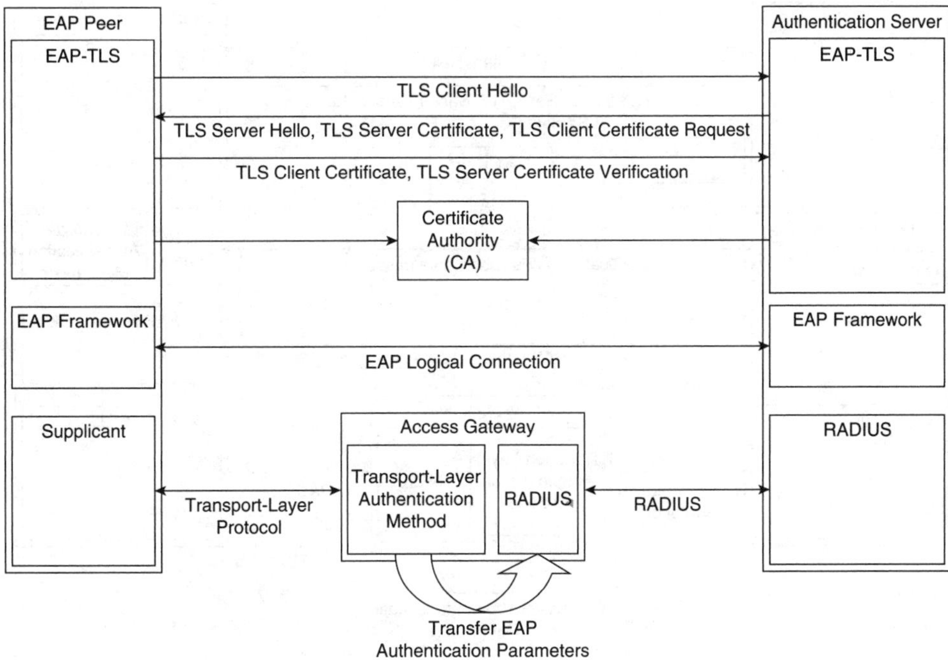

Figure 8-34 *EAP-TLS Message Communication*

EAP-TTLS

EAP-TTLS is defined in RFC 5281. Unlike EAP-TLS, which requires mutual authentication via PKI certificate, EAP-TTLS only requires that the server certificate be authenticated to the client. After this is complete, a secure tunnel is established between the client and server. This tunnel establishment may use any existing authentication protocol, including legacy password-based mechanisms. Because all client authentication is tunneled, EAP-TTLS provides mechanisms to protect against eavesdropping or man-in-the-middle attacks. Tunnel establishment also serves as the method by which the server authenticates the client.

EAP-TTLS was designed to solve the eavesdropping concerns that are common in challenge-response authentication mechanisms. With those mechanisms, an eavesdropper may listen to both challenge and response, and then apply various algorithms to determine the password used in the hash. This has been well-understood since the inception of challenge-response authentication, but has not been addressed because it has historically been unlikely to occur.

With the proliferation of wireless technologies, specifically WiFi and WiMAX, EAP-TTLS was designed to solve this problem. Wireless networks typically send passwords unencrypted and span domains (that is, the base station may reside in a visited operator, whereas the authentication server resides in the mobile subscriber's home operator), making the likelihood of eavesdropping considerably higher. With EAP-TTLS, all password transport is encrypted within TLS.

Figure 8-35 provides a functional diagram of EAP-TTLS.

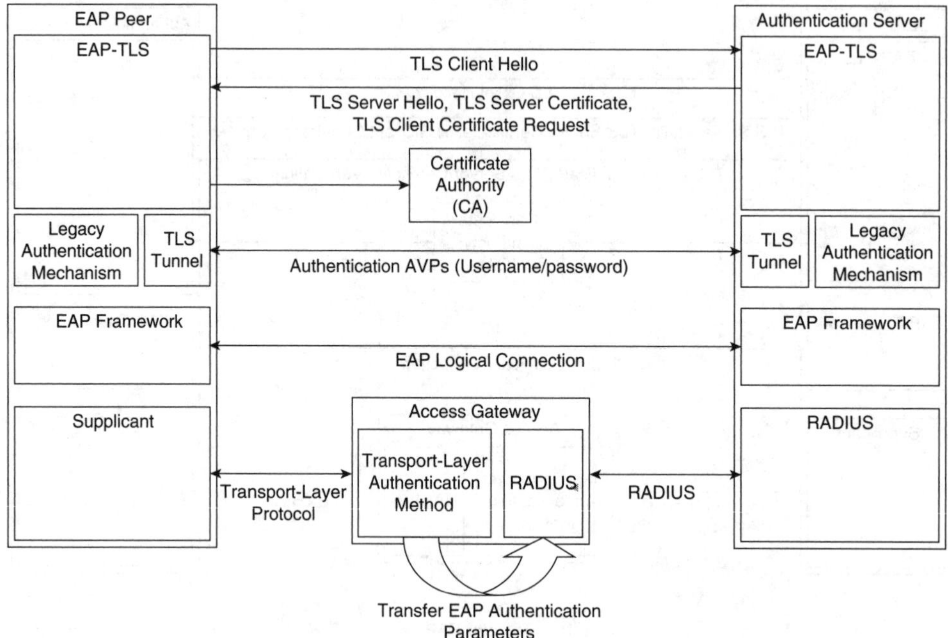

Figure 8-35 *EAP-TTLS Message Communication*

Diameter

Diameter, defined in RFC 3588, is a successor to RADIUS for AAA functions, driven partially by roaming and mobility concerns about the extensibility and scalability of RADIUS. Diameter is not intended to be a replacement of RADIUS in mobile networks, but instead to provide new capabilities above and beyond those that RADIUS was originally designed to provide. Table 8-13 highlights the differences between RADIUS and Diameter.

Table 8-13 *RADIUS Messages in Mobile Networks*

Message	RADIUS	Diameter
Transport	UDP (unreliable)	TCP/SCTP (reliable)
Encryption	Password-based	IPSec or TLS
AVP Length	8 bits	32 bits
Architecture	Client-Server	Peer-to-Peer
Communication	Port-based (configured)	Dynamic discovery
Capability Negotiation	No	Yes

The four functional elements in the Diameter infrastructure are as follows:

- **Clients:** Elements that originate Diameter requests for AAA.
- **Agents:** Nodes that act on the Diameter request and response, but do not request or respond directly to Diameter messages. Examples of agents include proxies, redirectors, or relays.
- **Servers:** Nodes that respond to Diameter requests locally. Servers perform authentication and authorization.

A Diameter node may simultaneously act as an agent and a server. For instance, a Diameter server may authenticate certain subscribers locally while redirecting other requests to a remote, or foreign, Diameter server.

Diameter specifications consist of three components:

- **Diameter BASE specification:** This specification defines the message formats, protocol capabilities, and generic functions. In general, the Diameter BASE specification includes the necessary subsystems for AAA.
- **Transport profile:** This specifies the transport layer functions, Diameter failover, and Diameter state machine.
- **Applications:** Numerous Diameter applications, or protocols leveraging the Diameter base and transport mechanisms with unique capabilities, have been defined.

Diameter BASE

Diameter BASE specification includes the following functions:

- **Peer discovery:** When a request comes in from a Diameter peer, the server uses peer discovery to locate an agent in a particular realm. The realm may be obtained from the NAI from the Diameter request. Diameter peer discovery is performed using either Service Location Protocol (SERVLOC) or Domain Name System (DNS).
- **Capabilities exchange:** When two Diameter peers establish a connection, a capabilities exchange process takes place. Capabilities include Diameter version number, security capabilities, Diameter applications, and vendor-specific capabilities. At least some of the security and application capabilities need to be the same on both the client and server in order for the Diameter session to stay established. Capabilities exchange messages cannot be proxied, relayed, or redirected.
- **Request/Answer:** Diameter may be used for all AAA functions, or only Accounting. Requests from the Diameter client are sent to the server, and Answers from the server are sent to the client. There may be intermediary agents, such as redirectors or relays, within the path. Figure 8-36 illustrates the Request/Answer mechanism.

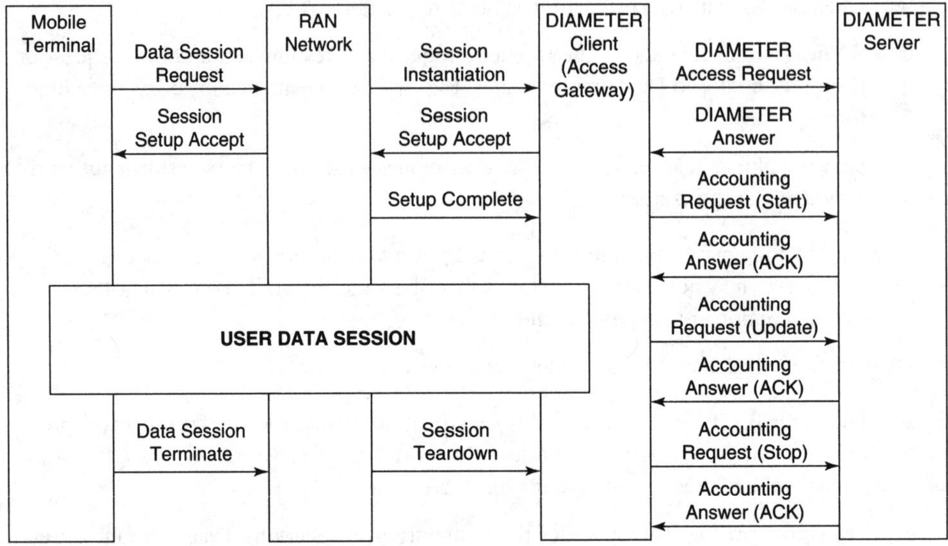

Figure 8-36 *Diameter Request/Answer*

Diameter Transport Profile

Diameter peers establish connections with each other. Each transport connection uses a single TCP connection. Because SCTP allows for a single connection to span interfaces, each transport connection may use multiple IP addresses. These connections are used to transport sessions. A session is an end-to-end logical communications channel between a Diameter client and Diameter server. Figure 8-37 illustrates Diameter connections and sessions.

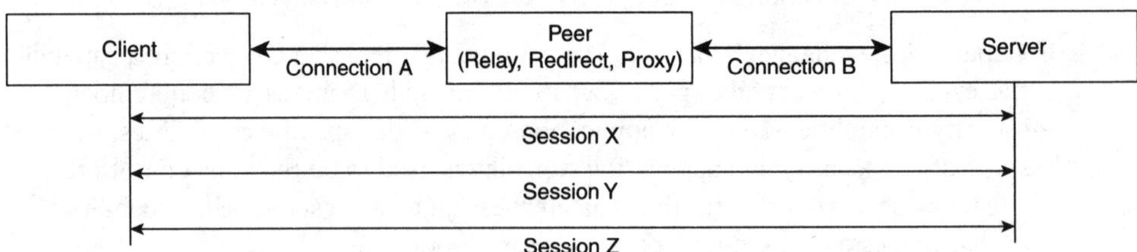

Figure 8-37 *Diameter Connections and Sessions*

Multiple simultaneous sessions between client and server may traverse a single Diameter connection. Each subscriber requires a unique session, with a unique session ID for each. This session may consist of multiple Request/Answer messages traversing the session, and all include the same session ID for correlation.

Diameter Applications

Diameter supports numerous "applications," which are protocols leveraging only the Diameter BASE defined in RFC 3588. Examples of Diameter applications include the following:

- **Diameter Network Access Server Application (NASREQ) (RFC 4005):** NASREQ was developed as a transitional application for migration from RADIUS to Diameter. NASREQ extends Diameter to support RADIUS attributes and avoid unnecessary attribute conversions.
- **Diameter Credit Control Application (DCCA) (RFC 4006):** DCCA was developed as a charging application for IMS-based networks.
- **Diameter Extensible Authentication Protocol (RFC 4072):** Diameter EAP was developed as an application for supporting EAP over Diameter, similar to RADIUS support discussed previously.
- **Diameter Mobile IPv4 (RFC 4004):** Diameter MIPv4 was developed as an application for AAA communication from Mobile IPv4 network elements. The Foreign Agent and Home Agent both use Diameter for communication with the AAA server of events such as MIP registration/deregistration, MIP binding updates, and so on.
- **IP Multimedia Subsystem (IMS) and Policy Applications:** 3GPP, 3GPP2, and WiMAX Forum use the Diameter protocol for transport of policy and charging rules between the Access Gateway and policy server. Chapter 8 discusses further the use of Diameter in IMS environment.

Location Awareness

Location awareness refers to the capability of a device or network to understand where it is located, either via geography or via proximity. Location awareness is used by mobile networks for basic functions (that is, to determine handover), as well as more advanced functions (that is, location-specific services). There are three main mechanisms in mobile networks for attaining location, as follows:

- Device-based mechanisms
- Network-based mechanisms
- Hybrid mechanisms

Device-Based Mechanisms

Device-based mechanisms involve hardware and/or software components on the device that can be used to locate the mobile device.

Low-granular techniques of device-based location awareness include signal strength calculations from multiple adjacent cells (similar to triangulation), cell positioning (the cell the device is located in), and signal strength calculation.

The most granular technique, Global Positioning System (GPS), uses precise coordinates from multiple (three or more) satellites to compute exact location. Each GPS satellite sends messages that include exact coordinates and the time the message was sent (to the microsecond). Four satellites are typically required to ensure accuracy, because most device-based clocks are not accurate enough to function at the microsecond level. However, in some instances, three satellites may be sufficient. In the GPS mechanism, latitude, longitude, and altitude are computed.

Network-Based Mechanisms

Network-based mechanisms use the mobile operator infrastructure to determine a user location with varying degrees of granularity.

The least granular mechanism is sector localization. At any given time, a mobile operator is aware of their cell tower locations and to which cell tower sector a subscriber is connected. With this information, a mobile operator can isolate subscribers to a specific sector, and therefore a specific geographic location.

Another low-granular mechanism is done via triangulation. In triangulation, the mobile operator is able to determine up to three cell towers of which a mobile subscriber is within range. With this information, the mobile network operator may use triangulation mechanisms, similar to a compass-and-map technique, to triangulate a subscriber within a triangle of range. Figure 8-38 illustrates triangulation with three cell towers.

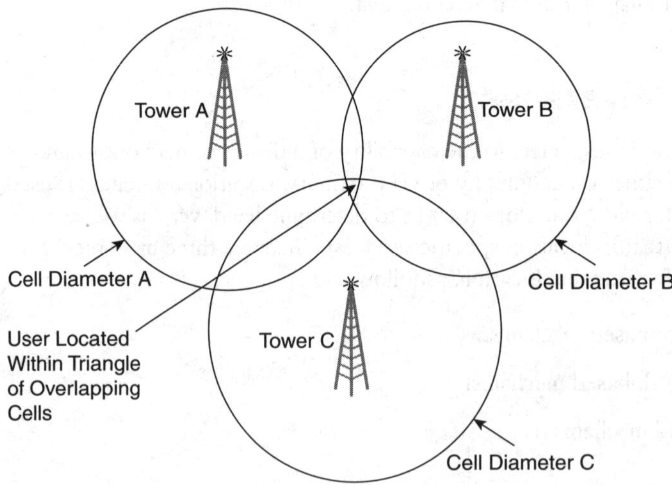

Figure 8-38 *Triangulation*

Similar to triangulation, GSM networks make use of trilateration, which takes into account the distance from a tower. This distance from a tower is calculated from the GSM Timing Advance parameter. Figure 8-39 illustrates trilateration with three cell towers.

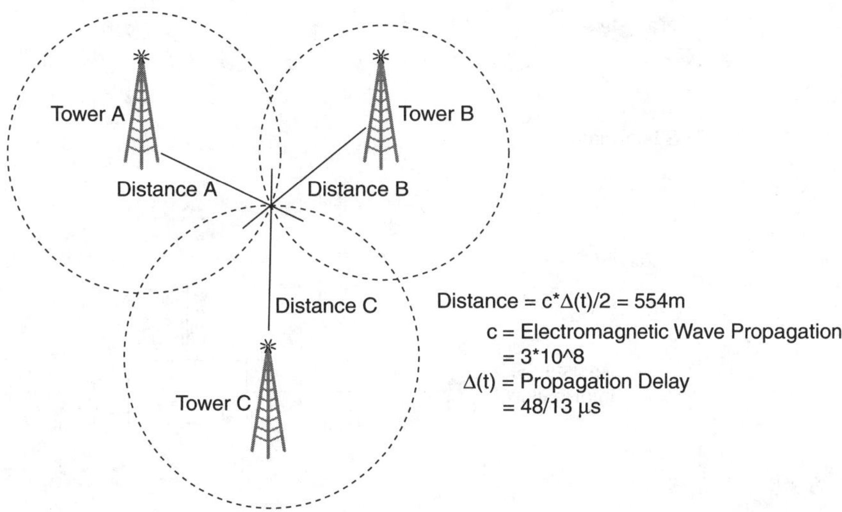

Figure 8-39 *Trilateration*

> **Note** UMTS Location Services (LCS) are based on triangulation, where distance from the tower is calculated by Observed Time Difference of Arrival (OTDoA). Uplink Time Difference of Arrival (UTDOA) is specified explicitly by GSMA for determining distance.

Accuracy of each distance is a function of electromagnetic propagation and propagation delay.[4] However, because distance is being measured simultaneously from the three cell towers, the accuracy is actually considerably greater.

Hybrid Mechanisms for User Location

Hybrid mechanisms have taken a leading role in accuracy of user location. Although these mechanisms use a combination of both device-based and network-based techniques to provide greater accuracy, they also inherit all limitations associated with both techniques.

The most prominent example of a hybrid mechanism is Assisted GPS (A-GPS). A-GPS leverages GPS devices in cellular networks, along with known cell ID to determine what GPS signal the mobile device will receive. This information is sent to the mobile device, and reduces the time-to-first-fix (TTFF), or the amount of time required for a GPS to find and "lock on" to three or more satellites.

Because the information computed by the network-based GPS system and the information received by handset-based GPS system are so similar, A-GPS allows for accurate positioning with as few as one cell tower and one satellite. This allows A-GPS to provide accurate information at times when standard GPS would be unable to, such as indoors.

Figure 8-40 illustrates how A-GPS complements the existing GPS capability.

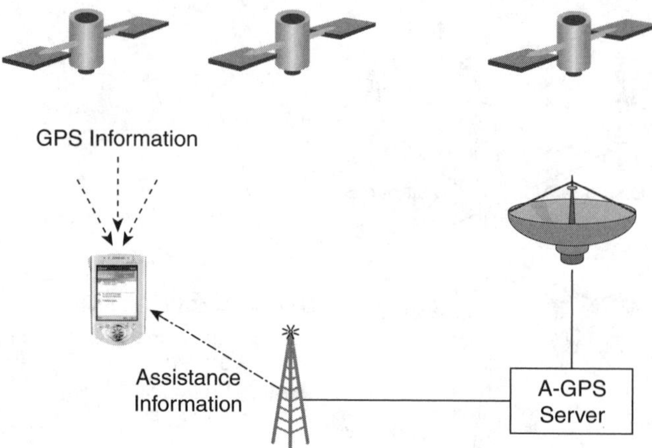

Figure 8-40 *A-GPS*

Summary

Today's mobile network QoS models are independently administrated and enforced. Figure 8-41 illustrates a QoS model of the independence of today's networks.

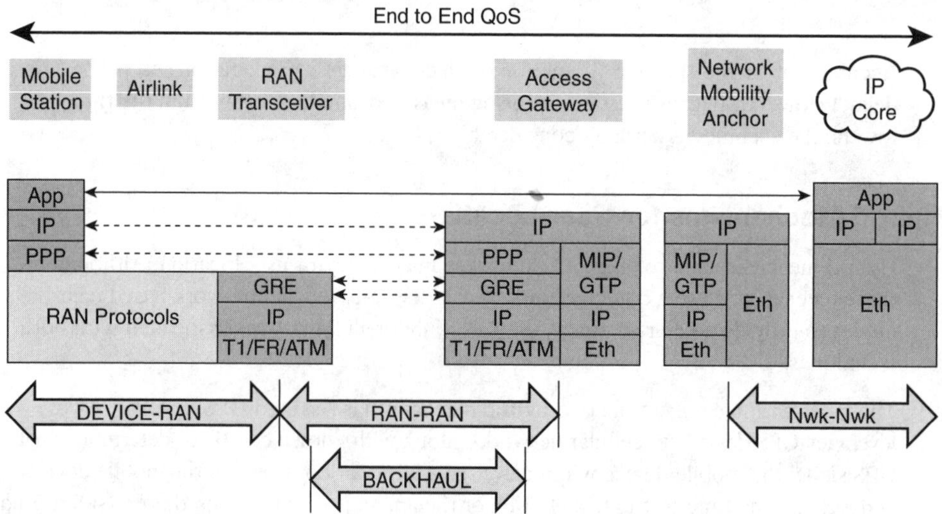

Figure 8-41 *Mobile Network QoS Model Today*

Specifically, this model illustrates four different QoS models working independently. These QoS models include the following:

- **RAN Scheduling algorithms:** See Chapter 1, "Introduction to Radio Systems."
- **Backhaul QoS algorithms:** See Chapter 5, "Connectivity and Transport."
- **RAN-to-Gateway Communication Channel:** See Chapter 2, "Cellular Access Systems."
- **Network to Network, or IP Core QoS algorithms:** See Chapter 5, "Connectivity and Transport."

As networks, services, user traffic models, and network intelligence improve, this model will eventually migrate to an interdependent model, where all mobile network elements work in a coordinated fashion to achieve end-to-end policy control, including charging, QoS, network admission control, and security functions. All IP architectures enable a widely-used model for enabling such an interdependent model.

Endnotes

[1]For 3GPP Standards, reference http://www.3gpp.org/ftp/Specs/archive/23_series/23.203/23203-100.zip.

[2]Mobile Identity Number is a 10-digit number, which is most commonly the subscriber's phone number.

[3]AES was first announced in the Federal Information Processing Standards Publication 197 on November 26, 2001. Detailed information on AES can be found in that announcement at the following link: http://www.csrc.nist.gov/publications/fips/fips197/fips-197.pdf.

[4]Location-Based Services for Satellite-Based Emergency Communication (http://www.wisecom-fp6.eu/papers/Paper_WRECOM_2007.pdf).

Chapter 9

Content and Services

Since the dawn of modern communications, consumer adoption and usage growth has been predicated on unique content, services, and applications. These services began with the first telephony networks, and have evolved to include video services such as broadcast television and video-on-demand, as well as data communications such as Internet browsing, instant messaging, and Voice over IP.

So, too, have wireless communications evolved from a voice-centric architecture and service offering to one in which users have access to browsing services (based on Wireless Application Protocol [WAP] or Hypertext Transfer Protocol [HTTP]), video (both live streaming video and video communications), and transactional services, all complemented with features and functions that only a mobile network and device can provide. With this, mobile services are unique in both content and experience.

This final chapter in this book explores how mobile network services, and corresponding service architectures, have evolved. This chapter provides an overview of the ever-changing mobile services architecture, beginning with Intelligent Networks (IN) as a means of providing advanced features over circuit-switched voice networks. In addition, this chapter explores voice and video service delivery over IP-enabled wireless networks, including the nuances associated with the wireless network itself.

Service Delivery Platforms

Service Delivery Platforms (SDP) provide a framework for the end-to-end delivery of a service to a subscriber. These services frameworks provide a common architecture and interface for new applications and content to be created, controlled, charged, and optimized. The most commonly-known SDP is the World Wide Web, which provides a common structure to request (http://), transport (HTTP over TCP), secure (HTTPS), and format (HTML) content to a subscriber device, or web browser.

In mobile networks, SDPs provide various functions, including delivery of extensible voice services (Intelligent Networks, or IN), IP Multimedia Services (IMS), and mobile TV services. Mobile SDPs enable service providers to both deliver existing services and deploy new services rapidly by leveraging common interfaces and integration points to existing infrastructure, such as Operations Support Systems (OSS). In some instances, mobile SDPs provide content re-formatting for devices that cannot support the native format. In other instances, mobile SDPs provide a full-service creation environment for building the entire service value chain.

SDPs also play a core role in regulatory compliance. Numerous regulatory agencies and laws, including the United States' Sarbanes-Oxley Act of 2002 and the United Kingdom's Combined Code of Corporate Governance, provide legislation and guidelines for the telecommunications service providers, including IT infrastructure management, data retention, network traffic monitoring and analysis, and accuracy of information. The SDP architecture outputs information that helps mobile service providers in a number of these areas.

This section explores the various elements involved in delivering services within the mobile SDP framework, from core components to overlay services.

SDP Core Components

SDP core components are those fundamental capabilities for delivering services to a subscriber. The SDP Alliance (www.thesdpalliance.com), a collaboration of software product companies that have architecturally defined the SDP core functions, categorize the SDP environment into five core components: capability and preference exposure, data integration, charging, mobile portal, and device portal. This chapter extends the SDP Alliance architecture further, by encompassing all elements in both the bearer and control plane within the SDP architecture.

Together, these core components provide an abstracted, access technology-independent mobile framework upon which any service may be delivered to a mobile device.

Figure 9-1 illustrates these core components and their internal and external logical connections.

Capability and Preference Exposure

The Capability and Preference Exposure layer of the SDP architecture enables mobile operators to provide a richer experience for their subscribers. A number of different functions may fall within the Capability and Preference Exposure layer, including the following:

- **Subscriber profile:** The subscriber profile identifies the subscriber, whether by username, IP address, MAC address, or some other unique identifier. Authentication of a subscriber based on this information is discussed in Chapter 8, "End-to-End Context Awareness."

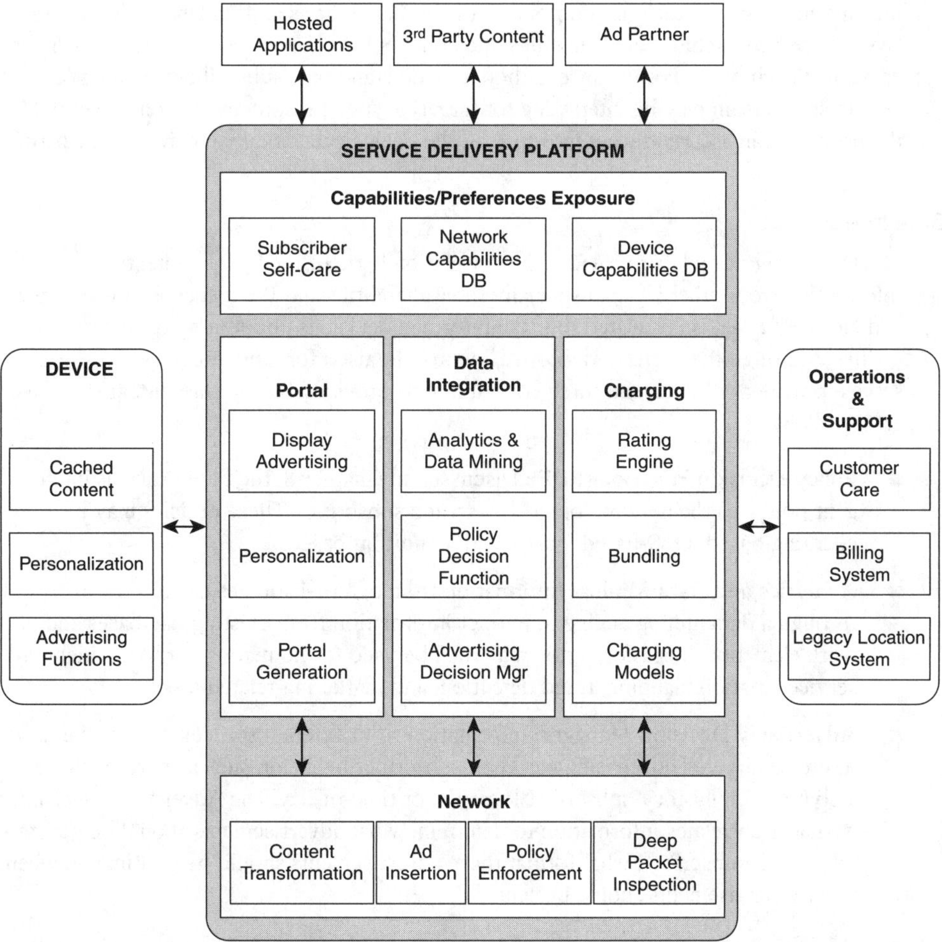

Figure 9-1 *SDP Core Components*

- **Network capabilities:** The network capabilities database maintains information on the capabilities of the network based on access technology. This may include the capabilities to support real-time protocols, Quality of Service (QoS), and multicast, as well as general network capabilities.
- **Device capabilities:** The device capabilities database maintains information on all devices that access the network. Information in the device capabilities database may include screen resolution, protocol support, video player, and buffering capabilities. The device capabilities database is useful to understand what applications and application formats can actually be understood by the mobile device.
- **Subscriber self-care:** The subscriber self-care database includes information entered by the subscriber. This information may include subscriber preferences, interests, spending limits, and sub-account preferences.

Information from the various components of the Capabilities and Preference Exposure layer of the SDP architecture is useful standalone, but even more powerful when correlated against each other. For instance, although understanding a subscriber's preference for a certain sports team may be interesting for targeting specific content, it is only useful if the operator can ascertain what information the device can actually receive and display.

Data Integration

The Data Integration layer provides the correlation logic of the SDP architecture. Information from other layers, especially the Capabilities and Preference Exposure layer and Network layer, is correlated to make informed decisions about how to treat the subscriber. Although the correlated information may be used for numerous purposes in a service provider environment, three core functions provided by the Data Integration layer are as follows:

- **Policy Decision Function (PDF):** Discussed in Chapter 8, the PDF provides intelligent policy to the network on how to treat a subscriber. These policies may be charging-based, QoS-based, or network condition-based.
- **Analytics and Data Mining:** Information from external sources can also be analyzed through a data mining engine to extract information from existing databases and network elements. This information may then be used for numerous purposes, including service creation planning, fraud detection, and marketing-related tasks.
- **Advertising Decision Manager:** Information from external sources can also be used to create targeted advertising based on subscriber behavior, such as purchasing or web browsing history, subscriber location, or time-of-day. The Advertising Decision Manager correlates information to determine what advertisements should be generated to each subscriber, what format these advertisements should be sent in, and when these advertisements should be sent.

The Data Integration layer is a core element in assisting an operator in monetizing their network. By extracting information from the network and existing databases, an operator can determine trends, usage patterns, and behavioral patterns across a broad set of demographics and use this information to create a better user experience.

Although the functions provided in the Data Integration layer are important tools for a service provider, numerous privacy and human rights concerns have been raised. In the United States, the American Civil Liberties Union (ACLU) has fought numerous legislations and issued many precautions about these human rights concerns (http://www.aclu.org/privacy/internet/index.html).

Charging

The Charging layer provides prepaid and postpaid charging rules and correlation functions to the SDP architecture. As part of the integrated SDP system, the Charging layer has exposure to information from all other layers that may be used for three main functions, as follows:

- **Rating:** A rating engine provides real-time valuation to services and content transported across the network, including both hosted services and third-party services. The rating engine may adapt this valuation based on time-of-day, location, content source, or subscriber billing plan.
- **Bundling:** Bundling is a mechanism that service providers use to upsell additional content and services to existing subscribers. Long-used in the cable and telecom industry, bundles also are a means of eliminating competition through a "Single Bill" model, where a subscriber receives a single bill for multiple services.
- **Charging models:** Each operator employs different charging models. These charging models, discussed in Chapter 8, "End-to-End Context Awareness," may be prepaid or postpaid, based on time, volume, or event, or some combination. The SDP Charging layer provides relevant information such that the OSS billing platform may represent the usage activity accurately on the customer bill. For example, for an event-based service, the SDP Charging layer would provide information on what event occurred, when the event occurred, what the rating for the event was, and so on.

The functions provided by the Charging layer have wide-ranging applicability within the SDP architecture, and these functions may be leveraged both within the SDP and externally. Charging provided by this layer is applicable to both hosted operator content and third-party content. The Charging layer also relies heavily on other layers of SDP, as well as external sources to accurately determine the applicable charging and rating.

Portal

The portal provides a customer-facing interface and starting point for many mobile transactions. Mobile service providers take many different factors into account in generating the mobile portal, including subscriber preferences and history, advertising relationships, subscriber location, time-of-day, and available content in building a personalized portal from which a subscriber may retrieve information (news stories, sports scores, and so on), personalize their device (ringtones, music downloads, and so on), or manage their account (pay bill, change billing plan, and so on). By leveraging information from within the SDP framework, a mobile operator may turn the static home page environment of the past into an adaptive web portal customized to a particular subscriber's needs.

Network

The network provides the underlying layer of the SDP framework, allowing a mobile operator to capture real-time usage (per-tower, per-subscriber, per-service, and so on) and enforce on-the-fly policy rules.

Discussed in Chapter 8, bearer-path network elements, including Deep Packet Inspection (DPI) systems and Policy Enforcement Points (PEP), are just some of the Network-layer functions that both send and receive information to upper layers of the SDP framework.

Other elements at the Network layer may include the following:

- **Content transformation engines:** Content transformation engines rely on information such as device capabilities, network capabilities, and network conditions to determine how to format content so that it can be displayed on the user's device. A content transformation engine for video, as an example, may provide transcoding and transrating of the video based on the processor and memory of a mobile device.

Note Special classes of content transformation engines, known as content optimization engines, further consider network conditions when optimizing delivery of content. These devices optimize mobile networks for the delivery of TCP-based applications and protocols.

TCP algorithms such as slow-start, congestion avoidance, windowing, and retransmit timers, which were originally designed to provide stability in wireline networks, are proving to be inefficient in wireless networks. High latency and packet loss in wireless networks cause these TCP inefficiencies to manifest themselves in numerous ways, including underutilization of the air interface and excessive retransmissions.

The IETF Performance Implications on Link Characteristics working group has summarized the reasons for the poor performance of TCP in wireless networks, as follows:

- Wireless networks tend to be asymmetrical (higher download speeds than upload), resulting in ACK bottlenecks.
- High latency, excessive delay spikes, and frequent jitter provide tradeoffs between reliability and capacity.
- Implementation of effective loss-recovery mechanisms is problematic because 2.5G wireless networks are long, thin networks (LTN), as specified by RFC 2757. LTNs are characterized by long and varying link delays, asymmetric bandwidth, and unusually high and inconsistent error rates.
- Effective use of 3G wireless bandwidth enhancements is difficult because the 3G wireless networks are long, fat networks (LFN). LFNs are characterized by large bandwidth and long delay.
- Underutilization is prevalent because TCP back-off algorithms do not accurately interpret packet loss in wireless networks; these packets tend to be lost because of corruption, rather than congestion as in wired networks.
- Delay spikes and corruption bursts increase during mobile inter-cell handoffs.

Because of the high latency and high packet loss inherent in 2.5G and 3G wireless networks, as well as the constant fluctuations in available bandwidth, content optimization engines are being used to provide network functions such as TCP optimization, image compression, HTML optimization, and caching.

- **Advertising Insertion Engine:** Advertising Insertion Engines provide a mobile operator with the ability to insert advertising real-time into various pieces of content. These advertisements take on numerous different forms depending on the content type and mobile service provider preference. For example, a video advertisement may be pre-roll (that is, shown prior to the content request by the subscriber), post-roll (shown following the content request by the subscriber), or spliced (shown at various intervals throughout the content request by the subscriber). In most instances, the Advertising Insertion Engine is responsible only for receiving and advertisement and inserting it into the content stream. Analytics from the Advertising Decision Manager are used for determining advertising placement.

SDP Overlay Services

SDP Overlay services are those that may be leveraged by any of the existing layers. Such services include functions such as presence and location.

Presence

Presence technology is capable of showing real-time information on a particular subscriber. The information allows other subscribers who want to contact that particular subscriber about their availability and willingness to communicate.

Instant Messaging (IM) is the most widely used form of presence technology today. Most, if not all, IM clients include the ability to set a status message. These status messages may be generic, such as "Available" or "Do Not Disturb," to more detailed, with information ranging from time zone to office location.

In mobile networks, presence technology is especially relevant for two reasons: The subscriber has Multiple Points of Presence (MPoP) and the subscriber device moves constantly.

MPoPs

In today's communications environment, a subscriber has multiple devices (mobile phone, desk phone, laptop, and so on), connects to multiple networks (3G, commercial WiFi, home WiFi, corporate WiFi, and so on), and has multiple "profiles" (corporate identity and preferences, personal identity and preferences, and so on). This creates an environment where a subscriber may be reachable via a wide array of technologies, such as Short Message Service (SMS), voice call, Instant Message, or email.

Presence becomes a very powerful tool when information about which PoP a subscriber is connected to, what device the subscriber is currently using, and what method is best for communication can be communicated, in real-time, to other subscribers.

Figure 9-2 provides a few examples of how presence in a mobile environment may be used.

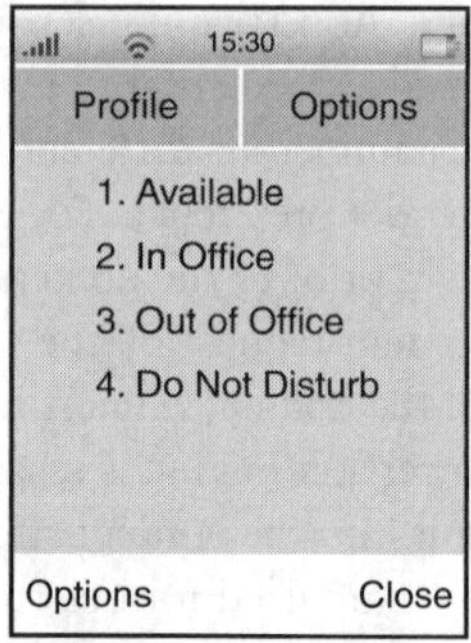

Figure 9-2 *Presence in a Mobile Environment*

Unified Communications (UC) environments provide tools for integrating and simplifying communications, relying heavily on presence. Although current UC has been an enterprise-hosted technology, hosted solutions that combine enterprise presence information and mobile service provider presence information through either network-based or device-based solutions are slowly emerging.

Figure 9-3 illustrates a mobile UC network environment.

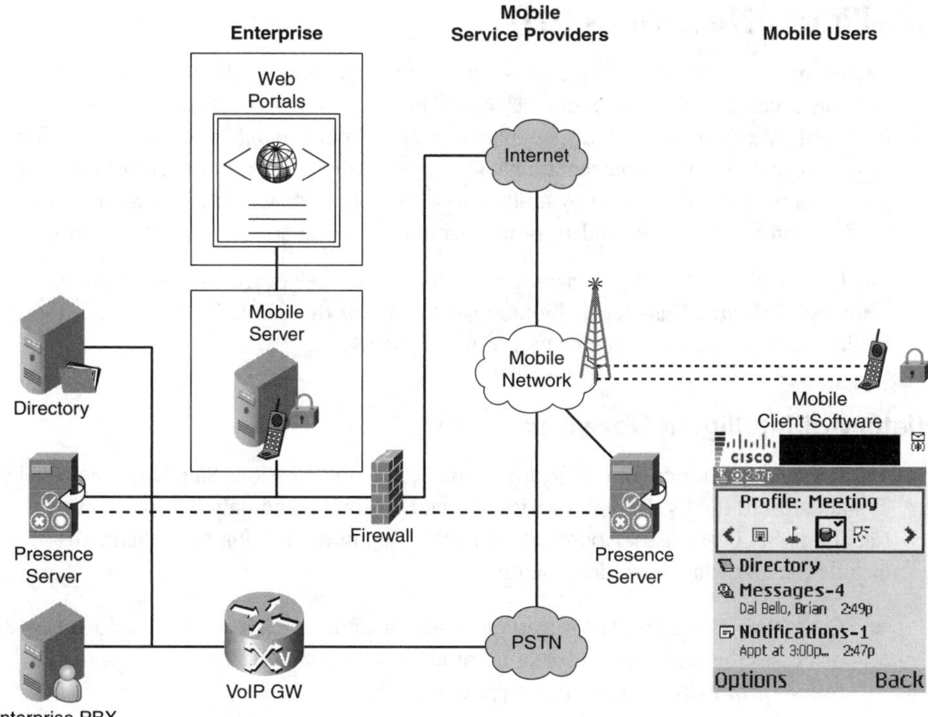

Figure 9-3 *Mobile Unified Communications*

Location

As discussed in the "Location Awareness" section of Chapter 8, a number of mechanisms are available for determining a mobile phone, and therefore a subscriber location. This location information allows mobile operators to enhance existing services such as mobile gaming, launch new services such as mobile dating, or monetize their network in new ways such as geomarketing.

Location awareness also allows a mobile operator to more-efficiently utilize resources within the SDP architecture, especially at the Network layer. By understanding where subscribers are and how they are moving, a mobile operator may proactively enforce QoS policies that maximize user Quality of Experience (QoE), pre-position content in a distributed cache environment, or transcode/transrate video content to available bandwidth.

Finally, location awareness helps mobile operators meet regulatory requirements for legal interception, such as the U.S.-based Communications Assistance to Law Enforcement Act (CALEA). The European Telecommunications Standards Institute (ETSI), in collaboration with the Third-Generation Partnership Project (3GPP), has defined TS 33.106 (http://www.3gpp.org/ftp/Specs/archive/33_series/33.106/), which defines requirements for legal interception. This specification requires that a mobile service provider be capable of sharing all location information and changes with the law enforcement agency.

Intelligent Networks (IN)

Intelligent Networks (IN) developed as a mechanism for adding advanced services to existing circuit switched telephony networks. Prior to IN models, all services were deployed directly into telephony switches, resulting in long integration times, complex solutions, and one-off implementations. Deploying contiguous services across all geographies was further complicated by multivendor environments, where integration to one vendor switch was an independent project from another vendor switch integration.

The IN, for all intents and purposes, can be considered one of the earliest mobile Service Delivery Platforms. This section looks at the history of the IN, the architecture and call model, and services that emerged as a result of the IN.

History of Intelligent Networks

The International Telecommunications Union Telecommunications Standards Sector (ITU-T) standardized the IN through a series of standards that commonly became known as Capability Set One (CS-1). Approved for publication in early 1994, these standards include the following seven documents:

- **Q.1210:** Q-Series Intelligent Network Recommendation Structure. This document discusses the organization structure of all documents in the CS-1 series and an overview of individual recommendations.
- **Q.1211:** Introduction to IN CS-1. This document defines the scope of the CS-1 standard, including a set of "benchmark" services upon which all CS-1 constructs would be tested.
- **Q.1213:** Global functional plane for CS-1. This document defines the Global Function Plane (GFP), which is the Service Logic layer of the IN.
- **Q.1214:** Distributed functional plane for CS-1. This document defines the Distributed Functional Plane (DFP) and the actual Functional Entities (FE), state model, and call/information flows.
- **Q.1215:** Physical plane for CS-1. This document defines how the individual FEs are interconnected.
- **Q.1218:** Intelligent Network Application Protocol for CS-1. This document defines the Intelligent Network Application Part (INAP), an ASN.1-based application layer-signaling protocol between IN elements.
- **Q.1219:** User guide for CS-1. This document provides service use-case examples and a more comprehensive understanding of the CS-1 implementation as a whole.

Since 1994, ETSI has further standardized and released CS-2 and CS-3 specifications. These specifications enhance the CS-1 protocols and features to allow for more advanced services to be deployed over the IN.

IN Architecture

The Intelligent Network is, first and foremost, an architecture. The IN, like the generic SDP architectures defined previously, focuses on the creation and provisioning of new services with the following guidelines:

- **The IN remains abstracted from the network type:** That is, the IN infrastructure is applicable to the Public Switched Telephone Network (PSTN), mobile networks, Integrated Services Digital Networks (ISDN), and various other types of telecommunications networks. The Physical Plane provides this abstraction layer.
- **The IN remains abstracted from the service:** That is, any service that can leverage the IN infrastructure, protocols, and capabilities may run as a service over the IN. The Global Functional Plane (GFP) provides this abstraction layer.
- **All network functions are modularized and reusable:** This eliminates the long integration cycles with existing core-switching systems. This is provided via the Distributed Functional Plane (DFP).
- **Flexibility and portability of functions between different physical entities:** As an architecture, IN does not define where functions must reside, or how functions may be combined—only that the functions are present.
- **Standardized communications:** Leveraging the INAP protocol and Signaling System 7 SS7 (discussed in this chapter) for communication between network functions.

Figure 9-4 illustrates the IN Conceptual Model (INCM), as defined in ITU-T Q.1201.

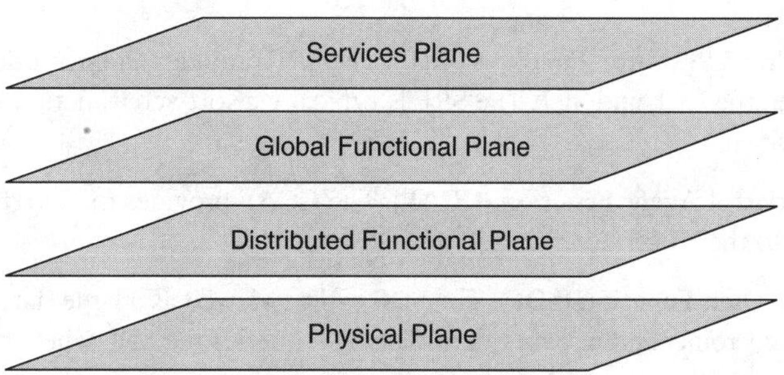

Figure 9-4 *IN Conceptual Model (INCM)*

The IN services plane decomposes commercial services into a set of service features. These service features encompass the 25 benchmark services defined in Q.1211, as well as numerous other services. The IN services plane includes functions that stretch from the SDP Capabilities/Preferences Exposure through the Network layer, although the services plane does not dictate how services are deployed within the network.

The IN global functional plane (GFP) describes Service Information Blocks (SIB) as part of the service creation process. These SIBs are abstracted functional units that link service features to network functions, and create a service model for how to combine service functions into an implementable network flow.

The bottom layers of the model—the distributed functional plane and physical plane—define the network functions and platforms responsible for execution of a service within the IN environment.

IN Distributed Functional Plane

The IN distributed functional plane (DFP) further decomposes a SIB into a series of network functions, known as Functional Entities (FE). Nine functional entities are defined as follows:

- **Call Control Function CCF:** The CCF can best be represented as a call exchange, responsible for all call and connection handling. The CCF also provides network connection services.
- **Service Switching Function (SSF):** The SSF is tightly coupled with the CCF. The SSF maintains a Basic Call State Machine (BCSM), representing the state of call from start to finish. When the SSF sees a service request from the CCF, the SSF interprets the request, determines the current call state, builds a query, and sends this query to the SCF.
- **Service Control Function (SCF):** The SCF is the "brains" of the IN. The SCF is responsible for all service logic execution and influences call logic on the CCF via the SRF.
- **Specialized Resource Function (SRF):** The SRF provides an interaction layer between the CCF and SCF. The SRF is typically a software function residing as part of the SSF.
- **Call Control Agent Function (CCAF):** The CCAF provides the interface for user access to the IN services.
- **Service Data Function (SDF):** The SDF can be viewed as a large database, responsible for customer and network data. The SCF queries the SDF when executing an IN service.
- **Service Creation Environment Function (SCEF):** The SCEF is the creation environment that allows an operator to develop, test, and deploy a new service function. The SCEF communicates to the IN network infrastructure through the SMF.
- **Service Management Function (SMF):** The SMF is the management environment that allows for deployment, provisioning, and ongoing management of a service function.
- **Service Management Access Function (SMAF):** The SMAF provides the interface for service managers to communicate and interact with the SMF.

Figure 9-5 depicts the IN DFP model described previously.

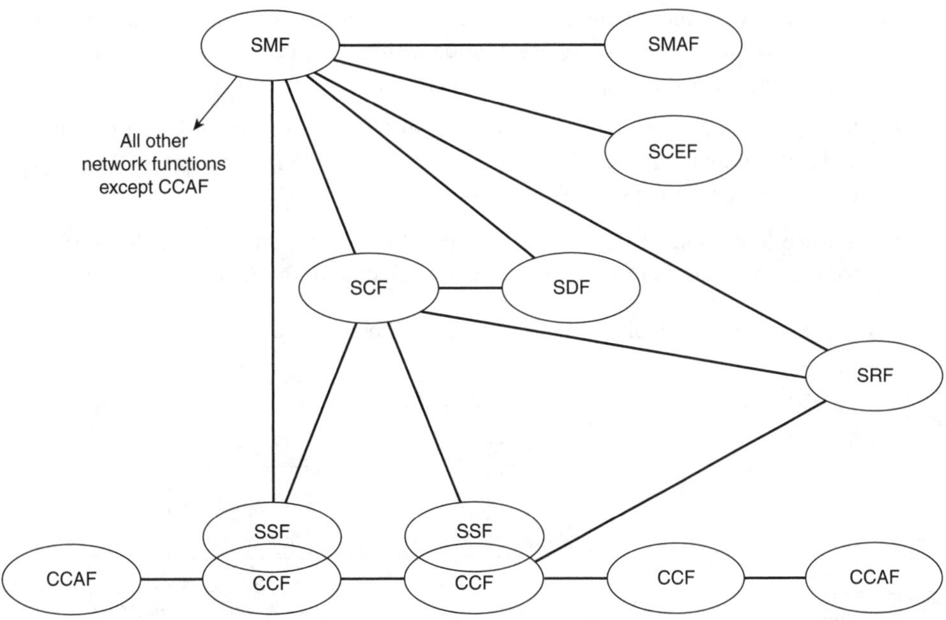

Figure 9-5 *IN DFP Model*

IN Physical Plane

The IN physical plane defines the actual IN architecture. Within this plane, each of the functional entities defined in the DFP are mapped into a physical entity (PE). The following PEs are defined within the IN architecture:

- **Service Control Point (SCP):** The SCP contains both the SCF and SDF. The SCP, therefore, inherently contains both the service logic and the call processing data required to implement an IN service. In a mobile network, the Home Location Register (HLR) is an example of a SCP.
- **Service Data Point (SDP):** The SDP provides the platform upon which the SDF resides. The SDP contains both customer and network data.
- **Service Switching Point (SSP):** The SSP contains both the SSF and CCF, in addition to optional CCAF and SRF. The SSP is the node responsible for all call processing and call routing within the IN. In a mobile network, the Mobile Switching Center (MSC) is an example of a SSP.
- **Network Access Point (NAP):** The NAP is an optional element that provides the CCF and CCAF as decomposed elements of the SSP. The NAP is nothing more than the traditional telephone exchange. The NAP has the ability to recognize which calls require IN services and route those calls appropriately to the SSP.

- **Intelligent Peripheral (IP):** The IP is composed of a SRF. The IP is the network element that interacts directly with the subscriber when invoking a service function.
- **Service Management Point (SMP):** The SMP is comprised of the SMF and SMAF, and is therefore the key management node within the IN architecture for provisioning, deploying, and managing service functions.
- **Service Creation Environment Point (SCEP):** The SCEP is comprised of the SCEF, and is therefore the key service creation node within the IN architecture for creating, testing, and deploying service functions.
- **Service Management Access Function (SMAF):** The SMAF provides the interface for service managers to communicate and interact with the SMF.

Figure 9-6 depicts the IN physical model described previously.

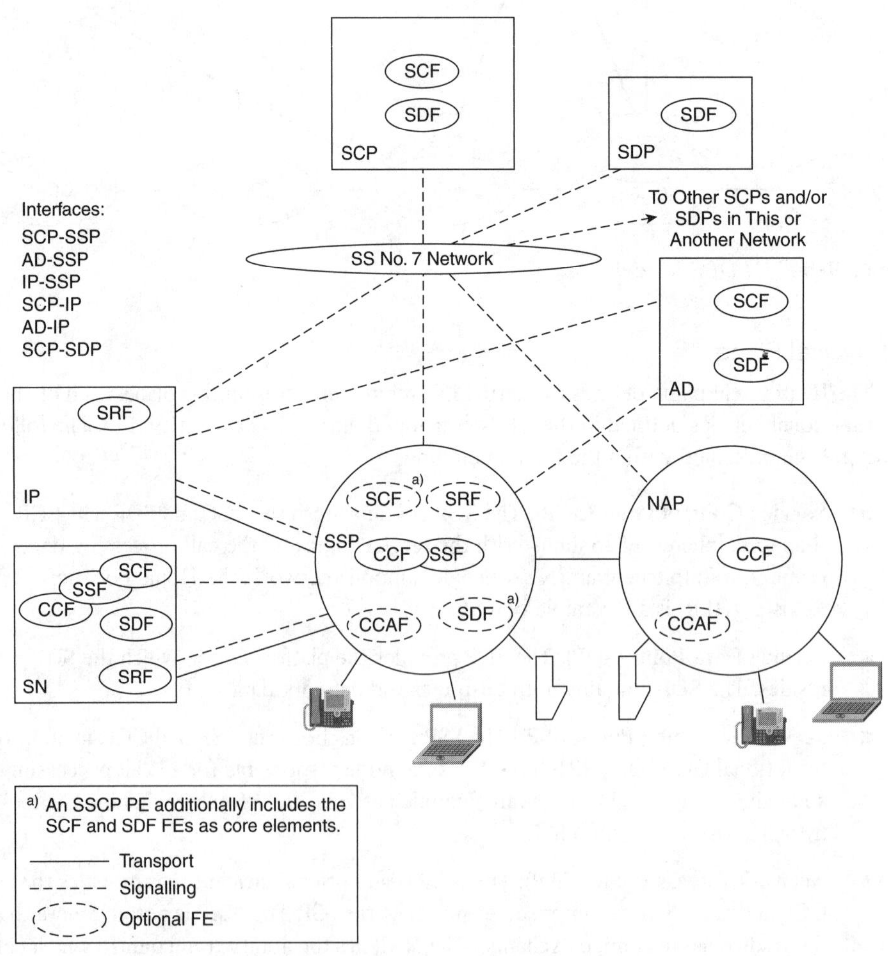

Figure 9-6 *IN Physical Model*

Elements within the IN infrastructure communicate with each other via the SS7 network, using the IN Application Part (INAP).

Mobile IN

Although IN has had moderate success in the wired world, the IN architecture and standards have played a key role in the evolution of mobile networks. Many GSM networks leverage INAP for operator-specific services, such as mobile Virtual Private Network (VPN), call screening, and virtual Private Branch Exchange (PBX). These INAP-based solutions have led to numerous problems, including challenges with supporting roaming subscribers.

In response, GSM standards (2.0 and 2.0+) began to include specifications for supplementary services. Standardization of supplementary services hurt operator capabilities for differentiation of services, leading many MSC vendors to build IN functions into their switches. This allows the MSC to function as an intelligent SSP with direct access to an IN SCP.

Figure 9-7 depicts this MSC/SSP integration model.

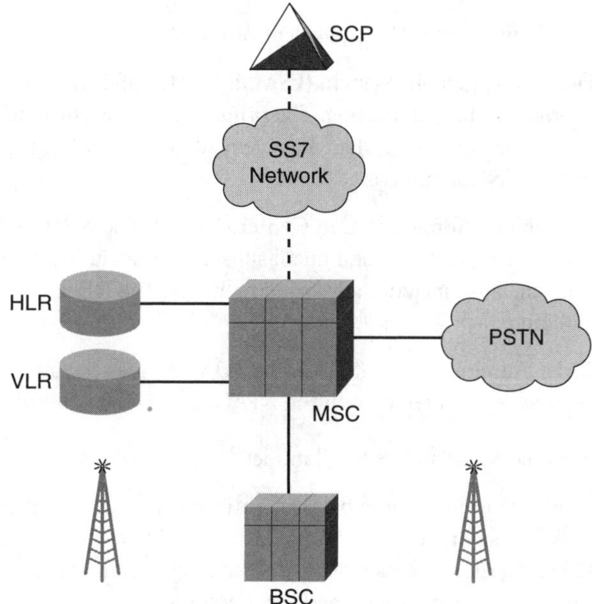

Figure 9-7 *MSC/SSP Integration Model*

The lack of a standard implementation model and operator-specific implementations of proprietary INAP solutions led to the publication of the GSM Customized Applications for Mobile network Enhanced Logic (CAMEL) standards. The CAMEL standards and architecture allows mobile operators to provide advanced IN services to both home and roaming subscribers. CAMEL functional evolution over time includes the inclusion of General Packet Radio Service (GPRS) control and CS-2-like features, such a Call Party Handling (CPH).

Local/Mobile Number Portability

Although numerous services have been deployed on existing IN architectures, implementation of a Local/Mobile Number Portability (LNP/MNP) solution is perhaps the most prevalent. LNP/MNP allows subscribers to move to a different operator without forcing them to change their phone number. After a few extensions, MNP was deployed in February 2002.

Architecturally, the components required for MNP include the following:

- MSC
- SCP
- **SCP Management Server:** The equivalent of the IN SMP.
- **Local Service Management System (LSMS):** The LSMS is the database that contains all information for call routing. The primary functions include subscription management, error processing, data management, and event logging. The LSMS is the SDF of the MNP architecture.
- **Number Portability Administration Center (NPAC):** The NPAC is a centralized database that includes information on all subscribers, including their current service provider. The database includes all ported numbers. The NPAC is the SMF of the MNP architecture.
- **Service Order Administration (SOA):** The SOA provides the interfaces that allow the service provider to interact with the NPAC. This is the equivalent of the SMAF.

Figure 9-8 depicts the MNP architectural model.

As mobile networks continue their evolution, both transport and control elements move into the IP domain. As such, newer technologies and architectures have evolved to supplant the IN. However, the principles of the IN remain intact, and are a reference point for understanding these new technologies and architectures.

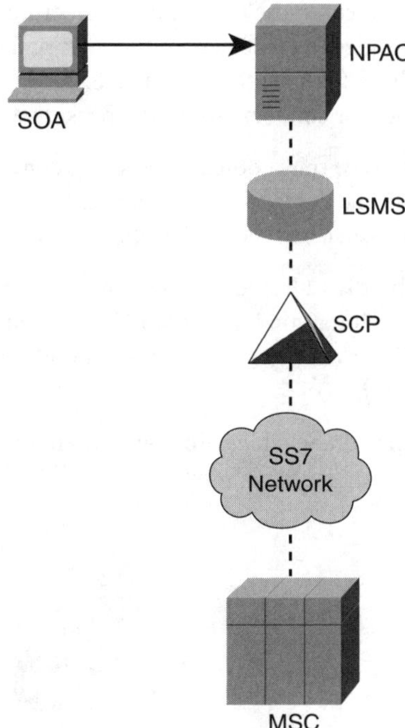

Figure 9-8 *MNP Architectural Model*

Softswitches

Softswitches are a transition mechanism in the evolution of a circuit-switched network to a packet-switched network. A softswitch provides call control intelligence for establishing, maintaining, routing, and terminating voice calls. The softswitch also provides an interface to enhanced service and application platforms, known as Feature Servers. These softswitches allow a mobile operator to leverage the inherent cost reductions of IP while seamlessly operating with the legacy circuit-switched infrastructure.

Today's architecture for this transition encompasses three elements: Call Agent, Media Gateway (MGW), and Feature Server.

The Call Agent is the control element in the transition architecture. The Call Agent is responsible for numerous control-path functions, including charging, call routing, and call signaling. On the northbound interface, the Call Agent interfaces with one or more Feature Server. On the southbound interface, the Call Agent interfaces and controls one or more Media Gateways.

The Feature Server is similar to the IN SCP. The Feature Server provides call-related functions that are triggered by the call-handling function of the Call Agent. When triggered, these functions are implemented in the bearer path by the MGW.

The MGW is the bearer element in the transition architecture. The MGW stitches together multiple access technologies to create a path for voice and data traffic. These interfaces may consist of T1/E1 for connectivity to the PSTN, ATM for connectivity to GSM BSCs or MSCs, or Ethernet for connectivity to the packet-switched or VoIP domains.

The MGW also performs voice transcoding or protocol conversion to allow an end-to-end call to span these multiple domains. In addition, the MGW also performs typical media-streaming functions, such as echo cancellation.

The MGW is controlled by the Call Agent using either Media Gateway Control Protocol (MGCP), H.248, or Session Initiation Protocol (SIP). H.248 and SIP are addressed later in this chapter. Because MGCP is not heavily used in a mobile environment, it will not be addressed.

Figure 9-9 depicts a mobile softswitch environment where both the Call Agent and Feature Server are embedded in a MSC Server.

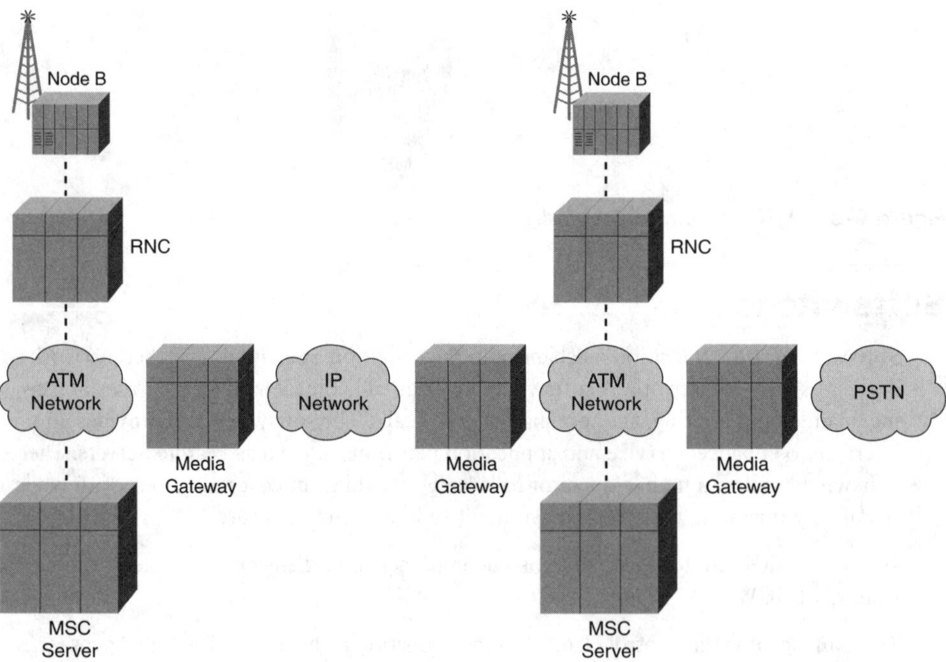

Figure 9-9 *Mobile Softswitch Environment*

Voice Over IP

Voice over IP (VoIP), as the name implies, is a mechanism for taking analog voice signals, digitizing them, and transporting them over a packet network. The circuit-switched networks upon which over 100 years of voice calls have occurred are being replaced by newer, packet-switched networks built on IP. This is occurring across all networks, from major residential phone providers (AT&T) to cable networks to over-the-top providers (such as Vonage). These packet-switched networks are cheaper to operate and more efficient, while providing the same or greater reliability (when properly implemented!) as the legacy telephony systems.

Voice Signaling

Voice signaling protocols are those used in the session establishment and teardown of voice calls. The information transported in these signaling messages are those relevant for call establishment, including dialed phone number, caller ID information, call waiting "beep," charging information, and so on. Even a dial tone itself is provided with signaling.

Signaling System #7 is the predominant signaling protocol used in the Public Switched Telephone Network (PSTN).

Signaling System #7 (SS7)

SS7 is an internationally-standardized protocol stack standardized by ITU for telephony signaling. Although ITU Q.700-series documents define a single SS7 protocol, national standards have evolved differently, creating numerous variants of the SS7 protocol, each with unique capabilities. Rather than discussing each of the national variants, this book focuses on the architectures, elements, and capabilities of SS7.

SS7 is an out-of-band signaling method. Out-of-band signaling uses a unique path through the network as bearer traffic. This allows for SS7 to communicate information between network elements via independent signaling links.

Note SS7 does not extend signaling to the end device; it is used only for communicating call information between network elements.

This out-of-band signaling network consists of three key elements: the previously discussed Signaling Switching Point (SSP) and the Signaling Control Point (SCP), and a third element, the Signaling Transfer Point (STP), which is the packet-switching element in the SS7 architecture. Although no messages originate from the STP, it provides message screening, firewalling, and routing of messages between intelligent endpoints.

Elements within SS7 communicate via either a TDM or ATM network. Each element is addressed via a unique Point Code (PC), similar to an IP address in the IP domain. Standard length of an International Signaling Point Code (ISPC) is 14 bits.

Note As noted earlier, each national standard varies. For example, PC length for North America and China is 24 bits, whereas Japanese PC length is 16 bits.

Figure 9-10 depicts an SS7 architecture, including SSPs, STPs, and SCPs.

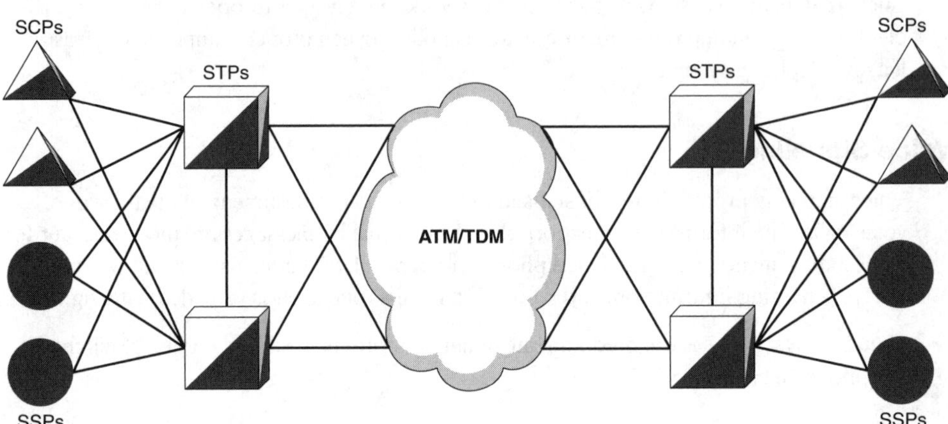

Figure 9-10 *SS7 Architecture*

The figure also highlights two important design considerations in the typical deployment model for STPs and SSPs, as follows:

- **Mated pairs:** Each signaling node in a mated pair performs the same functions. This provides platform resiliency to the SS7 network.
- **Quads:** STPs are interconnected with four sets of links. This provides link and path resiliency to the SS7 network.

SS7 Links

An SS7 link is the physical transmission that connects signaling nodes in the SS7 network. These links are typically serial (56 kbps or 64 kbps) links or DS0 channels. Six link types are defined, based on their role in the SS7 network. Although each of these links uses the same protocol stack, the information carried across the links, and the signaling nodes they interconnect, are different. The link types defined in SS7 are as follows:

- **Access Links (A-Links):** A-Links, illustrated in Figure 9-11, are used to interconnect the STP with signaling endpoints. These endpoints may be either the SSP or SCP. A-Links carry signaling information to these endpoints. Each signaling endpoint has a "home" STP for both ingress and egress traffic.

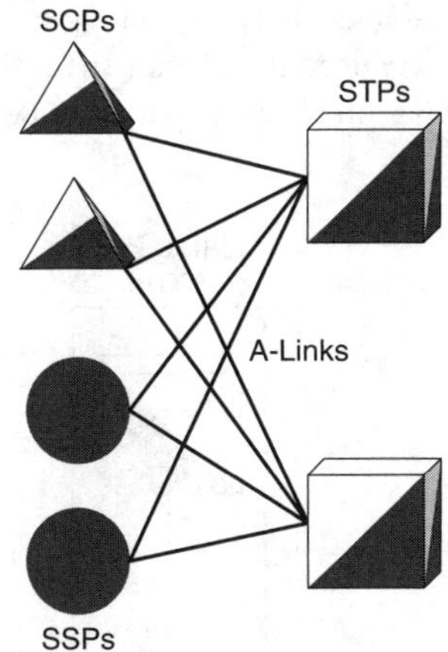

Figure 9-11 *A-Links*

- **Bridge Links (B-Links) and Diagonal Links (D-Links):** B-Links and D-Links, illustrated in Figure 9-12, are used to interconnect STPs (that is, Quads). B-Links are used to connect STPs at the same hierarchical level, whereas D-Links are used to connect STPs at different hierarchical levels.

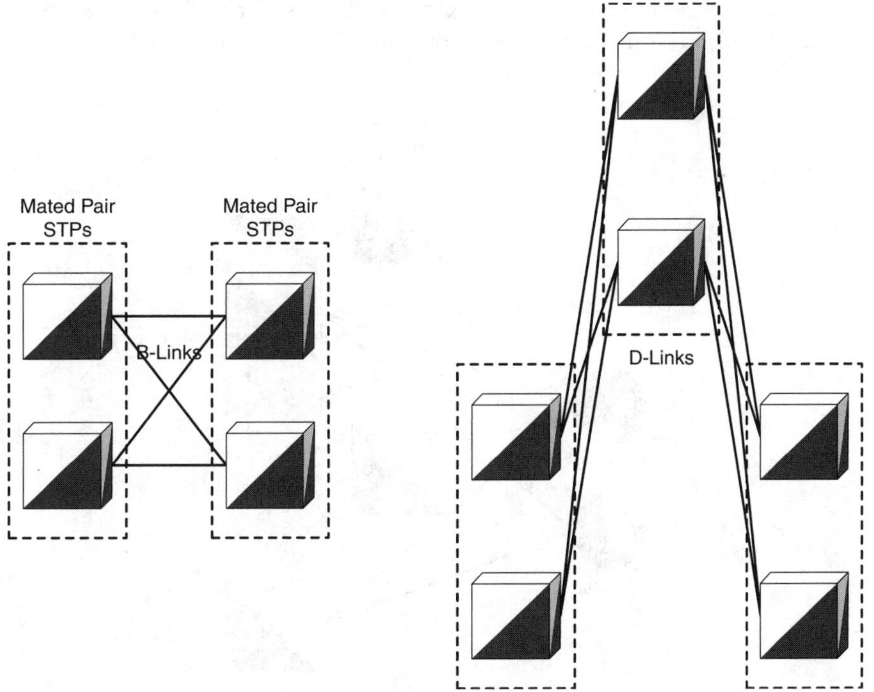

Figure 9-12 *B-Links and D-Links*

- **Cross Links (C-Links):** C-Links, illustrated in Figure 9-13, are the links between Mated STPs. These links are used to enhance the resiliency of the SS7 network and are only used if the STP has no alternate path to a destination code point.

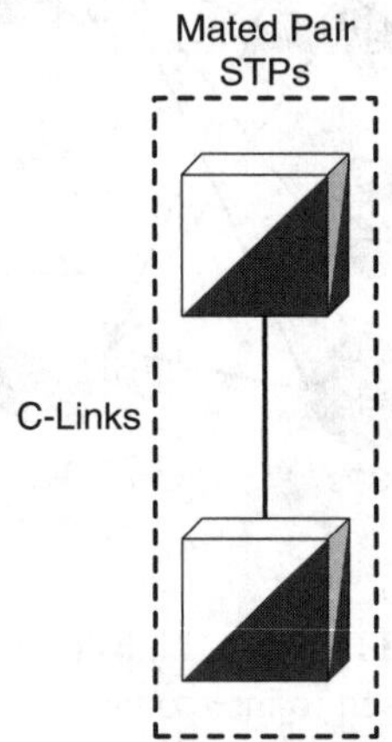

Figure 9-13 *C-Links*

- **Extended Links (E-Links):** E-Links, illustrated in Figure 9-14, are additional links used for resiliency that connect a SSP to a secondary pair of STPs. These links are used in the event that the A-links to the "home" STP are not available.

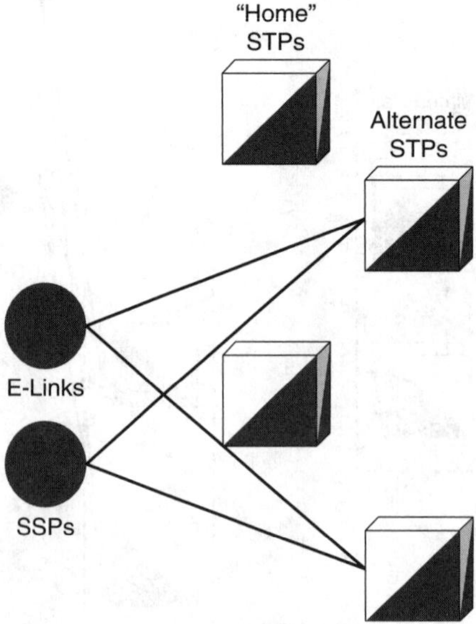

Figure 9-14 *E-Links*

- **Fully Associated Links (F-Links):** F-Links, illustrated in Figure 9-15, directly connect two signaling endpoints. These F-Links are typically not deployed in networks with STPs because they allow direct communication between endpoints, which bypasses the security features within the STP.

Figure 9-15 *F-Links*

SS7 Protocol Stack

The SS7 protocol is packet-switched and maps very closely to the OSI model discussed in Chapter 4. Figure 9-16 illustrates the SS7 protocol stack.

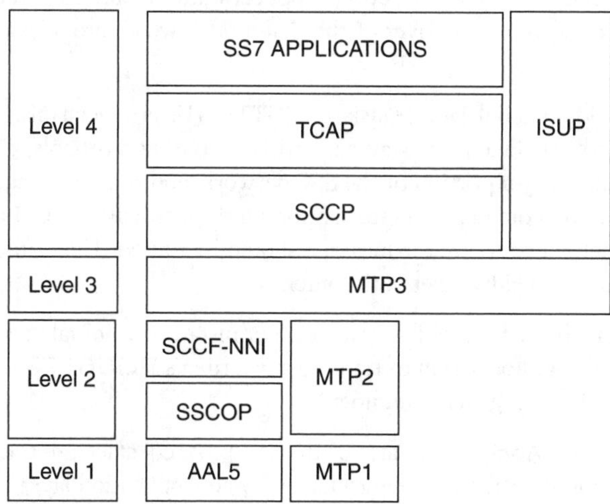

Figure 9-16 *SS7 Protocol Stack*

The SS7 protocol stack defines the following functions:

- **Level 1:** The Physical layer.
- **Level 2:** The Data Link layer.
- **Level 3:** The Network layer.
- **Level 4:** Higher-layer protocols, including User and Application functions.

Together, Level 1 through Level 3 are called the Message Transfer Part (MTP).

MTP MTP consists of three levels that map very closely to the Physical, Data Link, and Network layer of the OSI model. These layers provide the basic functions of network element connectivity and message exchange. All signaling nodes in the SS7 network implement the MTP.

MTP Level 1, or MTP-1, provides the physical layer attributes of the signaling links, such as electrical characteristics. The physical interfaces defined for SS7 include DS0, E1, DS1, DS0A, and V.35.

MTP Level 2, or MTP-2, provides the procedures for transmitting messages reliably across the signaling link. Functions such as flow control, message sequence validation, and error checking are performed at this layer.

MTP Level 3, or MTP-3, provides the functions for network transport. These functions include addressing (Point Codes), routing, convergence (re-routing in the event of a failure), and congestion control.

Signaling Connection Control Part (SCCP) SCCP, part of Level 4, provides specialized routing functions. SCCP is typically implemented in all SS7 signaling nodes. Although the MTP only defines how to route traffic to a particular signaling endpoint via PCs, SCCP provides more granular capabilities to route traffic to a particular application. This allows an endpoint to use the correct SS7 application for a particular message. This function is similar to the Transport layer of the OSI model, which provides protocol/port information.

SCCP also provides Global Title Translation (GTT). GTT is a mechanism of summarizing PCs across a network. Like route summarization in routing protocols, GTT allows signaling nodes to learn only a portion of the SS7 network, and route messages to other signaling nodes that have more detailed information on the destination PC. Each STP maintains a database to determine where the message should be routed. This database is similar to a routing table maintained by a network router.

GTT is a key capability for mobile networks. For instance, at initial network entry, GTT is used based on IMSI information to find the subscriber's HLR. GTT is also used to find a MSC/VLR based on a registered number.

Application Parts Application Parts of the SS7 protocol stack are transported using SCCP. Application Parts map closely to Layer 7 (the Application layer) of the OSI model, and enable enhanced or advanced functionality (such as IN services) over the SS7 network. Application Parts are typically implemented in signaling endpoints. STPs do not need to understand the Application Part to transport the message to the destination PC.

Some common examples of Application Parts include the following:

- **Transaction Capabilities Application Part (TCAP):** TCAP is used for database communication and to establish a transaction between two nodes. In the mobile network, these databases include the Home Location Register (HLR), Visitor Location Register (VLR), and Mobile Number Portability (MNP) database.

- **Mobile Application Part (MAP):** MAP is used to share mobile subscriber information, such as Mobile Identification Number (MIN) and serial number of the mobile device. This information is used by the IS-41 protocol (see Chapter 6, "Mobile Core Evolution") during roaming.

Note Many mobile operators use the Specialized Resource Function (SRF) in the STP to intercept and re-route MAP signaling messages to provide Mobile Number Portability.

- **Operations, Maintenance, and Administration Part (OMAP):** OMAP is used for diagnosing link troubles, validating routing tables, and performing other administrative tasks in the SS7 network. These OMAP messages may be transported over SCCP (when a particular signaling node application status is required), or over MTP (when signaling node status is required).

ISDN Signaling User Part (ISUP) ISUP is used in both the PSTN and ISDN networks for call session establishment over MTP-3. A standard voice call can be broken down into three phases: setup, conversation, and release. ISUP provides both call setup and release functions, as well as some mid-call signaling capabilities for invoking supplementary services.

Note Bearer Independent Call Control (BICC) is a signaling protocol based on ISUP, specified for call control and transport over any bearer network, including ATM and IP. 3GPP defines BICC for UMTS call control as part of 3GPP R4.

There are three message types used in call setup. These include the following:

- **Initial Address Message (IAM):** This message includes all information necessary to establish a call: calling party number, called party number, and information about the bearer circuit.
- **Address Complete Message (ACM):** This message is sent in response to the IAM to notify that the call can be completed, as requested.

Note After the ACM has been sent, ringing is applied at the destination and ring back is applied at the origination. Today, these ringback tones are customizable in part due to the Internet model discussed in the "SS7oIP/SIGTRAN" section of this chapter.

- **Answer Message (ANM):** This message is sent when the destination party answers the phone (phone off-hook). At this point, the call is fully established.

There are two message types used in call teardown. These include the following:

- **Release Message (REL):** When one of the parties hangs up the phone, the local SSP sends this message to the other party's SSP to notify that the bearer channel can be released.
- **Release Complete Message (RLC):** This message is sent as an acknowledgment to the REL message and signals that the circuit has been released.

Figure 9-17 illustrates both call setup and teardown ISUP messages.

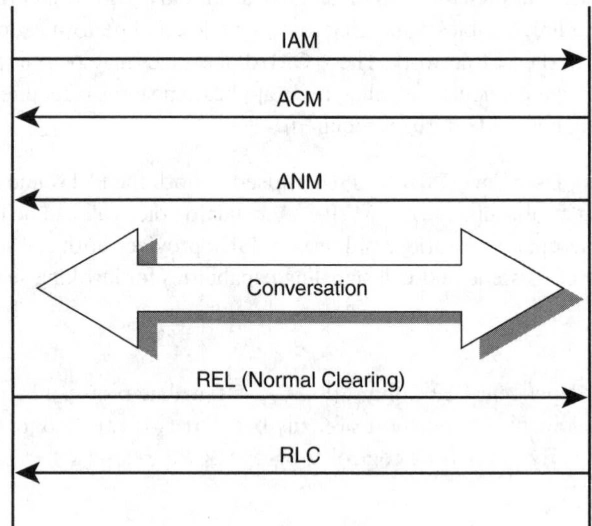

Figure 9-17 *ISUP Messages*

SS7 Signaling Units

Signaling Units (SU) are the messages used by the SS7 network for encapsulating signaling information. The SS7 protocol defines three SUs, as follows:

- **Message Signaling Units (MSUs):** MSUs are used in the SS7 network for transferring upper-level information, such as SCCP or Application Part information, throughout the network. All signaling associated with a call is sent via MSUs. In addition, MSUs are used for communicating route management information, such as route updates in the event of a failed signaling node. Because MSUs are transported across the entire SS7 network from originating PC to destination PC, each MSU contains information used in the routing process.

- **Link Status Signal Units (LSSUs):** LSSUs are used to bring links into alignment. Information on link status is communicated using LSSUs. After a link has achieved alignment, LSSUs are no longer sent. Because LSSUs are only used on a particular link, there is no addressing information associated with LSSUs.
- **Fill-In Signaling Units (FISUs):** FISUs are sent across idle links when there is no relevant signaling information to communicate. If no messages were being transported on a link, signaling nodes connected to that link have no way to detect link errors. FISUs are sent in order to detect link error information as quickly as possible to provide minimal interruption to service.

Short Message Service (SMS)

Aside from call setup/teardown and mobility/roaming, one of the most popular uses of the SS7 network for mobile operators is the transport of SMS messages. SMS relies on the SS7 MAP for transmission between subscribers.

A Short Message Service Center (SMSC) resides on the SS7 network for providing a store-and-forward function. When a message is received, the SMSC stores the message until it is able to successfully deliver the message. The SMSC relies on the Visiting Location Register (VLR) database to provide feature and user authentication, as well as subscriber location and routing information.

Figure 9-18 provides an architectural view of the SMS network.

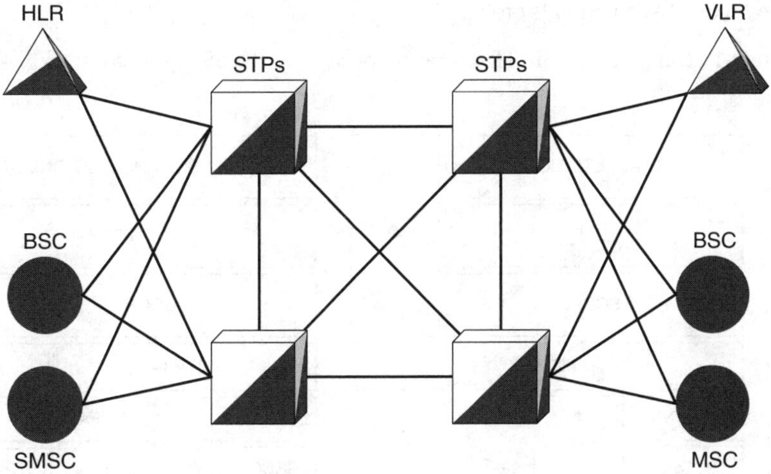

Figure 9-18 *SMS Architecture*

SS7oIP/SIGTRAN

Signaling Transport (SIGTRAN) is an IETF-defined standard that provides an architectural model for transporting signaling, such as SS7, over an IP network. SIGTRAN is an offload mechanism similar to those described in Chapter 7, "Offloading Traditional Networks with IP." SIGTRAN provides many of the common advantages that are seen with other circuit-to-packet transitions, including simplified deployment (SIGTRAN is an overlay on an existing IP network), CAPEX reductions (standard IP transport nodes can be used), scalability (IP networks scale better and are more efficient than circuit-switched networks), and the ability to deploy advanced IP services (via a signaling gateway, discussed later in this section).

SS7 networks have always had an inherent scalability challenge that was partially alleviated by creating *linksets*, or bundles of links, that act as a single communications path. With the dramatic increase in traffic over SS7 networks due to mobile devices and SMS, SIGTRAN provides mobile operators with a solution to this bandwidth problem. Signaling Gateways (SG), which provide an interface between the traditional SS7 network and the SIGTRAN network, allow an operator to transport SS7 traffic over IP networks without interrupting or upgrading existing signaling nodes (SCP, SSP, and so on).

The SIGTRAN architectural model is built on three components: an IP transport layer, the Stream Control Transmission Protocol (SCTP), and an Adaptation Protocol. These Adaptation Protocols allow the SG to transport upper-layer SS7 messages (MTP-3, SCCP) over a traditional IP network. Examples of Adaptation Protocols include MTP-2 Peer-to-Peer Adaptation (M2PA) layer, MTP-2 User Adaptation (M2UA) layer, and MTP-3 User Adaptation (M3UA) layer. These Adaptation Protocols are discussed layer in this chapter, in the section "Adaptation Protocols."

Figure 9-19 compares the SIGTRAN protocol stack to the SS7 protocol stack.

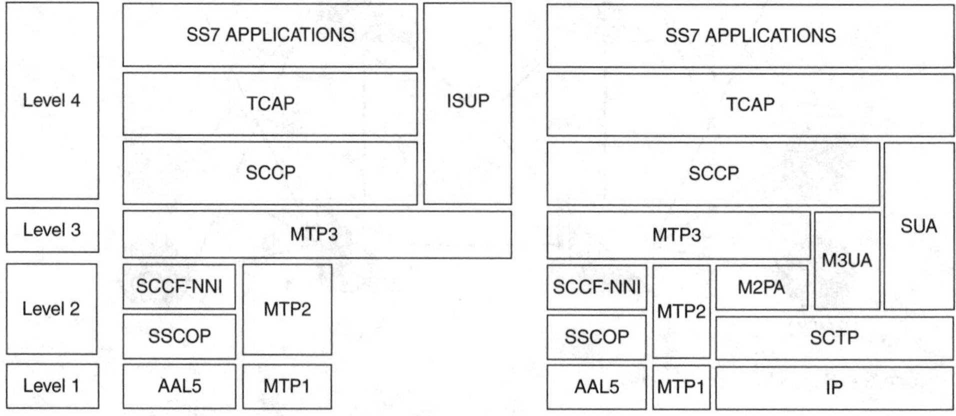

Figure 9-19 *SIGTRAN Protocol Stack vs. SS7 Protocol Stack*

Stream Control Transmission Protocol (SCTP)

SCTP (RFC 2960) was designed to transport SS7 signaling over IP networks in lieu of TCP. Although TCP has proven to be a reliable protocol for transporting data traffic, some fundamental limitations imposed by TCP made the protocol less-than-optimal for the transport of SS7 signaling messages. These limitations include the following:

- **Real-time transport:** As discussed in Chapter 4, "An IP Refresher," TCP is a reliable transport protocol. TCP uses acknowledgments as a mechanism to confirm delivery of packets and sequencing as a mechanism for ordered delivery. These mechanisms add unnecessary delay to message flows, resulting in sub-optimal delivery of real-time traffic, such as SS7.
- **Multihoming support:** TCP sockets are inflexible to multihoming of signaling nodes to create redundant paths.
- **Stream-oriented:** TCP is stream-oriented and does not respect the boundaries of actual messages carried. By transporting byte streams, TCP forces guarantees the reliability only of bytes rather than integrity of the original message.
- **Security issues:** TCP has numerous security vulnerabilities, including susceptibility to Denial-of-Service attacks.

Note Although SCTP was originally designed as a transport protocol for SIGTRAN, SCTP can also be used for other real-time transmissions. For instance, the DIAMETER protocol (see Chapter 8, "End-to-End Context Awareness") specifies SCTP as an optional transport layer.

SCTP protocol layer sits on top of the IP protocol, equivalent to the Transport layer of the OSI stack.

The primary function of SCTP is reliable transport of messages between SCTP endpoints. These endpoints form an association, or connection with each other prior to data transmission. Once this association is created, SCTP users, or Adaptation Protocols, may use the connection for transport of messages.

Figure 9-20 depicts a SCTP association.

SCTP Functions The SCTP protocol is split into a SIGTRAN protocol stack with various functions, as illustrated in Figure 9-21.

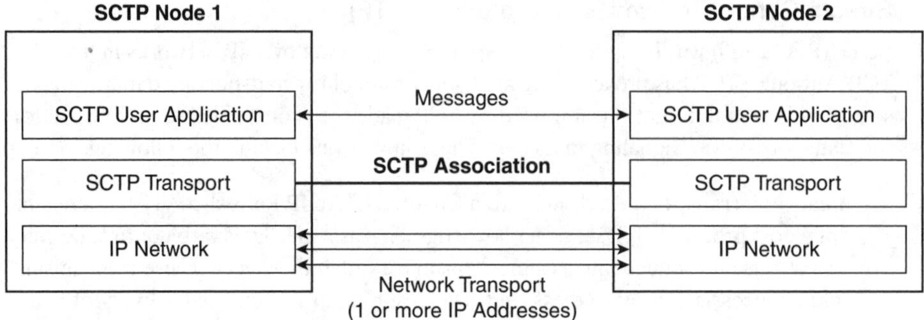

Figure 9-20 *SCTP Association*

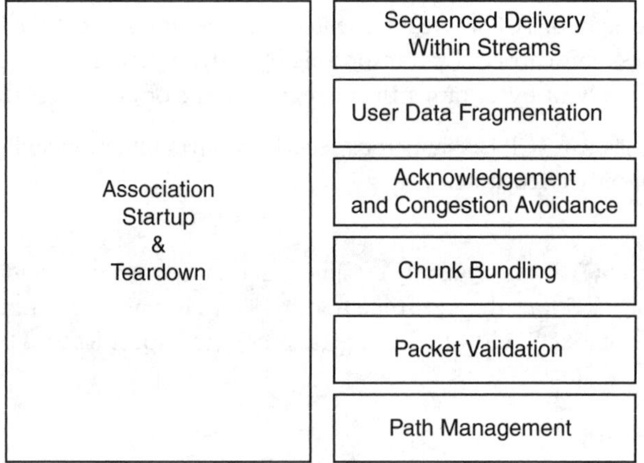

Figure 9-21 *SCTP Functional Diagram*

The functions provided by SCTP include the following:

- **Association startup and teardown:** When a SCTP user requests a connection, an association is established. This association startup uses a cookie that includes a four-way handshake. This four-way handshake provides a layer of security above the three-way handshake that TCP uses.

  The teardown process includes either a graceful or ungraceful close. A graceful close enables a SCTP user to complete a message transfer prior to closing the association. An ungraceful close forces the association to close immediately.

- **Sequenced delivery within streams:** A single association may include multiple streams. Each of these streams is the transmission of multiple messages, or transactions, between the SCTP users. SCTP ensures that a particular message within a stream is transmitted prior to other messages within the same stream.

- **User data fragmentation:** SCTP supports fragmentation in order to comply with path limits. SCTP will re-assemble these fragments into a complete message before passing to the SCTP user.
- **Acknowledgment and congestion avoidance:** Each message in a stream is assigned a Transaction Sequence Number (TSN). The receiving SCTP node acknowledges receipt of each TSN. This method ensures that transmission reliability includes message integrity.

Congestion avoidance mechanisms are similar to those used in TCP. These mechanisms are applied to the entire SCTP association, and not to individual streams. Functions such as SCTP slow-start and windowing are used to detect and avoid congestion. SCTP congestion avoidance mechanisms include:

- **Chunk bundling:** SCTP delivers packets within a single stream with a common header and one or more chunks. Each of the chunks for a particular message has the same TSN.
- **Packet validation:** Each packet includes a packet verification field as a security mechanism and a checksum to detect data corruption during transmission.
- **Path management:** At association startup, a primary network path (destination IP address) is determined. The path management function monitors each available path and notifies the SCTP user when one of these paths in not available.

Adaptation Protocols

There are numerous Adaptation Protocols that may leverage the services of SCTP. As illustrated in Figure 9-18, SIGTRAN includes three Adaptation Protocols: M2PA, M3UA, and SCCP User Adaptation (SUA).

M2PA M2PA provides a transport mechanism for MTP-3 to be transported over IP links. The MTP-3 layer is unaltered for transmission, and thinks it is communicating with a standard MTP-2 layer. M2PA is typically used in SS7oIP Core networks because all MTP-2 features are preserved, including acknowledgments and retransmissions.

Because MTP-3 is unaltered, all features and functions provided by MTP-3 in a traditional SS7 network, including high availability and routing, remain in the SS7 domain.

Note Because MTP-3 remains in the signaling node, each signaling node is addressable via a SS7 Point Code.

Figure 9-22 depicts a SG with M2PA.

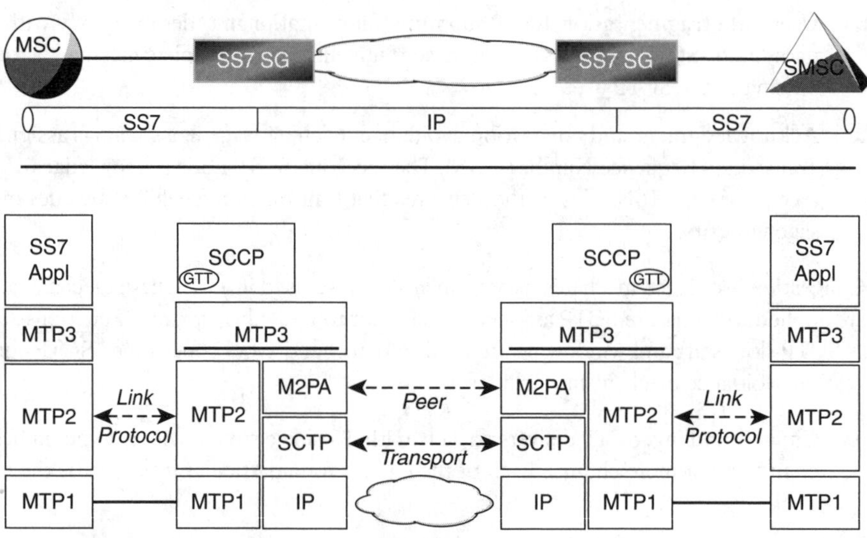

Figure 9-22 *Signaling Gateway with M2PA*

With M2PA, a mobile operator can leverage the efficiencies of IP transport without forcing expensive upgrades to existing TDM-based SS7 nodes, such as MSCs, HLRs, and VLRs. Figure 9-23 provides a deployment example where M2PA is used to transport SS7 traffic over an IP network.

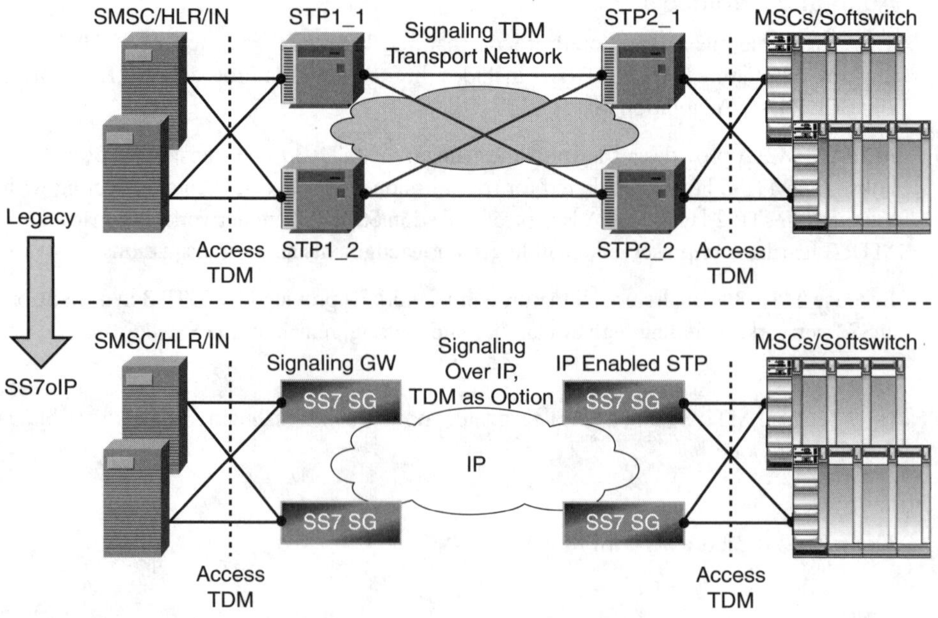

Figure 9-23 *M2PA Transport*

M3UA M3UA provides a mechanism for transporting MTP-3 signaling, such as SCCP or MAP, over an IP network. M3UA allows the SS7 network to communicate with non-SS7 entities and vice versa. With M3UA, the SG would be responsible for terminating SS7 links, converting messages to M3UA, and transmitting these messages over a SCTP/IP association via a Network Interworking Function (NIF). Figure 9-24 depicts an SG with M3UA.

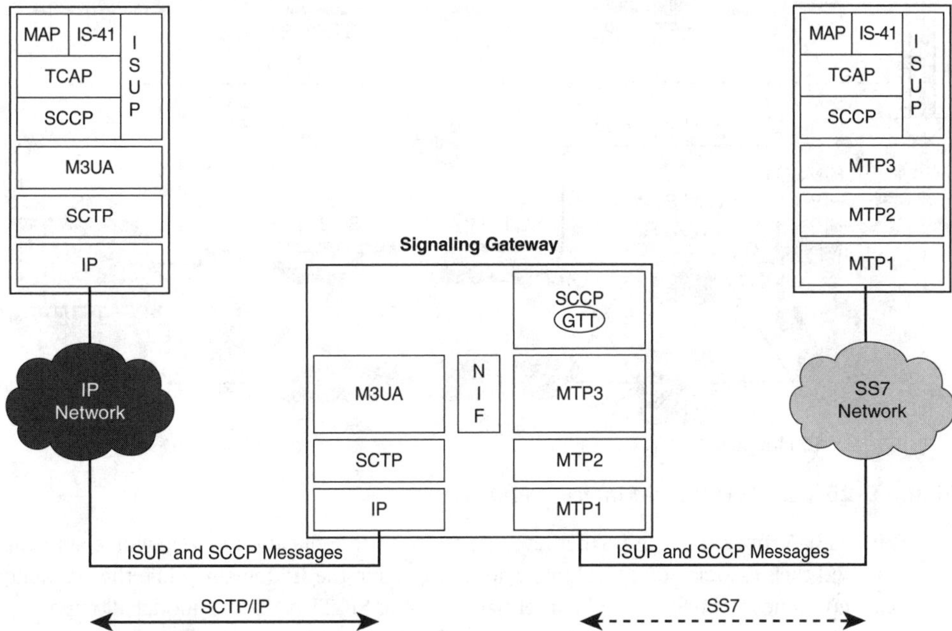

Figure 9-24 *Signaling Gateway with M3UA*

With M3UA, mobile operators can begin to migrate their legacy SS7 endpoints to IP-based endpoints, while still maintaining communication with TDM-based SS7 nodes. Application Server Processes (ASP) are IP endpoints that support M3UA for communication into the SS7 domain (via a SG). Various ASPs exist today, including IP HLRs, IP SCPs, and MGCs.

In essence, M3UA extends access to MTP-3 services to IP-based applications. Figure 9-25 provides a deployment example where M3UA is used to provide interworking between an IP-based node and a SS7-based node.

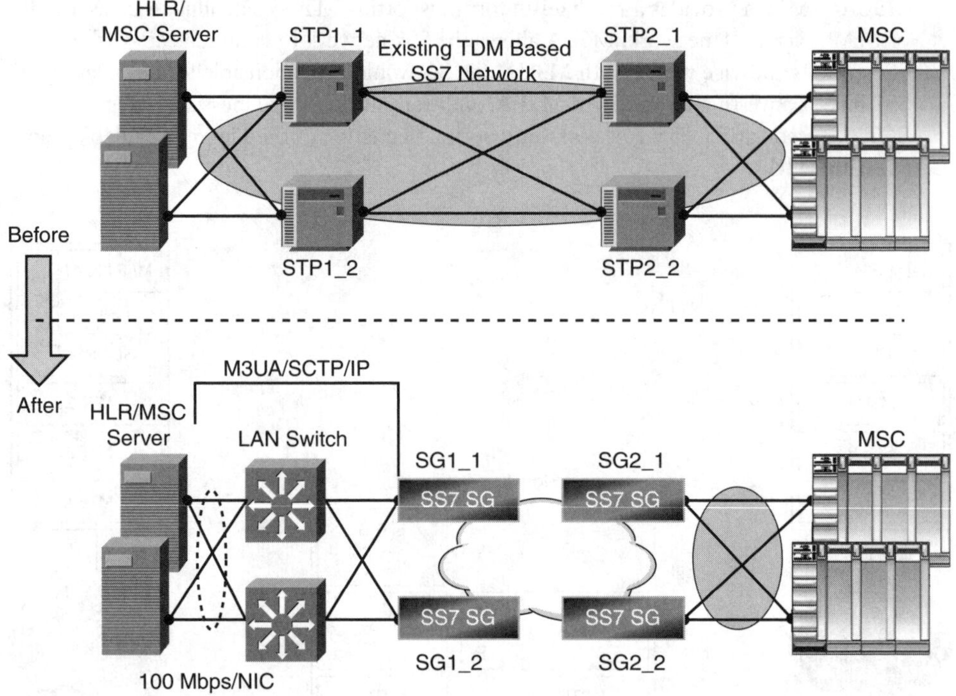

Figure 9-25 *M3UA IP/TDM Interworking*

With M3UA, operators can further leverage an Internet application model, where applications and their associated control plane are deployed in the IP domain, while the signaling plane continues to be SS7-based (either native SS7 or SIGTRAN). This model allows a mobile operator to migrate from the closed, restrictive conditions of SS7 architecture to an open, flexible Internet model.

Figure 9-26 provides a view of this decoupling of the application/control plane and the signaling plane into IP and SS7, respectively.

SCCP User Adaptation (SUA) SUA provides a mechanism for transporting any SCCP user signaling (TCAP, MAP, and so on) over an IP network. SUA sits further up the protocol stack than M3UA, therefore eliminating the need for IP-based applications to interwork with SS7 at all. This allows ASPs to interwork with the SS7 network without having to understand Point Codes, GTT, link provisioning, and so on.

Figure 9-27 depicts an SG with SUA.

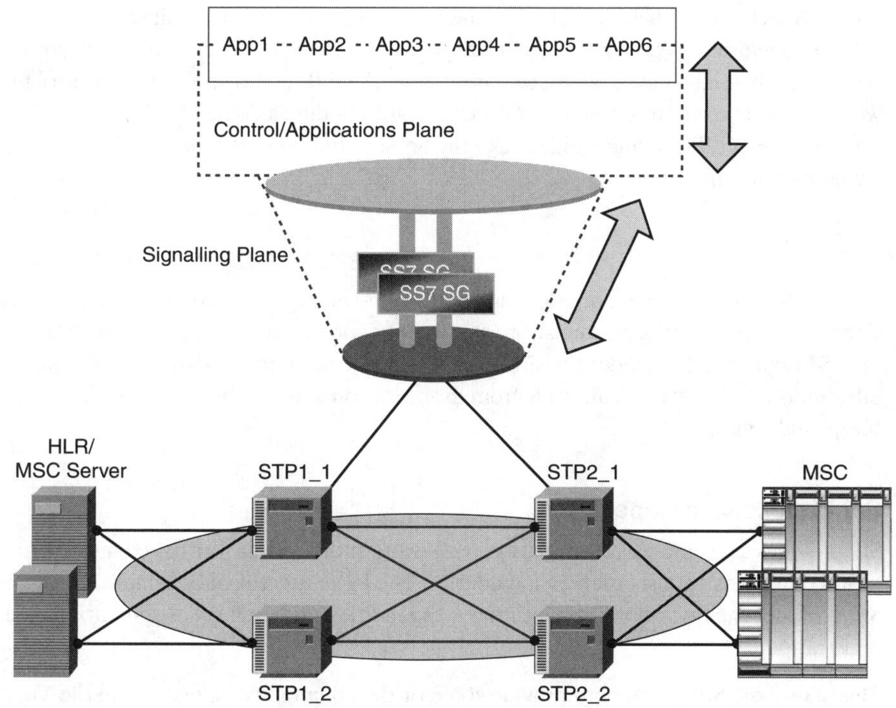

Figure 9-26 *Decoupling of Application/Control Plane and Signaling Plane*

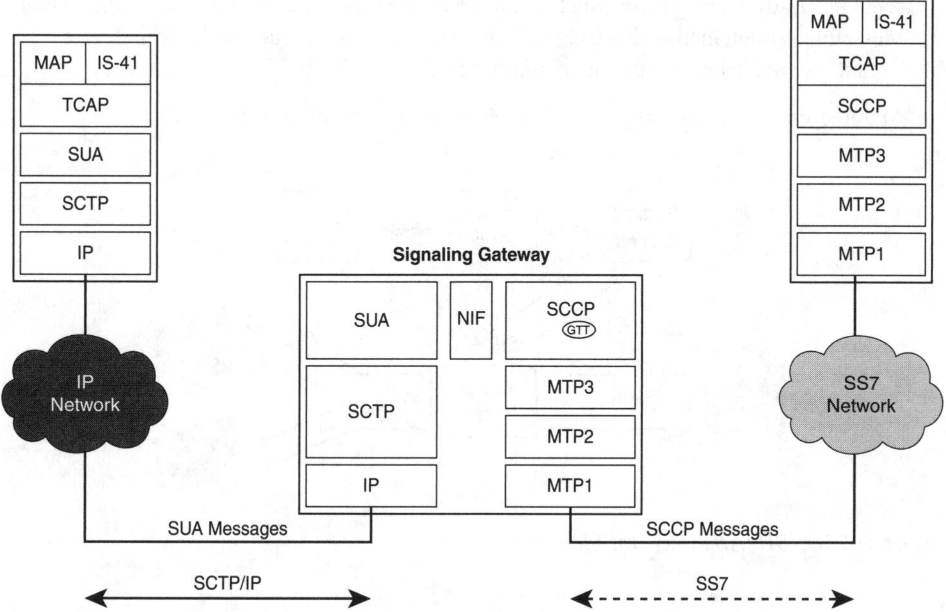

Figure 9-27 *Signaling Gateway with SUA*

The SUA architecture helps accomplish the transition to the All-IP architecture. With SUA, an operator can deploy the SS7 transport services of SCCP over an IP infrastructure. With this signaling infrastructure in place with an IP-based application/control network, a mobile operator takes the first step toward building a complete Voice over IP offering. This VoIP offering will leverage the Session Initiation Protocol (SIP) as the signaling mechanism.

SIP

Session Initiation Protocol, or SIP, is an application-layer control protocol that provides signaling for the creation, termination, and modification of sessions. Similar to ISUP in the SS7 domain, SIP provides the signaling for voice calls in the IP domain to enable VoIP. SIP supports all facets of VoIP calls from user location and capabilities to availability, call setup, and handling.

SIP Protocol and Capabilities

SIP provides a generic session initiation framework rather than a structured method and protocol for session instantiation and control. The basic functionality established by the SIP protocol can be summarized into three capabilities: addressing, session initiation, and registration.

This allows the SIP protocol to provide some of the common voice features in the VoIP world that are provided by an IN system in the telephony world. These features include supplementary services, such as call hold, call waiting, call transfer, call forwarding, and three-way calling. In addition, because of its roots in the IP domain, SIP also provides some more advanced features, such as Find-Me services (location identification), Instant Messaging, simultaneous ring (ring two phones at the same time), and in-call device handoff (switch from one phone to another mid-call).

Architecturally, SIP consists of five key elements, illustrated in Figure 9-28.

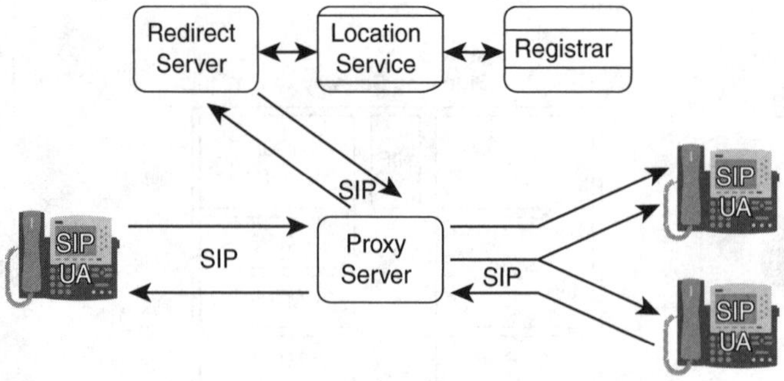

Figure 9-28 *SIP Architectural Elements*

These elements include the following:

- **SIP User Agent:** SIP relies on a client-server request-response mechanism for session initiation, as illustrated in Figure 9-29. A User Agent Client (UAC) initiates SIP requests. A User Agent Server (UAS) responds to SIP requests.

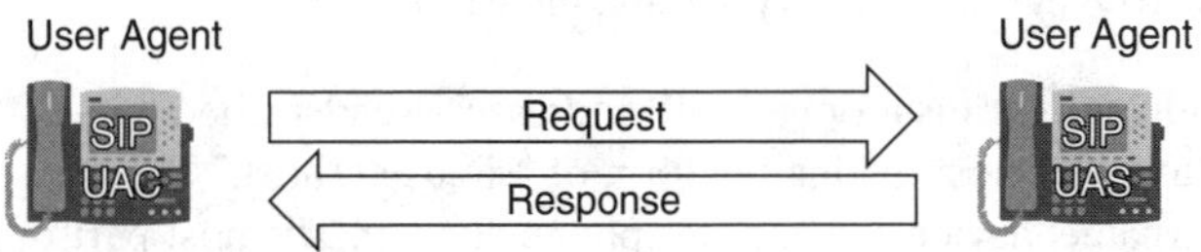

Figure 9-29 *User Agent Relationship*

- **Proxy server:** A proxy server acts as a signaling router, as illustrated in Figure 9-30. The proxy server may also provide security or authentication capabilities on the local network (via a client challenge mechanism) to ensure identity of a SIP client.

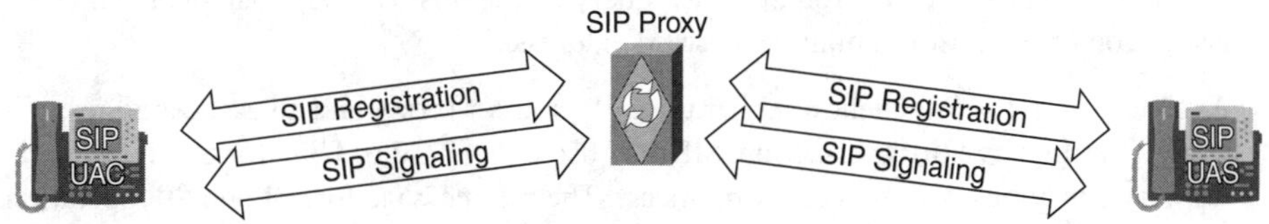

Figure 9-30 *SIP Proxy Server*

- **Registrar:** A registrar is an SIP component that accepts SIP user registrations. These registrations are used to establish reachability (that is, the registrar is informed of both subscriber identity and network address). Although the registrar itself is an optional component in a fixed SIP environment, mobile VoIP requires a SIP registrar.
- **Redirect server:** A redirect server may be used to redirect a SIP client session to a new destination.
- **Location/presence server:** Location and presence servers may be used to offer advanced supplementary services. These advanced services may take advantage of understanding the state and location of the user device. Methods for providing location and presence are discussed in Chapter 8.

These components function as a system to provide a core set of functionality, including the following:

- Identification/authentication of a calling party
- Identification of called party
- Registration (endpoint reachability)

- Call control functions:
  - Initiate, terminate, or redirect a call
  - Suspend/resume a call
  - Provide call progress information
  - Specify/negotiate/modify session media

SIP Addressing and Transactions SIP addresses are identified by a SIP URI. This URI references a user at a host, taking the form of "sip:user@host." The user part of the URI may be a username, device name, or telephone number. The host part of the URI is either a domain name or a numeric network address, such as an IP address.

After a SIP address has been determined, a SIP server is located by either using a SIP proxy, or using the host portion of the SIP address to locate a SIP server. In the former case, a local SIP proxy provides the remote session initiation on behalf of the SIP client. In this way, SIP signaling becomes a trusted network-to-network interaction rather than an untrusted client-to-foreign-network interaction. In the latter case, the SIP client may determine the host server through a DNS query (if the host is a DNS name) or simple inspection (if the host is a numeric network address).

A request from the SIP client to either the SIP server or proxy and all associated responses are classified as a SIP transaction. SIP may use either TCP or UDP for transport, and responses may be either unicast or multicast. The SIP message format and SIP operations are independent of the transport layer.

SIP Methods SIP protocol defines a number of methods, or requests and responses between SIP clients (or proxy servers) for call control. The basic methods for call setup, teardown, and registration are INVITE, BYE, and REGISTER, respectively.

Note The SIP RFC was intentionally vague in implementation to accommodate flexibility. For this reason, a large percentage of SIP methods are not defined in the RFC itself, but instead in ancillary specifications that provide additional capabilities. The following presents some examples and is not intended to be a comprehensive list of all SIP extensions:

- SUBSCRIBE/NOTIFY, which conveys presence information, is defined in RFC 3265.
- REFER, which enables call transfer, is defined in RFC 3515.
- MESSAGE, which is used for Instant Messaging, is defined in RFC 3428.
- UPDATE, which allows for a session to be modified, is defined in RFC 3311.
- 3GPP wireless extensions are defined in RFC 3455.

Figure 9-31 illustrates the use of the INVITE method for initiating a session. Figure 9-31 also illustrates how SIP can be used to signal bearer capabilities (with Session Description Protocol [SDP]), session QoS (with Resource Reservation Protocol [RSVP]), prior to bearer session establishment.

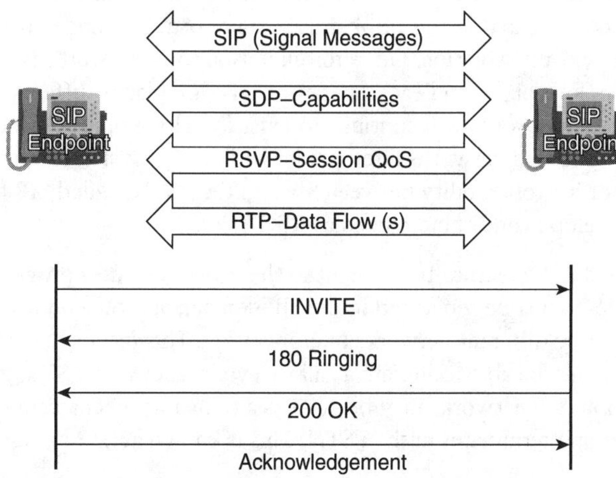

Figure 9-31 *INVITE Method*

There are many responses to the SIP INVITE, including message 100, indicating that the call is being tried, or message 180, indicating that the other party is ringing. Message 183 indicates that the call is ringing and allows the remote party to provide a ringback tone. Message 200 indicates an OK response.

The SIP BYE method is used to terminate a SIP session. Figure 9-32 illustrates the use of the BYE method.

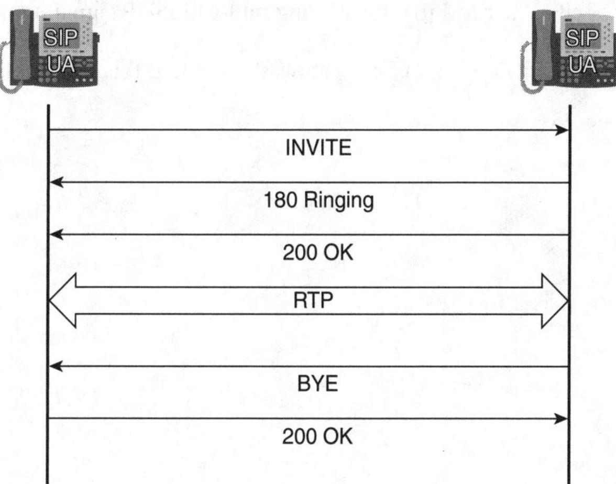

Figure 9-32 *BYE Method*

Later in this chapter, we explore how SIP is used in the IP Multimedia Subsystem (IMS) for providing VoIP and other IP-based services over wireless networks.

SIP-T

Although the benefits and efficiencies of deploying IP networks and services, such as VoIP, are well-documented in this book, it is also important to understand that these services cannot exist in isolation. Operator migration to IP networks is a process that does not happen overnight, and each operator transition plan is different. Therefore, traditional telephone networks will continue to exist for a long time. With this in mind, it is important that IP-based networks interoperate with legacy systems. In this context, a set of guidelines for interoperability between SIP and the PSTN, called SIP for Telephones (SIP-T), was developed and standardized as RFC 3372.

SIP-T is intended to be feature-transparent to the PSTN. Features provided in the PSTN, especially by SS7, must be replicated in the SIP domain, and the end user should have no knowledge of these different networks interoperating. This means that a VoIP user with SIP signaling should be able to initiate a call to a voice user with SS7 signaling, and vice versa. In addition, SIP networks may be used as a transport mechanism for a call that both originates and terminates in the PSTN. This is known as *SIP bridging*.

SIP-T provides this framework for interoperability between SIP and SS7 domains. To provide this function, PSTN gateways are leveraged that understand both SS7 and SIP messaging, and provide a combination of protocol translation and protocol encapsulation.

SIP-T provides three functions in the PSTN gateway, as follows:

- Encapsulation of SS7 ISUP messages in the SIP body to provide ISUP signaling transparency.
- Translation of ISUP messages into the SIP header to provide routability of SIP messages that are dependent on ISUP.
- Use of the INFO method for transferring mid-call ISUP signaling messages.

Figure 9-33 provides a view of a PSTN gateway providing this protocol interworking function.

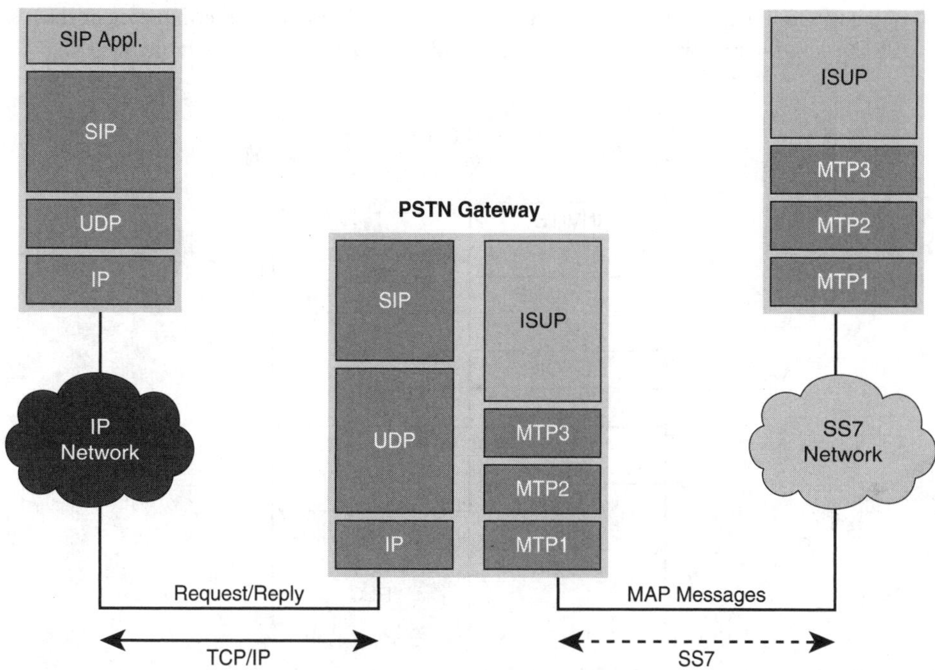

Figure 9-33 *PSTN Gateway Protocol Interworking Function*

Figure 9-34 illustrates a call flow originating from the PSTN and terminating at a SIP phone. This illustration shows how ISUP messages are converted into SIP methods.

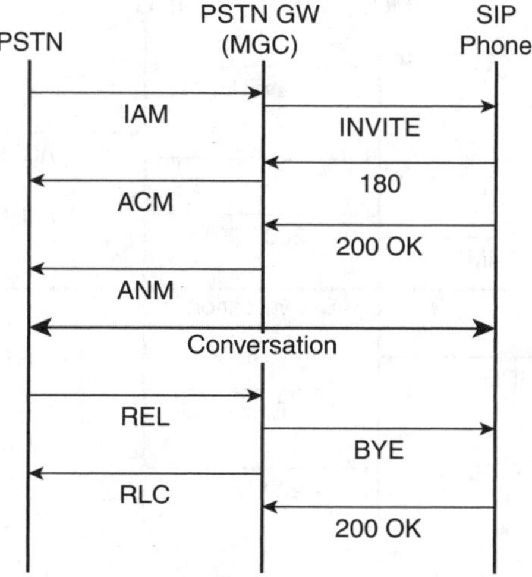

Figure 9-34 *PSTN to SIP Phone Call Flow*

Figure 9-35 illustrates a call flow originating from a SIP phone and terminating at the PSTN. This illustration shows how SIP methods are converted into ISUP messages.

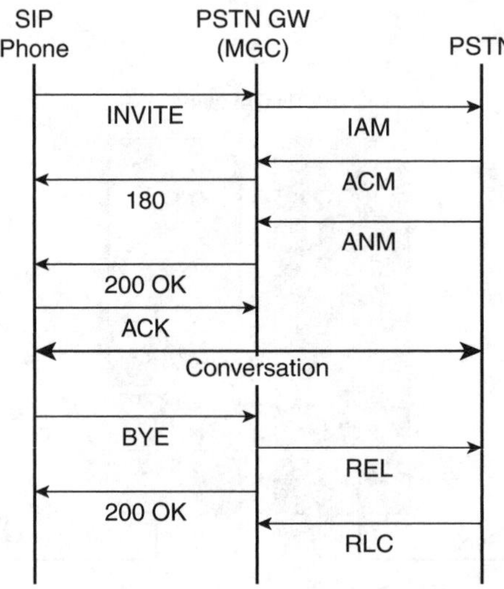

Figure 9-35 *SIP Phone to PSTN Call Flow*

For completeness, Figure 9-36 illustrates a call flow both originating and terminating in the PSTN, where SIP is used within the transport network between PSTN gateways.

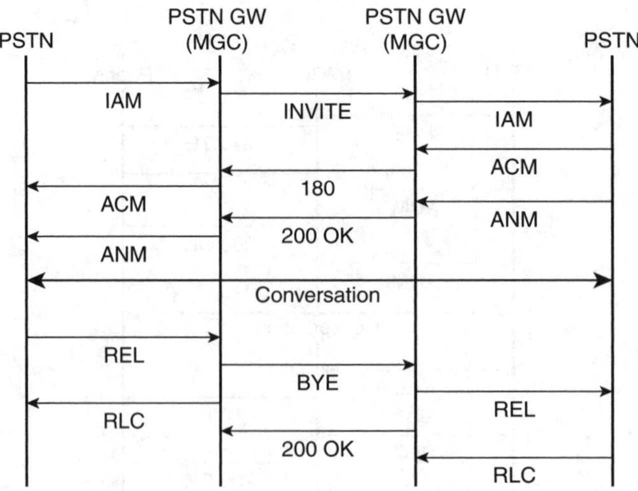

Figure 9-36 *PSTN to PSTN Call with SIP Transport Network*

SIP-I Although SIP-T provides the foundations for basic call control and mapping architecture between the PSTN and SIP domains, exact maps, procedures, and security implications were further defined by ITU-T, in Q.1912.5, and published under SIP-I. SIP-I provides a more detailed mapping and encapsulation document than RFC 3372, along with support for supplementary services defined in the IN.

Note The basic framework and architecture of protocol translation and encapsulation were explained in the previous section on SIP-T. An extensive list of mapping functions can be found in the relevant standards document.

VoIP Bearer Overview

VoIP bearer uses the Real-time Transport Protocol (RTP) for transport of the voice media stream. RTP is a UDP-based protocol that has become the de-facto standard for transporting audio and video over IP networks.

Note Although this book references UDP as the transport layer for RTP, the RTP standard is flexible to include Datagram Congestion Control Protocol (DCCP) and Stream Control Transport Protocol (SCTP) as other transport methods. These protocols and transport mechanisms are not discussed in this book.

RTP, defined in RFC 3550, provides the following services to the VoIP media stream:

- **Sequence numbering:** Because UDP does not provide sequencing, RTP provides this function. Sequencing is important to ensure that voice is processed in the correct order. Otherwise, it would be difficult to understand what is being said!
- **Timestamping:** These timestamps are used both for synchronization and jitter calculation.
- **INFO Method:** Use of the INFO method for transferring mid-call ISUP signaling messages

RTP is typically transported in small packet sizes based on the capabilities of the voice encoder. Most often, the payload is a multiple of 10 ms duration. With such small payloads, header compression tends to be used to counteract the ratio of header (RTP, UDP, IP) to payload.

Note Robust Header Compression (RoHC) is most widely used in wireless networks. RoHC is defined in RFC 3095.

With transport being standardized, two other key functions must be addressed when handling the voice media streams: transcoding and QoS, which have been previously discussed in this book.

IP Multimedia Subsystem (IMS)

IMS is another of the architectural visions that have swept over the telecommunications landscape for the last 20 or so years. Beginning with IN, then softswitching, and now IMS, the evolution of the services domain is similar to that of the network itself—with a focus on IP as the foundation.

The IMS framework was designed for deploying IP-based services over a circuit-switched network, such as 2G or 3G mobile networks. IMS was first standardized through 3GPP, but has since been extended into numerous standards organizations, including 3GPP2, WiMAX Forum, TiSPAN, and CableLabs.

The IMS standards leverage the SIP protocol for delivering real-time, peer-to-peer, and collaborative services such as VoIP, video calling, dual-mode voice services, and Push-to-Talk.

IMS defines a number of new elements for the mobile core. These functional elements, known as Call State Control Functions (CSCFs), are similar to many of the circuit-switched IN nodes discussed earlier in this chapter. The three new nodes defined for the packet core in IMS are the following:

Note The CSCFs defined for the packet core are logical functions that may be physically co-located or integrated with other network functions.

- **Proxy CSCF (P-CSCF):** The P-CSCF is the first contact for a mobile device within IMS. SIP signaling messages are exchanged between the mobile device and P-CSCF. The P-CSCF provides security functions (encryption of SIP session, Route Header analysis), and is responsible for communicating session information to the policy server. This information may then be used as part of the end-to-end policy framework for QoS, charging, or other functions.
- **Serving CSCF (S-CSCF):** The S-CSCF acts as a SIP registrar and SIP proxy, providing full session-control capabilities. This type of function is known as a Back-to-Back User Agent (B2BUA). As the interface to the services/applications, the S-CSCF is also responsible for service execution.
- **Interrogating CSCF (I-CSCF):** The I-CSCF sits at the edge of the mobile operator network for either inbound or outbound calls to other domains, or operators. The I-CSCF is the first contact for inbound signaling from another domain. The I-CSCF may also provide functions such as topology hiding.

In addition, the Home Subscriber Service (HSS) is defined as a database that combines the 2G HLR function and 3G User Data Server (UDS) function. Together, these functions in the HSS provide mobility management, identification handling, service authorization support, call/session establishment support, and application services support.

Figure 9-37 illustrates the IMS components.

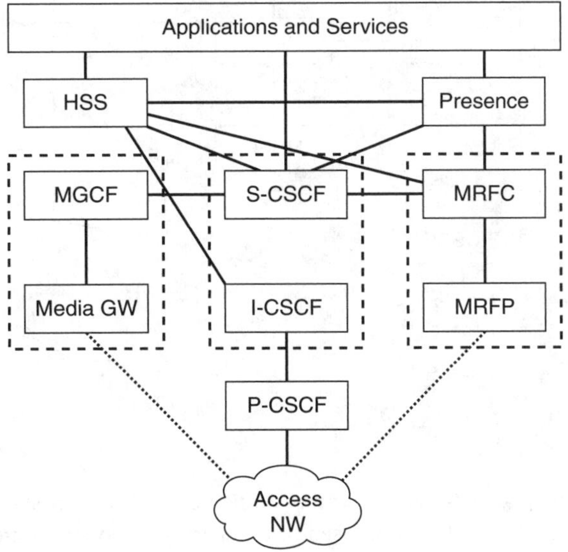

Figure 9-37 *IMS Components*

Application servers (AS) connect into the IMS network through the S-CSCF. These servers may be SIP application servers, presence servers, service capability servers, or even gateways to other service networks.

Note The IMS Service Switching Function (IM-SSF) is a CAMEL gateway designed to allow IMS subscribers access to existing IN services by providing an interface between these two domains. This allows an operator to migrate subscribers to IMS/IP without having to replicate all features provided by the IN.

Figure 9-38 illustrates the IM-SSF interworking.

continues

continued

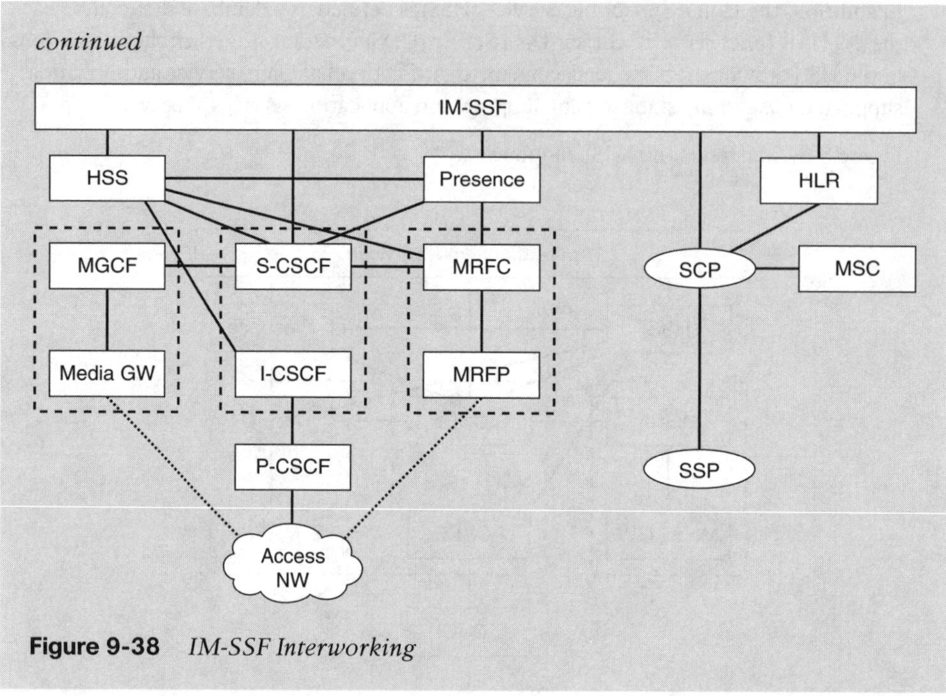

Figure 9-38 *IM-SSF Interworking*

One of the peripheral IMS elements is the Media Resource Function (MRF), responsible for conferencing. The MRF is composed of two parts: a Media Resource Function Control (MRFC) and Media Resource Function Processor (MRFP), which are the control and bearer functions, respectively. The MRF performs any media mixing or transcoding required for conferencing.

IMS Framework

The IMS framework provides a standard for all elements, protocols, and interworking reference points to enable IP-based services. Enabling these services includes allowing the following:

- A local IMS subscriber to contact another local IMS subscriber.
- A local IMS subscriber to contact a remote IMS subscriber.
- A roaming IMS subscriber to contact a local or remote IMS subscriber.
- A roaming or local IMS subscriber to contact a non-IMS subscriber (via PSTN).

Figure 9-39 illustrates the interfaces and elements required to enable these services. Note that SIP and DIAMETER are the main protocols in the IMS infrastructure for call signaling and policy control.

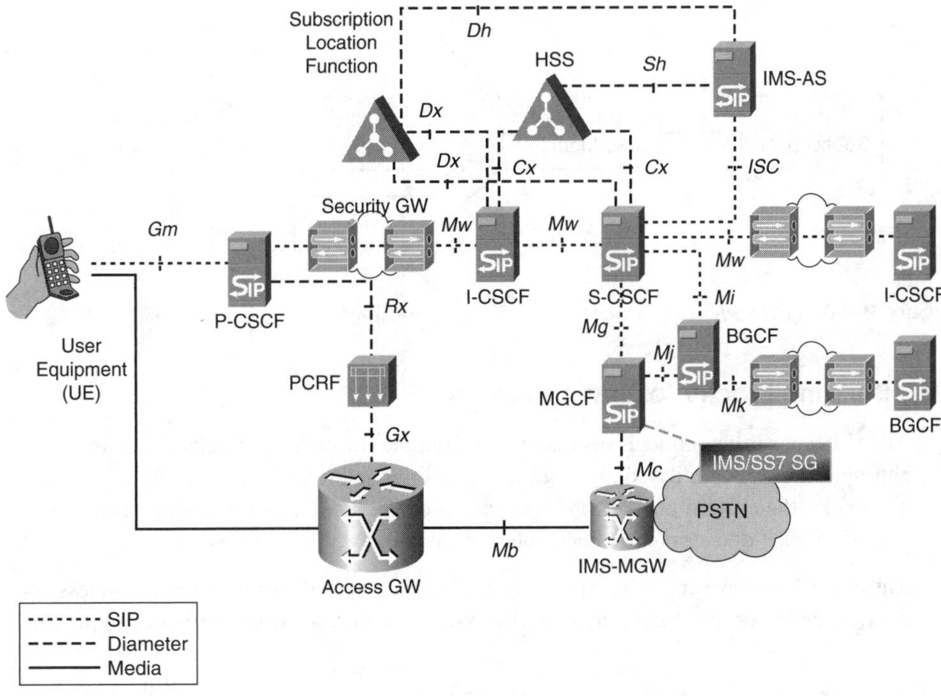

Figure 9-39 *IMS Interfaces and Elements*

IMS Identity/Subscriber Model

Each IMS subscriber is identified by a single IMS Private Identity (IMPI). This IMPI is linked to either the GSM SIM or other subscriber identity discussed in Chapter 8. The HSS stores a mapping of each subscriber's IMPI to one or more IMS Public Identities (IMPU). Each IMPU may have different service profiles associated with them.

When a subscriber registers (based on IMPI), these public identities are transferred to the S-CSCF, as illustrated in Figure 9-40. The S-CSCF uses the characteristics of the public identity to determine what services are enabled for that particular subscriber. These services may also depend on time or location parameters.

The IMPU is also used by the S-CSCF to trigger third-party registrations to one or more IMS AS. S-CSCF actions depend on a set of rules stored in the IMPU known as initial filter criteria (iFC). These iFC are assigned different priorities and are processed in order of priority by the S-CSCF.

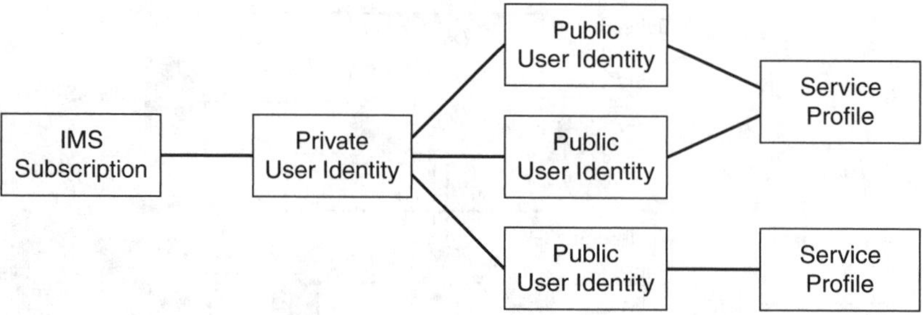

Figure 9-40 *IMS Identity Model*

IMS Building Blocks to New Services

The IMS subscriber model is dependent on a number of building blocks discussed throughout this book. By combining the capabilities of 3G and 4G Radio Access Networks, the evolved packet core, and end-to-end context awareness, all transported over IP, mobile operators have been able to launch innovative services.

These services may simply be replicas of those a subscriber uses over a non-wireless connection/device or may be differentiated services that only a mobile network can provide.

Video Delivery over Mobile Networks

Mobile networks have continued to enable new services. From offering only voice services to data to enhanced IP services, mobile networks have closed the gap with traditional fixed broadband networks in offering higher speed and more intriguing services. Video is the next wave of innovation sweeping the mobile (and fixed!) broadband industry.

Although numerous business and technical challenges remain unanswered, mobile video has had quite a bit of success around the world. Mobile video delivery has taken on numerous forms, including the following:

- Clipcasting, or short videos, usually one to two minutes in duration.
- Live TV, or offering broadcast television channels to the mobile device.
- Place-shifted content, or video retrieved from a fixed location (a home Set-Top Box, for example).
- Interactive TV, or video that includes the ability for a user to interact.
- Personalized TV, or video that has been tailored for a particular subscriber based on preference.

As exact subscriber requirements and usage patterns continue to change, a number of video-delivery mechanisms have emerged. These video-delivery mechanisms can be summarized into three categories: unicast, multicast, and broadcast.

Each of these technologies has both merits and disadvantages. As such, many mobile operators deploy a mixed strategy, in which unicast, multicast, and broadcast are used to deliver the optimal user experience.

Unicast Video Delivery

Unicast video delivery is the most prominent form of mobile video delivery today. As its name implies, unicast video delivery involves a single subscriber accessing a particular video via the mobile network.

Figure 9-41 illustrates a unicast video delivery model.

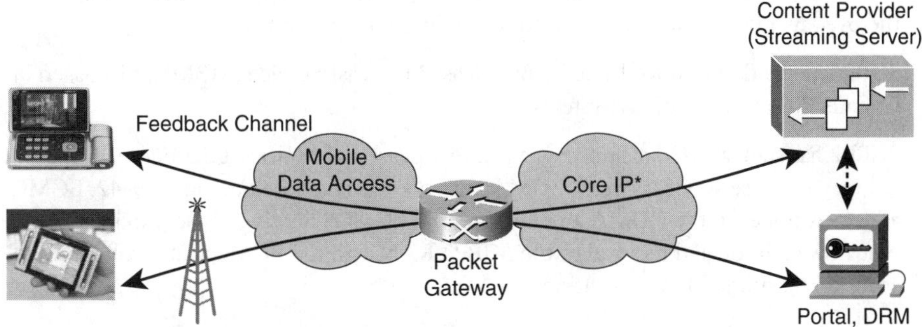

Figure 9-41 *Unicast Video Delivery*

Unicast video delivery tends to be best for delivering video that has limited mass appeal or enables interactivity. In addition, unicast allows a mobile operator to leverage existing authentication mechanisms, such as RADIUS-based AAA. Clipcasting, Video-on-Demand, and personalized video leverage a unicast video delivery model extensively. A number of operators, however, continue to offer live television services via unicast.

Unicast Video Delivery Challenges

Although this may sound simple, a number of challenges exist with unicast video delivery.

Throughout this book, one common theme has continually emerged: Mobile networks are shared resources. A single user can consume more than his fair share of available resources, whether that be radio time, backhaul bandwidth, network processing, or server memory. With video, the impact of this is amplified. Delivering individual video streams on a mass scale is resource-intensive.

Consider a mobile network consisting of 10,000 towers, and on each tower, three users are watching a 100-kbps video feed. At the tower, this is generating 300 kbps—not too much traffic. However, toward the mobile core, a simple use-case like this already shows the potential to generate very large amounts of aggregate traffic (3 Gbps in this model). As mobile video continues to grow in popularity, and the quality of mobile video improves (with potential for 1 Mbps video feeds over a 4G mobile network), core networks could see tens of Gbps of traffic from mobile video.

With this amount of bandwidth over shared resources, QoS become imperative. Implementations of video QoS are varied, ranging from bitrate starvation algorithms (adapting IP bitstreams) to transcoding/transrating (adapting video quality) to Call Admission Control (rejecting a new subscriber video request if the quality will degrade for existing subscribers). In most networks, a blend between these technologies is used.

Multicast Video Delivery

Multicast video delivery has been a focus for many standards organizations. In all cases, the existing unicast RAN is used for session authentication and key distribution, whereas the overlay multicast network is used for multicast bearer traffic.

3GPP has standardized Multimedia Broadcast Multicast Service (MBMS), discussed in Chapter 2, "Cellular Access Systems."

3GPP2 has standardized a similar service, Broadcast and Multicast Services (BCMCS), for delivery of these services over a CDMA network. As illustrated in Figure 9-42, BCMCS adds new nodes to the CDMA architecture, the BCMCS Serving Node provides IP multicast flow addition and removal to the 3GPP2 RAN, and the BCMCS Controller provides security/encryption key generation.

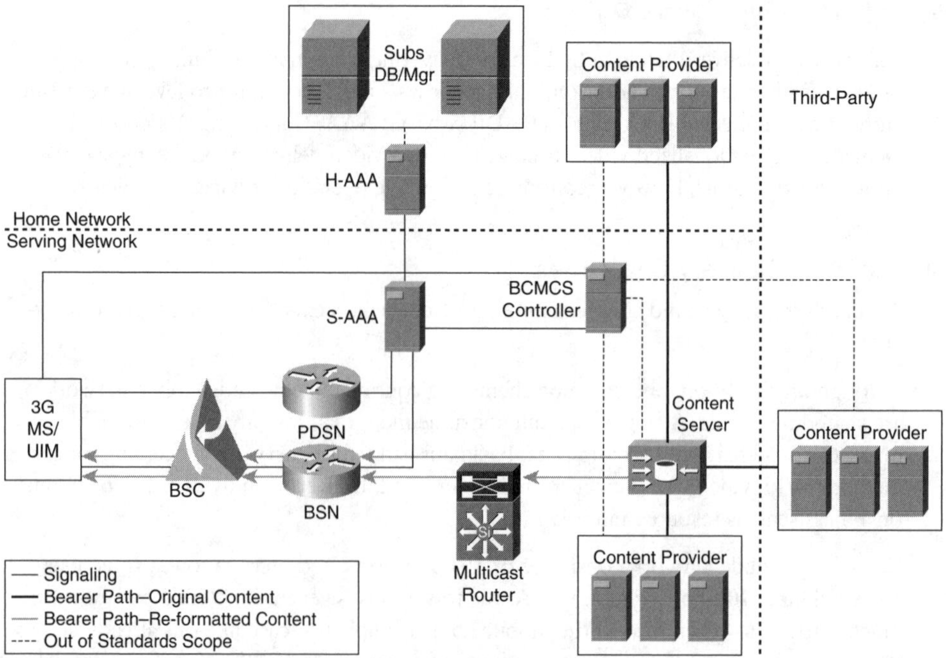

Figure 9-42 *BCMCS Architecture*

WiMAX Forum has developed the Multicast Broadcast Service (MBS) for delivery of video multicast within a cell. The MBS architecture adds the MBS Controller. This element provides the encapsulation of digital video into WiMAX MBS Frames and timing for synchronization and time slicing at the BTS receivers. The MBS interfaces to the ASNGW via the R4 interface. Figure 9-43 illustrates the WiMAX MBS architecture.

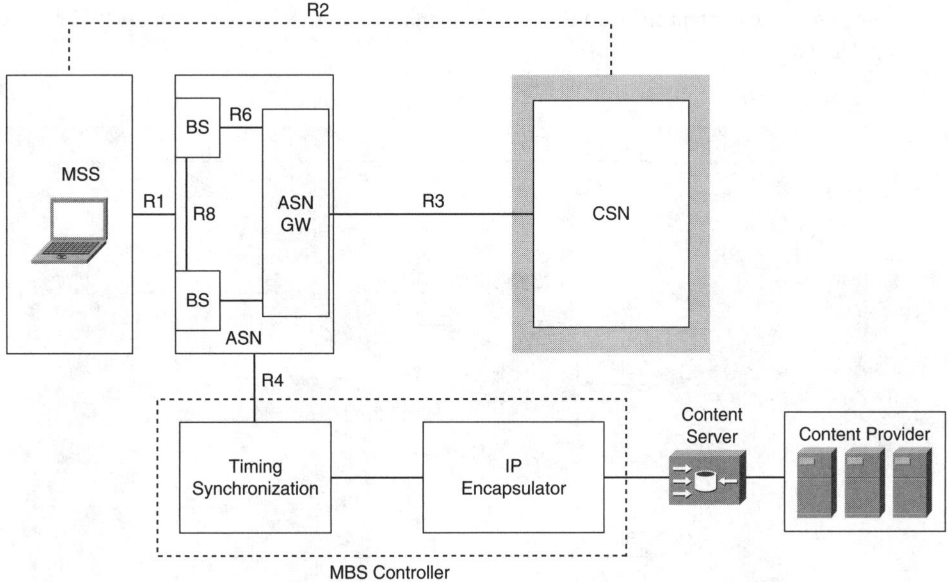

Figure 9-43 *WiMAX MBS Architecture*

These multicast networks, although standardized, have limited deployments thus far.

Overlay Broadcast Video Delivery

Overlay broadcast networks have seen varied success worldwide. These networks require additional spectrum and a new radio in the mobile terminal. These broadcast networks give mobile operators the ability to launch a large number of channels to mobile devices without the inherent challenges from a unicast model—shared access and QoS requirements. However, broadcast technologies provide new challenges on the handset: availability (there are relatively few handsets with the dual radios required), price (devices tend to be more expensive), and battery power (operating two radios is more power-intensive).

The two leading technologies in the overlay broadcast segment are Digital Video Broadcasting: Handheld (DVB-H) and Media Forward Link Only (MediaFLO).

DVB-H

DVB-H is an evolution of the DVB Terrestrial (DVB-T). Both DVB-T and DVB-H use Orthogonal Frequency Division Multiplexing (OFDM) with up to 64-QAM modulation. See Chapter 1, "Introduction to Radio Systems," for delivering digital video signals to devices. DVB-H is defined in ETSI EN 302 304.

DVB-H networks provide all components for a complete video SDP. These components stretch from the content itself to the mobile terminal. Figure 9-44 depicts a DVB-H functional architecture

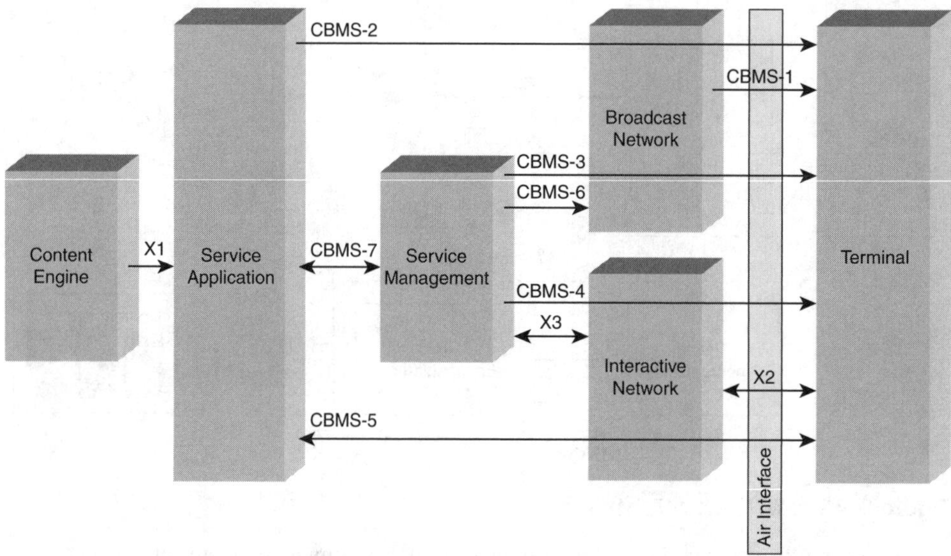

Figure 9-44 *DVB-H Functional Architecture*

DVB-H includes the following functions:

- **Service Application Function:** This function aggregates content from multiple sources, encodes the content to a form understood by the DVB-H device, and provides application logic.
- **Service Management Function:** This function provides service configuration, resource allocation, service guide provisioning, and service security.
- **Broadcast Network:** The broadcast network provides the assignment of IP flows to DVB-H timeslices for transmission.
- **Interactive Network:** The interactive network provides the mechanism for interactivity and access control. This interactive network is typically one of the existing mobile operator networks themselves (GSM, UMTS, CDMA, WiMAX, and so on) .

Video in DVB-H consists of IP datagrams transported using standard MPEG-2 coding, encapsulated using Multiprotocol Encapsulation (MPE).

Note MBE is a link-layer protocol defined by the Digital Video Broadcasters (DVB). The protocol is defined in ETSI EN 301 192.

Figure 9-45 provides a more complete view of the DVB-H protocol stack.

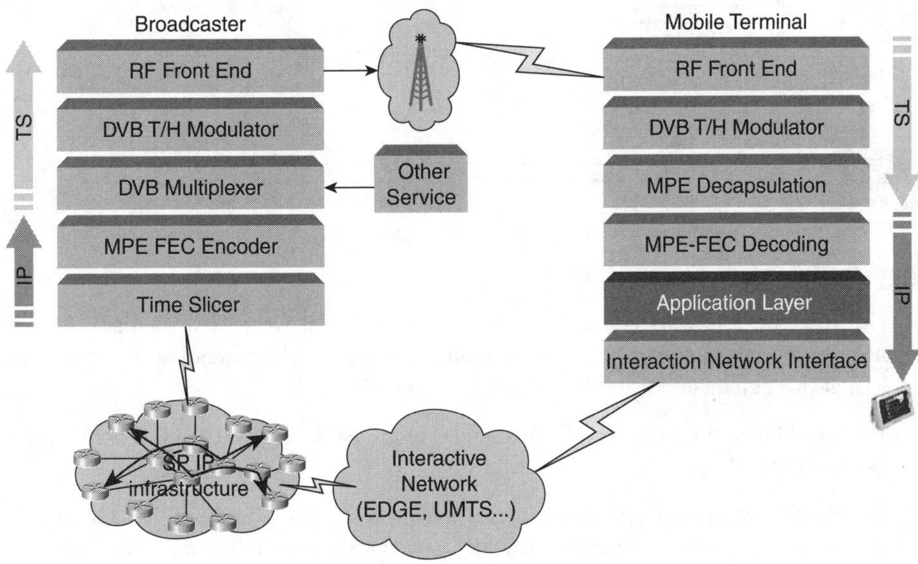

Figure 9-45 *DVB-H Protocol Stack*

DVB-H is approved by the European community for mobile TV broadcast. Over 20 DVB-H networks have been launched around the world (http://dvb-h.org). These networks have had varying degrees of success. For instance, although Crown Castle, a U.S. mobile TV provider, discontinued DVB-H service in the U.S. in 2007, DVB-H has had a large amount of success in Europe.

MediaFLO

MediaFLO (http://www.mediaflo.com) is a proprietary technology from Qualcomm, Inc. that provides an overlay OFDM-based broadcast media network. Qualcomm not only created MediaFLO, but also continues to operate networks worldwide based on MediaFLO technology.

Figure 9-46 provides an overview of the MediaFLO architecture.

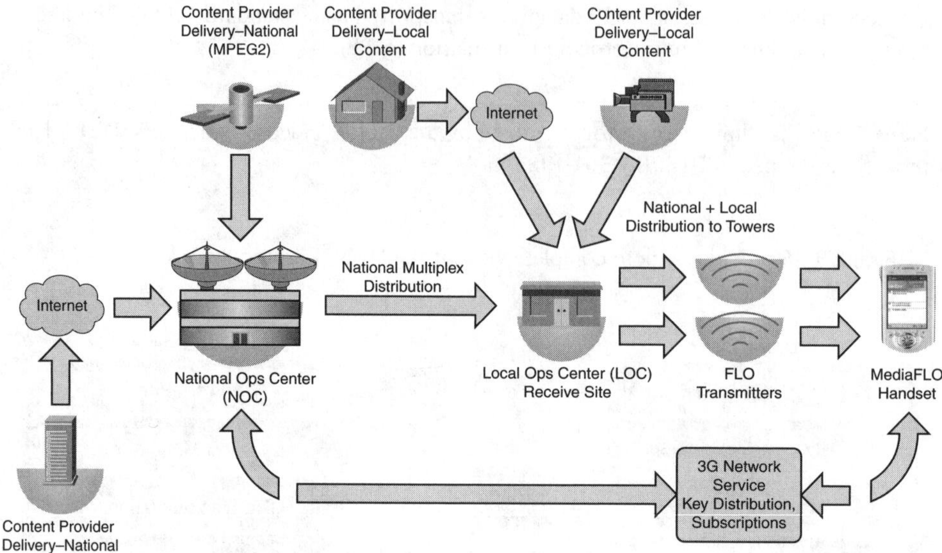

Figure 9-46 *MediaFLO Architecture*

The MediaFLO network consists of a Network Operations Center (NOC) that is responsible for receiving generic content from multiple sources and transcoding the content to a format that can be understood by the MediaFLO receivers.

The Local Operations Center (LOC) is similar to the NOC, except the LOC only receives local content.

The transmitter site receives the broadcast signal via satellite from both the LOC and NOC, and multiplexes the video into OFDM for transmission to the receiving device.

Note MediaFLO is a technology owned and licensed by Qualcomm, Inc. All information in this section is reproduced from Qualcomm documentation.

As with other broadcast technologies, a mobile network acts as a complement to the MediaFLO network, providing an interactivity channel, and non-broadcast video to mobile devices.

Service Security

In Chapter 8, we explored user confidentiality and security mechanisms for ensuring that a subscriber's profile, identity, and location are protected. In this section, we look at security from a service perspective. Mobile operators have implemented various levels of security as both a revenue-generating service and as a mechanism for protecting their own network infrastructure.

Many of the mechanisms used to protect mobile infrastructure are similar to those used to protect Internet infrastructure. Common security elements, such as firewalls and Intrusion Prevention Systems (IPS), are deployed in mobile operators to protect critical elements and databases, such as the AAA server. Common security techniques, such as heuristic analysis of data traffic to diagnose and mitigate Distributed Denial of Service (DDoS) attacks, are utilized as much in mobile core networks as in ISP networks. In fact, data mining, discussed earlier in this chapter as part of the SDP framework, also plays a key role in the overall operator security framework.

However, a mobile network does have nuances that require unique solutions. These solutions protect the mobile SDP framework itself. Two such solutions include the following:

- **SMS Spam filtering:** SMS Spam-filtering solutions alleviate the impact of large amounts of unsolicited SMS messages from impacting the SS7 network performance. These Spam filters reside in the SS7 network and interact with SMSCs for analyzing and categorizing SMS messages as Spam.
- **Blacklisting:** Blacklisting is used in various parts of the mobile network to block an abusive subscriber. As examples, the blacklists can be applied at the AAA to reject authorization of the subscriber, or at the SMSC to reject SMS originated by the subscriber. Blacklists can even be used in service gateways (WAP Gateway, P-CSCF, and so on) to reject requests to specific URLs or third parties.

There are numerous mobile-specific security companies and technologies under constant development to improve the service security of a mobile network. These security technologies seek to improve transaction service security so that credit cards may be used securely, browsing service security to prevent subscribers from browsing to unsecure websites, mitigate the impacts of mobile-targeted viruses, and VoIP security to prevent against SIP vulnerabilities.

As more and more subscribers join the mobile Internet, security concerns will force the adoption of more security standards that either integrate with or overlay the SDP frameworks described in this chapter. Today, however, these concerns have not been loud enough to elicit any immediate actions.

Summary

From the IN to IMS to video delivery, the SDP model has continually been revamped and redesigned to meet the needs of both a changing mobile subscriber base and enhanced mobile network. As operators migrate from 2G to 3G to 4G and evolve their networks to support newer, faster services and devices, the benefits to mobile subscribers is evident. The mobile network is one that is in constant flux, and a smooth transition of both network infrastructure and network services is important for business continuity. As such, the SDP framework has consistently provided an architectural model upon which a mobile operator may both deploy new services and interwork with existing services. As social interactions and business requirements change, it is clear that future services will be deployed on a services framework similar to those presented in this chapter.

Index

Numbers

A

B

C

D

E

F

G

H

I

J-K

L

M

N

O

P

Q

R

S

T

U

V

W-X-Y-Z